THE TEXTUAL TRADITION
OF
PLATO'S REPUBLIC

MNEMOSYNE
BIBLIOTHECA CLASSICA BATAVA

COLLEGERUNT

A.D. LEEMAN · H.W. PLEKET · C.J. RUIJGH

BIBLIOTHECAE FASCICULOS EDENDOS CURAVIT

C.J. RUIJGH, KLASSIEK SEMINARIUM, OUDE TURFMARKT 129, AMSTERDAM

SUPPLEMENTUM CENTESIMUM SEPTIMUM

GERARD BOTER

THE TEXTUAL TRADITION OF PLATO'S REPUBLIC

THE TEXTUAL TRADITION
OF
PLATO'S REPUBLIC

BY

GERARD BOTER

E.J. BRILL
LEIDEN · NEW YORK · KØBENHAVN · KÖLN
1989

Library of Congress Cataloging-in-Publication Data

Boter, Gerard.
    The textual tradition of Plato's Republic / by Gerard Boter.
       p.   cm.—(Mnemosyne, bibliotheca classica Batava.
Supplementum, ISSN 0169-8958; 107)
    Revision of thesis (doctoral)—Vrije Universiteit, Amsterdam,
1986.
    Bibliography: p.
    Includes indexes.
    ISBN 90-04-08787-7 (pbk.)
    1. Plato. Republic—Criticism, Textual. 2. Transmission of
texts. I. Title. II. Series.
PA4279.R7B68   1986
321'.07—dc19   88-24042
                                                        CIP

ISSN 0169-8958
ISBN 90 04 08787 7

© *Copyright 1989 by E. J. Brill, Leiden, The Netherlands*

All rights reserved. No part of this book may be reproduced or translated in any form by print, photoprint, microfilm, microfiche or any other means without written permission from the publisher

PRINTED IN THE NETHERLANDS BY E. J. BRILL

PARENTIBVS
VXORI

CONTENTS

Preface	XI
Note to the reader	XIII
Index siglorum	XV
Stemmas of the A-, D- and F-families	XVII
Introduction: Method of research	XIX

PART ONE

STATUS QUAESTIONIS 1

PART TWO

THE GREEK DIRECT TRADITION

Chapter One: Description of Manuscripts	25
Chapter Two: The primary Manuscripts	65
I. The relationship of ADF	65
1. The source of ADF	65
2. ADF are independent of each other	66
3. D and F derive from a common source	70
4. When did ADF part company	77
5. Contamination in ADF	78
II. The individual primary Manuscripts	80
1. A	80
2. D	91
3. F	99
Chapter Three: Affiliation of Manuscripts	111
I. The A-family	111
II. The D-family	169
III. The F-family	190
Chapter Four: The secondary Manuscripts	201
1. β	203
2. Vind.Bon.Sc.	214
3. Vind.Bon.	216

4. Sc.	217
5. Par.	222
6. TMγ	225
7. Mγ	226
8. N	231
9. VMatr.	234
10. αt	235
11. x$^{rec.}$	237
12. Par.$^{rec.}$	239
13. Other Manuscripts	240

Chapter Five: The sixteenth-century editions and Cornarius'
Eclogae 242
    1. The Aldine edition.. 242
    2. The first Basle edition 245
    3. The second Basle edition 245
    4. Cornarius' *Eclogae* 246
    5. Stephanus' edition 247

Chapter Six: The papyri 252

PART THREE

THE TRANSLATIONS

Chapter Seven: The fifteenth-century Latin translations 261
    1. The Chrysoloras-Uberto translation 261
    2. The translation by Pier Candido Decembrio 265
    3. The translation by Antonio Cassarino 268
    4. Ficino's translation 270

Chapter Eight: Translations into languages other than Latin 279
    I. Coptic translation.. 279
    II. Other languages.. 280
        1. Arabic... 280
        2. Persian.. 280
        3. Hebrew... 280

PART FOUR

THE INDIRECT TRADITION

I. Some general remarks on the indirect tradition.............. 285
    1. The Greek tradition 285

a. Direct quotations	285
b. References, imitations, etc.	286
c. The value of the Greek tradition	286
2. The Latin tradition	287
a. Direct quotations	287
b. *Verbatim* translations	287
c. References, imitations, etc.	287
3. The Arabic tradition	288
II. Index testimoniorum	290
III. Index auctorum Platonis Rempublicam laudantium	366
Bibliography	377
Index locorum potiorum	382

PREFACE

This book is a corrected version of my doctoral dissertation, which was submitted to the Vrije Universiteit, Amsterdam, in September 1986.

I wish to acknowledge my gratitude to the following persons and institutions. I have greatly benefited from the help I received from Prof. Dr D. M. Schenkeveld and Dr S. R. Slings, who have supervised my work on the text of Plato's *Republic*. Prof. Dr C. Datema and Mr G. Jonkers have read large portions of my work, and passed their comments on to me. Mrs M. L. Vaalburg-Darbon has undertaken to correct my English. The Netherlands Organization for the Advancement of Pure Research (Z. W. O.) has made my work financially possible. The Fondation Hardt at Vandoeuvres (Switzerland) has permitted me to complete the *index testimoniorum* during a fortnight's stay in the summer of 1985.

This book has been produced almost entirely by means of conversion from floppy-disks; the staff of E. J. Brill has constantly advised me in finding my way in the labyrinth of computer language. I am especially indebted to Mr J. D. Deahl. My parents have greatly helped me by placing a personal computer at my disposal.

Finally, I am grateful to the Editorial Board of Mnemosyne for accepting my book in the series of the *Mnemosyne Supplementa*.

NOTE TO THE READER

1. It may be convenient to explain at the outset which sigla are used for which MSS in this book. Alline 321-323 already complained about the divergencies in the use of different sigla; he accordingly proposed fixed sigla for a very restricted number of MSS. But even after his time (1915) new sigla were invented. The result is that in some cases different sigla are used to indicate the same MS, while in other cases the same siglum is attached to different MSS.

As a rule, I have accepted the sigla most currently used; thus I take over most of the sigla given by Bekker and Stallbaum, but in some cases I have departed from their sigla; for instance, Venetus 185 was christened **Π** by Bekker, but it is designated **D** by Schanz, who is followed by Burnet and most later scholars. For MSS which had not yet been given a siglum I have invented my own.

Throughout this book, I designate the MSS with my sigla, but I have not ventured to do so in direct quotations: whenever an author quoted by me uses a siglum different from mine, I add my own siglum in brackets. Further, the siglum **x** is used for Florentinus 85,7 in the text, but in the diagrams x is used for a hypothetical MS, while Flor. 85,7 is designated **Flor.x**.

A systematic *index siglorum* can be found on pp. XV-XVI; the order is: Roman upper case, Roman lower case, Greek upper case, Greek lower case, composite sigla. After the sigla I have added the number which a MS bears in my *Description of Manuscripts* (pp. 25-64), where the other sigla given to a MS are also recorded.

All MSS discussed in this book are Greek MSS, unless otherwise stated.

2. In the course of my study, I do not repeat the position of a particular MS in the stemma on each occurrence; in order to get an impression of a MS as quickly as possible, the reader may consult the stemmas of the A-, D- and F-families on pp. XVII-XVIII. For clarity's sake I have refrained from indicating the lines of contamination in these stemmas. Further, the reader may look up all the basic information concerning a particular MS in the *Description of Manuscripts* (pp. 25-64), where references are given to the pages where I hold a full discussion of the MS in question.

3. In quoting the readings of the MSS, I report as faithfully as possible; that is, I quote readings as accentuated in the MSS, even in places where the accentuation is obviously wrong, or deviates from modern practice (e.g. the accentuation of enclitics); other peculiarities, such as the omission of *iota subscriptum*, are also reported as they stand in the MSS.

4. Terms like *exemplar, apographon* etc. are used in a loose sense; that is, I use the term *exemplar* to indicate the nearest extant or reconstructible source of a MS, not necessarily its *direct* source.

All terms used by me will, I think, be self-evident to the classical scholar, with the possible exception of the verb *telescope*; following Clark, I use this term to indicate a specific type of parablepsis, namely those cases in which a scribe has left out one or more lines in his exemplar.

5. All references are to Burnet's 1905 Oxford edition.

6. In recording the readings of the MSS I use the following abbreviations:

X^{it}	=	lectio in textu scripta
X^{sl}	=	lectio supra lineam scripta
X^{im}	=	lectio in margine scripta
X^{ac}	=	lectio ante correctionem
X^{pc}	=	lectio post correctionem, a manu recentiore scripta (but for some MSS I use X^{pc} to indicate readings which have been added by the scribe after the text had been copied; this is the case with **A, M, N, a, c, Ambr.** and **Sc.**; in the case of these MSS, the same practice is followed with readings *supra lineam* and *in margine*)
X^{1pc}	=	lectio post correctionem, a prima manu scripta
X^{2pc}	=	lectio post correctionem, a secunda manu scripta
X^{ir}	=	lectio in rasura scripta
X^{Σ}	=	scholium vel glossema

INDEX SIGLORUM

A   Parisinus 1807 (32)
D   Venetus 185 (47)
D   lectio apographorum **D** (ubi deest **D** ipse)
E   Venetus 184 (46)
F   Vindobonensis Suppl. Gr. 39 (54)
K   Parisinus 1642 (31)
M   Caesenas D 28,4 (Malatestianus) (3)
N   Venetus 187 (48)
P   Vaticanus Palatinus 173 (43)
R   Vaticanus 1029 (39)
T   Venetus Append. Class. IV 1 (45)
V   Vindobonensis Phil. Gr. 1 (49)
W   Vindobonensis Suppl. Gr. 7 (53)

a   Florentinus Laurentianus 59,1 (10)
b   Florentinus Laurentianus 85,6 (13)
c   Florentinus Laurentianus 85,9 (15)
k   Vaticanus Urbinas 31 (44)
m   Vaticanus 61 (36)
n   Florentinus Laurentianus 85,14 (16)
p   Vaticanus 229 (38)
q   Monacensis 237 (25)
t   Ambrosianus 300 (22)
v   Angelicus 101 (35)
x   Florentinus Laurentianus 85,7 (14)

Θ   Vaticanus 226 (37)
Φ   Vindobonensis Phil. Gr. 109 (51)
Ψ   Scorialensis Ψ,1,1 (7)

α   Florentinus Laurentianus 80,7 (11)
β   Florentinus Laurentianus 80,19 (12)
γ   Florentinus Laurentianus Conventi Soppressi 42 (9)

Acq.   Florentinus Laurentianus Acquisti e Doni 37 (8)
Ambr.   Ambrosianus 329 (23)
Ambros.   Ambrosianus 778 (24)
Ath.   Athous Iviron 131 (1)
Bodl.   Bodleianus Misc. Gr. 104 (Auct. F.4.5) (29)
Bon.   Bononiensis 3630 (2)
Darmst.   Darmstadt 2773 Misc. Gr. (4)
Durh.   Durham C. IV.2 (5)
Hier.   Hierosolymitanus Τάφου 405 (18)
Lobc.   Prague, Narodni a Universitni Knihovna, Radnice VI Fa 1 (Lobcovicianus) (34)
Lond.   London, British Library, Royal MS 16 C. XXV (20)
Matr.   Matritensis 4573 (olim N 36) (21)
Matr.^{fr} Matritensis 4573 (olim N 36), fragmenta a manu recentiore addita (21)
Mon.   Monacensis 490 (26)
Neap.   Neapolitanus 340 (28)
Neapol.   Neapolitanus 233 (27)

Ott.	Vaticanus Ottobonianus 177 (41)
Ox.	Oxoniensis Corpus Christi College 96 (30)
Pal.	Vaticanus Palatinus 129 (Heidelberg) (42)
Par.	Parisinus 1810 (33)
Ricc.	Florentinus Riccardianus 66 (17)
Sc.	Scorialensis y,1,13 (6)
Vat.	Vaticanus 2196 (40)
Vind.	Vindobonensis Phil. Gr. 89 (50)
Vindob.	Vindobonensis Phil. Gr. 233 (52)
Voss.	Vossianus Gr. Q 54 (19)

STEMMA OF THE A-FAMILY (contamination not indicated)

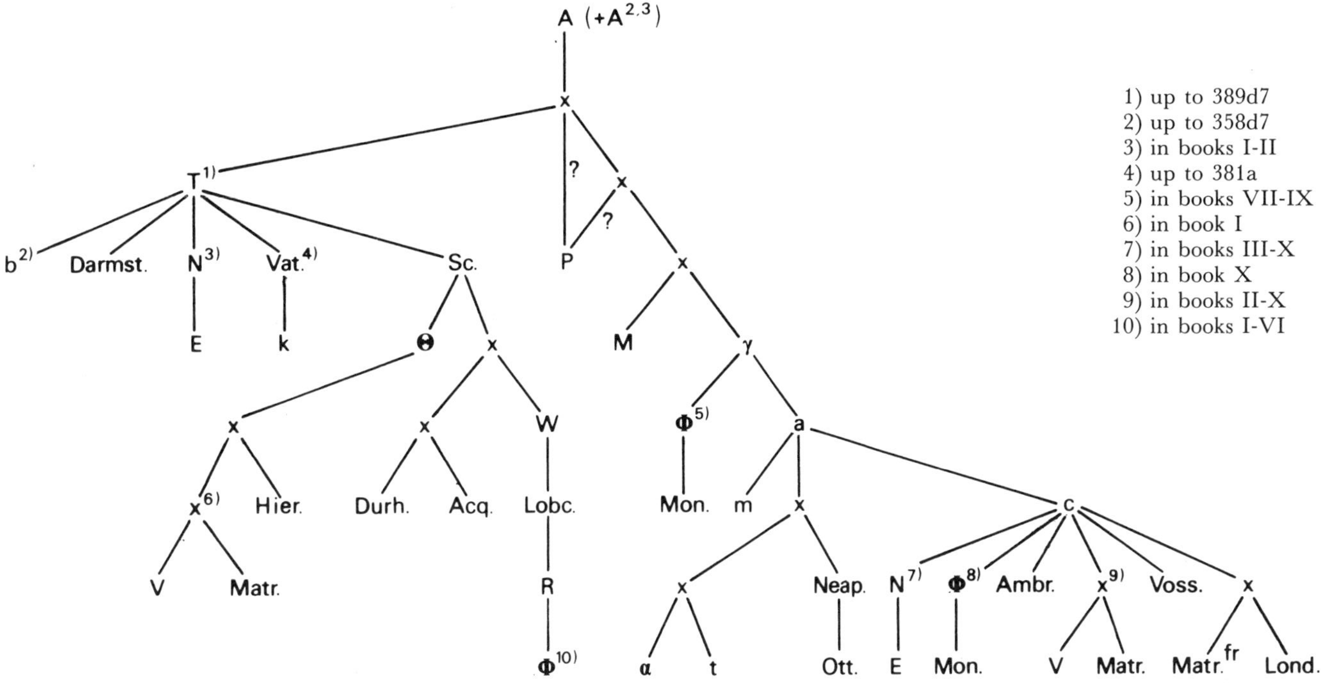

1) up to 389d7
2) up to 358d7
3) in books I-II
4) up to 381a
5) in books VII-IX
6) in book I
7) in books III-X
8) in book X
9) in books II-X
10) in books I-VI

STEMMA OF THE D-FAMILY (contamination not indicated)

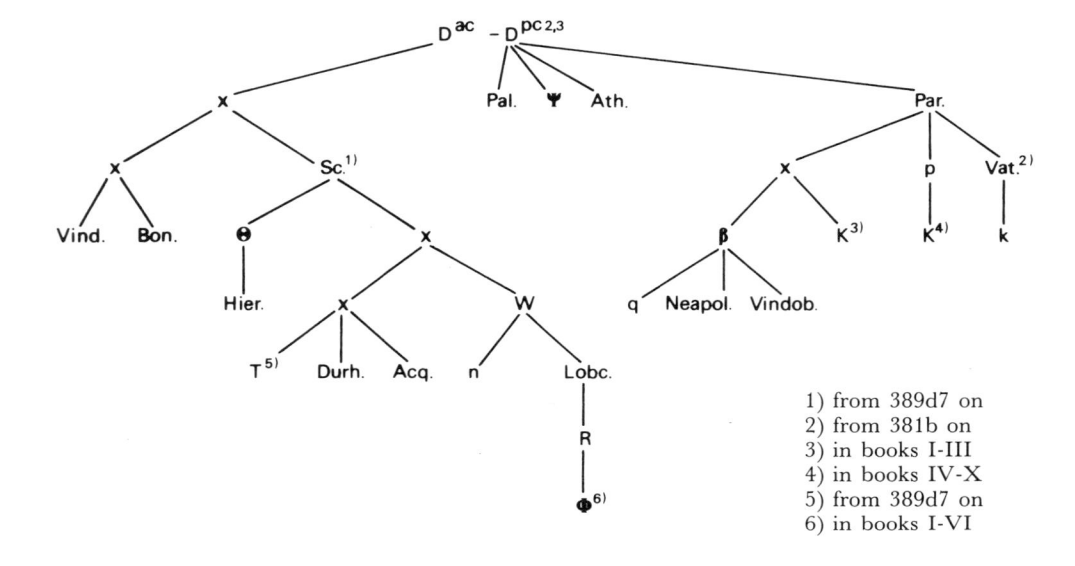

$D^{ac} - D^{pc\,2,3}$ — Pal. Ψ Ath. — Par.

Vind. Bon. — Sc.[1] — p Vat.[2]

Θ — β — K[3] — K[4] — k

Hier. — q Neapol. Vindob.

T[5] Durh. Acq. n W

Lobc.

R

Φ[6]

1) from 389d7 on
2) from 381b on
3) in books I-III
4) in books IV-X
5) from 389d7 on
6) in books I-VI

STEMMA OF THE F-FAMILY
(contamination not indicated)

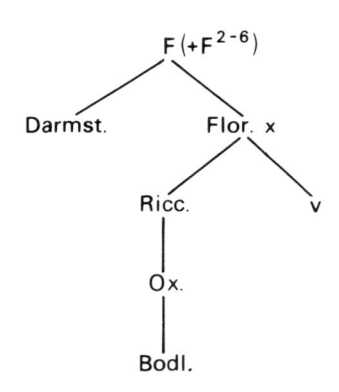

$F(+F^{2-6})$

Darmst. — Flor. x

Ricc. — v

Ox.

Bodl.

INTRODUCTION

METHOD OF RESEARCH

In 1978, Dr S. R. Slings, Lecturer of Greek at the Amsterdam Free University, inaugurated the project "Text Edition of Plato's eighth Tetralogy", a project executed under the aegis of the Netherlands Organization for the Advancement of Pure Research (Z. W. O.). The aim of this project is to prepare a new edition of Plato's eighth tetralogy, which contains the dialogues *Clitophon*, *Republic*, *Timaeus* and *Critias*.

In order to give the new edition of the eighth tetralogy as reliable a character as possible, it was decided that the text would be based on an exhaustive evaluation of the tradition. Some preparatory work was done by two assistants, Mrs. J. Raap and Mrs. B. A. Blokhuis, in the years 1978-1982. In 1981, Dr Slings published his dissertation, *A Commentary on the Platonic Clitophon*, in which he also discusses the tradition of the *Clitophon* and offers a new text, based on the examination of almost all extant MSS. In 1982, two Junior Fellows were appointed for a period of four years, one for the study of the *Republic*, the other for the study of the *Timaeus* and *Critias*; *Ti.* and *Criti.* were assigned to Mr. G. Jonkers, *R.* to myself.

The aim of the present study is to give a detailed exposition of the sources we have at our disposal for the constitution of the text of the *Republic*. These sources comprise the Greek medieval MSS, the papyri, the translations made before *ca.* 1500 A. D., the sixteenth-century editions, and the indirect tradition; I propose to investigate the mutual relationship of these sources and to assess their value for the constitution of the text.

It is not my purpose to give a full account of the history of the text of the *Republic*, let alone of the Platonic corpus as a whole; further, I do not claim to make any systematic contribution to the science of codicology, although I do pay attention to the distinguishing of later correcting hands, esp. in the primary MSS. Finally, I do not intend to go into much detail about the constitution of the text: this is the task of Dr Slings.

In the first part of this study, *Status Quaestionis*, I give a survey of previous work that has been done on the text of the *Republic*. I discuss the major editions, starting with Bekker's, and those studies which, directly or indirectly, concern the text of the *Republic*; with regard to the editions, I do not intend to give an evaluation of the text printed by the various editors, but only to discuss the use they make of the tradition.

Moreover, I give a brief survey of the different opinions on the history of the text of Plato, and on the value which is to be attached to our tradition.

Part II deals with the Greek direct tradition. In the first chapter I list and describe all extant MSS which contain (parts of) the *Republic*. I have taken my information about the extant MSS from the well-known lists of Platonic MSS composed by Post, Wilson and Brumbaugh-Wells. None of these is complete[1], but together they list 51 MSS. To these I have added **Vindob.**, which contains some excerpts of the *Republic*. Dr Paul Moore, of the Greek Index Project of the Pontifical Institute of Mediaeval Studies, Toronto, has kindly checked his systematic index of all published catalogues for the MSS of the *Republic*: he has found two MSS which are not recorded in the lists mentioned above, nor noticed by me, namely **Hier.** and **Lond.**, both of which contain various excerpts from the *Republic* (and of some other dialogues as well).

As a matter of fact, I think it more than likely that there are still some more MSS containing (parts of) the *Republic* (and, for that matter, of other dialogues as well) which have hitherto remained unnoticed because they have not been catalogued properly. Further, it is quite possible that there are still a number of MSS, maybe important or even primary witnesses, in the unexplored libraries of Greece and the Near and Middle East.

I have recorded such technical data about the MSS as were available to me from the secondary literature; therefore, there are considerable divergencies in the information about different (groups of) MSS.

In the second chapter I discuss the three primary witnesses, **ADF**. First, I try to establish the relationship of these MSS; further, I make some observations on the character of each MS.

In the third chapter I give an account of the relationship of all extant MSS. In establishing this relationship I rely almost exclusively on the internal evidence which can be gathered from the MSS, that is, I apply the method of stemmatic arrangement, based on *errores coniunctivi* and *separativi*, which is generally accepted among classical scholars nowadays[2]. But I believe that one should not only pay attention to errors,

---

[1] Post does not mention, e.g., **Ath.**; Wilson omits **Sc.** (which he does mention for other dialogues); Brumbaugh-Wells do not record **Matr.**

[2] The first systematic exposition of the stemmatic method is P. Maas' *Textkritik*, which originally appeared in 1927 as part 7 of Gercke-Norden, *Einleitung in die Altertumswissenschaft*, Band I, 3. Auflage; I have consulted the fourth edition of 1959. The most recent work in this field is West's *Textual Criticism and Editorial Technique* (see Bibliography), which is intended to supersede Maas' study. Nevertheless, I think that Maas' sensitive account should not fall into oblivion.

that is, to readings which are certainly wrong. In many cases agreement of a group of MSS in a manifestly correct reading, or in an ingenuous conjectural emendation which cannot simply be dismissed as an error, may be used as evidence for the affinity of these MSS. To give one instance: in some places **Par.** is the principal MS to preserve a true reading (see below, p. 224); the fact that these readings recur in **Vat.pβ(K)** is by no means a less important indication of the dependence of these MSS on **Par.** than the places in which they follow **Par.** in error (for the relationship of the **Par.**-group see pp. 176 ff.). Therefore I sometimes prefer to speak of "significant agreement" rather than "agreement in error".

Only in isolated cases do I make use of codicological evidence such as the dating or provenance of a particular MS. This is not because I underestimate the value of codicology, but because, even in the case of the most important Platonic MSS, hardly anything has been established beyond doubt. For instance, **T**, which is a primary witness in the first seven tetralogies, used to be assigned to the eleventh or twelfth century, until B. L. Fonkič and A. Diller showed that it was written by Ephraim Monachus, who was active as a scribe in the middle of the tenth century; see p. 55 f. Yet this earlier dating does not disturb the conclusions based on the internal evidence of the MSS, namely that **T** derives from **A**. Therefore, I believe that the stemmatic method in itself is sufficient to establish the affiliation of MSS in a satisfactory way; codicology will, in most cases, be able to supply additional evidence and to give a picture of the circumstances under which our MSS were written, but it will only rarely shake the conclusions reached by a stemmatologist. In some isolated cases, I have ventured to express disagreement with current datings of MSS, when these seemed to be untenable on stemmatic grounds.

As to the methods of stemmatology, it has been maintained that the affiliation of MSS can only be established when the transmission is strictly vertical, that is, when there is no contamination[3]. Now the tradition of Plato's works, including the *Republic*, is heavily contaminated.

With regard to the process of contamination I agree with the general account given by Maas 8 f.:

> Die Kontamination brauchen wir uns nicht so entstanden zu denken, daß ein Schreiber zwei Vorlagen vor sich hat und bald den Text der einen, bald

---

For some other theoretical expositions see, e.g., B. M. Metzger, *The Text of the New Testament* (Oxford 1968[2]), 149-185; R. D. Dawe, *The Collation and Investigation of Manuscripts of Aeschylus* (Cambridge 1964), 15-22.

[3] See e.g. Maas 8 f.; 30: "(...) und im Bereich einer Kontamination versagt die strenge Stemmatik"; "Gegen die Kontamination ist kein Kraut gewachsen."

den Text der anderen wiederholt; denn dies ist ein sehr mühseliges Verfahren. Vielmehr ist der Gang wohl meist so: in einer Handschrift, sagen wir F, werden die abweichenden Lesungen der anderen, die nicht deren Vorlage ist, sagen wir A, am Rand oder zwischen den Zeilen notiert. (Maas refers to the stemma on his p. 7-GJB)

In those cases in which corrections and variant readings have been added by a later hand, or by the scribe himself after the text was copied, we are as a rule entitled to assume that the corrections and variant readings come from a MS different from the exemplar. But this is not always the case: some of the corrections and variant readings in **Sc.** were added by the scribe at a time when the text had already been copied; yet at least some of these later additions appear to be borrowed from the exemplar; see p. 156. On the other hand, the corrections and variant readings in β were added by a scribe who did not copy the text itself, but it can be regarded as certain that at least some of the readings added by the corrector were borrowed from the exemplar; see pp. 185 ff. But generally speaking, when dealing with MSS provided at a later stage with corrections and variant readings, it is possible to distinguish between the exemplar from which the text was copied and the source of the corrections and variant readings; often the source of these readings is identifiable. See for instance **N**: in books III-X **N** follows **c** very closely and may well be a direct transcript; after the text had been copied, Bessarion added innumerable corrections and variant readings, at different stages and from different sources: I have been able to identify seven MSS which were consulted by Bessarion; see pp. 144 f. Of course many corrections and variant readings cannot be traced back to an extant source: some of these may go back to a MS now lost, others may be due to conjectural emendation.

The situation is more complicated with MSS deriving from sources provided with variant readings; there were no general rules for the ways in which scribes dealt with variant readings in their exemplaria. Some scribes copied the original reading plus the variant reading; other scribes had the habit of constantly choosing between the reading in the text and the alternative reading. In both cases one gets the general impression that the scribes took some trouble to assess the value of the variant readings they had before them: the scribe of **Lobc.**, for instance, usually copied both the original reading and the variant reading in his exemplar, **W**; in some cases he put the alternative reading in **W** in his text, relegating the reading in the text of **W** into the margin or writing it above the line; see p. 165.

But of course not all scribes handled the variant readings they found in their sources as scrupulously as the scribe of **Lobc.** To mention some instances: the scribe of **k** often wrote the original reading and the variant reading of his exemplar, **Vat.**, in the text, thus betraying that he did not bother to interpret the words he copied; see p. 181. The scribe of **v** even went so far as to misinterpret abbreviations intended to introduce a variant reading (e.g. ἄλλως) as forming part of the variant reading itself; see p. 195.

It is sometimes assumed that worthless readings are *a priori* not likely to have been disseminated through contamination; see for instance West 41. This is untrue. In the *Republic* I have noted many instances of worthless corrections which have been added at the expense of irreproachable readings; to give one instance: at 616c1 **M**^{ac} read τῶν *recte*; this unobjectionable reading is replaced by the worthless ἐκ, which is found in **R**, the source of the corrections in **M**; see p. 122.

On the possibility of making a stemmatic arrangement of contaminated MSS Maas 9 remarks:

> J folgt dann bald der ersten Lesung von F, bald der sekundären. Gehen dann A und F verloren, so werden die Abhängigkeitsverhältnisse von J unklar, weil J dann Sonderfehler von δ (aber nicht alle) wie solche von β (aber nicht alle) zeigen wird. (Again, Maas refers to the stemma on his p. 7-GJB)

I believe that this statement as such is somewhat exaggerated: only in very isolated cases is it likely that a MS has been contaminated to such a degree that it holds a position between its exemplar and the source of the contamination; as a rule a contaminated MS will basically follow its exemplar and exhibit a relatively restricted number of agreements with the source of contamination. To give an instance: α shows traces of contamination from various sources; nevertheless it is beyond doubt that α goes back to **a**, as is shown by the fact that α shares many distinctive readings of **a** and **a**^{pc}; see pp. 129 ff.

But the situation becomes more complicated when several intermediary MSS, all of which have been contaminated, have got lost. To return to α: it has been possible to demonstrate that α ultimately goes back to **A**; for my argumentation I have made use of the circumstance that α shares readings with **a**, **γa**, **Mγa**, **TMγa** and **ATMγa**; among these cases of agreement there are also readings added by later hands in **A**, **γ** and **a**, while it is certain that the sources of **Mγ** and **TMγ** have been contaminated. Now if all the intermediary MSS between α and **A** had got lost, it would have been very difficult indeed to furnish a clear proof of the dependence of α on **A**; see pp. 111-137.

Further, I believe that it is often possible to distinguish between readings which are the result of vertical transmission and those which are due to contamination. To give an instance: in a number of places **Par.**

agrees in a significant reading with **Sc.**; yet although both MSS derive from **D** (**Sc.** from 389d7 on), it is absolutely certain that some of these cases of agreement result from contamination and not from vertical transmission because 1. the cases of agreement occur both before and after 389d7, where **Sc.** changes its original exemplar **T** for **D**, and 2. **Sc.** follows **D**^{ac}, while **Par.** depends on **D** as corrected by **D**^{2} and **D**^{3}. In my opinion, the main difficulty in dealing with a contaminated tradition lies in establishing in what direction the contamination has taken place; often, this problem too can be resolved. To return to **Par.** and **Sc.**: the corrections by **D**^{2}, which recur in **Par.**, but not in **Sc.**, are for the greater part borrowed from **W**, a derivative of **Sc.**: therefore, **Par.** must be younger than **W**, and *a fortiori* younger than **Sc.**; the conclusion is that the contamination has taken place from **Sc.** to **Par.**, not *vice versa*. Of course, it is not possible to apply strict rules in every case: in each particular case we will have to judge according to circumstances[4].

In recent years, many attempts have been made to develop elaborate techniques, often with the help of computers, for unravelling the relations between MSS (for references see Reynolds-Wilson 249). With regard to the tradition of the *Republic* I have found that "nature's own computer, located between the ears of the investigator" (to borrow a phrase from Reynolds-Wilson 213) has been able to resolve most, if not all, problems in a satisfactory manner. This is not intended as an illiberal disparagement of a new field of science, but only to point out that more or less traditional methods do not become altogether worthless once new methods have been invented.

It goes without saying that my remarks on methodology have no claim to universal validity: what I have said applies to my treatment of the tradition of the *Republic*. I am fully aware that the state of affairs is different in the case of other authors (e.g. the tragedians), not to speak of texts in the vernacular languages.

The three primary witnesses have been collated in full by me from microfilm. I have also inspected them *in situ*, in order to remove doubts concerning particular readings and to establish the identity of the various correcting hands which have been at work in each MS.

My stemma of the secondary MSS is based in the first place on a fresh collation of all extant MSS for four sample passages, to wit 327a-333d, 386a-392e, 514a-520e, 614b-621d. These sample passages have been chosen at regular intervals, in order to give as representative a picture as possible. The reason for choosing the beginning of book III instead of

---

[4] West 12 f., 35 ff., makes some methodological remarks about the way in which a contaminated tradition may be dealt with.

book IV, was that the old part of **T** breaks off at 389d7; as it was *a priori* likely that **T** would have numerous progeny, collation of 386a-392e could be expected to show in which way the descendants of **T** behaved after having been bereaved of their original ancestor.

The first of the sample passages was collated twice by Mrs. Blokhuis and Dr Slings, the second once by Mrs. Blokhuis or Dr Slings and once by me; the third and fourth passages were collated twice by me, all from microfilm. I have inspected some secondary MSS *in situ*, mainly in order to distinguish later hands.

For each of the four sample passages I have constructed a separate stemma; subsequently, I have compared the results. As a rule, the results of the four passages coincided exactly. In cases where there were serious discrepancies among the separate stemmas, I have sought to remove the problems by collating further portions of text. In some cases this resulted in the conclusion that a MS had changed its exemplar in the course of the *Republic*; in other cases, the additional evidence supplied by the collation of further parts of text proved sufficient to remove all doubts.

In the second place, I have worked through Schneider's apparatus for the whole of the *Republic*; Schneider records readings of some 25 MSS, which represent most, if not all, families and sub-families of the MSS of the *Republic*. As a rule, the readings recorded by Schneider confirmed the stemma based upon the sample passages. In cases where I met serious difficulties, I have checked the MSS concerned on microfilm; usually, the difficulties proved to be the result of a wrong report of the MSS; in some cases I have been able to correct my stemma.

Finally, I have compared my results with the studies by Schanz, Jordan, and others, on the affiliation of Platonic MSS. I have found that their conclusions usually agree with mine; where they disagree, this has been due to errors in the report of MSS, to incomplete knowledge of all MSS, or to misinterpretation of the evidence. In the first place, Schanz *c.s.* do not take the trouble to unravel the complicated relations of contaminated MSS; further, they tend to regard the tradition of the Platonic corpus as a whole, that is, they tend to assume that a conclusion which is valid for, say, the *Gorgias*, must be valid for the *Republic* as well.

I believe that in this way I have met the fundamental objections which could be raised against the use of sample passages instead of collating all MSS for the whole of the *Republic* (for a justification of the use of sample passages see also Maas 18 f.). It may be possible that a few interesting readings escape our attention (although I do not think this very likely, because most groups of MSS, as has already been pointed out, are represented in Schneider's apparatus), but I deem it virtually impossible that my stemma would have to undergo serious modifications as the result of a full collation of all MSS.

Chapter four is devoted to those secondary MSS which, though deriving demonstrably from one of the primary witnesses, contain some readings which may go back to a lost ancient source, or which are interesting in other respects.

Chapter five is concerned with the sixteenth-century editions (Aldine, first and second Basle edition, Stephanus' edition) and Cornarius' *Eclogae*.

Finally, chapter six deals with the few papyrus fragments of the *Republic* which have come to light up to the present day.

Part three is devoted to the translations of the *Republic* made before *ca.* 1500.

In chapter seven I discuss the fifteenth-century Latin translations. Of the four translations made in that century, only Ficino's has been edited (*editio princeps* Florence 1484). Therefore, I have studied the others (Uberto Decembrio/Chrysoloras, Pier Candido Decembrio, Antonio Cassarino) in one MS only, on microfilm; this means that the text I have consulted is not founded on a critical basis. The Greek sources of the four translations are in all cases identifiable; Ficino's is the only one which contains some interesting readings, but they are almost certainly conjectural. The value of these translations for the constitution of the text is therefore very restricted.

The eighth chapter deals with the other translations, of which hardly anything is extant. In the first place, there is a fragment of a Coptic translation, found in the Nag Hammadi papyri. Because this translation is, in the words of the editor, J. Brashler, "a disastrous failure", it has no value for the text. Finally, I briefly mention those translations which are known to have existed, but which are no longer extant: Arabic, Persian and Hebrew.

Part IV is concerned with the indirect tradition. My primary aim in studying quotations, references etc. of the *Republic* was to collect readings in ancient authors which might be relevant to the text. I have not undertaken a full-scale study of the indirect tradition as such, because, as I have already stated at the beginning of this introduction (p. XIX), I do not propose to deal with the history of the text; moreover, A. Carlini has given a splendid general survey of the tradition of the Platonic corpus in antiquity in his authoritative study on the text of the *Phaedo*.

The collecting of quotations etc. of the *Republic* has not been exclusively my work; a start was made by Mrs. Raap; this work was continued by her successor, Mrs. Blokhuis; my completion of the work would not have been possible without the great help of Dr Slings and Mr. Jonkers.

In order to assess the value of the indirect tradition for the constitution of the text, I have made an apparatus criticus of the indirect tradition which is as complete as possible; considerations of space prevent me from publishing this collation[5]. Instead, I have thought it more helpful to add an *index testimoniorum*, which has a double purpose: in the first place, it enables the reader interested in textual matters to look up readings in a particular author for himself; in the second place, an *index testimoniorum* will also be very useful to scholars interested in other subjects related to the *Republic*, such as the history of Platonism.

The purpose of this *index* being twofold, I have tried to make it as complete as possible, but I do not flatter myself for a moment that I have been successful in recording each and every reference to the *Republic*. I think that the index of direct quotations is fairly complete, but I feel quite sure that I have missed many references, imitations etc. In the first place, many texts, especially of Byzantine authors, have not yet been properly edited; in the second place, many editions lack reliable indexes. There are great discrepancies among the indexes of different authors; some give too little (e.g. Philostratus), some give too much (e.g. Synesius, Choricius Gazaeus), some have no index at all (e.g. some volumes of *Sources Chrétiennes*). Moreover, it is quite possible that some authors, even important ones, have been overlooked by me: this will be especially true of Byzantine authors, some of whom can only be consulted in Migne.

Finally, I must mention that I have not been able to find a sound criterium for drawing a chronological limit: I have thought it fitting to end with Bessarion's *In Calumniatorem Platonis*, of which the original Greek version was finished in 1458, but I have not included references in all works written before 1458; for instance, I have omitted Plethon's *Comparatio Platonis et Aristotelis*, because the only edition of this work, the *editio princeps* of 1523, is hardly accessible. I have not included references in medieval Latin authors, partly because they will be few and far between, partly because they cannot be regarded as the result of independent study of Plato's text.

In collecting the references to the *Republic* I have usually relied on the indexes composed by the editors. In many cases I have gone beyond these indexes, but I have thought it superfluous to specify all authors with whom this has been the case, with the exception of Proclus' commentary, which I have studied in full myself. In all cases I have checked the references given in the indexes.

An *index locorum potiorum* and a bibliography complete the book.

---

[5] Those who wish to obtain a copy of my collation of the indirect tradition are requested to apply to Vrije Universiteit, Faculteit der Letteren, Vakgroep Grieks, Postbus 7161, 1007 MC Amsterdam.

PART ONE

STATUS QUAESTIONIS

Modern textual criticism of Plato's writings, including the *Republic*, begins with the monumental edition by Immanuel Bekker, which appeared in 1816-1818, supplemented by the *Commentaria Critica* in two volumes, published in 1823. Before his edition, editors relied almost exclusively on previous editions, especially the edition by Stephanus, published in 1578, which provided the basis for the so-called vulgate of Plato[1].

The Bipontine editors (1781-1787) published a collation of **K** for the text of *Smp.*, *Min.*, *R.*, and *Deff.*[2]. Ast, too, in his second edition of the *Republic* (1814), published readings from **K**; besides, he used collations of **D** for the earlier books of the *Republic*, made by Nürnberger[3], and of **Mon.**, which contains book VII and the beginning of book X, made by Krabinger. Further, he mentions many *testimonia*, of which he also records variant readings.

Bekker, however, was the first to make the collation of a considerable number of MSS the basis of his text. For the *Republic*, he collated 12 MSS: **A, Θ, E, D, Φ, Par., K, q, t, v, m, R**; the accuracy of these collations leaves much to be desired. Bekker does not explicitly expound his views on the MSS, but from the text he prints one can infer that he assigns the greatest authority to the oldest MS, **A**; however, he freely adopts readings from other MSS, esp. **D, Par., q** and **v**.

Ast's third edition of 1822 is not based on new MS evidence; therefore, I do not discuss it.

Next comes the edition by G. Stallbaum (1825). For the *Republic* he uses collations of the Florentine MSS **a, b, c, n, x, α, β, γ**, made for him by De Furia; like Bekker, De Furia is a rather careless collator; a specific drawback of his collations is that he does not pay any attention to the occurrence of later hands in a MS: readings by the first hand and by later hands are quoted indiscriminately. Further, Stallbaum mentions **Darmst.**, collations of which had been made by Creuzer[4].

In his 1825 edition, Stallbaum does not explain how he assesses the MSS, but in the 1829 edition of a number of dialogues, *in usum scholarum*, he states the following (vol. III, 1, p. LXXIX):

> Optimus omnium est Par. A. Non multum huic bonitate cedit Vat.Θ. Sequuntur deinde Π(= **D**)Ξ(= **E**)ΦD(= **Par.**)K., qui sunt mediocres. Sed

---

[1] For the vulgate of Plato, see below, p. 251.
[2] The collation of **K** can be found in vol. VII, 352-424; IX, 432-450, 482 f.
[3] Ast wrongly calls **D** "Ven. 150", as is pointed out by Immisch 55, n. 1, and Post 80. See Ast[2], *praefatio* IV.
[4] See Stallbaum, *Platonis Opera* XI, iv; XII, iii-x.

mediocribus hisce multis partibus longe sunt praestantiores Monacensis (= q) et Flor.β, qui libri, etsi passim habent lectiones deteriores, tamen plurimis locis soli veram scripturam conservarunt. Quocirca eorum auctoritati saepenumero obsequendum fuit.

He further remarks that β and q are very closely related; the same, according to Stallbaum, goes for v and α. About the other MSS he remarks: "(..) nullus est quin aliquid boni praebuerit."

In the 1829 edition Stallbaum also makes use of the indirect tradition, both in his apparatus and in his commentary.

The next edition is the most complete critical edition of the *Republic* which has ever been published: Schneider's three-volume *Platonis Civitas* (1830-1833). In his apparatus criticus, Schneider gives the collations of Bekker and De Furia, and adds his own collations of **VFVind.Lobc.**, which are very accurate[5]; further, he has made a fresh collation of **q**. In addition, he has recollated **Mon.** and large sections of **Φ**, and investigated **W**, which he considers to be very closely related to **Lobc.** (which is correct). He also mentions **Darmst.**, already referred to above, and **Pal.**, which contains among other Platonic excerpts R. 359c7-360b2; he also collated the fragments from books VIII-X in **P**. Further, he gives a collation of the great sixteenth-century editions: the Aldine, the two Basle editions and Stephanus' edition. His account of the indirect tradition is fuller and more systematic than Stallbaum's and Ast's.

Like Bekker and Stallbaum, Schneider regards **A** as the best MS (I xxviii: "optimus ille Regius A"); he recognizes the excellence of **D** (e.g. in his notes ad 534a4 and 567e3); occasionally, he relies on the authority of **F** (III 311, referring to his note ad 477b8, "unus non interpolatus"); among other MSS he assigns some value to β and q; about β he says (III 309): "cum Mon. B (= q) secundum corruptos codices emendatus"; nevertheless, referring to 454d1-2 he remarks that β "cum Mon. B (= q) verum tenuit". Occasionally, Schneider has recourse to readings found in other MSS. As a rule, Schneider hesitates to accept readings from secondary MSS like β and q; see for instance 341d10-11: Schneider approves of the addition in β, which recurs in q, but he prints the words between brackets because "codicis Monacensis minime ea indoles est, ut magis integram et genuinam recensionem, quam reliqui omnes, repraesentare videatur (...)".

Schneider makes many sharp observations concerning the affiliation of the MSS: ad 353a1 he notes that **Fxv** are "ex eodem fonte ducti"; he recognizes that **Par. Kqβ** form a group which derives from **D** (III 309:

---

[5] Schneider himself collated **F** for 327a-379b; the remainder of the *Republic* was collated for him by his pupil Endlicher; 371b-445e was recollated by Schneider.

"Mon. B (= q) cum Par. D(= **Par.**)KFlor. U(= β) ex Ven. C (= **D**) ductus"; cf. his note ad 540c4); he remarks that "Mon. C (= **Mon.**) cum Vind. B (= **Φ**) et Vat. H (= **m**) ex eodem fonte ductus" (III 310; cf. II xxxvii)[6]. Concerning **F** he makes the famous statement (III 311): "Veterem vulgatam repraesentat et fere cum Stobaeo, Eusebio etc. consentit." This hypothesis was to be developed at length by Burnet, who was the first editor to perceive the great value of **F** adequately (cf. pp. 12 f.).

Schneider is very reluctant to admit conjectures in his text; thus he sometimes retains readings which are clearly indefensible, e.g. 352e9 ἄν—φαμέν. Schneider's own conjectures, too, are to be found in his apparatus, not in his text; thus at 547b4-5, where the MSS give τὸ δ' αὖ τό, Schneider conjectures τὼ δ' αὖ τό, a correction which has met with general approval, but he prints τὸ δ' αὖ τό in his text.

A serious drawback of Schneider's edition is that he has introduced new sigla for nearly all MSS; he does not indicate his reasons for doing so. Despite this shortcoming, however, Schneider's edition must be judged excellent and indispensable for critical work on the text of the *Republic*.

Until the edition by Jowett and Campbell (1894), editors after Schneider rely on the editions of Bekker, Stallbaum and Schneider for their information about the MSS; the only MS which is recollated is **A**: Dübner made a new collation for Schneider's Didot edition, which appeared in 1846; Baiter consulted **A** for the 1847 Zürich edition; Hermann inspected **A** for the 1852 Teubner edition[7]. The Zürich edition of the complete Plato appeared in 1839; in this edition the editors do not reveal their views on the MSS; elsewhere, Orelli states that he relies more exclusively than Schneider had done on the authority of **A**; concerning "interpolated" MSS he remarks[8]:

> Interpolatorum autem codicum agmen ducunt Florentinus, quem Stallbaumius littera β, Schneiderus littera U signavit, et Monacensis, a Bekkero q, a Schneidero B appellatus. Quorum auctor id secutus est, ut abstrusiores Platonis sententias verbis clarioribus faciliores reddere conaretur, qua in re ingenii et doctrinae et sermonis elegentiae laus ei certe denegari non potest, ut mirandum non sit, viros vel doctissimos interdum ab eo decipi se passos esse.

---

[6] It should be realized that the method of stemmatic arrangement of MSS, which is usually associated with Lachmann, came into existence gradually. The first editor who presented what we call a stemma, is F. Ritschl, in his edition of Thomas Magister's *Ecloga Vocum Atticarum* (Halle 1832), xxx. See S. Timpanaro, *La genesi del metodo del Lachmann* (Padua 1981³). Schneider also uses the word *stemma*; see e.g. his note ad 540c4.

[7] See Schneider's preface to the Didot edition, p. III; Baiter's preface to the 1847 Zürich edition, viii ff.; Hermann's preface to vol. IV of the 1852 Teubner edition.

[8] I quote Orelli from Baiter's preface to the 1847 Zürich edition, p. vii f.

Thus Schneider's reluctance to adopt readings from "interpolated" MSS results in the conviction of Orelli (and others) that good readings in these MSS are nothing but conjectures, which in the best case are "not inept", but do not have any claim to high authority. Nevertheless, the Zürich editors do admit readings from "interpolated" MSS in some places.

The tendency to recognize **A** as the main or even sole authority for the text of the *Republic* becomes even stronger in the subsequent editions. Hermann, in his preface to the fourth volume of his Teubner edition of the complete Plato (1852), writes: "in hoc volumine ad eos (sc. dialogos–GJB) transgredimur, quorum recensio prae ceteris libris Parisino (= **A**) niti debet." He mentions no other MS authority; he bases his text upon Schneider's Didot edition and especially upon Baiter's 1847 Zürich edition; the only critical notes he gives are the places in which he departs from Baiter's edition.

The *ratio edendi* is now to start from **A**, and to emend the text with the help of other MSS, but preferably by means of conjectural emendation, in cases where the reading of **A** is obviously wrong. The most vigorous defence of the method of using **A** as the sole authority and emending its errors by conjecture is given by Cobet in his article *De Platonis codice Parisino A* (see Bibliography). After having given a full collation of **A** for the *Critias* he states (195) that MSS other than **A** give us "NIHIL, PRORSUS NIHIL (praeter levissimas quasdam correctiunculas, quas quilibet nostrum inter legendum nullo negotio statim reperisset) (...) quod ad Platonis scripturam aut recte constituendam, aut emendandam quidquam faciat, excepto uno lacunae supplemento pag. 112. A." Whence this lacuna was filled in these "utterly worthless" MSS, is a question that Cobet does not raise. On p. 198 he says: "Multum enim abest ut Parisinus A. mendis erroribusque careat"; subsequently, he shows (pp. 198-208) how successful conjectural emendation can be for the constitution of the text of the *Critias*. Nevertheless, it must be admitted that Cobet pays some attention to the indirect tradition.

In the eighteen-seventies Lachmannianism made its entrance in the field of Platonic textual criticism. The most important work on this subject was done by M. Schanz, whose work was supplemented and often corrected by the studies of A. Jordan. Schanz' aim in establishing the relationship of the MSS of Plato was to reduce to an absolute minimum the number of MSS which deserve consideration for the constitution of the text. His conclusions about the affiliation of MSS are often correct, but he is too rash in his elimination of apographa: according to Schanz, a MS that is interpolated is *qualitate qua* worthless; he does not consider for a moment the possibility that a MS may have been interpolated from an important source which is now lost[9]. Thus Schanz, *Republik* 178, concludes that **Par. Kq** should be eliminated because they derive from **D**; about the many interesting and correct readings in these MSS, especially in **q**, he does not say a word. Further, Schanz (like others) tends to assume that conclusions based upon one dialogue are valid for all the works contained in a particular MS; in reality, there are many instances of MSS which change their exemplar in different dialogues, some of them even within a dialogue.

With regard to the MSS of the *Republic* his conclusion is (*Republik* 181): "Für die Kritik der platonischen Republik kommen von den 12 von Bekker verglichenen Handschriften nur der Parisinus A und der Venetus Π (=**D**) in Betracht." Schanz does not include either Stallbaum's or Schneider's MSS in his discussion, but in other publications he shows (or believes he shows) that all these MSS derive from one of Bekker's MSS (Schanz regards **F** as the exemplar of **x** (*Platocodex* 105-107), which he considers to be derived from **a** (*Platocodex* 80)). Therefore, there are two families, the first family represented exclusively by **A**, and the second by **D** alone. Schanz' conclusions about the MSS of the *Republic* are accepted by Jordan, *Republik* 474.

It is to be regretted that Schanz did not produce a text of the *Republic*, from which we could have seen in how far he relied on the authority of **A** and **D** alone, supplemented by conjectures and readings from "worthless" MSS[10].

The years at the turn of the century show a great editorial activity in England: within eleven years, five critical editions of the *Republic* were produced by English scholars: one by Jowett and Campbell (1894), two by James Adam (1897 and 1902) and two by John Burnet (1902 and 1905).

The great three-volume edition by Jowett and Campbell marks the beginning of a new period in the textual criticism of the *Republic*. In the second Essay in vol. II, pp. 67-131, Campbell explains his views on the tradition.

Unlike the Zürich editors and Hermann, Campbell does not accept **A** as the only MS authority. Following Schanz he recognizes **D** as an independent witness besides **A**[11]; he even adds a third primary witness,

---

[9] For Schanz' attitude towards interpolated MSS see his remark *Republik* 180: "(...) und da v in noch höherem Grade als t von Interpolationen *heimgesucht* wird" (my italics).

[10] Wilamowitz 336 suggests that Schanz did not complete his edition "weil er sich nicht entschließen konnte, seinen Grundfehler offen einzugestehen."

[11] Campbell collated **A** himself; **D** and **E** were collated for him by Castellani; Rostagno collated **M** for him.

M, which he considers to be closely related to **A**, but not dependent on it; he goes to great lengths to illustrate this thesis (73-86). I will not discuss his argumentation here, because I shall speak in detail about **M** in the chapter on the **A**-family (see pp. 111-118); for the moment I will note that Campbell's arguments are not convincing and that **M** does derive from **A**.

A second point on which Campbell's opinions on the tradition differ from those of the Zürich editors and Hermann, Cobet, Schanz and others, is that he assigns some value to secondary MSS; on p. 91 he says: "(...) no text of the Republic can be constituted aright without placing some reliance on late MSS." To us, this sounds like a truism, but one should bear in mind that Campbell wrote these words only some twenty years after the havoc created by Schanz and Cobet among the *recentiores*, and that, therefore, it took some intellectual independence to arrive at this conclusion.

Scholars before Campbell were inclined to attribute good or plausible readings in apographa to Byzantine or Renaissance conjectural activity (see, e.g., Orelli's judgement on β and **q**, quoted above, p. 5); Campbell, on the contrary, believes that such readings have come into late MSS through contamination; p. 92: "MS. conjecture is generally traceable to some mis-writing having introduced obscurity which the scribe has instinctively sought to remove. This process (...) except in the removal of the simplest clerical errors, can seldom be credited with the restoration of an original text." On pp. 100 f. he even says: "On the one hand such MSS. (i.e. MSS which contain original readings taken from MSS now lost–GJB) must have been few and far between, but on the other hand the feebleness of conjecture at best, and especially in the infancy of criticism, makes it antecedently improbable that Rhosus or Cardinal Bessarion, for example, should have hit, by mere intuition, on readings which had been lost for sixteen centuries." It is remarkable that Campbell should not have thought of the possibility of contamination with regard to the good readings in **M**, instead of assuming that **M**, though very closely related to **A**, is an independent witness.

Among the apographa which contain good or plausible readings Campbell particularizes **R** (as a member of the group **Lobc.ΘV**) (p. 90 f.); **Par.** and **K** (p. 91 f.); **E** (p. 92-94); **x** (p. 94) and β/**q** (p. 94-96).

Campbell's treatment of the affiliation of the MSS is very defective; most of his errors in this field could have been prevented if he had taken the trouble to consult Wohlrab's splendid article (see Bibliography), which gives a lucid survey of the results of the work done up to 1887[12].

---

[12] In fact, Campbell, Adam and Burnet, like many 20th-century scholars, show some

I mention some instances of Campbell's nonchalance on this subject.

On p. 67, n. 4, Campbell states that in *R.* **W** derives from **Lobc.**; Schanz, *Platocodex* 62, 100, quoted by Wohlrab 714, proves that it is the other way round. It has already been noted above that Campbell attaches some importance to **x**; Schanz, *Platocodex* 105 f., quoted by Wohlrab 673, shows that **x** derives from **F**, so that Campbell would have done better to refer to **F** instead of **x**.

On p. 96, Campbell gives the following classification of the MSS:
1. **A b α γ**
2. (1) **D Par. q β K** (2) **R Φ Θ** (3) **V Vind. F**
3. **M E m a c x t v**

This classification is absolutely worthless, for the following reasons:

1) Campbell classifies **α** and **γ** in the first family, whereas on p. 73 he himself says that **acγ** belong to the sub-family **MEtv**; as to **α**, Schanz, *Platocodex* 79-81, quoted by Wohlrab 674, proves that **α** goes back to **a**.

2) Campbell lumps together in one group (the third sub-family of his second family) the three Vienna MSS **VVind.F**, which have absolutely nothing in common, except that they are in the same library. Schanz, *Platocodex* 102, n. 3, and Jordan, *Republik* 474, quoted by Wohlrab 719, state that **Vind.** goes back to **D**, so that **Vind.** belongs to the first sub-family of Campbell's second family. Jordan, *Republik* 475, states that **V** belongs to the group **ΘΦR** (which, in reality, is only the case in book I); thus Campbell should have included **V** in the second sub-family of his second family. It has already been noted that **x** derives from **F**: Campbell should therefore have included **F** in his third family (which in itself would be wrong, because **F** is a primary witness).

3) the second sub-family of Campbell's second family derives from **D** from 389d7 onward, as is shown by Schanz, *Platocodex* 78 f., 102, *Republik* 174, quoted by Wohlrab 682. Campbell should therefore have made **D** the head of his second family, with his first two sub-families both deriving from **D**.

4) Campbell does not indicate the relationship between the MSS within his families, which he could have found too in Wohlrab.

Another deficiency in Campbell's treatment of the text is that in the Essay on the text he does not say a word about the indirect tradition. Accordingly, in his apparatus criticus he hardly ever reports a reading

---

disregard, if not disdain, for the work done by Schanz, Jordan and others who study the affiliation of MSS. Adam, *Burnet* 218, even speaks of the "modern *cacoethes affiliandi*". Burnet, *Neglected MS* 98, praises Adam's "generally prudent and healthy scepticism as to theories of manuscript affiliation". The cause of this disregard, I think, is that many stemmatologists, and especially Schanz, completely eliminated those MSS which could be shown to derive from another extant MS, without reckoning with the possibility that these MSS might contain useful readings, whether through contamination or conjecture.

found in an author who quotes Plato, not even in places where a true reading found in a secondary MS is supported by the indirect tradition[13]. In the commentary Jowett-Campbell sometimes do refer to the indirect tradition.

The second part of Campbell's Essay is devoted to *Textual Errors and Emendations* (97-131), in which he makes many useful observations. The upshot of this discussion is that one should be very reluctant to adopt conjectures in preference to the tradition. Campbell is very extreme in his scepticism concerning conjectures; this attitude can be explained as a reaction to the practice of his predecessors, who freely adopted conjectures in their texts (cf. above, pp. 6 f.).

On balance, despite his obvious shortcomings, Campbell should be credited with having turned from the all-too-easy methods of textual criticism practised by his predecessors to a more prudent *ratio edendi*.

Adam first produced a text of the *Republic* in 1897, which was followed by his great edition with commentary in 1902. In the latter work, he alludes to an introductory volume, in which he proposes to "deal *inter alia* with the MSS." (p. x); however, he did not fulfil this promise, so that for his views on the tradition we have to resort to the preface to the 1897 edition, to the note on the text in the 1902 edition (xiii-xvi) and to his review of Burnet's 1902 edition.

In general, Adam's opinions on the tradition of the *Republic* are the same as those of Campbell. Adam recognizes two primary witnesses, **A** and **D**[14], as Schanz had done; he does not accept the primary status of **M**, vindicated by Campbell. He regards **A** as the primary authority and follows **A** wherever possible, but has recourse to **D** when **A** is wrong. In cases where neither **A** nor **D** give a satisfactory reading, he considers "in the first instance, the reading of all the other available MSS.; secondly, the evidence of ancient writers who quote or paraphrase parts of the *Republic*, and, thirdly, emendations" (1902 edition, xiii)[15].

As to the secondary MSS Adam holds the same opinion as Campbell; 1897 edition, ix: "Some of them (= good readings in apographa–GJB) are no doubt due to conjecture, but it would be rash to affirm that they

---

[13] See, e.g., 454d1, where τὸ—τείνον τὰ is read by β^{pc} and Galen, which Campbell could have read in Schneider's apparatus.

[14] Adam collated **A** himself; for **D**, **M** and **E** he consulted the collations which had been made for Campbell (see note 11 to this chapter).

[15] This method of using the evidence is criticised, rightly in my opinion, by Burnet, *Platonica I* 200: "this is a procedure which could only pass muster if our aim were to produce a readable rather than an authentic text."

are all arrived at in this way." Adam restricts himself as far as possible to **E** and **q**, "partly because I have found by experience that they come to the rescue oftenest when A and Π (= **D**) break down, and partly because they are among the few MSS. of the *Republic*, besides A and Π (= **D**), of which we possess thoroughly trustworthy collations." (1902 edition, xiii-xiv). If the four MSS **ADEq** fail to provide a satisfactory reading, Adam has recourse to **v**. Thus, like Campbell, Adam does not pay much attention to the work done by Schanz: he could have known that **v** derives from **x**, which in its turn derives from **F**, and that **q** derives from β (for **Fxv**, see above, p. 9; for **q** see Schanz, *Platocodex* 85, 103, quoted by Wohlrab 712). There are, however, cases where Adam adopts readings from other apographa, e.g. 354b3 ἐγώ μοι with ΘR against ἐγῶιμαι **AE** and ἐγὼ οἶμαι **Dq**; sometimes, he prints a reading found in an apographon without reporting it, e.g. 487c1 φέρωσιν **VMatr.**: φέρουσιν **rell**.

Adam proclaims to use the evidence of the indirect tradition only when all MSS are wrong (cf. above); the result is that, like Campbell, he hardly ever mentions readings taken from the indirect tradition in his critical notes or commentary.

Adam shows the same reluctance as Campbell as regards the adoption of conjectures in the text. He admits emendations only when all MSS and the other evidence available are unsatisfactory. In his 1902 edition, he shows himself even more conservative than in the 1897 edition.

Adam is very sceptical about the possibility of establishing the affiliation of all extant MSS; he argues (1897 edition, viii-ix) that such an affiliation will only be possible on the fulfilment of three conditions: "we must, in the first place, possess a thoroughly full and trustworthy collation of all the MSS. (...) The second requisite is a careful comparison of each of the later MSS with A and Π (= **D**)" (Adam follows Schanz in assuming that the MSS of the *Republic* are divided into two families); in the third place, the dependence of a MS on **A** or **D** will not be adequately proved "until every case of divergence between the copy and its supposed original has been explained by a theory which not only may, but must, be true."

As regards the treatment of the text and the evaluation of the tradition, Adam's editions are very close to the edition by Jowett and Campbell.

Burnet produced a separate edition of the *Republic* in 1902, which was superseded by vol. IV of *Platonis Opera*, published in 1905, containing the complete eighth tetralogy. Burnet expounds his views on the text in his prefaces and in a series of articles in CR 16 (1902)—19 (1905).

Burnet follows Campbell's classification of the MSS and accordingly recognizes **ADM** as primary witnesses[16]. The most important innovation in his edition is that he adds a fourth primary witness, **F**, which had been used by Schneider in his edition, and which was thought to derive from **a** by Schanz (see above p. 7). Burner argues that **F** "is derived, mediately or immediately, from an archetype of greater antiquity than any extant Platonic MS." and "that its archetype was independent of that of ADM." (*Neglected MS* 99). In the preface to his editions he quotes with approval Schneider's comment (already quoted above, p. 5) "Veterem vulgatam repraesentat et fere cum Stobaeo, Eusebio etc. consentit."

In the enthusiasm of his new and indeed extremely important discovery, however, Burnet makes a mistake in classifying **ADM** together against **F** (*l.c.*). He argues convincingly that **F** derives independently from a majuscule exemplar because it brims with errors which can only be explained as the result of misreading majuscule script. Yet in his list of such readings, he himself mentions four places where **D** agrees with **F** in readings caused by misreading majuscule script, which points to a common uncial source of **D** and **F**. What is more, on p. 99 f. Burnet illustrates that **F** often agrees with the indirect tradition against **ADM**, both in correct and wrong readings. If he had carried on this kind of investigation for **D**, he would have found 1. that in some places **D** agrees with **F** and the indirect tradition against **A** (and **M**, which in reality is no primary witness) and 2. that in other places **D** alone agrees with the indirect tradition against **AF(M)**. This indicates that **D**, too, goes back independently to antiquity, and that **D** cannot be classified with **A(M)** as the representative of one family, against **F** as the representative of another family. Therefore, Burnet's conclusion "that the agreement of F with D will in many cases outweigh the undoubted authority of A" (*o.c.* 100 f.) breaks down: I assume that Burnet makes this contention because he ranks **D** in the same family as **A** against **F**: on this hypothesis, in cases where **D** agrees with **F**, Burnet seems to suppose that **D** represents the original reading of the common ancestor of **AD** and that, accordingly, **A** must be wrong. In reality, **D** stands somewhere between **A** and **F** (and is probably closer to **F** than to **A**), so that in all cases we must weigh and not count.

Burnet's opinions on **F** were criticised vigorously by Stuart Jones, who objected to Burnet's concept of an ancient vulgate, and by Adam, who hesitated to accept the dependence of **xv** on **F**, and who criticised Burnet for holding a very low opinion of secondary MSS.

---

[16] Burnet did not collate any MS of the *Republic* himself; for his information about **A** he relies on Adam and Campbell; for **D** and **M** he uses the collations made for Campbell (see note 11 to this chapter); for **F** he uses Schneider's report.

Stuart Jones 388-391 argues against the existence of an ancient vulgate; for a discussion of the matter see below, pp. 104 f. Despite his denial of the existence of an ancient vulgate, however, Stuart Jones accepts Burnet's conclusion "that F must rank as a witness independent of ADM" (Stuart Jones 391).

Adam, in his review of Burnet's 1902 edition (see Bibliography), shows himself reluctant to accept the dependence of **xv** on **F**. He concentrates his criticism on Burnet's contention that it is "an appreciable gain" that by using **F** we can dispense with **E** and **q** (see Burnet, *Neglected MS* 101). Burnet's argument is that **F** is an "entirely unsophisticated document", whereas MSS like **E** and **q** are very likely to contain Byzantine and/or Renaissance conjectures.

With regard to the relationship of **Fxv** Adam argues (215 f.) that Burnet has not proved that "F is the ancestor, and not the elder brother of the other two MSS."; yet he adds: "Whichever of these alternatives is true, it is right that F, as the older member of the family, should henceforward be quoted rather than Ang. B (= **v**) for readings which are common to both." Burnet meets this objection (*Vind. F* 12) by referring to Schanz' studies.

In the second place, Adam, *Burnet* 216, argues that *on the whole* **A**, supplemented by **D**, is more trustworthy than **F**. Of course, it is true that if **A** were the only extant MS of the *Republic*, we would possess a better text than if **F** alone had been handed down to us, but this observation tells us absolutely nothing about particular readings in **F**: "usually wrong" does not imply "always wrong". But in fact Adam's criticism is completely irrelevant, because Burnet did not oppose **F** to **AD**, as Adam implies, but to **E** and **q**.

In the third place, Adam protests (218 f.) against the disparaging judgement expressed by Burnet on such secondary MSS as **E** and **q**. In the preface to the 1902 edition and in the article *Neglected MS* Burnet claimed that good readings in late MSS are due to conjecture; 1902 edition, *praefatio*: "illud ex eo lucramur, ut novicios et interpolatos codices Venetum Ξ (= **E**) et Monacensem q abicere possimus, nisi si quando scribae non ineruditi qui eos descripserunt felici coniectura in verum incidisse videntur"; *Neglected MS* 101: "(...) it is antecedently improbable that, where they depart from the earlier MSS. of their own family, they rest on anything better than conjecture. Of course, a few—a very few—of their conjectures are right." Adam argues against this supposition (*Burnet* 218): "(...) until we know more about the conditions under which MSS. were produced, we have assuredly no right to maintain that those admittedly right readings of Ξ (= **E**) and q (...) are *never* based on earlier MS. authority." Moreover, he points out (*l.c.*) that "in at least thirty-three places (...) he (Burnet–GJB) has recourse *nolens volens* to Ξ (= **E**) or q or both of these MSS. together for the reading which he himself adopts."

Burnet seems to have heeded this criticism, because in *Platonica I* 200 he states: "Of course we must admit the possibility that, even in the latest MSS., there may be stray fragments of genuine tradition." But even if he had to admit that his initial position was untenable, in his 1905 edition, too, he is rather careless in quoting secondary MSS, often lumped together by him as "scr.recc." (cf. Dodds, *Gorgias* 48).

Burnet's treatment of the text and his apparatus criticus differ conspicuously from those of Jowett-Campbell and Adam in that he makes a fairly extensive use of the indirect tradition; *Platonica I* 201: "The quotations from Plato in early writers are of great value when they agree with other independent testimony." In some places Burnet even adopts readings found in the indirect tradition against the agreement of **ADF(M)**, e.g. 331b5 ἐν γε **Stob.**: γε ἐν **ADF(M)**. In his apparatus criticus, he often records readings found in ancient authors, esp. Stobaeus, Eusebius, Theodoretus, Clement, Galen, Iamblichus and Proclus. In his preface to the 1905 edition he states that he quotes the indirect tradition "quantum id fieri potuit, e recentissimis editionibus". Yet I suspect that in some cases at least he contents himself with taking over Schneider's report; this is especially clear in the case of Galen: thus at 410b5 he reports γε μὴν as the reading of Galen, which he even admits in the text against **ADF(M)** who read μὴν; now in the edition of the *Thrasybulus* by Helmreich, published in 1893 (in *Scripta Minora III*), Burnet could have found that γε is only read by the Basle edition of Galen, not by the MSS. The same goes for the quotations from *De Placitis Hippocratis et Platonis*, which was edited in a very satisfactory way by I. Müller in 1874[17]; consultation of this edition would have taught him that the addition of ταῖς μὲν before ὡς at 451e1 is also only found in Galen's Basle edition.

Burnet does not express his fundamental attitude towards conjectural emendation, but judged from the text he prints he is less conservative than Jowett-Campbell and Adam; he sometimes admits conjectures in places where they are not absolutely necessary, e.g. 452a2 μὴν **H. Richards**: μὲν **ADF Gal.**; *ibid.* γε **H. Richards**: τε **ADF**: om. **Gal.** Burnet records a restricted number of conjectures in his apparatus.

It has already been mentioned (note 16) that for his information about

---

[17] Müller's edition is now superseded by the modern edition of Ph. de Lacy in *CMG* 5.4.1.2 (Berlin 1978-1979). De Lacy makes use of the Hamilton codex (**H**), which was inaccessible to Müller, who used **M** and the Aldine edition, both derived from **H**.

the MSS Burnet relies on the collations made by others; his report, however, is not always correct. Partly, this is due to errors in the collations at his disposal; partly, it is the result of carelessness on his part. For instance, he reports that at 557e6 the readings ἄρχειν and δικάζειν are found in scr.recc.; in reality, this goes for ἄρχειν and δικάζειν at 558a1, which makes all the difference. At 472a2 he attributes the reading στραγγευομένῳ to **F** (i.e. the scribe himself), whereas Schneider (on whom Burnet relies for his information about **F**) says that this reading has been written "ab antiqua manu", which is not the same.

In conclusion we may say that Burnet's treatment of the text has some defects, but that, on the other hand, he has done good service to the textual criticism of the *Republic* (and, for that matter, of other dialogues as well), by assigning **F** its due place; further, the use he makes of the indirect tradition is an important improvement upon the editions after Schneider's. Finally, with regard to the adoption of conjectures Burnet wisely takes an intermediary position between the hypercritical attitude of Baiter, Hermann etc. and the exaggerated conservatism of Jowett-Campbell and Adam.

After Burnet's 1905 Oxford edition only one critical edition of the *Republic* has been published: Chambry's Budé edition, which appeared in 1932-1934[18]. In part IV of the introduction in vol. I (pp. cxxxviii-cxlvi) Chambry discusses the tradition.

Chambry reduces the primary witnesses to **A** (which he makes the basis of his recension (cxli)) and **F**; thus he rejects the primary status of **M** and **D**, which he both considers to be contaminated from **A** and **F** (cxlii f.). For **M**, this is correct, as I will show myself; Chambry, however, does not bother to prove that **M** is not a primary witness. His rejection of **D** is clearly mistaken: he says that **D** (like **M**) is contaminated from **A** and **F**. Now, **D** is usually assigned to the twelfth century, while **F**, according to Hunger, belongs to the fourteenth century, so that contamination of **D** from **F** is impossible. But even if it be granted that **D** is contaminated from the **A** and **F** *traditions*, **D** is nevertheless to be reckoned among the primary witnesses: a primary MS is a MS which does not derive from another extant MS, whether it contains many

---

[18] I regret that I have not been able to see the three-volume edition (with Spanish translation) by J. M. Pabón and M. F. Galiano (Madrid 1949), but from a note by J. Fantini in Helmantica 1 (1950), 255 f., I understand that the text of this edition is based principally on **A**.

I do not discuss the Loeb edition by P. Shorey (London 1930-1935), which is mainly based on the Teubner edition (see vol. I, xlv).

original readings or not. Therefore Chambry's elimination of **D** is unjustified[19].

On the other hand, Chambry attaches much importance to the older part of **T**, of which he gives a rather full collation in his apparatus. This is all the more unintelligible as he regards **T** as a direct copy of **A**, borrowing some readings from the **F** tradition (cxlii). About the more recent part of **T** (from 389d7 on) he notes that it is "assez différente de D". He suggests that it derives from the same exemplar as **W**, which is correct; about **W**, however, he states on the same page that the part from 389d7 on is "apparentée à D." Now, if **T** and **W** derive from the same exemplar, either both are "assez différents de D" or both are "apparentés à D".

Chambry has gathered some readings from other MSS, notably **E** and **q**, "qui tous les deux ont été fortement corrigés par des copistes intelligents" (cxliv); yet he does not say whether he considers the interesting readings in these MSS the result of conjectural emendation or contamination from a lost primary source.

A novelty in Chambry's edition is the use he makes of four papyri which contain fragments of the *Republic*, about which he remarks (cxlv): "(...) les papyrus, d'où il n'y a rien à relever." I believe that it is somewhat exaggerated to say that the papyri confirm "l'excellence du texte de nos manuscrits" (cxliv).

Chambry has rightly followed Burnet's example in paying due attention to the indirect tradition; unlike Burnet, he had the complete Wachsmuth-Hense edition of Stobaeus at his disposal; like Burnet, he does not quote Galen from the best editions: Chambry repeats Burnet's errors in the places mentioned above (p. 14) and elsewhere.

With regard to conjectures Chambry says that the tradition is not sufficient to clear all the difficulties and that "il reste place aux conjectures des savants" (cxlvi). He shares the scepticism of Jowett-Campbell and Adam (and, to a lesser degree, Burnet) about the trustworthiness of conjectures (cxlvi): "Je n'ai admis dans le texte que celles qui sont à peu près incontestables, et je n'ai relevé dans l'apparat que les plus ingénieuses et les plus vraisemblables."

Chambry collated seven MSS himself (cliii): **A**, **D**, **F**, **W**, **T**, **Par.** and **K**. The full collation of **TWPar. K** is, in my opinion, nothing but waste of time: readings of **W** can also be found in **Lobc.**, whose readings are reported in the most satisfactory way by Schneider; from 389d7 on **T** is a gemellus of **W**, as Chambry himself has concluded, and a copy of **A** in book I-III 389d7; **Par.** has not very much to tell us that is not in Bek-

---

[19] The same conclusion is reached for *Clit.* by Slings 285.

ker's collation or in the apographa of **Par.**, namely β and **K**; and **K** derives from **Par.**, as Chambry himself says. Excessive zeal, however, is not something for which we should blame an editor; and Chambry's collation of **A** is decidedly better than Burnet's report of it, although Burnet did not collate **A** himself, as Chambry believes (cliii).

The case is different with his collation of **F**, of which he says (cliii, n. 1): "J'en donne pour la première fois, je crois, la collation complète". Now **F** had already been collated by Schneider and his pupil Endlicher in a fairly complete manner, so that Chambry's collation is certainly not the first one; what is worse, Chambry's collation is in reality by no means complete: I do not want to blame Chambry for overlooking some, or even many, readings in **F** (everyone who has collated a long text knows that it is virtually impossible to make a really complete collation), but he certainly should have compared his collation with Schneider's report, which would have saved him from many errors.

All in all, except for the better report of **A** and **F**, and the use of four papyri, Chambry's edition does not mark any progress on Burnet's edition.

Apart from the editions and studies mentioned, no full-scale study of the text of the *Republic* has been undertaken in our century. There are, however, many works on Platonic MSS, the tradition of the Platonic writings and editions of particular dialogues which have some bearing on the text of the *Republic* and its tradition. I mention the most important of these.

In his *Quaestiones Platonicae* (1910) L. Gadelle discusses the position of **D** in the *Republic*.

H. Alline, in his *Histoire du Texte de Platon* (1915), gives a general survey of the history of the text from the fourth century B. C. until the sixteenth century A. D. One cannot but agree with Carlini 7, n. 14: "L'opera dell'Alline, preziosa per il materiale raccolto, in alcune parti è piuttosto debole". As to his opinions on the MSS, Alline is certainly wrong in accepting Immisch' hypothesis of the "archetype with variant readings", for which see below (p. 19).

A. C. Clark devotes one chapter of his *The Descent of Manuscripts* (1918) to the MSS of Plato; of the MSS containing the *Republic* he discusses **A**, **D**, **F** and **T**, of which he studies the omissions. In the course of my study, I will refer to his work more than once.

E. Deneke, *De Platonis dialogorum libri Vindobonensis F memoria* (1922), studies the origin and importance of **F** for the text of the major dialogues it contains. He confirms Burnet's conclusion that **F** derives from a MS written in majuscules; in *R.*, he corrects Burnet's views on the relationship of **ADF** by pointing out that **D** and **F** share many readings against **A** (cf. above, p. 12). He believes that he has shown that **ADF** go back to a MS which belonged to T. Pomponius Atticus; the **F** tradition, according to Deneke, has possibly come into existence with the edition to which a preface was added by Thrasyllus, i.e. during the reign of Tiberius.

Although Deneke's study is very valuable on many points, I agree with Pasquali's comment (259): "Convien dire che i resultati (...) non sono altrettanto netti quanto sembra al Deneke."

In his authoritative general survey of the tradition of the classical authors (1934), G. Pasquali gives a comprehensive and sensitive account of the tradition of Plato (247-269)[20]. On p. 247 he remarks: "per Platone il lavoro critico, che nella seconda metà del secolo XIX aveva imboccato una via troppo facile, ma sbagliata, ha dovuto ricominciar di bel nuovo negli ultimi anni prima della guerra, ed è ancora ai principî."

L. A. Post, *The Vatican Plato and its Relations* (1934), is primarily concerned with Vat. 1 (**O**), which does not contain the *Republic*, but he gives a list of Platonic MSS, with a brief description, for the greater part borrowed from Schanz, Jordan and others.

E. R. Dodds, in his edition of the *Gorgias* (1959), and R. S. Bluck, in his edition of the *Meno* (1961), give an extensive description of the major MSS of these dialogues; for the *Republic*, their conclusions concerning **F** are of importance.

A. Carlini has published a masterly study on the tradition of the *Phaedo* (1972); the MSS which are of importance for the text of the *Phaedo*, are for the greater part not of much importance for the text of the *Republic*, **T** being a copy of **A** (which may also be partly true for **W**, cf. below, p. 20 and p. 120, n. 8), and **D** representing a different tradition in the *Republic* than in the *Phaedo*, as I will show (see p. 91 f.); Carlini's account of the history of the text of the *Phaedo* in antiquity, however, is of the greatest importance for the Platonic corpus as a whole, including the *Republic*.

Finally, in his *A Commentary on the Platonic Clitophon* (1981), S. R. Slings discusses the transmission of the *Clitophon*, which is adjacent to the *Republic*, on the basis of nearly all the MSS; because many MSS contain both *Clit.* and *R.*, I will often refer to his book.

The study of the history of the text of Plato has given cause to much debate. I have already stated that in this study I do not intend to go into much detail on this question, but I will give a brief survey of the most

---

[20] Pasquali's work originally appeared in 1934; I have consulted the second edition of 1952 (repr. 1971).

important opinions on the subject. For an excellent account see Carlini 3-141.

H. Usener[21] was the first to give an over-all account of the history of the text of Plato. His main thesis is that "unsere Platonüberlieferung (ist) eine einheitliche; gespalten hat sie sich erst im Mittelalter" (p. 155). This hypothesis he bases upon the work done by Schanz.

The studies of Schäffer, Diehl and Immisch[22] have shown that this hypothesis is untenable, because the indirect tradition agrees with different branches of the direct tradition in different places, both in right and wrong readings. Immisch, developing a suggestion made by Schanz (*Platonis Opera* IX, viii) and Král, advanced the theory of an archetype provided with variant readings (Immisch 13, n. 3; 19 f.). This theory was accepted by Alline 185 as "extrêmement vraisemblable".

Yet it had already been shown in the studies by Burnet and Stuart Jones (cf. above, pp. 12 f.; below, pp. 104 f.) that **F** directly continues an ancient tradition; this induced Pasquali 258 ff. to reject the hypothesis of the archetype with variant readings explicitly.

The fundamental unity of our tradition being beyond doubt (see Immisch 19; Pasquali 251 ff.), different answers have been given to the question as to when our extant sources part company.

Some scholars hold that ultimately our tradition goes back to an Academic edition, possibly made by Archelaus (*ca.* 250 B. C.); see e.g. Wilamowitz 324 ff.; Pasquali 261 ff.; E. Bickel, *Geschichte und Recensio des Platontextes*, RhM 92 (1943), 97-159); cf. Carlini 17 f. Others, like Jachmann 331 ff., defend the theory of an Alexandrine edition, possibly by Aristophanes; this, according to Jachmann, excludes the existence of an Academic edition, because such an edition would have made the critical work of the Alexandrine scholars superfluous. Bickel however (quoted with approval by Carlini 22-23) believes that the two do not exclude each other.

Others again, like Deneke, believe that the ramification of our tradition starts in the environment of T. Pomponius Atticus (cf. above, p. 18); for *R.*, see Deneke 32-40.

The last hypothesis I mention is the one put forward by Carlini for the MSS of the *Phaedo* (see Carlini 127-141). With great caution he suggests that the foundation of the imperial library in Byzantium by Constantius in the year 356 A. D. may have been the occasion for making a new

---

[21] *Unser Platontext*, NGG 1892, nr. 2, 25-50; nr. 6, 181-215; reprinted in *Kleine Schriften III* (Leipzig-Berlin 1914), 104-162; I refer to *Kleine Schriften*.
[22] A. Schäffer, *Quaestiones Platonicae* (Strassburg 1898); E. Diehl, *Der Timaiostext des Proklos*, RhM 58 (1903), 246-269; Immisch 10 ff.

recension of the text of many authors; for this hypothesis he refers to Themistius, *Or.* IV 59d, where Themistius expresses his joy at seeing the rebirth of Plato, Aristotle, Demosthenes, Isocrates, Thucydides and the other great authors of the past. Carlini does not claim that the putative recension of Plato made in Byzantium[23] is the "archetype" of our medieval tradition, but he confines himself to submitting that "l'esemplare platonico della Biblioteca di Bisanzio è l'antenato comune più vicino a noi dei rami tradizionali che nelle prime sei tetralogie hanno in B, in T, in W i loro principali rappresentanti" (134).

Even if this hypothesis is accepted, it has hardly any bearing on the tradition of the *Republic*, because of the three leading MSS in the first six tetralogies, only **T** and **W** have a counterpart in the *Republic*, viz. **A**[24]. On the other hand, the **F** tradition and, to a lesser degree, the **D** tradition, occupy an important place in the *Republic*, while they are absent in the *Phaedo* (as I have already noted above, p. 18, the tradition represented by **D** in the *Republic* differs from that represented by **D** in tetr. I-IV; see p. 91 f.).

In the course of my study, I will have something to say about the origin of the **A**, **D** and **F** traditions, but I will limit myself strictly to the *Republic* and only make use of the evidence which can be gathered from the tradition *itself*; accordingly, I will refrain from extending my conclusions about the tradition of the *Republic* to the Platonic corpus as a whole.

With regard to the value to be attached to secondary MSS, there is no more unanimity nowadays than in the days of Campbell, Adam and Burnet. I mention the basic positions together with some of their recent representatives, without claiming that my enumeration is even approximately complete.

Dodds, *Gorgias* 48-56, pays considerable attention to a number of secondary MSS which contain good or plausible readings. He ends his discussion with the conclusion (56): "It would be fantastic to suggest that these small scattered insights are the *disiecta membra* of an ancient tradition. They are the first-fruits of a new age, the work of men who were no longer content to copy a corrupt text but had enough confidence in their own scholarship to substitute one which they deemed better."

---

[23] For a different interpretation of the passage in Themistius, see Wilson, *Scholars* 50: "One point of considerable interest which is clear on a careful reading of the text is that the leading authors (...) are of such standing that they do not require official support in order to guarantee their position. In other words Themistius is saying what we are in any case entitled to infer, that the major school authors did not need any protection beyond their place in the school syllabus, which ensured that they would continue to be copied."

[24] For the relationship of **ATW**, see below, p. 120, n. 8.

G. Müller, in a review of Dodds' *Gorgias* (see Bibliography), 128, states that "byzantinische Eingriffe in den Text und antikes Gut nebeneinander stehen können." He adds: "Ein wirklich zwingendes Argument in dieser Frage kann nun aber in der Übereinstimmung von Sonderlesungen der recentiores mit Lesungen der Papyri oder der indirekten Überlieferung liegen."

Wilson, *Scholars* 237, remarks: "In practice modern scholars make a rough and ready distinction between readings that seem too good to be medieval conjectures and others that could easily have been suggested by men like Planudes. As a general rule, this distinction holds good (...)". But even if it be admitted that this holds good as a general rule, it tells us nothing in the case of particular readings or particular MSS. On p. 265 Wilson lays down another general rule, viz. that "manuscripts written in the second half of the fourteenth century and later are not valuable to editors." In the particular case of the *Republic*, however, this general rule cannot be applied, as I hope to show; see pp. 201-241.

In any case, whatever the origin of interesting readings in apographa may be, there is substantial agreement that an editor cannot dispense with them completely, although few scholars would go so far as Jachmann, who states (379): "In methodischer Hinsicht erweist sich die eklektische Kritik erneut als die einzig angebrachte." Müller 129 expresses himself rather more prudently: "In der Praxis kritischen Arbeitens am Platontext kommt man allerdings mit dem eklektischen Prinzip Immanuel Bekkers bei möglichst großer Zahl von Lesarten ziemlich weit." Cf. Wilamowitz 334: "Bekkers eklektische Kritik, die auf seiner seltenen Sprachkenntnis beruhte, hat Recht behalten."

A final word should be said about the different opinions on the reliability of our tradition as a whole. The prevailing opinion is that the transmission of the *Republic* is good; German scholars show themselves more sceptical, e.g. Wilamowitz 376: "Trotz Campbell-Jowetts langatmigen Beteuerungen ist die Überlieferung des Staates durchaus nicht vortrefflich, und die Konjektur hat gerade hier noch recht viel zu leisten." Jachmann is even more sceptical: he goes to great lengths to show that the tradition of Plato's writings was already disfigured by contemporaneous interpolations (see Jachmann *passim*). Accordingly, German scholars are as a rule more inclined to admit conjectures than their English, French and Italian colleagues (to mention only the major countries in which Platonic textual criticism is practised). Wilamowitz 335: "Nur wer Platons Worte für lauteres Gold hält, wird sich's nicht verdrießen lassen jedes Stäubchen abzublasen." Jachmann defends his advice to apply the eclectic principle as follows (382): "Die Handschriften als Stützen einer Kritik, die sich nicht nur unserer algemeinen Abhängigkeit vom Schatz der Manuskripte, sondern auch der Verantwortung vor dem Genius des größten Meisters hellenischer Sprache (...) bewußt ist, habe ich nicht angegriffen, wohl aber als Idole blinden Aberglaubens an den überlieferten Buchstaben.''

Such is the *Status Quaestionis* of the text of the *Republic* at the moment. Only two MSS are generally recognized as primary witnesses, about two others there is no unanimity. Some MSS are still completely unknown; the value of the secondary MSS for the constitution of the text has not yet been studied systematically. Since the studies of Schanz and Jordan no further work has been done on the affiliation of all the extant MSS of the *Republic*, so that the relation of the MSS to each other and to the indirect tradition is not clear. The inventarization of the indirect tradition is very unsatisfactory. Some sources, such as the Latin translations before Ficino's, have not yet been studied at all.

It is my aim in this book to remedy these defects.

PART TWO

THE GREEK DIRECT TRADITION

CHAPTER ONE

DESCRIPTION OF MANUSCRIPTS

In this chapter I give a description of all those MSS which contain (parts of) the *Republic*; the description falls into the following sections:

- **a)** *references* to catalogues (if available), and to the lists of Wohlrab, Post, Wilson and Brumbaugh-Wells. If more than one catalogue of a library has been published, I only refer to the most recent one.
- **b)** *date*: I mention all the assumptions for the date of a MS; I have ventured to express my disagreement with current datings only in those cases where they seem to be untenable on stemmatic grounds.
- **c)** *appearance*: I give the data which can be gathered from the secondary literature, but in some cases I add observations made by myself. Further, the scribes are specified and the presence of later correcting hands is mentioned. Finally, I record the presence of scholia, but I neglect such marginalia as ση, summaries of passages etc.
- **d)** *history*: whenever I have found any note concerning the history of a MS I mention it briefly. For many MSS, however, nothing is known about there vicissitudes.
- **e)** *contents of Platonic writings*: I confine myself to the works which belong to the tetralogical corpus and the *Spuria*, excluding such works as *Timaeus Locrus*, *Halcyon* etc.
- **f)** *sigla*: I mention all the sigla which have been given to a MS, indicating which is the one adopted by me.
- **g)** *collations*: I record collations of the *Republic* made by other scholars.
- **h)** *opinions of other scholars*: I give a summary of the conclusions arrived at by my predecessors; I do not intend to give a full bibliography for all the MSS, but I confine myself to those statements which affect the position of a MS in the *Republic*.
- **i)** *my opinion*: I briefly state my opinion on a MS, concerning its ancestor, derivatives and possible occurrence of interesting readings.

The manuscripts are mentioned in the alphabetical order of the cities where they are now, with the exception of **Pal.**, which, though preserved in the Heidelberg library, precedes it former room-mate **P**.

1. Athous Iviron 131

- **a)** Lambros 25, nr. 4251; Wilson nr. 1. This MS is not mentioned by Wohlrab, Post and Brumbaugh-Wells.

b) fifteenth century.
c) size: octavo; material: chartaceus; scribes: the text is written in one hand throughout. There are no later additions, and no scholia.
d) —
e) *R*. I
f) no siglum has been given to this MS; I designate it **Ath.**
g) uncollated.
h) —
i) **Ath.** derives from **D**, as corrected by **D²** and **D³**, via a copy of **D** which was corrected from another source.
See pp. 169 f., 174-176.

2. Bononiensis 3630

a) Olivieri-Festa 440 f. (= Samberger I 58 f.); Wohlrab 666; Post 66; Wilson nr. 5; Brumbaugh-Wells 33 f.
b) thirteenth-fourteenth century.
c) size: 24.1 × 16.5/15.5 cm.; material: chartaceus; scribes: Olivieri-Festa *l.c.*: "scripserunt duo librarii: a ff. 1-32. 35-50. 55-102. 197-250. 267 (a verbis πονηριάς εἴδεσιν οὔσας Civitas V p. 82, 1. 9 (449a5–GJB))-268 (παραθαρρύνειν λέγεις; ἔγωγ' ἔφη ib. p. 83 l. 15 (450d7–GJB)); b elegantius ff. 33-34. 51-54. 103-196. 251ᵛ-267 (usque ad v. κατασκευήν, ἐν τέτταρσι Civ. V p. 82 l. 9 (449a4–GJB), 268 (a v. πᾶν τοίνυν ἦν ib. p. 83 l. 15 (450d8–GJB)) usque ad finem." The folium which contains the beginning of the first book of the *Republic*, fol. 102ᵛ, has been displaced; it is written by the first scribe; the second scribe wrote the same part on fol. 196ᵛ, where it immediately precedes the second folium written by the first scribe.
There are no later additions, and no scholia.
d) —
e) *Euthph.*, *Ap.*, *Cri.*, *Phd.*, *R.* 327a1-c8 (fol. 102ᵛ: see section c), *Cra.*, *Tht.*, *Phdr.*, *Mx.*, *R.* I-V (i.e. the same dialogues in the same order as **Vind.**)
f) no siglum has been given to this MS; I designate it **Bon.**
g) uncollated.
h) according to Jordan, *Republik* 474 f., **Bon.** goes back to **D**; Jordan does not add any proof in favour of this thesis. Post 56 states that **ΔΘ** (Vat. 225 and 226, which form one MS, bound in two parts) in tetr. I is "very close to Vind. 89, which has the same contents as Bononiensis 3630 and in the same order."
i) **Bon.** is a gemellus of **Vind.**; their common ancestor derives from **D**ᵃᶜ, via a lost MS which also served as the exemplar of **Sc.** (from

389d7 on). **Bon.** and **Vind.** have some interesting readings; the same goes for the common source of **Bon. Vind. Sc.**
See pp. 169-174.

3. *Caesenas D 28,4 (Malatestianus)*

a) Mioni, *Ital.* 65 f.; Wohlrab 666; Post 56, 66; Wilson nr. 8; Brumbaugh-Wells 34. See further Rostagno 157-164.

b) Rostagno 157: "exeunte saeculo xii maiore ex parte, ut videtur, exaratus." Mioni assigns **M** to the early thirteenth century. Post 56: "but it (**M**-GJB) is copied in part from B (Par. 1808-GJB), so that it can hardly be older than the thirteenth century and it may, like u (Ang. 107-GJB), really be even later." E. Martin, LSKPh 19 (1899), 103, quoted by Post 56, n. 3, assigns **M** to the fourteenth century with a query. Maas, *apud* Dodds, *Gorgias* 49, assigns **M** to the thirteenth or fourteenth century. Slings 267 thinks that **M** may be even later than the fourteenth century.

As **M** is in part copied from **a** (see Slings 267 f.; Mr. Jonkers tells me that he has established the same relationship for *Criti.*), which in all probability belongs to the fifteenth century (see p. 32), I believe that Slings is right in assuming that **M** belongs to the fifteenth century.

c) size: 34 × 23.6 cm.; material: chartaceus; scribes: Rostagno 158 notes that **M** has been written by two scribes; on pp. 158-160 he specifies which folia have been written by which scribe. Mioni 65 remarks: "Liber, ut videtur, ab uno eodemque librario minuta scriptura accurate descriptus (...)". After having inspected **M** *in situ*, I am fully convinced that Rostagno is right in distinguishing two different scribes.

Rostagno does not speak about the corrections and variant readings; some of the variant readings have been written by the scribe during the copying of the text: these variant readings were in all probability in the exemplar, because they often occur in γ (a gemellus of **M**) as well. Other variant readings and all corrections have been written by the scribe after the text had been copied, as appears from the fact that they are usually written in a different ink. Further, Rostagno distinguishes three different hands which have added the scholia; I have not checked this. In *R*. I have noted some trivial marginal annotations, but hardly any substantial scholia; the A-scholia do not recur in **M**.

d) Mioni 65: "Codex, iudice Zazzeri, fuit olim Johannis Marci Ariminensis qui libris suis Conventum S. Francisci Caesenae anno

1474 donavit (cfr. *Inventario dei libri lasciati da Giovanni di Marco medico riminese*, apud L. Tonini, *Rimini...*, vol. V, Rimini 1882, pp. 262-267), sed in codice nullam notam possessionis inveni neque e verbis huius inventarii "*Plato...in chartis edinis cū fundo rubro*" facile liber noster recognosci potest."

e) tetr. I-VII; *Iust.*, *Virt.*, *Demod.*, *Sis.*, *Erx.*, *Ax.*, *Clit.*, *Ti.*, *Criti.*, *Min.*, *R*.
f) **M** (Campbell).
g) **M** was collated by Rostagno for the edition of Jowett and Campbell; this collation was also used by Adam and Burnet.
h) Campbell 73-90 argues at great length that **M** is a primary witness, very closely related to **A**, but not dependent on it. His conclusion is rejected by Adam (1902 edition, xiv), but accepted by Burnet (1905 edition, *praefatio*; *Neglected MS* 98). Nielsen 131 (quoted by Post 56, n. 4) states without proof that **M** derives from **γ**. Chambry cxliii does not accept the primary status of **M**, which he regards as contaminated from **A** and **F**.
i) **M** does derive from **A**; it goes back to the same source as **γ**; the exemplar of **Mγ**, which contained readings that can be partly traced back to the **D** and **F** traditions, and partly go back to an unknown source, derives from a lost MS that also served as the exemplar of **P** and of the older part of **T**. This MS, too, contained readings borrowed from other sources, notably the **F** tradition. In some places, **M** offers interesting readings, usually in combination with its gemellus **γ**.

See pp. 111, 113-118, 120-123, 225-231.

4. *Darmstadt 2773 miscellaneus Graecus*

a) there is no printed catalogue in which this MS is mentioned. See L. Voltz-W. Crönert, *Der Codex 2773 misc. graec.*, ZBB 14 (1897), 537-571; Wohlrab 710; Post 88; Wilson nr. 10; Brumbaugh-Wells 29.
b) thirteenth-fourteenth century, according to Wohlrab; fourteenth-fifteenth century, according to Post.
c) size: ? (judged from the microfilm, the size is quarto); material: chartaceus; scribes: the folia which I have inspected (on microfilm) appear to have been written by two, or even more, different hands; there are no scholia.
d) **Darmst.** turned up in Paris at the beginning of the nineteenth century. In 1810, Bast bought it in Paris for Ludwig I, at the price of 300 Livres tournois. Since then, it has been in the Darmstadt library.
e) excerpts from many Platonic dialogues.

f) no siglum has been given to this MS; I designate it **Darmst.**
g) collations of excerpts in **Darmst.** have been published by F. Creuzer, in *Plotini de pulchritudine* (Heidelberg 1810); a collation of the fragments from **R.** is found on pp. 516 f.
h) —
i) some fragments in **Darmst.** appear to derive from **T**; other fragments go back to **F**.
See pp. 111, 168 f., 190, 199 f.

5. Durham C IV.2

a) Rud 293 f.; Post 85; Wilson nr. 11; Brumbaugh-Wells 17 f.; see further J. R. Harris, *Further Researches into the History of the Ferrar-Group* (London 1900), 28-34. Not mentioned by Wohlrab.
b) fifteenth century.
c) size: quarto; material: membranaceus et chartaceus; scribes: the text is written in one hand throughout; corrections and variant readings have been added by the first hand; the scribe has been identified as Emmanuel Constantinopolitanus. There are no scholia.
d) —
e) *Men., Hi. Ma., Hi. Mi., Io, Mx., Clit., R.*
f) no siglum has been given to this MS; I designate it **Durh.**
g) uncollated.
h) the text of **Durh.** in **R.** has not yet been studied; Marg 45-48 shows that in *Timaeus Locrus* **Durh.** derives from **Sc.**
i) **Durh.** derives from the same MS as **Acq.** and (from 389d7 on) **T**: this lost MS is a gemellus of **W**; the lost common source of **W** and the exemplar of **Durh. Acq. T** goes back to **Sc.**
See pp. 111, 157, 161-163, 169.

6. El Escorial, Scorialensis y, 1, 13

a) De Andrés II 190 f.; Wohlrab 694; Post 81 f.; Brumbaugh-Wells 68 f.; **Sc.** is not mentioned for **R.** by Wilson, who quotes this MS (nr. 14) for other dialogues.
b) the oldest part of **Sc.** belongs to the early thirteenth century, according to De Andrés and Post. The part written by the second hand, which contains *Clit.* and **R.**, should be assigned to the fifteenth century, according to De Andrés; yet I believe that the part which contains **R.** must be older, and probably belongs to the thirteenth century; cf. p. 48, section b. Wohlrab and Post assign the whole MS to the thirteenth century. **R.** breaks off after 607d6 αὐτῆς.

c) size: 31.6 × 24.3 cm.; material: chartaceus; scribes: De Andrés: "copiado por tres manos diferentes, la segunda (ff. 254-318. 320ᵛ-321ᵛ) letra caligráfica"; *R.* has been written by the second scribe.

Some corrections and variant readings seem to have been written by a later hand; the majority, however, have been written in a darker ink than the text, by a hand which seems almost certainly to be identical with the scribe (but I have not seen **Sc.** *in situ*). Marg 19 says: "E (= **Sc.**) ist durchkorrigiert, z. T. mit Rasuren, ob von der gleichen Hand, ist nicht auszumachen, z. T. jedenfalls in anderer Tinte."

Sc. has the **A**- and **T**-scholia up to 389d7 (where its source **T** breaks off), and a few scholia after 389d7. The scholium on Ἡρόδικος at 406a appears for the first time in **Sc.**

d) **Sc.** once belonged to Juan Paéz de Castro (died 1570); in 1572, Philip II ordered that it should be placed in the library of the monastery of San Lorenzo in El Escorial. Marg 18, n. 2, questions De Andrés' remark that **Sc.** belonged to Demetrios Trivolis.

e) tetr. I-VII, *Clit.*, *R.*, *Ti.*

f) Marg has given the siglum **E** to this MS; because **E** is the siglum for the Platonic MS Ven. 184 (given by Schanz), I prefer to designate this MS **Sc.** (Marg's introducing of new sigla for some well-known Platonic MSS is one of the few objections one could make against his otherwise exemplary edition).

g) uncollated.

h) **Sc.** has not yet been studied for *R.*, but Schanz, RhM 34 (1879), 132 ff., argues that **Sc.** derives from **T** in *Euthph.*. Slings 261 f. tries to prove that in *Clit.* **Sc.** is a gemellus of **W**, because of the separative error 407b4 δικαίως] δικαίου in **Sc.** against **W**; in reality, **Sc.** does have δικαίως, but ως is written *per compendium*, so as to resemble ου.

i) in 327a1-389d7 **Sc.** derives from **T** (the older part of **T** breaks off at 389d7); after 389d7 **Sc.** derives from the same source as the exemplar of **Vind.** and **Bon.**, and thus goes back to **D**ᵃᶜ. Occasionally, **Sc.** has interesting readings; in some cases, such readings may go back to an ancient tradition, as there is incidental agreement with the indirect tradition.

Sc. is the exemplar of Θ and of the common source of **W** and **Durh. Acq. T** (**T** from 389d7 on).

See pp. 111, 150 f., 155-158, 160 f., 169-173, 214 f., 217-222.

7. El Escorial, Scorialensis Ψ, 1, 1

a) De Andrés III 1 f.; Post 82; Wilson nr. 15; Brumbaugh-Wells 69. Not mentioned by Wohlrab.

b) 1462 A. D. (note on fol. 207^v).
c) size: 38.1 × 27.8 cm.; material: chartaceus; scribes: written by Demetrios Trivolis (note on fol. 207^v); there are no corrections by later hands. Ψ has a few scholia.
d) from the subscription on fol. 207^v it appears that this MS was written in Corfu; it once belonged to Antonio Agustín, as appears from a note on fol. 1 (De Andrés, *l.c.*).
e) tetr. I, *Cra.*, *Phdr.*, *Grg.*, *Men.*, *Tht.*, *Sph.*, *Plt.*, *Prm.*, *Ti.*, *Phlb.*, *Smp.*, *Alc.1*, *Alc.2*, *Hipparch.*, *Am.*, *Clit.*, *Ax.*, *Iust.*, *Virt.*, *Dem.*, *Sis.*, *Erx.*, *Deff.*, *R.*, *Lg.*, *Epin.*, *Mx.*, *Epp.*
f) no siglum has been given to this MS: I designate it Ψ.
g) uncollated.
h) Slings 262 proves that in *Clit.* Ψ derives from **D**^{pc}; he suggests that it is a direct copy.
i) Ψ derives from **D**, as corrected by **D**^{2} and **D**^{3}; but Ψ cannot be a direct copy of **D**, as it agrees in many places with **Neapol.**; therefore, it must go back to a copy of **D** which was corrected from (a close relative of) **Neapol.**

See pp. 169 f., 174-176.

8. *Florentinus Laurentianus Acquisti e Doni 37*

a) Rostagno-Festa 197; Post 69: Wilson nr. 47; Brumbaugh-Wells 35; not mentioned by Wohlrab.
b) sixteenth century.
c) size: 15.6 × 10 cm.; material: chartaceus; scribes: written in one hand throughout; no later additions, no scholia.
d) —
e) fragments from *R.*, *Ap.* and *Phdr.*
f) no siglum has been given to this MS; I designate it **Acq.**
g) uncollated.
h) —
i) the fragments from *R.* derive from the same source as **Durh.** and (from 389d7 on) **T**; this common source is a gemellus of **W**; the lost exemplar of **W** and **TDurh. Acq.** (**T** from 389d7 on) derives from **Sc.**

See pp. 111, 157, 161-163, 169.

9. *Florentinus Laurentianus Conventi Soppressi 42*

a) Rostagno-Festa 142; Wohlrab 674; Post 68; Wilson nr. 40; Brumbaugh-Wells 35.

b) twelfth century, according to Rostagno-Festa; thirteenth century, according to Stallbaum (*Platonis Opera* XII, viii); "vielleicht aus dem 13. Jahrh." Wohlrab.
c) size: 25.6 × 19.2 cm.; material: membranaceus; scribes: the text has been written by one scribe throughout; I have distinguished six later hands. γ takes over some of the **A**-scholia; there are a few scholia by later hands.
d) γ once belonged to the Benedictine monastery in Florence.
e) R.
f) γ (Stallbaum, ego); **Flor. V** (Schneider).
g) collated for Stallbaum by De Furia.
h) according to Schanz, *Platocodex* 81 f., γ (with **a** and **m**) derives with **T** from **A**. This view is confirmed by Jordan, *Republik* 476 f. and 479, who, however, does not say that γ goes back to **A** *with* **T**, but *like* **T**. Post 36 f. states that γ is the source of **a**. Nielsen 131 (quoted by Post 56, n. 4) states, without adducing proof, that γ is the source of **M**.
i) γ goes back to the same source as **M**; the exemplar of **M**γ, which contained readings that can be partly traced back to the **D** and **F** traditions, and partly go back to an unknown source, derives from a lost MS that also served as the exemplar of **P** and the older part of **T**. This MS, too, contained readings borrowed from other sources, notably the **F** tradition. In some places, γ offers interesting readings, usually in combination with **M**.

γ is the source of **a** and (in books VII-IX) of **Φ**.
See pp. 111. 114-118, 120-126, 127-129, 225-231.

10. *Florentinus Laurentianus 59,1*

a) Bandini II 485-488; Wohlrab 666 f.; Post 66; Wilson nr. 22; Brumbaugh-Wells 37 f.
b) **a** is usually assigned to the fourteenth century. Yet there is some reason to suppose that **a** was written in Italy: **a** derives from γ, which in some places has a variant reading introduced by the abbreviation *al.* (*aliter* or *alibi*); such corrections must therefore have been been added in Italy; the fact that **a** takes over some of such readings suggests that **a** must have been copied in Italy; as the copying of Greek texts in Italy began *ca.* 1400, I believe that **a** should probably be assigned to the fifteenth century.
c) size: folio; material: chartaceus; scribes: the text is written in one hand throughout. The numerous corrections and variant readings are apparently written by the scribe himself, but added after the copying of the text, as appears from the fact that they are in a darker

ink; moreover, **m** always follows **a**^{ac}. According to Sicherl, *Ficino* 59, Ficino's hand is traceable in **a**; Sicherl himself states (*o.c.* 53, n. 28) that he has not noted any signs of Ficino's having used this MS, but Marcel 254 f. says that Ficino's hand is easily identifiable as the hand that added many variant readings and notes. I believe that Sicherl is right in denying the presence of Ficino's hand in **a**.

a has the **A**-scholia at the beginning of book I; there are no further substantial scholia.

d) according to Sicherl, *Platonismus* 554, **a** was given to Marsilio Ficino in 1462 by Cosimo de'Medici; Ficino had a copy made of **a**, namely **c**; cf. Sicherl's note 139. I have checked all references Sicherl gives, but nowhere have I found any proof that Ficino ordered **c** to be copied from **a**; therefore, Sicherl's statement should not be taken for granted.

e) **a** is the oldest extant complete Plato. Basically, the tetralogical order is observed, but there are some anomalies: *Ti.* comes before *Alc.1*; *Spp.* are inserted between *Mx.* and *Clit.*; some *Platonica* (*Timaeus Locrus*, Plutarch's *De Animi Procreatione in Timaeo Platonis* etc.) are inserted between the texts of the tetralogical corpus.

f) **a** (Stallbaum, ego); **Flor. A** (Schneider).

g) collated for Stallbaum by De Furia.

h) according to Schanz, *Platocodex* 81 f., *Nachträge* 364, **a** forms a group with γ and **m**, and thus goes back with **T** to **A**. Jordan, *Republik* 475, states that **Etvm** and **a** go back to γ. Post 36 f. illustrates that **a** derives from γ.

Post 39 states that **a** is the source of **c**; Schanz, *Platocodex* 80 f., claims that **x** derives from **a**; the same goes, according to Schanz, for α. In *Platocodex* 105 f. Schanz argues that **F** is the source of **x**, which implies that he believes **F** to be derived from **a**.

i) **a** derives from γ, and thus goes back to **A**. **a** is the source of **m**, **c**, and of the lost exemplar of αtNeap.

A few corrections in **a** are not found in other extant MSS, but they hardly deserve any attention.

See pp. 111, 125 f., 127-132.

11. *Florentinus Laurentianus 80,7*

a) Bandini III 185; Wohlrab 673 f.; Post 68; Wilson nr. 28; Brumbaugh-Wells 38.

b) fifteenth century.

c) size: folio; material: membranaceus; scribes: the text is written by Theodorus Gazaeus; there are corrections and variant readings by at least one later hand. α has a few scholia.

d) α was written for Francesco Filelfo.
e) *R.*, *Prm.*; Stallbaum, *Platonis Opera* XII, viii, wrongly states that α contains *Clit.*; cf. Slings 265 f.
f) α (Stallbaum, ego); **Flor. T** (Schneider).
g) collated for Stallbaum by De Furia.
h) Schanz, *Platocodex* 80 f., shows that α depends on **a**. Jordan, *Republik* 475 f., derives α from γ, and quotes Schanz with approval (476, n. 1). Schanz, *l.c.*, states that **t** derives from α.
i) α goes back to the same source as **t**; this common source derives from the same exemplar as **Neap.**; this lost MS, in its turn, derives from a^{pc}. The exemplar of α**tNeap.** was heavily contaminated; the same goes for the exemplar of α. In isolated cases, a reading in α deserves particular attention.
  See pp. 111, 129-137, 235-237.

12. Florentinus Laurentianus 80,19

a) Bandini III 203; Wohlrab 674; Post 68; Wilson nr. 30; Brumbaugh-Wells 39.
b) twelfth century, according to Bandini; fourteenth century, according to Post; late fourteenth or fifteenth century, according to Jordan, *Republik* 469.
c) size: quarto; material: membranaceus; scribes: the text of *R.* has been written by three different scribes: the first scribe has written 327a1-429a10, the second 429a11-505a7, the third 505a7-553d4; the remainder of *R.*, again, has been written by the first scribe. The very numerous corrections and variant readings have been added by yet another scribe, whose script is very similar to that of the first scribe. There are no scholia.
d) Dott. M. Vicanò of the Biblioteca Medicea Laurenziana has investigated β for me; he writes me (letter of 14/8/84) that it is possible that β was written in Sicily or Calabria, but he adds that no certain proof can be furnished.
e) *R.*, *Ti.*
f) β (Stallbaum, ego); **Flor. U** (Schneider).
g) collated for Stallbaum by De Furia.
h) Schanz, *Platocodex* 85, states that β derives from **K**, and that **q** stems from β. Editors since Bekker have adopted readings of β in their texts (Bekker took these readings from **q**, a derivative of β), although they differ in their opinions on the provenance of these readings; one group (e.g. Orelli, Burnet) regards good readings in β (and, for that matter, in all *recentiores*) as conjectures; the other group (e.g. Adam)

believes that these readings go back to an ancient source; cf. above, pp. 5-14, 20 f. From Campbell's edition on, editors quote **q** instead of β.

i) β derives from the same exemplar as **K** (**K** only in books I-III); this common source goes back to **Par.**

β is the source of **q**, **Neapol.** and **Vindob.**; β has been interpolated intensively, quite possibly from an ancient source, as there are striking cases of agreement with the indirect tradition. In any case, β has many good or plausible readings.

See pp. 169, 179, 183-189, 203-214.

13. Florentinus Laurentianus 85,6

a) Bandini III 251-253; Wohlrab 667 f.; Post 66; Wilson nr. 33; Brumbaugh-Wells 39.
b) twelfth century, according to Bandini; thirteenth century, according to Post; not later than 1355: see Dodds, *Gorgias* 48 (with note 3). *R.* II, from 358d8 πολλάκις on, has been added by a recent hand (sixteenth century).
c) size: folio; material: membranaceus; scribes: the old part is written in one hand throughout; the recent part has been added by a sixteenth-century hand (see section b). There are no later additions, no scholia.
d) —
e) tetr. I-VI; *Io, Clit., Ti., Hi. Ma., Hi. Mi., Mx., R.* I-II
f) **b** (Stallbaum, ego); **Flor. B** (Schneider).
g) collated for Stallbaum by De Furia.
h) Schanz, *Platocodex* 71, 81, shows that **b** derives from **T**. On pp. 56-58 he illustrates that **b** goes back to **T** via Par. 1808 in tetr. I-VII; this is confirmed for *Grg.* by Dodds, *Gorgias* 48-53. About the recent part of **b**, Schneider III 309 remarks: "cum Bas.a conspirat".
i) **b** derives from **T**; as Par. 1808 does not contain *R.*, **b** must go back to **T** either directly or via another copy of **T**; cf. Slings 264 f. for *Clit.* The recent part of **b** goes back to the first Basle edition.

See pp. 111, 150 f.

14. Florentinus Laurentianus 85,7

a) Bandini III 254; Wohlrab 673; Post 68; Wilson nr. 34; Brumbaugh-Wells 39 f.
b) Schanz, *Platocodex* 106, states without proof that **x** was written in 1420; this date is accepted by all subsequent scholars, but in fact it

c) is not certain at all. Yet **x** can be safely attributed to the fifteenth century.

c) size: folio; material: membranaceus; scribes: written in one hand throughout; I have distinguished four later hands. There are a few scholia.

d) **x** once belonged to the monastery Sanctae Crucis in Florence, before it came into the Laurenziana; on the last folium there is a note: "Gorus prior sanctae Crucis, Zamerarius generalis, & D. Lucensis Episc."

e) *Grg.*, *Men.*, *Hi. Ma.*, *Hi. Mi.*, *Mx.*, *Io*, *Clit.*, *R.*, *Ti.*, *Criti.*, *Min.*; i.e. the same dialogues in the same order as **F**.

f) **x** (Stallbaum, ego); **Flor. R** (Schneider).

g) collated for Stallbaum by De Furia.

h) Schanz, *Platocodex* 80 f., says that **x** derives from **a**; on pp. 105 f. he illustrates that **x** derives from **F**. Nowadays, **x** is almost generally assumed to be a copy of **F**; see Burnet, *Neglected MS* 99; —, *Vind. F* 12; —, *Platonica II* 99 f.; Dodds, *Gorgias* 44 f.; Bluck 140; Slings 266. Adam, *Burnet* 215 f., did not think that Burnet had shown "that F is the ancestor, and not the elder brother of the other two MSS. (**x** and **v**-GJB)". Immisch 84, n. 1, and W. Theiler, *Gorgias* (Editiones Helveticae, n.d.), 138, too, did not accept the dependence of **x** on **F**.

Campbell 94 states: "Flor. x is another MS. without which the apparatus criticus would be imperfect." If he had bothered to look at Schanz' and Wohlrab's report, he would probably have replaced **x** by **F**.

i) **x** derives from **F**, and is in all probability a direct transcript; sometimes, later hands in **x**, esp. **x**^{3}, offer interesting readings. **x** is the source of **Ricc.** and **v**.

See pp. 190-197, 237-239.

15. *Florentinus Laurentianus 85,9*

a) Bandini III 257-266; Wohlrab 669; Post 66; Wilson nr. 35; Brumbaugh-Wells 40 f.

b) thirteenth century, according to Bandini; Schanz, *Mittheilungen I* 174, rejects this dating, because **c** stems from **a**, which is usually assigned to the fourteenth century. Because **a** probably belongs to the fifteenth century (see above, p. 32), I conclude that **c** belongs to the fifteenth century as well. Sicherl, *Platonismus* 554, says that **c** was copied from **a** ca. 1462.

c) size: folio; material: membranaceus; scribes: written in one hand throughout; I believe that the scarce variant readings have been added by the scribe himself; Sicherl, *Ficino* 59, states that Ficino has supplied some lacunae in **c**; in *R.*, I have not noted such additions. **c** has the **A**-scholia at the beginning of book I; there are no further scholia.

d) Sicherl, *Platonismus* 554 (with n. 139) says that **c** was copied from **a** at the instigation of Ficino, who had received **a** from Cosimo de'Medici; yet the positive evidence for this hypothesis is very scanty.

e) **c** contains the complete Plato, as does its exemplar **a**; **c** has the dialogues in the same order as **a**, except that in **c** *Ti.* is in its proper place.

f) **c** (Stallbaum, ego); **Flor. C** (Schneider).

g) collated for Stallbaum by De Furia.

h) it is generally accepted that **c** is a copy of **a**; see, e.g., Schanz, *Mittheilungen I* 173 f.; —, *Platocodex* 60 f., 65, 74, 81, 86, 91, 95 f.; Post 39; Immisch 49, n. 1; Slings 266 f.; Slings, *l.c.*, expresses some doubts about the *direct* derivation of **c** from **a**.

i) **c** is a copy of **a**; in *R.*, I have not found any objections to the hypothesis that **c** is a direct copy of **a**; yet this is improbable for *Clit.* (see section h), and Mr. Jonkers tells me that he regards it as improbable that in *Criti.* **c** is a direct transcript of **a**.

c is the source of **N** (in books III-X), **Matr.** and **V** (in books II-X), Φ (in book X), **Voss.**, **Ambr.**, **Matr.**[fr] and **Lond.**

See pp. 111, 129-131, 137-140, 142-144, 147-148.

16. *Florentinus Laurentianus 85,14*

a) Bandini III 273 f.; Wohlrab 672; Post 67 f.; Wilson nr. 37; Brumbaugh-Wells 41.

b) fifteenth century.

c) size: quarto; material: chartaceus; scribes: written in one hand throughout; there are some scanty corrections by a recent hand ("recentissima manus" Bandini). There are no scholia.

d) on the frontispiece of the book there is a note: "Αὕτη ἡ βίβλος ἐστὶν Ἁρμονίου τοῦ Ἀθηναίου. ἔχει φλουρία ι'. *Hic liber est Harmonii Atheniensis emtus florenis x.*" This Harmonius was a nephew of Theodorus Gazaeus.

e) *Ti.*, *R.* 400c4-439a2, *Smp.*, *Alc.2*, *Hipparch.*, *Am.*, *Men.*

f) **n** (Stallbaum, ego); **Flor. L** (Schneider).

g) collated for Stallbaum by De Furia.

h) Schanz, *Platocodex* 68, 70 f., shows that **n** is closely related to **R**, and that **n** derives from **W** in the *Meno*; on p. 85 he states that in *R.* **n** belongs to the group **ΘΦRLobc.**, esp. to **R**. Jordan, *Republik* 475, says that in *R*. **n** belongs to the group **ΘΦRLobc.V**. Post 67 f. says that **n** derives "perhaps from R throughout"; he seems to have misinterpreted Schanz' remarks, *Platocodex* 68.

i) n derives from **W**.
See pp. 111, 164, 168, 169.

17. Florentinus Riccardianus 66

a) Vitelli 518 (= Samberger I 182); Wohlrab 675; Post 69; Wilson nr. 50; Brumbaugh-Wells 42.
b) "s. xv scripsit idem librarius qui codicem 67 exaravit" (Vitelli, *l.c.*).
c) size: 24 × 17 cm.; material: membranaceus; scribes: in one hand throughout. There are no later additions, no scholia.

The quinio 151-160, which contains 556e8-573e4, is wrongly inserted after the quinio 141-150; it should come before it. As **Ox.**, a sixteenth-century derivative of **Ricc.**, has the text in the right order, the displacement has probably taken place after *ca.* 1500.
d) —
e) R.
f) no siglum has been given to this MS; I designate it **Ricc**.
g) uncollated.
h) Jordan, *Republik* 475, n. 2, says: "Mit diesem Codex (v–GJB) stimmt der Riccard 66. in allem wesentlichen überein". Yet Jordan does not say on what this conclusion is based.
i) **Ricc.** derives from **x**, but it is not dependent on **v**; **Ricc.** and **v** are gemelli. The exemplar of **Ricc.** has been corrected from another source, probably a member of the **Mγ**-group.
Ricc. is the source of **Ox.**
See pp. 190, 194-198.

18. Hierosolymitanus Τάφου 405

a) Papadopoulos-Kerameus 408-411. This MS is not mentioned in any list of Platonic MSS; it was brought to my notice by Dr Paul Moore.
b) fourteenth century.
c) size: 15 × 22 cm.; material: chartaceus; scribes: in one hand throughout; the scribe has been identified as Manuel Kalekas. There are no later additions, no scholia.
d) —
e) excerpts from a number of Platonic dialogues.
f) no siglum has been given to this MS; I designate it **Hier**.

g) uncollated.
h) —
i) **Hier.** goes back to Θ^{pc}, via a lost MS which also served as the exemplar of the common source of **V** and **Matr.** in book I.
See pp. 111, 158 f., 169.

19. Leiden, Vossianus Q 54

a) De Meyier 163-172; Post 88; Wilson nr. 60; Brumbaugh-Wells 32 f.; not mentioned by Wohlrab.
b) fifteenth-sixteenth century.
c) size: 21 × 14 cm.; material: chartaceus; scribes: De Meyier 163: "Varii librarii scripserunt, qui saepe distingui vix possunt"; the Plato excerpts (fol. 431-460) are written in one hand throughout. There are no later additions, no scholia.
d) —
e) excerpts from a large number of dialogues.
f) no siglum has been given to this MS; I designate it **Voss.**
g) uncollated.
h) —
i) **Voss.** derives from **c**.
See pp. 111, 139, 147.

20. London, British Library, Royal MS 16 C. XXV

a) Warner-Gilson 187; this MS is not mentioned in any list of Platonic MSS; it was brought to my notice by Dr Paul Moore.
b) sixteenth century.
c) size: 9¼ in. × 6½ in.; material: chartaceus; scribes: the fragments from *R.* are written in one hand throughout; no later additions, no scholia.
d) Warner-Gilson: "Apparently belonged to Sir Robert Cotton and was transferred by him to the Royal Library on the same occasion as 15 B. vii (q.v.)."
e) excerpts from a large number of Platonic dialogues.
f) no siglum has been given to this MS; I designate it **Lond.**
g) uncollated.
h) —
i) the fragments from *R.* are exactly the same as those in **Matr.**^{fr} (the same may be valid for *all* the Platonic excerpts in these two MSS); **Lond.** and **Matr.**^{fr} derive from a lost common source which in all probability goes back to **c**.
See pp. 111, 139, 147-149.

21. Matritensis 4573 (olim N 36)

a) Iriarte 138-141; Wilson nr. 70; not mentioned by Wohlrab, Post and Brumbaugh-Wells.
b) *R.* and *Epp.* have been written in 1480 A. D.; the fragments at the end of the MS probably belong to the sixteenth century.
c) size: folio minor; material: chartaceus; scribes: the text of *R.* and *Epp.* is in one hand throughout, without any later additions; the excerpts at the end of the MS have been written by another scribe. The scribe of *R.* and *Epp.* has been identified as Constantinus Lascaris. There are no scholia.
d) **Matr.** was written at Messina.
e) *R.*, *Epp.*; excerpts from a large number of dialogues.
f) no siglum has been given to this MS; I designate it **Matr.**; the fragments which have been added by a later hand are designated **Matr.**^{fr}.
g) uncollated.
h) —
i) **Matr.** is a gemellus of **V**; in book I, the common source of **V** and **Matr.** derives from a copy of Θ^{pc} which also served as the exemplar of **Hier.**; in books II-X **VMatr.** go back to **c**.
   The fragments from *R.* in **Matr.**^{fr} are exactly the same as those in **Lond.** (the same may be valid for *all* the Platonic excerpts in these MSS); **Matr.**^{fr} and **Lond.** derive from a lost common source which in all probability goes back to **c**.
   See pp. 111, 139-142, 147-149, 159 f., 234 f.

22. Milan, Ambrosianus 300 (E 90 sup.)

a) Martini-Bassi I 338 f.; Wohlrab 676; Post 70; Wilson nr. 77; Brumbaugh-Wells 43.
b) "recens", according to Bekker, *Commentaria Critica* I, v; fifteenth century, according to Martini-Bassi.
c) size: 26.9 × 19.9 cm.; material: membranaceus; scribes: written in one hand throughout; there are a few later additions, no scholia.
d) in 1607 this MS belonged to Rovidius.
e) *R.*
f) **t** (Bekker, ego); **Amb. C** (Schneider).
g) collated by Bekker, up to 439e.
h) Schanz, *Republik* 174, says that **t** belongs to the group **AmEtv**. In *Platocodex* 80 he states that **t** derives from α.
i) **t** derives from the same exemplar as α; this common exemplar goes

back to the same source as **Neap.**; the exemplar of α**tNeap.** stems from **a**^{pc}.
See pp. 111, 129-137, 235-237.

23. Milan, Ambrosianus 329 (F 19 sup.)

a) Martini-Bassi I 375-378; Post 70 f.; Wilson nr. 80; Brumbaugh-Wells 43-45; not mentioned by Wohlrab.
b) fifteenth century, according to Martini-Bassi; as **Ambr.** is an autograph of Ficino's, it is most likely to have been written after *ca.* 1460.
c) size: 14.4 × 10.8 cm.; material: chartaceus; scribes: written by Ficino throughout; Ficino added corrections and variant readings after the copying of the text. On fol. 2^r there is a note: "Marsilij ficini florentinj".
d) —
e) excerpts from a large number of dialogues.
f) no siglum has been given to this MS; I designate it **Ambr.**
g) uncollated.
h) Post 71 remarks that in *Ep.* 2,313b **Ambr.** agrees with **c**.
i) **Ambr.** derives from **c**. In some places, variant readings in **Ambr.** are borrowed from **N** (Bessarion's working copy).
See pp. 111, 139, 147 f.

24. Milan, Ambrosianus 778 (& 146 sup.)

a) Martini-Bassi II 875; Post 71; Wilson nr. 88; Brumbaugh-Wells 42 (wrongly numbered 788); not mentioned by Wohlrab.
b) sixteenth century.
c) size: 22.5 × 16.3 cm.; material: chartaceus; scribes: the fragment from *R.* is in one hand, without later additions; there are no scholia.
d) —
e) excerpts from *Lg.*; *R.* 459d4-460b5.
f) no siglum has been given to this MS; I designate it **Ambros.**
g) uncollated.
h) —
i) **Ambros.** derives from one of the sixteenth-century editions, but it cannot be established from which edition.
See p. 200.

25. Monacensis 237

a) Hardt III 7-9; Wohlrab 711 f.; Post 89; Wilson nr. 95; Brumbaugh-Wells 29.
b) fifteenth century.
c) size: ? (judged from the microfilm, the size is quarto); material: chartaceus; scribes: from fol. 166^v on (557a3 τοὺς) the text is written by a second scribe. There are a few later additions and corrections; there are no scholia.
d) Schneider I xxxiii quotes I. Hardt, *Aretini Symbolae* IV (1805), 583 f.: "possessus a Demetrio Rhaul graeco, item a Nic. Dorcaborico, ex libris P. Victorii."
e) *Deff.*, *R.*, *Ti.*
f) q (Bekker, ego): **Mon. B** (Schneider).
g) collated by Bekker and Schneider.
h) Schanz, *Mittheilungen II* 115, remarks that **q** derives from **K**. In *Platocodex* 85, 103, he says that **q** depends on β (which he regards as a derivative of **K**); this is also stated by Jordan, *Republik* 468 f. Editors since Campbell quote **q** where they should have quoted β, β being the source of **q**.
i) **q** derives from β.
   See pp. 169, 187 f.

26. Monacensis 490

a) Hardt V 71 ff.; Wohlrab 712; Post 89; Wilson nr. 100; Brumbaugh-Wells 30.
b) fifteenth century.
c) size: ? (judged from the microfilm, the size is quarto); material: chartaceus; scribes: in one hand throughout; there are no later additions, no scholia.
d) —
e) excerpts from *Prm.*, *Ti.*, *Mx.*, *Men.*; *Lg.* 726a1-747e11; *R.* VII, X 595a1-604c1.
f) **Mon. C** (Schneider); **M** (Brumbaugh); **Mon.** (ego).
g) collated for Ast^2 by Krabinger (see Ast^2, *praefatio*, iv); recollated by Schneider.
h) Schneider II 37, III 310, remarks that **Mon.** is related to Φ and **m**; Schanz, *Platocodex* 102, n. 3, notes that **Mon.** is close to Φ.
i) **Mon.** depends on Φ, but probably derives from an apographon of Φ which was corrected from another source.
   See pp. 111, 127, 143.

27. Neapolitanus 233 (III B 9)

a) Cyrillus 311 f., 435 f.; Wohlrab 676 f.; Post 72; Wilson nr. 105; Brumbaugh-Wells 47.
b) fourteenth century, according to Cyrillus; fifteenth century, according to Wohlrab and Post.
c) size: ? (judged from the microfilm, the size is folio); material: bombycinus; scribes: in one hand throughout; there are no later additions, no scholia.
d) —
e) *R., Ti.*
f) no siglum has been given to this MS; I designate it **Neapol.**
g) uncollated.
h) Jordan, *Republik* 475, says that in *R.* **Neapol.** derives from **D**.
i) **Neapol.** derives from β.
   See pp. 169, 187-189.

28. Neapolitanus 340 (III E 18)

a) Cyrillus 451 f.; Wohlrab 677; Post 72 f.; Wilson nr. 108; Brumbaugh-Wells 48.
b) "sec. XIV ad finem vergentis", Cyrillus; fifteenth century, according to Wohlrab and Post.
c) size: quarto; material: membranaceus; scribes: *R.* in one hand throughout; there are no later additions, no scholia.
   The quaternion which contains 368b1-381c8 ἐx—ὦν has been displaced; it bears folium numbers 279-286, while it should come after fol. 16; judged from the microfilm, the correct order of the folia has now been restored.
d) —
e) *R., Cra., Alc.1, Alc.2, Tht., Sph.*
f) no siglum has been given to this MS; I designate it **Neap.**
g) uncollated.
h) Jordan, *Republik* 475, n. 3, remarks that **Neap.** forms a group with α and **t**.
i) **Neap.** is a gemellus of the common ancestor of α and **t**, and thus goes back to a^{pc}.
   Neap. is the source of **Ott.**
   See pp. 111, 129-137.

29. Oxford, Bodleianus miscellaneus 104 (Auct. F.4.5.)

a) Coxe, *Bodl.* 679 f.; Post 86; Wilson nr. 115; Brumbaugh-Wells 18; not mentioned by Wohlrab.

- **b)** sixteenth century.
- **c)** size: quarto; material: chartaceus; scribes: the fragment from *R.* is written in one hand, without later additions; there are no scholia.
- **d)** —
- **e)** *Grg.*, *Ti.* 27d6-43e1, 46a4-47b4; *R.* 328d6-330a7; *Ap.* 40c4-end.
- **f)** no siglum has been given to this MS; I designate it **Bodl.**
- **g)** uncollated.
- **h)** —
- **i)** **Bodl.** depends on **Ox.** and is quite probably a direct transcript, made in Oxford.
  See pp. 190, 199.

30. Oxford, Corpus Christi College 96

- **a)** Coxe, *Ox.* 34; Post 87; Wilson nr. 119; Brumbaugh-Wells 19; not mentioned by Wohlrab.
- **b)** fifteenth century.
- **c)** size: folio; material: chartaceus; scribes: *R.* is written in one hand throughout; Post 28 says that from *Lg.* 919a on there is a new hand to the end of *Epin.*; the variant readings and corrections in *R.* seem to have been made by the scribe himself, possibly after the text had been copied. There are no scholia.
- **d)** Post 87: "A gift of the first President of Corpus Christi, John Claymond (died 1537–GJB), who obtained it from the estate of William Grocyn."
- **e)** *R.*, *Ti.*, *Lg.*, *Epin.*
- **f)** **Ox.** (Post).
- **g)** uncollated.
- **h)** according to Post 28 f. **Ox.** goes back, in *Lg.*, to the same source as Ricc. 67 and Barb. 209; this common source derives from Flor. 80,17. **Ox.** has not been studied for *R.*
- **i)** **Ox.** derives from **Ricc.**; **Ox.** is the source of **Bodl.**
  See pp. 190, 198 f.

31. Parisinus 1642

- **a)** Omont, *Inventaire* 115; Wohlrab 701; Post 83; Wilson nr. 124; Brumbaugh-Wells 19.
- **b)** fifteenth century.
- **c)** size: folio; material: chartaceus; scribes: in one hand throughout; the few corrections and variant readings have been added by the scribe himself, probably during the copying of the text. There are no scholia.

d) —
e) R., Smp., Min., Deff.
f) **K** (Bekker).
g) first collated by the Bipontine editors (1781-1787); recollated by Bekker and Chambry.
h) Schanz, *Mittheilungen II* 114 f., notes that **K** derives from **Par.**, probably through **p**. In *Platocodex* 85 he remarks that **K** depends on **D** through intermediaries; on the same page he states that **K** is the source of β. In *Mittheilungen II* 115 he says that **K** is the source of **q**.
i) in books I-III **K** goes back to the same exemplar as β; this exemplar derives from **Par.**; in books IV-X **K** derives from **p**, and thus goes back to **Par.** as well. The common source of β and **K** contained a lot of interesting readings, some of which recur in **K**.
See pp. 169, 179, 182-185.

32. *Parisinus 1807*

a) Omont, *Inventaire* 145 f.; Wohlrab 696 f.; Post 82; Wilson nr. 127; Brumbaugh-Wells 20.
b) **A** is generally considered to be the oldest extant Plato MS, slightly older than the Bodleianus (895); Carlini 146 says that **A** is "attribuito al terzo quarto del sec. IX", but he does not adduce any proof in favour of this dating.
c) size: folio; material: membranaceus; scribes: the text is written in one hand throughout; the identity of the so-called *vetus diorthota* has been the subject of much dispute; see e.g. Burnet, 1905 edition, *praefatio*; Des Places ccix-ccxiv; Tarán 172. I conclude that both the corrections commonly attributed to the first hand and the corrections usually assigned to A^2 have been made by the scribe himself, after the text had been copied. The hand which is called A^3 by Des Places, and which is very frequent in *Lg.*, has added only a few variant readings in *R.*; a later hand, A^4, has busied himself with orthographical corrections; finally, a certain Constantinus (probably from Hierapolis in Phrygia) has added a number of corrections and variant readings (A^5). The hand of the scribe of **A** has been identified in three other philosophical MSS: see Allen *passim*. **A** is the source of almost all extant scholia on the *Republic*.
d) Carlini 146 says that **A** "è stato con buoni argomenti posto in relazione con l'ambiente foziano", but he does not mention the arguments on which this assumption is based. I have found the following indications.

1. Alline 213 refers to Immisch 49, n. 2, who suggests that the Constantine who added the subscription in **A** (my **A**^{5}, see section c) lived in Hierapolis in Sicily: Alline adds that this Constantine "a peut-être été le disciple (et plus tard l'adversaire) de Léon le philosophe, lui-même élève de Photios." This argument does not hold good, because it is now generally accepted that the Constantine who owned **A** lived in the Phrygian Hierapolis at the end of the twelfth century: cf. Des Places ccx, n. 2.

2. Further, I do not see any serious objections to the hypothesis that Arethas, a pupil of Photius, worked on **A** (see below), but this is not enough to show that **A** can be identified as the second volume of the complete Plato "prima dell'880 (...) commissionata, *forse da Fozio stesso*" (my italics), as Carlini, *l.c.*, states.

3. Finally, A. Diller, Traditio 10 (1954), 44 f., points out that some scholia on Strabo are identical with the **A**-scholia on Plato; Diller concludes (44): "This large lexicographical element not only connects the scholia on Strabo with the Paris Plato group, but also suggests an author for them, that is, the Patriarch Photius." As an additional argument Diller asks the rhetorical question (45): "Who else but Photius in the third quarter of the ninth century would have produced these magnificent codices, so outstanding alike in material, craft, and erudition?"

In my opinion, the connection of **A** with the circle of Photius can be neither proved nor disproved.

Allen *passim* places **A** in a group of ninth-century philosophical MSS. Des Places ccxii f., following Lenz 205 f., attributes the hand he calls **A**^{3} to Arethas himself. He is quoted with apparent approval by P. Lemerle, *Le premier humanisme byzantin* (Paris 1971), 215, n. 35, who mentions **A** in connection with Arethas. Lemerle is rebuked by Wilson, *Scholars* 129, n. 11, who, however, does not give any proof against the association of **A** with Arethas.

According to Diller, *Petrarch* (followed by E. Pellegrin, IMU 7 (1964), 487 f.; see also A. Diller, *Studies in Greek Manuscript Tradition* (Amsterdam 1983), 252), **A** is the Greek MS which once belonged to Petrarch; yet the evidence for this thesis is not very strong, and there are two weighty arguments against it:

1. **A** once belonged to Johannes Lascaris, who is known to have brought hundreds of Greek MSS from the East; Diller, *Petrarch* 271, remarks that "Lascaris was with the French in Milan in 1499 and 1500", but this does not explain how Lascaris managed to acquire this precious MS from the French, who had annexed the Visconti-Sforza library, where Petrarch's books were too.

2. in **R**., all the descendants of **A** go back to one lost MS, the exemplar of **Mγ** and the old part of **T**; in *Clit.* the situation is comparable (see Slings 287); if **A** had already been in Italy *ca.* 1400, it is extremely unlikely that nobody should have used it, because fifteenth-century scholars were very eager to use old MSS; Post 7 aptly remarks: "The copies made by George Hermonymus (Voss.) and George Valla (Est.) perhaps confirm the date *c.* 1490 for its arrival in Italy".

Diller, *Petrarch* 271, confesses that there is no positive proof; I conclude that the hypothesis that **A** belonged to Petrarch is attractive in itself, but cannot be proved or disproved.

In his introduction to the facsimile edition of **A**, Omont sketches the history of **A**. Johannes Lascaris, who made two journeys to the East in order to acquire MSS, mentions in his catalogue Πλάτων, περγαμηνόν; in a list of books that belonged to Lascaris, made by Matthieu Devaris shortly after Lascaris' death, we read: "93. Πλάτωνος διάλογοι τινὲς καὶ αἱ πολιτεῖαι, *in pergamena, in-folio grande, n° primo della prima* [*cassa*]." Cardinal Nicolas Ridolfi, who acquired Lascaris' books, records in his catalogue: "IN PHILOSOPHIA, *in cassa prima*: N° 1 Πλάτωνος Κλειτοφῶν ἢ προτρεπτικός" (there follows a list of all dialogues in **A**). In 1550, Ridolfi's heirs sold his books to Piero Strozzi; when Strozzi was killed at the siege of Thionville in 1558, his books passed to his relative Caterina de'Medici. In 1594, five years after her death, her books were taken to the library of the King of France, by J.-A. de Thou and P. Pithou. Our MS is mentioned in the successive catalogues of the King's library; in Rigault's catalogue (1622) and in the catalogue by P. and J. Dupuy (1645), it is numbered 94; in the catalogue by N. Clément (1682), it is numbered 2087; finally, in the catalogue of 1740, it received its present number, 1807. For a full discussion and references, see Omont, *Parisinus*, 1-3; cf. Alline 213 f.

e) tetr. VIII-IX, *Spp.*

f) **A** (Bekker).

g) Faesi was the first to note some readings from **A** (see Schneider I xxviii-xxx); since then, **A** has been collated several times, by the following scholars: Bekker, Dübner (who collated **A** for Schneider's Didot edition; his collation is published by Schneider in NJPhP 18 (1852), 485-520 and 19 (1853), 5-30 and 165-188), Baiter (for the 1847 Zürich edition), Hermann (for the 1852 Teubner edition), Campbell, Adam and Chambry.

h) the primary status of **A** has not been questioned by any scholar. Bekker, who was the first to make full use of **A** for an edition of the

Republic, does not express his opinions on the MSS explicitly, but from his text it is clear that he regards **A** as the most important of his MSS; the later nineteenth-century editors attached ever more importance to **A**, until it became virtually acknowledged as the only MS authority; since Schanz, *Republik*, proved that **D** is independent of **A**, editors have recognized that **A** is not the only primary witness to the text; Campbell added **M** (wrongly), Burnet **F** (rightly), while Chambry recognized only **A** and **F**.

For different opinions on the corrections and variant readings in **A**, see above, section c (p. 45).

Clark 386-395 studies the omissions in **A**. Most scholars believe that **A** is the source of the older part of **T**, e.g. Jordan, *Republik* 477-479; Chambry cxlii; Dodds, *Gorgias* 37 f.; Slings 268, 273. Some scholars, however, deny the dependence of **T** on **A**, for instance Burnet, *Vindiciae I* 231; Greene xxxiv f.; Giorgetti 203; I will discuss the matter when dealing with the **A**-family; see pp. 112-116.

γa and their derivatives are considered to be dependent on **A** by Jordan, *Republik* 476-479, and Schanz, *Nachträge* 364.

i) **A** is a primary witness; the corrections and variant readings usually ascribed to **A²** have been added by the scribe himself, after the text had been copied. **A** is the source of the exemplar of **TPMγ**.

See pp. 65-91, 111-120.

33. *Parisinus 1810*

a) Omont, *Inventaire* 146 f.; Wohlrab 698; Post 83; Wilson nr. 130; Brumbaugh-Wells 22.

b) thirteenth century, according to Omont. As **Par.** reproduces readings added by **D²**, which are for the greater part borrowed from **W**, **Par.** cannot be older than **W**, and must *a fortiori* be younger than **Sc.**, the source of **W**. **W** is assigned to the fourteenth century by Hunger: therefore, either **Par.** is dated too early, or **W** is dated too late.

c) size: folio; material: bombycinus; scribes: written in one hand throughout; I have distinguished at least six later hands. There are no scholia.

Some leaves, containing 429e1 δευσοποιόν-442d3 ἰδιώτου, are missing; as all the derivatives of **Par.** have the text which is lacking in **Par.**, these leaves must have got lost after the (ancestors of the) extant derivatives of **Par.** had been copied. At the bottom of fol. 248ᵛ (after which the lacuna begins) there is a note ἐντεῦθεν λείπει. Fol. 275, which contains 564b2 δουλοῦται-568c8 τιμῶνται, has been

wrongly inserted after fol. 274, which ends with 574b1 ἐπιτρέπωσιν.
- d) **Par.** once belonged to the bookprinter Franciscus Asulanus; see Bekker, *Platonis Dialogi* I, viii; Schanz, *Mittheilungen II* 112.
- e) *Euthph., Cri., Ap., Phdr., Prm., R., Smp.*
- f) **D** (Bekker); **Par.** (ego).
- g) collated by Bekker and Chambry.
- h) Schneider III 310 already observed that **Par.** derives from **D**. This is confirmed by Schanz, *Mittheilungen II* 112 f., 116; —, *Republik* 177 f.; Jordan, *Republik* 474. Chambry cxliv notes that **Par.** has been contaminated with **W**.
- i) **Par.** derives from **D**, as corrected by D^2 and D^3, through one or more intermediaries which had been contaminated with a member of the **Sc.**-group. Sometimes, **Par.** has interesting readings; the same goes for some later corrections in **Par.**

    Par. is the source of **p**, **Vat.** and the ancestor of β and **K** (**K** only in books I-III).
    See pp. 169, 174 f., 176-183, 222-225, 239 f.

34. Prague, Narodni a Universitni Knihovna, Radnice VI Fa 1 (Lobcovicianus)

- a) Olivier-Monégier du Sorbier 97-103; Wohlrab 714; Post 90; Wilson nr. 159; Brumbaugh-Wells 17.
- b) "Saec. XII ex. (?)" (Olivier-Monégier du Sorbier); fourteenth century, according to others.
- c) size: 36.2/36.5 × 28/28.5 cm.; material: membranaceus; scribes: the text is written in one hand throughout; there are a few later corrections; there are no scholia.
- d) Immisch 67 remarks: "(...) Lobcovicianus, quem exeunte saeculo XV intercedente Marsilio Ficino emit Boguslavius de Lobcowitz." It is a matter of controversy whether **Lobc.** is the same MS as the so-called Hassensteinianus, which was used by Cornarius for his *Eclogae* (1561); Fischer, in his separate edition of the *Eclogae* (1771), confirms that it is; this is denied by Schneider I xv. Wilson 393, n. 2, again confirms this hypothesis. Having compared the readings in the *Eclogae* with Schneider's apparatus, I agree with Schneider that there are no positive internal grounds for assuming that **Lobc.** was used by Cornarius, because none of his readings is actually found exclusively in **Lobc.**
- e) tetr. I-III, *Alc.1, Chrm., Prt., Grg., Men., Hi. Ma., Hi. Mi., Io, Euthd., Ly., La., Thg., Am., Hipparch., Mx., Clit., R., Ti.*
- f) **Lob.** (Schneider); **L** (Schanz); **Lobc.** (Slings, ego).

g) collated by Schneider.
h) Schneider I xvi f. remarks that **Lobc.** is virtually identical with **W**. Schanz, *Platocodex* 62, 100, says that **Lobc.** derives from **W**; Král 204 and Post 32-34, 90, arrive at the same conclusion. Schanz, *Platocodex* 100 f., says that **Lobc.** is the source of **R**; this is denied by Post 30-34, who believes that **Lobc.** and **R** are gemelli.
i) **Lobc.** derives from **W** and is the source of **R**.
   See pp. 111, 164-167, 169.

35. Rome, Angelicus 101 (olim C.1.7)

a) Franchi de'Cavalieri-Muccio 140 f. (= Samberger II 154 f.); Wohlrab 677; Post 73; Wilson nr. 161; Brumbaugh-Wells 48 f.
b) Franchi de'Cavalieri-Muccio: "s. fortasse XV (the older part–GJB), s. XVI (the later part–GJB)"; Post ascribes **v** to the fifteenth-sixteenth century; Wohlrab assigns **v** to the sixteenth century.
c) size: 35.5 × 20.5 cm.; material: "membran. usque ad f. 382, deinde chart." (Franchi de'Cavalieri-Muccio); scribes: "scripserunt duo librarii: *a* s. fortasse XV, ff. 1-153, *b* s. XVI cetera" (Franchi de'Cavalieri-Muccio). The part written by the first scribe contains *Grg.*, *Men.*, *Criti.*, *Min.*, *R.*, *Hi. Ma.*, *Hi. Mi.*, i.e. the same dialogues as **x** (without *Io*, *Mx.*, *Clit.*, *Ti.*) but in a different order. In *R.*, there are no later additions, and only a very few scholia.
d) —
e) *Grg.*, *Men.*, *Criti.*, *Min.*, *R.*, *Hi. Ma.*, *Hi. Mi.*, *Phdr.*, *Lg.*, *Alc.2*
f) **v** (Bekker, ego); **Ang. B** (Schneider).
g) collated by Bekker.
h) it is generally accepted that **v** derives from **x** and thus goes back to **F**; see Schanz, *Platocodex* 73, 79 f., 106 f.; Jordan, *Republik* 470, n. 1; Burnet, *Neglected MS* 99; —, *Vind. F* 12; —, *Platonica II* 99 f.; Post 37 f., 73. Schneider, in his note on 353a1, had already noted that **Fxv** are "ex eodem fonte ducti". The objections raised by Adam, *Burnet* 215 f., need not be taken seriously.
i) **v** is a (possibly direct) transcript of **x**.
   See pp. 190, 194 f.

36. Vaticanus 61

a) Mercati-Franchi de'Cavalieri 54 f.; Wohlrab 683; Post 77; Wilson nr. 193; Brumbaugh-Wells 50.
b) **m** is usually assigned to the thirteenth century; yet as **m** derives from **a**, which probably belongs to the fifteenth century (see above, p. 32), **m** too must be assigned to the fifteenth century.

c) size: 23.8 × 17 cm.; material: chartaceus; scribes: in one hand throughout; there are a very few later additions, no scholia.
d) —
e) *R.* II-X; *Grg.* (breaking off at 482b2); *Phdr.* 261b7-274a4.
f) gothic **m** (Bekker); **Vat. H** (Schneider); **m** (ego).
g) collated by Bekker.
h) Schanz, *Platocodex* 81 f., *Republik* 180 f., states that **m** ultimately goes back to **A**; in *Nachträge* 364 he says that **m** forms a group with **aγ**. Jordan, *Republik* 475-477, specifies that **mEvt** and **aFx** go back to **γ**. Campbell 73 f., 86-90, illustrates that **m** belongs to the same group as **M**, but is more corrupted.
i) **m** derives from **a**[ac].
    See pp. 111, 129 f.

37. *Vaticanus 226*

a) Mercati-Franchi de'Cavalieri 295-297; Wohlrab 681 f.; Post 77; Wilson nr. 196; Brumbaugh-Wells 51.
b) twelfth century, according to Mercati-Franchi de'Cavalieri; not older than the thirteenth century, according to Post 56, 77; Schanz, *Untersuchungen* 649, even attributes Θ to the fifteenth century. The script of this MS is highly archaizing, which complicates its dating. Θ derives from **Sc.**[ac]; because the corrections and variant readings in **Sc.** have probably been added by the scribe himself, after the text had been copied, Θ must be of about the same age as **Sc.**, which probably belongs to the thirteenth century. Because **Hier.**, written by Manuel Kalekas (died 1410), derives from Θ, Θ cannot be younger than *ca.* 1400.
c) size: 31.6 × 32 cm.; material: membranaceus; scribes: the text is written in one hand throughout; there are numerous corrections and variant readings added by a later hand, which uses a much lighter ink. There are no scholia.
d) Θ forms one MS together with Vaticanus 225 (**Δ**); Θ once belonged to Cristoforo Garatoni.
e) *Thg., Chrm., La., Ly., Euthd., Prt., Ti., Hi. Ma., Hi. Mi., Io, Mx., Spp., Clit., R.*
f) Θ (Bekker, ego); **Vat. B** (Schneider).
g) collated by Bekker.
h) Schneider III 309 notes that Θ goes back to **D**, and that **Lobc.** derives from Θ. Schanz, *Platocodex* 78 f., 102, says that Θ goes back, with **ΦRW**, to **T** up to 389d, and from there on to **D**. In *Republik* 174, Schanz had already stated that Θ belongs to the first class (**A**-family)

up to 389d, and to the second class (**D**-family) in the remainder of the *Republic*.

Stallbaum regarded Θ as only slightly inferior to **A** (see above, p. 3).

i) Θ derives from **Sc.**[ac]; it is a direct transcript. Θ is the source of a lost MS which served as the exemplar of **V** and **Matr.** in book I, and of the fragments in **Hier.**

See pp. 111, 157-160, 169.

38. Vaticanus 229

a) Mercati-Franchi de'Cavalieri 299; Wohlrab 684; Post 78; Wilson nr. 199; Brumbaugh-Wells 52.

b) fourteenth century.

c) size: 26.5 × 19.8 cm.; material: chartaceus; scribes: the text is written in one hand throughout; there are some corrections and variant readings, quite probably written by the scribe himself, but in a different ink, and therefore after the copying of the text. There are no scholia.

d) —

e) *Euthph., Cri., Ap., Phdr., Prm., R., Smp., Phd., Grg.*

f) gothic p (Bekker); **p** (ego).

g) uncollated.

h) **p** has not yet been studied for *R.*; Schanz, *Mittheilungen II* 113 f., *Untersuchungen* 650, *Platocodex* 63, says that in *Smp.* **p** goes back to **D** via **Par.**, and that **p** is the source of **K**. He suggests that the relationship is the same for *R*.

i) **p** derives from **Par.**; it is the source of **K** (in books IV-X).

See pp. 169, 179, 181-183.

39. Vaticanus 1029

a) there is no printed catalogue in which this MS is mentioned; Wohlrab 684 f.; Post 78; Wilson nr. 208; Brumbaugh-Wells 53 f.

b) late twelfth century, according to Hinck (*apud* Immisch 70); thirteenth century, according to Immisch 70; fourteenth century, according to Post 78. If the date usually given for **Lobc.** is correct, namely fourteenth century, **R** cannot be older than the fourteenth century, because it derives from **Lobc.**

c) size: folio; material: membranaceus; scribes: the text is written in one hand throughout; there are some scanty additions by a later hand. **R** has no scholia.

- **d)** there is a signature at the end of the MS ἰωάννης ἀργυρόπουλος. Yet it is not clear whether this is to indicate that Johannes Argyropoulos was the scribe or the owner; see G. Mercati, BZ 19 (1910), 580; —, Studi e Testi 46 (1926), 85 f.; cf. Post 33.
- **e)** tetr. I-III; *Alc.1*, *Chrm.*, *Prt.*, *Grg.*, *Men.*, *Hi. Ma.*, *Hi. Mi.*, *Io*, *Euthd.*, *Ly.*, *La.*, *Thg.*, *Am.*, *Hipparch.*, *Mx.*, *Alc.2*, *Clit.*, *R.*, *Ti.*, *Lg.*, *Epin.*, *Epp.*, *Deff.*, *Iust.*, *Virt.*, *Dem.*, *Sis.*, *Ax.*
- **f)** gothic **r** (Bekker); **Vat. M** (Schneider); **R** (Post, ego).
- **g)** collated by Bekker.
- **h)** Schneider III 310, and in his note ad 540c4, already noted that **R** derives from **Lobc.**; Schanz, *Platocodex* 100 f., says that in *R*. **R** derives from **Lobc.**, thus recanting his earlier view (*Republik* 176 f.) that **R** derives from Θ; in *Platocodex* 84 f. he notes that the later part of **T** (from 389d7 on) derives from the same source as **R**, and that this common source is related to Θ. In *Platocodex* 78 f. he notes that **ΘΦR** go back to **T** up to 389d, and to **D** in the rest of the *Republic*. Post 30-35 protests against Schanz' views, and tries to prove that **R** and **Lobc.** are gemelli.
- **i)** **R** derives from **Lobc.**; it is the source of **Φ** in books I-VI.
  See pp. 111, 165-168, 169.

40. Vaticanus 2196

- **a)** Lilla 128 f.; Post 79; Wilson nr. 219; Brumbaugh-Wells 55 f.; not mentioned by Wohlrab.
- **b)** second half of the fourteenth century, according to Lilla; fourteenth-fifteenth century, according to Post and Wilson.
- **c)** size: 26.1 × 18.2 cm.; material: membranaceus; scribes: the text is written in one hand throughout; there are a few later corrections; **Vat.** has no scholia.
- **d)** on fol. 2 there is a note "I<ohannes card. de Salviatis>" (all letters except the I have been erased, cf. G. Mercati, Studi e Testi 79 (Vatican City 1937), 201, n. 1).
- **e)** *Clit.*, *R.*, *La.*, *Ly.*, *Euthd.*, *Prt.*
- **f)** **Va.** (Slings): **Vat.** (ego).
- **g)** uncollated.
- **h)** **Vat.** has not yet been studied for *R*.; Slings 272 f. shows that in *Clit.* **Vat.** goes back to the same source as Par. 1809, and thus to **T**; heclaims that their common source was interpolated from a MS which was related to Themistius' copy of *Clit.*
- **i)** **Vat.** derives from **T** up to 381a; from there on it depends on **Par.**; **Vat.** is the source of **k**.
  See pp. 111, 150-153, 169, 179-181.

41. Vaticanus Ottobonianus 177

a) Feron-Battaglini 100; Wohlrab 679; Post 74; Wilson nr. 175; Brumbaugh-Wells 57 f.
b) sixteenth century.
c) size: 21 × 13.5 cm.; material: chartaceus; scribes: the text is written in one hand throughout; there are no later additions, no scholia.
d) —
e) excerpts from a large number of dialogues (*Alc.2* complete); *R.* 505a2-509d5, 514a1-520a5, 614a6-621d3.
f) no siglum has been given to this MS; I designate it **Ott**.
g) uncollated.
h) —
i) **Ott.** depends on **Neap**.
   See pp. 111, 137.

42. Heidelberg, Vaticanus Palatinus 129

a) Stevenson 61 f.; Wohlrab 710 f.; Post 88 f.; Wilson nr. 55; Brumbaugh-Wells 29.
b) fourteenth century, according to Wilson, *Scholars* 267; late fifteenth century, according to Stevenson.
c) size: octavo; material: chartaceus; scribes: the text is written in one hand throughout; the scribe has been identified as Nicephorus Gregoras by Wilson, *Scholars* 267. I have not noted any later additions in the fragment from *R.*; in this fragment, there are no scholia.
d) **Pal.** came to Heidelberg via Paris (cf. Stevenson).
e) excerpts from a large number of dialogues; from *R.* only 359c7-360b2.
f) no siglum has been given to this MS; I designate it **Pal**.
g) the fragment from *R.* was collated by F. Creuzer, *Meletemata e disciplina antiquitatis* 117; cf. Schneider I xxxvii.
h) —
i) **Pal.** depends on **D** as corrected by **D²**.
   See pp. 169, 189 f.

43. Vaticanus Palatinus 173

a) Stevenson 91; Wohlrab 679; Post 74 f.; Wilson nr. 178; Brumbaugh-Wells 58 f.
b) variously assigned to the tenth-eleventh century (Stevenson, Post); eleventh-twelfth century (Immisch 40, 65); twelfth century (Jordan, *Republik* 467, n. 1).

c) size: octavo; material: membranaceus; scribes: the text is written in one hand throughout, without later additions. There are some marginal notes and scholia, which may have been added by a later hand.
d) **P** once belonged to Gianozzo Manetti.
e) *Ap.*, *Phd.*, *Alc.1*, *Grg.*, *Men.*, *Hi. Ma.*; excerpts and paraphrases of a large number of dialogues; *Deff.*
f) gothic d (Bekker); **Pal. A** (Schneider): **P** (Burnet, ego).
g) the fragments from *R.* VIII-X have been collated by Schneider.
h) Schneider III cxvi says that the fragments from *R.* derive from **A** ("sequitur familiam optimi"); Burnet, 1905 edition, *praefatio*, argues that **P** is independent of **A** in *Ti.*; he believes that **A**^{2} has drawn on the source of **P**.
i) **P** derives from the same exemplar as **Mϒ** and the older part of **T**; this exemplar in its turn derives from **A**. There are some slight indications that **P** is a gemellus of **Mϒ**, so that **PMϒ** form one group against **T**.
See pp. 111, 119 f.

44. Vaticanus Urbinas 31

a) Stornajolo 37 f.; Wohlrab 681; Post 75 f.; Wilson nr. 185; Brumbaugh-Wells 61.
b) fifteenth-sixteenth century.
c) size: 29.1 × 19.2 cm.; material: membranaceus; scribes: the text is written in one hand throughout; there are no later corrections, no scholia.
d) —
e) *Clit.*, *R.*, *La.*, *Ly.*, *Euthd.*, *Prt.* (i.e. the same dialogues in the same order as **Vat.**).
f) gothic **k** (Bekker); **k** (ego).
g) uncollated.
h) Post 75 f. states that **k** derives from **Vat.**; this is confirmed for *Clit.* by Slings 271, who says that **k** is a direct transcript.
i) **k** derives from **Vat.** and may very well be a direct transcript.
See pp. 111, 153, 169, 180 f.

45. Venetus Appendix Classis IV,1 (coll. 542)

a) Mioni, *Ven. App.* 199; Wohlrab 691-693; Post 81; Wilson nr. 237; Brumbaugh-Wells 62 f.
b) the old part of **T** is usually assigned to the twelfth century, but Diller,

Codex T, and Fonkič 158 have shown that **T** was written by Ephraim Monachus, who was active as a scribe in the middle of the tenth century. I have compared a MS which bears Ephraim's subscription, Venetus 201 (which contains Aristotle's *Organon*), *in situ* with **T**, and I am fully convinced that the two MSS have been written by the same scribe (a specimen of Ven. 201 can be found in L. Th. Lefort and J. Cochez, *Palaeografisch Album* (Leuven 1932), plate 34 (= fol. 102^v)); Ven. 201 is dated A. D. 954 by Ephraim. Therefore, **T** must be dated about 950. The more recent part of *R.*, 389d7-end, has been added by a fifteenth-century hand; *Ti.* has been written by Caesar Strategus, and *Timaeus Locrus et alia* by Johannes Rhosus, both in the fifteenth century.

c) size: 29.4 × 37.2 cm.; material: membranaceus; scribes: the old part of **T**, as has already been noted, was written by Ephraim Monachus (see section b); there are two later hands in this part. The more recent part of *R.* is written in one hand, with a few later additions. The old part of **T** has almost all the scholia which are in **A**, and adds a few scholia of its own. The more recent part has no scholia.

d) in 1789, **T** came into the Marcian library from the monastery of SS. Giovanni e Paolo.

e) tetr. I-VII, *Clit.*, *R.*, *Ti.*

f) gothic t (Bekker); **T** (Burnet, ego).

g) collated for *R.* by Chambry, who gives a fairly full report of the older part of **T** in his apparatus.

h) the position of the older part of **T** has given rise to much debate (see above, description of **A**, section h, p. 48); I discuss the matter in the chapter on the **A**-family, pp. 112-118. Schanz, *Platocodex* 84 f., says that the more recent part of **T** is related to **R**; their common source, in its turn, is related to **Θ**.

i) the older part of **T** derives from the same exemplar as **PMγ**; this common source goes back to **A**. The more recent part derives from the same source as **Durh.** and **Acq.**; this lost MS is a gemellus of **W**, and thus goes back to **Sc.^{pc}**.

See pp. 111-118, 149-156, 160-163, 168 f., 225 f.

46. Venetus 184 (coll. 326)

a) Mioni, *Ven. Ant.* 295 f.; Wohlrab 686 f.; Post 80; Wilson nr. 224; Brumbaugh-Wells 63 f.

b) fifteenth century, probably about 1460.

c) size: 28.5 × 43 cm.; material: membranaceus; scribes: written by Johannes Rhosus for Bessarion; there are countless corrections and variant readings added by Bessarion. There are many pencil strokes in the margin and in the text; this same hand has added Ast's chapter numbers in the margin; the same hand has added the same signs in **D**; I therefore suppose that Bekker did not only collate with his eyes.

Up to 389d, **E** has most of the scholia which are in **T**; these scholia did not all come into **E** via **N**, because **E** has some scholia which are not in **N**, e.g. the long **T**-scholium on σαρδάνιον at 337a3. **E** has a long new scholium at 509-511.

d) in 1468, Bessarion gave all his books to the Marcian library in Venice; see Sabbadini 68.
e) **E** contains the complete tetralogical corpus and the *Spuria* in the tetralogical order.
f) Ξ (Bekker); **Ven. B** (Schneider); **E** (Schanz, ego).
g) collated by Bekker, and by C. Castellani for Campbell.
h) Hermann, *Platonis Dialogi* III, iii (Leipzig 1851), took **E** as the basis for his text of the seventh tetralogy (where **B** and **A** are both lacking); he is criticised by Schanz, *Studien zur Geschichte des platonischen Textes* (Würzburg 1874), 63-66;—, *Platocodex* 77. Schanz, *Platonis Opera* I, ix (Leipzig 1875), regarded **E** as the representative of his second family; he was rebuked severely by Jordan, Hermes 12 (1877), 172, and F. Susemihl, JAW 3 (1877), 325; Schanz admitted his error in *Untersuchungen* 662. I do not understand how Slings 274 can say that Bekker took **E** as the basis of his textual studies; his remark that "E is a very important MS. for the history of the Platonic text for s. xvi-xix" (*l.c.*) is strongly exaggerated.

Morelli 107, quoted by Jordan, *Cod. Auct.* 639, says that in *R.* **E** goes back to the same source as **N**. Schanz, *Platocodex* 97 f., says that **E** is a direct transcript of **T** up to 389d, and that **E** goes back to **c** for the rest. Post 40 f. shows that **E** derives from **N** in tetr. VIII 2-IX. **E** has long been regarded as the principal source of the Aldine edition (see e.g. Campbell 92 f.; Alline 316), but Post 22, 39, 41 f. has shown that **E** should be replaced by Ven. 186 and **N**.
i) **E** derives from **N**.
See pp. 111, 146, 155, 242 f.

47. Venetus 185 (coll. 576)

a) Mioni, *Ven. Ant.* 296 f.; Wohlrab 688 f.; Post 80; Wilson nr. 225; Brumbaugh-Wells 64 f.
b) twelfth century; but this dating is doubted by Jordan, NJPhP 46 (1876), 773, who, however, does not mention his motives for doubting the traditional dating of **D**. Dodds, *Gorgias* 46, n. 3, also expresses his doubts about the traditional dating of **D**.

c) size: 26 × 35 cm.; material: membranaceus; scribes: the text is written in one hand throughout; there are numerous corrections and variant readings in a very thick, dark-brown ink (**D²**), which must have been added quite early, because they recur in **Par.**, which is assigned to the thirteenth century; readings added by **D²** also recur in **Ath.**, **Pal.** and **Ψ**. A third hand (**D³**) has added a few corrections, which recur in **Par.**, **Ath.** and **Ψ**. There are a few corrections by a more recent hand, which do not recur in any of the apographa. For the pencil strokes in **D**, see above, description of **E**, section c, p. 57.

The first hand has added a very few scholia; **D²**, which draws on **W**, adds most of the A-scholia.

Some folia have got lost: the absence of 507e4-515d7 is due to the loss of two leaves; the MS ends at *R*. 612d7; it is impossible to tell whether **D** ever contained more works after *R*. The leaves were lost after all the apographa had been copied, because all of them have conjunctive errors in the places where the lacunae in **D** occur.

d) **D** once belonged to Bessarion (see Mioni); in 1468, Bessarion gave all his books to the Marcian library in Venice; see Sabbadini 68.

e) tetr. I-IV, *Clit.*, *R*.

f) Π (Bekker); **Ven. C** (Schneider); **D** (Schanz, ego).

g) collated by Bekker, Castellani (for Campbell) and Chambry.

h) Schneider regarded **D** as only slightly inferior to **A**; after a period in which **A** was unduly valued as the only MS authority, Schanz, *Republik*, proved that **D** is independent of **A**. This conclusion is accepted by all later scholars, with the exception of Chambry cxliii, who holds that **D** (like **M**) is contaminated from **A** and **F**.

In the first four tetralogies, **D** is now considered independent of **B**: see Carlini 151-158. It has been supposed that **D** represents the **B** tradition for *Clit.* and *R*.: see Alline 219, 288 f.; Clark 405-411 studies the omissions in **D**. Schanz, *Stichometrie* 313 (with n. 1), discusses the stichometric signs in **D**; his conclusions anticipate those of Berti 219 f.

Gadelle (see Bibliography) gives a thorough account of the position of **D** in *R*.

i) **D** is a primary witness; it is the exemplar of a number of MSS: the exemplar of **Vind. Bon. Sc.** (**Sc.** from 389d7 on), **Par.**, **Ath.**, **Pal.** and **Ψ**.

See pp. 65-79, 91-99, 169-173, 174-178, 189 f.

48. Venetus 187 (coll. 742)

a) Mioni, *Ven. Ant.* 299; Wohlrab 689; Post 80; Wilson nr. 227; Brumbaugh-Wells 66.

- **b)** fifteenth century, probably about 1460.
- **c)** size: 17.5 × 26 cm.; material: membranaceus; scribes: all in all, Mioni distinguishes four scribes in **N**: the first two books of *R.* have been written by Bessarion himself; the remainder of *R.* has been added by a second scribe; in the other works contained in **N**, Mioni distinguishes still two other scribes. Bessarion added very many corrections and variant readings at different stages, as is proved by the differences in the ink of many additions. **N** takes over a few scholia which are in **T**.
- **d)** in 1468, Bessarion gave all his books to the Marcian library in Venice; see Sabbadini 68.
- **e)** tetr. VIII 2-IX.
- **f)** **N** (Post).
- **g)** uncollated.
- **h)** Morelli 107 (quoted by Jordan, *Cod. Auct.* 639) says that in *R.* **N** goes back to the same source as **E**. Post 40 f. shows that **N** is the source of **E** in tetr. VIII 2-IX; he proves that **N** derives from **T** in books I-II, and from **c** in the remaining books. Post 22, 39, 41 f., shows that **N**, and not **E**, is the principal source of the Aldine edition in the *Republic*.
- **i)** **N** derives from **T** in books I-II, and from **c** in books III-X. It is the exemplar of **E**, and the primary source of the Aldine edition. In some cases, Bessarion has added very good or even manifestly correct readings.

   See pp. 111, 139, 143-146, 150, 153-155, 231-234, 242 f.

49. *Vindobonensis Phil. Gr. 1*

- **a)** Hunger, *Katalog* 137; Wohlrab 720; Post 92; Wilson nr. 241; Brumbaugh-Wells 13.
- **b)** first half of the sixteenth century.
- **c)** size: 28.3 × 43.8 cm.; material: chartaceus; scribes: the text is written in one hand throughout, which resembles that of Konstantinos Angelos (Hunger). There are no later corrections, no scholia. For 327a-379b and 399b-417a, Ficino's translation has been added in the margin.
- **d)** **V** once belonged to Johannes Sambucus.
- **e)** *R*.
- **f)** **Vind. E** (Schneider); **V** (ego).
- **g)** collated by Schneider.
- **h)** according to Jordan, *Republik* 475, **V** belongs to the group **ΘΦRnLobc.**, and thus derives from **T** and **D**.

i) **V** is a gemellus of **Matr.**; in book I, their common source goes back to a derivative of **Θp^c** which also served as the exemplar of **Hier.**; in books II-X, the common source of **VMatr.** depends on **c**.
  See pp. 111, 139-142, 159 f., 234 f.

50. Vindobonensis Phil. Gr. 89

a) Hunger, *Katalog* 199; Wohlrab 719; Post 91; Wilson nr. 246; Brumbaugh-Wells 13 f.
b) *ca.* 1500.
c) size: 29/29.3 × 21/21.5 cm.; material: chartaceus; scribes: the text is written in one hand throughout; there are a few later additions, no scholia.
d) **Vind.** was acquired in Constantinople by Ogier van Busbeck (notes on fol. II^r, 218^v).
e) *Euthph.*, *Ap.*, *Cri.*, *Phd.*, *Cra.*, *Tht.*, *Phdr.*, *Mx.*, *R.* I-V (i.e. the same dialogues in the same order as **Bon.**).
f) **Vind. D** (Schneider); **Vind. 4** (Stallbaum); **Vind.** (ego)
g) collated by Schneider.
h) Schneider III 310, referring to his note on 333b8, says that **Vind.** is related to **DPar.Kqβ**; he also mentions some affinity of **Vind.** with **Lobc.ΦR** (III 310).
  Schanz, *Platocodex* 102, n. 3, remarks that **Vind.** goes back to **D** up to *R.* 404 (he does not say anything on the position of **Vind.** after 404): Jordan, *Republik* 474, argues that **Vind.** derives from **D**, without any restrictions.
i) **Vind.** goes back to the same source as **Bon.**; their common ancestor is a gemellus of **Sc.**, and derives from **D^{ac}** (**Sc.** from 389d7 on); the common source of **Vind.Bon.Sc.** has been interpolated, partly from **Mγ**, partly from an unknown source; the same goes for the exemplar of **Vind.Bon.**
  See pp. 169-175, 214-217.

51. Vindobonensis Phil. Gr. 109

a) Hunger, *Katalog* 217 f.; Wohlrab 716; Post 91; Wilson nr. 247; Brumbaugh-Wells 14.
b) **Φ** is usually assigned to the fourteenth century; however, because in *R.* X **Φ** depends on **c**, which belongs to the fifteenth century (possibly *ca.* 1450-1460), **Φ** must also belong to the fifteenth century.
c) size: 27 × 18/18.5 cm.; material: chartaceus; scribes: the text is written in one hand throughout; there are some Latin and Greek

marginalia by later hands, but no corrections and variant readings by later hands; there are a very few scholia.
d) as appears from an Exlibris on fol. 2ʳ, Johannes Sambucus bought the MS for five ducats. Hunger (*l.c.*) says that the MS shows traces of having been used for printing; he suggests that this has been done for Stephanus' edition, but he does not adduce any argument in favour of this hypothesis.
e) *Ap., Cri., Phd., Ax., Mx., Phdr., Grg., R., Epp., Deff.*
f) **Φ** (Bekker, ego); **Vind. B** (Schneider); **Vind. 6** (Stallbaum).
g) collated by Bekker; large sections recollated by Schneider.
h) Stallbaum, *Platonis Opera* XII, vi, says that **Φ** is related to **W**. Schneider II xxxvii, III 310, draws attention to the affinity of **Φ** with **m** and **Mon.**; Schanz, *Republik* 174-176, *Platocodex* 78, says that **Φ** goes back to **R** in *R.* I-VI, and that in books VII-X **Φ** is closely related to **m**, but offers a more corrupt text. Schanz, *Platocodex* 102, n. 3, remarks that **Mon.** is closely related to **Φ**.
i) **Φ** derives from **R** in books I-VI, from γ in books VII-IX and from **c** in book X. It is the source of the parts of *R.* in **Mon.**
   See pp. 111, 125-127, 139, 142 f., 167 f.

52. Vindobonensis Phil. Gr. 233

a) Hunger, *Katalog* 342; this MS is not mentioned in any of the lists of Platonic MSS.
b) second half of the fifteenth century.
c) size: 14 × 21.5 cm.; material: chartaceus; scribes: the fragments from *R.* are written in one hand throughout, without later additions and without scholia.
d) —
e) fragments from *R.*
f) no siglum has been given to this MS; I designate it **Vindob.**
g) uncollated.
h) —
i) **Vindob.** derives from β.
   See pp. 169, 187, 189.

53. Vindobonensis Suppl. Gr. 7

a) Hunger, *Supplementum* 13 f.; Wohlrab 716-718; Post 90; Wilson nr. 257; Brumbaugh-Wells 14 f.
b) **W** consists of three parts: the first part (fol. 1-514) is assigned to the eleventh century by Hunger, the second part (fol. 515-631, which

contains *Clit.*, *R.*, *Ti.*) to the fourteenth century and the third part (fol. 632-637) to the fifteenth century. For the relative dates of **W** and **Par.**, see above, description of **Par.**, section b, p. 48.

c) size: 24.5/26 × 34.5/35 cm.; material: membranaceus; scribes: *R.* is written in one hand throughout; there are no later additions. **W** has most of the **A**-scholia, plus the **T**-scholia, via **Sc.**

d) in 1478, Donato Nerio Acciaiuoli bequeathed **W** to the Carthusian convent near Florence; Immisch 68, following Kollar, believes that Donato received **W** from his father's family, but Post 33 thinks it more probable that "it came from his maternal grandfather Palla Strozza". In 1725, Alexander Riccardi (prefect of the Palatina Vindobonensis 1723-1726) acquired the MS for the Hofbibliothek in Vienna.

e) the old part of **W** contains the dialogues of tetr. I-VII (except *Alc.2*) in a characteristic order, the so-called **W**-order: tetr. I-III, *Alc.1*, *Chrm.*, *Prt.*, *Grg.*, *Men.*, *Hi. Ma.*, *Hi. Mi.*, *Io*, *Euthd.*, *Ly.*, *La.*, *Thg.*, *Am.*, *Hipparch.*, *Mx.*; the second part contains *Clit.*, *R.*, *Ti.*; the third part *Timaeus Locrus*.

f) **Vind. 1** (Stallbaum): **V** (Schanz); **W** (Schanz, ego).

g) collated by Chambry.

h) the oldest part of **W** is now generally considered to be a primary witness for the works it contains. As to the text of *R.*, Schneider I xvi f. already noted that **W** is very closely related to **Lobc.**; Schanz, *Platocodex* 62, 100-102, says that **Lobc.** is a derivative of **W** (this is confirmed by Král 204); **W**, he continues, goes back to the same source as **Θ**; the common source of **ΘW**, according to Schanz, goes back to **T** up to 389d, and to **D** for the rest of the *Republic*. Campbell 67, n. 4, wrongly states that **W** is derived from **Lobc.**

i) **W** goes back to the same lost MS as the common source of **Durh. Acq.T** (**T** from 389d7 on); this lost MS derives from **Sc.**[pc]. **W** is the source of **Lobc.** and **n**.

See pp. 111, 157, 160-162, 164 f., 168, 169.

54. *Vindobonensis Suppl. Gr. 39*

a) Hunger, *Supplementum* 33; Wohlrab 720 f.; Post 92; Wilson nr. 259; Brumbaugh-Wells 15 f.

b) fourteenth century, according to Hunger; possibly thirteenth century, according to Maas, *apud* Dodds, *Gorgias* 45.

c) size: 17.5 × 27.2 cm.; material: chartaceus; scribes: the text is written in one hand throughout; in *R.*, I have distinguished five later hands. The first hand adds some glosses, but no scholia. There are a few scholia by later hands.

d) in 1420, **F** belonged to Francesco Barbaro (Exlibris on fol. 262^v). In May 1723, A. Zeno bestowed **F** on the Emperor Karl VI. Since then it has been in the Hofbibliothek in Vienna.

e) *Grg.*, *Men.*, *Hi. Ma.*, *Hi. Mi.*, *Mx.*, *Io*, *Clit.*, *R.*, *Ti.*, *Criti.*, *Min.*

f) **Vind. F** (Schneider); **F** (Burnet, ego).

g) for *R.*, **F** was collated by Schneider and his pupil Endlicher; some parts collated by Endlicher have been recollated by Schneider himself; further collations have been made by Schanz. Chambry collated **F** for his Budé edition.

h) Schneider I 91 (in his note ad 353a1), III 311, already noted that **Fxv** form a group. Schanz, *Platocodex* 105-107, says that **F** is the source of **x**; on p. 80 he says that **x** derives from **a**; therefore, he implicitly concludes that **F** derives from **a**. Jordan, *Republik* 470, n. 1, says that **F** is the source of **x**, which is the source of **v**; on p. 475 he says that **Fxv** derive from **a**. Burnet was the first to assign **F** its due place, namely that of a primary witness (1902 edition, *praefatio*; *Platonis Opera* III (Oxford 1903), *praefatio*; 1905 edition, *praefatio*; *Neglected MS*; *Vind. F*), for Burnet's debate with Adam and Stuart Jones, see above, pp. 12-14; below, pp. 104 f. The primary status of **F** has been accepted by everyone.

Clark 414-417 studies the omissions in **F**; he submits that an ancestor of **F** had *ca.* 35 letters per line. Deneke (see Bibliography) studies **F** for the major dialogues it contains; he corrects Burnet's view on the relationship of **F** to **AD** (cf. above, pp. 17 f.). Dodds, *Gorgias* 41-47, gives an important account of **F** for *Grg.*; in *Notes* 24-27 he makes some further observations; he suggests that the exemplar of **F** had *ca.* 1200 letters per page, namely 31,5 lines of 38 letters each. Stating the opinion of C. H. Roberts, he argues that these dimensions "would suit very well the type of cheap papyrus *codex* which was manufactured in quantity in and after the third century A. D.". Following a suggestion of W. Theiler, Dodds states that the corrector of **F** drew on **b**; thus he recognizes only one later hand; the same conclusion is arrived at by Slings 265 for *Clit.*; yet both in *Grg.* and *Clit.* there are at least two different later hands, maybe even more (I have not studied this in detail). Bluck 135-140 discusses **F** for the *Meno*; he confirms Dodds' conclusions. The only point in which he differs from Dodds is that he believes (138, n. 3) that the mechanical injury in **F**'s exemplar was due to damp, not to wormholes, as Dodds, *Notes* 26, suggested, because the scribe of **F** often made an attempt to read his exemplar in places where it was damaged.

i) **F** is a primary witness; it is the source of **x** and of some of the fragments in **Darmst.**

See pp. 65-79, 99-110, 190-192.

CHAPTER TWO

THE PRIMARY MANUSCRIPTS

As I have already noted in the *Status Quaestionis* (see pp. 6 ff.), there are four MSS for which a primary status has been vindicated: **ADFM**. The primary status of **A** and **F** has not been questioned by any scholar; **D** was discarded as a primary witness by Chambry cxliii, but I will show that **D** must be ranked as a primary source. The hypothesis that **M** is a gemellus of **A** was put forward by Campbell 73-90; it was accepted by Burnet, but rejected by Adam and Chambry. In the chapter on the stemma of the **A**-family (see pp. 113-116), I will demonstrate that **M** goes back to **A**.

The position of **T** has given rise to much debate; some scholars maintain that **T** is dependent on **A**, others deny this and regard **T** as a gemellus of **A**; if the dependence of **T** on **A** is not accepted, **T** must necessarily be regarded as a primary witness. In the chapter on the stemma of the **A**-family (see pp. 112-116), I will prove that **T** does derive from **A**, and cannot therefore be considered a primary source.

I have not found any new primary MS; all extant MSS besides **ADF** ultimately derive from one of these three MSS, as I will show below (pp. 111-200).

In the first part of this chapter, I discuss the mutual relationship of **ADF**; in the second part, I give a description of the individual MSS.

I. The relationship of ADF

1. The source of ADF

That **A**, **D** and **F** ultimately go back to a common ancestor which must be later than Plato's autograph, appears from the fact that they have a considerable number of conjunctive errors; the character and the number of their common errors exclude the possibility that all these readings came into **ADF** as the result of contamination or coincidence. I quote some places where the reading of **ADF** is certainly corrupt (cf. Deneke 22 f.):

336e9 οἵου γε σύ **Bekker**: οἵου τε σύ **ADF**
354b3 ἐγώ μοι **Sc.**: ἐγῷμαι **AF**: ἐγὼ οἶμαι **D**
370a6 ῥᾶον β^pc: ῥᾴδιον **ADF**
386d4 τὶς **T**: τι **ADF**

387c2   ὡς οἴεται ADF
407c1   τινὰς Par.: τινὸς ADF
411e4   ἐπὶ δὴ βᵖᶜ: ἐπειδὴ ADF
429c7   γεγονυίας βᵖᶜ: γεγονυῖαν ADF
431b6   οὗ βᵖᶜ: οὖν ADF
435d3   ἄλλη α Gal.: ἀλλὰ ADF
437d11   ἑνὶ λόγῳ Cornarius: ἐν ὀλίγῳ(ι) ADF Ath.
440c7   ζεῖ βᵖᶜ Gal.: ζητεῖ ADF
444b5   τῷ δ' οὐ Burnet (vix recte): τοῦ δ' αὖ ADF
451b9   τότε xᵖᶜ: ποτε ADF
461b10   ἀφήσομεν Eus. Thdt.: φήσομεν ADF
468a10   ἐλοῦσι Van Leeuwen: θέλουσι ADF
493b3   ἑκάστας Groen van Prinsterer: ἕκαστος ADF
494b5   παισὶν De Geer: πᾶσιν ADF
504c6   προσδεῖ Par.: προσδεῖται ADF
544c7   διαφέρουσα xᵖᶜ Stob.: διαφεύγουσα ADF
553b2   τιν' Mγ: τὴν ADF
554b6   ἐτίμα μάλιστα Schneider: ἔτι μάλιστα ADF
571b2   ἐν καλῷ Mγ: ἐγκαλῶ ADF
580d4   λογιστικὸν om. Sc.ᵖᶜ recte: habent ADF falso
581d10   τί οἰώμεθα Graser: ποιώμεθα ADF
590e1   βούλεται xᵖᶜ Iambl. Stob.: βουλεύεται ADF
604c7   αἱρεῖ βᵖᶜ Plu. Stob. (uno loco): ἔρρει DF: ἐρεῖ A Stob. (altero loco)
610d3   τούτου βᵖᶜ Π¹¹: τοῦτο ADF

Especially remarkable is the reading at 581d10, which finds its origin in misreading majuscule script (ΤΙ > Π).

An additional argument for the hypothesis that **ADF** go back to a common ancestor later than Plato's autograph is supplied by the circumstance that they all observe the tetralogical order of the dialogues (cf. Pasquali 251 f.).

2. *ADF are independent of each other*

A, being the oldest extant Plato MS, is *qualitate qua* a primary witness. Nevertheless, I shall quote a number of places where **A** agrees with the indirect tradition against **DF**, or where an error in **A** is due to misreading majuscule script or wrong word-division, in order to demonstrate that **A** goes back to antiquity *linea recta* and does not derive from a Byzantine predecessor of **D** or **F**.

It is remarkable that there are only a very few places where **A** agrees with the indirect tradition in manifest error; even so, I mention some cases of agreement between **A** and the indirect tradition:

352a10   δέ habent A Stob.: om. DF
383a3   ποιεῖν habent A Eus.: ἀκούειν DF
409a1   ψυχῇ habent A Stob.: om. DF
413c7   ἀεὶ habent A Stob.: ἅ F: ἃ D

436a9   μὲν habent **A Stob.**: om. **DF**
439d8   ἑταῖρον **DF Gal.**: ἕτερον **A Stob.** (a rather common error)
441a1   ἐπικουρητικόν habent **A Gal. Stob.**: ἐπικουρικόν **DF**
509d7   τὸ *DF*: om. **A Plu.**
510b4   μιμηθεῖσιν habent **A Procl.**: τιμηθεῖσιν **F**: τμηθεῖσιν *D*
525a7   τοῦτο **DF**: τούτωι **A Iambl.**
590c9   ἐκείνου **A Stob.**: καὶ ἐκείνου **DF**
604c7   αἱρεῖ β^pc **Plu. Stob.** (uno loco): ἐρεῖ **A Stob.** (altero loco): ἔρρει **DF**

I have noted a very few places where **A** has an error which seems to be due to misreading majuscule script:

342a5   δεῖ] δεῖ ἀεὶ **A** (αἰεὶ **A**^pc), i.e. ΔΕΙ > ΑΕΙ, deinde ΔΕΙ supra lineam vel in margine; duae lectiones in textum irrepserunt.
367d5   ἀποδεχοίμην] ἀποσχοίμην **A** (confusion of Ε and Σ): ἀποδεχοίμην **A**^1im
596c4   Οὔπω] οὔτω **A** (confusion of Π and Τ): corr. **A**²

The places where **A** has a wrong word-division against **DF** are also very few: some instances:

402d8   δὴ ὅτι] διότι
403b4   νομοθετήσεις] νομοθέτης εἷς
526c2   ἂν εὕροις] ἀνεύροις
589b8-c1   ἀληθῆ ἄν] ἀλήθειαν
595b10   ἔοικε μὲν] ἐοίκαμεν (corr. **A**)

The readings quoted above are sufficient, in my opinion, to suggest that **A** does not go back to a Byzantine predecessor of **D** or **F**, although this hypothesis cannot be refuted altogether: it is certain that **A** represents a ninth-century recension for which an intensive study of the text was undertaken; this is illustrated by the provenance of the readings added by **A**¹ and **A**², for which see below (pp. 88-91). Therefore, it is possible that a predecessor of **A** originally had much more affinity with the **D** and/or **F** traditions than **A** itself; many errors common to the **A**, **D** and **F** traditions, then, were removed from **A** through conjecture or contamination. But I believe that the first explanation offered by me, viz. that the **A** tradition is independent of the **D** and **F** traditions, is by far the more probable.

The primary status of **F** is generally accepted nowadays; the main arguments for this position of **F** are the numerous cases of agreement between **F** and the indirect tradition and the fact that **F** has countless errors which are due to the misreading of majuscule script.
I will list some selected places where **F** significantly agrees with the indirect tradition (cf. Burnet, *Neglected MS* 100; Deneke 29-32):

329e5   παραμύθιά φασιν **AD**: φασὶ παραμύθια **F Stob.**

331a3   ὡς] ὥσπερ F Iust. Stob.
360b6   τολμήσειεν] θέλοι F Prisc.
378e5   ταῦτα om. F Eus.
381b9   δῆλον ἔφη ὅτι AD: δῆλον ὅτι ἔφη F: δηλονότι ἔφη Eus.
405c3   παρασχεῖν] παρέχειν F Phot. Suid.
430a1   μηδὲν] καὶ μηδὲν F Stob.
439e4   ἂν εἴη] εἴη ἂν F Gal.
467a10 μαχεῖται AD: μάχεται F Stob.
508c1   τοῦτο om. F Eus. Iul.
522b1   νῦν om. F Eus.
617a6   τῷ om. F Theon Sm.

Some instances of errors in **F** which are due to misreading majuscule script (cf. Burnet, *Neglected MS* 99):

339b2   μεγάλη] μέγα δὴ
351b4   γε ἡ ἀρίστη] γ' ἐπαρίστη
353a9   ἠρώτων] πρῶτον
371b4-5 μεταδώσουσιν ὧν] μεγάλως οὐσιῶν
394e2   ἢ οὔ] ποῦ
420a5   οὐδ' ἀναλίσκειν] οὐδὰν ἀδικεῖν
487e6   δέ γε] λέγε
521d3   εἴη, ὦ] εἴπω
576d7   ἀθλιότητος] δολιότητος
584b6   προλυπηθέντι] προλυτηθέντι
588c9   φύειν] φύσιν

Some instances of errors due to wrong word-division:

339b2   ἀλλ' ὅτι] ἄλλο τι
340c5   οὕτω σε φῶμεν] οὕτως ἔφωμεν
378d8   ἀλλ' ἃ] ἀλλὰ
395e2   ἐχομένην] ἔχομεν ἥν
423d8   ὦ ἀγαθὲ] ὦγ' ἀθὲ
470a8   ἀποφαινομένου] ἀποφαίνομεν οὐ
515b7   δ' εἰ] δεῖ
547b7   ἡγέτην] ἦγε τὴν
588b2   δι' ἃ δεῦρ' ἥκομεν] διαδευρήκομεν
604a7   ἃ εἴ] ἀεί

The primary status of **D** was vindicated by Schanz, *Republik* (Schanz did not notice the value of **F**, because in his article *Republik* he only deals with Bekker's MSS); Schanz was followed by Campbell, Adam and Burnet. Chambry cxliii argues that **D** can be dispensed with, since the great value of **F** has been discovered by Burnet; **D**, according to Chambry, is contaminated from **A** and **F**. However, if the datings usually given for **D** and **F** are even approximately correct (**D** is assigned to the twelfth century, **F** to the thirteenth or fourteenth century), this hypothesis is untenable: a MS cannot be contaminated with a source which is younger than itself; cf. Dodds, *Gorgias* 46, n. 3; Slings 275[1]. More important is the fact that in a number of places **D** significantly agrees with the indirect tradition (cf. Gadelle 26 f.); I have noted the following cases:

353a8	μὲν om. **D** Stobaei **MA** (habet Stobaei **S**)
375b2	ἐστι om. **D** Stob.
377e1	κακῶς οὐσίαν Eus. (uno loco): κακῶ οὐσίαν **D**: οὐσίαν κακῶς **F**: κακῶς **A** Eus. (altero loco) recte
405c2	λυγιζόμενος **A**: λογιζόμενος **D** Stob.: αὖ λογιζόμενος **F**
411c1	ἀκράχολοι habet **D** et legisse videtur **Plu.**: ἀκρόχολοι **AF** Them. Plot.
439e9	αὖ om. **D** Gal. Stob.
464e2	καὶ] ἢ **D** Stob.
620b4	ἔχθρᾳ] ἐχθρὰν *D* Eus.

Some cases of more trivial agreement:

379b1	γε om. **D** Eus. Thdt. Georg. Mon.
381b4	γε habent **D** Eus.: τε **AF**
473a3	πότερον] πρότερον **D** Stob.
473b7	ἔλθοι] ἔλθη **D** Stob.
544d7	τρόπων] τρόπον **D** Stob.

In the third place, **D** has a lot of errors against **AF** which result from a wrong word-division, and which therefore are likely to have originated in a majuscule MS; some instances:

331d5	χρὴ Σιμωνίδῃ] χρήσιμονίδη (sic)
337e2	ἄλλου] ἀλλ' οὐ
371a11	δέ εἰσιν] δέησιν
377a12-b1	ἄλλως τε] ἄλλῶστε (sic)
390d4	ἠνίπαπε] ἠνείπαπε **A**: ἦν εἴπαπε **D**
408a6	δ' ἔχρην] δὲ χρῆν
435a4	καθ' ὁδόν] κάθοδόν
480a4	ἀνέχεσθαι] ἂν ἔχεσθαι
528e7	σὺ μετέρχῃ] συμμετέρχει
547e1-2	ἄγειν ἄτε] ἀγείνατε
559a4	δὲ καὶ] δέκα
585b14	καὶ νοῦ] καινοῦ
601e2	ὑπηρετήσει] ὑπηρέτης εἶ

---

[1] Slings' additional argument (276) "It is not very likely that the scribe of D or its exemplar should have picked out a MS. so difficult to consult (the exemplar of **F**-GJB) for contamination", which seems to be based on Dodds' argument (*Gorgias* 46) "had the F tradition been made available at an earlier date we might expect to find some trace of its influence in our older medieval MSS.", is not valid: the fact that the exemplar of **F** *itself* may have been rather difficult to read, does not necessarily imply that there were no other MSS of the **F** tradition ("uncles" of **F**) circulating in the Byzantine world. Against Dodds' argument I would argue that **F** has left some trace in our older MSS: the common ancestor of **TMγ** (**T** was written *ca.* 950) was contaminated from a MS of the **F** tradition; see below, pp. 117 f.

Further, **D** has two errors against **AF** which result from misreading majuscule script:

394c1   ὅλη] ὁ δή (sic)
559d10-e1   που οἴου] πουσίου

Finally, if **D** derived mainly from **A** (or a congener of **A**), we would have to assume that most (if not all) cases of agreement with **F** must be due to contamination or coincidence; I will illustrate below (see pp. 72-74) that this is virtually excluded, because of the character of some of the readings common to **D** and **F**. On the other hand, if **D** derived mainly from a MS which even remotely resembled **F** as we have it, with its innumerable errors, we would expect to find many more cases of agreement between **D** and **F** than we do find in reality.

The conclusion is that **D** goes back to an ancient source independent of **A** and **F**.

The fact that **ADF** go back to an ancient tradition independently indicates that more than one MS has survived the Dark Ages: accordingly, the hypothesis of the archetype with variant readings (for which see above, p. 19) is untenable for *R*.

3. D and F derive from a common source

Thus there are three primary witnesses, **ADF**, which ultimately go back to a common ancestor, later than Plato's autograph. Therefore, there are two possibilities for the relationship of **ADF**: 1. all three MSS go back to their common source *linea recta*; 2. two of the three MSS derive from a common ancestor, which can be regarded as a gemellus of the third one.

It has already been noted (p. 65 and p. 68) that Chambry contended that **D** is to be dismissed as a primary source because, according to him, **D** is contaminated from **A** and **F**. Although this hypothesis as such has been shown to be untenable, Chambry was right in maintaining that **D** holds a position somewhere between **A** and **F**: **D** sometimes sides with **A**, sometimes with **F**, both in right and wrong readings. Moreover, the cases are very few in which **D** alone preserves a manifestly correct reading (cf. Gadelle 50-52); I have noted the following cases (I discount those places where a good reading in **D** has been anticipated by the corrector of **A**; further, I leave aside the indirect tradition for the moment):

328d7   γε **D**: τε **F**: om. **A**
330b8   Οὔ τοι] οὔτοι (sic) **D**: οὔτοι **A**: τούτου **F**
337c5   ἀποκρινεῖσθαι **D**: ἀποκρίνεσθαι **AF**
352a1   ποιεῖν **D**: ποιεῖ **AF**

381b4 γε **D**: τε **AF**
411c1 ἀκράχολοι **D**: ἀκρόχολοι **AF**
422e9 πολέμια **D** (which is correct, but for the accent): πολέμιαι **AF** (errat Burnet)
472a8 λέγης **D**: λέγεις **AF** (corr. **A⁴**, errat Burnet)
526d9 προιὸν **D**: προιὼν **F** (o supra lineam **F¹**): προσιὸν **A**
543c4 ἀλλ' ἄγε **D**: ἀλλά γ' **AF**
561b2 ἑαυτὸν **D**: ἑαυτῶ(ι) **AF**

With regard to **D**'s reading εἰ πάρεργον at 411e7, mentioned by Gadelle 51 as the one good reading for which **D** alone is responsible, I must note that εἰ πάρεργον (sic, nisi fallor) was also the reading of **Aᵖᶜ** (εὔπερεργον **Aᵃᶜ**): εἰ was changed into ᾖι by **A⁴**.

The good readings in **D** are all very easy corrections (or, for that matter, very easily made errors in **AF**).

Further, I have counted nine places where **AF** have an error due to wrong word-division or erroneous accentuation, e.g. 521d13 γυμναστικὴ—μουσικὴ **AF**; 559b8 ἤ] ἡ **AF**; 602d1 αὕτη] αὐτὴ **AF**.

In the few places where Burnet prints words which are in **D** but not in **AF**, I believe that the words in **D** are better omitted; they seem to be deliberate interpolations, added in order to clarify the sense (cf. below, p. 98):

333b8 οἰκοδομικοῦ τε καὶ **D**: om. **AF**
346a6 τούτων **D**: om. **AF**
370d3 ἢ οὔ **D**: om. **AF**
374b7-8 ἀλλὰ σκυτοτόμον **D**: om. **AF**

Thus the independent value of **D** is restricted; **D** serves mainly to control the readings of **AF**. In order to appreciate how **D** can be used in this way, it is necessary to investigate the relationship of **D** to **A** and **F** respectively.

Chambry cxliii says that **D** is more closely related to **F** than to **A**, and I believe that this statement is basically correct. I will try to prove that **D** and **F** go back to a common source, which is, to all practical intents and purposes, a gemellus of **A**; this implies that **ADF** do not all go back to their common ancestor *linea recta*.

First, I will discuss the common errors of **DF** against **A**: I will argue that these errors cannot all be explained as the result of coincidence or contamination. In the second place, I will deal with the common errors of **AD** against **F**: I will show that these can be ascribed to coincidence or contamination, while in many cases the reading of **AD** is to be preferred to the reading of **F** adopted by Burnet.

Before embarking on the discussion of the relationship of **ADF**, I wish to draw attention to the general methodological consideration that in dealing with the relationship of MSS of which the primary status has been proved convincingly, stemmatological evidence should be used much more cautiously than in dealing with secondary MSS. In the case of secondary MSS, their ultimate source is still extant, which is *qualitate qua* not the case with primary MSS; because, in the case of the *Republic*, it is certain that intensive contamination has taken place in antiquity, the agreement of two MSS against the third one may be due to contamination and does not necessarily prove that these two MSS derive from a common source. Further, in the course of time, many trivial errors may have originated in different branches of the tradition independently. Therefore, only agreement in very significant readings can be used as evidence for the closer relationship of two MSS against the third one.

I state in advance that I do not pay attention to word order for stemmatic purposes, because in places where **ADF** are not unanimous the correct word order can hardly ever be established beyond doubt. I may note in passing that there are only five places where **A** differs from **DF** in word order, and only seven places where **D** deviates from the word order of **AF**. **F** differs from **AD** in word order in countless places.

Errors of DF against A

1. In quite a few places, **DF** share an error which is made easily and which, accordingly, may have originated in **D** and **F** independently.

a. often, **DF** have an error which is due to wrong word-division; some instances:

351a7   τῇδέ πῃ σκέψασθαι **A Stob.**: τῇδ' ἐπισκέψασθαι **D**: τί δ' ἐπισκέψασθαι **F**
414d4   ἄρ'ἄ] ἄρα **DF**
445c2   ἅ γε **A Stob.**: ἄγε **DF**
489a9   δίδασκέ τε] διδάσκετε **D**: διδάσκεται **F**
533e4   'Αλλ' ὅ] ἄλλο
579a7   λαμβάνοιεν] λαμβάνοι ἐν

b. some other trivial errors:

334c4   ἡγῆται] ἡγεῖται
338a3   καὶ prius om.
347d4   νυνὶ] νῦν
371d2   αὖ om.
395a7   γε om.
409a1   ψυχῇ om.
435e5   ἐγγεγονέναι **A**: ἐκγεγονέναι **Stob.**: γεγονέναι **DF**
489c5   ἐλέγομεν ναυταῖς] ἐλέγομεν αὐταῖς
538c3   μέλειν] μέλλειν
576b10   διαδεξάμενος] δεξάμενος
607b2   ὅτι] ὅτε

THE PRIMARY MANUSCRIPTS

2. In other places, however, **DF** agree in significant error.

a. the most significant errors common to **DF** are, in my opinion, those which result from misreading majuscule script (cf. Deneke 25):

398d5	ᾀδομένου] διδομένου	(A > Δ)
399c5	νυνδὴ] νῦν ἄν	(ΔΗ > ΑΝ)
401c8	αὔρα] λύρα	(Α > Λ)
440b6	σαυτῷ] ἑαυτῷ (et A²ˢˡ Gal.)	(Σ > Ε)
581a10	ἀεὶ] δεῖ	(Α > Δ)

It is true that **F** brims with errors which have been caused by misreading majuscule script; on the other hand, in **D** I have found only two such errors (see above, p. 70); this makes it all the more improbable that the five majuscule errors quoted above have originated in **D** and **F** independently. That these readings passed from one tradition into the other as the result of contamination is virtually impossible because in all five cases the reading of **DF** is markedly inferior to the correct reading of **A**, but it is admitted that this possibility cannot be excluded altogether (in fact, ἑαυτῷ at 440b6 is added by A²ˢˡ).

b. some other errors common to **DF** which can hardly be coincidental:

359d8	οὐδέν] ἔχειν οὐδέν (a deliberate interpolation)
377c1	μῦθον habent **DF** falso: om. **A Eus.** recte
377e1	οὐσίαν habent **DF Eus.** (uno loco) falso: om. **A Eus.** (altero loco) recte
383a3	ποιεῖν **A Eus.**: ἀκούειν **DF**
401a7	κακοηθείας] κακονοίας
407c6	Εἰκός γε, ἔφη om.
461b6	φήσομεν] θήσομεν
470a2	φοβησόμεθα] φοβηθησόμεθα
506a9	τελέως] παντελῶς (glossema ?)
549a5	ἀλλ' ἀπὸ ἔργων] ἀλλὰ πρὸ ἔργων **F**: ἀλλὰ προέργων **D**
552c1	ἐδόκει om.
554b5	χοροῦ] χρόνου
560b10	θεοφιλῶν om.
574c9	Πάνυ] οὐ πάνυ
587e2	ἥδιον] ἥδιστον
597a6	κλινουργοῦ] δημιουργοῦ
621a7-8	τοὺς—μέτρου om. **DF**

Now there are two possible explanations for such common errors: either the agreement of **DF** is the result of contamination, or these readings are conjunctive errors of **D** and **F**, which prove that **D** and **F** go back to the same exemplar.

The hypothesis of contamination may hold good for such cases as 359d8 οὐδέν] ἔχειν οὐδέν, or 597a6 κλινουργοῦ] δημιουργοῦ; but there are some places where contamination can hardly be accepted as the explanation for the agreement of **DF**, namely those places where the reading of **DF** is so inferior to the reading of **A**, that it is hard to imagine that a scribe who had the text of **A** before him should have added the reading of **DF** as a variant reading, let alone that he (or a scribe who found both readings in his exemplar) should have preferred it to the reading of **A**. This is especially clear in the case of omissions which are common to **D** and **F**: see for instance:

407c6   Εἰκός γε, ἔφη om.
552c1   ἐδόκει om.
560b10 θεοφιλῶν om.
621a7-8 τοὺς—μέτρου om. **DF**

It could perhaps be argued that the omission of one word may have occurred in **D** and **F** independently; this may hold good for such words as μέν, γε etc. (in fact, **DF** sometimes do omit such words, see above, p. 72), but the omission of such vital words as 552c1 ἐδόκει and 560b10 θεοφιλῶν in **DF** is too much of a coincidence, nor is it likely that a scribe should have deleted such words intentionally. This goes *a fortiori* for the omission of 407c6 Εἰκός γε, ἔφη and of 621a7-8 τοὺς—μέτρου.

An analogous argument can be adduced with regard to many other readings, such as 401a7 κακοηθείας] κακονοίας; 549a5 ἀλλ' ἀπὸ ἔργων] ἀλλὰ πρὸ ἔργων **F**: ἀλλὰ προέργων **D**; 574c9 Πάνυ] οὐ πάνυ. But as I have already stated in the *Introduction* (see p. XXIII), the possibility that worthless readings were disseminated through contamination cannot be altogether excluded.

Thus, because **D** and **F** have 1. errors which are due to misreading majuscule script and 2. a lot of significant errors which can hardly be due to coincidence or contamination, I conclude that **D** and **F** go back to a common ancestor, which can be regarded as a gemellus of **A**.

Errors of AD against F

If the hypothesis that **D** and **F** derive from the same exemplar is correct, then the cases where **A** and **D** agree in error against **F** cannot possibly be conjunctive errors of **AD**, and must therefore be explained either as coincidence or as the result of contamination.

1. Often, **AD** share a trivial error against **F**:

a. in the whole of the *Republic*, I have found only four places where **AD** have a wrong word-division against **F**:

352d5   δ' ἔτι] δέ τι **AD**: δὲ ἔτι **F**
420b9   ἂν εὑρεῖν] ἀνευρεῖν **AD**
439a6   οὐδ' ἑνὶ] οὐδενὶ **AD**: οὐδὲ ἑνὶ **F**

550a5-6 αὖ τούς] αὐτούς **AD**

b. in two places, a wrong reading in **AD** differs from the correct reading in **F** only in accent and/or breathing, namely:

330b1 Ποῖ'] ποῖ **A**: ποι **D**
391e8 ὧν **F** Strabo: ὢν **AD**

c. often, **A** and **D** have an error which is easily made, and which, therefore, may have originated in **A** and **D** independently; some instances:

333d3 δέη] δέοι **A**: δὲ οἱ **D**
365d3 ἑταιρίας] ἑταιρείας
390d4 ἠνίπαπε] ἠνείπαπε **A** Gal.: ἢν εἴπαπε **D**
412a5 μετριώτατα] μετριότατα
438d2 οἰκίας] οἰκείας **A**: οὐκείας **D**
453e5 κατηγορεῖται] κατηγορεῖτε
466a3 σκεφοίμεθα] σκεψώμεθα
529b2 νοήσει] νοήσειν
565e3 προεστώς] προσεστώς
581c3 λέγομεν] λέγωμεν

2. In many places, the reading of **F** adopted by Burnet in preference to the reading of **AD** is far from certain:

a. **F** is notorious for the addition (and omission) of particles: I have counted some thirty places where Burnet adds a particle from **F**, while it is missing in **AD**; it is questionable, to say the least, whether Burnet is right in following **F** in all these places; at any rate, the omission of such particles in **A** and **D** cannot be considered an indication that **A** and **D** go back to a common ancestor. Some instances:

348c7 γε **F**: om. **AD**
428d11 οὖν **F**: om. **AD**
454e5 γ' **F** Gal.: om. **AD**
526d5 τε **F**: om. **AD**
544b9 γε **F**: om. **AD**

b. some other readings:

360b2 οὕτω **F**: om. **AD**; οὕτω is quite unnecessary.
366e6 τί δρᾷ **F**: ἐν **AD**; I think that τί δρᾷ is an interpolation, added in order to "improve" the grammatical structure of the sentence.
422a2 ἐμποιοῦντος **F** Eus. Stob.: ποιοῦντος **AD**; the reading of **AD** is certainly not inferior to that of **F**; see Adam ad loc.
535d2 ὄντα **F**: om. **AD** Stob.; ὄντα can easily be dispensed with.

3. **AD** do not have omissions of any length against **F**, nor omissions of vital words. **AD** have no common errors which are due to misreading majuscule script.

4. I quote some places where the reading of **AD** deserves more attention:

335a8-9   ὅτι ἔστιν δίκαιον **AD**: om. **F**
349b9   ἡγοῖτο **F** Stob.: ἡγοῖτο δίκαιον **AD**
352a5   ταυτὰ ταῦτα **F**: ταῦτα πάντα **AD**: ταῦτα Stob.
365e3   νόμων **F**: λόγων **AD** Cyr.
375b10   ἄλλοις **F** Stobaei MA: ἀλλοτρίοις **AD**: ἀλλήλοις Stobaei S
378b6   δοκεῖ **F** Eus. Thdt.: δοκῶ **AD**
388e6   ἐφιῇ Bekker: ἐφίη **F** Stob.: ἔφη **D**: ἔφην **A**
390a2   νεανιεύματα **F** Phot.: νεανιχεύματα **AD**
392b2   πολλοὶ **F**: δὲ πολλοὶ **AD** (recte ?)
416a3   ποιμέσι **F**: που ποιμέσι **AD**
442c6   ἐπιστήμην **F** Stob.: ἐπὶ ἐπιστήμην **AD** (corr. **A**)
463c5   ἢ **F**: τις ἢ **AD** (recte ?)
515b5   νομίζειν **F**: νομίζειν ὀνομάζειν **AD**: ὀνομάζειν Iambl.
522a7   ἔθη **F** Eus.: ἔφη **AD**
530c1   ἀχρήστου **F**: ἀρχῆς τοῦ **AD** (corr. **A**)
562b4   πλοῦτος **F**: ὑπέρπλουτος **AD**
579b1   εἴη **F**: εἰ εἴη **AD** (corr. **A**)

Two of these errors result from dittography (442c6 and 579b1) and may have come into **A** and **D** independently; at 392b2 and 463c5, **AD** add a word which is not in **F**, but which may very well be correct. At 349b9, the addition of δίκαιον (if indeed it is wrong) repeats ἡγοῖτο δίκαιον which precedes immediately. The addition of που at 416a3 may be a repetition of που before πάντων in the same line. The readings at 352a5, 375b10 and 522a7 are remarkable, but they could have originated in **A** and **D** independently. At 388e6, I suppose that, if ἐφιῇ is the correct reading, ἐφιῇ was corrupted into ἔφη, whether it originated in the **A** and **D** traditions independently, or came from the one into the other through contamination; subsequently, it was changed into ἔφην in **A**. It is also possible that we should read ἐφῇ, which is actually found in p^pc (ut vid.) (*a prima manu*).

The reading of **AD** at 335a8-9 ὅτι ἔστιν δίκαιον (**F** omits these words) is regarded as an interpolation by Dr Slings; this may be true. At 365e3 νόμων was likely to be corrupted into λόγων, as it is immediately followed by τῶν (...) ποιητῶν; the occurrence of λόγων in **A** and **D** (and Cyrillus) may be due to contamination, but it may well have originated in **A** and **D** independently.

At 515b5, I believe that Iamblichus' reading ὀνομάζειν must be correct, because of διαλέγεσθαι at b4; ὀνομάζειν and νομίζειν are often confused: I guess that the common source of **ADF** read νομίζειν for ὀνομάζειν; the reading νομίζειν ὀνομάζειν in **AD**, then, is due to the addition of ὀνομάζειν as a variant reading for νομίζειν; subsequently, both readings have been adopted in the text. For other views on this difficult phrase, see Adam, Appendix IV to book VII, II 179 f.; Wilamowitz 342.

The readings at 390a2 and 562b4 can hardly be coincidental, but the agreement of **A** and **D** may well be due to contamination in these places (this goes, of course, for many other readings quoted above as well). With regard to the reading ἀρχῆς τοῦ at 530c1, it should be noted that ἀρχῆς τοῦ was corrected by the scribe of **A**, so that it is possible that ἀρχῆς τοῦ is just an error made by the scribe of **A** when he copied the text: the error involves only the transposition of χ and ρ; of course, it is also possible that the exemplar of **A** had ἀρχῆς τοῦ, and that the scribe borrowed the correct reading from another source. Another possibility is that in this place (and in many other places as well) an error common to **ADF** was corrected in an ancestor of **F** (**ADF** all show traces of contamination, see below, pp. 78 f.).

All in all, I conclude that the places where **AD** agree in manifest error, are comparatively few; most of these readings can be explained as coincidence or as the result of contamination. Thus there are no objections to the hypothesis that **D** and **F** stem from a common source, which is a gemellus of **A**.

4. When did ADF part company?

I am not stating anything new when I remark that **F** often agrees with the indirect tradition (see Schneider III 311; Burnet, *Neglected MS* 100; Deneke 28-32; cf. above, pp. 67 f.). There are cases of agreement with ancient authors from different periods, among whom are also authors of the second century A. D., notably Galen; I quote some cases of significant agreement:

330d7 ἔμπροσθεν] ἐν τῷ πρόσθεν **F Iust.** (Stob.)
372c6 γε habent **F Ath.**: om. **AD**
407b4 γέ τι] τι γε (sic) **F**: τί γε **Gal.**
411b2 δὴ habent **F Demetr.**: om. **AD**
420a3 λαμβάνοντες ὥσπερ οἱ ἄλλοι] ὥσπερ οἱ ἄλλοι λαμβάνοντες **F**: ὥσπερ οἱ ἄλλοι λαβόντες **Ath.**
436e6 ἐγκλίνῃ] ἐκκλίνη **F**: ἐκκλίνει **Gal.**
439e4 ἂν εἴη] εἴη ἂν **F Gal.**
439e10 μὲν habent **F Gal.** (Stob.): om. **AD**
454d5 γε habent **F Gal.**: om. **AD**
454e5 γ' habent **F Gal.**: om. **AD**
617a6 τῷ om. **F Theon Sm.**

Some cases of rather trivial agreement:

436d8 ἑαυτῶν] αὐτῶν **F Gal.**
453b4 ὡμολογεῖτε] ὁμολογεῖτε **F Gal.**
455a9 δεώμεθα] δεόμεθα **F Gal.**

In one place, I have noted agreement of **F** with a papyrus, namely 414c9 δέ **AD**: γε **F Π⁴** (**Π⁴** belongs to the late second or early third century A. D.). Although the cases of agreement of **F** with second-century authors are not very striking in themselves, they do suggest that the bifurcation of the **D** and **F** traditions had already taken place in the second century A. D.; cf. Deneke 32 f.; Dodds, *Gorgias* 42, argues that the **F** tradition of *Grg.* already existed in the second century A. D.; Mr. G. Jonkers tells me that he has found many cases of agreement between **F** and authors before *ca.* 200 A. D. in the *Timaeus*; cf. Deneke 9-12, 15 f. If my hypothesis about the relationship of **ADF** is correct, the sources of **DF** and **ADF** will be older still. Deneke 32 f. goes on to establish the times at which the common sources of **ADF(M)** and **DF** originated; with regard to **F** Deneke 33 submits: "Quid obstat, ne memoriam F ex eadem editione Thrasylli temporibus facta, quam in Timaeo suspicati sumus, derivemus?" As regards the common ancestor of our tradition as a whole, Deneke suggests that it goes back to an edition made by Pomponius Atticus (Deneke 21, 40). The **FY** tradition of the *Timaeus* (which he regards as equivalent to the **FD** tradition in the *Republic*) came into existence *ca.* 10 B. C., according to Deneke 21. It is hardly necessary to remark that the evidence Deneke adduces for his hypotheses is very shaky and in fact wholly arbitrary. I think it is safest to admit that we are unable to tell at what time before the second century A. D. and under what circumstances the different branches of the medieval tradition came into existence.

5. *Contamination in ADF*

Although it has been possible to set up a stemma of **ADF**, it is impossible to apply a rigorous stemmatic method of choosing between variant readings in **ADF**, because all three MSS have been contaminated. I give some instances to prove this:

A	342a5	δεῖ] δεῖ ἀεί **A** (ex ἀεί fecit αἰεί **A**^{pc}) (this reading might also result from dittography)
	461a6	φύς, ἅς] φύσας **DF**: φύσας ἅς **A** (ἅς in rasura **A**, nescio quid ante fuerit)
	496a11	ἔφην ἐγώ] ἔφη, ἦν δ' ἐγώ **A**
D	358e2	τί ὄν τε **A**: οἷόν τε **F**: τί οἷόν τε **D** (cf. Gadelle 46)
	389d9	τοιάδε] τοιαῦτα δέ **D** (et **Stobaei A**)
	395c2	δὴ δέοι] δη δει δέοι (sic) **D**
	547c9	μεταβήσεται **A**: μεταθήσεται **F**: μεταβηθήσεται **D**
F	405c2	λυγιζόμενος **A** Phot. Suid. sch. Pl. ad loc. : λογιζόμενος **D** Stob.: αὖ λογιζόμενος **F** (i.e. addidit ΛΥ supra ΛΟ, quod corruptum in ΑΥ; cf. Schneider ad loc.)
	474a4	τωθαζόμενος] τωθαυμαζόμενος **F**
	549a9	μὲν ὦν **A**: μένων **D**: μένων ὦν **F**

For an instance of contamination of **A** in *Clit.*, see *Clit.* 408a1: δὴ **F**: ἂν **D**: ἂν δὴ **A**; cf. Slings 276.

Thus, it is impossible to state that if either **D** or **F** agrees with **A**, this must certainly represent the original reading of **ADF**: in some cases, agreement between **A** and **D** or **F** may be due to contamination. The same goes for the cases of agreement between **ADF** and the indirect tradition: as a rule, we can assume that where **AD** agree with the indirect tradition against **F**, the reading of **F** will be wrong (**F** brims with errors of every type, see below, pp. 105-110), but this is not always so: for instance, at 440e8 **F** has τούτου *recte*, while **AD Stob.** read τοῦτο; cf. Deneke 39[2]. Deneke explains such cases by assuming that "Has emendationes post Stobaeum factas esse verisimile est." Another explanation is that the tradition upon which Stobaeus drew was contaminated with a predecessor of **A** or **D**, or that the errors came into **AD** and Stobaeus independently.

At any rate, it appears impossible to apply a stemmatic method of shifting readings of any type in **ADF** (and, for that matter, of the indirect tradition): each variant reading must be judged on its own merits.

The only cases in which a stemmatic principle has any validity, I think, are those cases in which the order of words is concerned, or where particles are added or omitted in **F**.

In numerous places, **F** gives some words in an order different from that of **AD**; on the other hand, the places are very few where **A** has a transposition against **DF**, and where **D** has a word order different from that of **AF**; thus whenever **AD** agree in word order against **F**, we may infer with some confidence that **AD** have the words in the correct order[3]. The same principle can be applied in the few places in which **AF** agree in word order against **D**.

As regards the particles, it has already been noted that **F** often adds or omits them (see above, p. 75; below, pp. 106 f.); therefore, I believe that only in those cases where the reading in **F** concerning particles is markedly superior to the reading of **AD**, we should adopt **F**'s reading; the same goes for pronouns, articles, prepositions, etc.: cf. below, pp. 106 f. In cases where the readings in **AD** and **F** are equally good, we should do wise to follow **AD**, without however flattering ourselves with the conviction that **AD** undoubtedly give what Plato wrote.

---

[2] In the two other places quoted by Deneke, 472a2 στραγγευομένῳ and 604c7 αἱρεῖ, Deneke has been led astray by Burnet's apparatus: in both cases the reading has been added by a later hand in **F**.

[3] In three places Burnet prefers **F**'s word order to that of **AD**: 365b5 μὴ καὶ **F**: καὶ μὴ **AD**; 427a1 γέ τι **F**: τί γε **AD**; 472a6-7 λόγον λέγειν **F**: λέγειν λόγον **AD**. At 427a1, **AD**'s reading τί γε sounds slightly abnormal, but at 365b5 and 472a6-7 I believe that **AD**'s word order is equivalent if not superior to that of **F** (cf. Adam ad locc.).

II. The Individual Primary Manuscripts

The description of the primary MSS falls into four parts: first I make some remarks about the appearance of the MS under discussion, then I note what can be inferred about its exemplar; in the third place, I discuss the correcting hands, and finally I make some observations on the character of the MS.

1. A

a. appearance

A is written in two columns per page; each column contains 44 lines of 18-26 letters, with an average of 22-23 letters (cf. Clark 386 f.). Abbreviations are very few; at the end of a line we regularly find the compendium for ν. As punctuation signs **A** uses the comma (placed half way up the letters) and the single point (placed on the line, a little above the line, or half way up the letters). The change of speaker is indicated by a double point (dicolon) and by a horizontal stroke in the margin (paragraphos); cf. Andrieu 288 f. Sometimes a comma has been added below a dicolon (in all probability by a later hand), as an interrogation mark.

A usually writes iota adscriptum, which is often replaced by a iota suprascriptum by the corrector (see below, p. 84); iota subscriptum, of course, is never found.

b. the exemplar of A

The omissions in **A** have been studied in detail by Clark 386-395, who confirms some conclusions arrived at by Schanz, *Parisinus* 305 f.[4]. Clark notes six places where 15-21 letters have been telescoped; omissions of 17 letters are the most frequent (eleven). This brings Clark to the assumption that the average length of a line in **A**'s exemplar was 17 letters. There are two long omissions, of 700 and 717 letters; Schanz, *l.c.*, suggests that **A** has omitted a column of its exemplar in these cases; Clark argues that "omission of columns is less common than that of folios, and it is possible that folios of a remote ancestor have been lost." If this is correct, it follows that **A**'s exemplar had some 700 letters per folio, i.e.

---

[4] Although Clark's analyses are sometimes useful, the reader must be warned that Clark tends to assume automatically that an omission must correspond to one or more lines in the exemplar. The absurdity of this way of using the evidence is shown by the case of 528c1: **A** omits the words οὐκ—μεγαλοφρονούμενοι, which correspond exactly to one line of text in Burnet's edition; it would be rash to assume that **A** were copied from the Oxford text !

some twenty lines of 17 letters per page. If, however, we follow Schanz' suggestion, we may conclude that **A**'s exemplar had columns of *ca.* 42 lines, with about 17 letters each; in this case, **A** would resemble its exemplar rather closely. I have a slight preference for Schanz' explanation, because a codex with 20 lines of 17 letters per page must have been unusually small. Further, one should realize that what is said above does not necessarily apply to the *direct* source of **A**; the omissions mentioned may also have originated in a remote ancestor of **A**.

c. the corrections in A

The distinguishing of later hands in **A** is a problem which has caused much trouble. The main difficulty concerns the distinction of **A**, **A**^{pc} and **A**^{2}. I will deal with this problem first.

Burnet, 1905 edition, *praefatio* and *index siglorum*, suggests that **A**^{2} is identical with the scribe of the text ("A^2 = idem post diorthosin (ab eadem manu ut videtur)"). This is denied by Des Places ccix-ccxii, with the argument (borrowed from Post 6 f.) that readings of **A**^{pc} which are not found in **O** (Vaticanus 1, which from *Lg.* 746b8 on is a direct copy of **A**) have been added by a later hand in **A**^{5}.

A careful study of the corrections in **A** *in situ* has convinced me that Burnet is right in attributing the corrections usually assigned to **A**^{2}, to the scribe himself. The most conspicuous feature of most of the variant readings commonly ascribed to **A**^{2} is that they are written in the (semi-)majuscule script which is also used for the scholia; Schanz, *Parisinus* 305, already noted that most of the scholia in **A** have been written by the scribe himself. That the hand of the scholia is identical with **A**^{2} appears from the fact that the ink of the scholia has the same colour as the **A**^{2} readings. It frequently happens that **A** adds a reading in the margin at a later stage (whether a variant reading or a suppletion of an omission) in a script exactly similar to that of the text itself, but in an obviously different ink from that in which the text is written. Especially in the later books of the *Republic*, the correction-ink is much lighter than the text-ink. It is decisive for the identification of **A**^{2} (that is, the variant readings in majuscules)[6] with the scribe of the text, that readings by **A**^{2}

---

[5] Thus Des Places distinguishes between corrections and variant readings added by the first hand (**A**^{1}) and corrections and variant readings added by a somewhat later hand (**A**^{2}). Post is also followed by Tarán 172: "Conversely, those readings in A which are different from those of O and which are corrections by a somewhat later hand which used a pale brown ink similar to the one used by A, will be called A^2".

[6] Editors use the siglum **A**^{2} for all the corrections and variant readings which are supposed to have been added after the text had been written, both in majuscule and

are written in the same ink as the scholia and the additions by A^1 (i.e. additions in minuscules) as opposed to the ink used for the text. Nowhere have I found an addition in minuscules (A^1), written in exactly the same colour as the text, but clearly different from the ink of the variant readings in majuscules (A^2); yet it cannot be excluded altogether that in some places A^1 has added some marginalia *during* the copying of the text, because in the earlier books of the *Republic* it is often very difficult to distinguish the correction-ink from the text-ink.

I quote some places where **A** has added a reading in minuscule script in the correction-ink, clearly differing from the ink of the text[7]:

471c7 (fol. 57ᵛ)	αὕτη om., add. in margine
486c10 (fol. 62ᵛ)	ἀνόνητα] ἀνόητα: γρ. ἀνόνητα in margine
528c1 (fol. 78ᵛ)	οὐκ—μεγαλοφρονούμενοι om.: add. in margine
601a8-9 (fol. 105ʳ)	ἐν—λέγεσθαι om.: add. in margine
613e2 (fol. 110ᵛ)	λέγων εἶτα habet: γρ. λέγοντα in margine

For some instances of scholia written in the correction-ink, see the scholium on 424a1-2 (fol. 39ᵛ) and the scholia on foll. 104ᵛ and 105ʳ.

I conclude 1. that A^2 is identical with the scribe, and 2. that most, if not all, additions and corrections, both in majuscule and minuscule script, have been made after the text had been copied.

As frequently happens, the solution of one problem creates another: why did the scribe of **A** use minuscule script in some places, and majuscule script in others ? I note some further differences between the majuscule and minuscule additions:

1. the minuscule variant readings are usually preceded by γρ. (but this is not always the case: e.g. 484b3 (fol. 61ᵛ) ἑξῆς habet: ἐξ ἀρχῆς without γρ. in the margin, in minuscules); this never occurs with the majuscule variant readings.

2. suppletions of longer omissions are always in minuscules, without γρ.

3. minuscule variant readings are usually in full, while the majuscule variant readings only give the letters which are different. Yet sometimes a variant reading is added above the line in minuscule script, e.g. 587c7 (fol. 100ᵛ) δημοτικὸς **A**: add. χρα supra lineam **A** litteris minusculis (in the

minuscule script. I reserve A^2 for the variant readings in majuscule script, and designate all the other readings added by the scribe with A^{pc} (or A^{im}, A^{sl}). Against this practice, it could be objected that it might be better to designate *all* variant readings and corrections by the first hand with the same siglum; yet I believe that it may be useful to distinguish between the readings in majuscule and minuscule script; although I myself am unable to tell what the difference is between the two types of variant readings, future scholars may find a criterium for assigning a different status to the readings in majuscule and minuscule script.

[7] The reader who wishes to check my observations will only be able to do so adequately by studying **A** *in situ*; Omont's facsimile, which reproduces **A** in black and white, does not bring out the differences in the colour of the text-ink and the correction-ink.

correction-ink). Majuscule additions are usually written *supra lineam* or *in margine*.

I can offer no explanation for the alternation of minuscules and majuscules in variant readings. One might be inclined to think that the use of a different type of script indicates that the scribe attached a different value to readings in minuscule and majuscule script; in this respect, the case of 608e6 (fol. 108ᵛ) is very interesting: τι καί] τι **A**: add. καί supra lineam litteris minusculis: ante καί add. δὲ litteris maiusculis; both καί and δὲ are written in the correction-ink, and must therefore have been added at the same time. Yet I have not been able to assign a different status to readings in minuscule and majuscule script; in both types of script there are readings which are found in other branches of the tradition, and readings which are not found elsewhere.

Most, if not all, accents and breathings in **A** have been added in the correction-ink (cf. Campbell 71; Burnet, 1905 edition, *praefatio*). As a rule, the accent is in accordance with the reading *post correctionem*:

501a3 (fol. 68ᵛ)   πρωτων **A**ᵃᶜ: πρῶτον **A**ᵖᶜ
591e2 (fol. 102ᵛ) πληθους **A**ᵃᶜ: πλῆθος **A**ᵖᶜ
599c7 (fol. 104ᵛ) πολεμον **A**ᵃᶜ: πολέμων **A**ᵖᶜ

Yet it also happens that a reading *ante correctionem* already had an accent, so that the correction involves the change of the accent and one or more letters; see for instance:

348a8 (fol. 11ᵛ)   αὖ] ἂν **A**ᵃᶜ: αὖ **A**ᵖᶜ
352c1 (fol. 13ʳ)   δὴ καὶ οὕς **A**ᵖᶜ: δικαίους **A**ᵃᶜ

In other places, only the accent itself has been changed, e.g. 380d3 and d4 (fol. 23ᵛ) τότε **A**ᵃᶜ: τοτὲ **A**ᵖᶜ.

In such cases we must assume that the accent was first placed on the erroneously written word (after the text had been copied) and that the word plus the accent were corrected subsequently.

It sometimes happens that there was a variant reading in the margin and that the reading in the text and the marginal reading have been interchanged; see for instance 437d8 (fol. 45ʳ) (τινός) που (sic) **A**ⁱᵗ: γρ. η ου (sic, nisi fallor) **A**ⁱᵐ: (τινος) ἢ οὐ **A**ⁱᵗᵖᶜ: γρ. που **A**ⁱᵐᵖᶜ. The original accent on τινός shows that the readings were interchanged after the accents in the text had been added.

In some places where a correction is made, the original reading in the text has been relegated to the margin as a variant reading; see for instance 555b10 (fol. 88ʳ) πλουσιώτατον: ου in rasura **A**ᵖᶜ: πλη in margine **A** litteris maiusculis; here, πλησιώτατον must have been the original reading in the text; moreover, πλη in the margin has been noted with dots, which seems to indicate that the scribe regarded this reading as inferior.

Whenever a correction is written *in rasura*, it is often impossible to decide with absolute certainty whether it was written during the copying of the text or afterwards when variant readings and accents were added. From the instances I have discussed above, I think we may conclude that, as a rule, readings *in rasura* have been written after the text had been copied.

A rasura is often filled up with a horizontal stroke with one dot above and one below it (in longer rasurae, this sign occurs repeatedly); this sign is also found in places where there is no rasura; in such cases it may serve to indicate a lacuna in the exemplar.

A number of other activities of **A** in the correction-ink:

> 1. often a iota suprascriptum has been added; sometimes a iota adscriptum is replaced by a iota suprascriptum; in such cases only the lower part of the original iota is erased. 2. sometimes a iota adscriptum is added. 3. between the elements of compound words (e.g. Θρασύμαχος), and between words which belong closely together (e.g. ἐπ' αὐτοφόρῳ), **A** often adds the so-called hyphen, for which see Dionysius Thrax, *Ars Grammatica, Suppl. I* (*Grammatici Graeci* I 1,113,5-114,1 Uhlig). 4. often δέ is changed into δαί.

On the basis of the observations made above, we may infer that accents and breathings, variant readings and corrections were all added at the same time, after the text had been copied. Most (but not all) of the accents and breathings were written first; then followed the variant readings and corrections, which sometimes involved the change of the accent which had just been added; finally, in some cases the variant reading in the margin appeared to the scribe, on second thoughts, to be superior and was interchanged with the reading in the text.

So much for the external features of **A** and **A²**. I may add that I have refuted Des Places implicitly: I do not intend to hold a full discussion on his argumentation, but I confine myself to exposing some weak spots:

> 1. when **O** has a word which has been erased in **A**, Des Places usually ascribes the erasure to **A²**; of course, in such cases the erasure may also have been made by a later correcting hand (**A³**, Constantine etc.); see for instance *Lg.* 758b4 τὸν **AO**: "τὸ A² (ν erasum)" Des Places.
> 2. when **A²** adds an alternative reading, the fact that **O** follows the reading in the text of **A** does not imply that the variant reading was not yet in **A** at the time when **O** was copied from **A**.
> 3. often Des Places errs in attributing a particular reading to a particular hand; see for instance 759c6 γρ. δευτερην **A**ⁱᵐ; Des Places attributes this reading to **A²**, but it is clearly written in the same minuscule script as the text.

For an account of the sources of the corrections and variant readings in **A**, see below, pp. 88-91.

There are several later hands in **A**. The first of these, **A³**, is especially active in tetr. IX; Des Places ccxii f. (following Lenz 205 f.) attributes this hand to Arethas. In isolated places, I have found readings added by **A³** in *R*.: 327c10 (fol. 3ʳ) γρ. ἓν λείπεται has been added by **A³** (not by **A**, as Burnet and Chambry wrongly note); at 329e1 (fol. 3ᵛ) σε may also have been added above the line by **A³** (or by **A²**; in any case not by **rec. a**, as Burnet reports). A number of scholia in the first two books of *R*. also seem to have been added by **A³** (e.g. some scholia on foll. 3, 4, 14). The reading 327c10 ἓν λείπεται recurs in **TMγ**, which provides us with a *terminus ante quem* of *ca*. 950 for **A³** (**T** was written at about that time); the attribution of **A³** to Arethas may therefore be correct.

Another hand, **A⁴**, is especially active in constantly changing the ending —ει of the second person indicative middle into —ηι, the ending —ῆς of the nominative plural of nouns in —εὺς into —εῖς etc. The commas below the dicolon, which have sometimes been added to make a query, seem to have been added by **A⁴** as well. Sometimes **A⁴** changes an accent (e.g. 437e8 (fol. 45ʳ) τοιοῦ (bis) **A**: τοίου **A⁴ᵖᶜ**), or adds breathings on — ρρ— (e.g. 453a1 (fol. 50ʳ) ἄῤῥενος).

A⁴ writes in a pale ink; **A⁴** has been active after the exemplar of **TMγ** was copied from **A**, because readings by **A⁴** do not recur in **T** (the places where **Mγ** agree with **A⁴** must be due to correction or corruption of the exemplar of **Mγ**).

The hand which I designate **A⁵** is usually called **a**, but I prefer to avoid the use of minuscule letters to indicate recent hands in MSS. **A⁵** is easily recognizable because of its red ink, as was already observed by Schanz, *Parisinus* 304. **A⁵** has added a subscription on the last folium ὠρθώθη ἡ βίβλος αὕτη ὑπὸ Κωνσταντίνου μητροπολίτου Ἱεραπόλεως τοῦ καὶ ὠνησαμένου. According to Des Places ccx (with n. 2) this Constantine lived in the twelfth century. Constantine adds some marginal notes, and repeats some words from the text in the margin; occasionally he corrects a reading in the text (e.g. 365a8 (fol. 17ʳ) ἐφιπτάμενοι **A⁵ᵖᶜ**). Further, he sometimes writes an extra accent on μὲν and δὲ, adds punctuation signs, and writes breathings on —ρρ— (e.g. 368d3 (fol. 18ᵛ) πόῤῥωθεν) and the like. Constantine has often been scolded for his stupidity: Cobet 159: "Constantinus ille Hierapolitanus Metropolita unus est ex illis correctorculis, qui ea quae emendare conantur depravare solent"; Burnet, 1905 edition, *praefatio*: "Constantinus (...) correctiunculis ineptis librum deformans". Yet in some places Constantine is responsible for a good reading not found in **ADF**; thus at 462b1 and b2 (fol. 54ʳ) Constantine has corrected the wrong reading ποιεῖ of **A** (and **DF Stob.**) into ποιῆι (Burnet's apparatus is wrong) ! There are some indications that **A⁵** comes after **A⁴**: in a number of places, **A⁴** adds a reading in the margin which has been written in the text by Constantine, e.g. 605b4 (fol. 107ʳ) ποιῶν] ποιοῦν A⁴ⁱᵐ (nisi fallor): ποιοῦν A⁵ⁱᵗᵖᶜ. Further, Constantine has the habit of changing ὤ/σπερ into ὤσ/περ.

I have not found any noteworthy readings in R. by the hands which are called a² and a³ by Burnet, Post and Des Places. There are a few scattered marginalia by still other hands than those specified above, but I have not thought it worthwhile to investigate these thoroughly. From fol. 19ᵛ on, we often encounter pencil strokes in the margin; Dr Slings tells me that he has observed similar pencil strokes in *Clit.*, on fol. 2ᵛ. Because these signs are also found in **E** and **D** (also collated by Bekker), I presume that they were added in **A**, when it was collated by Bekker.

d. the character of A

Nowadays scholars rightly avoid the use of the term *codex optimus*, but it is not surprising that **A** was designated as such by earlier scholars: if the text of the *Republic* had been handed down to us in **A** alone, we would possess a much better text than if only **D**, not to speak of **F**, had been preserved. Of course, this does not imply that **A** is free from errors, or that **A** should be followed wherever **A**'s reading is possible (Adam's *ratio edendi*, cf. p. 10).

In studying the text of **A**, we must distinguish between the text of **A** and the corrections and variant readings which have been added by the scribe after the text had been written. I will first discuss the text of **A**ᵃᶜ.

1. Omissions are found occasionally in **A**; I have distinguished three different types.

a. in many cases, an omission in **A** concerns one word only, often a particle or pronoun; see for instance:

328d7   γε om.
342a4   αὐτὰ om.
359d6   ἃ om.
362d3   ἔφη om.
373a4   καὶ prius om.
376c2   φιλόσοφον om. (add. p.c.)
378c8   λεκτέα om.
395c7   μὴ om.
404b5   ἁπλῆς om.
449a6   ἔφη om.
490d3   μὲν om.
526b2   τῇ om.
536a5   πάντῃ om.
597b6   ἐν om.
613b6   ἄττ' om.

THE PRIMARY MANUSCRIPTS

b. sometimes, more than one word has been omitted; often, such omissions concern a coherent set of words, sometimes a complete clause; this suggests that the scribe used to read a self-contained set of words in his exemplar, which he copied from his memory at one go; in this way, other self-contained portions of text were more likely to be left out without being noticed. Omissions of this type are remarkably frequent in the second book and the beginning of the third book, from which we may perhaps infer that the scribe had an off-day when he copied these parts. Some instances:

328d6	ὡς παρὰ φίλους τε om. (add. p.c.)
358a8	ἀδικία δ' ἐπαινεῖται om.
360a8	τῶν παρὰ τὸν βασιλέα om. (add. p.c.)
366a7	αὖ μέγα δύνανται om.
373a7	καὶ τὴν ποικιλίαν om.
376d2-3	ἵνα—διεξίωμεν om. (add. p.c.)
379b7-9	μή—γε om. (homoioteleuton ?; add. p.c.)
380e4	καὶ prius—τε alterum om. (homoioteleuton ?; add. p.c.)
381a7	καὶ ἀμφιέσματα om.
382e9-10	οὔτε κατὰ φαντασίας om.
386c6	ᾧ—εἴη om.
493d2-3	εἴτε—ὁμιλῇ om. (add. p.c.)
552d7	Δῆλον, ἔφη om.
601a8-9	ἐν—λέγεσθαι om. (add. p.c.)

c. in one place in *R.*, a line in the exemplar seems to have been telescoped: 400a7 —μι ποῖα δὲ ὁποίου βίου om.; yet this omission may also be due to parablepsis (εἴποιμι—μιμήματα).

2. Many errors in **A** have been caused by (inner) dictation, usually itacism; some instances:

338a6	εὐδοκιμήσειεν] εὐδοκημήσειεν (corr. **A**)
352c1	δὴ καὶ οὕς] δικαίους (corr. **A**)
364a7	δημοσίᾳ] διμοσίᾳ (corr. **A**)
389d4	κολάσει ὡς] κολάσεως
400b8	τιν'] τὴν (corr. **A**)
443a9	μὴν] μὲν
469e2	βάλλοντος] βαλόντος
516e3	ὁ τοιοῦτος] ὅτι οὗτος
568e5	ἑταίρους] ἑτέρους
589b8-c1	ἀληθῆ ἄν] ἀλήθειαν

3. Often an error is due to carelesness (esp. as regards the ending of words) or mental association; see for instance:

351d7	διαφέρωμαι] διαφέρωμεν
360c4	ταῦτ' ἄν] ταὐτὸν

374c2 ἀπεργάσεσθαι] ἀπεργάζεσθαι
387c3 ὑπέρ] ὑπὸ
432b8 θάμνον] θάμνων
450c4 οὖν] ἄν
472d1 μοῖραν] μοῖραν ἄν (dittography; ἄν del. A^pc)
506a5 πολλοῦ τινος] πολλοὺς τινὰς (corr. A)
516b9 οὗτος] αὐτὸς
529c2 νέων] μὲν
537e2 κακόν] καλὸν
558c3 Ταῦτά] ταῦτα τά (dittography)
601a6 ἀλλ' ἤ] ἀλλὰ
610b1 μή ποτε] μήτε

4. Occasionally a small word (preposition, article, particle) has been added; some instances:

339b8 δίκαιον] καὶ δίκαιον
382e9 λόγῳ] ἐν λόγῳ (possible)
404a10 τε] τε καὶ
533e7 οὖν] γ' οὖν (possible)
544c6 πασῶν] ἡ πασῶν

5. There are five places where **A** differs from **DF** in word order:

414b4 δὴ νῦν **A**: νῦν δὴ **DF**
443d7 καὶ εἰ **A**: εἰ καὶ **DF**
472b3 τόδε χρὴ **A**: χρὴ τόδε **DF**
600d2 ἐπιστατήσωσι τῆς παιδείας **A**: τῆς παιδείας ἐπιστατήσωσι **DF**
616a4 ὅτι εἰς **DF**: εἰς ὅτι **A**

At 616a4 the word order of **A** is certainly wrong, but in the remaining four cases the correct word order cannot be established beyond doubt.

6. Interpolations seem to be very rare in **A**; the addition of ἀρχομένοις at 340a6 has all the appearance of having been made conjecturally, to match ἄρχοντας at a5. For the case of 335a8-9 ὅτι ἔστιν δίκαιον, see above, p. 76.

It has already been noted that the **A** tradition shows traces of contamination (see pp. 78 f.).

The readings of A^pc

With regard to the source of the corrections in **A**, Campbell 70 remarks: "The question whether the first diorthotes, who seems to have been a careful person, had before him any other MS. than that from which the first hand had copied, is important, but can hardly be resolved." Slings 269 states without proof that "the older corrections in A appear to be derived from another source with independent value."

Readings added by **A^pc** (in this section I treat readings in minuscule and majuscule script together) are sometimes found in the other primary MSS as well, sometimes in either **D** or **F**, and sometimes in the indirect tradition, but not in **DF**. I quote some instances of all of these groups.

A^pc = DF

346a7 οἷον **A^pcDF**: οἷοι **A^ac**
351c7 σὺ **A^imDF**: σοι **A^it**
359d4 τι habent **A^slDF**: om. **A^ac**
440b6 σαυτῷ **A^it**: ἑαυτῷ **A^slDF** Gal.
461c5 μηδέ γ' ἕν **A**: μηδὲν **A^pcDF** Eus. Thdt. Phlp.
475e1 μαθητικοὺς **A**: μαθηματικοὺς **A^slDF** Clem. Thdt. Cyr.
486c10 ἀνόνητα **A^imDF**: ἀνόητα **A^it**
580b9 ὁ habent **A^slDF**: om. **A^ac**
608e4 δὲ habent **A^slDF**: om. **A^ac**

A^pc = D

330e5 ἠδίκησεν **A^slD** Iust.: ἠδίκηκεν **AF** Stob.
347e7 ἔγωγε **A^acF**: ἔγωγ' ἔφη **A^slD**
366d3 ὡς δὲ **A^pcD**: ὡδὲ **A^acF**
370a1 σίτου **A^acF**: σιτίου **A^pcD**
376c2 φιλόσοφον habent **A^imD** Stob.: om. **A^acF**
473c2 μεταβαλόντος **AF** Stob.: μεταβάλλοντος **A^slD**
556d2 ἰσχνὸς **A^pcD**: ἰχνὸς **A^ac**: ἴχνος **F**

A^pc = F

364d3 καὶ τραχεῖαν habent **A^imF**: om. **AD**
397b9 σμικραὶ **A^pcF**: σμικρὰ **A^acD**
415c6 σιδηροῦς **A^pcF** Eus.: σίδηρος **A^acD**
425e4 διήλθομεν **A^pcF**: ἤλθομεν **A^ac** (sic, nisi fallor): ἤλθομεν **D**
475c8 φήσομεν **AD**: θήσομεν **A^slF**
505b1 εἶναι **A^pcF**: εἰδέναι **A^acD**
525d9 αὖ Burnet: δύο **A^acD**: om. **A^pcF**
530c1 ἀχρήστου **A^pcF**: ἀρχῆς τοῦ **A^acD**

A^pc = indirect tradition

457b2 ἀτελῆ **ADF**: ἄτε δὴ **A^im** Eus. et legisse videtur **Thdt**.
470b4 ταῦτα **ADF**: ταῦτα τὰ **A^sl** Stob.
474d8 ἐπαινεθήσεται **ADF**: ἐπαινεῖται **A^sl** Aristaenet.
537a2 ὃ **ADF**: ὧι **A^sl** Stob.
613e2 λέγων εἶτα **ADF**: λέγοντα **A^im** Stob.
616b6 προσφερῆ **ADF**: προσφερὲς **A^sl** Simp. Procl.

Thus it appears that **A^pc** is not confined to one particular branch of the tradition; that the readings of **A^pc** do have primary value, goes without saying, because **A^pc** is contemporary with **A** itself, and therefore much older than **D** and **F**.

The fact that all the corrections and variant readings in **A** have been written in the same ink (see above, pp. 81-84), proves that they were added at the same time. Thus there are two explanations which offer themselves: 1. all the corrections and variant readings were noted in the exemplar; 2. the scribe consulted several MSS simultaneously when he added the corrections and variant readings.

The first possibility is not very attractive in itself: if it were true, we should have to suppose that the scribe, when copying the text, did not pay any attention to the numerous variant readings in his exemplar: it is, for instance, hard to believe that when confronted with the choice between ἀχρήστου and ἀρχῆς τοῦ at 530c1, the scribe should first have preferred the nonsensical ἀρχῆς τοῦ and changed it afterwards. Yet this procedure is not unparalleled: I will show that the scribe of β must have worked in almost exactly this way (except that the corrections and variant readings in β were added not by the scribe himself, but by someone else, yet from the same source from which the text was copied); see below, p. 185. Therefore the possibility that the exemplar of **A** was a MS with variant readings cannot be excluded altogether. Even so, I am inclined to believe that the scribe himself took the corrections and variant readings from various sources.

Besides the readings in which **A^pc** agrees with other attested branches of the tradition, there are quite a few readings which are not found elsewhere. Some of these readings are certainly correct: see for instance:

333e1   οὐκ ἂν οὖν **A^im**: οὐκοῦν **ADF**
511c3   οὔ **A^pc**: οὖν **ADF**
576d2   ἀρετῆι **A^im**: ἆρα ἡ **DF**: ἄρα ἡ **A**

Of course, it is possible that the new readings added by **A^pc** were taken from a source which is now lost. Yet some of the readings added by **A^pc** have all the appearance of being conjectures; see for instance:

328e7   αὐτὸ **ADF Stob.**: αὐτὸς **A^sl** (σὺ precedes immediately)
420b5   εἰσιν **ADF**: εἶεν **A^sl** (εἴη precedes in the same line)
538d8   ἤκουεν **ADF**: ἤκουσεν **A^sl** and ἐξελέγχῃ **ADF**: ἐξελέγξῃι **A^sl** (possibly because of the aorist participle ἀποκριναμένου at d7)
559e4   μετέβαλλε **ADF**: μεταβάλλει **A^sl** (μεταβάλλει follows at e6)
568d8   ἀποδομένων **ADF**: ἀπολομένων **A^sl** (this might also be an error caused by misreading majuscule script, but ἀποδομένων is certainly wrong, because the passive voice is needed)
607d4   μέτρῳ **ADF**: γρ. τρόπῳ **A^im**

However, it cannot be excluded that these readings, too, were actually found in a MS, whether as errors, genuine readings or conjectures; I am unable to tell whether the note γρ. in **A** always indicates that a reading was actually found in another MS; in the case of Bessarion (fifteenth century) we can be fairly certain that γρ. was also used to introduce conjectures. Be that as it may, the readings of **A**^{pc} do have primary value, whatever may have been their source[8].

2. D

a. appearance

D is written in one column per page; each page contains 40 lines. I have counted the letters on fol. 313^r: the minimum is 44, the maximum 57; the average length of a line is 52 letters.

As punctuation signs **D** uses the single point (on the line, a little above the line and half way up the letters); the comma, which is said by Slings 275 to occur rarely in **D**, seems to me to have been added by **D**^{2} (or **D**^{4}), judging from the microfilm (but I have not checked this *in situ*); yet some commas may have been written by the first hand. The dicolon serves to indicate the change of speaker; the paragraphos, which is said to occur in **D** by Andrieu 289, is in fact not found in **D**: I suppose that Andrieu was deceived by the numerous pencil strokes which are found in the margin of **D**, and which appear to have been added by Bekker (see below, p. 94).

Compendia are used only rarely; I have noted compendia for —ν, —ων, —ος and —αι, always at the end of a line. Adscript iota is found regularly; subscript and suprascript iota are never found.

There are two longer omissions in **D**, due to the loss of some leaves: 507e4-515d7 and 612e7-621d3.

b. the exemplar of D

The studies of, a.o., Carlini 151-158 and Berti 219 f. have established that **D** is a primary witness in tetr. I-IV, closely related to **B**, but not dependent on it (the stichometric studies of Berti were anticipated by Schanz, *Stichometrie* 313, n. 1).

The opinion held by, a.o., Alline 219, that **D** represents the **B** tradition in *R.*, is untenable: we have seen that in *R.* **D** and **F** go back to a common ancestor; now if **D** indeed represented the **B** tradition in *R.*, we should expect to find similar agreement between **B** and **F** against **T** (which, in some dialogues accompanied by **WP**, represents the **A** tradi-

---

[8] In a sense, the attempt to distinguish between readings invented by the scribe of **A** himself and readings conjectured by earlier scribes, is comparable to the famous statement (quoted by W. K. C. Guthrie, *A History of Greek Philosophy I* (Cambridge 1962), 176, n. 1) "that the *Iliad* was not written by Homer, but by another poet of the same name."

tion in tetr. I-VII; see below, p. 120, n. 8) in those dialogues which are in **BTWPF**, namely *Grg.* and *Men.*; yet Dodds, *Gorgias* 35-42, and Bluck 129-136 have shown that in these dialogues **BT** form one group, together with **WP**, against **F**.

Clark 409 notes that in the *Republic* there are two telescoped passages in **D**, one of 45 letters and one of 48 letters. He concludes, plausibly enough, that these omissions represent one line in a previous MS (N.B. not necessarily **D**'s *direct* source). For the rest, Clark's impressive list of 45 omissions and dittographies in **D** is misleading: only six cases (apart from the two telescoped passages just mentioned) do *not* result from homoioteleuton ! Therefore Clark's argumentation on pp. 409-411 breaks down completely (Gadelle 29 makes the same mistake). The only valid inference to be drawn from the omissions in **D** is the one already mentioned above, viz. that an ancestor of **D** had about 45 letters per line. As a rule, the lines in majuscule MSS are much shorter; if we combine this with the observation that **D** has some (not very many) errors which may be due to misreading minuscule script, we may suppose that **D** does not go back directly to a majuscule MS; some instances of errors in **D** which seem to be due to misreading minuscule script:

543c7   διεληλυθώς] διελήλυθας
562e4   ἐμφυομένην] εὐφυομένην
568e8   ἡβῶντα] ἡμῶν τὰ

N. B. Most of the instances quoted by Gadelle 30 f. can also be explained in another way.

c. the corrections in D

In some places, the scribe of **D** noticed an error he had made, and corrected it himself. The scribe of **D** does not add material from other sources.

The most prominent later hand, **D²**, is easily recognizable by its very dark-brown ink. **D²** pays much attention to accents and breathings, which are often omitted or wrongly placed in **D**; **D²** also adds numerous scholia.

The source of the readings added by **D²** can be traced exactly: in *Phd.* **D²** draws on a MS related to **W** (see Carlini 158, n. 16); in *R.*, most of the readings added by **D²** are found in the **Sc.**-group[9] (to which **W** belongs in *R.*), some of them only in **W** (and its derivatives); **D²** also

---

[9] This is also the case in *Clit.*; see Slings 277.

adds the scholia as they stand in **W**. Because **W** belongs to different traditions in *Phd.* and *R.*, **D²** cannot have drawn on an ancestor of **W** (*R.* has been written by a later hand in **W**); because the extant derivatives of **W** (**Lobc.** and its apographon **R**) do not contain the scholia, we may conclude that **D²** drew on **W** itself (or a lost apographon of **W**). I quote some instances of agreement between **D²** and **W**:

373e9   οὔ τι] ὄντι D²pcW
391d5   ἡμῖν] ἡμᾶς D²slSc.W
402b9   ὃ λέγω] ὁ λέγων D²pcSc.W
476b7   τὴν φύσιν] τὸν νοῦν D²pcSc.W
526b6   φύονται] φαίνονται D²slSc.W
539a9   τρόπῳ] λόγῳ D²imSc.W
579b2   φρουρούμενος] φορούμενος D²pcW
582a10 ἐμπειρότατος habent DSc.W: τερο D²slW¹sl
603e7   ἀχθέσεται] ἀχθεσθήσεται D²pcSc.W

A number of readings added by **D²** are not found elsewhere; see for instance:

343d3   πανταχοῦ] παντελῶς D²sl
348b9   τελέαν] τελευταίαν D²sl
402c1   φαμεν] ἔφαμεν D²sl
516a6   καθορῷ] καθορᾷ D²pc
525a1   ἀγωγῶν] ἀναγωγῶν D²pc
585a3   πληρώσει—ἡδονῇ] πλήρωσιν—ἡδονὴν D²pc

The readings of **D²** do not recur in **Vind.Bon.Sc.**, but they are found in all the other derivatives of **D** (**Par.**, **Ψ**, **Pal.** and **Ath.**).

D³ writes in a pale, bluish ink; it adds only a few readings, almost exclusively in the first book, but, e.g., 531b8 ἐρήσεσθαι (for which **D** has αἱρήσεσθαι (sic)) seems to have been added by **D³** as well. I have not been able to determine the source of **D³**; some readings appear to be new; see for instance:

342a1   πονηρά] πονηρία D³sl
343e5   ἀπεχθέσθαι] ἀπέχεσθαι DF: ἀπέχθεσθαι (sic) D³pc
347a10 βελτίστων] βέλτιστον D³sl (N. B. **D** has τούτων for τὸν τῶν)

The readings added by **D³** recur in **Par.**, **Ath.** and **Ψ**, but not in **Vind.Bon.Sc.** (**D³** does not add any readings in the fragment which is in **Pal.**).

D⁴ writes in a rather pale brown ink, and is especially active in book VII, possibly also in a number of places in book VI (e.g. 484b5 παντοίως] πάντως D: γρ. παντοίως D⁴im). Some of the readings added by **D⁴** can be traced to the **F**-family, e.g.:

524c3 καὶ prius] καὶ ἡ FD⁴ᵖᶜ
530d7 ὡς] οὕτως F: οὕτω D⁴ᵖᶜ

A few other readings of **D⁴** appear to be new, e.g.:

527c2 καλλιπόλει] καλῇ πόλει D⁴ˢˡ
530b1 οἴει] εἰ οἴει D⁴ˢˡ

The readings of **D⁴** do not recur in the extant apographa of **D**.

Finally, a very recent hand, **Dʳᵉᶜ·**, writing with a pencil, has been active in **D**. This hand adds numerous horizontal strokes in the margin, adds Ast's chapter numbers, and writes some marginal notes; e.g. at 327c3 ὡς is added in the margin by **Dʳᵉᶜ·** (om. **D**); at 351d4 the words καὶ μίση are repeated in the margin. On fol. 313ʳ, the notes "duo folia abscisa" and "Πολιτεία Ζ" have been written by **Dʳᵉᶜ·**. As the same horizontal pencil strokes and chapter numbers are found in **E** (the horizontal strokes also in **A**), I assume that **Dʳᵉᶜ·** can be identified as the hand of Bekker, who collated these MSS.

d. the character of D

With regard to the character of the text, **D** holds a position somewhere between **A** and **F**: **D**'s text is not as good as that of **A**, but it has been transmitted with much greater care than the text of **F**. A useful discussion of the readings in **D** is given by Gadelle 27-51; my account is based partly on his, partly on my own observations.

Accents and breathings are often wrongly placed or omitted altogether, esp. on such words as ἐστι/ἔστι, ἐξαιρειν and the like. Some prepositions, used as prefixes, bear an accent, e.g. 523c3 προσπίπτουσα] πρὸς πίπτουσα; 458b6 συνδιασκοπεῖσθαι] σὺν διασκοπεῖσθαι.

1. Many longer omissions have been caused by homoioteleuton, to which the scribe of **D** was particularly susceptible; I have noted the following cases:

328d1-2	ἀλλ' —ἰέναι om.
330a5-6	πάνυ—ἐπιεικὴς om.
335b8-11	ἢ—ἵππων] ἀλλ' οὐκ εἰς τὴν τῶν ἵππων
335c9-12	ἀμούσους—ἱππικῇ om.
335d6-7	πάνυ—ἐναντίου om.
340e6	καὶ ὁ ἄρχων ἥμαρτεν om.
353b5-8	Ἔστιν—ἔργον om.
394d7-8	ἐγώ—δὴ om.
410c10-d1	ὅσοι—αὖ om.
462c6-7	Κομιδῇ—ταὐτὰ om.

479c8-d1   μὴ alterum—μᾶλλον om.
534a1-2   μέν—συναμφότερα om.
554d8-10   Καί—ἐπιθυμίας om.
563e4-5   ὅθεν—Νεανικὴ om.
583d10-e3 καί—"Ισως om.
588c4-5   λέγονται—γενέσθαι om.
602a2-3   Πάνυ—ἐπιστήμην om.

Conversely, at 516d5-6 the words πεπονθέναι—ἀκλήρῳ (πεπονθέναι preceded by καὶ ὁτιοῦν) have been written twice as the result of homoioteleuton. In addition, this passage shows the carelessness with which the scribe of **D** did his work: in writing this passage for the first time, **D** has βουλεύεσθαι; writing it for the second time, he writes βούλεσθαι, which is the correct reading (Burnet's apparatus is misleading here). There are still some other places where **D** has written a passage twice, as the result of homoioteleuton, e.g. 431e10-432a1 καὶ ἡ—ἀνδρείαν; 543d1-544a1 τόν—ἄνδρα.

2. There are many omissions in **D** which have not been caused by homoioteleuton; such omissions concern only one or a few words:

a. ἦν (in ἦν δ' ἐγώ), ἔφη etc., and assentory formulae or questions are sometimes omitted, e.g.:

341c3   ἔφη om.
405d7   ὡς οἶμαι om.
415e9   ἦν om.
492e2   ἦν δ' ἐγώ om.
507b8   Ἔστι ταῦτα om.
522e5   εἶπον om.
526e5   λέγεις om.
536a8   ἔφη om.
558d8   ἦν om.
578b8   Πῶς; ἦ δ' ὅς om.
612b7   ἦν om.

b. particles, prepositions, pronouns, articles, negations, conjunctions etc. are often omitted; see for instance:

327c3   ὡς om.
331e6   γὰρ om.
336a10 ἂν om.
351d10 ἐν om.
388d5   αὐτῷ om.
395d3   κατὰ prius om.
427e1   οὐ om.
462c8   οὐκ om.
486c3   τι om.
495b8   μὲν om.
540a1   εἰ om.

559c9 τῶν om.
576c11 καί om.
606a1 εἰ om.

c. some other omissions:

343d2 Σώκρατες om.
364d2 ἔθηκαν om.
405c3 δίκην om.
460d2 γάλα om.
533a5 ἰδεῖν om.
557a2 γίγνεται om.
566a5 ἀνάγκη om.

3. Many errors in **D** have been caused by anticipation or perseveration; some instances:

336d1 δέον] δίκαιον (repeated from c6)
343c8 ποιοῦσιν] ποιοῦντες (followed by ὑπηρετοῦντες)
377d5 μύθους] μύθοις (followed by τοῖς ἀνθρώποις)
422a2 τῆς] τοῦ (cf. τοῦ μὲν a1)
443e7 ταύτῃ] ταύτην (preceded by τὴν ἐπιστατήσουσαν)
452d6 τοῦτο] τούτου (preceded by ἀρίστου)
487d4 ὑπό] ἐπί (followed by τοῦ ἐπιτηδεύματος)
554e7 μήν] μοι (preceded by δοκεῖ μοι at e6)
562d2 αὐτῆς] αὐτοῦ (preceded by ἀκράτου)
583d3 τῶν] περὶ τῶν (followed by περιωδυνίᾳ; περὶ del. **D**¹)
611a1 ἀεί] εἶναι (followed by ὄν εἶναι)

4. Sometimes words have been repeated from the direct context, e.g.:

396d5 μὴ ἄρα] μὴ ἄρα μή
401a3 αὖ] ἡ τοιαύτη δημιουργία καί (repeated, through homoioteleuton, from a2)
422a3 πρὸς τῷ νεωτερισμῷ] καὶ νεωτερισμὸν ποιοῦντος (repeated, through homoioteleuton, from a2)
440e9 δύο εἴδη] δύο εἴδη δύο
562d9 ἆρ' οὐκ] οὐκ ἆρ' οὐκ
579e1 ἐπιθυμίας] ἐπιθυμίας καὶ δουλείας (repeated, through homoioteleuton, from d10 θωπείας καὶ δουλείας)

5. In some places, one or more words have been written twice without homoioteleuton; see for instance:

343a3 Εἰπέ μοι ἔφη bis scripsit; prius del. **D**³
382b4 πάντες bis scripsit; alterum del. **D**², ut vid.
408e1 καὶ εἶεν bis scripsit; prius del. **D**¹ vel **D**²
504b4 ἔφατε bis scripsit
561b1 μέρη—ἐκπεσόντων bis scripsit (primo ἐπελθόντων pro ἐκπεσόντων praebens)
575a3 ὅθεν bis scripsit

6. Many errors are due to (inner) dictation, e.g.:

330d6	φροντὶς]	φροντῆς
338b9	εὖ ἐρεῖν]	εὑρεῖν
351d4	Στάσεις]	στάσις
371a11	δέ εἰσιν]	δέησιν
393c1	ὥς τις]	ὅστις
397b4	εἴδη]	ἤδη
419a9	νομίζεται]	νομίζετε
469d2	κυπτάζωσι]	κτυπτάζωσι
476b4	φιλήκooι]	φιλίκooι
494e4	δ' ἔπος]	δὲ πρὸς
525c1	μεθέξειν]	μέθεξιν
540a4	ἔτη]	ἔτι
541b2	οἱ λόγοι]	ὀλίγοι
554b4	ὁ τοιοῦτος]	ὅτι οὗτος
578b2	πόλιν]	πόλλην (sic)
599b5	πειρῷτο]	πρῶτον

Once an error apparently caused by itacism, could also be explained as a proof of misogyny on the part of the scribe: at 457d1 **D** reads κυνάς (sic) for κοινάς (sc. τὰς γυναῖκας (...) πάσας εἶναι)!

7. It is remarkable that **D** often omits or adds a final —ν (sometimes a —ς); see for instance:

330e2	τῆς]	τῇ
334b8-9	ὠφελεῖν—βλάπτειν]	ὠφελεῖ—βλάπτει
348e2	ἐθαύμασα]	ἐθαύμασαν
359a1	λυσιτελεῖν]	λυσιτελεῖ
420e3	κελεύειν]	κελεύει
429c4	ἔφη]	ἔφην
465b12	μὴν]	μὴ
472a5	συγγνώμην]	συγγνώμη
498b7	ἐπιτείνειν]	ἐπιτείνει
523e5	αὐτῶν]	αὐτῷ
540b2	φιλοσοφία]	φιλοσοφίαν
550a3	καλουμένους]	καλουμένου
572a1	ἐᾷ]	ἐὰν (sic)
589c6	ἁμαρτάνει]	ἁμαρτάνειν
612d4	δικαιοσύνης]	δικαιοσύνη

8. Many errors are due to mere negligence or mental association, e.g.:

330e7	θαμὰ]	θαυμὰ (sic)
361b1	παρεσκευακέναι]	παρεσκευασμέναι
365c2	ἀλάθειαν]	ἀλήθειαν
386a3	ἀλλήλων]	ἄλλην
397d2	ἀκράτων]	ἀκροατῶν
407a11	πότερον]	πρότερον

428b9 Δῆλον] δηλονότι (etiam 444a12)
437a7 εἰς] ὡς
479d7 τοιοῦτον] τοῦτον
502d4 σοφόν] σῶφρον (cf. 582d4 φρονήσεως] σωφρονήσεως)
516b5 φαντάσματα] φαστάσματα
528d5 μετὰ ταύτην] μετ' αὐτήν
540b1 κοσμεῖν] κατακοσμεῖν
540c4 ἀνδριαντοποιός] τοποιὸς
577d3 ἀνελευθερίας] ἐλευθερίας
590a5 πάλαι] πάλιν

9. Transpositions are very few; it is noteworthy that in four places **D** has ταῦτα πάντα where **AF** have πάντα ταῦτα (452d1, 530e3, 534d2, 603d5); the other transpositions are:

349c6 πλέον ἔχειν] ἔχειν πλέον
450a1 πάντα ὥσπερ] ὥσπερ πάντα
564b5 ἡγούμενον αὐτῶν] αὐτῶν ἡγούμενον

10. Sometimes, letters within a word are transposed, e.g.:

328b6 Καλχηδόνιον] χαλκηδόνιον
378a2 ῥᾳδίως] ῥῳδίας
400a7 εἴποιμι] ἐπίοιμι
439d4 ἀξιώσομεν] ἀξίωσόν με

11. In a number of places, **D** adds some words which are not in **AF**.

a. additions which are not simply dittographies are usually restricted to small words (particles, pronouns etc.) and do not occur very frequently; some instances:

331e6 ἀνήρ] ὁ ἀνήρ
359c6 βίᾳ] καὶ βίᾳ
366c6 ἔχει] μὴ ἔχει
393e2 αὐτοὺς] αὐτοὺς δὲ
397d7 παισί] καὶ παισί
423e7 κτῆσιν] τὴν κτῆσιν
463a1 πόλεσιν] πόλεσίν τε
490d4 τῆς] τῆς ἤδη
527c7 τε] τε καὶ
572a5 ἐλθών] ἐλθὼν καὶ

b. some additions, however, appear to be deliberate interpolations; I have noted the following instances:

333b8 οἰκοδομικοῦ τε καὶ: a reminiscence of b5.
346a6 τούτων: this word is cumbersome and quite superfluous.
370d3 ἢ οὔ: added to mark the end of Socrates' speech.
374a3 ἱκανοί] ἱκανοὶ διαμάχεσθαι: repeats διαμαχεῖται in the preceding line.
374b7-8 ἀλλὰ σκυτοτόμον: a quite unnecessary repetition of σκυτοτόμον at b6.

12. Deliberate conjectures appear to be very few in **D**; see for instance:

366e1 ὑμῶν—φατὲ] ἡμῶν—φαμέν τε: first, ὑμῶν was corrupted into ἡμῶν; then μεν was added above φατε, which resulted in φαμεν τὲ; cf. Gadelle 46.
429a2 ἦν] καὶ: an obvious simplification.
510b4 μιμηθεῖσιν] τμηθεῖσιν **D** (**F** has τιμηθεῖσιν); cf. 511a8 τετιμημένοις **F**A[pc]: τετιμημένοις **D**A[ac].
514b4 παρ' ἦν ἰδὲ] παρ' ἦ ἦν ἰδεῖν **D**: conjecture or error ?

13. Once, a reading in **D** is a gloss which has replaced the original reading: 339a1 καθεστηκυίας] οἰκείας. At 335d3 **D** adds τοῦ ἀδίκου after ἐναντίου. Because **D** omits 335d6-7 Πάνυ—ἐναντίου as the result of homoioteleuton, I guess that τοῦ ἀδίκου was originally a gloss on τοῦ ἐναντίου at d7; as an explanation of τοῦ ἐναντίου at d5 it is, of course, quite out of place.

It has already been noted that the **D** tradition shows traces of contamination; see above, pp. 78 f.

3. F

a. appearance

F is written in one column per page; each page has 32-35 lines. I have counted the letters on fol. 81[r]: the number of letters per line varies from 38 to 52, with an average of 44.

As punctuation signs, **F** uses the single point (on the line, a little above the line and half way up the letters) and the comma; the dicolon is used to mark the change of speaker; further, **F** uses the interrogation mark. Adscript, subscript and suprascript iota are never found.

Often, **F** writes some letters above the line; this is especially the case with the endings of words. **F** rarely uses compendia; the few compendia which do occur are found anywhere in the line (not only at the end); I have noted compendia for —ης, —αι, —εν, —ως, —οις, —ον, —ους, καὶ (but there may be more of them).

The accentuation of **F** is very careless.

b. the exemplar of F

The studies of Burnet and Deneke have established that **F** goes back, directly or indirectly, to a MS written in majuscule script: **F** has numerous errors which result from misreading majuscules; see above, p. 68.

Clark, who was the first to study the omissions in **F** (see Clark 414-417), notes that there is a remarkable number of omissions of 33-38 letters; he concludes (416): "It seems probable that we are here on the track of an ancestor."

The omissions in **F** were studied in more detail by Dodds, *Notes* 26 f., *Gorgias* 45-47, and Bluck 136-138. On the basis of a number of omissions which occur at regular intervals, Dodds concludes that the exemplar of **F** must have suffered from mechanical injury, for which he suggests wormholes. Dodds plausibly suggests that the intervals between the lacunae "represent pages of the exemplar" (*Notes* 26). He calculates that this exemplar had about 1200 letters per page; as there is a telescoped passage of 38 letters at *Grg.* 506c1, which must correspond to a line in the exemplar (this is in accordance with Clark's conclusions), he argues that the exemplar of **F** must have had some 31,5 lines of about 38 letters per page[10]. This again suggests that the exemplar of **F** was an uncial codex; Dodds remarks that C. H. Roberts "has noticed that the dimensions I have calculated would suit very well the type of cheap papyrus *codex* which was manufactured in quantity in and after the third century A.D." That this majuscule MS was the *direct* source of **F**, is suggested by the fact that **F** leaves a blank at the lacunae mentioned above (Dodds, *Notes* 26). Bluck 138, n. 3, notes that the scribe sometimes makes an attempt to decipher what was still left visible in the damaged place; this leads him to the hypothesis that the exemplar of **F** was injured not by wormholes, but by damp[11]. Bluck, *l.c.*, remarks that the lacunae "virtually come to an end" after the earlier pages of the *Hippias Maior*. In *R.*, there are some omissions and errors which must be due to illegibility of the exemplar, but such cases occur with much less frequency than in *Grg.* and *Men.*, and not at regular intervals. Probably, Dodds' worms had eaten their fill by the time they had struggled through *Grg.* and *Men.*; alternatively, they may have lost courage when they realized the huge task of devouring and savouring the whole of the *Republic*.

I list the places in *R.* where **F** leaves a blank when omitting some letters or words:

433c6   ἀρχόντων] ἀρχῇ, spatium vacuum post ἀρχῇ
435c3   Πᾶσα] ἴσα (sic), spatium vacuum ante ἄσα
442d4   γε om., spatio vacuo relicto
471d6   ταύτῃ om., spatio vacuo relicto
488d5   πέρι om., spatio vacuo relicto

---

[10] In *Notes* 26, n. 12, Dodds states that **F** is written in two columns per page; this must be an error, because it is simply untrue.

[11] This argument is not cogent: worms do not necessarily eat complete words; in some places they may have satisfied their hunger with just parts of some letters, leaving something behind for the scribe of **F** to guess at.

For bookworms in general, see now N. Hickin, *Bookworms: The Insect Pests of Books* (London 1986).

547a4   οὗ ἄν om., spatio vacuo relicto
553d6   ἑνὶ om., spatio vacuo relicto
562c4   ᾖα om., spatio vacuo relicto
567a7   ἀπολλύῃ] ἀπολυ**ει (sic, sine accentu)
604d10 ante καὶ prius spatium vacuum III litterarum
608d13 'Αγαθόν] θόν, spatium vacuum III litterarum ante θόν

Some other readings, too, may result from injury of the exemplar, e.g. 522a8-b1 τι ἄγον] τιαγ (sic, in fine lineae); 606a1 εἰ ἐκείνη] εἰεκείν (sic).

c. the corrections in F

Most editors use the siglum **f** to indicate recent hands in **F** (see, e.g., Burnet, Dodds, Bluck, Slings). My chief general objection to the practice of using minuscules to indicate recent hands in MSS is that it creates the impression that only one later hand has been at work in a particular MS. The validity of this objection is shown in the case of **F**: editors since Dodds (see Dodds, *Gorgias* 43 f.; Bluck 140; Slings 265) agree in assuming that there is only one later hand in **F**; in *R.*, however, I have distinguished five later hands; although I have not studied **F** for *Grg.*, *Men.* and *Clit.* in detail, it is certain that in these dialogues too the assumption that there is only one later hand is untenable. The following account is, of course, only valid for *R*.

Sometimes, the scribe corrects an error which he had made himself and which he had noticed during the copying; this goes especially for diacritics etc.

The hand which I have called **F²** writes with an ink which is somewhat brighter than that of **F¹**: the script is rather robust and slants slightly to the left. For an instance of **F²** see the addition of 354a4-7 Ὁ μὲν—Πῶς γὰρ οὔ at the top of fol. 95ʳ. **F²** is almost exclusively active in the first two books of the *Republic* (it is also found in *Grg.*, e.g. fol. 24ᵛ, and *Clit.*, e.g. fol. 80ᵛ). I have noted two cases of agreement between **F²** and **b**, to wit 339a3 αὐτό] αὐτοῦ **F²ˢˡb** and 352a5 ἐνοῦσα] ἐν οὖσα **F²ˢˡb**[12].

F³ writes in an ink of almost the same colour as **F¹**, but its script is much tinier, sometimes even almost illegible. For some instances, see the beginning of book III (fol. 108ᵛ). **F³** is mainly active in the earlier books of the *Republic*; it is not found in books VII-X. The readings added by **F³** can be partly traced to the **Par.**-group; see for instance:

---

[12] Dodds, *Gorgias* 44, following a suggestion by Theiler, notes that most corrections by **f** (as he designates the later corrections in **F**) are also found in **b**; the same conclusion is reached for *Clit.* by Slings 265.

334b2 πάντας] εἰς πάντας F³ˢˡPar.
337a7 ἀποκρινοῖο] ἀποκρίναιο F³ˢˡPar.
345d7 ἀρχή] ἄρχε. F³ˢˡPar.
349e6 ἅπερ] ὅνπερ F³ˢˡPar.
362d7 ἐπάμυνε] ἐπάμυναι F³ˢˡPar.
386a3 ἀλλήλων] ἕλλην F³ⁱᵐDPar.
389a8 σὺ] δὲ F³ˢˡPar.
420a4 ἑταίραις] ἑτέροις F³ˢˡD²Par. (Sc. W)

In a few places, **F³** adds a reading which is not found elsewhere, e.g.:

386c5   x'] καὶ F³ˢˡ
389a8   ἐμὸν] ἐμὸν τὸν λόγον F³ˢˡ
496d6-e2 λαβών—ἔχων—πράττων—ἀποστάς—ὁρῶν—ἀγαπᾳ—αὐτὸς—καθαρός—βιώσεται—αὐτοῦ—ἵλεως—εὐμενής—ἀπαλλάξεται] λαβόντες-—ἔχοντες—πράττοντες—ἀποστάντες—ὁρῶντες—ἀγαπῶσιν—αὐτοὶ—καθαροί—βιώσονται—αὐτῶν—ἵλεωι—εὐμενεῖς—ἀπαλλάξονται F³ˢˡ

F⁴ has a very bold script, sometimes even rough. The ink is very dark, sometimes almost black; only in the second half of the first book is the ink much lighter. For some instances of **F⁴**, see 354b5 (fol. 95ʳ) ὁρμῆσαι] ὥρμημαι, 407e4 (fol. 119ᵛ) δεικνοῖεν in margine.

A number of readings added by **F⁴** are traceable to the **Par.**-group (as is also the case with **F³**); some instances:

347a3   ὧν] οὗ F⁴ᵖᶜDPar.
354b5   ὁρμῆσαι] ὥρμημαι F⁴ˢˡPar.
407e4   ante ὅτι add. δεικνοῖεν F⁴ⁱᵐPar.
409a1   ψυχῆς] ψυχῆι F⁴⁽ᵘ·ᵛ·⁾ᵖᶜPar. (N. B. ψυχῇ om. DF)

A number of readings written by **F⁴** are not found in any other extant MS (except, of course, the apographa of **F**); some instances:

343b4   post καὶ prius add. οὐ F⁴ˢˡ
344e4   ante ἄλλως add. μὴ F⁴ˢˡ
347c1   post μέλλουσιν add. μὴ F⁴ˢˡ
476d5   γνώμην] γνῶσιν F⁴ᵖᶜ
487b5   ante τῶν add. δὲ F⁴ˢˡ
501a3   ὃ] ὅθεν F⁴ᵖᶜ
546b3   supra οὐ add. οὓς F⁴⁽ᵘ·ᵛ·⁾ˢˡ
549b10 supra πόλει add. καὶ πολιτεία F⁴ (cf. 449a1; an glossema est ?)

F⁵ writes in a blue-grey ink; the script is very tiny, almost microscopic, in some places simply illegible. It occurs for the first time on fol. 113ʳ (395e1) with a marginal note ἐντεῦθεν ἠρξάμεθα τῆς διορθώσεως ἀντιγράφου χωρὶς καὶ μὴ ζήτει αὐτὴν τελέαν (but I cannot vouch for the correct decipherment of these words); on fol. 143ᵛ (460e1) **F⁵** writes in the margin εἰς δεῦρο διωρθώθη. Indeed, almost all the readings added by **F⁵** are found between 395e and 460e, but **F⁵** turns up again in a few places in book X. For some instances of the script of **F⁵**, see the marginal notes on foll. 113ʳ and 143ᵛ, just mentioned.

Like **F³** and **F⁴**, **F⁵** has used a MS of the **Par.**-group; in some places **F⁵** shows remarkable agreement with β, an apographon of **Par.**; some instances:

402b5   εἰκόνας] εἰ εἰκόνας **F⁵ˢˡPar.**
402c1   φαμεν] ἔφαμεν **F⁵ˢˡD²Par.**
403b1,3 προσοιστέον] προσοιστέα **F⁵ˢˡPar.**
411d1   αὐτοῦ] αὐτῷ **F⁵ˢˡPar.**
436e5   δεξιὰν—ἀριστερὰν] δεξιὰ—ἀριστερὰ **F⁵ˢˡβᵖᶜ**
437c5   ἐρωτῶντος] ἐρῶντος **F⁵ˢˡPar.** (et βᵃᶜ !)
604c7   αἱρεῖ habent **F⁵ˢˡβᵖᶜ**

The fact that the reading ἐρῶντος at 437c5 is found in βᵃᶜ, but not in βᵖᶜ, seems to plead against the supposition that β itself was used by **F⁵**; as many of the corrections in β come from its exemplar (see below, p. 185), we are perhaps entitled to assume that **F⁵** consulted an ancestor of β; this hypothesis is corroborated by the observation that in two places in book III **F⁵** agrees with **K** (which, in books I-III, is a gemellus of β; see below, pp. 183-185): 407d1 ἀποκεκριμένον] ἀποκεκρυμμένον **F⁵ˢˡK**; 414b9 δὴ νῦν] νῦν δὴ **F⁵ˢˡK**.

I have found two cases of agreement between **F⁵** and **W** (452a8 περὶ] παρὰ **F⁵ˢˡSc.W** and 459c3 ἰατρὸν] ἰατρῶν **F⁵ˢˡW**) and one with **γ** (450b8 ᾖ] εἰ **F⁵ˢˡγ**). These cases of agreement may well be coincidental.

F⁵ has also added a considerable number of readings which are not found elsewhere; in two places, **F⁵** is the earliest MS authority for a correct reading: 407c2 διατάσεις **F⁵ˢˡ** (et Galenus) and 411c2 ἔμπλεωι **F⁵ˢˡ**. At 443a6 Burnet conjectures ὁπωστιοῦν γ' ἄν; this conjecture was anticipated by **F⁵**, who adds ἄν above ὅπως τί γε οὖν (but Burnet did not know this reading, which was not noticed by Schneider).

Some further readings:

399b6   ἄλλῳ] ἄλλων **F⁵ˢˡ**
404d4   δοκῶ] δοκεῖ **F⁵ˢˡ**
407a7   δεῖν] ἡδὺ **F⁵ˢˡ**
411e1   διαπράττεται] διαταράττεται **F⁵ˢˡ**
427e6   ante οἴμαι add. ἀνάγκη **F⁵ˢˡ**
433c7-8 δόξης—σωτηρίᾳ] δόξα—σωτηρίας **F⁵ˢˡ**
449d5   ὅλον] ὅλως **F⁵ˢˡ**
454a8   ἔριδι, οὐ] ἐριδίου **F**: γραιδίου **F⁵ˢˡ** (a charming conjecture !)

F⁶ writes in an ink of almost exactly the same colour as **F³**, but the script is different. Readings added by **F⁶** occur only sporadically; for an instance of **F⁶**, see fol. 108ᵛ, 387b1 παρακαλέσομεν **F⁶ˢˡ**. I believe that the excellent reading στραγγευομένῳ at 472a2 is due to **F⁶** (στραγγευ at the bottom of the page; Burnet is wrong in attributing this reading to the first hand of **F**); it was also conjectured by Orelli.

With regard to the chronological order of the several correcting hands in **F**, it can only be concluded that **F⁵** comes after **F³** and **F⁴**. That **F⁵** is later than **F³** appears from the case of 404b1-2 (fol. 117ᵛ): **F³** adds in the margin γρ. μὴ ἀκροσφαλὴς (sic), **F⁵** changes ἡ into εἰ, and adds a λ above the ν in the text (**F** has μὴ ἀκρὸς φανείς). That **F⁵** is later than **F⁴** is shown by the case of 407e4 (fol. 119ᵛ): **F⁴** adds δεικνοῖεν before ὅτι in the margin, **F⁵** erases νοῖ and writes ποιοῖ above δεικ (= ποιοῖεν).

The corrections by all the later hands in **F** recur in **x** and **Darmst**. (**Darmst.** depends on **F** for a few fragments from *R*.; **x** is the source of all the other derivatives of **F** in *R*.).

d. the character of F

In his first article on **F**, *Neglected MS*, Burnet argues that **F** must be considered a representative of an "ancient vulgate" of Plato's text; he quotes Schneider's statement (III 311) "Veterem vulgatam repraesentat, et fere cum Stobaeo, Eusebio etc. consentit" with approval. Burnet contends that the agreement between **F** and the indirect tradition "extends even to small details" (*l.c.* 100). In support of his thesis he notes some twenty cases of agreement between **F** and Eusebius in the passage 377c-383c, which is quoted in full by Eusebius. Burnet argues that similar cases of agreement between **F** with Iamblichus, Stobaeus and other writers can be found as well.

Stuart Jones (see Bibliography) protests against Burnet's postulation of an "ancient vulgate". He starts his criticism by giving a definition of the term "vulgate"; I quote (Stuart Jones 388): "As applied to printed books the word denotes a 'commercial' text reproduced in successive editions with no pretence at critical revision. The distinguishing mark of such a text is naturally its uniformity." As an instance, Stuart Jones mentions the vulgate of Homer's text. He goes on to demonstrate that the text used by the writers of the first centuries A. D. does not by any means present a uniform picture (388 ff.); he concludes (390): "the cases of agreement between FEus. and FStob. are *much* less frequent and less important than those in which they differ." Moreover, Stuart Jones examines in detail some passages quoted by Galen and Iamblichus, and shows that the places where these authors disagree with **F** are far more numerous than those in which they are in accordance with **F**.

Stuart Jones concludes (390 f.): "the text to which Eus. and Stob. bear witness is on the whole very inferior to that of our MSS. I should not, it is true, describe it as an 'ancient vulgate', but I should at any rate assert that it represents the 'commercial' texts which circulated amongst the reading public rather than the more scholarly editions in the hands of Galen and Iamblichus."

Although Burnet refused to abandon the hypothesis of an ancient vulgate *expressis verbis* (*Vind. F* 12), his remark in the preface to the 1905 edition "nec puto Schneiderum de *vetere vulgata* sua ita sensisse ut crederet textum quemdam ob omnibus receptum unquam fuisse" is, I think, a tacit recantation of his earlier position.

Dodds, *Gorgias* 46, *Notes* 27, quotes with approval Stuart Jones' words (390 f.) just cited by me, but he wrongly supposes that Stuart Jones speaks about **F**, while in fact he deals with "the text to which Eus. and Stob. bear witness". Nevertheless, the statement that **F** "represents a commercial text" will hold good as such; it is fully confirmed by the character of **F**'s text in the *Republic*: **F** brims with errors of every type, and is very careless in the addition or omission of particles, prepositions etc.; for a brief account of errors in **F**, see Deneke 29-31, 37 f.

Despite its countless errors, **F** has more value for the constitution of the text than **D**, because **D** is more heavily contaminated with the **A** tradition than **F**; although I believe that Burnet follows **F** in too many places (cf. above, p. 75), there are quite a few places where **F** (sometimes supported by the indirect tradition) is the only primary MS to preserve a true reading.

I propose now to discuss the different types of **F**'s errors in the *Republic*.

1. In some places, an omission in **F** is due to homoioteleuton; see for instance:

354a4-7   Ὁ—οὗ om.
367b8-c1 οὐδὲ—δοκεῖν om.
421c1   ποιεῖν καὶ πειστέον om.
438a6   λέγειν ὁ ταῦτα om.
457d6   Οὐκ—ὠφελίμου om.
463e5   ὅτι prius—ἤ om.
510e1-2   γράφουσιν—καὶ prius om.
585b2-4   Τί—ἕξεως om.

Conversely, **F** sometimes repeats some words as the result of homoioteleuton, e.g.:

350d5-7   κακίαν—ἀδικίαν bis scripsit
465d8-e1 σωτηρίαν—πόλεως bis scripsit
506d3-6   ἀρκέσει—καὶ μάλα bis scripsit
532d3-4   εἶναι—ἀποδέχεσθαι bis scripsit

There are also dittographies which have not been caused by homoioteleuton, e.g. 386b8 ὡς ἔοικεν bis scripsit (alterum del. **F¹**).

2. There are also a number of omissions which have not been caused by homoioteleuton; in quite a few places, a vital word (sometimes an assentory formula) is omitted: some instances:

380d2   φαντάζεσθαι om.
399c3   σωφρόνων om.
411a4   Καὶ μάλα om.
462a1   ἦ δ' ὅς om.
486d8   Ἐμμετρίᾳ om.
508a11   ἥλιος om.
526d2   προσήκει om.
580d8   ἰδίᾳ om
602c2-3 ἦ γάρ; Ναί. om.

3. There are many glosses to be found in **F**; the first hand has added a number of supralinear glosses; some instances:

331a7   ἀτάλλοισα: τρέφουσα **F¹ˢˡ**
332e6   μὴ κάμνουσί: μὴ νοσοῦσι **F¹ˢˡ**
359a7   τιμωρεῖσθαι: κολάζειν **F¹ˢˡ**
364d4   παραγωγῆς: περιστροφῆς **F¹ˢˡ**
386c6   παρ' ἀκλήρῳ: ἤτοι πένητα μὴ ἔχοντα κλῆρον **F¹ˢˡ**

It is remarkable that such glosses occur mainly in the earlier books of the *Republic*.

In many places, a gloss (or scholium) has intruded into the text, sometimes at the expense of the original reading:

332e3   ἐν τίνι πράξει] ἐν τῷ τί πράττειν (ἐν τίνι πράξει **F¹ⁱᵐ**)
333e3   δεινότατος] δυνατώτατος
345c3   πιαίνειν] παχύνει (παχύνειν **F³ᵖᶜ**)
360b6   τολμήσειεν] θέλοι
362c1   εὖ ποιεῖν] εὐεργετεῖν
366b3   ἂν πρὸ] ἀντὶ (ἂν omitted through haplography)
368e8-
369a1   ἐν ταῖς πόλεσι ζητήσωμεν] ἐν τῷ μείζονι ζητήσωμεν ἐν ταῖς πόλεσι
382c6   τῷ] τῷ τινὶ (sic)
530d7   ὡς] οὕτως
563a4   θωπεύει] θεραπεύει
575c4   βάλλει] ἐγγύς ἐστι δὲ ***οιμια ὥσπερ καὶ τὸ οὐδ' ἴκταρ ἥκεις βάλλει

Such cases, too, are mainly found in the earlier books.

4. **F** is very careless in the addition and omission of particles, articles, pronouns, prepositions etc.; some instances:

327c3   ἄλλοι] ἄλλοι πολλοὶ
334e6   ἐχθρὸν] τὸν ἐχθρὸν
337c7   σὺ] σὺ οὖν
353d1   αὐτὸν] αὐτὸν τοῦτον
359d4   ἔνεμεν] ἐκεῖνος ἔνεμεν
361c1   ἔσονται] καὶ ἔσονται
367a3   ἦν] ἂν ἦν
383c7   χρώμην] αὐτοῖς χρώμην
389e5   Ὁμήρῳ] παρ' ὁμήρῳ
390a1   ἄλλα] ἄλλα τοιαῦτα
410a3   τὴν om.
444c5   Ὅτι] ὅτι δὴ
462d4   αὐτὸς] αὐτός τε
486a4   Μή] μή γε
524c3   ὄψις] ἡ ὄψις
524c10   πρῶτον] πρῶτον μὲν
534c4   αὐτὸ om.
564c9   Τριχῇ] τριχὴ (sic) δὲ
586d7   ἂν om.
604d9   οὐκ] οὖν οὐκ
610b1   αὖ om.

5. Errors concerning the endings of verbs and nouns etc. are very frequent; some instances:

337e3   λαμβάνῃ—ἐλέγχῃ] λαμβάνει—ἐλέγχει
358d5   ἀκούειν] ἀκοῦσαι
381c7   θεῷ] θεὸν
392b3   λανθάνῃ] λάθη
400d4   λόγος] λόγους
412a5   φαῖμεν] φαμὲν
479b7   φήσωμεν] φήσομεν
526d8   ἐξαρχοῖ] ἐξαρχεῖ
560a6   ἐγγενομένης] ἐγγενόμενος
597a10   θαυμάζωμεν] θαυμάζομεν

6. In innumerable places, words have been transposed; see for instance:

339c7   ἔστι τίθεσθαι] τίθεσθαι ἔστιν
370b7-8   παρῇ ἔργου] ἔργου παρῇ
407e3   ἔφη, λέγεις] λέγεις ἔφη
420a3   λαμβάνοντες ὥσπερ οἱ ἄλλοι] ὥσπερ οἱ ἄλλοι λαμβάνοντες
470c6   πολεμεῖν μαχομένους] μαχομένους πολεμεῖν
493c1-2   πάντα ταῦτα] ταῦτα πάντα
528b4   δοκεῖ οὔπω] οὔπω δοκεῖ
558c3   τούτων ἄλλα] ἄλλα τούτων
616d3   μεγάλῳ σφονδύλῳ] σφονδύλῳ μεγάλῳ

7. Many errors are due to (inner) dictation, often itacism; see for instance:

365b3 δίχα] δὴ καὶ
388d5 ἐπίοι] ἐποίο.
435a2 πυρείων] πυρίων
474d7 ποιεῖτε] ποιεῖται
501d9 φήσει] φύσει
502a5 τις ἀμφισβτήσει, ὡς] τῆς ἀμφισβητήσεως
522a6 κατὰ ῥυθμὸν] κατ' ἀριθμὸν
546a8 ὑμετέρου] ἡμετέρου
556d4 ἴδῃ] ἤδη
563c5 πείθοιτο] πύθοιτο

8. **F** has a lot of errors which are due to anticipation or perseveration, and to mental association; some instances:

335b1 καλῶς] οὕτως (οὕτως precedes in the same line)
344a2 ὅσῳ] ὅσον (μᾶλλον follows immediately)
360d7 ἀδικεῖσθαι] ἐξαπατᾶσθαι (ἐξαπατῶντες precedes at d6)
362d9 βοηθεῖν] βοηθῆσαι (ποιῆσαι precedes immediately)
451a3 φίλους] ἄλλους (ἀλλὰ precedes in the same line)
489c1 ἰέναι] εἶναι (εἶναι precedes in the same line)
517b1 ἅπασαν] ἅπασι (immediately followed by τοῖς λεγομένοις)
529c1 ἀλλὰ] οὔτε (οὔτε also two words earlier)
559d4 ὡς] πάλιν ὡς (πάλιν precedes in the same line)
581c10 ἥδιστος] ἕκαστος (ἕκαστος follows a few words later)

9. Sometimes, a word is replaced by another word through mere carelessness, or *lapsus memoriae*; see for instances:

358d8 καὶ] ἢ
374c6 κυβευτικὸς] κυβερνευτικὸς
398b3 τύποις] τόποις
413c4 ἀπατᾷ] ἀγαπᾶται
459e2 λανθάνειν] λαμβάνειν
466b4 ἔλεγον] ἐλέγομεν
502d7 γίγνεσθαι] λέγεσθαι
524d5 ὁριζόμενος] ἐργαζόμενος
527a6 μάλα] μάλιστα
530b4 ἀλήθειαν] βοήθειαν
550b8 δοκεῖς] λέγεις
558c1 μόνον] μᾶλλον
619c7 προτέρῳ] δευτέρῳ

10. Often, a comparatively rare word (or form of a word) has been replaced by a more common one; some instances:

344e7 ὠγαθέ] ὦ ἀγαθὲ
348b2 διακρινούντων] διακρινόντων
350a1 ἰατρικές] ἰατρὸς
361c7 ἴτω] ἔσται
366e9 ἴσχει] ἔχει
439e8 δημίῳ] δήμῳ
457b4 λελέξεται] λέξεται

470e4   Ἑλληνὶς] ἕλληνες
519c6   ἀπῳκίσθαι] ἀποχεῖσθαι
526d3   ἐκτάσεις] ἐκτὸς
531a3   ἀνήνυτα] ἀνόνητα (glossema ?)
547e2   ἀτενεῖς] ἀσθενεῖς
553b5   ἀτιμωθέντα] ἀτιμασθέντα
607b7   κραυγάζουσα] κράζουσα (glossema ?)

11. In a few cases, a word has been wrongly understood as an abbreviation:

508b9   οὖν οὐ] οὐρανοῦ (nomen sacrum)
511b3   με] μετὰ

12. In a number of places, the text of **F** exhibits interpolations and conjectures.

a. often, one or two words have been added in order to clarify the construction of a sentence, especially forms of εἶναι and φάναι; some instances:

348e4   πάνυ] πάνυ ἔφη
358a9   δυσμαθής] δυσμαθὴς εἶναι
359c5   ἀγαθόν] ἀγαθὸν ὄν
360b2   οὕτω **F**: om. **AD**
363e2   ἀδίκων] ἀδίκων εἶναι
364d6   αὐτοί] αὐτοί εἰσι
365a7   εὐφυεῖς] εὐφυεῖς εἰσι
367b7   τὰς alterum] ἀλλὰ τὰς μὲν
368a1   ὑμᾶς] ὑμᾶς ἔχει
375d6   λέγεις] λέγεις ἔφη
444d1   ἄδικα] ἄδικα πράττειν (repeated from c10)
532b1   ἐπ'] τότε δὴ ἐπ'

b. in some places, the text has been changed or interpolated in order to simplify the grammatical structure or to give a different meaning; some of such conjectures destroy the sense completely; some instances:

330a5   πάνυ] οὐ πάνυ
330c6   κατὰ] οὐ κατὰ
344a3   ἄδικον—δίκαιον] τῶν ἀδίκων εἶναι ἢ τῶν δικαίων
366e6   τί δρᾷ **F**: ἐν **AD** (a clumsy attempt at simplifying the syntax, which should not have been adopted by Burnet; cf. Deneke 38)
376a5   χαλεπαίνει] μισεῖ καὶ χαλεπαίνει (the absence of a verb which governs ὄν—ἄγνωτα directly was felt to be intolerable by the scribe who made this addition)
376c8   καὶ ἆρά] ἐννοεῖν χρὴ εἴ
386d7   οἵῳ πεπνῦσθαι] οἷος (sic) πέπνυται
405b3   καὶ] ὡς
407a7   πῶς] ὅς

Interpolations and conjectures are mainly found in the earlier books. It has already been shown that the **F** tradition shows traces of contamination; see above, pp. 78 f.

CHAPTER THREE

AFFILIATION OF MANUSCRIPTS

In this chapter I discuss the affiliation of all extant MSS of the *Republic*; the first part deals with the **A**-family, the second part with the **D**-family and the third part with the **F**-family.

I. THE A-FAMILY

Apart from **A** itself, the **A**-family consists of the following MSS: **E**, **M**, **N**, **P**, **R** (up to 389d7), **T** (up to 389d7), **V**, **W** (up to 389d7), **a**, **b** (up to 358d7), **c**, **k** (up to 381a), **m**, **t**, **Θ** (up to 389d7), **Φ** (up to 389d7), **α**, **γ**, **Acq.** (up to 389d7), **Ambr.**, **Darmst.** (in some fragments only), **Durh.** (up to 389d7), **Hier.** (up to 389d7), **Lobc.** (up to 389d7), **Lond.**, **Matr.**, **Matr.**[fr], **Mon.**, **Neap.**, **Ott.**, **Sc.** (up to 389d7), **Vat.** (up to 381a), **Voss.**

I shall quote a number of readings which occur in all the MSS of the **A**-family against **DF** (I do not specify the presence or absence of excerpt MSS; moreover, it should be noted that the places where *all* the MSS of the **A**-family have the same reading are relatively few, because of the numerous stages of contamination):

328d5 νεανίσκοις **DF**: νεανίαις **A** etc.
329a6 τε alterum **DF**: om. **A** etc.
388d5 τι **DF**: om. **A** etc.
391d1 ἄλλον **DF**: ἄλλων **A** etc.
516b9 οὗτος **DF**: αὐτὸς **A** etc.
615a7 ὅσους **A**[ac]***DF***: οὓς **A**[pc] etc.
616a4 ὅτι εἰς ***DF***: εἰς ὅτι **A** etc.
616a6 τοῦτον **A**[ac]***DF***: τούτων **A**[pc] etc.

All the descendants of **A** ultimately derive from a lost copy of **A** which can be reconstructed from the agreement between **T** (that is, the older part of **T**), the lost exemplar of **Mγ**, and (for the fragments it contains) **P**. **T** has numerous offspring, one of **γ**'s derivatives, **a**, has also been very fertile, while **M** and **P** have remained childless.

T is generally considered an important MS, being a primary witness in the first seven tetralogies; **M** is regarded as a primary witness by Campbell and Burnet. Therefore I have collated **TMγ** in full for 327a1-389d7 (where the older part of **T** breaks off), in order to use all the evidence available for establishing the relationship of these MSS. For **P**, I have collated all the fragments from the *Republic*.

In my discussion, I shall first concentrate upon **TMγ**, and discuss **P** afterwards, because **P** has only a few fragments from 327a1-389d7, in all amounting to about two Stephanus pages, so that a comparison of **P** with **T** is hardly possible.

The relation of **T** to **A** has been the subject of much controversy[1]. That **T** and **A** are closely related, already appears from the fact that after *Mx.* (the last dialogue of tetr. VII), **T** has a subscription τέλος τοῦ α' βιβλίου. This indicates that the exemplar of **T** was a two-volume edition of Plato. Now **A** (which contains tetr. VIII-IX and *Spp.*) is evidently the second volume of such an edition. Moreover, in both **T** and **A** *Clit.* is numbered xθ', which points to a complete edition.

Schanz, *Platocodex* 78, says: "Diese Stellen legen den Schluß nahe, daß T aus A stammt." Yet in note 1 on the same page he adds: "Allerdings bleiben einige Stellen übrig, die gegen unsere Ansicht zu sprechen scheinen." (Schanz mentions 328c7 ἦ habet **T**: ἦν **A**; 339b8 δίκαιον] καὶ δίκαιον **A**: δίκαιον **T**, addito καὶ supra lineam a prima manu; 342a5 δεῖ habet **T**: δεῖ ἀεὶ **A**: ex ἀεὶ fecit αἰεὶ **A**ᵖᶜ (for my opinion on such errors of **A** against **T**, see below, p. 118). In *Parisinus* 305 Schanz remarks that the comparison of the scholia in **T** and **A** "verstärkt aber die Bedenken, die sich der Annahme, daß die Republik im Venet. aus dem Paris. stamme, entgegenstellen (...)". Jordan, *Republik* 477-479 (quoted by Greene xxxiv), illustrates that a number of errors in the T-scholia can be explained as the result of misreading the script of **A**; he therefore concludes that **T** does depend on **A**; cf. below, p. 116.

The hypothesis that **T** is a (direct) transcript of **A** has been accepted by a majority of scholars (e.g. Alline 214 f.; Chambry cxli f.; Dodds, *Gorgias* 37-39; Carlini 160).

Others, however, refuse to accept the dependence of **T** on **A**, for different reasons.

Some scholars (Burnet, *Vindiciae I* 231; Greene xxxiv f.), following Schanz (see above), conclude that **T** cannot derive from **A** because **T** has some scholia which are not in **A**, and because in some places **T** has the obviously correct reading in a scholium against **A**. I will deal with this problem below, p. 118, with n. 7.

Clark 411-413 notices that **T** has hardly any omissions of *ca.* 22 letters, the average length of a line in **A**; he therefore concludes that **T** does not go back to **A**. I do not find Clark's argumentation very convincing: on the basis of the fact that **T** has two omissions of 34/35 letters, and one

---

[1] My account of the relationship between **ATMγ** has also been published separately, in a somewhat different form, in Mnem. IV 39 (1986), 102-111.

omission of 64 letters, he suggests that the average length of a line in **T**'s exemplar may have been *ca.* 35 letters. About the eight omissions of 19-24 letters he remarks: "The few which occur seem to belong to an early period in the transmission of the text." It is true that in three of these eight cases the omission also occurs in another primary witness (*Phlb.* 43b5 ἅπαν δὴ τοὐναντίον om. **T¹B**; *Hi. Mi.* 365e7 ὅτι ποιοῦσιν ἢ ἐπίστανται om. **TW**; *Grg.* 514b1 τὴν τέχνην ἢ οὐκ ἐπιστάμεθα om. **T¹B**), but in all these three cases the omission is due to homoioteleuton and may have originated in two MSS independently; the other five omissions in **T** are not necessarily early. I suggest that, if the omissions in **T** are to be explained by the length of a line in the exemplar at all, some of the omissions of 19-24 letters may have arisen when the exemplar of **T** was copied from the lost first volume of **A**; the omissions of 34, 35 and 64 letters, then, may have arisen when **T** was copied from its exemplar; of course, this is by no means certain. All the omissions mentioned by Clark occur in the first seven tetralogies, so that **A** itself cannot be compared.

Sauvantidis[2] concludes, on the basis of a fresh collation of **T**, **A** and **M**, that **T** and **A** are gemelli, and that the common ancestor of **T** and **A** is a gemellus of **M**. This classification, however, does not account for the conjunctive errors of **T** and **M** (and **γ**) against **A**, for which see below, p. 116.

Finally, Giorgetti 203 says that **T**'s reading τῶν εἴτε for τὸ μήτε at 359b3 shows that **T** must derive from a codex "written in capital script, with the words still undivided". It is, however, much more probable that the error has been caused by inner dictation, because—and this Giorgetti wrongly fails to report—**T** has τῶν εἴτε—εἴτε for τὸ μήτε—μήτε; it is extremely unlikely that the scribe of **T** should have misread the same word twice in the same way.

With regard to **M**, it has been argued at length by Campbell 73-86 that **M** is closely related to **A**, but not dependent on it. His conclusions are accepted by Burnet; Sauvantidis (see above) arrives at the same conclusion, although I am unable to tell what his arguments are for drawing up his stemma. Therefore, I will confine myself to a discussion of Campbell's argumentation, and expose its weak spots.

In the first place, Campbell remarks that **M** often agrees with **A**[pc]. The obvious explanation for this fact, namely that **M** has taken over these readings from **A**, is not accepted by him, because **M** does not take over certain other readings added by **A**[pc] (p. 85; cf. p. 79). He admits that "the argument is not a strong one"; in fact, it is not cogent at all:

---

[2] I have not been able to see Sauvantidis' study, but I have found a resumé of his views in a review of his book by V. Atsalos in Hellenika 24 (1971), 409-412.

only if **M** agreed with **A**^{ac} in some cases and with **A**^{pc} in others, in places where correction has made the original reading of **A** invisible[3], could it be concluded that **M** were independent of **A**; as it is, **M** takes over all the corrections made by the scribe in the text of **A**, but chooses between readings of **A** in the text and variant readings added above the line or in the margin; from the fact that a scribe does not accept variant readings which we regard as superior, we cannot infer that he did not have these readings before him[4].

Another weak point is Campbell's discussion of the agreement of **M** and **D**. His first argument against the supposition that **M** (or rather an ancestor of **M**) has been corrected from a MS of the **D** tradition is analogous to the argument he uses against the dependence of **M** on **A** as corrected by **A**^{2} (see above): "the supposition that they (the readings where **M** agrees with **D** against A–GJB) are borrowed by M from Π (= **D**) is weakened by the fact that the not less plausible additions (follow some instances–GJB) have not been similarly borrowed." (p. 82).

His second argument is still weaker (p. 86): "It (**M**–GJB) is not sufficiently removed from Π (= **D**) in point of time to make it probable that in these places it has been altered through contamination with derivatives of Π (= **D**)." To this thesis, the following objections can be raised:

1. One or two months of strenuous work will be enough for an intelligent and zealous scribe to introduce hundreds of variant readings into one MS from one or more other MSS.

2. Even if it be admitted that **M** has not been contaminated with *derivatives* of **D**, this does not imply that it cannot have been contaminated with an *ancestor* of **D** (or, for that matter, with **D** itself).

3. Campbell relied on Rostagno's judgement for his belief that **M** belongs to the twelfth century. Subsequent scholars have attributed **M** to the late thirteenth or fourteenth century; I believe that **M** even belongs to the fifteenth century: see above, p. 27.

$$\begin{array}{c} A \\ | \\ | \\ TM\gamma \end{array}$$

I shall now adduce some positive evidence for the dependence of **TMγ** on **A**.

---

[3] Of course, the term "invisible" should not be taken too literally: often some traces of an erased letter are left, permitting the restoration of this letter; it also happens that the way in which the parchment (or paper) has been damaged provides a clue for the reconstruction of the original reading. In other places a deleted reading can be found in those derivatives which go back to their exemplar^{ac}.

[4] With regard to the case of 383b1, where ἐνδυτεῖσθαι is read by **A**^{ac}**TMγ**, while **A**^{pc} has ἐνδατεῖσθαι, mentioned by Campbell 78, it should be noted that the υ has been corrected into an α in such a way that both υ and α can be understood.

In the first place, **TMγ** agree almost everywhere with **A** against **DF**, both in right and wrong readings; some instances:

328d5	νεανίσκοις **DF**: νεανίαις **ATMγ**
329a6	τε alterum **DF**: om. **ATMγ**
334d9	ἀδίκους **ATMγ**: ἀδικοῦντας **DF**
340a6	τοῖς δὲ **DF**: τοῖς δὲ ἀρχομένοις **ATMγ**
342a4	αὐτὰ **DF**: om. **ATMγ**
348e1	ὃ **DF**: ὅτι **ATMγ**
351d7	διαφέρωμαι **DF**: διαφέρωμεν **ATMγ**
352a10	δέ **ATMγ**: om. **DF**
360c4	ταὔτ' ἂν **F**: ταῦτ' ἂν **D**: ταὐτὸν **ATMγ**
366a7	αὖ μέγα δύνανται **DF**: om. **ATMγ**
367e3	καὶ **DF**: om. **ATMγ**
371d2	αὖ **ATMγ**: om. **DF**
374c2	ἀπεργάσεσθαι **DF**: ἀπεργάζεσθαι **ATMγ**
376a5	ὅτι **DF**: om. **ATMγ**
379a8-9	ἐάντε ἐν μέλεσιν **DF**: om. **ATMγ**
382e9-10	οὔτε κατὰ φαντασίας **DF**: om. **ATMγ**

Further, **TMγ** almost everywhere agree with **A** as corrected by the scribe of **A** himself (**A²**) and by **A³**. In the cases where a trivial error in **A** is corrected or where a correct reading in **A^pc** occurs in **DF** as well, the fact that **TMγ** follow **A^pc** does not provide positive evidence for the dependence of **TMγ** on **A**. In some cases, however, **TMγ** reproduce readings added by **A^pc** or **A³**, which are not merely corrections of obvious errors and which do not occur in **DF**. It has to be admitted that the readings of **A^pc** (and **A²**) have been written by the scribe himself, after the text had been copied, so that it cannot be excluded that these readings derive from the exemplar of **A** itself. The readings, or rather the one reading in *R.*, added by **A³**, however, is conclusive: 327c10 ἐλλείπεται **ATMγDF**: ἓν λείπεται **A³imT1imM1imγ1im**.

Nevertheless, I give some instances of corrections in **A**, added by the scribe, which recur in **TMγ**:

329e1	σου **ATDF**: σε **A²sl**(an **A³** ?)**Mγ1pc**
347e7	ἔγωγε **A^acF**: ἔγωγ' ἔφη **A^pcTMγD**
353d4	πράξαις **A^pcTMγDF**: πράξαιο **A^acA^sl(pc)T1sl**
361c7	ἴτω **A^ac**: ἰτῶι (sic) revera **D**: ἤτω **A^pcTMγ**: ἔσται **F**
364d6	λιστοὶ δέ τε] λιστοὶ δὲ στρεπτοί τε **A^ac**: λιστοὶ δὲ στρεπτοὶ δέ τε **A^pc**(δέ addito supra lineam)**TMγ**: στρεπτοὶ δέ τε **DF**
370a1	σίτου **A^acF**: σιτίου **A^pcTMγD**

At 375a6 the scribe of **A** has written the gloss διώκειν in the margin, to explain the rare form διωκάθειν; **T** has taken this as a variant reading and put it into the text.

In 327a1-389d7, **A** has only two real errors against **TMγ**, to wit 342a5 δεῖ] δεῖ ἀεὶ **A** (ex ἀεὶ fecit αἰεὶ **A^pc**) and 347b9 δή] δὲ **A** (I do not believe that Burnet is justified in preferring the reading of **TMγ** πράξει at 370b2 to πρᾶξιν of **ADF**). These errors of **A** against **TMγ** will be accounted for below, p. 118.

Thus, because **TMγ** follow **A** almost everywhere, and agree with **A** as corrected by the scribe himself and by **A³**, I conclude that **TMγ** derive from **A**, the more so because all of them have a considerable number of errors against **A** (see below, pp. 116 f.). **T**, in addition, reproduces nearly all the scholia which are in **A**; as has already been noted (p. 112), Jordan, *Republik* 477-479, plausibly explains some erroneous readings in the T-scholia as the result of misreading the script of **A**. To mention one instance: in the scholium on 364e, the ending —άτων of the word μειλιγμάτων is written by means of the compendium for ων above the μ and a τ between this compendium and the μ; Jordan, *l.c.*: "Der Schreiber des Venetus übersah das zwischen das M und das Compendium für ων hineingesetzte kleine τ, und so bietet dieser Codex καὶ μειλιγμῶν."

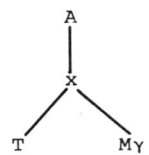

```
        A
        |
        x
       / \
      T   Mγ
```

The dependence of **TMγ** on **A** being certain, there are, theoretically speaking, four possibilities for a stemma of these MSS (**M** and **γ** go back to a lost common ancestor; this will be proved below, pp. 121 f.), viz. 1. **T** and the exemplar of **Mγ** go back to **A** independently; 2. **T** depends on the exemplar of **Mγ**; 3. the exemplar of **Mγ** depends on **T**; 4. **T** and the exemplar of **Mγ** go back to a common ancestor, which derives from **A**.

The first possibility is ruled out by the fact that **T** and **Mγ** have many readings in common against **A** (and **DF**), whether simply errors or possible readings; I quote some instances:

328b7   Χαρμαντίδην **ADF**: χαρματίδην **TMγ**
332e5   ἐν τῷ συμμαχεῖν **ADF**: συμμαχεῖν **TMγ**
340e2   ἀκριβῆ **ADF**: om. **TMγ**
343c1   ὠφελήσονται **ADF**: ὠφεληθήσονται **TMγ**
351b6   τόδε **ADF**: τό γε **TMγ**
358a2   ἀπ' **ADF**: ὑπ' **TMγ**
359b3   τὸ μήτε—μήτε **ADF**: τῶν εἴτε—εἴτε **T**ᵃᶜ**Mγ** (corr. T³)
362b3   βούληται prius **ADF**: βούλοιτο **TMγ**
372e8   θεωρήσωμεν **ADF**: θεωρήσομεν **TMγ**
377a6   μύθοις **ADF**: μύθους **TMγ**

The second possibility is disproved by the circumstance that **Mγ** have many readings in common which separate them from **T** (and from **ADF**); some instances:

329c8   γίγνεται **ADFT**: γίγνεται καὶ **Mγ**
335b3   ἀνθρώπων **ADFT**: τῶν ἀνθρώπων **Mγ**
340a4   γὰρ **ADFT**: om. **Mγ**
350d6   ἡμῖν οὕτω κείσθω **ADFT**: οὕτω κείσθω ἡμῖν **Mγ**
362a2   ἀνασχινδυλευθήσεται **ADFT**: ἀνασκινδαλευθήσεται **Mγ**[1pc]
363e1   ἄγοντες **ADFT**: ἄγεσθαι **Mγ**
366e2   ὅσων **ADFT**: ὅσον **Mγ**
373a1   ἐξαρκέσει **ADFT**: ἀρκέσει **Mγ**
378b1   οὐ **ADFT**: οἱ **Mγ**
380c1   μήτε ἄνευ **ADFT**: μὴ ἄνευ **Mγ**

The third possibility is to be rejected on the ground that **T** has some readings which have separative value against **Mγ** (and **ADF**). Some instances:

335e1   φησίν **AMγDF**: φήσει **T**
338c5   φὴς **AMγDF**: om. **T**
351b6   οὗτος ἦν **AMγDF**: ἦν οὗτος **T**
358c6   οὔ τι **AMγDF**: ὅτι οὐ **T**
360d7   οὖν **AMγDF**: om. **T**
374c1   σχολὴν ἄγων **AMγDF**: om. **T** (add. **T**[3])
382d11 τοὺς **AMγDF**: τοὺς μὲν **T**
383a2   δεύτερον τύπον **AMγDF**: τύπον δεύτερον **T**
386b6   δουλείας **AMγDF**: δειλίας **T**

The conclusion therefore is that **T** and **Mγ** go back independently to a common ancestor, itself a derivative of **A**, whether direct or not; on the other hand, it has become clear that **T** cannot possibly be a *direct* copy of **A**, as has been supposed by a number of scholars (e.g. Alline 214 f.; Chambry cxli f.; Dodds, *Gorgias* 37-39; Slings 268, 273).

In some places, **T** and **Mγ** show traces of contamination with the **F** tradition (sometimes the **D** tradition as well); I will cite some places where the agreement of **TMγ** with **F** and/or **D** can hardly be explained as coincidence: **Mγ** show traces of contamination with the **F** tradition (sometimes the **D** tradition as well); I will cite some places where the agreement of **TMγ** with **F** and/or **D** can hardly be explained as coincidence:

329c3   ἀσμενέστατα **AMγF**: ἀσμεναίτατα **TD**
333d7   μηδὲν **AT**[1sl]: μὴ **TMγDF**
339b8   δίκαιον **TMγDF**: καὶ δίκαιον **AT**[1sl]
341e4   ἡ alterum **AD**: om. **TMγF**
343a4   τίτθη **A**: τίθη **D**: τηθή **TMγF**
347a2   οὐδ' ἐπιτάττει **AD**: om. **TMγF** (add. **F**[4(u.v.)])

349e6   καὶ A: om. TMγDF
360c8   ἀδικεῖν ἀδικεῖν AD: ἀδικεῖν ἀδικεῖ TMγF
368c8   ᾧ AD: ὃ TMγF
374e11 παρείκῃ AD: παρήκει F: παρήκη(ι) TMγ
376c2   δεῖν AD: δεῖ TMγF

That omissions which are common to F(D) and TMγ, too, must be explained as the result of contamination, and not as coincidence, is shown by the case of 339b8: here A has καὶ δίκαιον, Mγ read δίκαιον with DF, T has δίκα.ον with καὶ added *supra lineam* by the first hand[5]. The explanation is that in the common ancestor of T and Mγ, the word καὶ was deleted, but not made illegible; the scribe of T, then, seeing that according to the corrector of his exemplar καὶ did not belong in the text, but existed as a variant reading, put it *supra lineam* to indicate this; Mγ omit the word altogether. The case of 333d7 can be explained in the same way; here, A has μηδὲν, DF^ac TMγ read μὴ (μηδὲν fecit F²), but T¹ has added δὲν *supra lineam*; apparently both readings were in the exemplar, as Mγ have μὴ.

Accordingly, the places where A has an error against TMγ can also be explained by the correction of the common source of T and Mγ from another MS[6]. It is possible that the extra scholia in T are due to contamination as well, although this cannot be settled beyond doubt[7].

---

[5] Chambry, in his apparatus, states that καὶ has been added by T²; I have inspected T *in situ*, and it is beyond doubt that the word has been added (*per compendium*) by the first hand. The same goes for δὲν at 333d7, which is discussed below.

[6] Dodds, *Gorgias* 38 f., suspects that in some cases the agreement of B and T must be explained as the result of contamination. His supposition is confirmed by my conclusions: in some places in *Grg*. T may have been corrected from a MS of the B tradition.

[7] Diller, *Codex T* 324, remarks that the four important plus scholia in T are all about proverbs; he suggests that Ephraim added them *suo Marte*, which is possible. Yet if Ephraim added them, I suppose that he borrowed at least parts of them from another source; thus in the scholium on ἀδελφὸς ἀνδρὶ παρείη at 362d6, the explanation ὅτι προτιμητέον τοὺς οἰκείους εἰς βοήθειαν can be found in substantially the same form in Suid. α 442, Macar. I 29, Apostol. I 36 and Diogenian. I 91.

The correct readings in the T-scholia against A cannot possibly all be due to conjectural emendation. In the scholium at 329e8 T has οἱ δ' ἐξ αὐτῆς (sc. Σερίφου) σερίφιοι, where A offers αὐτῶν for αὐτῆς; at 347a T has τὸ ὑπὸ πονηροτέρων ἄρχεσθαι, while A has πονητέρων for πονηροτέρων; at 357b, in the subdivision of pleasures, under the heading αὐτὸ αὑτοῦ ἕνεκα, T has χαίρειν ἀβλαβέσιν ἡδοναῖς, while A has χαίρειν ἢ λαβεῖν ἡδονήν; at 360e T reads in the scholium ὡς ἀναγκαῖον ἀλλ' οὐχ ὡς ἀγαθόν, where A offers ἄλλοις for ἀλλ'. In *R.*, T has a scholium on βούβρωστις at 379d; T offers a much longer version of the scholium on σαρδάνιον at 337a. Further, there are two scholia, mentioned by Diller, *l.c.*, on *Clit*. 407a and *Spp*. 374a (the scholium on *Spp*. 374a is found in Par. 1808, which goes back to T, as is shown by Schanz, *Platocodex* 47-51; the part of T which contained *Spp.* is now lost; cf. Diller, *l.c.*; of course, it is possible that Par. 1808 does not go back to the lost part of T in *Spp.*, but borrowed *Spp.* from another source; it is also possible that the scholium on *Spp.* 374a does not go back to T, but was added by a later scribe).

The fragments in P

Before embarking on the discussion of **T**, **Mγ** and their derivatives, I shall deal with **P**.

In the fragments from *R.*, **P** follows **A** very closely; I shall list some readings where **P** agrees with **A** (and usually with **TMγ** as well) against **DF**:

378c8	λεκτέα μᾶλλον **DMγ**^{1im}: μᾶλλον λεκτέα **F**: μᾶλλον **ATP**
379a8-9	ἐάντε ἐν μέλεσιν **DF**: om. **ATMγP**
382e9-10	οὔτε κατὰ φαντασίας **DF**: om. **ATMγP**
534a4	ἐπιστήμην **A**^{ac}**DF**: ἐπιστήμη **A**^{pc}**MγP**
615a7	ὅσους **A**^{ac}**DF**: οὓς **A**^{pc}**MγP**
615b2-3	εἴ τινες **AMγP**: οἵτινες **DF**
616a4	ὅτι εἰς **DF**: εἰς ὅτι **AMγP**
621a7-8	τοὺς—μέτρου **AMγP**: om. **DF**

The only place where **P** agrees with **DF** against **ATMγ** is 382e9 λόγῳ **PDF**: ἐν λόγῳ **ATMγ**; I do not believe that this reading has separative value.

Moreover, **P** follows the readings of **A**^{pc}; some instances:

591e2	πλῆθος **A**^{pc}**PMγ**: πλήθους **A**^{ac}**DF**
617e7	ἒ δὲ] ε δε (sic) **A**^{ac}: ἔδει **A**^{pc}**PMγ**
619b4	νῷ] ῶ (sic) **F**: om. **A**^{ac}: νῶ(ι) **A**^{pc}**PMγΘW** (deest **Sc.**): τῶ **Par**.

Therefore, the dependence of **P** on **A** can be regarded as certain, the more so because **P** has many separative errors against **A** (and against **TMγ**); some instances:

379a8	αὐτὸν om. **P**
382e8	θεός] θεὸς ἀμετάβλητος **P**
533d4	πολλάκις om. **P**
567d6	ταῦτα δρῶν om. **P**
614d2	διακελεύοιντό] διεκελεύοντο **P**

In the parts of books I and II which are in **P**, there are no conjunctive errors of **PTMγ** against **A**, nor separative errors of **T** and/or **Mγ** against **AP**. There is one (slight) conjunctive error of **PMγ** against **AT**, to wit 380b5 δὲ **ATDF**: om. **PMγ**. In the sample passage of book X, however, **P** has four errors in common with **Mγ**:

616c3	συνέχον τὴν] συνεχομένην **PMγ**
616e3	τὸν] τὸ **PMγ**
617a7-8	αὐτῶν δὲ τούτων] αὐτὸν δὲ τοῦτον **PMγ**
621c3	ψυχὴν] τὴν ψυχὴν **PMγ**

Further, I have noted the reading 588e3 Λέγωμεν] λέγομεν **PMγ**, but this can hardly be called a conjunctive error.

I conclude that **P** derives from the common ancestor of **T** and **Mγ**; the reading at 380b5 suggests (but no more than that) that **P** and **Mγ** go back to a gemellus of **T**. In a diagram, the possibilities can be depicted as follows:

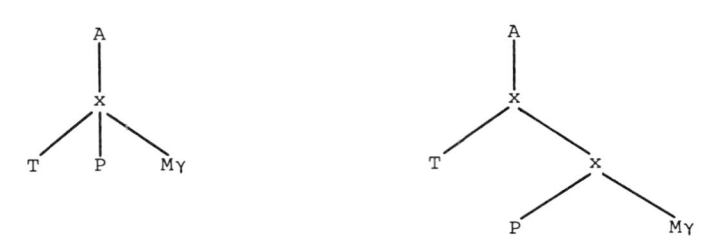

Mr. Jonkers tells me that in *Ti.* too **P** derives from **A**. Therefore, **P** can be discarded as a primary witness in both *R.* and *Ti.*[8].

The Mγ-group

I will first discuss the **Mγ**-group, then the **T**-group.

After books I and II, **Mγ** maintain the position they held before: they usually follow **A**, and have separative errors of their own. I list some errors of **Mγ** in the sample passages of books III, VII and X:

388b6   κυλινδόμενον] κυλινδούμενον
388d4   ἄνθρωπον] αὐτὸν ἄνθρωπον
388e2   ἐσήμαινεν] ἐσήμανεν
390b6   Δία] βία
392a8   εἴη ἄν] ἂν εἴη
516e3   τόδε] τότε
517a1   τὰ ὄμματα] τὸ ὄμμα
518d5   αὐτῷ] αὐτὸ
519d9   ὂν ἄμεινον] ἄμεινον ὄν
614d2   διακελεύοιντό] διακελεύοιτό
615e4   ἄνδρες, ἔφη, ἄγριοι] ἄγριοι ἔφη ἄνδρες (**M**^{pc}: ἔφη ἄγριοι ἄνδρες **M**^{ac})
617a4   τὸν ἕκτον] τῶν ἕκτων
617c7   χρόνον] χρόνῳ
619c1   βρώσεις] βρῶσις
620e5   ἐπικλωσθέντα] ἐπικλωθέντα

The exemplar of **Mγ** was provided with variant readings which can be partly traced back to another source, and are partly new; see for instance:

---

[8] Dodds, *Gorgias* 39-41, states that **PW** form a group apart from **T** (and **B**); the fact that in *R.* **P** goes back to the same source as **T** strongly suggests that in *Grg.* **TPW** should be considered one group against **B**; the same goes for the position of **P** in other dialogues which are also in **TW**, e.g. *Men.* (Bluck accepts Dodds' stemma). See my article *The Vindobonensis W of Plato*, to be published in *Codices Manuscripti*.

THE AFFILIATION OF MANUSCRIPTS   121

328b6   Καλχηδόνιον] καρχηδόνιον M¹ˢˡγ¹ˢˡF
334b2   ante πάντας add. ὑπὲρ M¹ˢˡγ¹ˢˡ: habet Fⁱᵗ
342b6   ἕωσπερ ἂν ᾖ] ἢ ὡς ἡ σφαῖρα M¹ⁱᵐγ³⁽ᵘ·ᵛ·⁾ˢˡ
616a6-7   μὴ—ἀναβαίνοι] τὸν φόβον εἰ μυκήσαιτο τὸ στόμιον Mⁱᵗγ³ⁱᵐ (cf. Procl., in R. II 183,27-29 K.)
          (For γ³ see below, pp. 123 f.).

The following readings may also be due to contamination of the exemplar of **Mγ**:

329e7   οἴονται] οἷόν τε **MγF**
332a12   τῳ] τὸ **MγF**
337a3   σαρδάνιον] σαρδόνιον **MγF**
341e6   τούτῳ] τοῦτο **MγF**
367c4   αὑτῷ] αὐτὸ **MγF**
387c3   ὑπὲρ **MγDF**: ὑπὸ **AT** falso
420c5   τις] ἄν τις **γF** (non ita **M**)
568b6   συγγιγνώσκουσιν] καὶ συγγιγνώσκουσιν **MγF**

In some places, **Mγ** are the most important MSS to preserve a true reading; I will discuss interesting readings in **Mγ** in the chapter on the secondary MSS, pp. 226-231.

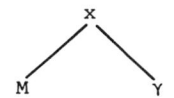

```
        x
       / \
      M   γ
```

That **M** and **γ** are gemelli is proved by the fact that they both have separative errors against each other; I will first record some separative errors of **M**:

327c5   ἄστυ] τὸ ἄστυ (et **F**)
332a2   παρακατέθετο] παρεκατέθετο
391c4   ἀλλήλοιν] ἀλλήλοις
392d8   ἔοικα διδάσκαλος] διδάσκαλος ἔοικα
519a5   βλέπῃ] βλέποι
614d6   τὼ ἑτέρω] τὸ ἕτερον

Some errors in books I-II, outside the sample passages:

339e2   ὡμολογῆσθαι] ὁμολογεῖσθαί
340e7   νυνδή] νῦν
342c7   ἔφη, οὕτως] οὕτως ἔφη
348e6   εἴπῃ] εἴποι
352b1   θεοῖς] τοῖς θεοῖς
357b3   εἶπον om.
368a3   περὶ] παρὰ
369c1   τὸν] τῇ
374a6   καλῶς om.
380b4   κολάσεως] κολάσεων

Some separative errors of γ:

328c7 χρῆν] χρή
388b7 ἐξονομακλήδην] ἐξονομακλήνδην
391b2 αὖ τάς] αὐτάς
392c2 διομολογησόμεθα] διωμολογησάμεθα
516e2 δέξασθαι] μᾶλλον δέξασθαι
616c6 ἀδάμαντος] ἀδάμοντος
620e5 ἄγειν] ἄγει

Some distinctive readings of γ in books I-II, outside the sample passages:

340c9 ὡμολόγεις] ὁμολογεῖς
342b6 ἕωσπερ ἂν ᾖ] ἕως ἑσπέρα ἦ
350a1 πόσει] πόση
363b1 μέν τε] μέντοι
365a3 θύσαντας] θύσαντες
367a1 ὑμῶν] ἡμῶν
370a2 οἰκίας] οἰκείας
374a5 ὡμολογοῦμεν] ὁμολογοῦμεν
382d5 χρήσιμον] τὸ χρήσιμον

M does not show significant traces of contamination against γ; but at 425d2 **M** reads λήξεως *recte* with **Lobc.**^{pc}**Par.** against λήξεις of **ADFγ**; this may be a conjectural emendation in **M**, but it is also possible that **M** has λήξεως *post correctionem*, although on the microfilm I see no traces of correction (**M**^{pc} draws on **R**, which is a derivative of **Lobc.**; see below).

It must be pointed out that Rostagno's collation, or at any rate Campbell's report of **M** is not always accurate; it happens rather frequently that a reading is attributed to **M** which in reality is not be found in **M** at all; e.g. the probably correct reading ἂν ἀναγκαῖαι at 558e1 is ascribed to **M** by Campbell and Burnet (Campbell adds **V**), while in fact it is only found in **V**, and not in **M**.

M has been provided with variant readings and corrections; although the ink of these corrections and variant readings is usually a bit darker than the ink of the text, I believe that they have been written by the scribe himself, after the copying of the text, because the script is exactly similar (I have inspected **M** *in situ*). Campbell 91 points out that the corrections and variant readings in **M** (like the supplementary leaves) are frequently in agreement with **R**; this is confirmed by my collations: **M**^{pc} often agrees with the **Sc.**-group, to which **R** belongs; incidentally, **M**^{pc} agrees with **R** alone, for instance 390a10 παρὰ πλεῖαι] περὶ πλεῖαι **M**^{sl}**RΦ** (Φ is an apographon of **R** in books I-VI); 616c1 τῶν] ἐκ **M**^{pc}**R**.

It appears that the corrections and variant readings in **M** are never original, but always derive from other sources, *i.c.* **R**; therefore, they do not deserve attention (of course, this does not apply to those variant readings in **M** which come from the exemplar of **Mγ** and which have been written in the same colour ink as the text).

M has no extant descendants in *R*.

Like **M**, γ does not show significant traces of contamination against its gemellus.

γ has many corrections and variant readings. Some of these have been written by the first hand, quite probably during the copying of the text; they appear to stem from the exemplar, e.g. 358a8 ἀδικία δ' ἐπαινεῖται om. **AT**: habet in margine γ¹, habet in textu **M**. In other places, the scribe corrected an error of his own, as at 354a4-7 Ὁ—οὗ om. γ, add. γ¹ⁱᵐ.

Unlike **M**, γ has been corrected and provided with variant readings by various later hands. The distinguishing of these later hands is an extremely complicated problem; I have studied γ for some hours *in situ*, in order to check my conclusions based on the study of a microfilm, but I do not claim that my account is exhaustive.

The hand which I have called γ² has supplied the long omission 496c2-498c9 ἡ δὲ—διάβαλλε on foll. 142-143. This omission in γ must be due to the loss of some leaves in γ itself, not in one of its ancestors, because the last word on fol. 141, φιλοσοφίας, immediately precedes the omission, while the first word on fol. 144, ἦν δ' ἐγώ, immediately follows it. There is a note in the lower corner of fol. 141ᵛ ζήτει τὸ λεῖπον ἐντεῦθεν; the script of this note looks exactly like the script of the scholia, which have been written by the scribe himself, but probably after the copying of the text; I therefore conclude that the folia in question were lost between the copying of the text and the writing of the scholia, so that the scribe noticed the omission and added the note. As the text on foll. 142-143 is usually in agreement with **M**, and is followed by **a**, an apographon of γ, I submit that the text has been supplied in the scriptorium in which the whole of γ was written, from the same source, but by another scribe. γ² writes in a dark blue-black ink; the parchment of foll. 142-143 is very thin.

γ³ writes in rather large, round letters, with a light bluish ink. γ³ is especially active at the end of book X, and seems to draw on the exemplar of γ, because readings of γ³ also occur in the text of **M**; see the famous variant reading 616a6-7 μὴ—ἀναβαίνοι] τὸν φόβον εἰ μυκήσαιτο τὸ στόμιον **Mⁱᵗ**γ³ⁱᵐ; 619e4 χθονίαν] χρονίαν **M**: χθονίαν γᵃᶜ: χρονίαν, addito θ supra ρ, γ³ᵖᶜ. In book I, the reading 342b6 ἔωσπερ ἂν ᾖ] ἢ ὡς ἡ σφαῖρα, which occurs in **M¹ⁱᵐ**, is found in γˢˡ; it appears to have been written by γ³.

These readings also occur in **a**, so that γ^3 must have been at work before (an ancestor of) **a** was copied from γ. Because γ^3 agrees with **M** against all the other MSS, it is probable that γ^3, like γ^2, was active in the scriptorium where γ was copied, and that it drew on the exemplar of γ.

γ^4 writes with a very dark, almost black ink, in a somewhat spotty script. It is curious that γ^4 introduces some variant readings on the foll. 142-143, which have been written by γ^2. Still more curious is the fact that some of these variant readings are preceded by the abbreviation *al.*, which stands for *aliter* or *alibi*; this proves that these variant readings were written when the MS was already in Italy; therefore, γ^4 probably belongs to the fifteenth century. Some instances of γ^4:

386b5 αἱρήσεσθαι] ἐρήσεσθαι γ^{ac}: αἱρήσεσθαι γ^{4pc}
492c6 ᾗ] οἳ γ^{4pc}
498b7 ἐπιτείνειν] ἐπιτείνει γ^{4sl}
498b7 ἐκείνης] ἐκείνων γ^{4sl}
543c4 τοῦτ'] ταῦτ' γ^{4pc}

Readings of γ^4 recur in **a**, and therefore have been written before **a** was copied from γ. Some of the readings of γ^4 appear to be new.

γ^5 uses a light brown ink and draws on a MS of the **Sc.**-group; some instances:

445a7 μετὰ om. γ^{ac}: add. γ^{5im}
472e8 δυνατώτατ'] δυνατόν τ' γ^5Vind. Bon. Sc.
544d7 τρόπῳ] τρόπον τινα γ^{5im}Sc.

This hand also wrote the note ζήτει τὸ λεῖπον ἐντεῦ[θεν (here the leaf is cut off) on fol. 159^r, to indicate the lacuna 524e5-528c6.

Readings of γ^5 do not recur in **a**, and therefore have been added after **a** was copied from γ.

γ^6 writes in a grey-blue ink, of varying intensity. It draws on **x** (or a descendant of **x**): see for instance:

330c6 καὶ] καὶ οὐ γ^{6im}F**x**
386a4 ποιησομένοις] ποιησομένοις οἴει γ^{6im}**x**^{3im}
544c7 διαφέρουσα recte γ^{6sl}**x**^{pc} (nescio quae manus)

That the readings which are common to γ^6 and **x**^{pc} by a later hand came from **x** into γ and not the other way round is clear from the case of 386a4, mentioned above: for ποιησομένοις **F** and **x** read ποιησομένοις οἷς (dittography): οἴει looks unmistakably like a conjectural emendation of οἷς.

There is some reason to assume that γ⁶ draws on (a close relative of) **Ricc.** (which is a derivative of **x^Pc**): at 331a7, where γ has ἀτάλλουσα, γ⁶ writes ἀτάλλοισα *supra lineam*, which is in **Ricc.** (and many other MSS as well) but not in **x**.

Readings added by γ⁶ do not recur in **a**.

γ⁷ supplies the lacunae 440a5-441a8 σημαί]νει—γενόμενα on fol. 98; 445c1-449c3 ὅσα—ἵνα on fol. 103; 524e5-528c6 αὐτῷ—ταῦτα on foll. 165-168. The first two of these lacunae are due to the loss of a leaf in γ; the last one was already in a predecessor of γ, because the last word before the lacuna and the first word after it do not correspond with the last word of a folium in γ before the lacuna, or the first word of a folium after it. The omission does not occur in **M**.

The ink of γ⁷ looks very similar to that of the first hand; the script is very characteristic, and somewhat angular.

The lacuna 524e5-528c6 also occurs in **a**, which proves that γ⁷ was active after **a** had been copied from γ. At the other two lacunae supplied by γ⁷, **a** has some readings in common with **M**, which proves that the folia which contained these passages were lost in γ after **a** had been copied from γ.

The notes on fol. 102ᵛ ζήτει ὅτι φῦλλον ἓν λείπεται and on fol. 97ᵛ ζήτει φῦλλον ἓν ὅτι λείπεται have been written by hands which I have not found elsewhere in γ.

Finally, there are some recent hands which write ση in the margin (esp. at the end of book X); on foll. 242ʳ and 243ʳ there are scholia by two different hands which tell us that the passage in question (the Myth of Er) is referred to by Justin Martyr.

```
      γ
     / \
    Φ   a
```

Two MSS, **Φ** and **a**, derive from γ; I will quote some places where **Φa** share a distinctive reading of γ (**Φ** only in book VII):

328c7	χρῆν] χρὴ
391b2	αὖ τὰς] αὐτὰς
392c2	διομολογησόμεθα] διωμολογησάμεθα
517d6	γελοῖος] γελοίως (γελοῖος Φ^Pc, prima manus, ut vid.)
518a6	ἂν ἀλογίστως] ἀναλογίστως
524e5-528c6	αὐτῷ—ταῦτα om.
620d6	ἡρῆσθαι] εἰρῆσθαι (γ^4pc)
620e5	ἄγειν] ἄγει

Φ and **a** go back to γ independently, because they have no conjunctive errors, while each of them has separative errors against the other and against γ. First, I discuss Φ.

Φ is the most adulterous of all MSS of the *Republic*: in books I-VI it derives from **R**, in books VII-IX it goes back to γ, and in book X it is dependent on **c**.

The dependence of Φ on γ in books VII-IX is proved by the fact that in the sample passage of book VII Φ follows γ almost everywhere, and adds some separative errors of its own; some instances:

514b6 παραφράγματα] παραδείγματα
515a5 Ὁμοίους ἡμῖν, ἦν δ' ἐγώ] ἦν δ' ἐγὼ ὁμοίους ἡμῖν
515d8 Πολύ] πάνυ
519e2 ἐν πόλει διαφερόντως] διαφερόντως ἐν πόλει

That Φ changes its exemplar at the beginning of book VII is proved by some conjunctive errors of **R**Φ at the end of book VI:

511d3 τὴν alterum om. **R**Φ
511d4 οὐ νοῦν] οὖν **R**Φ

Corrections by later hands in γ do not recur in Φ: the passage added by γ[2] (496c2-498c9) is found in book VI, where Φ derives from **R**; γ[3] is especially active in book X, where Φ depends on **c**; the reading ταῦτ' for τοῦτ' at 543c4, written by γ[4pc], is not in Φ, but it does recur in **a**; therefore, Φ goes back to an earlier phase of γ than **a**.

That Φ changes γ for **c** at the beginning of book X is illustrated by some readings at the end of book IX and at the beginning of book X:

590b3 αὐτοῦ habent γΦ: om. **c**
590e4-
591a1 καὶ—ἀντικαταστήσωμεν habent γΦ: om. **c**

596d8 χαλεπός habet γ: χαλεπῶς **ac**Φ (**a** is the source of **c**)
597a1 οὐ habent γ**a**: οὐδὲ **a**[sl]**c**Φ
597c5 μὴ φυῶσιν habent γ**a**: μὴν φύσι **c**: μὴν φύσει Φ

In some places Φ has been corrected by what seems to be the first hand (but I have not studied Φ *in situ*), e.g. 517d6 γελοίως γΦ[ac]: γελοῖος Φ[pc] *recte*.

In books VII-IX Φ does not show clear traces of contamination with other MSS; at 516e2 Φ has δέξασθαι *recte* against μᾶλλον δέξασθαι of γ, but this is an obvious correction. At 520b4 Φ reads ὀφείλειν for ὀφεῖλον, a reading which is also found in **VMatr.**; yet this reading may have originated in Φ and the exemplar of **VMatr.** independently as the result of anticipation of ἐκτίνειν which follows immediately. At 529d7 Φ has παραδείγματι for παραδείγμασι with **Sc.ᵖᶜ**; again, the agreement may well be coincidental.

```
        Φ
        │
       Mon.
```

Φ is the source of the parts of books VII and X which are in **Mon.**; I mention some cases of agreement of **Mon.** with a distinctive reading of **Φ**:

514b6 παραφράγματα] παραδείγματα
515a5 Ὁμοίους ἡμῖν, ἦν δ' ἐγώ] ἦν δ' ἐγὼ ὁμοίους ἡμῖν
515d8 Πολύ] πάνυ
516a8 τῷ om.
519e2 ἐν πόλει διαφερόντως] διαφερόντως ἐν πόλει

Mon. takes over most of the readings of **Φ** and has some separative errors of its own; some instances in book VII:

514a1 εἶπον] εἶπον ἐγώ
516d5 καὶ σφόδρα om.
517a6 καὶ om.
518e1 ἐμποιεῖσθαι] ἐμπεσεῖσθαι
519d8 χεῖρον] χείρω
520a9 μὲν om.

In some places **Mon.** shows traces of contamination; see for instance:

515e7 ἀνείη] ἀνίοι **Φ**: ἀνίη, addito οι supra lineam a prima manu, **Mon.**
529d7 παραδείγμασι] παραδείγματι **ΦMon.**¹ˢˡ: παραδείγμασι **Mon.**ⁱᵗ

Moreover, at 516a6 **Φ** reads τὰς σκολιὰς for τὰς σκιὰς (with **γa** (*deficit* **M**)), while **Mon.** has τὰς σκιὰς *recte*. (That the reading of **Mon.** at 517c9 αὐτῶν αἱ ψυχαὶ] αἱ ψυχαὶ αὐτῶν is also found in **VMatr.** is, I think, due to coincidence.) Therefore I conclude that **Mon.** stems from an apographon of **Φ** which was corrected from another source.

In some places **Mon.** has variant readings added by the first hand, e.g. 517b1 λεγομένοις] εἰρημένοις **Mon.**, λεγο in margine **Mon.**¹. The first hand also made some corrections, e.g. 518c2 ὄψιν] ὄχιν **Mon.**ᵃᶜ: φ per χ **Mon.**¹.

Mon. has not been corrected by later hands, and has no extant derivatives.

The second derivative of **γ** is **a**; **a** follows **γ** in most readings while adding a number of separative errors of its own; some instances:

330b8 μοι] μὴ
331d6 ὑμῖν] ἡμῖν
387b5 δεῖ] δὴ
391c4 νοσήματε] νοσήματά τε
514b6 δεικνύασιν] δεικνύουσιν
516d4 τὸ om.
517b5 τῆς ψυχῆς om.
520e3 ἐν om.
614d5 δικασθείη] διαδικασθείη
615b3 προδόντες] προδιδόντες
618b7 ἀνθρώπῳ] ἀνθρώπων
620a7 κύκνον] κύκνου

a corrects some slight and obvious errors in **γ**; some instances:
332b5 τύχη habet **a**: τύχοι **γ**
333d3 δέη habet **a**: δέοι **γ**
386c5 ἐπάρουρος habet **a**: ἐπ' ἄρουρος **γ**
388b2 αἰθαλόεσσαν habet **a**: αἰθαλόεσαν **γ**
389c6 τις habet **a**: τις τῆς **γ**
616c6 ἀδάμαντος habet **a**: ἀδάμοντος **γ**
619e2 ἀπαγγελλομένων habet **a**: ἀπαγγελομένων **γ**

a takes over readings of $γ^2$, $γ^3$ and $γ^4$ (see above, pp. 123-124); some instances:

$γ^2$: the text of the lacuna 496c2-498c9 on foll. 142-143 in **γ**.
$γ^3$: the readings at the end of book X, e.g. 616a6-7 μὴ—ἀναβαίνοι] τὸν φόβον εἰ μυκήσαιτο τὸ στόμιον $γ^{3im}a^{it}$.
$γ^4$: some variant readings on the folia written by $γ^2$, e.g. 498b7 ἐπιτείνειν] ἐπιτείνει $γ^{4sl}a^{it}$; ibid. ἐκείνης] ἐκείνων $γ^{4sl}a^{it}$.

It has already been pointed out (p. 124) that the variant readings by $γ^4$ are sometimes preceded by al., which implies that they have been written in Italy. Therefore, we may safely conclude that **a** was copied in Italy and probably belongs to the fifteenth century, not to the fourteenth century, as is usually assumed. The corrections by $γ^5$, $γ^6$ and $γ^7$ do not recur in **a**.

The text of **a** does not show any traces of contamination. There are, however, many corrections and variant readings; these are written in ochreous ink, in contrast to the text, which is written in greyish ink (I have inspected **a** in situ); however, the script of the corrections and variant readings is so similar to that of the text, that I believe that they have been added by the scribe himself, after the text had been copied. That some time elapsed between the copying of the text and the adding of the corrections and variant readings is suggested by the fact that **m**, a derivative of **a**, is always in accordance with a^{ac}, also in places where correction has made the original reading in **a** invisible.

The corrections and variant readings in **a** are mainly borrowed from the **F** tradition; this is in full accordance with the fact that in the dialogues which precede and follow *R.* in **a**, *Clit.* and *Criti.*, **a** is a close copy of **F** (for *Clit.* see Slings 263 f.; for *Criti.* I rely on the information given to me by Mr. Jonkers). **a** takes over numerous readings from **F**, even when these readings are clearly wrong or even nonsensical; see for instance:

519e3 ἐγγενέσθαι] ἐπαινεῖσθαι **a**[sl]**F**
520c6 ὕπαρ] παρ' **a**[im]**F**
615b4 ἐμβεβληκότες] ἐμβεβηκότες **a**[sl]**F**

F has been corrected by five later hands (see above, pp. 101-104); there is an indication that not all these later hands had been at work in **F** at the time when the scribe of **a** borrowed readings from **F**: 490a1 εἰ νῷ] ἐν ᾧ **F**[ac]**a**[im]: εἰ ἐν νῷ **F**[4pc]; 493a6 οὕς] ὅτε **F**[ac]**a**[sl]: οὕς τε **F**[4(u.v.)pc]. This proves that the corrections in **a** cannot have been borrowed from **x**, because **x** shares readings added by all the later hands in **F**.

Other variant readings in **a** are taken over from **γ**, e.g. 619e4 χθονίαν habet **γ**[ac]: χρονίαν **γ**[3pcit]**a**[it]: χθονίαν **γ**[3sl]**a**[1sl]. Such variant readings are written in the same ink as the text, in contrast to the corrections and variant readings which come from **F**.

In some cases a variant reading in **a** is not found in **γ** or **F**, or any other extant MS (except, of course, the apographa of **a**), e.g. 619e4 πορεύεσθαι] πορεύσεσθαι **a**[pc].

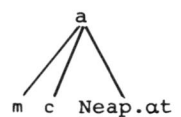

```
          a
         /|\
        / | \
       m  c  Neap.αt
```

The offspring of **a** can be divided into three branches: **m**, **c**, and the common source of **Neap.** and **αt**.

I will quote some places where **m**, **c** and **Neap.αt** share a distinctive reading of **a** (**m** is absent in book I):

329b2 τούτῳ] τοῦτο
389a3 ἀποδεξόμεθα] ἀποδεξώμεθα
514b6 δεικνύασιν] δεικνύουσιν
516a2 οὐδ' ἂν ἕν] οὐδὲν ἂν
517b5 τῆς ψυχῆς om.
519c10 πρόσθεν] ἔμπροσθεν
520e1 δὴ om.
520e3 ἐν om.
615b3 προδόντες] προδιδόντες
617e8 ὁπόστος] ὁπόσος (et **F**)
618b7 ἀνθρώπῳ] ἀνθρώπων

That **m, c** and the common ancestor of **Neap.** and **αt** go back to **a** independently, is proved by the fact that they do not have any conjunctive errors, while each of them has separative errors against the others and against **a**. First, I discuss **m**.

It has already been noted (p. 128) that **m** derives from **a** before **a** was corrected and provided with variant readings; this can be proved easily, as **m** follows **a**^{ac} almost everywhere, and adds some separative errors of its own; some instances:

390b6 τῶν] σῶν
515c3 Πολλὴ ἀνάγκη] πολλὴ ἂν ἀνάγκη
516d4 ἢ τὸ om.
518d9 κινδυνεύουσιν] κινδεύουσιν
614b3 μὲν om.
614b5 διεφθαρμένων] διεφθαλμένων
617a1 τὸ om.
618e1 ἐκεῖσε] ἐκεῖ

m follows **a** very closely, and even takes over many trivial errors, e.g. 517c6 Συνοίομαι] ξυνίομαι **a**^{ac}**m**.

In two places (in the sample passages) **m** has the correct reading against **a**:

391c4 νοσήματε habet **m**: νοσήματά τε **a**
518a2 διτταὶ habet **m**: διττὰς **a**

Yet these are two easy corrections, which need not be explained as the result of contamination.

m never takes over later corrections and variant readings in **a**, and always agrees with **a**^{ac}; some instances:

524e5-
528c6 αὐτῷ—ταῦτα om. γ**a**^{ac}**m**(Φ): add. **a**^{pc}
614d2 διακελεύοιντό] διακελεύοιτό Μγ**a**^{ac}**m**: διακελεύοιντό **a**^{pc}
619c2 σκέψασθαι om. **M**^{ac}γ^{ac}**a**^{ac}**m**: add. **a**^{pc}

Because **m** follows **a** so closely, shows no traces of contamination and has only a few errors against **a**, it is quite possible that **m** is a direct transcript of **a**^{ac}.

In some cases, the scribe of **m** corrected an error of his own, e.g. 615d4 οὖν om. **m**^{ac}: add. **m**^{1sl}. Very rarely, **m** has a correction by a later hand, e.g. 491d1 ἐγγείων] ἀγγείων **am**: add. ε supra α **m**^{2}.

m does not have extant derivatives.

In contrast to **m, c** and the exemplar of **Neap.** and **αt** derive from **a**^{pc}; see for instance:

328b6 Καλχηδόνιον habent **am**: καρχηδόνιον a^sl^c**Neap.αt**
330a5 ἐπιεικής habent **am**: ἐπιεικῆς οὐ a^sl^c**Neap.αt**
386a3 τε prius om. a^ac^m: habent a^pc^c**Neap.αt**
386c6 ᾧ—εἴη om. a^ac^m: habent a^sl^c**Neap.αt**
392a13 ἐρεῖν habent **am**: εὑρεῖν a^sl^c**Neap.αt**
524e5-
528c6 αὐτῷ—ταῦτα om. a^ac^m: habent a^pc^c**Neap.αt**
614d6 τὼ ἑτέρω] τῶ ἑτέρω (sic) γ**am**: τὸ ἕτερον a^sl^c**Neap.αt**
619c2 σκέψασθαι om. M^ac^γ^ac^a^ac^m: habent a^pc^c**Neap.αt**
621d1 οἱ om. a^ac^m: habent a^pc^c**Neap.αt**

I shall first discuss the group **Neap.αt**. Some separative errors of this group against **c** (and **a**):

327c4-5 πρὸς ἄστυ ὡρμῆσθαι ὡς ἀπιόντες] ὡς ἀπιόντες πρὸς τὸ ἄστυ ὡρμῆσθαι
328a9 τε] γε
329a1 ἐρῶ, ὦ Σώκρατες] ὦ σώκρατες ἐρῶ
386a1 ὡς om.
389e1 αὐτοὺς δὲ ἄρχοντας] ἄρχοντας δὲ αὐτοὺς (αt addunt ἂν post δὲ)
392a4 οἵους] οἷς οὓς
515d5-e1 ἐρωτῶν—ἀναγκάζοι om.
516d7-e1 ἢ—πεπονθέναι om.
614b8 οὗ om.
615a2 γῆς] γῆν
617c3 Κλωθὼ καὶ Ἄτροπον] ἄτροπον καὶ κλωθὼ
617e7-8 πλὴν—ἐᾶν om.

In many places, however, **Neap.αt** do not follow **a**; I will list a number of places where **Neap.αt** have the correct reading against **a** and **c** (and often **M**γ or γ as well):

386d2 τά τε habent **Neap.αt**: τά γε **ac**
387b5 δεῖ habent **Neap.αt**: δὴ **ac**
391d3 προσαναγκάζωμεν habent **Neap.αt**: προσαναγκάζομεν **ac**
516a6 τὰς σκιὰς habent **Neap.αt**: τὰς σκολιὰς γ**ac** (deficit **M**)
517d6 γελοῖος habent **Neap.αt**: γελοίως γ**ac**
615e6 διαλαβόντες habent **Neap.αt**: ἰδίᾳ λαβόντες A^pc^**M**γ**ac**
617a5 στρεφόμενον habent **Neap.αt**: στεφόμενον **M**γ**ac**

Such correct readings of **Neap.αt** against **a** (and the ancestors of **a**) must be explained as the result of contamination: I will show that the common source of **Neap.** and αt was heavily contaminated from other sources. The alternative explanation, that the exemplar of **Neap.** and αt does not derive from **a**, is to be rejected for the following reasons:

1. If the correct readings in **Neap.αt** against **a** are not regarded as the result of contamination, it must be assumed that the exemplar of **Neap.** and αt is a gemellus of the exemplar of **M**γ, because **Neap.αt** do not only have correct readings against **a**, but also against **M**γ**a**, as has been illustrated above; in that case, we cannot account for the conjunctive errors of **Neap.αt** with **a**, γ**a** and **M**γ**a**.

2. In some places, **Neap.αt** agree with readings added by later hands in **γ**, e.g. 498b7 ἐκείνων γ⁴ˢˡᵃᶜNeap.αt, and with readings which have been added by the scribe of **a** after the text had been copied.

Therefore, the dependence of **Neap.αt** on **a** is certain. After having discussed the relationship of **Neap.αt** towards each other, I will come to speak again about the contamination in this group.

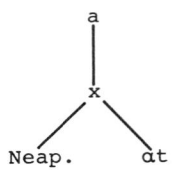

```
         a
         |
         x
        / \
     Neap. αt
```

That **Neap.** and the lost exemplar of **αt** are gemelli, is proved by the fact that they both have separative errors against each other; first, I will list some separative errors of **Neap.**:

328e2	ὥσπερ] οἵσπερ
515d2	λέγοι] λέγει
518b2	αὐτῇ] αὐτῷ
518c10-d1	φαμεν τἀγαθόν] τἀγαθόν φαμεν
518d4	τε om.

Some separative errors of **αt**:

331a3-7	ὡς—γηροτρόφος om.
387e1	ἑτέρου] ἑταίρου
391a5	αὖ ὡς] ὡς αὖ
392c1	περί γε] καὶ περὶ
617d7	ἀρχὴ] ἀρχῆς
618d5	ἄλληλα om.

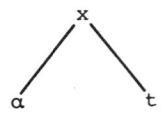

```
         x
        / \
       /   \
      a     t
```

α and **t** are gemelli, because they both have separative errors against each other; some errors of **α**:

331c8	πάντα ἐθέλων] ταῦτα λέγων
387a1	τὸ om.
387b5	θανάτου] πρὸ θανάτου
390d1	πρὸς ἅπαντα om.
391b3	ἱερὰς τρίχας] τρίχας ἱερὰς
514b8	φέροντας ἀνθρώπους] ἀνθρώπους φέροντας
517a8	τοίνυν om.
519e3	τοῦτο] τούτῳ

614b4 ὅς] ὡς
615c5 ἐρωτωμένῳ ἑτέρῳ] ἑτέρῳ ἐρωτωμένῳ
617d1 ἑκατέρας om.
621a6 μὲν om.

Some separative errors of **t**:

329a7 ἔχεται] ἔρχεται
331c5 πᾶς] πῶς
333d6 Φήσεις] φύσεις
387c1 ἐνέρους] ἐνέργους
389e11 Καλῶς] καλλῶς (sic)
392a3 λόγων] λέγων
515a9 ἔχειν] ἔχειν ἡ (sic)
516e5 ἥκων] εἴκων
517c5-
519b2 τὸν—ἡδοναῖς om. (add. t²)
616d1 τοῦ] τὴν
617c6 τῇ] τῇδε

t has very many orthographical errors; some instances:

387c1 τύπου] τίπου
388b3 κλαίοντα] κλέοντα
392d8 Γελοῖος] γελεῖος
616c7 σφόνδυλον] σφόνδηλον
617e1 λήξεται] λύξεται

I shall now discuss the contamination of **Neap.αt**. There are many cases where **Neap.αt** agree with other branches of the tradition in readings which cannot be the result of coincidence.

In the first place, there are many readings in **Neap.αt** which also occur in the **F** tradition, esp. **Ricc.**; some instances:

330b7 ἤ] ὧν Neap.αtx³ⁱᵐRicc.
332c5 ἦν δ' ἐγώ post ἤρετο Neap.αtRicc.
332c11 ἀποδιδοῦσα] ἀποδιδοῦσα τέχνη Neap.αtRicc.
332c12 τέχνη om. Neap.αtRicc.
388e6 γέλωτι] γέλωτι χρῆται Neap.αtx³ⁱᵐRicc.
614e3 κατασκηνᾶσθαι] κατασκηνοῦσθαι Neap.αtxRicc.
619b5 μήτε] μήτε οὖν Neap.αtRicc.ˢˡ

In isolated cases, **αt** agree with the **F** tradition against **Neap.**, e.g.:

519a5 ἐργαζόμενον] ἐργάσεται αtx³ⁱᵐRicc.
519c6 ἀπῳκίσθαι] ἀποκεῖσθαι αtFxRicc.
520c4 ὄψεσθε] ἄψεσθε αFxRicc.ᵃᶜ: ἄψεσθαι t

In other cases, again, **α** alone agrees with **FxRicc.**, **xRicc.** or **Ricc.**; some instances:

330c7 ἀλλ'] ἄλλο αRicc.
387c1 ἐνέρους] κερβέρους αx^{2pc}(nisi fallor)Ricc.
390c7 δι'] ἦ αFxRicc.
391c8 Μή] καὶ αx^{3im}Ricc.
514a5 τὸ σπήλαιον] τοῦ σπηλαίου αx^{3pc}(nisi fallor)Ricc.
519e1 τοῦτο] τούτω αRicc.
619b4 νῷ] τῶ αxRicc. (et **Par**.)

I think that the most natural explanation for the occurrence of readings of **FxRicc.**, **xRicc.** and **Ricc.** in this group is that the common ancestor of **Neap.** and **αt** has been provided with variant readings from **Ricc.** (or rather an ancestor of **Ricc.**, as I will illustrate); some of these readings have then been taken over by **Neap.** and the exemplar of **αt**; other readings have been neglected by **Neap.** but passed into the common source of **αt**; some of these have been taken over by both **α** and **t**, others by **α** alone (**t** hardly ever agrees with other MSS against **α** and/or **Neap.**); of course, we cannot exclude the possibility that readings of **Ricc.α** against **tNeap.** were brought into the exemplar of **α**, but in that case we should have to assume two, or even three, stages of contamination from the same source, which in itself is not particularly attractive, but not impossible.

Hitherto, I have assumed without proof that the agreement of **Neap.αt** and **FxRicc.** is the result of contamination of the exemplar of **Neap.** and **αt** with **Ricc.**; the opposite explanation, that the exemplar of **Neap.** and **αt** is the source of these readings, is to be excluded because in that case it should be assumed that not only **Ricc.** and **x**, but also **F** were contaminated from **Neap.αt**; this is impossible for the following reasons:

> 1. **Neap.αt** stem from **a**^{pc}, as I have shown; now in some dialogues at least **a** derives from **F** (see above, p. 129), while the corrections in **a** in *R*. derive from **F** as well. It is impossible that a predecessor of **F** was contaminated with one of **F**'s grandchildren.
> 2. It is universally accepted that **F** is a direct or almost direct transcript of a majuscule exemplar (cf. p. 99); this makes the theory of contamination of (an ancestor of) **F** with an ancestor of **Neap.αt** extremely unattractive.
> 3. We should have to assume three subsequent stages of contamination: of **F** itself, of **x** and of **Ricc.**, all from the same source, namely **α**; now **α** was written for Francesco Filelfo, and thus belongs to the fifteenth century, while **F** is assigned to the late thirteenth or to the fourteenth century.

I believe that the source of the variant readings borrowed from the **F** tradition can be localized between **x** and **Ricc.**, because of the reading at 328b7: here **x** reads χαρμαντίδην *recte*; a later hand deleted the letters αντ by marking them with dots. **Neap.αt** read χαρμίδην (as does **x**^{pc}), but **Ricc.** has χαρμαντίδην. Yet it is certain that the source of the **F** readings in **Neap.αt** is closely related to **Ricc.**, because there are many cases of agreement between **Ricc.** and **Neap.αt** (see above, p. 133); the explanation is, I think, that an ancestor of **Ricc.** read χαρμίδην, with x^pc; the **F** readings in **Neap.αt**, then, were taken from this source; subsequently, χαρμίδην was corrected into χαρμαντίδην in an ancestor of **Ricc.** (I will show that **Ricc.** stems from a corrected derivative of **x**; see below, pp. 194-197).

In the second place, there are two cases of agreement of **Neap.αt** with **Lobc.**, to wit 328e5 ἤδη om. **Neap.αtSc. WLobc.** and 614c5 δεξιάν] δεξιά and c7 ἀριστεράν] ἀριστερά **Neap.αtLobc.**; as these are the only instances from the sample passages, and as these readings are not very distinctive in themselves, I am inclined to dismiss them as coincidental.

So much for the contamination of the common source of **Neap.αt**. **Neap.** does not show traces of contamination against **αt**, but the case is different with **αt**, and especially with **α**.

To start with, **αt** sometimes have the correct reading against **aNeap.**; some instances:

517c8 οἱ habent **αt**: om. **aNeap.**
518c5 ὦ habent **αt**: ὁ **aNeap.**

Further, in some places **αt** agree with the **Sc.**-group, notably **W**; see for instance:

517c7 τοίνυν om. **αtSc.W**
517e2 μὴ πώποτε] μήποτε **αtSc.W**
518a2 γίγνονται] γίγνοιντ' ἄν **αtSc.W**
518a6 γελῷ—ἐπισκοποῖ] γελώη—ἐπισκοποίη **αtSc.W**
518a7 ἀηθείας] ἀληθείας **αtD^acSc.W**
518b1 ἄν om. **αtSc.W**
518e2 παντὸς μᾶλλον] μᾶλλον παντὸς **αtSc.W**
519b3 εἰ om. **αtW**

It is remarkable that both correct readings in **αt** against **aNeap.** and cases of agreement of **αt** with (**Sc.**)**W** against **aNeap.** occur only in the sample passage of book VII (the same goes, by the way, for the agreement of **αt** with the **F** tradition against **Neap.**; see p. 133); this suggests that the scribe who added the corrections and variant readings in the exemplar of **αt** which are in both **α** and **t**, was not active in the whole of the *Republic* but only in the environs of book VII.

I have already noted that **t** hardly ever agrees with other MSS against **aNeap.α** (see p. 134); the only instances (in the sample passages) are:

388b1 ἀμφοτέραισιν] ἀμφοτέροισι **tSc.**
388d5 ἐπίοι] ἐποίοι **tFx^ac** (non ita **Ricc.**)

518b1 εὐδαιμονίσειεν habent tPar.PcR: εὐδαιμονήσειε(ν) rell.
621b8 οὕτως] οὗτος t*D*

None of these cases is such as cannot be explained as coincidence.

α, on the other hand, shows traces of intensive contamination. In many places, **α** has the correct reading against **aNeap.t**; in these cases, of course, the source of the corrections cannot be specified; some instances:

389a6 ἴδον habet α: εἶδον aNeap.t
516e3 ὁ τοιοῦτος habet α: ὅτι οὗτος AMγaNeap.t
517a6 ἄν habet α: αὖ MγaNeap.t
620a7 κύκνον habet α: κύκνου aNeap.t
620e5 ἄγειν habet α: ἄγει γaNeap.t

The agreement of **α** with **Ricc.** has already been mentioned above (pp. 133 f.). There are also some places where **α** shares a reading with the **Sc.**-group, esp. **WLobc.R**; some instances:

388c2 μήτοι] μήτι α^{ac}R
614d2 διακελεύοιντό] διακελεύειν τε αΘWLobc.R (deficit Sc.)
616a4 τε] τε ταῦτα ὑπομένοιεν αTWLobc.R (deficit Sc.)
621b7 ἐπί] ἐν αWLobc.R

On one occasion, there is agreement with β: 386b5 ἀδεῆ] ἀδεᾶ αβ^{pc}, but this may be coincidental.

We cannot decide whether these readings were already in the common source of **αt**, or came into a MS between this common source and **α** itself; it is also possible that they were brought into the exemplar of **αt** when **t** had already been copied from its exemplar.

Neap. has not been corrected by later hands. In **t** there are some corrections by a later hand; this hand has also supplied the lacuna 517c5-519b2 τὸν—ἡδοναῖς.

α has been corrected and provided with variant readings by the first hand and by at least one later hand. Scholia have been added by the first hand in red ink (I have examined **α** for a short while *in situ*). The later hand (α²) uses ink of almost the same colour as the ink of α¹; its script is very characteristic, with upright letters; see e.g. the addition at 331a3-7 ὡς—γηροτρόφος. It is possible that some of the corrections and variant readings are by yet another hand, but this is not certain.

Some of the corrections in **α** can be traced to other branches of the tradition; in the first place, there is some agreement with the **Sc.**-group, esp. **W**; some instances:

328d5	σύνισθι] ξύνιθι α^ir Sc.W
329c2	συγγίγνεσθαι] συμμίγνυσθαι α^2(u.v.)sl Sc.W (Par.)
331c8	οὐδ'] ὁδ' α^2pc W
614d5-6	κατὰ δὲ τὼ ἑτέρω erasit α^pc: om. ΘW (deficit Sc.)
618c8	εἰδέναι] καὶ εἰδέναι α^1(u.v.)sl ΘWPar. (deficiunt DSc.)

I have noted one case of agreement with β: 387c2 οἴεται] οἷόν τε α^1im β^pc.

In other places α adds readings which are not found elsewhere; see for instance:

328e7	post χαλεπὸν add. τὸ α^1sl
619d7	καὶ punctis del. α^1 vel α^2

Outside the sample passages, α (sometimes in combination with its gemellus t) occasionally has interesting readings, which sometimes agree with the indirect tradition; such readings will be discussed in the chapter on the secondary MSS; see pp. 235-237.

```
    Neap.
      |
      |
    Ott.
```

α and t do not have extant derivatives; **Neap.** is the source of **Ott.**, which contains 505a2-509d5, 514a1-520a5 and 614a6-621d3. I will mention some cases of agreement of **Ott.** with distinctive readings in **Neap.**:

515d2	λέγοι] λέγει
518b2	αὐτῇ] αὐτῶ
518c10-d1	φαμεν τἀγαθόν] τἀγαθόν φαμεν
518d4	τε om.

Ott. follows **Neap.** everywhere, and has two, admittedly very slight, errors against **Neap.**:

518a1	ἔχοι] ἔχει
617e1	αἱρήσεσθε] αἱρήσεσθαι

Ott. does not show any traces of contamination in comparison with **Neap.**, and may well be a direct transcript. There are no later hands in **Ott.**; **Ott.** has no extant derivatives.

The second derivative of **a^pc** is **c**: **c** follows **a** almost everywhere, and adds some separative errors of its own against **a** (and against **Neap.αt**); some instances of readings peculiar to **c**:

329a6	τἀφροδίσια] ἀφροδίσια
330a2	ὧν om. (et **Fxv**)

332a1	ἐστιν τοῦτο] τοῦτό ἐστιν
387c1	τούτου τοῦ τύπου] τοῦ τύπου τούτου
389a8	ἔφη, βούλει] βούλει ἔφη
391b2	αὖ τὰς] αὐτὰς τὰς (αὐτὰς γa)
516d2-3	αὐτὸν et αὐτῶν transposuit
516d5	ἐπάρουρον] ἄρουραν (ἐπ' ἄρουραν γa)
614d5	δικασθείη] καταδικασθείη
614e4	ἀλλήλας] ἀλλήλαις
616c1	αὐτοῦ post δεσμῶν
619b8-9	καὶ prius-ἑλέσθαι om.

c follows a very closely; in some places c corrects an error in a, e.g.:

330a7	πλείω habet c: πλέω AMγa
391a7	ἤ σ' habet c: ἧς γa
392a3-4	πέρι ὁριζομένοις] περιοριζομένοις οἷς a: περιοριζομένοις c (which is correct, but for the accent)
616e3	τὸν habet c: τὸ Mγa

These are, however, all very easy corrections, which need not be explained by contamination. c takes over some variant readings in a; c sometimes admits such readings in the text, or records them as variant readings above the line or in the margin; many variant readings in a do not recur in c.

The alternative explanation for the correct readings in c against a, viz. that c does not depend on a, would imply that c were independent of AMγ as well; this is impossible because of the conjunctive errors of c with AMγa, Mγa, γa and a, and because of the fact that c reproduces variant readings added by γ², γ³, γ⁴ and a^pc.

In one case (in the sample passages) a reading in c can be explained as having been caused by misreading the script of a: 329b1 προπηλακίσεις] προπηλακίσεις εἰς TMγa, sed εἰς credas ἐκ in a: προπηλακίσεις ἐκ c.

c does not show traces of contamination against a; as to the text of *R.*, I do not see any objections to the hypothesis that c is a direct transcript of a; this is regarded as improbable for *Clit.* by Slings 266 f., and for *Criti.* by Mr. Jonkers. Sicherl, *Platonismus* 554, states that c was copied from a at the instigation of Ficino, but the evidence on which this assumption is based is very slight indeed; see above, pp. 33 and 37.

In some places, c has been corrected by the scribe himself; yet the corrections by the scribe are sometimes written in a lighter ink; some instances:

386d7	πεπνῦσθαι] πέπνυσθον c^pc
514a3	ἀναπεπταμένην habet c^pc: ἀναπεπταμένη γac^ac

Some of the readings *post correctionem* occur only in a (and sometimes F); such readings therefore stem from a; see for instance 386d5 οὐκ ἔνι] οὐκέτι a^sl c^sl F. Other readings, e.g. 386d7 πεπνῦσθαι] πέπνυσθον appear to be new.

Marcel 253 f. and Sicherl, *Ficino* 59, say that Ficino's hand has been identified in c, e.g. as the hand that wrote *Deest hic ferme folium* on fol. 333^r and added some corrections. I have not checked this, but I must note that in R. I have not noted any variant reading which seems to be due to a hand different from that of the scribe.

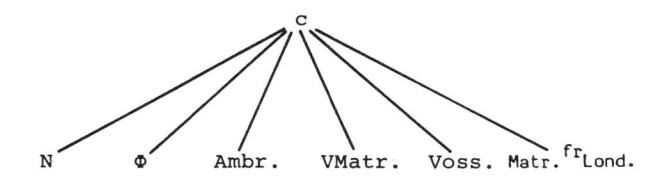

```
                    c
       ╱  ╱  ╱  │  ╲   ╲
      ╱  ╱  ╱   │    ╲   ╲
     N   Φ  Ambr. VMatr. Voss. Matr.^fr Lond.
```

c is the source of six other MSS: **N** (in books III-X), **Φ** (in book X), **Ambr.**, the exemplar of **V** and **Matr.** (in books II-X), **Voss.** and the exemplar of **Matr.**^fr and **Lond.** The corrections and variant readings in c recur in the apographa. I will quote some places where **NΦVMatr. Voss.Ambr.Matr.**^fr**Lond.** agree with distinctive readings in c (Φ in book X only; the presence or absence of the excerpt MSS is not specified):

386d7	πεπνῦσθαι] πέπνυσθον
387c1	τούτου τοῦ τύπου] τοῦ τύπου τούτου
389a8	ἔφη βούλει] βούλει ἔφη
391b2	αὖ τὰς] αὐτὰς τὰς
516d5	ἐπάρουρον] ἄρουραν
614d5	δικασθείη] καταδικασθείη
616c1	αὐτοῦ τῶν δεσμῶν] τῶν δεσμῶν αὐτοῦ
619b8-9	καὶ prius-ἑλέσθαι om.

That all these MSS go back to c independently, appears from the fact that they do not have any conjunctive errors, while each of them has separative errors against the others (and against c).

The exemplar of **V** and **Matr.** derives from Θ in book I (see below, pp. 159 f.); that it changes its exemplar Θ for c at the beginning of book II, is illustrated by some readings at the end of book I and at the beginning of book II:

353d9	οὐ habet **c**: om. **ΘVMatr.**
354b8	οὐx alterum habent **ΘVMatr.**: om. **c**
354c3	ἢ habet **c**: ἢ οὐx **ΘVMatr.**
357b8	διὰ ταύτας habent **cVMatr.**: om. Θ
358a6	ὂν habet Θ: ἦν **cVMatr.**

I will list some separative errors of **VMatr.** against **c** (and against the other derivatives of **c**):

387e10	καὶ—σπουδαίαις om.
388a1	ἡμῖν] μὴ
388e2	Δεῖ δέ γε οὐχ] οὐ δεῖ δέ γε
391c1-2	καὶ Πηλέως om.
515a5	Ὁμοίους] ὁμοίως
516d4	τοῦ om.
519a9	κοπτόμενον] περικοπτόμενον
520c3	θεάσασθαι] θεᾶσθαι
614c1	ἀφικνεῖσθαι] ἀφικέσθαι
616a5	φόβων] πολλῶν
617b1	καὶ ἕκτον om.
621a1	δι'] δὴ

V and **Matr.** follow **c** in most places, but not everywhere. That this must be due to contamination of the exemplar of **V** and **Matr.** and should not be regarded as an indication that **VMatr.** do not depend on **c**, is proved by those places where **VMatr.** have the correct reading not only against **c**, but also against **ac**, **γac**, **Mγac** and **AMγac**: if it is assumed that **VMatr.** are independent of **c**, it should also be assumed that they are independent of **a** and **AMγ**; this is out of the question because of the conjunctive errors of **VMatr.** with **c**, **ac**, **γac**, **Mγac** and **AMγac**. Moreover, **VMatr.** reproduce readings by later hands in **γ** and by **a**[pc] and **c**[pc].

Further, in other places **VMatr.** show unmistakable traces of contamination with other MSS.

Some instances of correct readings in **VMatr.** against **c**:

386c7	καταφθιμένοισιν habent **VMatr.**: καταφθινομένοισι **Fa**[sl]**c**
387b5	δεῖ habent **VMatr.**: δὴ **ac**
387b5	μᾶλλον habent **VMatr.**: om. **Mγac**
390a2	νεανιεύματα habent **VMatr.**: νεανισκεύματα **Mγac** (νεανιχεύματα **A**)
515b9	παριοῦσαν habent **VMatr.**: παροῦσαν **γac** (deficit **M**)
515e3	δύναται habent **VMatr.**: δύνανται **γac** (deficit **M**)
516d2-3	αὐτὸν et αὐτῶν hoc ordine habent **VMatr.**: transposuit **c**
516e3	ὁ τοιοῦτος habent **VMatr.**: ὅτι οὗτος **AMγac**
518c5	ᾧ habent **VMatr.**: ὃ **Mγac**
619c1	βρώσεις habent **VMatr.**: βρῶσις **Mγac**
620a7	κύκνον habent **VMatr.**: κύκνου **ac**
620e5	ἄγειν habent **VMatr.**: ἄγει **γac**

The exemplar of **V** and **Matr.** has been contaminated from various sources:

1. In some places, **VMatr.** agree with the **F**-family, esp. **x**; some instances:

349c8   ἁπάντων] ἂν πάντων **Fx**: ἂν ἁπάντων **VMatr.**
366e6   τί δρᾷ **Fx**: ἐν **AD**: τί δρᾷ ἐν **VMatr.**
387a6   ἐπεί] ἐπὴν **Matr.Fx**: ἐπεὶν **V**
486d11 εὐάγωγον] καὶ εὐάγωγον **VMatr.x**
509c5   ἀλλὰ] ἄλλο **VMatr.x**[3sl]
511c8   αἰσθήσεσιν] αἰσθήσει **VMatr.x**[3pc]
527d6   τό] τοῦτο **VMatr.x**
544c7   διαφέρουσα habent **VMatr.x**[pc](nescio quae manus) (γ[6])
598d1-2 τῷ τοιούτῳ] τὸν τοιοῦτον **VMatr.x**

2. In other places, there is agreement between **VMatr.** and the **Par.**-group, esp. β; some instances:

362a1 ἐκκαυθήσεται] ἐκκοπήσεται **VMatr.βP**[c]**K**
395d3 τὴν om. **VMatr.βK**
519b2 περὶ κάτω] περὶ τὰ κάτω **VMatr.βPar.**

3. Further, there are some cases of agreement with **N** and its derivative **E**; see for instance:

461c1 ᾧ] ἢ **VMatr.N**[pc]**E**
554e7 ἰδίᾳ om. **VMatr.N**[pc]**E**

I believe that in such cases **N** (or **E**) is the source of these readings in **VMatr.**, and not the other way round, because of the age of these MSS: both **N** and **VMatr.** are derivatives of **c**, but **N** has been written at the latest in the sixties of the fifteenth century, like its direct transcript **E**, while **Matr.** has been written in 1480, and **V** even belongs to the sixteenth century.

On one occasion, **VMatr.** have the obviously correct reading against all the other MSS: 487c1 φέρωσιν **VMatr.**: φέρουσιν **rell.**; I shall discuss some interesting readings in **VMatr.** in the chapter on the secondary MSS; see pp. 234 f.

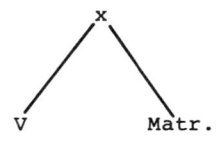

```
        x
       / \
      /   \
     V    Matr.
```

That **V** and **Matr.** are gemelli is proved by the fact that they both have separative errors against each other; some errors of **Matr.**:

389a1 ἀποδεκτέον] ἀποδεικτέον
390e4 τοῦ om.
391d3 νῦν om.
516a8 ὕστερον] ὕστερα
518d7 διαμηχανήσασθαι] δεῖ μηχανήσεσθαι (δεῖ μηχανήσασθαι **V**: δὴ
       μηχανήσασθαι **Mγac**)
614e5 τῆς om.

616a3 σημαίνοντες] ὑποσημαίνοντες
616d5 καθάπερ] ὥσπερ (glossema ?)
617d2 δεῖν] ἰδεῖν

Some errors of **V**:

388c7 μοι] μὴ
390c8 τὸν om.
391c5 αὖ om.
515c2 τὰς] καὶ τὰς
517c9 διατρίβειν] ἀεὶ διατρίβειν
520a6 εἶπον] εἶπεν
615a5 δ' οὖν om.
619c5 δαίμονας] εὐδαίμονας
621b4 ἄττοντας] ἅπτοντας

In some places **V** shows traces of contamination with other MSS against **Matr.**; see for instance:

370c9 καλὸν] κάλλιον **Vx**
591d2 συμφωνίας] ἀρμονίας **Φ**: συμφωνίας ἀρμονίας **V**

Of course, it is quite possible that these readings were already in the exemplar of **V** and **Matr.**, but have been neglected by **Matr.**

Occasionally, **V** alone has an interesting or good reading, e.g. 558e1 ἂν habet **V**: om. rell. (etiam **M**, errat Burnet).

Matr. shows no traces of contamination against **V**. Neither of the two MSS has been corrected by later hands, and neither of them has any extant derivatives.

The second MS which derives from **c** is **Φ**: it has already been argued that in books I-VI **Φ** is dependent on **R**, while in books VII-IX it derives from **γ** (see above, pp. 125-127). Thus it is only in book X that **Φ** derives from **c**.

In book X, **Φ** follows **c** almost everywhere, and adds some errors of its own, which have separative value; some instances:

615b4 δουλείας] δουλείαν
615e3 ἀνιάτως ἐχόντων] ἐχόντων ἀνιάτως
617a5 ὅλον] ὅλην
619a1 ἔχοντα] ἔχοντι
620a7 μεταβάλλοντα] μεταβάλλουσαν (this looks like an intelligent conjecture, caused by the preceding κύκνου of **acΦ**)

In some places **Φ** has the correct reading against **c**. Since in some of these places the wrong reading occurs in **a**, **γa**, or **Μγa** as well, this cannot be used as an argument against the dependence of **Φ** on **c**.

Some instances of correct readings in **Φ** against **c**:

617a5 στρεφόμενον habet **Φ**: στεφόμενον **Μγac**
620e5 ἐπικλωσθέντα habet **Φ**: ἐπικλωθέντα **Μγac**
621a1 ἐκείνου habet **Φ**: ἐκεῖνον **ac**

In the sample passage of book X, Φ has two variant readings added by the first hand:

617e1 λήξεται] λήψεται Φ¹ˢˡ
620e6 ποιοῦντα] ποιοῦσαν Φ¹ˢˡ (this reading is also found in **P**, but **P** can hardly be the source of the corrections in Φ, as it contains only fragments)

I tend to regard the readings in Φ just mentioned as conjectural emendations; yet the possibility remains that in some cases Φ has been contaminated.

In book X there are no corrections by later hands.

```
    Φ
    |
   Mon.
```

As in book VII, Φ is the source of **Mon.** in book X (**Mon.** only has 595a1-604c1 of book X); some common errors of ΦMon.:

596d3   δοκεῖ] δοκῇ **Mon.**¹ᵖᶜΦ (δοκεῖ **Mon.**ᵃᶜ)
597a10 τι] τε
597a10 τυγχάνει] τυγχάνοι

However, in a number of places **Mon.** has the correct reading against Φ, so that the conclusion drawn on the basis of the sample passage of book VII, namely that **Mon.** derives from a contaminated derivative of Φ, is confirmed by the part of book X in **Mon.** (cf. p. 127); the case of 597b12 is illustrative: for Ἔστω, Φ reads ἔσται, **Mon.** has ἔσται with ω added above αι by the first hand; see also 597a2 ποιεῖ] ποιοῖ **F**: ποιεῖ **Mon.**, addito οι supra ει a prima manu.

The third MS that goes back to c is **N**, in books III-X. In books I-II **N** depends on **T**, as will be shown below (see pp. 153-155). Post 41 notes that **N** "leaves a blank at the end of book II (not elsewhere), thus betraying the change of manuscript." What is more, after book II the text is written by another scribe. I will cite some readings at the end of book II and at the beginning of book III which illustrate that **N** exchanges **T** for c from 386a1 on:

378a6 ὅπως ὅτι habet c: ὅτι ὅπως **NT**
383a2 δεύτερον τύπον habet c: τύπον δεύτερον **NT**
386b6 δουλείας habent c**N**: δειλίας **T**
387c1 τούτου τοῦ τύπου habet **T**: τοῦ τύπου τούτου c**N**

N follows c almost everywhere, even in the smallest details; the only places in the sample passages where N has the correct reading against c concern trivial orthographical errors in c:

618b2   ταῦτα habet N: ταυτὰ (sic) c
618c5   διαγιγνώσκοντα habet N: διαγινώσκοντα c

N has a number of separative errors against c (and against the other derivatives of c); some instances:

387c8   Ναί] δικαίως
390e7   οὐδ' prius] μηδ'
392c1   λόγους] λέγειν
515c6   συμβαίνοι] ξυμβαίνει
615a6   τινα ἠδίκησαν] ἠδίκησάν τινα
615c6   εἴη] ἂν εἴη
615e4   διάπυροι] καὶ διάπυροι
616b5   μάλιστα] καὶ μάλιστα
621a7   εἶναι om.

The text of N does not show traces of contamination, and N is in all probability a direct transcript of c.

After the text had been written, N was corrected and provided with variant readings from various sources; all these readings are written by Bessarion himself, but at different stages, as is proved by the different colours of the ink in which the corrections and variant readings are written (I have inspected N *in situ*).

Post's remark (42) that Bessarion "may well have had manuscript authority for his corrections" proves to be an understatement: I have identified seven extant MSS with which N^{pc} agrees.

The first MS used by Bessarion for his corrections is $Θ^{pc}$; see for instance:

399b1   ἐν] καὶ ἐν $N^{sl}Θ$
422e9   ᾖ] εἶεν $N^{pc}Θ^{pc}$
423a5   χρήσῃ] χρήσαιο $N^{pc}Θ^{pc}$
449c4   οἰηθῆναι] οἴει $N^{pc}Θ^{pc}$
497e7   πόλιν] πάλιν $N^{im}Θ^{pc}$
550b1   λογιστικὸν] λογικὸν $N^{pc}Θ$
555e3   δοκοῦντες] δοκοῦσι $N^{pc}Θ$
559b4   ὠφέλιμος] καὶ ὠφέλιμος $N^{sl}Θ^{2sl}$

A second MS from which Bessarion borrowed a number of variant readings is x (or a derivative of x); see for instance:

519a5   ἐργαζόμενον] ἐργάσεται $N^{sl}x^{3im}$
558a8   περινοστεῖ] περινοστεῖ ὁ καταψηφισθεὶς $N^{sl}x^{3im}$

Thirdly, Bessarion consulted (a derivative of) β; some instances:

360e1 αὐτήν] αὐτοῖν N^sl β^pc
454d1 τὸ—τεῖνον τὰ habet β^pc: τὸ—τεῖνον N^pc (τὰ eraso): τὰ—τείνοντα rell.
519e1 νόμῳ] νομοθέτῃ N^sl β^im
554b5 χοροῦ] βίου N^sl β^pc

In the fourth place, I have noted a few cases of agreement with the more recent part of **T**:

516a6 καθορῷ] καθορώῃ **N^pcTDurh.**
516a9 ἂν ante τὸν οὐρανὸν **N^pcTDurh.**

The fifth MS from which readings have been borrowed by Bessarion is **R**; some instances:

471b4 ἀλγούντων] ἀλγοῦντες **N^slLobc.R**
501c9 εἰ σωφρονοῦσιν] ἢν σωφρονῶσι **N^slR** (ἢν σωφρονοῦσι **Lobc.**)
526d2 καταλήψεις] τὰς καταλήψεις **N^slSc.Lobc.R**

The numerous readings in which **N^pc** agrees with **Sc.** may come from **Θ, T** or **R**; some instances:

472b1 εἰπεῖν] λέγειν **N^imSc.**
488d8 δὲ] τε **N^slSc.**
603a11 ὂν] οὖσα **N^pcSc.**

Number six of the MSS which provided variant readings for **N** is **α**; see for instance:

504b8 μὴν] δὲ **N^pcα**
598c3 ἐξαπατῳ] ἐξαπατώῃ **N^slα**

Finally, I have noted one case of agreement with **p**:

602c10 ταὐτά] τὰ **N^pcp**

In the discussion of **V** and **Matr.** it has already been noted (p. 141) that these MSS sometimes agree with **N**; I have already stated that I believe that in these cases the exemplar of **VMatr.** has drawn on **N** (or **E**); I mention a number of cases of agreement between **NE** and **VMatr.** (N. B. not **N^pc**):

360e8 διαισθάνεται] διαισθάνεσθαι **NEVMatr.**
387c7 Ἀφαιρετέα] ἀφαιρετέον **NEVMatr.**
496a11 ἔφην ἐγώ] ἔφη ἦν δ' ἐγὼ c: ἦν δ' ἐγὼ **NEVMatr.**

A number of corrections and variant readings in **N** are not found elsewhere; in some cases, these readings deserve particular attention; they will be discussed in the chapter on the secondary MSS; see pp. 231-234.

N
|
E

N is the source of **E**, undoubtedly its direct source (**N** is partly Bessarion's autograph, **E** was written for him by Johannes Rhosus). I will note a number of places where **E** shares a characteristic reading of **N**:

387c8   Ναί] δικαίως
390e7   οὐδ' prius] μηδ'
515c6   συμβαίνοι] ξυμβαίνει
517c3   νοητῷ] τῶ νοητῶ N^sl E
519e1   τοῦτο] τούτου N^pc E
615a6   τινα ἠδίκησαν] ἠδίκησάν τινα
615c6   εἴη] ἂν εἴη
621a7   εἶναι om.

E follows **N** everywhere, and takes over many corrections and variant readings in **N**; whenever Rhosus accepts a variant reading in **N**, he usually puts it into the text, and hardly ever adds it in the margin or above the line in **E**.

E is a very accurate transcript; in the sample passages of books III, VII and X its only errors are:

390c5   φίλους om. E^ac
391b2   Σπερχειοῦ] σπερχιοῦ
518a3   μεθισταμένων] μεθισταμένω
616c6   ἀδάμαντος] ἀδάνμαντος

Like **N**, **E** has been corrected and provided with variant readings by Bessarion (**E²**). In some cases, a correction or variant reading is written by Bessarion in both **N** and **E**; this suggests that he sometimes worked on **N** and **E** simultaneously; see for instance:

471b4   ἀλγούντων] ἀλγοῦντες N^sl E^2sl Lobc.R
529b6   συμμεμυκώς] νενευκώς N^sl E^2pc Θ^2sl
558a8   περινοστεῖ] περινοστεῖ ὁ καταψηφισθεὶς N^sl E^2sl x^3im

In other places a correction or variant reading in **E** does not occur in **N**; some instances:

558b1   συγγνώμη] σοι γνώμη E^pc Θ^pc
585d11 φύσει] τῇ φύσει E^pc R
590e1   βούλεται habent E^2sl x^3pc

It hardly ever happens that **E** (or **E^pc**) has a reading which is not found in any other MS. **E** has no extant derivatives.

Another derivative of **N**, though not a MS, is the Aldine edition, which will be discussed in the chapter on the sixteenth-century editions; see pp. 242 f.

Finally, there are four excerpt MSS which derive from **c**: **Voss.**, **Ambr.**, **Matr.**^{fr} and **Lond.**; I shall first discuss **Voss.**

Voss. has all the characteristic readings of **a**^{pc} and **c**, and adds some errors of its own. Some cases of agreement between **Voss.** and (**AMγ**)ac:

328d4 τε om. **Voss. M**γac
328d7 γε om. **Voss.AM**γac
330c6 καὶ] καὶ οὐ **Voss.**a^{sl}cF
330e7 δειμαίνει] ἀεὶ δειμαίνει **Voss.**a^{sl}cF

I have noted one conjunctive error of **Voss.c**:

609a8-b1 ἑκάστου—τό γε om. **Voss.c**

Some errors of **Voss.**:

328d7 χαίρω] ἐγὼ χαίρω
330e1 δή] δεῖ
519b8 μήτε] οὔτε

Moreover, in the shorter fragments **Voss.** often omits assentory formulae, like 335d4 Ναί, 335d10 Πάνυ γε, or names, e.g. 331a3 ὦ Σώκρατες. In other cases, the text is paraphrased rather than copied exactly. These phenomena can also be observed in other excerpt MSS. **Voss.** has not been corrected by later hands and has no extant derivatives.

The second excerpt MS depending on **c** is **Ambr.**, an autograph of Ficino's. **Ambr.** follows **c** everywhere; I will quote some places where **Ambr.** shares a characteristic reading of **c**:

516d2-3 αὐτὸν et αὐτῶν transposuerunt
614d5   δικασθείη] καταδικασθείη
616c1   αὐτοῦ post δεσμῶν
619b8-9 καὶ prius-ἑλέσθαι om.

Ambr. has a number of errors of its own; some instances:

518b8 φασὶ δέ που] φασί τινες
617c1 τῆς om.
617c8 τὰς] τὰ
617d5 τι] τὸ
618b2 δὲ] τε
618c8 κραθὲν] κρασθὲν
619a4 ἐργάσηται] ἐργάσεται

Like **Voss.**, **Ambr.** often omits assentory formulae and the like.
In a number of places, **Ambr.** has corrections and variant readings by Ficino, written after the text had been copied; some instances:

518d5 οὐ τοῦ] αὑτοῦ **Ambr.ac**: οὐ τοῦ **Ambr.**^{im}a^{sl}
614d6 τὼ ἑτέρω] τὸ ἕτερον **Ambr.**a^{sl}c: τῶ ἑτέρω (sic) **Ambr.**^{pc}γa

Such corrections and variant readings may have been borrowed from a^{pc}.

At 616e5-8 Ficino has added three variant readings which otherwise only occur in **N**^{sl}: e5 ἕκτου] πέμπτου **Ambr.**^{sl}**N**^{sl}; e7 πέμπτου] δευτέρου **Ambr.**^{sl}**N**^{sl} (et ***D***); e8 δευτέρου] ἕκτου **Ambr.**^{sl}**N**^{sl}; cf. below, p. 234.

Ambr. has no extant derivatives.

Finally, the fragments in **Matr.**^{fr} and **Lond.** appear to derive from **c**; I have noted the following cases of agreement between **Matr.**^{fr}**Lond.** and **c**:

352c2 κοινῇ πρᾶξαι] πρᾶξαι κοινῇ **Matr.**^{fr}**Lond.c**
377a12 μέγιστον] τὸ μέγιστον **Matr.**^{fr}**Lond.ac**
377b1 δὴ om. **Matr.**^{fr}**Lond.ac**
491d1 ἐγγείων] ἀγγείων ac: ἀγγεῖον **Matr.**^{frac}(u.v.)**Lond.**^{ac}(u.v.): ἀγγείου **Matr.**^{frpc}(u.v.)**Lond.**^{pc}(u.v.)
535b6 τοι] τι **Matr.**^{fr}**Lond.ac**

Yet in some places **c** has an error against **Matr.**^{fr}**Lond.**:

352c2 οὐ habent **Matr.**^{fr}**Lond.**: ἢ γac
491d3 ἐρρωμενέστερον habent **Matr.**^{fr}**Lond.**: ἐρρωμενέστερος ac

Moreover, at 328e4 **Matr.**^{fr}**Lond.** have εὔκολος for εὔπορος, with **Vind.Bon.Darmst.**; yet such cases may be due to conjectural emendation.

On the basis of the fragments from *R.* in **Matr.**^{fr} and **Lond.** it is impossible to place the fragments in these MSS in the stemma with full confidence; as far as the evidence goes, it suggests that the source of the fragments is **c**. I have not found any conjunctive errors of **Matr.**^{fr}**Lond.** with other derivatives of **c**.

It remains for me to deal with the relationship of **Matr.**^{fr} and **Lond.** to each other. That these two MSS are very closely related, already appears from the fact that the fragments from *R.* contained in these MSS are exactly identical (the same may be true for *all* the Platonic excerpts in **Matr.**^{fr} and **Lond.**, but I have not checked this); moreover, they have a number of conjunctive errors; some instances:

352c6 ἐπὶ om.
491d1 εἴτε] εἴτε καὶ
491d3 μηδ' ὥρας om.
491e2 τυχούσας] τυγχανούσας
595c10 πολλά] πολλοὶ πολλά
596a1 βλεπόντων] ὁρώντων

613a7 ὑπό γε θεῶν ποτε ἀμελεῖται] ἀμελεῖται ποτὲ ὑπὸ τῶν θεῶν
613b2 γ', ἔφη] γὰρ

Each of the two MSS has a few, very slight, errors against the other; the errors of **Matr.**^{fr} are:

377b1 ὁτῳοῦν] οὕτω οὖν
519a3 τέτραπται] τέθραπται

Lond. has the following errors:

424a5 παίδευσις] πέδευσις (δ incertum)
539b6 σπαράττειν] σπαράττει

It is therefore probable that **Matr.**^{fr} and **Lond.** go back to a lost common source, although it is not excluded that **Matr.**^{fr} derives from **Lond.**, because in some places a reading in **Matr.**^{fr} seems to have been caused by misreading the script of **Lond.**: at 352c7 **Lond.** has ἡμιμόχθηροι *recte*, but the ι seems to have been written *post correctionem*, and it could easily be mistaken for a ν; **Matr.**^{fr} does read ἡμιμόχθηρον. At 491e2 **Lond.** has εὐφυιεστάτας for εὐφυεστάτας; the ligature of υι could easily be misinterpreted as ελ: now **Matr.**^{fr} does read εὐφελεστάτας. But I think it is safest to admit that the exact relationship of **Matr.**^{fr} and **Lond.** cannot be established on the basis of the fragments from *R*. in these MSS.

Neither in **Matr.**^{fr} nor in **Lond.** have I found any later additions; neither of the two MSS has any extant derivatives.

The T-group

The second branch of the **A**-family is the **T**-group, that is, the MSS which derive from the old part of **T**, which breaks off at 389d7. For the origin of the old part of **T** itself, see above, pp. 112-118.

I will first make some observations on **T** itself. The scribe of **T** often corrects his own errors; he often transposes words, and indicates the right order by writing transposition marks above the words concerned (cf. Dodds, *Gorgias* 38); there are also variant readings written by the first hand, which come from the exemplar (see above, p. 118).

In five places, there is agreement in trivial readings with **D** or **F**:

329c3 ἀσμενέστατα] ἀσμεναίτατα **TD**
364a8 καὶ] τε καὶ **TF**
365c2 ἀλάθειαν] ἀλήθειαν **TD**
370d5 δή] δὲ **TF**
371a7 δή] δεῖ **TF**

I believe that at 364a8, 365c2, 370d5 and 371a7 the agreement of **T** with **D/F** is coincidental, but the reading ἀσμεναίτατα at 329c3 may well be due to contamination (it is also found in Philox. Gramm., *EM* and *Et. Sym.*).

There are two later hands in the old part of **T**; the first of these uses a very light brown ink and has a very tiny script; the second uses very dark ink and writes in thickish letters.

T² (the hand with the light ink) seems to draw on **Θᵖᶜ**:

330c6 καὶ] καὶ οὐ **T²ⁱᵐΘ²ᵖᶜFaⁱᵐ**
347a3 ὤν] ὦι **Tᵃᶜ**: οὗ **T²ᵖᶜΘ** (alii)
360e4 μηδέν] εἰ μηδέν **T²ˢˡΘ²ˢˡ** (εἰ pro μηδέν **x³⁽ᵘ·ᵛ·⁾ᵖᶜ**)

Occasionally, **T²** has a new reading, e.g. 379a5 θεολογίας] μυθολογίας **T²ˢˡ**.

T³ seems to borrow readings from a member of the **Mγ**-group; see for instance:

362a1 ἐκκαυθήσεται] ἐκκοπήσεται **T³ˢˡMγ**

At 367d5 **T³**'s reading ἀνασχοίμην for ἀποδεχοίμην also occurs in one of **T**'s derivatives, **Sc.**; yet **T³** must have been at work after (a predecessor of) **Sc.** was copied from **T**, because at 359b3 **Sc.** reads τῶν εἴτε—εἴτε for τὸ μήτε—μήτε with **Tᵃᶜ**, while **T³** has corrected this to τὸ μήτε—μήτε, making the reading of **Tᵃᶜ** illegible. Readings of **T²** and **T³** do not recur in **T**'s apographa, except **N**.

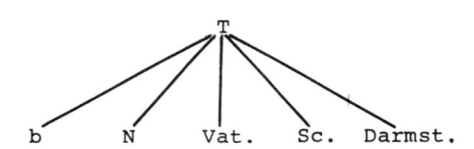

```
            T
         /∕|∖∖
        / / | \ \
       b  N Vat. Sc. Darmst.
```

The offspring of **T** can be divided into five branches, represented by **b**, **N**, **Vat.**, **Sc.** and **Darmst.**; that these five MSS go back to **T** independently is proved by the fact that they have no conjunctive errors, while each of them has separative errors against the others (and against **T**); **b** follows **T** up to 358d7 μᾶλλον (where the old part of **b** breaks off); **N** depends on **T** in books I-II; **Vat.** follows **T** up to 381a; **Sc.** derives from **T** until the old part of **T** breaks off, i.e. up to 389d7, and **Darmst.** depends on **T** in some fragments only.

As **T** does not have many separative errors in the sample passage of book I, I have checked the separative errors of **T** in books I and II in the apographa.

Some instances of conjunctive errors of **TbVat. NSc.** (**b** up to 358d7, **Vat.** up to 381a):

335e1 φησίν] φήσει
336b1 μὲν om.
344c5 καὶ prius om.
360d7 οὖν om.
375a6 διωκάθειν] διώκειν
378a6 ὅπως ὅτι] ὅτι ὅπως
383a2 δεύτερον τύπον] τύπον δεύτερον

First, I shall discuss **b**. Up to 358d7 **b** follows **T** everywhere, and adds some errors of its own; some instances:

327c9 τοίνυν τούτων] τούτων τοίνυν
331a10 οὖν om.

Sometimes, **b** neglects a correction by the first hand in **T**: 344a1 νυνδή] δὴ νῦν **Tb**: add. signa transpositionis **T**[1].

b does not reproduce corrections by **T**[2]; all the corrections by **T**[3] occur after 358d7, where the old part of **b** breaks off.

In some places **b** has been corrected by the first hand, e.g. 330d5 ἔφη om. **b**: add. **b**[1sl]. There are no later corrections in **b**. Slings 264 f. shows that **b** goes back to a derivative of **T** which also served as the exemplar of **R** in *Clit.*

The old part of **b** breaks off after 358d7 μᾶλλον; the rest of book II has been added by a sixteenth-century hand. It derives from the first Basle edition (1534), as appears from the fact that **b** usually follows the Aldine edition (the source of the first Basle edition, see p. 245), and in some cases agrees with the first Basle edition against all the MSS and the other editions (Aldine, second Basle edition, Stephanus); some instances of agreement between **b** and the first Basle edition:

359c1   δόντες] δέοντες **b** **Bas.**[1] (δόντες **Ald. Bas.**[2] **Steph.**)
360d7   ταῦτα] ταῦτα τὰ **b** **Ald. Bas.**[1,2] (ταῦτα **Steph.**)
361b4   δέηται] δεήσεται **b** **Bas.**[1] (δέηται **Bas.**[2] **Steph.**)
373d8-9 αὖ τῆς] αὐτοῖς **b** **Bas.**[1] (αὖ τῆς **Ald. Bas.**[2] **Steph.**)

The agreement of the recent part of **b** with the first Basle edition was already noticed by Schneider III 309.

At 373a1 editors quote **b** for the reading αὕτη against αὐτή of all the other MSS; in reality, αὕτη is read by β[pc], not by **b**; the confusion is due to Stallbaum.

b has no extant derivatives.

The second MS that derives from **T** is **Vat.**; up to 381a **Vat.** follows **T** everywhere and adds a number of errors of its own; some separative errors of **Vat.**:

327a5   πρέπειν] πρέπον
327c11 ὡς om.
328c5   οὖν με ἰδών] μὲν οὖν ἰδών με
328d1   ἰέναι] εἶναι
329a7   ἀγανακτοῦσιν] ἀγανακτοῦντες
330a1   ὅτι om.
330d7   περὶ] παρὰ
331a8   μάλιστα] κάλλιστα
331d9   γε] μὲν οὖν
332d10 φίλους εὖ ποιεῖν] εὖ ποιεῖν φίλους
333b1   κοινωνὸς] κοινὸς

In a number of places **Vat.** does not follow **T**, but these are trivial errors or variant readings in **T**; in the sample passage of book I, I have noted the following cases:

328a3   ἦν habet **Vat.**: ἦ **T**
329c3   ἀσμενέστατα (sic) habet **Vat.**: ἀσμεναίτατα **T**
330c6   ἧπερ habet **Vat.**: ἤπερ **T**
333d3   δέῃ habet **Vat.**: δέοι **T**

Readings added by **T²** and **T³** do not recur in **Vat.**

In books I-II **Vat.** does not show traces of contamination; yet because of the enormous number of errors in **Vat.**, it can hardly be assumed that **Vat.** is a direct transcript of **T**. Slings 272 f. shows that in *Clit.* **Vat.** goes back to **T** via a derivative of **T** which also served as the exemplar of Parisinus 1809.

In some places **Vat.** has been corrected by a later hand, e.g. 373c2-4 ἢ—προσδεησόμεθα om. **Vat.**: add. **Vat.**[2im]. For some readings at least, **Vat.**[2] draws on a MS of the **D**-family; see 374b7-8 ἀλλὰ σκυτοτόμον add. **Vat.**[2im]: habet **D**: om. **AF**.

Vat. changes its exemplar suddenly somewhere between 381a7 and 381b4, from which point it belongs to the **D**-family, and undoubtedly derives from **Par.**, as it does in the sample passages of books III, VII and X (see below, pp. 179 f.); this is illustrated by the following readings:

378a6   ὅπως ὅτι] ὅτι ὅπως **Vat.T**
379a8-9   ἐάντε ἐν μέλεσιν om. **Vat.AT**
381a7   καὶ ἀμφιέσματα om. **Vat.AT**

381b4   γε habent **Vat.D**: τε **ATF**
382b10   ἐστὶν **ATF**: om. **Vat.D**
382e9-10   οὔτε κατὰ φαντασίας **Vat.DF**: om. **AT**
383a3   ποιεῖν **AT**: ἀκούειν **Vat.DF**

THE AFFILIATION OF MANUSCRIPTS 153

Vat.
|
k

Vat. is the source of **k**; I will quote some distinctive readings of **Vat.** shared by **k**:

327c4   ῏Ω Σώκρατες om.
328c8   τοῦ] τῶ
328e2   ἦν om.
330d5   ἔφη, ὦ Σώκρατες] ὦ Σώκρατες ἔφη
331d9   γε] μὲν οὖν
331e3   ἑκάστῳ] ἕκαστα
332d10 φίλους εὖ ποιεῖν] εὖ ποιεῖν φίλους

k follows **Vat.** everywhere and adds a lot of errors of its own; some instances:

328d1   πυκνότερον] πικρότερον
329e8   λοιδορουμένῳ] λοιδουμένω
330a4   ἔχει] ἔχεις
331d3   ἃ] εὖ
332a3   Ναί] καὶ
332a11 Μανθάνω] μανθάνων
333a8   κτῆσιν] κτῆσις

k often overlooks a correction in **Vat.**, e.g. 332b7 οἶμαι] οἶμαι παρά γε οἶμαι **Vat.k**, sed παρά γε οἶμαι linea del. **Vat.**[1]. Corrections by **Vat.**[2] recur in **k**, e.g. 373c2-4 ἢ—προσδεησόμεθα om. **Vat.**: add. **Vat.**[2im]: habet **k**[it].

k shows no traces of contamination against **Vat.** and may well be a direct transcript; **k** has not been corrected by later hands, and has no extant derivatives.

The third MS that goes back to **T** is **N**, in books I-II (*R*. I-II were written by Bessarion himself); it has already been noted (p. 143) that in books III-X **N** derives from **c**. **N** has most of the characteristic readings of **T**, and adds some errors of its own; some instances:

329b6   ἔγωγε] ἐγώ
331b3   ἐκεῖσε ἀπιέναι] ἀπιέναι ἐκεῖσε
331d8   ἔφη] ἔφην
333c8   δέη] δέοι

As to **T**[2], I have not found cases of agreement of **N** with **T**[2] in readings which do not occur elsewhere; in some cases **N** has the correct reading with **T**[2], but Bessarion may have taken such correct readings from another source as well. At 347a3 **T** has ᾧ for ὧν, which is altered into οὗ by **T**[2], in such a way that both readings can be understood; **N** has ὧν, with οὗ added above the line, possibly during the copying of the text. Yet the fact that **N** does not take over the words τε καὶ δικαιοσύνη at 364a2, added by **T²**, suggests that **T²** was at work after **N** had been copied from **T**, but this is not certain. **N** does take over readings added by **T³**, e.g. 367d5 ἀποδεχοίμην] ἀνασχοίμην **T³ˢˡN**.

Yet the relationship of **N** and **T** in books I-II is very complicated, because in a good many places **N** does not follow **T** (or **TMγ** and **ATMγ**); some instances of correct readings in **N** against **T**:

338c5   φῂς habet **N**: om. **T**
340e2   ἀκριβῆ habet **N**: om. **TMγ**
351b6   οὗτος ἦν habet **N**: ἦν οὗτος **T**
351d7   διαφέρωμαι habet **N**: διαφέρωμεν **ATMγ**
359d2   τότε habet **N**: τε **T**
368c8   ᾦ habet **N**: ὃ **TMγ**
379a3   ἐπιτρεπτέον habet **N**: ἐπιστρεπτέον **TMγ**
382d11   τοὺς habet **N**: τοὺς μὲν **T**

In some places, **N** agrees with other MSS, notably **ac**, against **T**; some instances:

328b6   Καλχηδόνιον] καρχηδόνιον **NˢˡcF**
329c7   ἐπειδὰν] ἐπειδὰν γὰρ **NMγac**
334b2   πάντας] ὑπὲρ πάντας **NMˢˡγˢˡacF**
337a3   σαρδάνιον] σαρδόνιον **NMγacFᵃᶜ**

In some cases, a correct reading in **N** occurs in **ac**, but not in **TMγ**; some instances:

340e2   ἀκριβῆ habent **Nˢˡc**: om. **TMγ**
357d3   ἔφην habent **Nˢˡc**: ἔφη **TMγ**
358a2   ἀπ' habent **Nˢˡc**: ὑπ' **TMγ**

On one occasion, a correct reading in **N** is found in **c** against **TMγa**:

377a6   μύθοις habent **Nc**: μύθους **TMγa**

Since **N** is a copy of **c** in books III-X, I infer that in books I-II Bessarion also made use of **c** to correct **T**, his principal source. If this should be true, the transposition τοῦτο ἔστιν at 332a1 which occurs in **c** and **N**, may not be fortuitous (at 351b6 **T** has ἦν οὗτος; **N** and **c** read οὗτος ἦν *recte*).

Nevertheless, there remain a number of places where **N** has the correct reading against **Tc** (and **Mγa**); in some cases, these are easy corrections:

351b6   τόδε habet **N**: τό γε **TMγac**
379a3   ἐπιτρεπτέον habet **N**: ἐπιστρεπτέον **TMγac**

In a few other cases, however, the correction is less obvious, but we should bear in mind that Bessarion had a great insight into Platonic Greek; it is, however, possible that Bessarion used yet another MS besides **T** and **c**; some instances:

354b4 ὃ τὸ habet **N**: ὅτῳ **TMγac**
363e4 οὗτος habet **N**: οὕτως **TMγac**
368c8 ᾧ habet **N**: ὃ **TMγac**

The corrections and variant readings in **N** have already been discussed (pp. 144 f.).

```
      N
      |
      |
      E
```

As in books III-X (see p. 146), **E** is a very close copy of **N**; I shall quote some places where **E** shares a distinctive reading of **N** in the sample passage of book I:

329b6 ἔγωγε] ἐγώ
331b3 ἐκεῖσε ἀπιέναι] ἀπιέναι ἐκεῖσε
331d8 ἔφη] ἔφην
333c8 δέῃ] δέοι

E follows **N** everywhere and adds very few errors of its own:

330c9 ἔφη om.
331d2 ὅρος om. (add. **E²**)

The corrections in **E** have already been discussed (p. 146).
As in books III-X, **E** has no extant derivatives in the first two books.

The fourth MS which derives from **T** is **Sc.**; **Sc.** follows **T** until the old part of **T** breaks off after 389d7 δεήσει. **Sc.** has numerous progeny, and the relationship of the members of the **Sc.**-group remains the same after 389d7, from which point **Sc.** belongs to the **D**-family. I will therefore discuss the **Sc.**-group here for all the sample passages, in order to avoid treading the same ground twice.

Sc. takes over all the characteristic readings of **T**, and adds a number of separative errors of its own; some instances:

328a2 ἀφ' ἵππων τῇ θεῷ] τῇ θεῷ ἀφ' ἵππων
328c6 τὸν om.
328e5 ἤδη om.
329c2 συγγίγνεσθαι] συμμίγνυσθαι
330b4 οὐσίαν] οἰκίαν
330d2 οἴει ἀγαθὸν] ἀγαθὸν οἴει
331c2 αὐτὸ om.
331c2 εἶναι om.
331c8 πάντα ἐθέλων] ἐθέλων πάντα
333c2 Φαίνεται] ναί
386b8 ἡμᾶς om.
386b9 λοιδορεῖν] λοιδορεῖσθαι

388c2 οὖν] οὐ
388d2 φίλε om.

Sc. does not take over readings added by T^2 and T^3.

In some places **Sc.** has the correct reading against **T**; some instances:

328a3 ἦν habet **Sc.**: ἦ **T**
329c3 ἀσμενέστατα (sic) habet **Sc.**: ἀσμεναίτατα **T**
359d2 τότε habet **Sc.**: τε **T**

There are some traces of contamination of **Sc.** with other (groups of) MSS, notably the **Mγ**-group and the **F**-family; see for instance:

329c7 ἐπειδάν] ἐπειδάν γάρ **Sc.**[1sl]**Mγ**
329e1 σου] σε **Sc.**[1sl]**A**[2(vel 3)sl]**Mγ**[1pc] (non ita **T**)
388e6 γέλωτι] γέλωτι ἀλῶ **Sc.**[1sl]**M**[1sl]γ[1sl]

349b9 ἡγοῖτο **Sc.F**: ἡγοῖτο δίκαιον **ATMγD**
361c2 οὖν] οὐ **Sc.F**

There are many corrections and variant readings in **Sc.**; some of these appear to have been written during the copying of the text, and are therefore likely to derive from the exemplar of **Sc.**, e.g. 329e1 σου habet: σε **Sc.**[1sl]. Many other readings are written in a much darker ink; yet the script is so similar to that of the text, that I believe that these readings have been written by the scribe himself, but after the copying of the text. The fact that Θ, one of the derivatives of **Sc.**, always follows **Sc.**[ac] suggests that some time elapsed between the copying of the text and the writing of the corrections and variant readings (we have already observed the same phenomenon in the case of **a** and its derivative **m**; see pp. 128, 130), However, the reader should be warned that I have not seen **Sc.** *in situ*, and that the microfilm I have used is of a very poor quality, so that the distinction made between readings which have been added immediately and readings that have been added afterwards is far from certain.

Some of the corrections and variant readings written in dark ink (i.e. after the copying of the text) are certain to derive from **Sc.**'s exemplar: e.g. at 427c2 **Sc.** has πατρίω, with γρ. πατρώω in the margin (in dark ink); the same variant reading is found in **Vind.**[1sl] and **Bon.**[1sl]; **Vind.** and **Bon.** go back to the same source as **Sc.** (from 389d7 on), which proves that the variant reading πατρώω goes back to this common source of **Sc.** and **Vind.Bon.** At 426a3 καί is omitted in **Vind.Bon.** and deleted in **Sc.**[pc].

Some corrections and variant readings in **Sc.** are certainly conjectures; see for instance:

519d9-e1 αὐτοῖς—οὐ om. **Sc.D**: ἀλλ' οὐ τούτου ἦν δ' ἐγὼ μέλει **Sc.**[pc] (δυνατὸν deleto)
598e1 ἐπίστανται om. **Sc.D**: ἴσασι add. **Sc.**[pc]

In some cases **Sc.** is the principal MS to preserve a true reading; in many other cases a reading in **Sc.** deserves particular attention. Such readings will be discussed in the chapter on the secondary MSS; see pp. 217-222.

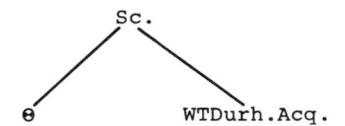

```
              Sc.
             /   \
            /     \
           Θ       WTDurh.Acq.
```

From **Sc.** derive two MSS, **Θ** and the lost exemplar of **W** and **TDurh. Acq.** (**T** from 389d7 on). These two MSS go back to **Sc.** independently, because they have no conjunctive errors, while each has separative errors against the other and against **Sc.** I will quote some places where **TDurh. Acq.WΘ** agree with distinctive readings of **Sc.** (the presence or absence of **Acq.**, which has only fragments, is not specified; **T** from 389d7 on; **Sc.** is absent in book X):

328a2	ἀφ' ἵππων τῇ θεῷ] τῇ θεῷ ἀφ' ἵππων
328c6	τὸν om.
328e5	ἤδη om.
329c2	συγγίγνεσθαι] συμμίγνυσθαι
330d2	οἴει ἀγαθὸν] ἀγαθὸν οἴει
331c8	πάντα ἐθέλων] ἐθέλων πάντα
386b8	ἡμᾶς om.
388c2	οὖν] οὐ
388d2	φίλε om.
388d3	μὴ] δὴ
391a3	ἦν δ' ἐγώ, δι' Ὅμηρον] δι' ὅμηρον ἦν δ' ἐγὼ
391b7	εἰρῆσθαι] εἶναι
514b7	Ὁρῶ] ὀρθῶς
516e7	μάλα γ'] μάλ'
517e2	μὴ πώποτε] μήποτε
518a2	γίγνονται] γίγνοιντ' ἄν
520c3	βέλτιον] βέλτιονι

First, I shall discuss **Θ**. **Θ** follows **Sc.** everywhere, and adds a number of separative errors of its own; some instances:

327c11	ἡμᾶς om.
387b2	ποιητὰς om.
387c9	Τὸν δὲ ἐναντίον τύπον] τοῦ δὲ ἐναντίου τύπου
517c8	οἱ] εἰ
520b4	τὰ om.
520d6	ἡμῖν om.
616b5	τεταμένον] τεταγμένον
616e5	ἕκτου om.
618d4	τοιαῦτα om.

Θ is always in accordance with **Sc.**^ac, that is, the corrections and variant readings written in **Sc.** with the dark ink (cf. above, p. 156) do not recur in Θ.

There is a strong indication that Θ is a direct transcript of **Sc.**: Θ omits the words 386b8-9 ὡς—λοιδορεῖν, which correspond exactly to one line in **Sc.**; the words have been added in the margin of Θ by the first hand. The explanation is that the scribe of Θ telescoped one line in his exemplar, **Sc.**, but noticed the omission himself and added the missing words in the margin.

In some cases, an error in Θ can be explained as having been caused by misunderstanding a compendium in **Sc.** (**Sc.** often uses compendia); see for instance 388b2 χευάμενον: ον is written *per compendium* by the scribe of **Sc.**, Θ has overlooked the compendium and reads χευάμεν (*sic*)[9].

Θ shows no traces of contamination, as is only to be expected in a direct transcript.

Θ has been corrected and provided with variant readings by a later hand; this hand uses a much lighter ink, and writes in a minute script. In some cases, readings of Θ² are borrowed from the **F** tradition; see for instance:

330c6 καί] καὶ οὐ Θ²pcF
368a3 εὐδοκιμήσαντας] εὐδοκιμήσαντος Θ²pcF
378c8 λεκτέα om. Θ: add. post μᾶλλον Θ²pc: habet ita **F**
477a10 δὲ habent Θ²pcF⁴(u.v.)

In some cases, a correction by Θ² is also found in **x**, added by a later hand, e.g. 582c4 τιμὴ μὲν habent x³(u.v.)pcΘ²pc. This would seem to suggest that Θ² has drawn on **x**; yet this hypothesis does not hold good, because the common source of **VMatr.Hier.**, which derives from Θpc, must belong to the fourteenth century (**Hier.** was written by Manuel Kalekas, who lived in that century), while **x** must have been written in Italy, and therefore should be assigned to the fifteenth century. Therefore I assume that in such cases a corrector of **x** has consulted (a derivative of) Θ.

In some cases a correction in Θ is not found elsewhere; some of these corrections deserve some attention; yet because of their scantiness I have refrained from discussing such readings in the chapter on the secondary manuscripts.

---

[9] This phenomenon has already been observed by Slings 262; yet Slings himself was once deceived by a compendium in **Sc.** in the same way as the scribe of Θ: he reports that at *Clit.* 407b4 **Sc.** and Θ read δικαίου instead of δικαίως; in reality, **Sc.** has δικαίως, but the combination of the acute accent and the compendium for ως could easily be mistaken for ου. Thus there are no objections to the dependence of Θ on **Sc.** in *Clit.*; cf. S. R. Slings, Mnem. IV 40 (1987), 39.

THE AFFILIATION OF MANUSCRIPTS

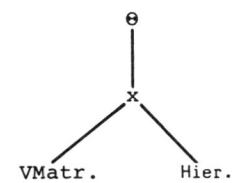

```
      Θ
      |
      x
     / \
  VMatr. Hier.
```

Θ is the source of a lost MS which served as the exemplar of the lost common ancestor of **V** and **Matr.**, and of the fragments in **Hier.**; **VMatr.** go back to Θ only in book I; in books II-X they depend on **c**, as has already been shown (see pp. 139 f.). **Hier.** and **VMatr.** follow Θ almost everywhere; some cases of agreement in the sample passages of book I:

327c11   ἡμᾶς om.
329e4   πολλήν] πολλή

Corrections by Θ² recur in the common source of **Hier.** and **VMatr.**; see for instance:

330b8   Οὔ τοι] οὗτοι ATSc.Θ^ac: τούτου Θ²pcVMatr.F (deest **Hier.**)
330c6   καί] καὶ οὐ Θ²VMatr.F (deest **Hier.**)

That **VMatr.** and **Hier.** do not go back to Θ independently, but derive from a common ancestor which depends on Θ, is proved by the two conjunctive errors of **VMatr.** and **Hier.** that I have found in the fragments in **Hier.** from book I:

327c14   ἀκουσομένων] ἀκουσομένων ἔφη
329b8   ἔφη om.

I shall mention some cases of agreement between **Hier.** and Θ in the sample passages of books III and VII (**Hier.** does not have fragments from the Myth of Er):

386c6   ᾧ—εἴη om. ASc.ΘHier.
387b2   ποιητάς om. ΘHier.
514b6   δεικνύασιν] δεικνύουσιν Sc.ΘHier.
515a4   ἔφη om. Sc.ΘHier.
518e2   παντὸς μᾶλλον] μᾶλλον παντός Sc.ΘHier.
520b4   τά om. ΘHier.

Some separative errors of **Hier.**:

327c7   ὅσοι] ὁπόσοι
387b5   δουλείαν] δειλίαν
515a4   ἀτόπους] ἀνθρώπους
520d2   ἄρχειν] ἄρξειν

VMatr. have a number of separative errors against Θ; some instances (N. B. in all these cases **Hier.** is absent):

328c1 ἐστεφανωμένος om.
329d3 οὐ τὸ γῆρας, ὦ Σώκρατες] ὦ σώκρατες οὐ τὸ γῆρας
330e4 μεστός] φοβερός (glossema ?)
332c11 καί] τε καί

In the sample passage of book I **VMatr.** do not show traces of contamination with other MSS. The reading φοβερός for μεστός at 330e4 may originally have been a gloss on δείματος μεστός.

```
        x
       / \
      /   \
     V    Matr.
```

The relationship of **V** and **Matr.** in book I is the same as in books II-X (see pp. 141 f.), that is, they are gemelli: both have separative errors against the other; some errors of **Matr.**:

330b1 τις] τε
330d8 ἐκεῖ om.
333a8 ἄν οἶμαι φαίης] φαίης ἄν οἶμαι

Some errors of **V**:

329d2 καί prius om.
330b5-6 αὐτήν—ἐλάττω om.
332d10 κάμνοντας φίλους] φίλους κάμνοντας φίλους

In some places **Matr.** has been corrected by the first hand; see for instance:

327c2 Νικίου] νικηράτου **Matr.**[ac]: corr. **Matr.**[1]
330c6 καί] καὶ οὐ **VMatr.** (F, alii): οὐ del. **Matr.**[1]

Neither **Matr.** nor **V** has been corrected by later hands; **Matr.** has some marginal annotations which seem to have been added by the scribe himself, but in a different ink (but I have not seen **Matr.** *in situ*).

Neither **Matr.** nor **V** has extant derivatives.

The second MS which depends on **Sc.** is the exemplar of **W** and of the lost common ancestor of **T** (from 389d7 on), **Durh.** and **Acq.** (which has only fragments).

Unlike Θ, these MSS follow **Sc.**[pc]; for instance, at 519d9-e1 **Sc.** omits the words αὐτοῖς—οὐ (like its source **D**[ac]); **Sc.**[pc] (dark ink) has ἀλλ' οὐ τούτου ἦν δ' ἐγὼ μέλει, while δυνατόν is erased; this is also the reading of

TDurh. and **W** (**Acq.** is absent), but Θ agrees with **Sc.**ac.

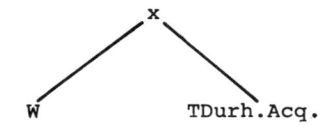

```
            x
           / \
          /   \
         W    TDurh.Acq.
```

TDurh.Acq. and **W** have a number of conjunctive errors which separate them from **Sc.** and Θ; some instances (**T** only from 389d7 on; **Durh.** is absent in book X; **Acq.** has only a few fragments from the sample passages):

330a2   ἐγένετο] γένοιτο **Durh.Acq.W**
331c8   οὐδ'] ὀδ' **Durh.**: ὀδ' **W** (deest **Acq.**)
387d5   ὁ om. **Durh.W** (deest **Acq.**)
617a2   παραπλήσια] παραπλησίως **TW** (desunt **Durh.Acq.**)
618d6   αὐτῶν] αὐτὸν **TW** (desunt **Durh.Acq.**)

On one occasion (in the sample passages) **TW** have a reading which seems to be due to contamination or deliberate conjecture: 616a4 τε] τε ταῦτα ὑπομένοιεν **TW** (desunt **Durh.Acq.**) (this reading is also found in **M**pc (which draws on **R**, a derivative of **Lobc.**, which depends on **W**), **Par.**im (manus recentior) and **E**2im); Θ has τε. Yet it is possible that this reading was already in **Sc.**pc, because this part of **Sc.** is now lost (Θ derives from **Sc.**ac).

Further, the exemplar of **TDurh.Acq.** and **W** does not show traces of contamination.

That the common ancestor of **TDurh.Acq.** and **W** are gemelli, is proved by the fact that they both have separative errors against the other. Some errors of **TDurh.Acq.** (**T** from 389d7 on; **Durh.** is absent in book X; **Acq.** has only fragments):

331a4   τὸν βίον] τοῦ βίου **Durh.**
331c7   χρὴ τὰ] χρήματα **Durh.**
388a2   ποιεῖν om. **Durh.**
388a7   αὖτε] ἂν **Durh.Acq.**
389b3   τῷ] τῶν **Durh.**
391e5   συγγνώμην] συγνώμην **TDurh.**
515d4   ὀρθότερον] ὀρθότατα **TDurh.**
517e1   αὐτὴν] αὐτῶν **TDurh.**
519b2   ἡδοναῖς τε om. **TDurh.**
616c7-d1   μεικτὸν—σφονδύλου om. **T**
619d1   ἀρετῆς] ἀρετῶν **T**

Some separative errors of **W**:

327b5 Καὶ] καὶ γὰρ
329c6 γε om.
330b8 μοι] μὴ
386a2 τοῖς] τοὺς
390a4 εἷς] εἴ
515c1 τι om.
519b3 εἰ om.
520b3 τό γε] τότε
614c1 πολλῶν] τῶν πολλῶν
618a3 τε om.
620a8 ἀνθρωπίνου] ἀνθρωπείου

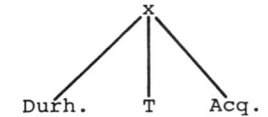

```
         x
        /|\
       / | \
      /  |  \
   Durh. T  Acq.
```

The common source of **TDurh.Acq.** does not show traces of contamination. That **T**, **Durh.** and **Acq.** go back to their common ancestor independently is proved by the fact that they all have separative errors against the others; some errors of **Durh.**:

329b4 κἂν] οὐκ ἂν
390d5 τέτλαθι] τέτληθι
391c3 τοσαύτης bis deinceps
516a6 τὰς om.
516d4 ἐνδυναστεύοντας] δυναστεύοντας
517e3 θαυμαστόν] τὶ θαυμαστὸν

Some errors of **T**:

389d7 ἡμῖν] ὑμῖν
392c6 τὸ] τὰ
514b1 δὲ] δὴ
516a3 ἀληθῶν] ἀγαθῶν
516a6 ῥᾷστα] ῥᾷστον

Some errors of **Acq.**:

328c2 τεθυκὼς] τετυχὼς Acq.[ac]: τετυχὼς Acq.[1pc]
328e5 τοῦτο] τοῦτον

That **Acq.** does belong to this group is proved by the fact that it follows **Sc.** everywhere, and takes over many readings which are in **T** and/or **Durh.**; that it does not depend on either of these, is proved by the separative errors of **T** and **Durh.**

In some places **Acq.** has been corrected by the first hand, e.g. 516a6 καθορῷ] καθορῶν **Acq.**ᵃᶜ: καθορώη **Acq.**¹ᵖᶜ**TDurh.**; **Acq.** has no extant derivatives.

Durh. does not show traces of independent contamination; there are some variant readings by the first hand, which come from the exemplar, e.g.:

329e1   σου] σε **Durh.**¹ˢˡ**Sc.**¹ˢˡ**W**¹ˢˡ
516c9   καθορῶντι] καθορᾶν τι **Durh.**¹ˢˡ**Sc.**¹ˢˡ**W**¹ˢˡ

In some places, the scribe corrected his own errors, e.g. 519a9 περιεκόπη] περιεσκόπη **Durh.**ᵃᶜ: corr. **Durh.**¹.

Once (in the sample passages) **Durh.** has the correct reading against the other members of its group: 390e6 ἐπαμύνειν habet **Durh.**: ἀπαμύνειν **Sc.**; this is an easy correction.

Durh. has not been corrected by later hands, and has no extant derivatives.

In some places in the sample passages, **T** shows a possible trace of contamination: at 617e8 **ΘW** read δηλονότι ὁ παιστὸς ἤλεγχε for δῆλον εἶναι ὁπόστος εἰλήχει (deest **Sc.**); **T** has δηλονότι ὁ παιστὸς εἴληχε. Yet the correction of ἤλεγχε into εἴληχε may be due to conjectural emendation; if (an ancestor of) **T** borrowed the reading εἴληχε from another MS, it is strange that he should have left ὁ παιστὸς unchanged. Another explanation for this reading in **T** is that **Sc.** had both readings, and that **W** chose ἤλεγχε, while **T** preferred εἴληχε.

Moreover, **T** has the correct reading ἥξει at 615d3 against ἥξοι of its fellows, and λαχέσεως at 617d4 and d6 against λάχεως of the other members of the group. Again, these readings do not prove beyond doubt that (an ancestor of) **T** was corrected.

In some places **T** has been corrected by a later hand; this hand seems to be different from the correcting hands that have been at work in the old part of **T** (for which see above, p. 150), but I have not checked this *in situ*. Some instances:

514b2   πυρὸς om. **T**ᵃᶜ: add. **T**²ˢˡ
616c7-d1   μεικτὸν—σφονδύλου om. **T**ᵃᶜ: add. **T**²ⁱᵐ

T has no extant derivatives (of course, I am only speaking about the recent part of **T**), but Arlenius has borrowed some readings from **T** for the second Basle edition (1556); this will be illustrated in the chapter on the sixteenth-century editions; see p. 245.

W has many variant readings by the first hand; these derive nearly always from **Sc.**; some instances:

386b9 λοιδορεῖν] λοιδορεῖσθαι **Sc.W**: λοιδορεῖν **Sc.**[sl]**W**[1sl]
517b1 ἅπασαν] ἅπασι **Sc.**[sl]**W**[1sl]**Durh.**[1sl]**F**

In a few places **W** has the correct reading against **Sc.** and **Durh.** **T(Acq.)**, e.g. 516b6 κατιδεῖν habet **W**: καὶ κατιδεῖν **Sc.TDurh.Acq.** Such good readings in **W** may be due to conjectural emendation, but it is possible that they are the result of contamination.

Occasionally, **W** has been corrected by the first hand, e.g. 328a2 ἔσται πρὸς ἑσπέραν] πρὸς ἑσπέραν ἔσται **W**: add. signa transpositionis **W**[1].

There are no corrections by later hands.

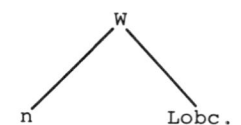

Two MSS, **Lobc.** and **n**, derive from **W** (**n** has only 400c4-439a2). These MSS go back to **W** independently, because they have no conjunctive errors, while each of them has separative errors against the other and against **W**. I will quote some places where **Lobc.** and **n** agree with a distinctive reading of **W** (**n** only in the places quoted from book IV):

327b5 Καὶ] καὶ γὰρ
329c6 γε om.
386a2 τοῖς] τοὺς
390a4 εἴς] εἴ
420a5 ποι] πη
421b5 εὐδαιμονία] εὐδαιμονίας
437e5 ἄλλου] ἄλλη
437e7 μόνον] μόνου
517a5 εἴ πως] ὅπως
518a1 μεμνῆτ'] οὐ μέμνητ'
519b3 εἰ om.
520d2 ἢ om.
614c1 πολλῶν] τῶν πολλῶν
620b4 ἀνθρωπίνου] ἀνθρωπείου
621b7 ἐπὶ] ἐν

Lobc. follows **W** almost everywhere and adds some separative errors of its own; some instances:

332b9 ὡς ἔοικεν om.
332c1 φαίνεται] ἔοικεν
388d2 τὰ om.

388e5   γε] τε
391a7   τισαίμην] τησαίμην
515d3   καὶ om.
619a5   γνῷ τὸν] γνωτὸν
619c2   κακά] πολλὰ

The only places in the sample passages where **Lobc.** has the correct reading against **W** are all quotations from Homer; in all these places the reading of **W** is metrically impossible:

386d10   γοόωσα habet **Lobc.**: γοῶσα **W**
386d10   λιποῦσ' habet **Lobc.**: λιποῦσα **W**
391a6   μ' habet **Lobc.**: με **W**

Therefore it is all the more remarkable that at 620b2 **Lobc.** reads τελαμωνιάδαο for Τελαμωνίου (the reading of **W** and all the other MSS): evidently, the scribe of **Lobc.** was thoroughly acquainted with Homer.

Lobc. has a number of variant readings by the first hand; these derive from **W**. Sometimes, **Lobc.** switches the reading in the text and the variant reading, e.g. 331a7 γηροτρόφος **W**, addito ον supra lineam a prima manu: γηροτρόφον **Lobc.**, addito ος supra lineam a prima manu.

On one occasion, **Lobc.** shows some slight traces of contamination: 516e3 τόδε] τότε and 516e4 θᾶκον] θῶκον; both these readings also occur in **Mγ**. Yet, as these readings are the only instances, they may be coincidental.

Very rarely, **Lobc.** has a correction or variant reading added by a later hand; this hand writes with very faint ink; some instances:

359d1   Γύγου] γύγη **Lobc.**[2pc]
425d2   λήξεως habet **Lobc.**[2pc]: λήξεις **ADF**
583d9   οὐ] ὂν **Lobc.**[2pc]

For the identification of **Lobc.** as the Greek MS used by Cornarius for his *Eclogae*, see below, pp. 246 f.

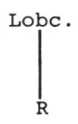

Lobc.
|
R

Lobc. is source of **R**; I shall quote some places where **R** agrees with a distinctive reading of **Lobc.**:

332b9   ὡς ἔοικεν om.
332c1   φαίνεται] ἔοικεν
388d2   τὰ om.
388e5   γε] τε
391a7   τισαίμην] τησαίμην

515d3 καὶ om.
515d3 τετραμμένος] τεθραμμένος
614c5 δεξιάν] δεξιά
614c7 ἀριστεράν] ἀριστερά
619c2 κακά] πολλὰ
620b2 Τελαμωνίου] τελαμωνιάδαο

R follows Lobc. almost everywhere, and adds some separative errors of its own; some instances:

327c14 οὕτω om.
330b1 ἔφη, ὦ Σώκρατες] ὦ σώκρατες ἔφη
330e5 καὶ prius-ἠδίκησεν om.
386b2 δεῖμα] δεῖγμα
387c4 τῆς om.
391b3 ἱερὰς om.
514b1 μόνον om.
518c1 ἐπιστήμης] ἐπιστήμη
519c7 ἔφη] λέγεις
614b6 μέλλων] καὶ μέλλων
616c1 τῶν] ἐκ
618b1 ἀρεταῖς] ἀρετὰς

The few readings added by Lobc.[2] recur in R.

In some places R has the correct reading against Lobc.; as this also happens in places where W has the same reading as Lobc., this cannot be used as an indication that R does not derive from Lobc., as Post 33 f. does (Post's remark, *l.c.*, that at 330c2 WR have οἱ ἄλλοι against ἄλλοι Lobc. is wrong: in reality R omits οἱ with Lobc.). In all cases, the corrections are simple; I have noted the following cases in the sample passages:

328a7 ποιήσουσιν habent WR: ποιήσασιν Lobc. (but the α may very well have been intended as ου)
331a5 διαγάγῃ habet R: διαγάγοι WLobc.
331d3 λάβῃ habet R: λάβοι WLobc.
332b5 τύχῃ habet R: τύχοι WLobc.
333d3 δέῃ habet R: δέοι WLobc.
518a4 ταὐτὰ habet R: ταῦτα WLobc.
520a3 ὅπῃ habet R: ὅποι WLobc.
616c3 συνέχον habet R: συνέχων WLobc.
620d8 ξυμπέμπειν habent WR: ξυμπέπειν Lobc.

That the scribe of R sought to remove errors in his exemplar by means of conjecture, appears from the case of 519a1: for ἐννενόηκας WLobc. read ἐννενόησας, a non-existent form; R has the correct aorist form ἐνενόησας, which is not found in any other MS.

Therefore, the dependence of R on Lobc. is certain; it has already been noted that R reproduces the readings added by Lobc.[2], which is another indication of the dependence of R on Lobc. As R does not show any trace of contamination against **Lobc.**, it may well be a direct copy, the more so because it resembles **Lobc.** very much in appearance (cf. Post 32 f.). In addition, I may note that **Lobc.** occasionally takes over double readings in **W**, whereas this is hardly ever the case in **R**.

In isolated places **R** has been corrected by a later hand; see for instance 527c10-11 Δεύτερον—ἔφη om. **R**: add. **R**^{2im}.

```
        R
        |
        Φ
```

In books I-VI **R** is the source of **Φ**; I list some places where **Φ** agrees with a distinctive reading of **R**:

327c14 οὕτω om.
330b1   ἔφη, ὦ Σώκρατες] ὦ σώκρατες ἔφη
330b6   καταλίπω] καταλείπω
330e5   καὶ prius-ἠδίκησεν om.
332b1   βλαβερὰ] φανερὰ
333a8   ἂν om.
386b2   δεῖμα] δεῖγμα
387c4   τῆς om.
390a4   σωφροσύνην] σωφροσύνη
390a10 παρά] περὶ
391b3   ἱερὰς om.
391c2   ἀπὸ om.

Φ follows **R** almost everywhere, and adds a number of separative errors of its own; some instances:

328e7   ἐξαγγέλλεις] ἐρεῖς (glossema ?)
329d6   χαλεπή] χαλεπὰ
330c1   τὸ] ἐπὶ
330c2   αὐτοὶ] σφόδρα
386a3   τε prius om.
391e8   ὦν] ὄντες
392d7   ἔτι δέομαι σαφέστερον] σαφέστερον ἔτι δέομαι

Φ does not follow **R** in the following places:
331c5   λάβοι habet **Φ**: λάβῃ **R**
387a7   ἀλλήλησιν habet **Φ**: ἀλλήλοισιν **R**

These are very obvious corrections.

Φ occasionally has corrections and variant readings by what is probably the first hand (but I have not studied **Φ** *in situ*); these readings seem to be borrowed from the **F**-family or **a**^{sl}; see for instance:

330a5   ἐπιεικής] ἐπιεικὴς οὐ Φ¹ˢˡFaˢˡ
330b8   Οὔ τοι] τούτου Φ¹ˢˡFaˢˡ

In book V I have noted some striking cases of agreement between **Φ** and **Vind.Bon.**; see for instance:

464b9   ἰδίας] οἰκείας ΦVind.Bon.
465b9   ἡ] καὶ ΦVind.Bon.
470e10 ὧνπερ] ὥσπερ ΦVind.Bon.
473c8   δὲ] δὴ ΦVind.Bon.
477a10 μεταξὺ prius] μεταξὺ ἄρα ΦVind.Bon.

If the date of **Bon.** given by Olivieri-Festa, viz. thirteenth-fourteenth century, is correct, these readings must have come through contamination from (an ancestor of) **Vind.Bon.** into **Φ**, as **Φ** belongs to the fifteenth century.

The reading ἐρεῖς for ἐξαγγέλλεις at 328e7, probably a gloss, suggests that **Φ** derives from a contaminated apographon of **R**, not from **R** *linea recta*.

That **Φ** follows **R** up to book VI inclusive, has already been demonstrated above (p. 126).

Φ has not been corrected by later hands, but there are some marginalia by a later hand, e.g. 331a2 ἡδεῖα ἐλπὶς ἀγαθὴ γηροτρόφος *in margine*.

In books I-VI **Φ** has no extant derivatives.

The second MS that depends on **W** is **n**, which contains only 400c4-439a2. As this section falls outside the sample passages, I have collated two fragments, 419a1-421c6 and 437d8-439a2.

n proves to be a derivative of **W**, because it follows **W** everywhere, and adds some separative errors of its own; some instances:

420a4-5 ἰδίᾳ—βούλωνται om.
420e4   δεξιά] τὰ δεξιά
421a1   ὁ om.
421b6   θεατέον] θετέον
437d8-9 πλέονος—ἐστὶ om.
438a1   θορυβήσῃ] θορυβούσῃ
438d9   τε om.
438e9   δοκεῖ] δοκεῖν
439a1   τῶν om.

n shows no traces of contamination, has not been corrected by later hands, and has no extant derivatives.

Finally, I must say something about the fragments in **Darmst.**; that the fragment 328b8-329d6 in **Darmst.** goes back to a MS of the **A**-family, probably **T**, is proved by the fact that it follows **ATMγ** closely; see for instance:

328d5 νεανίσκοις] νεανίαις **ATMγDarmst.**
329a6 τε alterum om. **ATMγDarmst.**
329b1 προπηλακίσεις] προπηλακίσεις εἰς **TMγDarmst.**
329c3 ἀσμενέστατα] ἀσμεναίτατα **TDarmst.**[ac]

All the other derivatives of **T** have separative errors against **Darmst.**, so that we are left with the conclusion that **Darmst.** goes back to **T** itself (or to a lost derivative of **T**).

In the fragment 341a3-c4 there are no separative errors of **ATMγ** against **DF**; **DF**, however, have separative errors against **Darmst.**, so that it is likely that in this fragment too **Darmst.** goes back to **T**. The other fragments all come from **F**, except 376a11-b1, where **F** has μὴν που for μὴν, which is read by **Darmst.**; see the chapter on the **F**-family, pp. 199 f.

II. THE D-FAMILY

Apart from **D** itself, the **D**-family consists of the following MSS: **K**, **R** (from 389d7 on), **T** (from 389d7 on), **W** (from 389d7 on), **k** (from 381b on), **n**, **p**, **q**, **Θ** (from 389d7 on), **Φ** (in 389d7-511e5), **Ψ**, **β**, **Acq.** (from 389d7 on), **Ath.**, **Bon.**, **Durh.** (from 389d7 on), **Hier.** (from 389d7 on), **Lobc.** (from 389d7 on), **Neapol.**, **Pal.**, **Par.**, **Sc.** (from 389d7 on), **Vat.** (from 381b on), **Vind.**, **Vindob.**

I list some places where all the MSS of this family share a distinctive reading against the other two primary witnesses, **A** and **F** (the presence or absence of excerpt MSS is not recorded; **Vat.** and **k** join the **D**-family from 381b on; **Sc.** and its derivatives depend on **D** from 389d7 on. I also quote places in the passages where **D** itself is absent, as the result of the loss of some leaves, to wit 507e4-515d7 and 612e7-621d3):

328b6 καλχηδόνιον **A**: καρχηδόνιον **F**: χαλκηδόνιον **D** etc.
328d1-2 ἀλλ' —ἰέναι **AF**: om. **D** etc.
331e8 ὅτι **AF**: om. **D** etc.
386a3 ἀλλήλων **AF**: ἄλλην **D** etc.
388d5 αὐτῷ **AF**: om. **D** etc.
514b4 παρ' ἦν ἴδε (sic) **A**: παρ' ἤνιδε **F**: παρ' ἦ ἦν ἰδεῖν *D*
515a5 μὲν **AF**: om. *D*
517d2 τοῦτ' **AF**: ταῦτ' *D* etc.
614d5 αὐταῖς δικασθείη **AF**: αὐτοῦ δικασθεῖεν *D*
615b7 ταῦτα **AF**: ταύτην *D*
616c2-3 εἶναι—ὑποζώματα **AF**: εἶτα *D*
621b8 οὕτως **AF**: οὗτος *D*

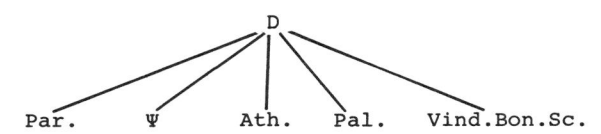

```
                    D
          ╱    ╱   │   ╲    ╲
        Par.  Ψ   Ath. Pal. Vind.Bon.Sc.
```

The descendants of **D** can be divided into five groups, represented by the following MSS: **Par.**, **Ψ**, **Ath.**, **Pal.** and the lost MS which can be reconstructed from the agreement of **Sc.** and the common source of **Vind.** and **Bon.**

The common ancestor of **Vind.Bon.** and **Sc.** goes back to **D**^{ac}, the other four MSS derive from **D** as corrected by **D**^{2} and **D**^{3}.

That these five MSS go back to **D** independently, is proved by the fact that they have no conjunctive errors, while each of them has separative errors against the others (and against **D**).

I shall first discuss the common source of **Vind.Bon.** and **Sc.** As has already been illustrated in the chapter on the **A**-family (see pp. 150 f.; 155 f.), **Sc.** follows the old part of **T** until it breaks off suddenly at 389d7; from there on **Sc.** follows **D**^{ac}. I do not discuss the derivatives of **Sc.** here, because the relationship of the members of the **Sc.**-group is the same in 389d7-621d3 as in 327a1-389d7; for the discussion of the derivatives of **Sc.** see pp. 155-168.

After 389d7, **Sc.** goes back to the same source as **Vind.** and **Bon.**; these MSS follow **D**^{ac} and have conjunctive errors which separate them from **D** (and from the other derivatives of **D**). Some instances of conjunctive errors of **Vind.Bon.Sc.** (N. B. the part of the *Republic* where **Vind. Bon.** and **Sc.** go back to the same source falls almost completely outside the sample passages, **Sc.** belonging to the **D**-family only from 389d7 on and **Vind.Bon.** containing books I-V only; I will therefore quote readings from books III, IV and V, taken from Schneider's apparatus and checked by me on microfilm):

393b1	ποιῆσαι] πεῖσαι
395a5	ἄρτι τούτῳ] ἀντὶ τούτων
396b7	αὖ om.
420c5	εἰ om.
422a6	κἂν om.
423e7	γάμων] γάμον
424c1	τις οἴηται] οἴηταί τις
424d3	ἔφη, ῥᾳδίως αὕτη] αὕτη ῥᾳδίως ἔφη
426b8	ὅλη om.
429d7	προπαρασκευάζουσιν] παρασκευάζουσιν
430e7-9	ὥς φασι—λέγεται] καὶ ὥς φασι διὰ ταῦτα καὶ ἀλλ' ἄττα τοιαῦτα ὥσπερ ἴχνη αὐτῆς ὄντα κρείττων αὐτὴ ἑαυτῆς φαίνεταί τε καὶ λέγεται **Vind.**^{it}**Bon.**^{it}**Sc.**^{1im} (+ καὶ τὰ ἑξῆς **Sc.**)
472b7	ἐστι om.
473c6	δή om.
476a7	πανταχοῦ] πολλαχοῦ
476d9	οὐκ ἀληθῆ] οὐ καλῶς
477a10	καὶ om.
480a6	καλοῦντες αὐτούς] αὐτοὺς καλοῦντες

Bon. and Vind. follow D from the beginning of book I; I will quote some conjunctive errors of Vind.Bon. against D (and the other apographa of D) in the sample passages of books I and III:

327c10	ἔτι] ὅτι
329b4	αἴτιον prius om.
331c3	παρά του om.
332c7-12	ἰατρικὴ—τέχνη om.
333b12	ἤ] καὶ
387d12	αὐτὸς om.
388b6	κυλινδόμενον] καλινδούμενον

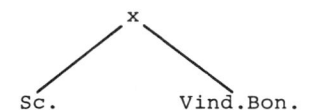

```
        x
       / \
      /   \
    Sc.   Vind.Bon.
```

Sc. and Vind.Bon. are gemelli, as is proved by the fact that they have separative errors against each other; some errors of Vind.Bon.:

394c6	ἔφη] φησὶν
394e9	ἐν] σὺ
399b7	ἐκ τούτων] ἐν τούτω
420a3	πρὸς] ἐν
422e9	ᾗ om.
424b2	γ'] γὰρ
428c3	κλητέα] λεκτέα
472c5	οἷόν ἐστι] εἶναι
478a6	Ἐπιστήμη μὲν] ἐπιστήμην
479c4	δυνατὸν om.

Some separative errors of Sc.:

394c2	ἀπαγγελίας] ἐπαγγελίας
394c8	ἔτι σκεπτέον] ἐπισκεπτέον
396e9	τὸν τύπον εἶναι] εἶναι τὸν τύπον
398e10	αὖ] τοιαῦταί
399d5	ὄντα om.
428d4	Ἔστι μέντοι om.
472b1	εἰπεῖν] λέγειν
474c7	ἔφη] τοίνυν
478d12-e1	Πέφανται—ἔοικε τὸ om.
479c1	τῷ alterum] ἔοικε

To illustrate my thesis that Vind.Bon.Sc. go back to D^{ac}, I quote some cases of agreement between D^{ac} and Vind.Bon. (in 327a1-389d7), Vind.Bon.Sc. (in 389d7-480a13), and Sc. (in books VI-X) (in those places where D^2 adds a correction in the text, at the expense of the original reading, the original reading is as a rule practically illegible):

329e8	σεραφίω D^{ac}Vind.Bon.: σεριφίω D^{2pc} recte
331a8	θνάτονον D^{ac}Vind.Bon.: θνάτων D^{2pc} recte
335c9-12	ἀμούσους—ἱππικῇ om. D^{ac}Vind.Bon.: add. D^{2im}
339a1	καθεστηκυίας] οἰκείας D^{ac}Vind.Bon.: καθεστηκυίας D^{2pc}
343d2	Σώκρατες om. D^{ac}Vind.Bon.: add. D^2
350a2	πλεονεκτεῖ D^{ac}Vind.Bon.: πλεονεκτεῖν D^{2pc} recte
361a6	ἄδικοι D^{ac}Vind.Bon.: ἀδίκω D^{2pc} recte
364c1	ἀκεῖσθε D^{ac}Vind.Bon.: ἀκεῖσθαι D^{2pc} recte
367d1-2	φρονεῖν—τῇ om. D^{ac}Vind.Bon.: add. D^{2im}
387a2	καπνός] καὶ πρὸς D^{ac}Vind.Bon.: καπνὸς D^{2pc}
402c1	φαμεν habent D^{ac}Vind.Bon.Sc.: ἔφαμεν D^{2pc}
403c9	θρεπτέοι habent D^{ac}Vind.Bon.Sc.: θρεπτέον D^{2pc}
428e1	ἐνέσεσθαι habent D^{ac}Vind.Bon.Sc.: ἔσεσθαι D^{2pc}
516a6	καθορῶ habent D^{ac}Sc.: καθορᾷ D^{2pc}
519a7	Πάνυ] πᾶν D^{ac}Sc.: πάνυ D^{2pc}
525a1	ἀγωγῶν habent D^{ac}Sc.: ἀναγωγῶν D^{2pc}
530b4	αὐτῷ D^{ac}Sc.: αὐτῶν D^{2pc} recte
585a3	πληρώσει—ἡδονῇ habent D^{ac}Sc.: πλήρωσιν—ἡδονὴν D^{2pc}

In many places **Sc.** agrees with D^2 (in some cases **Vind.Bon.** do as well); the explanation is that D^2 has drawn upon **W** (an apographon of **Sc.**); this has already been illustrated above, pp. 92 f.

The exemplar of **Vind.Bon.Sc.** was corrected and provided with variant readings; in some places **Vind.Bon.Sc.** have the correct reading against **D**; some instances:

330e2	τῆς habent **Vind.Bon.**: τῇ **D**
333d8	ὁπλιτικὴν habent **Vind.Bon.**: ὁπλητικὴν **D**
429a2	σοφίαν habent **Vind.Bon.Sc.** D^{2pc}: σοφία D^{ac}
450d1	ὄκνος habent **Vind.Bon.Sc.** D^{2pc}: ὀκνῶ D^{ac}

Some further instances of contamination:

411c1	ἀκράχολοι habet **D**: ἀκρόχολοι, addito α supra lineam, **Vind.Bon.Sc.**
458a1	εἰώθασιν] εἰώθεσαν **Vind.**^{1sl}**Bon.**^{1sl}**Sc.**^{it}
467e3	διδαξαμένους] διδαχθέντας **Vind.**^{1sl}**Bon.**^{1sl}**Sc.**^{it}

In some cases **Vind.Bon.Sc.** have readings which deserve some interest; there is occasional agreement with the indirect tradition; such cases will be discussed in the chapter on the secondary MSS; see pp. 214 f.

It appears that the exemplar of **Vind.Bon.** has been contaminated independently against **Sc.**: the source of the contamination belongs to the **Mγ**-group; some instances:

454c9	μόνον] μόνον ὂν A^{2sl}**MγVind.Bon.**
458d9	μείγνυσθαι] γυμνοῦσθαι **AM**^{1im}γ^{it}**Vind.**^{1im}**Bon.**^{1im}
461a6	φύς, ἃς] θύσας ἃς **Vind.Bon.Mγ**
461a7	ἐφ' om. **Vind.Bon.Mγ**: habent **Vind.**^{1im}**Bon.**^{1im}

Cases of agreement between **Vind.Bon.** and the **Mγ**-group are mainly found in book V. In a few places **Vind.Bon.** have a reading which deserves some attention; I will discuss such readings in the chapter on the secondary MSS; see pp. 216 f.

Sc. too seems to have undergone further contamination against its gemellus; this already appears from those places in which **Sc.** has the correct reading against **D^acVind.Bon.**, such as 392a1 ἐντίκτασι **D^acVind. Bon.**: ἐντίκτωσι **Sc. D²pc**.

In many places **Sc.** agrees with the **Mγ**-group; some instances:

496c5   γενόμενοι] γευόμενοι **Sc.^1slMγ**
497a5   μετὰ—κοινὰ] τὰ—καὶ τὰ τῶν κοινῶν **Sc.Mγ**
497a10 αὐτῇ] αὐτοῖς **Sc.Mγ**
497b6   ἦθος] εἶδος **Sc.Mγ** (**Par.**)
571b2   ἐν καλῷ habent **Sc.Mγ**: ἐγκαλῶ **ADF**

As both **Vind.Bon.** and **Sc.** show signs of contamination with the **Mγ**-group, it is possible that the readings of **Mγ** were not received independently, but were added in the common source of **Vind.Bon.** and **Sc.**, although the fact that cases of agreement between **Vind.Bon.** and the **Mγ**-group are found almost exclusively in book V seems to plead against this hypothesis; moreover, I have not found places where **Vind. Bon. Sc.** all agree with **Mγ**.

In some places **Sc.** has a reading which is undoubtedly due to conjectural emendation, e.g. 392c2 λέγεσθαι habet **Vind.**: ἐλεγεσθαι (sic) **D^ac Bon.**: ἐλέσθαι **Sc. D²pc**.

In some cases **Sc.** is the principal source for a true reading; such readings and readings which ask for attention in other respects will be discussed in the chapter on the secondary MSS; see pp. 217-222.

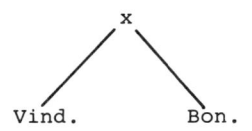

```
        x
       / \
      /   \
   Vind.  Bon.
```

That **Vind.** and **Bon.** are gemelli is proved by the fact that they both have separative errors against each other; some errors of **Bon.**:

328a1   ἴστε] ἴσθι
330b4   παραλαβὼν] περιλαβὼν
386a5   οἶμαί] οἶμε
386c5   x' om. (et **Fk**)
387c1   ἀλίβαντας] ἀλύβαντας
390b1   μέθυ] μέθη
390e3   βασιλῆας] βασιλέας

Some errors of **Vind.**:

328e3 ἴσως] ἴσθι
331b5 γε] τε
386b8 καὶ om.
388a5 ποιητῶν om.
388a8 δὲ] δὴ

Vind. has a number of corrections and variant readings by a later hand; some of these appear to derive from the **F** tradition or from **a**[pc]; see for instance:

332a12 τῳ] τὸ **Vind.**[2sl]**FM**γ**a**
391c4 πλέως] ἔμπλεως **Vind.**[2sl]**Fa**[sl]

Some other readings are also found in γ[pc] and its derivatives, e.g.:

387c2 οἴεται] οἷόν τε **Vind.**[2pc]γ[pc]α[im]**N**[sl]
388e6 γέλωτι] γέλωτι ἁλῶ **Vind**[2(u.v.)im]β[pc]α[sl]x[3im]**Sc.**[1sl]**M**[1sl]γ[1sl]

Vind. does not show traces of contamination against **Bon.**; at 392c2 **Vind.** has λέγεσθαι *recte* against ἐλεγεσθαι **D**[ac]**Bon.**; this is probably due to conjectural emendation. **Vind.** has no extant derivatives.

Bon. has some corrections by the first hand; usually these are simply corrections of a *lapsus calami*. In some places the first hand has added a variant reading; see for instance:

329b2 post ἐπὶ add. δὲ **Bon.**[1sl]
387a7 πέτρης habet **Bon.**: supra ε add. α (= πάτρης) **Bon.**[1sl]

Yet these readings do not seem to deserve particular attention.
Bon. has not been corrected by later hands; **Bon.** shows no traces of independent contamination against **Vind.**; **Bon.** has no extant derivatives.

The other derivatives of **D**, viz. **Par.**, **Ψ**, **Ath.** (I leave **Pal.** out of account for the moment, because it contains only a tiny fragment), derive from **D** as corrected by **D**[2]; I will quote some places where **D**[2]**Par.ΨAth.** (**Ath.** has only book I) agree against **D**[ac]**Vind.Bon.Sc.** (**Vind.Bon.** only in books I-V, **Sc.** from 389d7 on):

329c7 ἐπειδὰν habent **D**[ac]**Vind.Bon.**: ἐπειδὰν γὰρ **D**[2pc]**Par.ΨAth.**
329e8 σεραφίῳ **D**[ac]**Vind.Bon.**: σεριφίῳ **D**[2pc]**Par.ΨAth.** recte
333e7 δεινότατος habent **D**[ac]**Vind.Bon.**: δεινότατος καὶ **D**[2pc]**Par.ΨAth.**
339a1 καθεστηκυίας] οἰκείας **D**[ac]**Vind.Bon.**: καθεστηκυίας **D**[2pc]**Par.ΨAth.**
343d2 Σώκρατες om. **D**[ac]**Vind.Bon.**: habent **D**[2]**Par.ΨAth.**
367b2 κατατείνας] κατατίνας **D**[ac]**Vind.Bon.**: κατατείνας **D**[2pc]**Par.Ψ**
387a2 καπνός] καὶ πρὸς **D**[ac]**Vind.Bon.**: καπνὸς **D**[2pc]**Par.Ψ**

402c1 φαμὲν habent D^acVind.Bon.Sc.: ἔφαμεν D^2pcPar.Ψ
428e1 ἐνέσεσθαι habent D^acVind.Bon.Sc.: ἔσεσθαι D^2pcPar.Ψ
516a6 καθορῶ habent D^acSc.: καθορᾶ D^2pcPar.Ψ
519a7 Πάνυ] πᾶν D^acSc.: πάνυ D^2pcPar.Ψ
525a1 ἀγωγῶν habent D^acSc.: ἀναγωγῶν D^2pcPar.Ψ
530b4 αὐτῶ D^acSc.: αὐτῶν habent D^2pcPar.Ψ
585a3 πληρώσει—ἡδονῇ habent D^acSc.: πλήρωσιν—ἡδονὴν D^2pcPar.Ψ

The few corrections and variant readings added by **D³** recur also in **Par.**, **Ath.** and **Ψ** (**D³** does not add any readings in the fragment which is in **Pal.**); some instances:

341e5 ηὑρημένη] ἐξευρημένη D^3imAth.Ψ: εὑρημένη D^itPar.Vind.Bon.
343b5 οἳ habent D^3pcPar.ΨAth.: ἢ D^acVind.Bon.
344c5 καὶ prius del. D³: om. Par.ΨAth.

The corrections by **D³** do not recur in **Vind.Bon.**; **D³** does not add any readings after 389d7, from which point **Sc.** joins the **D**-family.

Corrections by **D⁴** and **D^rec.** do not recur in any of the derivatives of **D**.

First, I shall discuss **Ψ**[1]. **Ψ** follows **D**, as corrected by **D²** and **D³**, fairly closely and adds many errors of its own; some instances:

327b6 τε] μὲν
330a3 Ἀθηναῖος] ἀθηναῖος ἦν
331d7 ἱερῶν] ἰδίων
333c5 κοινῇ χρῆσθαι] χρῆσθαι κοινῇ
389c6 συνναυτῶν] ναυτῶν
390b1 μέθυ] μέου
391d2 ἥρω] ἥρωα
515a7 καταντικρὺ] κατανκρὺ
517b2 τῇ] τὴν
520b7 πεπαιδευμένους] πεπαιδευμένα

Yet **Ψ** does not go back to **D** *linea recta*, but stems from a derivative of **D** which was corrected from another source. The source on which the corrector of an ancestor of **Ψ** drew, is **Neapol.**, itself a derivative of **β^pc**, which in its turn derives from **Par.**; some instances:

386d1 οἰκία] οἰκεῖα Ψ: οἰκεία Neapol.
514b4 τειχίον] τοιχίον Ψ^1slβ^pcNeapol.
515e7 ἀνείη] ἀνίοι ΨβNeapol.
516c8 εἴ τινες] αἵτινες ΨNeapol.
517c6 ἐγώ—δύναμαι] ἕπομαι ἐς ὅσον κατ' ἐμόν γε δὴ τρόπον δύναμαι Ψβ^pcNeapol.

---

[1] It has taken me a lot of trouble to obtain microfilms from the monastery in El Escorial; unfortunately, the microfilm I received of **Ψ** proved to be incomplete (as the result of an inaccurate description in Brumbaugh-Wells); therefore I am unable to cite readings of **Ψ** in the sample passage of book X.

The cases of 386d1 and 516c8 prove that **Neapol.** was the source of the contamination.

In some cases the scribe has added a variant reading (e.g. 514b4 τειχίον habet Ψ, addito οι supra lineam a prima manu) or corrected a *lapsus calami* (e.g. 330a7 δ' om. Ψ; add. Ψ1sl).

I do not believe that Ψ has been corrected by later hands; but the reader should be warned that I have not seen Ψ *in situ*, but have only been able to work on a microfilm of rather poor quality.

The scholia in Ψ appear to have been written by another hand, but they may have been added by the scribe after the copying of the text.

Ψ has no extant derivatives.

The second apographon of **D**pc is **Ath.**; **Ath.** follows **D** (as corrected by **D**² and **D**³) closely, and adds many errors of its own; some instances:

328b3	εἰ δοκεῖ] ἦν δοκῇ
329a4	συνιόντες] ξυνιέντες
330c1	οἵ] οἱ ἄνθρωποι
332c3	ὠνόμασεν] ὠνομάσθη
332c7	τέχνη ἰατρικὴ om.
333b4	ὁ δίκαιος om.

Ath. does not go back to **D** *linea recta*, but derives from an apographon of **D** which was corrected from another source; this appears from the reading of **Ath.** at 331d9: τὰ ἱερά] τὰ ἱέναι **D**: τὰ ἱερὰ ἱέναι **Ath.**

The source of the contamination of **Ath.** cannot be identified on the basis of the sample passage of book I. I have deemed it superfluous to collate further parts of book I in order to clarify this problem.

Ath. has not been corrected by later hands, and has no extant derivatives.

The third MS that depends on **D**, as corrected by **D**² and **D**³, is **Par.**; **Par.** follows **D** in most places, but not everywhere, and adds some errors of its own; some instances:

330c4	τε] γε
331b5	πολλάς] τινάς
331c2	αὐτὸ φήσομεν εἶναι] εἶναι αὐτὸ φήσομεν
387b8	τά alterum om.
389a8	σύ] δὲ
390a1	ἄλλα om.
390e5	ὡς] ὅς
515a5	Ὁμοίους] ὁμοὺς
517e3	Οὐδ'] μηδ'
519c9	ἀφικέσθαι] ἐφικέσθαι
520c8	τοῦ] τὸ

614b3   Ἡρὸς] ἥρωος
616c3   συνέχον] συνέχοντα
617e7-8   ἓ δὲ οὐκ ἐᾶν] ἥδε οὐκ ἐᾶ
619c6   τῶν—ἡκόντων] τὸν—ἥκοντα
621a6   στέγειν] στέγει
621d3   πράττωμεν] πράττοντες

In the following places (in the sample passages) **Par.** does not share an error of **D**:

328a9   καὶ habet **Par.**: om. **D**
330e2   τῆς habet **Par.**: τῇ **D**
331a9   κυβερνᾷ habet **Par.**: κυβερνᾶν **D**
388e3   πειστέον habet **Par.**: πιστέον **D**
390d4   ἠνίπαπε habet **Par.**: ἦν εἴπαπε **D**
518b7   ἐπαγγελλόμενοι habet **Par.**: ἐπαγγελόμενοι **D**

Partly, these are obvious corrections; yet the addition of καὶ at 328a9 may well be due to contamination; the same goes for the readings at 330e2 and 331a9. There are other indications that an ancestor of **Par.** was indeed corrected from another source; thus there is occasional agreement with the **Sc.**-group; some instances:

329c2   συγγίγνεσθαι] συμμίγνυσθαι **Par.Sc.**
412d6   οἴοιτο] οἷόν τε **Par.Sc.**
460a4   πολέμους] πολεμίους **Par.Sc.Vind.Bon.**
461a6   γεννήσεται] γενήσεται **Par.Sc.Vind.Bon.**
466d7   ὥσπερ] ὥσπερ καὶ **Par.Sc.Vind.Bon.**
488d5   ἐπαΐοντες] ἐπαΐοντας **Par.Sc.** (et **F²**)
523a2   ὤν] ὃ **Par.Sc.** (et **V**)
547b3   γένει] γένη **Par.Sc.** (et **x**)
612d6   ἃ ante ἀπὸ **Par.Sc.** (om. **D**)

In some isolated places, there is agreement of **Par.** with **Mγ**:

424a1   τὰ] τῶν **Mγ**: τὰ τῶν **Par.**
477a10 μὴ] τῷ μὴ **Par.MγVind.Bon.**

Such cases of agreement may well be coincidental.

That readings which are common to **Par.** and **Sc.** are the result of contamination of an ancestor of **Par.** from a member of the **Sc.**-group and not *vice versa*, appears from the following considerations:

1. From 389d7 on, **Sc.** stems from D^{ac}.
2. The corrections in **D** added by D^2 go back to (a lost derivative of) **W**, which depends on **Sc.** (see pp. 92 f.).
3. **Par.** stems from **D** as corrected by D^2 (and D^3).

Therefore, **Par.** must be younger than **W**, and *a fortiori* younger than **Sc.**; it is impossible that an ancestor of **Sc.** (or **Sc.** itself) was contaminated from a MS that is younger than one of **Sc.**'s derivatives.

The alternative explanation for the cases of agreement between **Par.** and **Sc.**, namely that they derive from a common ancestor, breaks down because **Vind.Bon.Sc.** follow **D**ac, while **Par.** is in constant agreement with **D**pc; moreover, in that case **Par.** should also share at least some conjunctive errors with **Vind.Bon.Sc.**; finally, **Sc.** changes its exemplar after 389d7, while cases of agreement between **Par.** and **Sc.** occur both before and after 389d7.

The fact that an ancestor of **Par.** was contaminated from one or more other MSS also accounts for the correct readings in **Par.** against **D**.

In some cases **Par.** is the principal MS to preserve a true reading; in other places **Par.** has a reading which calls for attention in other respects; there is occasional agreement with the indirect tradition. I will discuss interesting readings in **Par.** in the chapter on the secondary MSS; see pp. 222-226.

Par. has been corrected by several later hands. The distinguishing of these later hands is extremely complicated; I have seen **Par.** *in situ* only for a short time, in order to check my observations made on the basis of a microfilm; I have distinguished six later hands.

For some hands, the occurrence of a reading of **Par.**pc in the apographa will decide the attribution to a particular hand. Therefore I state in advance what I intend to prove presently, to wit that **Par.** has three derivatives, viz. **Vat.** (from 381b on), **p**, and the lost common ancestor of β and **K** (**K** only in books I-III).

The hand which I call **Par.**[2] writes with very dark ink; its readings recur in **p** and β**K**, but not in **Vat.**; therefore **Vat.** represents the oldest derivative of **Par.** (the age of **Vat.** itself, of course, is irrelevant). See for instance 518a7 ἀηθείας] ἀληθείας **Par.**acVat.: ἀμαθίας **Par.**[2]pcβp.

The hand which I designate **Par.**[3] uses a very light ink; its readings recur in β(**K**), but not in **Vat.p**. This proves that **Par.**[3] is later than **Par.**[2], and that **p** represents a later derivative of **Par.** than **Vat.**, but older than β(**K**). See for instance 419a3 ὧν ἔστι] ἔνεστι **Par.**acVat.p: ὧν ἔστι **Par.**[3]pcβ.

Par.[4] writes, like **Par.**[3], in a very pale ink; its readings do not seem to recur in the apographa. See for instance 330a5-6 πάνυ—ἐπιεικής om. **DPar.**β**Kp** (here **Vat.** derives from **T**): add. **Par.**[4]im. However, it is possible that these words were added in the margin of **Par.** before the exemplar of β**K** was copied from **Par.**, because the words have been added in the margin of β by the corrector, who in all probability drew upon the exemplar of β (see below, p. 185).

Readings added by **Par.**[5], **Par.**[6] and **Par.**[7] do not recur in the apographa of **Par.**

Par.[5] writes with the same colour ink as that of the text; see for instance 614e5 τάς] τά **Par.**[ac]**Vat.βp**: τάς **Par.**[5pc] *recte*. **Par.**[5] is responsible for the excellent reading πολλοῖς at 615b3, which is written in the margin (Burnet's apparatus is misleading here); **Par.** has πολλοὶ in the text with **AF**; **ΘW** read πολλῶν (**Sc.** is absent here).

Par.[6] uses a very dark ink, and writes in a careless script; see for instance 619c2 σκέψασθαι] σκέψαιτο **Par.**[ac]**Vat.βp**: σκέψασθαι **Par.**[6pc] *recte*.

Par.[7], finally, writes in very dark, almost black ink, with a very thin pen. See for instance 386a3 γονέας **codd. omnes** (et **Par.**[ac]): πατέρας

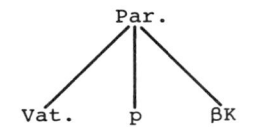

```
            Par.
           / | \
          /  |  \
        Vat. p  βK
```

I have already stated (p. 178) that **Par.** is the source of three MSS: **Vat.** (from 381b on), **p**, and the lost common ancestor of β and **K** (**K** in books I-III only).

I will list some places where **Vat.β(K)p** share a distinctive reading of **Par.** (**Vat.** in books III, VII and X only; **K** in books I-III only):

331b5 πολλάς] τινάς
331c2 αὐτὸ φήσομεν εἶναι] εἶναι αὐτὸ φήσομεν
333c1 ἐγὼ οἶμαι] ἐγῶμαι
389a8 σύ] δὲ
390a1 ἄλλα om.
390c8 ἐπιτήδειον] ἐπιτήδεια
515a5 Ὁμοίους] ὁμοὺς
517e3 Οὐδ'] μηδ'
519c9 ἀφικέσθαι] ἐφικέσθαι
520c8 τοῦ] τὸ
614b3 Ἡρὸς] ἥρωος
616c3 συνέχον] συνέχοντα
617e7 ἒ δὲ οὐκ ἐᾶν] ἤδε οὐκ ἐᾶ
619b3 τελευταίῳ] τελευταῖον
621a6 στέγειν] στέγει
621d3 πράττωμεν] πράττοντες

Vat., **p** and **β(K)** go back to **Par.** independently, because they have no conjunctive errors against **Par.**, while each of them has separative errors against the others (and against **Par.**).

Vat. derives from **T** up to 381a (see above, pp. 151 f.); from there on **Vat.** follows **Par.** very closely and adds an enormous number of errors of its own, many of these orthographical. **Vat.** goes back to **Par.**

before **Par.** had been corrected by later hands (see p. 178). Some instances of separative errors of **Vat.**:

386c5	θητευέμεν] θητεύωμεν
387a5	θεσπεσίοιο] θεσπέσιοι
387b9	Κωκυτούς] κωκκυτούς
387e3-4	ἢ χρημάτων om.
388c1	ὤμοι alterum] ὤμοι ἐγὼ
390e4	παιδαγωγὸν] ἀδελφὸν
515b5	τὰ] τοὺς
515e7	πρὶν] πρὶν ἂν
518b8	δέ] δὴ
614d2	ἀνθρώποις] ἀνθρώπους
618b5	τὰ δὲ νόσοις bis deinceps
621c4	μὲν] μοι

Vat. does not show traces of contamination. In some places **Vat.** has been corrected by a later hand; for some corrections, this hand draws on a MS of the **F** tradition, in all probability **x**; some instances:

386c1	ἔσεσθαι] γενέσθαι **Vat.**^{2sl}**Fx**
388e6	γέλωτι] γέλωτι ἁλῷ **Vat.**^{2im}**x**^{3im} (et alii)
389a8	ἔφη] ἔφην **Vat.**^{2pc}**x**^{3sl}
391c4	πλέως] ἔμπλεως **Vat.**^{2pc}**Fx**

In other places the corrector of **Vat.** has consulted a MS of the **D** tradition; see p. 152.

I have not found corrections by later hands in the sample passages of books VII and X.

```
Vat.
 |
 |
 k
```

Vat. is the source of **k**, as has already been shown for the sample passage of book I (see p. 153). I will quote some places where **k** shares a distinctive reading of **Vat.**:

387e3-4	ἢ χρημάτων om.
390e4	παιδαγωγὸν] ἀδελφὸν
391a4	ἄλλων] τῶν ἄλλων
516c9	παριόντα] πάντα
519e2	ὅπως] ὅπως μὴ
520a1-2	τὸ κοινὸν δυνατοὶ ὦσιν] δυνατοὶ ὦσιν τὸ κοινὸν
618a8	ἐπὶ om.
620c4	τὴν] τοῦ
621c4	μὲν] μοι

As in book I, **k** follows **Vat.** everywhere and adds many errors of its own; some instances:

388d3   καταγελῷεν] καταγελῶν ἐν
390d1   εἴ πού] εἶπον
391b4   νεκρῷ] νεκρῶν
514b4   τειχίον] ταχίον
517b1   λεγομένοις] λεγομένοιν
519b6   Εἰκός] οἰκὸς
614e4-5 πυνθάνεσθαι—καὶ om.
616d6   γὰρ] καὶ
619a1   τὴν om.
621a4   φύει] φύσει

The corrections by **Vat.**[2] recur in **k**, e.g. 388e6 γέλωτι] γέλωτι ἀλῶ **Vat.**[2im]**k**[it].

Sometimes **k** puts a double reading of **Vat.** into the text, e.g. 386a3 ἀλλήλων φιλίαν] ἄλλην φιλανθρωπίαν **Vat.**: ἀλλήλων φιλίαν **Vat.**[2im]: ἄλλην ἀλλήλων φιλίαν φιλανθρωπίαν **k**.

k does not show traces of contamination, has not been corrected by later hands, and has no extant derivatives.

The second MS that depends on **Par.** is **p**; **p** follows **Par.** almost everywhere, and adds a number of errors of its own; some instances:

329a6   περὶ om.
330d2   ἀγαθὸν om.
389e4   δή] δὲ δὴ
392b2   ὡς] ὡς οὐ
517b6   ἐπειδὴ] ἐπεὶ
614c5   τὴν εἰς] εἰς τὴν
619d3   τῶν] τοὺς
621c6   αὐτοῖς om.

p follows **Par.** everywhere, except in the following places (in the sample passages):

517a3   ἥκει habet **p**: ἥκοι **Par.**
518a4   ταὐτὰ habet **p**: ταῦτα **Par.**
520a3   ἀφίη habet **p**: ἀφίει **Par.**
620c6   περιιοῦσαν habet **p**: περιοῦσαν **Par.**

These are all very easy corrections, which do not prove that **p** stems from a corrected apographon of **Par.**

p does not show traces of contamination; at 619a5 **Par.** reads τὸν τοιοῦτον βίον for τῶν τοιούτων βίον; **p** has τῶν τοιούτων βίων, which, I think, is a conjectural emendation of the reading of **Par.**

It has already been mentioned (p. 178) that **p** derives from **Par.** as corrected by **Par.**[2], while later readings in **Par.** do not recur in **p**.

In some places **p** has been corrected by what is probably the first hand (but I have not seen **p** *in situ*); such corrections are sometimes written in a different ink, which suggests that the scribe added them after the text had been copied; see for instance:

390d7 μέν] μὴν p¹ᵖᶜ
515a5 Ὁμοίους] ὁμοὺς Par.pᵃᶜ: ὁμοίους p¹ᵖᶜ

At 580d4 the words ἐπιθυμητικὸν θυμικὸν have been added above the line by the scribe himself with lighter ink (editors assign this reading to **K**, a derivative of **p**; Campbell 91 even regards this reading as "manifestly anterior" to the reading of **ADF**).

At 388e6 **p**ᵖᶜ reads ἐφῆ, a very intelligent correction of ἔφη, which is read by **p**ᵃᶜ**DPar.**; ἐφῆ may very well be the correct reading in this place.

There are no corrections by later hands, but there are some marginal notes by a later hand, e.g. on fol. 82ᵛ ad 379b.

p
|
K

p is the source of **K** in books IV-X (in books I-III **K** goes back to the same source as β, as will be illustrated below; see pp. 183-185.

I will mention some places where **K** shares a distinctive reading of **p**:

517b6 ἐπειδὴ] ἐπεὶ
614c5 τὴν εἰς] εἰς τὴν
614d1 ἑαυτοῦ δὲ προσελθόντος] ἑαυτὸν δὲ προσελθόντα
617e7 ἀναιρεῖσθαι] αἱρεῖσθαι
619d3 τῶν] τοὺς
621c6 αὐτοῖς om.

That **K** changes its exemplar at the beginning of book IV appears from some readings at the end of book III and the beginning of book IV:

417b4 πλείω habet **p**: πλεῖον β**K**
419a3 ἑαυτούς habent **Par.**β**p**ᵃᶜ: αυτοὺς (sic) **p**ᵖᶜ: αὐτοὺς **K**
419a3 ὧν ἔστι habent **Par.**³ᵖᶜβ: ἔνεστι **Par.**ᵃᶜp**K**

K follows **p** almost everywhere and adds some separative errors of its own; some instances:

515d5 ἀποκρίνεσθαι] ἀποκρίνασθαι
516a8 τῷ om. (et Φ**Mon.**)
614c2 δύ' εἶναι] εἶναι δύο
616e6-8 πέμπτον—τρίτου om.
618a8 κάλλη] κάλλους

The only places (in the sample passages) where **K** does not follow **p** are:

616d3 ἐξεγλυμμένῳ habet **K**: ἐξεγλυμένῳ **p**
618b4 γίγνεσθαι habet **K**: γίνεσθαι **p**

These are two very easy corrections.

In one case (in the sample passages of books VII and X) **K** has a variant reading added by the first hand: 519c8 Ἡμέτερον] ὑμέτερον **K**[1sl].

K shows no traces of contamination, has not been corrected by later hands, and has no extant derivatives.

The third MS that derives from **Par.** is the lost common ancestor of β and **K** (**K** in books I-III only; see above, p. 182).

The relationship of β and **K** is a very complicated problem; as β is one of the most important secondary MSS, I will deal with this relationship in detail. Because the evidence that could be gathered from the sample passages of books I and III proved insufficient to clear all difficulties, I have made a full collation of β and **K** for the whole of book I.

That β and **K** go back to **Par.** is shown by the fact that they follow **Par.** almost everywhere. Yet if we throw a glance at Schneider's apparatus, we see many places where **Par.** is reported to have an error, often in conjunction with **K**, against β; the explanation is that β has been corrected in countless places; β[ac] is usually in accordance with **Par.** and **K**.

Further, β**K** sometimes have readings written by later hands in **Par.**, e.g. 386d2 τά τε] τὰ δὲ **Par.**[ac]**Vat.p**: τά τε **Par.**[3pc]β**K**.

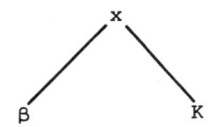

```
        x
       / \
      /   \
     β     K
```

That β and **K** do not go back to **Par.** independently, is shown by their conjunctive errors; some instances:

331a3   τοι om.
335b2   ἄρα] οὖν ἄρα
336a2   φάναι] φάμενον
336d2   μηδ' ὅτι το συμφέρον om.
339b1   ἴσως ἔφη] ἔφη ἴσως
344a2   οὖν om.
348e1   μέν] μὲν οὖν
351b9   αὐτῇ] αὐτὴν
352e9   ταῦτα τούτων φαμὲν] φαμεν ταῦτα τούτων
388b3   τε] γε
388b6   κόπρον] κόπρου

β cannot be dependent on **K**, as **K** has separative errors against β: some instances:

327a4	μοι om.
329d1	ἐστι καὶ μαινομένων] καὶ μαινομένων ἐστι
332d4-5	ἔμπροσθεν εἰρημένοις] εἰρημένοις ἔμπροσθεν
334d5	μηδὲν] μὲν
340e7	οὖν om.
344b2	τε om.
347b8	αὐτοὶ] αὐτὸ
350b9	Ἔοικεν ἔφη et b12 Φαίνεται transposuit
352c6	δὲ] γὰρ
391a2	ἔφη om.
392d3	μελλόντων] μὴ ὄντων

In book I, there are only two separative errors of β against **K**:

340e7	σοι] σε
354a13	μέντοι] μέν τι

In books II and III I have noted the following separative errors of β against **K**:

358b1	δοκῇ] δοκοῖ
373e4	λέγωμεν] λέγομεν
376e11	διττὸν] διττῶν
383a4	ἑαυτοὺς] αὐτοὺς
404a7	οὗτοι οἱ] οἱ τοιοῦτοι
404d2-3	δοκεῖ ὀρθῶς] ὀρθῶς δοκεῖ
409a5	σῶμα] τὸ σῶμα
412c9	αὐτοὺς ἀρίστους δεῖ] ἀρίστους δεῖ αὐτοὺς
413c1	μὴν] μὲν
414a8	πῃ] που
416b5-6	ἄν εἶεν] εἶεν ἄν

Few as these errors may be, they are enough to separate β from **K**. Yet their extreme scantiness requires an explanation.

I have already noted that β has been corrected in many places (p. 183); these corrections have been written by a hand which is fairly similar to that of the first scribe, yet not identical with it (cf. p. 34).

In the first book I have counted 115 places where β has been corrected (I do not claim that I have seen each and every correction); in 53 cases, the reading of βpc is also found in **K**. This too pleads against the dependence of **K** on β: all the corrections in β have been written by the same hand (I have inspected β *in situ*), so that, in order to keep up the hypothesis of the dependence of **K** on β, we should be compelled to assume that the corrector of β wrote the corrections at two different stages, between which **K** was copied from β, a hypothesis which is not particularly attractive. Further, it appears that of the 53 corrections in β which occur in **K** too, 43 are found in most, if not all, other MSS, so that these readings do not tell us anything whatsoever about the relationship of β and **K**. The ten remaining cases will be dealt with below.

For the sake of completeness, I record that in some places **K** has a variant reading written by the first hand, which does not occur in β, e.g. 329d6 χαλεπή habent β**K** (**codd. omnes**): ἃ **K**[1sl] (= χαλεπά); 363a1 αὐτὸ habent β**K** (**codd. omnes**): ἥν **K**[1sl] (= αὐτήν).

Therefore we must conclude that β and **K** go back to a common ancestor, itself a derivative of **Par**.

With regard to the corrections in β, I think it can be proved that the corrector of β drew on the exemplar of β**K** for at least some of these corrections: in ten places a reading of β[pc] also occurs in **K**[it], but not in **Par**.; in seven of these cases the reading of β[pc]**K** against **Par**. is clearly correct, and is also found in most other MSS; some instances:

329b8 ἐρωτωμένῳ] ἐρωτώμενος **DPar**.β[ac]: ἐρωτωμένῳ β[pc]**K**
338b9 εὖ ἐρεῖν] εὑρεῖν **DPar**.β[ac]: εὖ ἐρεῖν β[pc]**K**

In three cases a reading of β[pc]**K** is not found in any other extant MS (except, of course, the apographa of β):

336e9 οἵου γε σύ **Bekker**: οἵου τε σύ **ADF**: οἵου σύ **Par**.β[ac]: μὴ οἵου σύ β[pc]**K**
337a4 'κείνη habent **Par**.β[ac]: ἐκείνη β[pc]**K**
351b1 φαίης habent **Par**.β[ac]: φαίην β[pc]**K**

The explanation is, I think, that the exemplar of β**K** had double readings: the scribe of β chose the reading which was in the text of the exemplar (i.e. the reading of **Par**.), while **K** chose the variant reading; afterwards, the corrector of β adopted the variant reading from the exemplar. The alternative explanation, that **K** and β[pc] got these readings from independent sources, is to be excluded because of the readings at 336e9 and 351b1, where the agreement of β[pc] and **K** can hardly be coincidental.

The fact that β was corrected from its own exemplar accounts for the extremely low number of separative errors of β against **K**: most errors that were in β originally, have subsequently been removed. In this respect, it is remarkable that most separative errors of β against **K** occur at the end of book III: it appears that the corrector of β became less keen on errors of β as the work went on.

K has some variant readings written by the first hand (see above); in all probability, these variant readings derive from the exemplar; some further instances:

341b6 ἀκριβεῖ] ἀκριβῇ β[ac]**K**[it]: ἀκριβεῖ β[pc]**K**[1sl]
370e1 βοῦς habent β[it]**K**[1sl]: βόας **K**[it]

K does not show traces of independent contamination against β, has not been corrected by later hands, and has no extant derivatives.

The text of β has been written by three different scribes (see p. 34). In some cases the scribe of β has written a variant reading in the margin, which has afterwards been put into the text by the corrector; in other places the scribe of β noticed an error he had made, and corrected this error by writing the correct word or, in the case of an omission, the omitted word(s), above the line or in the margin, or by placing transposition marks above transposed words; the corrector subsequently erased wrong reading and correction, and wrote the correct reading *in rasura*.

The corrections in β (which, as has been demonstrated, sometimes occur in **K** too) deserve much attention. Some of them are clearly conjectural emendations, often very intelligent; see for instance:

331e8 ὅτι om. **DPar.**β^(ac)**K**: ὡς β^(pc)
346e4-5 ἀλλ' —παρασκευάζει om. **DPar.**β^(ac)**K**: ἀλλ' ἐκεῖνο σκοπεῖ ἐφ' ᾧ τέτακται β^(im)

Some corrections have been borrowed from the **Sc.**-group; some instances:

433c8 ἢ ἡ habent β^(pc)**Sc.M**γ
441c6 ἑνὸς habent β^(pc)**Sc.Vind.Bon.**
455c6 μακρολογῶμεν] μακρολογοῦμεν β^(pc)**Sc.**
565c9 δῆμος] ὁ δῆμος β^(pc)**Sc.**
571b2 ἐν καλῷ habent β^(pc)**Sc.M**γ
580d1 δὲ ἰδὲ **Adam**: δεῖ δὲ **ADF**: δὲ δεῖ β^(pc)**Sc.**
586c1 σφοδροὺς] σφοδρὰς β^(pc)**Sc.**^(sl)
606c7 ἀνιεῖς] ἀνίης β^(pc)**Sc.**

In some cases β^(pc) agrees with Θ or Θ²; some instances:

502d7 γίγνεσθαι] γίγνεται β^(pc)Θ
575a5 αὐτῶν] αὐτοῦ β^(pc)Θ²^(pc)
604c7 αἱρεῖ habent β^(pc)Θ²^(sl)F⁵^(sl)

Other corrections seem to derive from the **M**γ-group, e.g. 516e4 θᾶκον] θῶκον β^(pc)**M**γ; the readings at 433c8 and 571b2, quoted above, may also have been borrowed from the **M**γ-group.

There are, however, a lot of corrections and variant readings which do not occur in other extant MSS (except, of course, the derivatives of β); sometimes there is significant agreement with the indirect tradition; many corrections in β are manifestly correct or at least very interesting; such readings will be discussed in detail in the chapter on the secondary manuscripts; see pp. 203-214.

```
          β
       ╱ │ ╲
  Neapol.  q  Vindob.
```

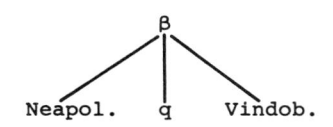

β^pc is the source of three other MSS; **Neapol.**, **q** and **Vindob.**; **Vindob.** contains only fragments, among which is also the beginning of the Myth of Er.

I shall list some places where **q** and **Neapol.** (at the beginning of the sample passage of book X **Vindob.** as well) share distinctive readings of β and β^pc:

327c14	ἀκουσομένων] ἀκουσομένων ἔφη (β^pc)
328e3	τραχεῖα] πότερον τραχεῖα (β^pc)
331e9	ἀπαιτοῦντι] ἀπαιτοῦντος (β^pc)
386a1	δὴ] οὖν (δὴ om. **K**)
387e9	θρήνους] θρήνους τοὺς (β^pc)
514a1	τοιούτῳ] τοιῶδε (β^pc)
516e4	καθίζοιτο] καθέζοιτο
517c6	ἐγώ, ὅν] ἕπομαι ἐς ὅσον κατ' ἐμόν (β^pc) (ἐς om. q)
518c2	ἐντιθέντες] ἐντιθέντας
519a3	ὡς] ἄτε (β^pc) (εἴτε **Neapol.**)
614d4	καθ' ἑκάτερον] κατὰ θάτερον (β^pc)
615b5	δεκαπλασίας] δεκαπλασίους
616e2	περὶ—δὲ] τὴν δ' ἠλακάτην ἐκείνην (β^pc)
617b1	τὸν om. (β^pc)
617e2	πρῶτος alterum] πρῶτον
618a3-4	ζῴων—ἅπαντας om. (β^pc)
619d3	τῆς om.
619e6-620d5	Ταύτην—μείγνυσθαι om. (β^pc)

q, **Neapol.** and **Vindob.** go back to β independently, because they have no conjunctive errors, while each of them has separative errors against the others (and against β).

q follows β^pc everywhere and has a number of separative errors of its own; some instances:

329c7	κατατείνουσαι om.
333a10	πρὸς—κτῆσιν om.
386b6	θάνατον om.
386b8	δή] δὲ
392c8	ἐσκέψεται] εὖ σκέψεται
518e1	ὕστερον om.
614b5	δεκαταίων τῶν om.
614d3	δὴ] δὲ
621c4	μὲν κακὰ om.

q does not show traces of contamination and may well be a direct transcript of β.

In some cases the scribe noticed an error he had made himself and corrected it immediately, e.g. 387a7 ἔχοντας q^{ac}: ἔχονται q^{1pc}.

In some places **q** has been corrected by a later hand; some of these later corrections are clearly conjectural; some instances:

332d11   κακῶς om. q: add. βλάπτειν q²ˢˡ
387e6   καὶ] χρὴ q²ᵖᶜ

Other corrections are traceable to other MSS, e.g.:

351c1   ἔχει] ἔστιν q²ᵖᶜN
417a3   αὐτὸν] αὐτῶν q²ᵖᶜx
470c6   πολεμεῖν μαχομένους] μαχομένους πολεμεῖν q²ᵖᶜF
501b3   τὸ] ὃ q²ⁱᵐNᵖᶜ
532b1   αὐτῇ] αὐτῇ τῇ q²ˢˡNˢˡ
535b8   αὐταῖς] αὐτοῖς q²ˢˡF
537e4   ἐμπίμπλανται] ἐμπίπλασθαι q²ᵖᶜVMatr.
543c7   ὡς om. q²ᵖᶜNᵖᶜ
583e3   ἔφη del. q²: om. Sc.

Therefore, q² seems to have drawn upon various sources.

q does not have extant derivatives.

Neapol. follows β everywhere and has many separative errors of its own; some instances:

328c6   καταβαίνων] καταβαῖνον
331a4   ὅς] ὡς
333b8   οἰκοδομικοῦ] οἰκονομικοῦ
387a7   ἔχονται om.
387d8   ὑπέρ] εἴπερ
390e8   παρὰ] περὶ
515c4   αὐτῶν om.
520e1   δικαίοις] δικαίης
615b1   τοσούτου om.
618d2-5 καὶ τί—ἐργάζεται om.
619d4   ἄλλους] ἀλλήλους

Sometimes **Neapol.** misinterprets a marginal note in β; e.g. at 329e5 β has two dots above φασιν, which refer to the marginal note παροιμία (also found in **Par.**); yet the word παροιμία is written in such a way as to look like παρεῖν or παρεῖναι; **Neapol.** has παρεῖν εἶναι in the text for φασιν εἶναι.

Neapol. does not show any traces of contamination; yet because of the large number of errors in **Neapol.** I do not think it very likely that **Neapol.** is a direct transcript.

In some places the first hand has corrected an error, e.g. 387c2 δή] δεῖ **Neapol.**^{ac}: δή **Neapol.**^{1pc}.

There are no corrections by later hands; **Neapol.** has no extant derivatives.

Vindob., which contains some excerpts from *R.*, follows β everywhere and has some separative errors of its own. I will quote some places where **Vindob.** shares a significant reading with β:

614c2 χάσματα] χάσματε (β^{pc})
614d4 καθ'ἑκάτερον] κατὰ θάτερον (β^{pc})
615b5 δεκαπλασίας] δεκαπλασίους

Vindob. cannot be derived from q or **Neapol.**, because these MSS have separative errors against **Vindob.**; some errors in q:

614b5 δεκαταίων τῶν om.
614d3 δή] δὲ
615d5 ἦμεν om.

Some errors of **Neapol.**:

614d4 τε om.
615a6 τινα om.
615b1 τοσούτου om.
615e3 ἀνιάτως om.

Some separative errors of **Vindob.**:

614b5 μὲν om.
614b7 τῇ om.
614d2-3 οἱ ἀκούειν τε om.
615b4 τινος] τινες

Some cases of agreement between **Vindob.** and β in the other fragments in **Vindob.**:

360a6 οὕτω] ἀεὶ οὕτω (β^{pc})
609a3 τε] τι (β^{pc})

Vindob. does not show traces of contamination, has not been corrected by later hands, and has no extant derivatives.

The fragment 359c7-360b2 in **Pal.** remains to be discussed. I mention the places from which it becomes clear that **Pal.** goes back to **D**^{2pc}:

359d8 οὐδέν **A**: ἔχειν οὐδέν **Pal.DF**
359e2 εἰωθότος **A**: εἰωθότως **Pal.DF**
359e6 πρὸς ἑαυτόν] πρὸς σεαυτόν **Pal.D**^{2pc}
360a6 οὕτω **AF**: οὕτω καὶ οὕτω **Pal.D**
360b2 οὕτω **F**: om. **Pal.AD**

Pal. does not go back to one of the other derivatives of **D**, because each of these has separative errors against **Pal.**:

360a1   καὶ om. Ψ
360a2   τὸν om. **Vind.Bon.**
360a5   ἔχοι] ἔχει **Par.**Ψ

Therefore **Pal.** goes back to **D** independently. **Pal.** has one error of its own, namely 360a8 παρά] περί (et **N**[sl]).

In some places **Pal.** has been corrected by the first hand; there are no later corrections; **Pal.** has no extant derivatives.

III. THE F-FAMILY

Apart from **F** itself, the **F**-family consists of **x**, **v**, **Ricc.**, **Ox.** and **Bodl.**; in addition, some of the fragments in **Darmst.** appear to be derived from a MS belonging to the **F**-family.

I will mention some distinctive readings of the **F**-family against the other MSS:

327b3   δραμόντα τὸν παῖδα] τὸν παῖδα δραμόντα
327c3   ἄλλοι] ἄλλοι πολλοί
328d2   ὅτι om.
330c5   περί om.
387b2   ἄλλους om.
388a2   φυλακῇ] τῇ φυλακῇ
389b7   προσήκει] προσῆκε
391e1   πού] τουθ'
515a9   ἔχειν om.
516d6   ὁτιοῦν] ὅτι
517c7   ἦν δ' ἐγώ post τόδε
518a1   μεμνῇτ' ἄν] μέμνημαι
520d7   ἐν prius om.
616d3   μεγάλῳ σφονδύλῳ] σφονδύλῳ μεγάλῳ
617a6   τῷ om.
618a8   κατὰ κάλλη] κάλλει
619a4   αὐτὸς μείζω] μείζω αὐτός

Of **F**'s apographa only **x**, and some of the fragments in **Darmst.**, go back back to **F** *linea recta*; the other MSS all depend on **x**.

That **x** derives from **F** appears from the fact that **x** follows **F** everywhere, even in the smallest details and in the most obvious errors, and that **x** has separative errors of its own. In the four sample passages the only place where **x** has the correct reading against **F** is 517b1 ἔμπροσθεν habet **x**: ἔμπροσθε **F**; but it is possible that the final —ν has been added in **x** *post correctionem*; I have not been able to decide this on the basis of the microfilm.

Some separative errors of **x** against **F**:

389a1 ἐάν] ἄν
515e4 σαφέστερα] σαφέστερον
520c4 γνώσεσθε] γνώσεσθαι
614e3 κατασκηνᾶσθαι] κατασκηνοῦσθαι
616b3 τῇ ὀγδόῃ] τὴν ὀγδόην
618a3 γὰρ om.

Moreover, there are some codicological indications for the dependence of **x** on **F**:

1. In two cases (in the sample passages) an omission in **x** corresponds exactly to one line in **F**: 388e6 ὅταν—ζητεῖ om. **x** (add. **x**^{3im}) and 389a5-6 γέλως—ποιπνύοντα om. **x** (add. **x**^{3im}); in these cases the scribe has telescoped one line in his exemplar, **F**.

2. In some places, words or parts of words have become illegible in **F** because they have faded. Often these letters or words are omitted altogether in **x**; some instances:

597e5 μὲν evanuit in **F**: om. **x**
600b2 τε evanuit in **F**: om. **x**
601c15 οὐ evanuit in **F**: om. **x**
602c12 ταραχὴ] χὴ evanuit in **F**: ταρα (sic) **x**^{ac} (corr. **x**^{3})
604d10 τε evanuit in **F**: om. **x** (add. **x**^{3})

3. In some cases the scribe of **F** leaves a blank, presumably because he could not decipher some letters or words in his exemplar (cf. pp. 100 f.). Usually, **x** copies the words that are separated in **F** by a lacuna, without leaving an open space, as at 488d5, where **F** omits the word πέρι *spatio vacuo relicto*, while **x** writes μηδ᾽ immediately after κυβερνήτου. In other cases **x** leaves a blank, as **F** does; e.g. 442d4 γε om. **Fx** *spatio vacuo relicto* (add. **x**^{3} *in lacuna*).

4. Finally, **x** shares readings added by later hands in **F**, also in places where such a reading does not occur in other MSS (except, of course, the apographa of **x**). I will give some instances of such unique readings:

347c1 ante ἐθέλειν add. μὴ **F**^{4sl}: μὴ ἐθέλειν **x**^{it}
375c3 φθήσονται] φθίσονται **F**^{4pc}**x**^{ac} (corr. **x**^{3})
399c10 τριγώνων] τριβώνων **F**^{5sl}**x**^{ac} (corr. **x**^{3})
415a4 ante πλάττων add. ὁ **F**^{5sl}: ὁ πλάττων **x**^{it}
453b3 δεῖ] δὲ **F**^{ac}: δέον **F**^{5pc}**x**
476d5 γνώμην] γνῶσιν **F**^{4pc}**x**
501a3 ὃ] ὅθεν **F**^{4pc}**x**
549b10 supra πόλει add. καὶ πολιτεία **F**$^{4(u.v.)sl}$: πόλει καὶ πολιτεία **x**^{it}

I believe that I have distinguished five later hands in **F** (see pp. 101-104); **x** shares readings with all of these hands:

F^2: 354a4-7 Ὁ μὲν—οὔ om. **F**: add. **F**^{2}: habet **x**^{it}
F^3: 386a3 ἀλλήλων] ἄλλην **F**^{3im}**x**^{it}
F^4: 354b5 ὁρμῆσαι] ὥρμημαι **F**^{4sl}**x**^{it}

F^5:   415a4   ante πλάττων add. ὁ F^{5sl}: ὁ πλάττων x^{it}
F^6:   387b1   παραιτησόμεθα] παρακαλέσομεν F^{6sl} (glossema, ut videtur): παρακαλέσομεν x^{1sl} (atramento rubro)

Scholia and glosses in **F** are copied in **x** in red ink (I have inspected **x** *in situ*); this is also the case with scholia and glosses written by later hands in **F**, e.g. 387b1 παρακαλέσομεν (just quoted above), and the scholium on ἀνδρείαν at 429b2, written by F^5.

x may very well be a direct transcript, although this cannot be settled with absolute certainty.

I have discussed the dependence of **x** on **F** at length, because some scholars have assumed that **x** should be regarded as a gemellus of **F**; see p. 36.

The first hand in **x** corrects some *lapsus calami*, like 333b11 χρῆσαι x^{ac}: χρῆσθαι x^{1pc}; sometimes a very obvious error in **F** is corrected by the scribe of **x** himself, e.g. 387c3 ὑμεῖς Fx^{ac}: ἡμεῖς x^{1pc}.

Whenever **x** takes over a variant reading from **F** (whether by F^1 or by a later hand), **x** inserts this reading into the text, that is, **x** does not record the variant readings in **F** as such.

It has already been noted that x^1 adds glosses and scholia in red ink; the script of these notes looks a bit thinner than that of the text, but this may be due to the use of a different pen; besides, in writing scholia many scribes use a type of script different from that in which the text is written.

I believe that at least four later hands can be distinguished in **x**.

The first of these later hands, x^2, writes in a fairly light grey-brown ink; the script is upright and neat, somewhat angular; some instances:

332c5   post ὦ prius add. σώκρατες x^{2im}
335a6   ἡμᾶς] ἡμᾶς ἄλλο x^{2im}
521a6   οἰόμενοι] ἰώμενοι Fx: οἰόμενοι x^{im}
531b1   προστησάμενοι] προησάμενοι x^{2im}

It is possible that many of the corrections in the text are also due to x^2; as I have not been able to check this *in situ* on all occasions, the possibility remains that in some cases such corrections may have been made by the first hand, because the ink of x^1 and x^2 looks very similar on microfilm.

Another hand, x^3, writes in a greyish ink; the script is somewhat more flowing than that of x^2; some instances:

337c4   τῷ ἐρωτηθέντι] τῷ ἐρωτωμένῳ x^{3im}
519a5   ἐργαζόμενον] ἄλλως ἐργάσεται x^{3im}

x^3 occurs rather frequently and introduces some interesting readings, e.g. 330b7 ἤ] ὧν x^{3im}.

The next hand, x^4, uses light-brown ink, and writes in large letters; see for instance:

526a8 ἦν om. **Fx**: add. x^{4im}

This hand sometimes adds γνώ in the margin (e.g. fol. 149^v, fol. 156^v (bis)); x^4 is not very frequent.

Finally, x^5 writes in a very light greyish ink, in very thick letters; some instances:

539b1 συχνή] μεγίστη x^{5sl} (glossema ut vid.)
558a9 πολλούς] πολύ x^{5sl} (et **Θ**: πολύς **D**)
559d9 δεινοῖς] πανουργοῖς x^{5im} (glossema ut vid.)

At 546c there is a marginal note *numero platonis obscurius* by yet another hand.

Sicherl, *Ficino* 59, states that Ficino's hand has been detected in **x**; on the basis of a comparison of a microfilm of **Ambr.** (Ficino's autograph) and **x**, I am unable to tell whether or not this is true; at any rate, I do not find the likeness between Ficino's hand and any of the correcting hands in **x** very striking.

In many cases, readings added by later hands in **x** are simple corrections of quite obvious errors, which may be due to conjectural emendation or contamination; see for instance:

388d5 ἐπίοι] ἐποίοι Fx^{ac}: ἐπίοι $x^{3(u.v.)pc}$
519a9 κοπτόμενον] σκοπτόμενον Fx^{ac}: κοπτόμενον x^{pc} (nescio quae manus)
617c3 Λάχεσίν] λάχεσι Fx^{ac}: λάχεσιν $x^{3(u.v.)pc}$

In a number of other cases, particular readings are traceable to other branches of the tradition, esp. in the case of x^3; see for instance:

388e6 γέλωτι] γέλωτι ἀλῶ $M^{1sl}γ^{1sl}ax^{3im}$
430b6 ὀρθήν] αὐτήν ax^{3im}
516d1 καὶ prius om. γa: del. $x^{3(u.v.)}$
616a6-7 μὴ—ἀναβαίνοι] τὸν φόβον εἰ μυκήσαιτο τὸ στόμιον $Mγ^{3im}ax^{3im}$

Therefore I believe that x^3 draws at least partially on **a**.

At 620b4 x^{3im} has ἐχθράν for ἔχθρᾳ, with the **D**-family; some corrections in **x** come from β, e.g. 456a1 οὔ, οὐδέ] καὶ $β^{pc}x^{3(u.v.)pc}$. Thus β may have been another source for the readings added by x^3.

In addition, there are many corrections which cannot be the result of conjectural emendation, and which accordingly must go back to other MSS; some instances:

332b8 προσήκει, κακόν] κακὸν προσήκει Fx^{ac}: signis transposuit x^2
391c3 ταραχῆς] ἀρετῆς Fx^{ac}: ταραχῆς x^{3pc}
520a4 ἐπί] ἐν ᾗ Fx^{ac}: ἐπί x^{3pc}

Other readings, again, look unmistakably like conjectural emendations of corrupt readings in **Fx**^{ac}; see for instance:

386a4 ποιησομένοις] ποιησομένοις οἷς **Fx**: οἴει x^3 vel x^5 in margine

Finally, there are a number of readings which do not occur in other MSS; whether these readings are the result of conjecture or of comparison with another MS now lost, it is impossible to decide; there are also instances of agreement with the indirect tradition. See for instance:

330b7 ἤ] ὧν x^{3im}
389e2 ἡδονῶν] ἡδονῶν ἀπέχεσθαι x^{5im}
519a5 ἐργαζόμενον] ἄλλως ἐργάσεται x^{3im} (et ὥστε del.)
590e1 βούλεται habent x$^{3(u.v.)pc}$ **Iambl. Stob.**: βουλεύεται **AD** et revera **F**

Some interesting readings added by later hands in **x** will be discussed in the chapter on the secondary manuscripts; see pp. 237-239.

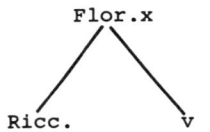

```
         Flor.x
         /    \
        /      \
     Ricc.      v
```

Two MSS, **Ricc.** and **v**, derive from **x**; I will quote a number of places where **Ricc.** and **v** share a distinctive reading of **x** (or **x**^{pc}):

330b7 ἤ] ὧν (x^{3pc})
387c1 ἐνέρους] κερβέρους (x$^{3(u.v.)pc}$)
389a1 ἐάν] ἄν
391e4 ἑαυτῷ] αὐτῷ
515e4 σαφέστερα] σαφέστερον
519c1 ἐπιτροπεῦσαι] ἐπιτροπεύσειν
615b5 κακουχίας] κακουργίας (x^{5sl})
616b3 τῇ ὀγδόῃ] τὴν ὀγδόην
618a3 γὰρ om.

That **Ricc.** and **v** go back to **x** independently, appears from the fact that they have no conjunctive errors, while they both have separative errors against each other (and against **x**).

First, I will discuss **v**. **v** follows **x** very closely; **x** has no separative errors against **v**, whereas **v** has many errors with separative value against **x** (and **Ricc.**); some instances:

328b9 γὰρ om.
329b5 γήρως] γήνως
331d6 ὁ] ὦ
388c7 φίλτατον] φιλτάτων
392e1 μέρος] μένος

515e4   τῶν] τῷ
520a2   καὶ om.
616c4   'Ανάγκης] ἀνάγκη
620a2   καὶ om.

In some cases an error in **v** is due to a misreading of the script of **x**, e.g. 391e2 κακά: the final —ά can be read as an —ώ in **x**: **v** has κακώ.

In other places **v** misinterprets a correction in **x**; some instances:

328b7   Χαρμαντίδην] χαρμίδην x^{pc} (punctis additis infra αντ a nescio qua manu): χαρμαντίδην (sic, punctis additis a prima manu) **v**
519a5   ἐργαζόμενον habet **x**: ἄλλως ἐργάσεται x^{3im} (et ὥστε del.): ἄλλως ἐργάσεται v^{it}; in this case the scribe of **v** did not recognize ἄλλως as a formula to introduce a variant reading, but regarded it as a part of the variant reading.
616b2   τοῖς] τοὺς **x**: add. οἷς x^{3sl} (supra τ): οἵ τοὺς **v**
619b9-c1 ἀλλ' αὐτὸν] ἀλλὰ τοῦτον **x**: αὐτὸν x^{3im}, signo ∶ addito in textu inter ο et υ: ἀλλὰ τοαὐτὸν (sic) **v**

Schanz, *Platocodex* 80, gives some more instances; he accordingly calls the scribe of **v** "ganz stupide", a judgement he had already passed in *Untersuchungen* 668.

v was copied from **x** when **x** had already been corrected by all the later hands which I have specified above (see pp. 192 f.); some instances:

332c5   post ὦ prius add. σώκρατες x^{2im}: ὦ σώκρατες v^{it}
519a5   ἐργαζόμενον] ἄλλως ἐργάσεται $x^{3im}v^{it}$
526a8   ἦν om. **Fx**: add. x^{4im}: habet v^{it}
559d9   δεινοῖς] πανουργοῖς $x^{5sl}v^{it}$

The first hand sometimes corrects his own errors, e.g. 398b8 ὡς λεκτέον om.: add. in margine v^1. Sometimes the first hand copies variant readings found in the margin of **x**, e.g. 349b5 εὐήθης] εὖ ποιεῖν **F**: εὖ ποιεῖς $F^{2pc}xv$: εὐήθης $x^{3im}v^{1im}$. The same goes for some glosses in **x**, e.g. 331a7 ἀτάλλοισα] τρέφουσα $F^{1sl}x^{1sl}v^{1sl}$; as the ink of this word in **v** is a little bit brighter than the ink of the text, it is possible that the word is written in red ink (as is the case in **x**), but I have not seen **v** *in situ*.

I have not noted any corrections by later hands; in some places there are some marginal notes by a later hand, e.g. 345c2 τὸν ὡς ἀληθῶς ποιμένα: ποιμένα ἀληθῶς v^{2im}; 416e5 χρυσίον θεῖον v^{2im}.

v shows no traces of contamination and may very well be a direct transcript of **x**; **v** has no extant derivatives.

Ricc., too, derives from **x**, because it shares most of the readings of **Fx**, and readings added by later hands in **F** and **x**. **Ricc.** never takes over the reading of Fx^{ac} when this reading is illegible in x^{pc}.

Ricc. has some separative errors against **x** (and **v**):

329d4   γὰρ om.
330b5   αὐτὴν ἐποίησε] ἐποίησεν αὐτὴν
330b8   μοι om.
330c5   περὶ τὰ χρήματα om. (περὶ om. etiam **Fx**)
332c11 ἀποδιδοῦσα] ἀποδιδοῦσα τέχνη
387d5   δὲ om.
390b6   τῶν om.
392c8   ἐσκέψεται] ἐσκέφεσται
519e1   τοῦτο] τούτω
620a7   μεταβάλλοντα] μεταβαλόντα

Ricc. shares readings with all four later hands in **x**; see for instance:

335a6   post ἡμᾶς add. ἄλλο x^{2im}: ἡμᾶς ἄλλο **Ricc.**^{it}
337c4   ἐρωτηθέντι] ἐρωτωμένω x^{3im}**Ricc.**^{it}
526d3   ἐκτάσεις] ἐκτὸς **FxRicc.**: ἐκτάσεις x^{4im}: ἄλλως ἐκτάσεις **Ricc.**^{1im}
389e2   post ἡδονῶν add. ἀπέχεσθαι x^{5im}: ἡδονῶν ἀπέχεσθαι **Ricc.**^{it}

However, **Ricc.** does not share all the errors of (**F**)**x**; in some cases the correction is very easy and may be due to conjectural emendation; see for instance:

329e3   σε ῥαδίως habet **Ricc.**: σε ῥαδίως σε **Fxv**
332a10 μέν τι habet **Ricc.**: μέντοι **Fxv**
387b5   μᾶλλον habet **Ricc.**: μᾶλον **xv**
616b2   ἀναστάντας habet **Ricc.**: ἀναστάντες **xv**
617e1   ὑμᾶς habet **Ricc.**: ἡμᾶς **xv**

In other cases a correct reading in **Ricc.** against **x** must be due to contamination; see for instance:

329e5   παραμύθιά φασιν habet **Ricc.**: φασι παραμύθια **Fxv**
330a2   ὧν habet **Ricc.**: om. **Fxv**
330d2   οἴει habet **Ricc.**: εἴη **Fxv**

Finally, in a number of places **Ricc.** agrees with other branches of the tradition in readings where the agreement can hardly be coincidental; some instances:

329e1   σου] σε **Ricc.** A^{3sl}(an A^2 ?)**MγSc.WDurh.**
330a2   ἐγένετο] γένοιτο **Ricc.WDurh.**
331c2   αὐτὸ om. **Ricc.Sc.WDurh.**

Therefore I conclude that **Ricc.** derives from an apographon of **x** which was corrected from another source; although the evidence is rather slight, I would guess that this source belongs to the **WDurh.**-group.

It is remarkable that the cases of agreement between **Ricc.** and other branches of the tradition in specific readings occur (in the sample passages) only in book I. The situation is comparable with regard to the distribution of correct readings in **Ricc.** against (**F**)**x**: in book I there are some fifteen cases, in book III only two (both very slight errors in **x**: 387b5 μᾶλλον] μᾶλον **x** and 389b2 πολλοῦ] πολοῦ **x**), in book VII none and in book X five (all of them very slight: 616b2 ἀναστάντας] ἀναστάντες **x**; 616e6 ὀγδόου] ὀγδώου **x**; 616e6 πέμπτον] πέμπον **x**; 617c2 στέμματα] στέματα **x**; 617e1 ὑμᾶς] ἡμᾶς **x**). This suggests that the corrector of an ancestor of **Ricc.** became less active as the work proceeded, a phenomenon which we encounter frequently.

The alternative explanation for the correct readings in **Ricc.** against **x** and **F**, viz. that **Ricc.** is not dependent on **x**, is untenable for the following reasons:

    1. If **Ricc.** is regarded as a gemellus of **F**, the conjunctive errors of **Ricc.x**, which separate **xRicc.** from **F**, cannot be accounted for.
    2. **Ricc.** has readings in the text which have been added in **F** by F^{2-6}, and in **x** by x^{2-5}; if **Ricc.** were independent of **Fx**, we should have to assume that the exemplar of **Ricc.** received these readings, added in **F** and **x** by nine different scribes, from another source; this would be absurd.

About the frequent agreement between **Ricc.** and the group **Neap.αt** (esp. **α**), I have already spoken at length in the chapter on the **A**-family (see above, pp. 133-135).

In isolated places **Ricc.** has variant readings, all of them added by the first hand. In some cases these variant readings go back to **x**, e.g.:

519a5 ἐργαζόμενον] ἄλλως ἐργάσεται x^{3im}**Ricc.**^{1im}
526d3 ἐκτάσεις] ἐκτὸς **FxRicc.**: ἐκτάσεις x^{4im}**Ricc.**^{1im}

Some other readings appear to go back to other MSS:

328c6 θαμίζεις] συχνάζεις $A^Σγ^Σa^Σ$**Ricc.**^{1im}
390c7 δι' ἕτερα] ἢ ἕτερα **FxRicc.**: δι' ἕτερα **Ricc.**^{1im}**AD**
518a1 μεμνῆτ'] μέμνοιτ' **Ricc.**$^{1im}Θ^{2sl}$**VMatr.**
617c7 χρόνον habet **Ricc.**: ω supra ον **Ricc.**^{1}: χρόνῳ **Mγa**

In other places, a variant reading is found only in **Ricc.**, and may result from conjecture or contamination with a MS now lost; see for instance:

332e4 βλάπτειν] βλάστειν **Ricc.**^{1im}
619b5 μήτε prius] μήτε οὖν **Ricc.**^{1sl}

In none of these cases can it be decided whether the readings come from the exemplar of **Ricc.**, or have been introduced by the scribe of **Ricc.** himself.

In some places **Ricc.** has been corrected, probably by the first hand (but I have not seen **Ricc.** *in situ*). In one case a correction is traceable to another group of MSS: 518a7 ἀηθείας] ἀληθείας **Ricc.**^{1pc} (λ addito supra lineam)Sc. D^(ac)Par.^(ac)Vat. (the λ in **Ricc.** is written in a somewhat lighter ink, but even so I believe that it should be attributed to the first hand, possibly after the text had been copied).

```
    Ricc.
      |
      |
     Ox.
```

Ricc. is the source of **Ox.**; I will quote some places where **Ox.** shares a characteristic reading of **Ricc.**:

329d4	γάρ om.
331a10	θαυμαστῶς] θαυμαστὸς
332c5	ἦν δ' ἐγὼ post ἤρετο
387d5	δὲ om.
390b6	τῶν om.
519e1	τοῦτο] τούτῳ
619b5	μήτε prius] μήτε οὖν **Ricc.**^(1sl)**Ox.**^(it)

Ox. follows **Ricc.** everywhere and adds a number of errors of its own; some instances:

328e4	ἡδέως] ἰδέως
331e4	λέγειν] λέγεις
391c8	τάδε] τὰ
391d1	ἐπὶ] ἐπεὶ
515c1	δή] δὲ
518a3	σκότους] σκότως
617c5	τὴν] τῶν
619b2	ὁ] οὐ

In one instance, an omission in **Ox.** corresponds exactly to one line in **Ricc.**: 514c1-515a1 ἀνδριάντας—καὶ alterum om. **Ox.**; the words have been added in the margin by what I believe to be the first hand (see below); this suggests that **Ox.** is a direct transcript of **Ricc.**

Many errors have been corrected by the first hand, presumably during the copying of the text.

There are also many corrections and additions written in a lighter ink and with what appears to be a thinner pen; nevertheless, I believe that these readings have been written by the first hand, after the text had been copied (but I have not seen **Ox.** *in situ*).

Ox. does not show traces of contamination, which accords with the hypothesis that **Ox.** is a direct transcript of **Ricc.**

Ox.
|
Bodl.

Ox. is the source of the fragment from *R.* in **Bodl.**, 328d7-330a6. I will quote the places where **Bodl.** takes over a distinctive reading from **Ox.**:

328e4 ἡδέως] ἰδέως
329e8 λοιδορουμένῳ] λοιδωρουμένῳ

Bodl. has hardly any errors of its own:

328e3 ποία] ποῖα
329a5 ἐν] ἐν ἐν

Bodl. shows no traces of contamination and may well be a direct transcript of **Ox.**, especially because **Ox.** was already in Oxford in 1537 at the latest, while **Bodl.** dates from the sixteenth century (see p. 44).

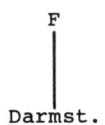

F
|
Darmst.

In the chapter on the **A**-family I have already noted that some of the fragments in **Darmst.** go back to **T**, while others belong to the **F** tradition (see pp. 168 f.).

Two longer fragments (359d1-e6, 393c5-394d6) exhibit many cases of agreement with the **F**-family; some instances:

359d4 ἔνεμεν] ἐκεῖνος ἔνεμεν
359d8 οὐδέν] ἔχειν οὐδέν (et **D**)
359e2 γενομένου] γιγνομένου
393e2 αὐτούς] αὐτοὺς δέ (**F³**)
394a3 τε] γε
394a4 εἴ τι] εἴτε
394b5 καταλείπῃ] καταλίπῃ

But **Darmst.** does not follow **F** on all occasions: at 359e2 **F** has εἰωθότως (with **D**), while **Darmst.** has the correct reading εἰωθότος with the **A**-family; at 394a3 **F** has τά, but **Darmst.** reads τῷ *recte*. Even so, we may safely conclude that **Darmst.** ultimately goes back to **F**: the agreement with **F³** at 393e2 excludes the possibility that **Darmst.** goes back to an ancestor or a gemellus of **F**. I have not found any conjunctive errors of **Darmst.** with (the derivatives of) **x**; in some places **x** has separative errors against **Darmst.**, but the two cases I have noted both concern readings added in **x** by a later hand:

393e1   ἑλόντας] ἑλεῖν x^pc (nescio quae manus)
393e8   μετὰ οὗ] μετ' αὐτοῦ x^pc (nescio quae manus)

Therefore it is not altogether impossible that **Darmst.** derives from x^ac.

There are also some cases of agreement with **F** in the other fragments; see for instance:

372b5   κατακλινέντες] κατακλινάντες
605d2   ἢ om.

Other fragments do not exhibit distinctive readings and cannot be classified within a group of MSS.

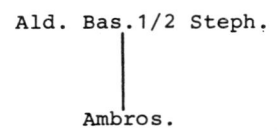

```
        Ald. Bas.1/2 Steph.
                |
                |
             Ambros.
```

There is one MS which has not yet been discussed, because it does not belong to the **A**-, **D**- or **F**-family: it is **Ambros.**, which contains only one fragment from *R.*, 459d4-460b5. This MS does not derive from another MS, but depends on one of the sixteenth-century editions. This is proved by the following readings:

459d5   γίγνεσθαι] γενέσθαι **Ambros. Ald.** etc.
459e5   νομοθετητέαι] νομοθετητέαι ἔσονται **Ambros. N^sl Ald.** etc.

There is no saying from which of the four editions **Ambros.** derives, because none of these editions (Aldine, first and second Basle edition, Stephanus) has separative errors against **Ambros.** in this fragment.

Ambros. has some errors of its own, e.g.:

460a8   τινες om.
460a9   τύχην] τὴν τύχην

Ambros. usually omits assentory formulae and the like, e.g. 459e4 Ὀρθότατα, ἔφη om.; 460a7 Ὀρθῶς, ἔφη om.; this practice is also observed in other excerpt MSS.

Ambros. shows no traces of contamination, has not been corrected by later hands, and has no extant derivatives.

CHAPTER FOUR

THE SECONDARY MANUSCRIPTS

In the chapter on the affiliation of MSS I have often remarked that a particular secondary MS contains readings which in some respect call for attention. In this chapter I will discuss some of these MSS in more detail. The discussion falls into three sections:
I. In the first section, I will discuss the possibility of the presence in secondary MSS of readings derived from a primary source now lost. Generally speaking, there are three ways of testing whether a secondary MS contains ancient material: 1. comparison with the indirect tradition; 2. comparison with the papyri; 3. comparison with younger primary MSS (which may yield indications of contamination from a lost member of another branch of the tradition, the oldest extant representative of which is younger than the secondary MS in question). I do not believe that the presence of excellent readings in a secondary MS necessarily points to contamination with a lost primary source: as I will show, many Byzantine scholars were capable of making very intelligent conjectures.

Before I go on to discuss these three ways of testing the evidence, I wish to draw attention to the general methodological consideration that the statement that a particular secondary MS has been interpolated from a lost primary source is not falsifiable: even if we are unable to adduce positive evidence in favour of the thesis that a particular secondary MS has readings which already existed in antiquity, we cannot exclude this possibility with absolute certainty. Thus because negative proof can never be given, I will concentrate in my discussion upon those readings which do furnish positive indications of the contamination of secondary MSS with an ancient source.

With regard to the comparison of secondary MSS with the papyri I can be brief: I have noted only one case of agreement between a secondary MS and a papyrus: 610d3 τοῦτο habent β^{pc} Π^{11}: τούτου **ADF**.

As regards the contamination of older secondary MSS with lost members of another branch of the tradition, I can say in advance that this applies only to **TMγ**, whose common source was contaminated with a MS belonging to the **F** tradition (a number of readings in **T** are also found in the **D** tradition); to **Mγ**, whose exemplar, too, was interpolated from a MS of the **F** tradition; and maybe to **Sc.**, which has a very few readings in common with **F**. The exemplar of **TMγ** must be older than *ca.* 950, because **T** was written about that time; the common source of **Mγ** must belong to the twelfth century at the latest, because **γ** was written in that century; **Sc.** is attributed to the fifteenth century by De Andrés, but I believe that it is much older, and may belong to the thirteenth century (cf. p. 29); **F** is assigned to the fourteenth century by Hunger (but, except in the case of **T**, none of these datings is very firm).

Thus the only test we can apply to the majority of MSS is the comparison with the indirect tradition; but I stress that this test must be applied with extreme caution, for the following reasons:

1. It should be realized that in a sense it is misleading to speak of *the* indirect tradition. This term suggests that the indirect tradition can be regarded as one coherent entity, which of course is not true. I have collected references, quotations etc. in more than 200 Greek, Latin, Arabic and Byzantine authors, over a period from the fourth century B. C. to the fifteenth century A. D. Each author has his own textual tradition; even within the works of one single author we can often determine that the author in question used different sources at different stages in his work (see, e.g., 377e1, where Eusebius in one place has οὐσίαν with **DF**, while in another place he omits the word with **A**). It is impossible to tell with any degree of reliability how many copies of the *Republic* circulated in the ancient world, but their number must have been considerable, as may be guessed from the number of authors who quote from the *Republic*, and from the divergencies in their texts. Thus whenever a particular secondary MS agrees remarkably often with one particular ancient author, it is all the more probable that the MS in question was interpolated from an ancient source, whether (a congener of) the Plato MS used by this author, or the text of this author himself.

2. The indirect tradition does not cover all of the *Republic*, which implies that in places where the indirect tradition is absent, we are simply unable to apply the test of comparison.

3. Agreement in very plausible or manifestly correct readings does not tell us very much: from my discussion it will appear that many of the scribes were gifted philologists, who must have been capable of conjecturing numerous good readings.

4. Agreement in trivial error, on the other hand, also fails to produce positive evidence for contamination from an ancient source; if, e.g., at 410a3 both **K** and Stobaeus add τε before καὶ, it would be absurd to conclude automatically that the addition of τε in **K** must be due to contamination from an ancient source related to Stobaeus' copy of Plato.

5. In some cases, the tradition of an author who quotes Plato has been interpolated from the direct tradition; this is the case, e.g., with the Parisinus A of Stobaeus.

6. It may occasionally have happened that a Plato MS was contaminated from the indirect tradition. In the time of Stephanus, at any rate, the habit of comparing the indirect tradition was regularly practised (see below, p. 251): Stephanus often refers to such authors as Galen and Justin Martyr. Already in the scholia on Plato traces of Proclus' influence can be found.

For these reasons I believe that only in those cases where a secondary MS agrees with the indirect tradition in demonstrably wrong readings or in such readings as can hardly be explained as conjectural emendations or simple errors, can we conclude with a high degree of certainty that the Platonic MS in question has been interpolated from a source which contained ancient material, whether the indirect tradition itself or a lost primary MS.

In order to find cases of agreement between the indirect tradition and the secondary MSS, I have compared my apparatus of the indirect tradition with Schneider's report of the MSS. Therefore I may have missed some cases of agreement, either through negligence on my part, or through insufficient report of the MSS in Schneider's edition. As a rule, I have checked Schneider's report on microfilm.

II. In the second section, I will mention those places where a particular secondary MS is the principal or sole MS authority for an authentic or highly probable reading; when necessary, I will add a brief discussion of these readings.

III. In the third section, I will discuss a selection of readings found in a particular MS; I will try to distinguish between the different types of variant readings, such as additions, omissions, grammatical corrections etc.; further, I will try to explain why a certain reading was introduced, and I will discuss its merits.

The order in which the secondary MSS are discussed is determined by their importance; but, although **Sc.** should be assigned the second place, **Vind.Bon.Sc.** and **Vind.Bon.** precede **Sc.**, because of the stemmatic relationship of these MSS.

In quoting readings found in the indirect tradition, my report is as full as possible, that is, I also quote authors who are known to rely on other extant authors for their quotations from the *Republic*, as is the case with, e.g., Theodoretus, who, in some places at least, draws on Clement or Eusebius for his Platonic quotations; see E. des Places, *Le Platon de Théodoret*, REG 68 (1955), 171 ff.; P. Canivet, *Histoire d'une entreprise apologétique au V*^{e} *siècle* (Paris 1958), 257 ff.

1. β

1. In the following places I have noted agreement between β and the indirect tradition (I will list readings of β and β^{pc} together, because, as I have proved in the chapter on the **D**-family (see p. 185), many corrections in β come from the exemplar. Therefore readings in the original text of β may also represent corrections or variant readings in the

exemplar. Of course, it is possible that the corrector of β consulted other MSS besides β's exemplar):

331a3	τοι om. βK Stob.
343a3	ἀποκρίνεσθαι] ἀποκρίνασθαι β^pc Alexandri Aldina (ἀποκρίνεσθαι Alexandri AI)
351b9	αὐτῇ] αὐτὴν βK Stob.
353c8	γε om. βK Stob.
354a11	Βενδιδίοις] βενδιδείοις β Hsch.
361b8	ἐθέλοντα] θέλοντα βK: θέλει Aeschylus
362a1	ἐκκαυθήσεται] ἐκκοπήσεται β^im K Clem. Eus. Thdt. (ἐκκοφθήσεται Mγ)
362a1	τώφθαλμώ] τὼ ὀφθαλμὼ βK Clem. Eus. Thdt.
375d7	ἐννενοήκαμεν] ἐνενοήσαμεν β^pc Stob.
413c6	τοῦτο] τοῦ β^pc Stob.
436d8	ἀποδεχοίμεθα habent β^pc Gal.: ἀποδεχώμεθα ADF
436e5	δεξιὰν—ἀριστερὰν] δεξιὰ—ἀριστερὰ β^pc Gal.
436e6	ἔστιν om. β^pc Gal.
440c7	ζεῖ τε habent β^pc Gal., hunc locum interpretatus: ζητεῖ τε ADF: ζητεῖται Galeni H: ζητεῖν τε Galeni L, hunc locum afferentis
441d8	πῃ] πω β^pc Stob.
442b2	προσῆκον] προσῆκεν β^pc Stob.
443a1	τοῦτον αὐτὸ] τοῦτο αὐτὸν β^pc Stob.
445e1	ἐγγενόμενοι] ἐγγενόμενος β^pc Stob. (errat Burnet)
454d1	τὸ—τεῖνον τὰ habent β^pc Gal.: τὰ—τείνοντα ADF
462e6	αὐτή] αὕτη β^pc Stob.
486a8	῞Ηι] ᾧ β^pc Antonini T: ἡ Antonini A
524a7	αὕτη] αὐτὴ β Iambl.
600a5	τινας ἄλλας] τινες ἄλλαι β Aristid.
601b3	αὐτῶν] ἑαυτῶν β Eus.
604c7	αἱρεῖ habent β^pc Plu. Stob. (uno loco): ἐρεῖ Stob. (altero loco): ἔρρει DF
604d2	ἰατρικῇ habent β^pc Plu. Stob. (bis): ἰατρικὴν ADF
617b1	τὸν om. β^pc Theon Sm. Simp.

Further, at 610d3 β^pc has τοῦτο with Π[11], against τούτω(ι) ADF.

In studying the cases of agreement between β and the indirect tradition, we must bear in mind that the corrector of β (or rather of the exemplar of β) was a gifted scholar, who made countless conjectures, many of which were extremely intelligent; see below, pp. 206-214. Therefore it is sometimes possible that a striking case of agreement with the indirect tradition in a true reading may not be due to contamination, but to conjecture.

When we look at the list of cases of agreement between β and the indirect tradition, it strikes us immediately that two authors are prominent: Galen and Stobaeus.

Most cases of agreement with Galen occur between 436d and 440c, and three of them within seven lines of text (but Galen has only a few quotations from other parts of the *Republic*). This is additional proof that these readings came into β through contamination, even if, taken by themselves, some of them might be explained as resulting from conjectural emendation. Yet we cannot conclude with certainty that β drew upon a lost primary MS: all the cases of agreement with Galen are found in his *De Placitis Hippocratis et Platonis*; accordingly, it is not to be excluded that β took these readings from Galen himself, not from a lost primary Plato MS. If this should be true, the readings in β have no primary value.

The cases of agreement with Stobaeus are scattered throughout the *Republic*, but there are some readings which occur closely together, e.g. the four readings at 441d8, 442b2, 443a1 and 445e1, and the two excellent readings at 604c7 and 604d2 (which are also in Plutarch). Again, it is impossible to decide whether these readings are borrowed from the direct or the indirect tradition, but in dealing with Stobaeus we are perhaps entitled to use an *argumentum e silentio*: if β had had a copy of Stobaeus at his disposal, we would certainly expect to find many more cases of agreement, as Stobaeus has many excerpts from *R.*, taken from all parts of the work. The passages in which cases of agreement between β and Stobaeus are found are quoted in different places in Stobaeus (but they are all in books III and IV, as is the case with most of the quotations from *R.*); this is an additional indication that the corrector of β did not consult a copy of Stobaeus.

Many other cases of agreement with other authors are rather trivial and do not tell us very much; this goes for the readings at 331a3, 343a3, 353c8, 354a11, 362a1 (τὼ ὀφθαλμώ), 462e6, 524a7, 600a5 and 601b3. As regards the case of 361b8 it is possible that the scribe who introduced this reading consulted a MS of Aeschylus, although I regard the agreement as coincidental.

The reading ἐκκοπήσεται at 362a1, also found in Clement, Eusebius and Theodoretus, is very remarkable indeed, but a similar reading ἐκκοφθήσεται is found in **Mγ** (see the discussion of it there, p. 228); therefore it is possible that β took over and adapted the reading ἐκκοφθήσεται from **Mγ**, replacing —φθ— by the regular —π—. But β may also have borrowed the reading from an ancient source, whether direct or indirect.

At 486a8 β^pc has ὦ for ˉΗι with cod. **T** of Antoninus; yet the hypothesis that this reading came into β through contamination is weakened by the observation that Antoninus has διάνοια μεγαλοπρέπης, while β has διανοίας μεγαλοπρέπεια.

Finally, the deletion of τὸν at 617b1, which makes β agree with Theon Smyrnaeus and Simplicius, is a splendid correction, with which the corrector of β can certainly be credited.

I conclude that there are some indications that β drew upon an ancient source, but we can only guess at the character of this source (direct or indirect), while it is beyond doubt that β contains many conjectures (see below, pp. 206-214).

2. In the following places β is the principal or sole MS to preserve a true reading:

337a7	ἀποκρινοῖο β^{pc}: ἀποκρίνοιο **AF**: ἀποκρίναιο **D**
337b4	ἀποκρινοῖτο β^{pc}: ἀποκρίνοιτο **ADF**
342a4	ἐκποριούσης β^{pc}: ἐκποριζούσης **ADF**
370a6	ῥᾶον β^{pc}: ῥά(ι)διον **ADF**
370e12	ἴη β^{pc}: εἴη **ADF**
373a1	αὕτη β^{pc} (editors wrongly attribute this reading to **b**): αὐτὴ **ADF**
414e3	δεῖ β^{pc}: δὴ **ADF** (Burnet's apparatus is wrong: δεῖ is written by **F**^{5})
429c7	γεγονυίας β^{pc}: γεγονυῖαν **ADF** Stob.
431b6	οὗ β^{pc}: οὖν **ADF** Stob.
436d8	ἀποδεχοίμεθα β^{pc} Gal.: ἀποδεχώμεθα **ADF**
436e6	ἔστιν om. β^{pc} Gal. recte: habent **ADF** falso
440c7	ζεῖ τε β^{pc} Gal., hunc locum interpretatus: ζητεῖ τε **ADF**: ζητεῖται Galeni **H**: ζητεῖν τε Galeni **L**, hunc locum afferentis
442b6	φυλαττοίτην β^{pc}: φυλάττοι τὴν **ADF** Stob.
452e4	αὐτῶν β^{pc}: αὐτὸν **ADF** (αὐτῶν revera **F**^{2} vel **F**^{3} supra lineam)
454d1	τὸ—τεῖνον τὰ β^{pc} Gal.: τὰ—τείνοντα **ADF**
498c1	στρατειῶν β^{pc}: στρατιῶν **ADF**
501a5	διενέγκοιεν β^{pc}: διενεγκεῖν **ADF**: διενέγκαι ἂν **Eus.**
548d9	φιλονικίας β^{pc} (et saepius): φιλονεικίας **ADF**
559b4	μὴ add. β^{pc}: om. **ADF**
604c7	αἱρεῖ β^{pc} **Plu. Stob.** (uno loco): ἐρεῖ **A Stob.** (altero loco): ἔρρει **DF**
604d2	ἰατρικῇ β^{pc} **Plu. Stob.** (bis): ἰατρικὴν **ADF**
610d3	τοῦτο β^{pc} Π^{11}: τούτου **ADF**
611c3	διαθεατέον β^{pc} (θεατέον **Mγ**): διαθετέον **ADF**
617b1	τὸν om. β^{pc} **Theon Sm. Simp.** recte: habent **ADF** falso

In some cases (337a7, 337b4, 373a1, 442b6) the reading of β involves only the change of the accent and/or breathing; at 337a7, 337b4, 342a4, 436d8, 501a5, the corrections concern the ending of a verb; at 498c1 and 548d9 (*et alibi*) β gives the correct forms of words which are constantly corrupted in our MSS; the remaining readings are good or brilliant conjectures, but some of them may be due to contamination.

The addition of μὴ at 559b4 is, of course, not certain, but it makes good sense; Dr Slings tells me that he accepts Baiter's conjecture ᾗ τε παῦσαι ζῶντ' ἀδύνατον; Wilamowitz 385 f. suggests ᾗ τε παύσασθαι ζῶντος ἀδυνατεῖ.

3. β has an enormous number of corrections, many of which prove that the scribe who introduced these readings took much trouble to arrive at

the correct interpretation of the text he had before him. In the chapter on the **D**-family I have already noted (p. 186) that β borrowed some readings from **Sc.**, and others from **Mγ**; in section 1 (pp. 203-206) I have argued that in some places β may have been interpolated from an ancient source.

That many readings in β are conjectural, appears most clearly from those places in which β has tried to restore a corrupt text in its exemplar or to fill up a lacuna; see for instance:

346e4-5   ἀλλ'—παρασκευάζει om. **DPar.**β: ἀλλ' ἐκεῖνο σκοπεῖ ἐφ' ᾧ τέτακται β^{im}

375a5   Οἷον—αἴσθησιν om. **DPar.**β: ὀξύν που εἶναι δεῖ πρὸς τὸ αἰσθάνεσθαι β^{im}

410c10-d1   ἢ αὖ—καὶ αὖ] ἢ αὖ **DPar.**β: ἢ τοὐναντίον δυσκολίας τε καὶ ἀγριότητος ἢ αὖ β^{im}

479c8-d1   πρὸς—ὄντος om. **DPar.**β: οὔτε τοῦ ὄντος φανώτερα β^{im}

517e2-3   ἰδόντων; Οὐδ' ὁπωστιοῦν θαυμαστόν, ἔφη] ἰδόντων μηδ' ὁπωστιοῦν; θαυμαστὸν ἔφη **Par.**: ἰδόντων μηδ' ὁπωστιοῦν; οὐ θαυμαστὸν ἔφη β^{pc}

607a4   ὕμνους—παραδεκτέον] ὑκτέον **D**: ἐκτέον **Par.**: οὐχ ἐκτέον β^{pc}

The cases where a lacuna has been filled up suffice to show that the scribe who introduced these readings had a great ability to recognize a lacuna and to supply words which perfectly express the sense required.

In my discussion of the variant readings in β, I will distinguish between the several types of variant readings.

a. fillings of alleged lacunae

In quite a few places β adds words to fill up a supposed lacuna; some of these additions are quite interesting:

341d11 ἢ—εἶναι] οὗ προσδεῖται, ἢ ἐξαρκεῖ ἑκάστη αὐτὴ αὑτῇ, ὥστε ὅτι μάλιστα τελέαν εἶναι β^{im}: Schneider and Adam ad loc. hold that these words are absolutely necessary for the argumentation, but they both hesitate to accept the words in the text; that the text printed by Burnet cannot be correct, appears from the sequel: if Socrates had aimed at giving an explanation of the words d10-11 as they stand in Burnet's text, he would have had to explain "quid esset quam maxime perfecta ars, si forte hoc Thrasymachus non intellexisset, vel demonstrare, quicquid utile sit arti, ita utile esse, si perfectionem artis adiuvet: aliam utilitatem ei afferri non posse" (Schneider). The explanation Socrates gives at e2-8 has absolutely nothing to do with the question at d10-11. Reconstructing from e2-8, we would expect to read at d10-11 something like: "does every τέχνη have some advantage for which it needs something else, or is it able to realize its own advantage by itself?" Therefore I would suggest expanding the addition in β and reading (...) ἔστιν τι συμφέρον ἐφ' (or πρὸς) ὃ ἄλλου (του) προσδεῖται ἢ ἐξαρκεῖ ἑκάστη αὐτὴ αὑτῇ, ὥστε ὅτι μάλιστα τελέαν εἶναι: at e2-8,

Socrates does not speak about an advantage which is necessary, but about something which is necessary to realize this advantage. Of course, I do not claim that this addition is exactly what Plato wrote, but I feel fairly confident that he wrote something which gives the same general sense.

506a7 post ἱκανῶς add. πρὶν ἂν περὶ τἀγαθοῦ ὅ ἐστι γνῶ β^im. This addition must have been made in order to give a complement to πρότερον. Schneider ad loc. rightly observes that "ad πρότερον ex superioribus supplendum est πρὶν ἂν ὅπῃ ποτὲ ἀγαθά ἐστι γνῷ." He remarks that the addition in β "glossema ineptum est. Nam ipsam boni naturam Socrates et supra p. 505. A. satis perspectam hominibus negavit et infra D. E. explicare recusat."

529b5-6 ἐάν—τι] ἐάν τέ τις ἄνω κεχηνὼς ἢ κάτω συμμεμυκὼς τούτων τι μανθάνῃ· ἐὰν δ' ἄνω που κεχηνὼς ὁτιοῦν τῶν αἰσθητῶν β^im. This reading is accepted by Bekker and Stallbaum[2]. The scribe who added these words probably thought that it was impossible to study the movements of the heavenly bodies while looking downward (κάτω συμμεμυκώς), while for the student of τὸ ὄν it does not make any difference; only ἄνω κεχηνώς, then, is considered appropriate for astronomical studies. To my mind, the addition is quite superfluous.

544a4 ἔχειν καὶ] ἔχειν ὧν καὶ δεῖν ἐπιμνησθῆναί τε καὶ β^im: as Schneider ad loc. rightly notes, this addition appears to be a reminiscence of 445c7.

557c7 καὶ prius] φαίνοιτο γὰρ ἦ δ' ὅς τοιαύτη τις (Adimanto tribuens). καὶ β^im: the repetition of ἦν δ' ἐγώ in this position justifiably puzzled the scribe who made this addition. His addition is a bold attempt to avoid this repetition.

b. shorter additions

b.1. In many places β adds one or more words which serve to make the sentence run more smoothly; some instances:

327c14 ἀκουσομένων] ἀκουσομένων ἔφη (sc. Πολέμαρχος) β^pc.
347d3 εἶναι] εἶναι ἐν αὐτῇ (= ἐν πόλει ἀνδρῶν ἀγαθῶν) β^pc.
351a6 οὐδείς] οὐδεὶς γάρ β^pc: γάρ serves to isolate the parenthesis from the main sentence.
375d1 ἀδύνατον] ἀδύνατον εἶναι β^pc: εἶναι is probably introduced to make it clear that the gender of ἀδύνατον is neuter: "and thus it happens to be impossible that a good guardian will come into existence."
400d4 ἐλέγετο] ἐλέγετο ἀκολουθεῖ β^pc: ἀκολουθεῖ is repeated from 400c8.
407c7 Οὐκοῦν] οὐκοῦν ἦν δ' ἐγώ β^pc: a quite superfluous addition, introduced in order to mark the change of speaker.
409a1 δέ γε] δέ γε ἦν δ' ἐγώ β^pc: cf. 407c7.
426b8 τοιοῦτον] τοιοῦτόν τι β^pc: τι makes it clear that τοιοῦτον is used substantively; τι is regarded as necessary by J. J. Hartman 243.
469a6 ἂν ἐξηγῆται] ἐκεῖνος ἐξηγεῖται β^pc: ἐκεῖνος refers to τοῦ θεοῦ (a4).
530a3 Τῷ] τὸν τῷ β^pc: τὸν serves to indicate that ἀστρονομικὸν ὄντα is used substantively.
540d3 ἤ] ἢ ἤ β^pc: a quite unnecessary addition.
608c7 πάντα] τὸν πάντα β^pc: the addition of τὸν makes it impossible to misinterpret πάντα as a neuter plural.

b.2. Other small additions are intended to normalize the construction or to emend a passage which was supposed to be corrupt; some instances:

328e3 τραχεῖα] πότερον τραχεῖα βˢᵖᶜ: the scribe who added πότερον thought the omission of this word intolerable; in fact, it is not uncommon, cf. KG II 532, Anm. 11.

354b4 πρίν] πρὶν ἤ βᵖᶜ: KG II 445, Anm. 2, remark that πρὶν ἤ is very rare in Attic authors.

428b4 οὐχί] ἤ οὐχί βᵖᶜ: at the end of a sentence, οὐχί alone is not very frequent.

436a9 ἄλλο ἄλλῳ] ἄλλῳ ἄλλο καὶ βᵖᶜ: ἄλλο and ἄλλῳ are probably transposed in order to place ἄλλῳ immediately after τρισὶν οὖσιν while καὶ has been added to make μανθάνομεν κτέ dependent on εἰ.

439a2 ἔστι δὲ δήπου δίψος] καὶ ἔστι δήπου τὸ δῖψος δῖψός του βᵖᶜ: unfinished questions do not occur often in Plato (in *R*., see for instance 567e3, another vexed place), and the reading of β aims at completing Socrates' question (for a discussion of the various interpretations and conjectures proposed, see Adam ad loc., and his Appendix III to book IV (I 270 f.).

451b1 εὖ] οὐκ εὖ βᵖᶜ: the addition of οὐκ shows that the scribe who added οὐκ failed to appreciate Socrates' irony here; the same worthless conjecture was made by Cornarius.

452e1 καὶ alterum] καὶ οὐ βᵖᶜ: an intelligent solution for this difficult passage (cf. my discussion of this passage in the section on **Sc.**, pp. 220 f.).

457c6 ἴδω] ὡς ἴδω βᵖᶜ: in phrases like this, the adhortative subjunctive instead of a final clause introduced by ἵνα, ὡς or ὅπως, is quite normal; see KG I 219 f.; J. J. Hartman 251 suggests ἵν' ἴδω: C. G. Cobet, *Variae Lectiones* (Leiden 1873²), 53, conjectures Φέρε for Λέγε.

477a9 ἐπί] εἰ ἐπὶ βᵖᶜ: in the MSS (except **F⁴ᵖᶜ**: Burnet's apparatus is wrong) δὲ at a10 is omitted; the addition of εἰ is an alternative solution. Stallbaum follows βᵖᶜ in adding εἰ after Οὐκοῦν at a9, reading ἐπὶ τῷ μεταξὺ (without δὲ) at a10; Wilamowitz 381 conjecturally adds καὶ before the second ἐπί at a10 and deletes καὶ before ζητητέον in the same line.

492a6 τινὰς] μέν τινας βᵖᶜ: μέν is introduced to match δὲ at a7.

c. deletions and omissions

In some cases, one or more words are deleted in β; some instances:

360a8 τὸν del.: βασιλέα is often used without the article, but this is especially the case when the Persian King, or one of the Spartan kings, is meant; see KG I 602-604.

410d2 ἦν δ' ἐγώ del.: as Schneider ad loc. notes: "nec facile alibi ἦν δ' ἐγώ aut ἦ δ' ὅς in fine orationis inveniuntur, nisi ubi sententia brevior et verbis interpellationem respuentibus expressa est." Burnet follows Schneider's suggestion "nostro loco suspicari licet Socratem aliquid additurum fuisse" and prints a horizontal stroke to indicate this.

412a9 τοῦ del.: the combination ὁ τοιοῦτός τις seems to be unparalleled, see Adam ad loc.; yet the explanation of Jowett-Campbell ad loc. sounds attractive: "τοῦ τοιούτου refers to the class which is definite, τινὸς to the individual who is undefined". But the omission of the article may be correct.

421a8 μὲν prius del.: the corrector probably took offence at the double occurrence of μέν; besides, the first μέν is not answered by a corresponding δέ. H. van Herwerden, Mnem. II 11 (1883), 344, proposes reading ᾗ μὲν οὖν ἡμεῖς <λέγο>μεν φύλακας κτέ; Richards 1893, 252, wishes to delete the first μὲν with β^pc; Vollgraff 137 suggests μέλλομεν for the second μὲν, while reading ᾗ for εἰ with Van Herwerden (see above).

459b11 εἶναι om.: the text as it stands is a contamination of δεῖ ἄκρων τῶν ἀρχόντων and δεῖ τοὺς ἄρχοντας ἄκρους εἶναι; cf. Schneider ad loc., and KG II 577. There seems to be no reason to doubt the phrase.

In the Myth of Er, the corrector of β seems to have been scandalized by the notion that human souls can be reincarnated as animals: the passages 618a3-4 ζῴων—ἅπαντας and 619e6-620d5 Ταύτην—μείγνυσθαι have been erased completely!

d. other variant readings

d.1. In some cases a variant reading concerns the spelling of a (rare) word; see for instance:

362a2   ἀνασχινδυλευθήσεται] ἀνασχιλινδευθήσεται β^pc
495e1   ἀποτεθρυμμένοι] ἀποτεθραυσμένοι β^pc

d.2. In other cases, β gives an alternative form for the declension or conjugation of a word; some instances:

386b5   ἀδεῇ] ἀδεᾶ β^pc
460b2   ἀφθονεστέρα] ἀφθονωτέρα β^pc
466a4   εἷμεν] εἴημεν β^pc
582a1   εἰδεῖμεν] εἰδοῖμεν β^pc

d.3. Sometimes the form of a word is changed in order to facilitate or normalize the syntactical structure:

387b4 ἀκουστέον] ἀκουστέα β^pc: the corrector interpreted ταῦτα κτέ at b1 ff. as nominatives.

403b1 et b3 προσοιστέον (bis)] προσοιστέα (bis) β^pc: thus προσοιστέα corresponds in case and gender with ἡδονή.

440a2 ὑμῖν] ὑμεῖς β^pc: corresponds with ὦ κακοδαίμονες, and is the subject of ἐμπλησθῆτε.

442b2 γένει] γενῶν β^pc: taken with ὧν.

445e1 ἐγγενόμενοι] ἐγγενόμενος β^pc (et Stobaeus): introduced because the verb κινήσειεν is also in the singular (congruent with εἷς). Indeed, when two subjects are linked by οὔτε—οὔτε, the predicate usually accords with the nearest subject (see KG I 81), so that one would expect to find ἐγγενόμενος κινήσειεν (the reading of β^pc and Stobaeus); yet ἐγγενόμενοι κινήσειαν would be equally possible, but it is perhaps safest to accept the anomaly as it stands, especially because it is not easy to explain how ἐγγενόμενος should have been corrupted into ἐγγενόμενοι, immediately after εἷς; in favour of κινήσειαν for κινήσειεν it could perhaps be argued that —αν was changed into —εν in order to avoid the cacophonous (but not uncommon) repetition —αν ἄν. ἐγγενόμενος is accepted by many editors, e.g. Bekker, Schneider, Jowett-Campbell, Adam.

472d5 οἷον] οἷος βᵖᶜ: congruent in gender with ὁ—ἄνθρωπος.

506a6 μηδένα] μηδ' ἂν ἕνα βᵖᶜ: this leads to the dubious combination future + ἄν; see KG I 209.

508b12 φάναι] φάθι βᵖᶜ: of course we expect to find an imperative, but infinitive for imperative is not uncommon, especially with φάναι; cf. Adam ad 473a8, KG II 21.

508d6 ἔχειν] ἔχον βᵖᶜ: obviously, the scribe was not content with the conclusion that the soul appears to have intelligence: he wants the soul to prove it !

514a1 τοιούτῳ] τοιῶδε βᵖᶜ: usually, οὗτος and its compounds are used to point backwards, ὅδε and its compounds to point forwards. The failure to recognize that this is by no means always so (see KG I 646), has led the corrector of β to the harmless but unnecessary conjecture τοιῶδε.

519a3 ὡς] ἅτε βᵖᶜ: ὡς usually involves a subjective element, which is absent when ἅτε is used. As at 508d6, the corrector of β does not admit any doubt !

536c3 ἀγανακτήσας] ἀγανακτῆσαι βᵖᶜ: this simplification has undoubtedly been introduced because of καὶ at c4: ἀγανακτῆσαι is linked with εἰπεῖν at c5.

537a11 ἐγκριτέον] ἐγκριτέος βᵖᶜ: congruent with <οὗτος> ὃς-φαίνηται.

545d3 ἀδύνατον] ἀδύνατος βᵖᶜ: congruent with πολιτεία.

573e3 μὲν τὰς] τὰς μὲν βᵖᶜ: symmetrical with τοὺς δ' at e5.

586e1 ἑπομένων] ἑπομένας βᵖᶜ: congruent with τὰς ἡδονὰς (d6-7).

599b1 ἔχοντα] ὅν βᵖᶜ: ἔχοντα has caused some problems (see Schneider and Adam ad loc.), but Adam is no doubt right in accepting Schleiermacher's translation: "als das beste was er habe".

612c8 δυνατὸν] δυνατὰ βᵖᶜ: the scribe probably took ταῦτα as a nominative. Cf. the similar corrections at 387b4 and 403b1,3.

614c2 χάσματα] χάσματε βᵖᶜ: the combination of dual and plural, especially after δύο, is quite normal Attic idiom (see Adam ad loc.; KG I 70), but was intolerable to the corrector of β.

d.4. In many places a variant reading in β seriously affects the interpretation of a passage:

333e6 λαθεῖν] μὴ παθεῖν βᵖᶜ: the MSS have λαθεῖν—ἐμποιῆσαι; ἐμποιῆσαι was changed into ἐμποιήσας by Schneider (Apelt 340 f., Vretska 76 f., and Tucker ad loc. propose reading λαθὼν—ἐμποιῆσαι). μὴ παθεῖν is an attempt to make the sentence run regularly, but λαθεῖν cannot be dispensed with, as the notion of acting unnoticed becomes prominent at 334a1 ff.; moreover, μὴ παθεῖν is tautological after φυλάξασθαι; as an alternative for μὴ παθεῖν, Naber 280 proposes deleting καὶ λαθεῖν. See Adam ad loc. and his Appendix II to book I (I 62 f.).

336e9 οἴου γε σύ **Bekker**: οἴου τε σύ **ADF**: μὴ οἴου σύ βᵖᶜKⁱᵗ: Bekker's conjecture οἴου γε σύ is not free from objection: the phrase οἴεσθαί γε χρή, found at Cri. 53d1, Phd. 68b2 and Prt. 325c4, is usually quoted in support of οἴου γε σύ, sc. ἡμᾶς σπουδάζειν ὅτι μάλιστα φανῆναι αὐτό (see, e.g., Jowett-Campbell ad loc.; Adam, Appendix IV to book I (I 64)), but here οἴου γε σύ comes very awkward after μὴ οἴου at e4. The reading μὴ οἴου σύ is an obvious conjecture, which makes perfect sense; however, the corruption of μὴ οἴου σύ to οἴου τε σύ cannot be accounted for. Wilamowitz 377 proposes reading ἀλλ' οἶμαι οὐ δυνάμεθα, οἴου τε σύ, ὦ φίλε.

352e9 φαμὲν] φαῖμεν βᵖᶜ (editors attribute this reading to Stephanus, but it is already found in βᵖᶜ): the reading ἂν—φαμὲν cannot be retained (see Adam's objections to Schneider's interpretation); in phrases like this, the optative with ἂν is regular; see for instance *R.* 353d6-7, *R.* 558d11-e1, *R.* 605a8, *Cra.* 410b7-8, c8, *Grg.* 454a7-8.

358e2 τί—δικαιοσύνη] τί οἴονται καὶ ὅθεν γεγονέναι δικαιοσύνην βᵖᶜ: **DPar.**β have τί οἷόν τε, which is clearly a conflation of the readings of **A** (τί ὄν τε) and **F** (οἷόν τε); therefore the correction οἴονται for οἷόν τε, which in itself is quite attractive (see Adam ad loc., Schneider ad 329e7), is to be rejected. For other solutions, see Adam ad loc.; after Adam, the following emendations have been proposed: τί ὄν τε] ὁποῖόν τε G. E. Vasmanolis, Platon 16 (1964), 189; τί ὄν τε] οἷόν τε vel οἷόν τοι K. I. Logothetis, Platon 18 (1966), 4 f.

365d8 τί καὶ ἡμῖν] οὐδ' ἡμῖν βᵖᶜ (καὶ ἡμῖν **DPar.**βᵃᶜ): an intelligent conjecture, in full accordance with the general sense of the passage, but the reading of **F** is of course to be preferred.

408a5 ἐκμυζήσαντες **F**: ἐκμυζήσαντ' **AD**: ἐκμύζησάν τ' βᵖᶜ: this reading was also conjectured by Adam, who did not think it worth while to put it into the text.

436c2 Εἶεν] καὶ βᵖᶜ: by reading καὶ, β makes b8-c3 a continuous speech by Socrates, uninterrupted by the tame Εἶεν.

444b5 τῷ—ὄντι] τὼ δ' αὖ δουλεύειν ἀρχικοῦ γένους ὄντε βᵖᶜ: I must confess that I do not see what sense can be extracted from this attempt at correcting this much disputed passage (see the discussion of this place on p. 215 and p. 235).

454d2 ἰατρικὴν] ἰατρικὸν βᵖᶜ: this correction is accepted by Stallbaum, Schneider and Jowett-Campbell; the main difficulty, of course, is the repetition of ἰατρικὸν; Schneider argues that ἰατρικὸν means someone who practises the art of medicine, while ἰατρικὸν τὴν ψυχὴν ὄντα indicates someone who has the ability to practise medicine, but does not necessarily do so. Jowett-Campbell state that "the repetition simply emphasizes identity in order to prepare for the contrast between identity and difference." Neither explanation seems quite convincing to me, nor does any other solution proposed for this undoubtedly corrupt phrase; Adam may well be right in cancelling the words τὴν ψυχὴν ὄντα, although his explanation that "τὴν ψυχὴν ὄντα (is) a relic of ἰατρὸν τὴν ψυχὴν ὄντα, a marginal annotation on ἰατρικόν" is far-fetched. Some other solutions: ἰατρικὸν] ἰατρὸν Cornarius (in De Lacy's edition of Galen's *PHP*, p. 554, app. crit. ad l. 13); ἰατρικὴν—ὄντα] "—κὸν vel ἔχοντα lege pro ὄντα" Cornarius, *ibid.*; ὄντα secl. Burnet (N.B. both Θ and Galen read ὄντα, not ἔχοντα, as Burnet wrongly reports). See further the discussion by S. B. Pomeroy, *Plato and the female physician*, AJPh 99 (1978), 496-500.

456a1 δ' del. et οὔ, οὐδὲ] καὶ βᵖᶜ; **a2** φιλογυμναστική] γυμναστική βᵖᶜ: there is a great variety of MS readings in this place; the corrections in β form one of the boldest solutions for this undoubtedly corrupt phrase; β's reading is accepted by Stallbaum. Although it is hard to believe that the sentence as it stands in β^pc represents exactly what Plato wrote, it has at least the merit of making good sense: the substitution of καί for οὔ, οὐδὲ brings out the antithesis between the first and the second part of the sentence, corresponding to the antitheses at 455e6-7 and 456a4-5 (although in these places the antitheses are juxtaposed in single pairs). As the text stands in **ADF**, γυμναστικὴ οὔ is equivalent to οὐ φιλογυμναστική, while οὐδὲ πολεμική is synonymous with ἀπόλεμος. The explanation given by Schneider and Jowett-Campbell, among others, viz. that both οὔ and οὐδὲ serve to introduce a question to which a positive answer is expected, seems unnatural to me. J. J. Hartman 250 proposes reading γυμναστικὴ δ' ἄρα (sic) οὐ οὐδὲ πολεμική; H. Wolf, ap. A. Gennadios, Philologus 10 (1855), 347 ff., suggests ἡ δὲ for οὐδέ.

471b6 ἐναντίους] ἕλληνας and **b9** φύλαξι] ἕλλησι β^pc: obviously introduced to emphasize the different kinds of warfare against Greeks and barbarians.

479a6 οὐχ] οὐ καὶ β^pc: the addition of καί brings out more elegantly the idea that the same thing cannot be beautiful and ugly at the same time. It is surprising that the same correction has not been made with οὐκ at a7.

504d2 μάλιστα] μόνου β^pc: here the corrector was not content to hear that the study of the Form of the Good is a most fitting one; according to him, it is the only fitting subject for serious study; cf. the corrections at 508d6 ἔχειν] ἔχον and at 519a3 ὡς] ἄτε, discussed above (p. 211).

544c6 καὶ alterum] ἐκ β^pc: the reading διαφέρουσα at c7 is found in x^pc and Stobaeus; ἐκ for καί aims to give some sense to the reading διαφεύγουσα in the other MSS.

554b5 χοροῦ] βίου β^pc: the corrector apparently did not understand the metaphor, for which see (with Adam) 490c3 and 560e3.

554b6-7 καὶ—σκόπει] καὶ ὅτι μάλιστα αὖ ἦν δ' ἐγὼ τῇδε δὴ σκόπει β^pc: Schneider's brilliant conjecture ἐτί <μα> μάλιστα for ἔτι μάλιστα **ADF**, has been generally accepted by modern editors, but Dr Slings tells me that he is inclined to reject it, because εὖ alone, used as an affirmative answer, is unparalleled in Plato. The reading in β is an intelligent attempt to emend this phrase, which is undoubtedly corrupt; yet the sentence remains clumsy, and a satisfactory solution for this difficult phrase remains to be proposed.

567e3 Τίς] τί β^pc: although in β there is no interrogation mark after τί δέ, this would be an easy solution for the difficult τίς; τί is accepted by all editors, with the exception of Burnet. Richards 1894, 293, suggests Τί δέ; αὐτόθεν ἄρ' οὐκ ἂν ἐθελήσειέ πως τοὺς δούλους κτέ. Dr Slings tells me that he believes that the difficulties are mainly caused by Πῶς, not by Τίς.

585c7 οὖν ἀεὶ] δὲ τοῦ μηδέποτε β^pc: Adam ad loc. calls this passage one of "the most perplexing in the whole of the *Republic*, or indeed in the whole of Plato's writings"; see also his Appendix VI to book IX (II 381-383). Indeed, one is puzzled to read ἀεὶ ὁμοίου at c7, instead of ἀεὶ ἀνομοίου (Adam's emendation), μὴ ἀεὶ ὁμοίου (x^pc) or τοῦ μηδέποτε ὁμοίου (β^pc). If ἀεί is indeed corrupt, the error may have been caused by the preceding ἀεὶ ὁμοίου at c6; τοῦ μηδέποτε is apparently borrowed from c3-4. A host of conjectures have been proposed for this phrase; apart from those recorded in Adam's Appendix, the following deserve to be mentioned: ἡ—οὐσία οὐσίας—ἡ] ἡ—οὐσία, οὐσίας—[ἡ] H. W. Garrod, CR 20 (1906), 210; ἀεὶ ὁμοίου οὐσία secl. et ἡ] ἤ (ἤ οὖν ?) C. Ritter, JAW 161 (1913), 54 f.; ἡ οὖν ἀεὶ ὁμοία οὐσία οὐσίας τι μᾶλλον ἢ ἐπιστήμης μετέχει K. Vretska, WS 71 (1958), 52-54; Apelt 348-350 proposes reading c6-9 as follows: "(Glaukon spricht) Πολύ, ἔφη, διαφέρει τὸ τοῦ ἀεὶ ὁμοίου ἢ (mit dem Lobk.) οὐκ ἀεὶ ὁμοίου οὐσία. Darauf Sokrates: Οὐσίας τι μᾶλλον ἢ ἐπιστήμης μετέχει; Glaukon: Οὐδαμῶς κ.τ.λ.''.

604a1 πότερον] πότε β[pc]: inspired by the following temporal clauses ὅταν—ὁμοίων and ὅταν—γίγνηται.

609a3 τε] τι β[pc]: serves to make κακόν substantival (cf. the addition of τι after τοιοῦτον at 426b8, mentioned on p. 208).

e. glosses

In at least one case, a gloss seems to have replaced the original reading: 440a5 τὴν ὀργὴν] τὸν θυμὸν.

2. Vind.Bon.Sc.

The common ancestor of **Vind.Bon.Sc.** can only be reconstructed in 389d7-480a13: until 389d7 **Sc.** depends on **T**, while **Vind.Bon.** have only books I-V.

1. In a very few places I have noted agreement between **Vind.Bon.Sc.** and the indirect tradition:

413e5 ὧν om. **Vind.Bon.Sc. Stob.**
415a6 τε om. **Vind.Bon.Sc. Clem. Eus.** (bis)
423c6 γε om. **Vind.Bon.Sc. Phot. Suid.** *EM*
429d8 δέξεται] δέξηται **Vind.Bon.Sc. Theon Sm.**
445c1 καὶ alterum om. **Vind.Bon.Sc. (Mγ) Stob.**
462a6 νυνδὴ] νῦν **Vind.Bon.Sc. Stob.**
473b2 ἂν om. **Vind.Bon.Sc. Stob.**

I believe that all these readings are simple errors which have come into **Vind.Bon.Sc.** and the indirect tradition independently.

2. In a few places **Vind.Bon.Sc.** are the most important MSS to preserve a true reading:

441c6 ἑνὸς **Vind.Bon.Sc.**: ἑνὶ **ADF Stob.** (ἑνὸς et M[pc], non **M**; errat Burnet)
461d6 ἐκεῖνα αὖ **Vind.Bon.Sc.**: ἐκείνου αὖ **ADF**
462b2 ξυνδῇ **Vind.Bon.Sc.**[1sl](**M**): ξυδῇ **F**: ξυνδεῖ **AD**

None of these readings is such as cannot be ascribed to conjectural emendation.

3. In some places **Vind.Bon.Sc.** show traces of intentional change of the transmitted text; some of these corrections are very intelligent.

423e7 γάμων] γάμον: this looks like a simple conjecture, introduced in order to make γάμον depend on παραλείπομεν, in line with κτῆσιν; cf. Adam ad loc.; Vollgraff 140 suggests καὶ παίδων for καὶ γάμων καὶ παιδοποιίας.

426a3 καὶ om. **Vind.Bon.Sc.**^pc: καὶ, if retained (= *idque* (Stallbaum)), is a bit puzzling (cf. Adam ad loc.); the sentence runs more smoothly if καὶ is omitted; the omission may be correct (interpolation of καὶ is rather frequent).

444b5 τῷ δ' οὐ δουλεύειν **Burnet**: τοῦ δ' αὖ δουλεύειν **ADF Stob.**: τῶ τοῦ **Vind.Bon.Sc.**: a rather bold correction of this vexed passage, accepted by most editors, among whom Jowett-Campbell, Adam and Chambry. It does make sense, although the phrase is awkward, but the insertion of δουλεύειν in **ADF Stob.** is very hard to account for. At any rate, this reading shows that the passage has been interpreted carefully by the scribe who introduced it. For a discussion of this passage see Adam ad loc.; two recent emendations: τὸ δ' αὖ δουλεύηι ἀρχικοῦ γένους ὄντι Wilamowitz 380; τοῦ δ' αὖ δουλοῦσθαι ἀρχικοῦ γένους ὄντος S. R. Slings, Mnem. IV 31 (1978), 246-252. See also the readings of β (p. 212) and **VMatr.** (p. 235).

454d2 ἰατρικὸν—ὄντα] ἰατρικὸν μὲν τὴν ψυχὴν ὄντα: in this difficult place (cf. β's solution, p. 212), the omission of καὶ ἰατρικὴν in **Vind.Bon.Sc.** must be deliberate, but cannot possibly be correct.

458a5 εἶναι om.: if ὑπάρχον is taken in the normal sense "be", "exist", εἶναι is indeed superfluous; Schneider's attempt to save εἶναι (taking ὑπάρχον in the sense "be"), viz. that εἶναι ὃ βούλονται goes with θέντες (accepted by Adam) does not sound very attractive to me; Schneider translates: "das Dasein des gewünschten als gegeben annehmend". However, I believe that εἶναι can be retained if we take ὑπάρχειν in the sense "be allowed", "be possible" (LSJ s.v. B, V 2) and translate: "assuming that their wish can possibly be fulfilled".

467e3 διδαξαμένους q^pc: διδαξομένους **ADF**: διδαχθησομένους **Vind.**^it**Bon.**^it: διδαχθέντας **Vind.**^1sl**Bon.**^1sl**Sc.**^it: I suppose that the scribe who introduced the readings διδαχθησομένους and διδαχθέντας wrongly supposed that διδαξομένους is middle, and not passive; on this hypothesis, he must have argued that, if διδαξομένους is retained, we must supply something like τοὺς πατέρας; the fathers, however, are the agents of ἀκτέον, so that we would expect the dative instead of the accusative; in Attic, the substitution of the accusative for the dative to express the agent is not uncommon (KG I 448, Anm. 2), but in this case it might cause some ambiguity, because we must supply τοὺς νεανίας or the like as the object. The two readings in **Vind.Bon.Sc.** have, I think, been introduced in order to evade this ambiguity. But I do not see any objections to διδαξομένους of **ADF**, provided that it is rightly taken as a passive.

471c8 ἀγαθὰ πόλει] ἀγαθὴ πόλις **Vind.Bon.Sc.**^1sl: this reading avoids the somewhat awkward change of subject: εἰ γένοιτο (sc. ἡ πολιτεία), εἴη (sc. πάντα), ᾗ γένοιτο (sc. ἡ πόλις). J. J. Hartman 254 hesitantly submits that ἐν be supplied before ᾗ γένοιτο.

476b7 τὴν φύσιν] τὸν νοῦν: I suppose that this may originally have been a gloss.

3. Vind.Bon.

1. I have noted the following cases of agreement between **Vind.Bon.** and the indirect tradition:

337a3	σαρδάνιον] σαρδώνιον **Vind.Bon.** (**Par.**) **Tim. Iul. Zenobii B Zach. Mit.**	
361c7	ἴτω] ἔστω **Vind.Bon. Eus. Thdt. Georg. Mon.**	
376a6	προπεπονθώς] πεπονθώς **Vind.Bon. Stob.**	
381c9	ἀεὶ om. **Vind. Procl.** (semel) **Simp.** (habent **Bon.**, **Procl.** altero loco)	
403a11	ὀρθῷ] ὀρθῶς **Vind.Bon. Stob.**	
416c2	ἥμεροι] ἥμερον **Vind.Bon. Stob.**	
433c1	ἐν ᾗ] ἥ **Vind.Bon. Stob.**	
436d7	αὐτῇ] αὐτοῦ **Vind. Gal.** (non ita **Bon.**)	
457b1	γυναιξί] ταῖς γυναιξὶ **Vind.Bon.** (**M**) **Eus. Thdt.**	
469e1	οἷς om. **Vind.Bon. Stob.**	

The agreement with Eusebius and Theodoretus at 361c7 and 457b1 is remarkable at first sight; yet the reading ἔστω may be due to conjectural emendation, or it may be a conflation of ἴτω and ἔσται, which is found in **F** (I suppose that ἔσται in **F** is a further corruption of ἔστω in Eusebius and Theodoretus, which in its turn is a corruption of ἴτω; **A**[2] reads ἤτω, while **D**[ac] has ἴτωι (*sic*)); with regard to the addition of the article at 457b1 it must be noted that in such phrases the article is added more than once in **Vind.Bon.** (as in many other secondary MSS); some instances in *R.*: 364a2 καί] καὶ ἡ; 438e2 νοσωδῶν] τῶν νοσωδῶν; 456e6 πόλει] τῇ πόλει.

At 337a3 the reading σαρδώνιον (also found in **Par.**) may be due to contamination, but it may also be nothing more than an error.

The one case of agreement with Simplicius, 381c9 ἀεὶ om., is not very striking, nor is the agreement with Galen at 436d7 αὐτῇ] αὐτοῦ (for the phrase ἐν τῇ αὐτοῦ ἕδρᾳ cf. 516b6 ἐν τῇ αὐτοῦ χώρᾳ), the more so because in these two places only **Vind.** (and not **Bon.**) agrees with Simplicius and Galen respectively.

Of the places where **Vind.Bon.** agree with Stobaeus, 376a6 and 433c1 are simple errors; 416c2 ἥμεροι] ἥμερον is a simplification; 403a11 ὀρθῶς is not very remarkable; the omission of οἷς at 469e1 looks like an error caused by haplography (λίθοις οἷς).

I conclude that there are no strong indications that the exemplar of **Vind.Bon.** was contaminated with a lost primary source.

2. There are no places where **Vind.Bon.** alone preserve a manifestly true or highly probable reading.

3. In some places a reading of **Vind.Bon.** deserves some attention (I shall also discuss some readings of **Vind.ᵖᶜ**):

345a7 πείθει] πείθεις **Vind.** (non ita **Bon.**): a quite possible reading, probably introduced in order to avoid the slight difficulty that the subject of πείθει must be supplied from the preceding sentence (cf. Jowett-Campbell and Adam ad loc.); Ficino translates *suades*.

364a1 ἐξ] ὡς ἐξ: ὡς has probably been added in order to introduce the metaphor.

394c7 μὲν] μὲν μὴ **Vind.** (non ita **Bon.**): in itself this reading is possible, because Socrates has spoken at greater length about the kind of tales that should not be told, than about those which are admissible. Yet the reference to 392c7-8 establishes beyond doubt that the reading of **ADF** is correct.

399b3 τύχην] ψυχὴν: the confusion of these two words is not unique (cf. 366c2 ψυχῆς] τύ **A²ⁱᵐ**); here the reading ψυχὴν makes excellent sense. If the reading is not simply an error but a deliberate emendation, the scribe who introduced it may have reasoned that it is impossible to escape one's fate, and that, accordingly, it would be useless to fight against fate.

403a6 μανικωτέραν] μαλακωτέραν **Vind.** (non ita **Bon.**): again, the confusion of these words is not without precedent: cf. *Smp.* 173d8. In itself the condemnation of weakness is not out of place here, but the mentioning of frenzy (ἔκφρονα) at 402e5 which is the result of pleasure, makes it clear that here the reading μανικωτέραν is certainly right.

414e2 καὶ del. **Vind.ᵖᶜ** (habent **Vind.ᵃᶜBon.**): καὶ has also puzzled modern scholars (see Adam ad loc.): Ast deletes the word, Hermann changes it into ὡς; Adam himself accepts the transmitted text, but adds that "exact parallels are rare". At first sight, the reader naturally interprets καὶ as connecting ἐπειδὴ—ἦσαν with ἡ γῆ—ἀνῆκεν, but this is contrary to the general sense of the passage. The solution offered by Jowett-Campbell, that "καί helps to mark the correspondence of the clauses" does not seem very attractive to me, but I agree with Adam that "If the text is sound, it must be explained in this way". At any rate, the excision of καὶ is an intelligent conjecture.

420c7-8 οἱ γὰρ ὀφθαλμοί—εἶεν] τὸν γὰρ ὀφθαλμὸν—εἶμεν **Vind.** (non ita **Bon.**): probably an attempt to make the parenthesis run syntactically parallel to the preceding clause; in itself, the reading is not unattractive.

Sometimes a reading in **Vind.Bon.** may originally have been a gloss, e.g. 457a7 ἀμφιέσονται] ἐνδύσονται.

4. Sc.

1. In the following places I have noted agreement between **Sc.** and the indirect tradition:

328d5 σύνισθι] ξύνιθι **Sc. Thom. Mag.**
329e7 γε om. **Sc. Stob.**
358b7 ἐπανανεώσομαι] ἐπὰν ἀνανεώσομαι **Sc.**: ἐπὰν ἀνανεώσωμαι **Φ Thom. Mag.**
394c8 ἔτι σκεπτέον] ἐπισκεπτέον **Sc. Prisc.**

441c6   γένη habent **Sc. Stob.**: γένει **ADF**
550e8   ῥέποντε] ῥέποντος **Sc. Stob.** (uno loco; ῥέποντε habet **Stob.** altero loco)
551a1   δή] δὲ **Sc. Stobaei A** (δὴ habent **Stobaei SM** et **Stob.** altero loco)
572a7   τ' om. **Sc. Stob.**
572a8   παράνομοι] παρανομεῖ **Sc. Stob.**
572b2   οἶμαι om. **Sc. Stob.**
612d6   ἃ ante ἀπὸ **Sc. Stob.** (ἃ om. **D**)
614b8   οὗ] οἱ **Eus. Thdt.**: οἱ οὗ **TW** (non ita Θ: deficit **Sc.**)
615c3   ἀσεβείας τε καὶ εὐσεβείας] εὐσεβείας τε καὶ ἀσεβείας **ΘW** (deficit **Sc.**) **Procl.**

Of these cases, the readings at 329e7, 551a1, 572a7 and 615c3 do not tell us anything at all, in my opinion.

The reading ἐπισκεπτέον at 394c8, also found in Priscianus, may be due to confusion of Τ and Π, a confusion which seems to find its origin in the misreading of majuscule script (a glance at Hertz' apparatus teaches us that some scribes of Priscianus contented themselves with simply drawing Greek letters, without making any attempt at understanding the text they copied).

With regard to the cases of agreement with Thomas Magister at 328d5 and 358b7, it should be noted that it is not very likely that Thomas Magister (*ca.* 1300 A. D.) used a primary source unknown to us; I guess that for *R.* he consulted a MS of the **Sc.**-group.

At 550e8, ῥέποντος (also found once in Stobaeus) is clearly provoked by the preceding genitives.

The three cases of agreement with Stobaeus at 572a7, a8, b2, although not very significant in themselves, are remarkable, because they occur so close together. The omission of τ' in itself is not very significant, and the same could be said of the omission of οἶμαι at b2; as to the reading παρανομεῖ for παράνομοι, it must be noted that **D** (the source of **Sc.**) reads παρανομοῖ; therefore I think that in this case too the agreement between **Sc.** and Stobaeus is coincidental.

More interesting is the case of 614b8 οὗ] οἱ **Eus. Thdt.**: οἱ οὗ **TW** (non ita Θ: deficit **Sc.**): because this reading occurs in **TW**, but not in Θ, I assume that it was added by the scribe of **Sc.** after Θ had been copied from **Sc.** (cf. p. 156); that οἱ was added deliberately, appears from the fact that both readings are in the text of **TW**.

In a few places I have noted agreement between **Sc.** and **F** (see p. 156), but in these few places the agreement may well be due to coincidence. Yet if these readings are the result of contamination, they may have come into **Sc.** from an ancestor of **F**, because **Sc.** may belong to the thirteenth century (see p. 29), while **F** is assigned to the fourteenth century by Hunger; but neither of these datings is very firm.

I conclude that certain indications for contamination of **Sc.** with a lost primary source are very slight indeed.

2. In the following places **Sc.** is the only or principal MS to preserve a true or highly probable reading:

354b3   ἐγώ μοι **Sc.**: ἐγῶ(ι)μαι **AF**: ἐγὼ οἶμαι **D**
399c3   ἁρμονίας om. **Sc.**
441c6   γένη **Sc. Stob.**: γένει **ADF**
460c6   μέλλει **Sc.**: μέλλοι **ADF**
461a6   φὺς ἃς **Sc.**: φύσας ἃς **A**: φύσας **DF**
527c2   ἀφέξονται **Sc.**: ἀφέξωνται **ADF**
553c4   ξυλλέγεται **Sc.**: ξυλλέγηται **ADF**
580d4   λογιστικὸν del. **Sc.**[1pc]: habent **ADF**
606c7   ἀνίης **Sc.**: ἂν εἴης **AF**: ἀνείης **D**
607b1   ἀπολελογήσθω **Sc.** (et **M** (non γ) **Par.**): ἀπολελογίσθω **AD**: ἀπολελογείσθω **F**

At 477e7 **ADF** have ποτέ τις, while Burnet prints τις; ποτέ is actually omitted in **Sc.**, but Burnet is silent in his apparatus. One might naturally think that the omission of ποτέ in the OCT is due to a typographical error, but the fact that Jowett-Campbell too omit the word without any note makes one suspect that Burnet relies on Jowett-Campbell in this place.

It is remarkable that three of the true readings in **Sc.** concern the correct form of a verb (460c6, 527c2, 553c4): in the next section I will illustrate that **Sc.** pays much attention to such matters as orthography, moods, tenses etc. (see p. 222).

The reading ἀπολελογήσθω at 607b1 is a very easy correction of ἀπολελογίσθω, which is read by **AD** (ἀπολελογείσθω **F**); cf. 518b1 εὐδαιμονίσειεν *recte* **tRPar.**[pc]: εὐδαιμονήσειε(ν) **ADF**. At 399c3 the word ἁρμονίας, omitted by **Sc.**, is bracketed by most editors; the repetition of ἁρμονίας, immediately after ἁρμονίας at c2, is harsh, but not impossible; the repetition is avoided by deleting the word either at c2 (as does β[pc]) or at c3 (as does **Sc.**); Van Herwerden even proposes deleting the word in both places. At 580d4 λογιστικὸν is cancelled by most editors; the word is deleted by **Sc.**[1pc].

The remaining four readings are certainly correct. If they are conjectures (as I tend to believe), they are brilliant.

3. In a good many places **Sc.** has an interesting reading. In some cases the reading of **Sc.** is certainly conjectural; this is proved by those cases where **Sc.** has sought to emend an error in its exemplar; some instances:

392c2   λέγεσθαι] ἐλεγεσθαι **D**[ac]: ἐλέσθαι **Sc.** (et inde **D**[2pc])
559d10-e1   που οἴου] πουσίου **D**: πλουσίου **Sc.**

I will discuss the different types of variant readings in **Sc.**

a. In some cases words are added to clarify the sense, or because the scribe felt that there was a lacuna:

398e10 αὖ] καὶ τοιαῦταί: an obvious attempt to remove the initially confusing usage of τινες; cf. Adam ad loc.

407e4 ὅτι] δεικνύοιεν ἂν ὅτι: as the text stands, the position of the words ὅτι τοιοῦτος ἦν is puzzling; the insertion of δεικνύοιεν ἂν solves this difficulty, but should of course not be accepted as the genuine reading; cf. Jowett-Campbell and Adam ad loc.; Adam accepts Schneider's proposal, which consists in transposing καὶ οἱ παῖδες αὐτοῦ after ὅτι τοιοῦτος ἦν; ὅτι τοιοῦτος ἦν is deleted by Wallies 41 f.

435b7 ἀλλ' ἄττα] καὶ οὐ κατ' ἀλλ' ἄττα Sc.pc: the scribe interpreted ἀλλ' ἄττα πάθη τε καὶ ἕξεις as "different from those just mentioned" (i.e. δίκαιος, σώφρων, ἀνδρεῖος, σοφός), which would be contrary to the general sense of this passage. The correction is devised to exclude this interpretation.

508b13 ὅτιπερ] ὅτιπερ γὰρ Sc.[1sl]: the addition of γὰρ makes the sentence run more smoothly, but is definitely to be rejected; cf. the addition of γὰρ after ἐπειδὰν at 329c7 in **Mγ** and **Sc.**

508d2 ἐνοῦσα] ὄψις ἐνοῦσα Sc.[1sl]: the addition of ὄψις is correct in itself: ὄψις καθαρὰ should be supplied from c7; yet as Adam ad loc. says: "the feminine inflexion (of ἐνοῦσα—GJB) prevents the possibility of mistake". H. van Herwerden, Mnem. II 12 (1884), 323, suggests <ὄψις> ἐνοῦσα <σαφής>; J. L. V. Hartman 41, who gives a number of earlier conjectures, proposes ὄμμασιν ὄψις ἐναργὴς ἐνοῦσα.

518a4 νομίσας] νομίσας τις Sc.[1sl]: repeats τις at a1, and can easily be dispensed with.

580d10 ἦν] ἦν δ' ἐγώ: by the addition of δ' ἐγὼ **Sc.** kills two birds with one stone: φαμεν is used in the general sense of "we usually say", and the idiomatic usage of the imperfect (for which see KG I 145 f.) is avoided. Yet the text as it stands is perfectly satisfactory.

581e1 νομίζειν] νομίζειν οὐδέν: almost all editors have accepted Graser's brilliant conjecture τί οἰώμεθα for ποιώμεθα of the MSS at d10. If ποιώμεθα is retained, the absence of an object dependent on νομίζειν is intolerable; the addition of οὐδέν after νομίζειν is a very intelligent solution for this problem; one might object, as Adam does (see his Appendix III to book IX (II 376 f.)), that ποιεῖσθαι in the sense "deem" cannot be used absolutely (cf. LSJ s.v. A. V.).

599c2 τίνας] τίνας γὰρ: cf. the case of 508b13, discussed above.

616a4 τε] τε ταῦτα ὑπομένοιεν **TW**: this reading is not found in Θ, while **Sc.** itself is absent; I therefore suspect that the words were added in **Sc.** after Θ had been copied (cf. p. 156). This accretion has its origin in the conciseness of diction: ἄγοιντο depends on both ὧν ἕνεκα and ὅτι, as Adam ad loc. rightly explains; the addition of ταῦτα ὑπομένοιεν makes the sentence run more fluently.

b. In a few cases some words are omitted or deleted:

452e1 καὶ καλοῦ αὖ om.: this passage has given rise to much debate, and many interpretations and emendations have been proposed (see Adam's Appendix II to book V (I 355-357)); if the text of the MSS is retained, there are two obvious ways of constructing the sentence; the first of these is to make μάταιός <ἐστι> and ὁ γελωτοποιεῖν ἐπιχειρῶν σπουδάζει both depend on ὅτι; this is the solution proposed by Adam (see the translation he gives in his note ad loc.); in the second interpretation all three ὅς—κακόν, ὁ—κακοῦ and <ὃς> καλοῦ αὖ σπουδάζει κτέ depend on μάταιος; this is the interpretation of Jowett-Campbell (accepted by Shorey). In objection to the first interpretation it could be said that καὶ—αὖ is completely unintelligible, while the position of καλοῦ is extremely misleading; in the second interpretation, the sequence relative clause-substantively used participle-relative clause is, to say the least, rather unusual; neither does the fact that at e1 ὅς should be supplied from d6, after the participle clause, recommend it. I believe that both interpretations should be rejected, and that the text is corrupt. Although the solution given by **Sc.** is, of course, not certain, it makes excellent sense: Chambry, who omits καὶ καλοῦ αὖ with **Sc.**, translates: "et que celui qui cherche à faire rire en ridiculisant tout autre spectacle que celui de la folie et du vice poursuit sérieusement une autre fin que le bien." Besides, the omission of καὶ καλοῦ αὖ brings out the fine paradox ὁ γελωτοποιεῖν ἐπιχειρῶν σπουδάζει. Yet the insertion of καὶ καλοῦ αὖ in **ADF** is difficult to account for. To the conjectures mentioned by Adam, the following may be added: e1 κακοῦ—πρός] κακοῦ <οὐδὲν ἄλλο ποιεῖ ἢ> καὶ καλοῦ αὖ <ὁ> σπουδάζει <ν> προσ<ποιούμενος> Vretska 89-91; e1 σπουδάζει πρός] <ὃς> σπουδάζει Wallies 42. I have refrained from including the puzzling words d8 ὡς γελοίου and e1-2 πρός—στησάμενος in my discussion; cf. Adam I 355-357.

505a3 καὶ δίκαια del.: as the text stands, τἄλλα means "beauty, courage etc.", i.e. virtues other than justice; if καὶ δίκαια is dropped, τἄλλα means "everything else (besides the good itself)", which gives a more general meaning to the sentence. The words are better retained. **Sc.**'s reading is accepted by J. L. V. Hartman, Mnem. II 45 (1917), 414, who discusses the other solutions for this phrase as well.

547b4-5 τὼ δ' αὖ, τὸ] τὸ δ' αὖ (τὼ is Schneider's correction of τὸ which is read by the MSS): an easy and not unattractive conjecture for the senseless reading of **ADF**, but Schneider's conjecture is superior.

567e3 ἄρ' om.: an intelligent attempt to emend this puzzling sentence; see also the reading of β^pc (p. 213).

c. In many places **Sc.** offers a variant reading which looks like a deliberate change of the transmitted text:

410e5-6 τούτω τὼ] ταῦτα τῇ: a superficial simplification.

411a6 καταχεῖν] κατηχεῖν (**Sc.**^pc, ut vid.): probably introduced to form a counterpart of the musical verb καταυλεῖν; but καταχεῖν is certainly correct.

471b4 ἀλγούντων] ἀλγοῦντες **Sc.**^1sl: this reading indicates the result of the punishment inflicted upon the war-makers, instead of the suffering undergone by their innocent victims.

495e1 ἀποτεθρυμμένοι] ἀποτεθραυμένοι **Sc.**^1sl: a possible variant reading, which gives the same sense as ἀποτεθρυμμένοι.

530d8 εἶναι] εἰσίν: gives an easier construction, because, as the text stands, κινδυνεύουσι must be supplied to εἶναι from κινδυνεύει at d6 (which, of course, is a quite normal idiom).

545c6 γέ τοι ἄν, ἔφη] ἔφη ἂν γένοιτο εἰ: a charming anagram (with νο and εἰ added), but the text is unobjectionable.

580d1 δὲ ἰδὲ Adam: δεῖ δὲ **ADF**: δὲ δεῖ **Sc.**: an attempt to emend this corrupt phrase, which was corrected brilliantly by Adam.

d. In section 2 (p. 219) I have already noted that **Sc.** pays considerable attention to verbs. First I will note some orthographical variant readings.

Often the forms of the imperfect of ἰέναι are given in the long form: 328b4 Ἧιμεν] ἤειμεν **Sc.**[1sl]; 489e4 διῇμεν] διήειμεν.

The optative, too, often has the longer form: 349b8 ἀξιοῖ] ἀξιοίη; 549b1 καταφρονοῖ] καταφρονοίη; 582a1 εἰδεῖμεν] εἰδείημεν.

At 527c2 **Sc.** preserves the future indicative in a complementary final clause; at 553c4 **Sc.** restores the indicative where **ADF** have the subjunctive. At 615d3 **ΘW** (**Sc.** itself is absent) have ἥξοι for ἥξει of the primary MSS; in Attic, the future indicative + ἄν is very rare (see KG I 209), but the reading ἥξοι throws us from the frying-pan into the fire: the future optative with ἄν in a principal clause never occurs, and Chambry should not have adopted this reading. I wonder if all difficulties cannot be evaded by accepting H. Jackson's simple emendation (JPh 4 (1872), 148 f.) ἀνήξει, which involves only a change of accentuation, and makes perfect sense: "no, he has not come, nor will he come up again": the unjust are punished below the earth (614c7) and after having expiated their sins they come up from below the earth (614d6).

Although the moods are often confused in our MSS, there are some places where **Sc.** seems to have changed a mood deliberately, e.g. 518a2 γίγνονται] γίγνοιντ' ἄν; 596d3 δοκεῖ] δοκοῖ (ἄν precedes).

Tenses are also often confused in our MSS; sometimes the change seems to be intentional in **Sc.**, e.g. 337a6 ἀποκρίνασθαι] ἀποκρίνεσθαι (possible); 503b5 καθιστάναι] καθεστάναι (possible, but not superior to καθιστάναι).

e. Finally, there are a few readings in **Sc.** which may originally have been glosses, e.g. 393e8 οὗ] αὐτοῦ; 503c5 βεβαιότητος] ἡμερότητος; 569a1 κατέστησεν] ἔθρεψεν.

5. Par.

1. In the following places I have noted agreement between Par. and the indirect tradition:

337a3   σαρδάνιον] σαρδώνιον **Par.** (et **Vind.Bon.**) **Tim. Iul. Zenobii B Zach. Mit.**
341c4   (etiam 541b2) Ἅδην] ἄδδην **Par. Did.**
379d6   τε] γε **Par. Eus.**
414b3   βουλήσονται—δυνήσονται] βουλήσωνται—δυνήσωνται **Par. Stobaei A**

429d8 δέξεται] δέξηται βVat.p (deficit Par.) Theon Sm.
438b2 μόνον] μόνου βVat.p (deficit Par.) Gal.
439b4 θηρίον habent βVat.p (deficit Par.) Stob.: θηρίου ADF Gal. (errat Burnet)
441c5 ὡμολόγηνται habent βVat.p (deficit Par.) Stob.: ὁμολογεῖται ADF
444a1 αὖ] ἂν Par. Stob.
464e6 ἐπιμελείᾳ] ἐπιμελείας Par. Stob.
475e2 μὲν om. Par. Thdt.
519b2 περὶ] περὶ τὰ Par. Iambl.
527d5 Ἡδὺς] ὡς ἡδὺς Par. Nicom.
572a8 παράνομοι] παρανομεῖ Par. (et Sc.) Stob.
586a4 ἀληθῶς] ἀληθὲς Par. Longin.
614b3 Ἡρὸς] ἥρωος Par. Theodoreti LMV
616a4 τε] γε Par. Iustini codd. plerique
616b7 προελθόντες] προελθόντας Par. Theon Sm.

Of these readings, the cases of 379d6, 414b3, 429d8, 438b2, 586a4, 616a4 and 616b7 are simple errors. The reading at 572a8 παρανομεῖ is also found in **Sc.**; because an ancestor of **Par.** was contaminated from a member of the **Sc.**-group, this reading too may have come into **Par.** from a member of the **Sc.**-group, but the change of —οι (**D** has παρανομοῖ) into —ει may also have occurred in **Par.** and **Sc.** independently, as the result of itacism (for the contamination of **Par.** from **Sc.**, see pp. 177 f.).

At 337a3, the reading σαρδώνιον may be due to contamination, but it could very well have been borrowed from a lexicographer; it might also be a conjecture or an error.

The reading ἄδδην at 341c4 and 541b2 may have been borrowed from a lexicographer, if it is not simply an error. As regards the reading ἂν for αὖ at 444a1, also found in Stobaeus, one should bear in mind that ἂν and αὖ are constantly confused in our MSS.

The agreement with Stobaeus at 464e6 is very remarkable, although the fact that **Par.** has ἀνάγκη for ἀνάγκην (with **D**) makes one suspect that ἐπιμελείας in **Par.** may be due to conjectural emendation.

Equally remarkable are the readings 439b4 θηρίον and 441c5 ὡμολόγηνται, which are also found in Stobaeus; both readings are accepted by Burnet. Yet the latter reading may well be an intelligent conjecture, introduced to match the preceding διανενεύκαμεν (an analogous case is 564b6, where **Par.** has ἀφωμοιοῦμεν, following the imperfect ἔλεγον at b4); for θηρίον at 439b4 too conjectural emendation cannot be excluded as the explanation for the occurrence of this reading in **Par.**

The addition of τὰ at 519b2 has all the appearance of being a conjecture, introduced in order to make κάτω substantival.

The addition of ὡς at 527d5 may be deliberate, but it could have originated conjecturally as well as through contamination.

The omission of μὲν at 475e2 may be intentional (cf. below, section 3, p. 225): it may well be due to contamination.

At 614b3, the reading ἥρως is remarkable; yet it is found in only three of the leading MSS of Theodoretus, the other three having corrupt readings which derive from Ἡρὸς (ἡ ῥάστου **K**: ἡδοστοῦ **SC**).

I conclude that only the readings at 439b4 and 464e6 give some positive evidence of the contamination of **Par.** from an ancient source, but the evidence is rather slight.

2. In the following places **Par.** is the principal or sole MS to preserve a true reading:

407c1 τινας **Par.**: τινος **ADF Gal.**
411d2 γευόμενον **Par.** (fort. p.c.): γευομένου **DF**: γενομένου **A**
425d2 λήξεως **Par.**: λήξεις **ADF**
439b4 θηρίον β**Vat.p** (deficit **Par.**) Stob.: θηρίου **ADF Gal.**
504c6 προσδεῖ **Par.** (προσδεῖται **Par.**^ac: φ vocis sequentis φύλακι per ται scripsit prima manus): προσδεῖται **ADF** (et **D**: errat Burnet)
510b7 τῶν περὶ **Par.** (ὧν περὶ **Par.**^ac: τῶν περὶ **Par.**^pc a prima manu, ut vid.): ὧνπερ **AD**: ὧν περὶ **F** (τῶν περὶ non habet **F**, ut perhibet Burnet, sed **F**^4pc)
558a1 ἄρχειν καὶ δικάζειν **Par.**: ἀρχῆς καὶ δικάζη(ι)ς **A**^ac**F**^ac: ἀρχη(ι)ς καὶ δικάζη(ι)ς **A**^pc**F**^pc: ἀρχὴ καὶ δικάζεις **D**^ac: ἀρχῆς καὶ δικάζης **D**^2pc

I believe that all these readings can be regarded as certain, with the exception of 510b7: τῶν περὶ for ὧνπερ has all the appearance of an emendation, admittedly a very ingenuous one; ὧνπερ is rightly explained and defended by Jowett-Campbell and Adam ad loc.; τῶν περὶ is based on ὧν περὶ, the reading of **F** and **Par.**^ac.

3. In many cases it is obvious that **Par.** has sought to emend the text conjecturally; this becomes especially clear in those places where **D** (the source of **Par.**) has a corrupt reading; some instances:

403c9 θρεπτέοι] θρεπτέον **D**^2**Par.**: θρεπτέον is impossible in combination with οἱ νεανίαι; accordingly, **Par.** reads τοὺς νεανίας.
547c9 Μεταβήσεται] μεταβηθήσεται **D**: μεταβληθήσεται **Par.**: an admirable conjecture, which suits the sense perfectly.
607a4 ὕμνους—παραδεκτέον] ὑκτέον **D**: ὑκτέον is a *vox nihili*, for which **Par.** gives ἑκτέον, which at least has the appearance of being Greek.

I will now discuss some further variant readings in **Par.**

344a3 τὸ om.: the omission of τὸ has as a result that δίκαιον is adjective masculine, on one line with ἄδικον; of course, no such change is necessary.
346a5 ἑτέρα] ἑτέραν: ἑτέρα involves the ellipse of ἔστιν; ἑτέραν repeats the first ἑτέραν at a2, dependent on φαμέν. In itself, ἑτέραν is unobjectionable, but not necessarily better than ἑτέρα. Vollgraff 6 deletes ἑτέρα.

416d1 αὐτούς om.: at c7, the MSS and Stobaeus have τοὺς for τοῦ, which is a conjecture by Cobet; if τοὺς is retained, αὐτούς seems to be superfluous, which must have been the reason for omitting it.

441c5 ὡμολόγηται βVat.p (deficit **Par.**) **Stob.**: ὁμολογεῖται **ADF** et 564b6 ἀφομοιοῦμεν] ἀφωμοιοῦμεν **Par.**: see above, p. 223.

452c9 πρῶτοι] πρῶτον: the change of πρῶτοι into πρῶτον must have been provoked by the immediately following adverb ἔπειτα.

475e2 μὲν om. (et **Thdt.**): the scribe who deleted μὲν probably took offence at μέν, not followed by δέ, although this is by no means an uncommon idiom; cf. Adam ad loc.; Denniston, *GP* 378.

502b11 ἄπερ] ὅπερ: this reading seems to have been introduced because of the following singulars θαυμαστόν and ἀδύνατον.

521c7 οὖσαν] ἰούσης: οὖσαν has been doubted by many scholars, and various solutions have been proposed: see Adam's Appendix VI to book VII (II 182 f.) and Jowett-Campbell ad loc.; ἰούσης is an intelligent attempt at emendation, although it involves a rather inelegant hyperbaton.

603a12 ἀπεργάζεται] ἀσπάζεται: if not a simple clerical error, this reading may have been introduced in order to avoid the pleonastic ἔργον ἀπεργάζεται; for this use of ἀσπάζεσθαι cf. 330c3. Of course, the text as it stands need not be doubted.

621d3 πράττωμεν] πράττοντες: if this is a deliberate change (as I think it is), I guess that the reason for introducing it is the way in which the five καί's and the one τε at c6-d2 are taken: the scribe who conjectured πράττοντες took the two καί's at c6 as one pair, τε—καί at c7 as another pair, with καί—καί at d1-2 as the third pair; this involves a harsh asyndeton of ὦμεν and πράττωμεν, which is avoided by changing πράττωμεν into πράττοντες. Richards 1894, 395, proposes reading τε καί for καί at d2.

In a few places, a gloss has replaced the original reading; see for instance: 400a6 ὅθεν] ἐξ ὧν; 414a4 γέρα] δῶρα.

6. ΤΜγ

1. In the chapter on the **A**-family (pp. 117 f.) I have already shown that the common source of **ΤΜγ** was interpolated from a MS belonging to the **F** tradition; because the exemplar of **ΤΜγ** must be dated to the first half of the tenth century, the source of these corrections cannot have been **F** itself, because **F** belongs to the late thirteenth or fourteenth century. In one place **T** agrees significantly with **D**: 329c3 ἀσμενέστατα] ἀσμεναίτατα **TD**; neither can this reading be derived from **D** itself, because **D** belongs to the twelfth century, while **T** was written about 950. Therefore **ΤΜγ** must have borrowed readings from a lost primary source; the question whether this source contained ancient material which is not found in **D** and **F** themselves, can only be answered by comparing **ΤΜγ** with the indirect tradition.

I have not found any case of agreement between **ΤΜγ** and the indirect tradition against **ADF**; thus there is no positive evidence that **ΤΜγ** were interpolated from a source independent of the **ADF** traditions.

2. In two places, the reading of **TMγ** is accepted by Burnet in preference to the reading of **ADF**: 342b5 αὐτὴ **TMγ**: αὕτη **ADF**; 370b2 πράξει **TMγ**: πρᾶξιν **ADF**. The reading αὐτὴ at 342b5 is certainly correct, but I do not believe that Burnet is justified in reading πράξει at 370b2. In one place, **T** alone is responsible for a good reading: 386d4 τις **T**: τι **ADFMγ**.

3. **TMγ** have a very few readings which deserve any attention:

> 332e5 ἐν τῷ συμμαχεῖν] συμμαχεῖν: possible, but certainly not superior to the reading of **ADF**.
> 343c1 ὠφελήσονται] ὠφεληθήσονται: the middle voice is markedly better than the passive here.
> 358a2 ἀπ'] ὑπ': a possible reading, but ἀπ' is much better.

All these readings are probably nothing more than simple clerical errors.

I do not hold a separate discussion on **T**, which has hardly anything to tell us; **Mγ**, on the other hand, contain interesting readings not found in **T**; the next section therefore is devoted to **Mγ**.

7. Mγ

1. In the chapter on the **A**-family (pp. 120 f.) it has already been shown that the exemplar of **Mγ** was contaminated with a MS belonging to the **F** tradition; the source of the contamination cannot have been **F** itself, because **F** belongs to the late thirteenth or fourteenth century, while **γ** is assigned to the twelfth century. In order to ascertain whether the source of the corrections in the exemplar of **Mγ** contained any material not found in the **F** tradition, it is necessary to compare **Mγ** with the indirect tradition.

In the following places I have noted agreement between **Mγ** and the indirect tradition:

354b8	οὐκ alterum om. **Mγ** *Lex. Vind.* **Prisciani C**
362a1	ἐκκαυθήσεται] ἐκκοφθήσεται **Mγ**: ἐκκοπήσεται **Clem. Eus. Thdt.** (β^pc)
362a2	ἀνασχινδυλευθήσεται] ἀνασκινδαλευθήσεται **Mγ Phot.** (bis) **Suid. Theodoreti codd. aliquot**
405c2	διεξελθών] διελθών β **Mγ Phot. Suid.**
425c2	ὂν om. **Mγ Stob.**
430a7	χαλεστραίου] χαλαστραίου **Mγ Stob. Poll. Tim. sch. Pl. ad loc.**
433c8	ἢ ἡ habent **M^isl γ Stob.**: ἢ **ADF**
439e6	τούτῳ] τοῦτο **Mγ Stob. Gal.**
445c1	καὶ alterum om. **Mγ Stob.** (etiam **Vind.Bon.Sc.**)
457b1	γυναιξί] ταῖς γυναιξὶ **M** (non ita **γ**) **Eus. Thdt.** (etiam **Vind. Bon.**)
465d2	τε prius] δὲ **Mγ Stobaei M**

523d5	ἐσήμηνεν] ἐσήμαινε **Mγ** Iambl.
524a7	αὕτη] αὐτὴ **Mγ** Iambl.
544e1	ῥέψαντα] ῥεύσαντα **Mγ** Hsch.
547a5	γενεῆς habent **Mγ** Procl. (errat Burnet): γενεᾶς ADF Plot.
588e3	Λέγωμεν] λέγομεν **Mγ**(P) Eusebii ND
591c7	ζήσει habent **Mγ** Iambl. *AB* Phot. (ut vid.): ζώσει A: ζώση D: ζῶ F
600d6	ὀνῆσαι Aristidis A: ὀνῆναι **γ** Aristidis codd. quinque Eusebii N: ὀνίναι A^pcM Eusebii IO Aristidis U: ὀνεῖναι A^acDF^1pc: ὂν εἶναι F^ac
614d6	τῷ ἑτέρῳ] τῶ ἑτέρω **γ** Stob. (τὸ ἕτερον **M**)
616a3	κνάμπτοντες] κνάπτοντες **Mγ** Procl. Phot. Theodoreti codd. plerique
616a6-7	μὴ—ἀναβαίνοι] τὸν φόβον εἰ μυκήσαιτο τὸ στόμιον **Mγ**^3im et sic fere **Proclus** hunc locum interpretatus
620e5	ἄγειν] ἄγει **γ** Stobaei P (non ita **M** et Stobaei F)

Some of these readings are trivial errors and do not tell us anything at all about contamination of **Mγ**; these cases are 354b8, 405c2, 588e3, 600d6, 616a3 and 620e5. With regard to the reading ῥεύσαντα at 544e1, one should realize that ῥεύσαντα and ῥέψαντα are pronounced in the same way; the erroneous form is especially quoted by Hesychius.

Some of the other readings, however, are very interesting. The place where **Mγ** agree most conspicuously with the indirect tradition is 616a6-7. In his paraphrase of this passage Proclus writes (II 183,27-29 Kroll): παντοδαπῶν γὰρ αὐτοῖς γενομένων δειμάτων τοῦτον ὑπερβάλλειν τὸν φόβον μὴ μυκῆται τὸ στόμιον καὶ αὐτῶν ἀνιόντων κτέ; **M**^it and **γ**^3im have ἔνθα δὴ φόβων, ἔφη, πολλῶν καὶ παντοδαπῶν σφίσι γεγονότων τούτων ὑπερβάλλειν τὸν φόβον εἰ μυκήσαιτο τὸ στόμιον κτέ: both the addition of τὸν φόβον and the variant reading εἰ μυκήσαιτο τὸ στόμιον for μὴ—ἀναβαίνοι are clearly taken from either Proclus himself or a common source of Proclus and the ancestor of **Mγ**. However, it must be noted that Proclus has τὸν φόβον μὴ (which is correct), while **Mγ** have τὸν φόβον εἰ, which is equivalent to τὸν φόβον μὴ οὐ; yet this may be an error due to carelessness (the change could have been caused by itacism); the reading μυκήσαιτο in **Mγ** for Proclus' μυκῆται may be the result of dittography of τὸ; subsequently, μυκῆται τὸ τὸ was changed into μυκήσαιτο τὸ.

I do not think it very likely that the reading originated in Proclus and **Mγ** independently. Now the hypothesis that the common source of **Mγ** drew upon Proclus for this reading is by far the most attractive, because the sentence as it stands in Proclus is a paraphrase of the type which we encounter frequently in his commentary. We may assume that someone who read the *Republic* in a predecessor of **Mγ** also consulted Proclus' commentary, and was struck by the paraphrase he found in Proclus; accordingly, he noted the words in the margin of his Plato MS (probably as a scholium), from where they passed into the text of **M** and the margin of **γ** (**γ**^3 draws upon the exemplar of **γ**; see pp. 123 f.).

The one other case of agreement with Proclus, 547a5, may also come from Proclus' commentary, but the agreement may just as well be coincidental.

At 362a1, the reading of **Μγ** ἐκκοφθήσεται agrees substantially with ἐκκοπήσεται of Clement, Eusebius and Theodoretus (which is actually found in βp^c); it is hard to believe that the agreement is coincidental, but it should be noted that —υθ— was pronounced in the same way as —φθ—, so that the changing of ἐκκαυθήσεται into ἐκκοφθήσεται may be due to inner dictation. That ἐκκαυθήσεται is the correct reading, is certain on the basis of ἐκκαυθήσονται at 613e2, where Plato expressly refers to 362a. Yet it is difficult to establish which readings circulated in antiquity. Cicero, in his imitation of this passage (*Rep.* III 17,27 = 94,6-10 Ziegler), has *effodiantur oculi, vinciatur, uratur*; Clement, Eusebius and Theodoretus, as has been pointed out, read ἐκκοπήσεται τὼ ὀφθαλμὼ κτέ; but in another place, when paraphrasing the same passage, Clement has ἐξορύττηται, which again recalls Cicero's *effodiantur*; thus it looks as if in Cicero's time there was a variant reading ἐκκοπήσεται or ἐξορυχθήσεται (both ἐκκόπτειν and ἐξορύττειν can be used in this context; see LSJ s.v. ἐκκόπτω 1, s.v. ἐξορύττω II 2); it is imaginable that Cicero's copy contained both readings, which would account for his translation *effodiantur-uratur*; of course, this explanation is highly speculative. Be that as it may, it is more than likely that the reading of **Μγ** goes back to some ancient source, whether a lost copy of Plato or one of the Fathers.

At 362a2 the reading ἀνασκινδαλευθήσεται is also found in Photius, Suidas and some of the MSS of Theodoretus, which suggests that this reading and the variant reading at 362a1 were taken from Theodoretus, but agreement here may well be fortuitous.

At 457b1 the addition of ταῖς before γυναιξί in **M** (not **γ**) is also found in Eusebius and Theodoretus (and **Vind.Bon.**); I believe that this agreement is coincidental, because (as I have already noted above, p. 216) the article is often added or omitted in our MSS.

The two cases of agreement with Iamblichus at 523d5 and 524a7 are not very striking in themselves, but it is remarkable that they are found so close together.

At 591c7 **Μγ** have ζήσει with Iamblichus against ζώσει **A** (ζώση **D**: ζῶ **F**), but I do not think that this reading is necessarily due to contamination of **Μγ** with an ancient source.

There remain some cases of agreement with Stobaeus, none of which, however, is fully convincing. I will give a brief discussion of the passages in question.

> **425c2** ὄν om. **Μγ Stob.**: the omission of ὄν does not seriously affect the sense, and may result from haplography, ὅμοιον preceding. Moreover, ὄν

is also omitted in **F**ac, so that the omission in **Μγ** may also be the result of contamination with an ancestor of **F**.

430a7 χαλεστραίου] χαλαστραίου **Μγ Stob. Tim. Poll. sch. Pl. ad loc.**: given the fact that this reading is also found in the scholium in **A**, the most obvious explanation for its occurrence in **Μγ** is that an ancestor of **Μγ** placed the reading of the scholium in the text; the fact that **M** and **γ** reproduce only a very restricted number of the **A**-scholia does not exclude the possibility that their common source did have them (the **A**-scholia do recur in **T**, which is a gemellus of **Μγ**). In general, χαλαστραῖος is better attested than χαλεστραῖος; see LSJ s.v. Χαλαστραῖος.

The addition of ἡ at **433c8** may be due to conjecture as well as to contamination.

439e6 τούτῳ] τοῦτο **Μγ Stob. Gal.**: this reading seems to have been provoked by the preceding τι.

445c1 καὶ alterum om. **Μγ Stob.** (et **Vind.Bon.Sc.**): καὶ can be dispensed with, and it is easily omitted.

465d2 τε prius] δὲ **Μγ Stob.**: τε is markedly superior to δὲ, corresponding with τε after ζήσουσί, and δὲ is easily substituted for τε, at the beginning of a sentence.

614d6 τὼ ἑτέρω] τῶ ἑτέρω **γ Stob.** (τὸ ἕτερον **M**): this is nothing more than a very simple error, only involving the change of the accent.

I conclude that there are no really convincing cases of agreement between **Μγ** and Stobaeus; yet it is remarkable that those cases which occur are found all (except one) within some forty Stephanus pages (425-465); if the agreement of **Μγ** with Stobaeus is the result of contamination, this suggests 1. that an ancestor of **Μγ** drew on a Plato MS and not on a MS of Stobaeus; 2. that the contamination with this MS was restricted roughly to books IV-V.

All in all, we have found some indications that **Μγ** contain a number of readings which may go back to antiquity; the most striking cases, however, are probably derived from the indirect tradition.

2. In quite a few places **Μγ** (sometimes **M** or **γ** alone) are the principal or sole MSS to preserve a true or highly probable reading:

425d4	παράπαν **Μγ**: πάμπαν **ADF**
428c12	ἤ **γ** (non ita **M**): ἡ **D**: ἡ **AM**: ἤ **F**
433c8	ἤ ἡ **M**1sl**γ Stob.**: ἤ **AF**: ἡ **D**
497c8	ἐνεῖναι **Μγ**: ἐν εἶναι **AF**: εν εἶναι (sic) **D**
547a5	γενεῆς **Μγ Procl.**: γενεᾶς **ADF Plot.**
548a3	ἴδια **Μγ**: ἰδία(ι) **ADF**
553b2	ἤ τιν' **γ**: ἤ τινα **M**: ἤ τὴν **ADF**
558c2	γενναία **M** (non ita **γ**): γενναῖα **ADF**
571b2	ἐν καλῶ **Μγ**: ἐγκαλῶ **ADF**
578a4	τε **Μγ**: γε **ADF**
591c7	ζήσει **Μγ Iambl.**: ζώσει **A**: ζώση **D**: ζῶ **F**
611c3	θεατέον **Μγ** (διαθεατέον β^pc): διαθετέον **ADF**

In four of these cases the correction in **Mγ** only involves changing an accent and/or breathing: 428c12, 497c8, 548a3 and 558c2.

The readings 547a5 γενεῆς and 591c7 have already been mentioned in section 1 (p. 228); in fact, I do not believe that γενεῆς is certainly correct against γενεᾶς of **ADF** and Plotinus; J. Labarbe, *L'Homère de Platon* (Liège 1949), 324 f., believes that Plato wrote γενεῆς.

The readings of **Mγ** at 425d4, 433c8, 553b2, 571b2 and 611c3 are decidedly better than the readings of **ADF**; whether they are due to contamination or to conjecture, it is impossible to decide; the reading παράπαν at 425d4 may also have come into **Mγ** by mere chance.

Finally, the reading at 578a4 is an obvious correction, which may have been made unconsciously.

3. There are only few places where a reading in **Mγ** is obviously a deliberate attempt to improve the text; one such case is 469e5 διακωλύσεις] σκυλεύσεις **M¹ˢˡγ¹ˢˡ** (nisi forte διασκυλεύσεις intellegendum): this conjecture is probably based on σκυλεύειν at 469c8 (διασκυλεύσεις can hardly have been intended, because this word is not found in extant Greek). Another case is found on the same page: 469c9 ἔχει; ἢ οὔ; ἔχει ἢ οὔ; ἢ **Mγ¹ˢˡ**. Further, the reading χθονίαν] χρονίαν at 619e4 must have been a double reading in the exemplar of **Mγ**, as **γ** has both readings.

In a good many places, the reading of **Mγ** is clearly a simplification of the transmitted reading; some instances:

329c7   ἐπειδάν] ἐπειδὰν γὰρ
329d1   δεσποτῶν] καὶ δεσποτῶν
436a11 γέννησιν] γένεσιν
472b1   γίγνεσθαι] γίγνεται
475b1   τιμᾶσθαι] τιμῶνται
494b6   προσφερής] προσφερὲς
497a5   μετὰ τῶν ἰδίων τὰ κοινά] τὰ τῶν ἰδίων καὶ τὰ τῶν κοινῶν
535d4   διά om.
550e2   ἀπηργάσαντο] ἀπειργάσατο

In some places, an explanatory gloss seems to have crept into the text; see for instance:

393e2   οἵ] οἱ αὐτῷ
439b3   τι prius] τι ὁ λόγος

Some readings result from perseveration or anticipation; some instances:

496a1   διαφέρει] διαφέρειν (cf. διαφέρειν 495e4)
496c5   γενόμενοι] γευόμενοι (cf. γευσάμενοι c6; but this reading may also be due to confusion of υ and ν)

I conclude that, apart from the readings mentioned in sections 1 and 2 (pp. 226-230), **M γ** do not contain many important readings; the readings which cannot be explained as errors or simplifications, are very few.

8. N

1. In the following places I have noted agreement between **N** and the indirect tradition:

415a2   δή om. **N Clem. Eus.** (uno loco; habet **Eus.** altero loco): add. **N**^pc
435e7   τὸν **N**^pc **Stob.**: περὶ τὸν rell. (*** τῶν **N**^pc: ex τῶν fecit τὸν, et deinde iterum add. περὶ in rasura: τὸν (sic) **E**^ac: περὶ τὸν **E**^2pc)
452b1   καὶ ἤδη] ἤδη καὶ **N**^pc **Eus.**
458c7   ἐξέλεξας del. **N**: om. **Eus. Thdt.**
581e6   Ὅτε] ὅτι **N**^pc **Galeni H** (ὅ** **Galeni L**)

The case of 415a2 is, I think, a mere coincidence (note that it is a reading of **N**, not of **N**^pc): the other four cases are indeed surprising, but I guess that they may be due to conjectural emendation on the part of Bessarion: the deletion of ἐξέλεξας at 458c7 is an attempt to avoid the repetition ἐξέλεξας—ἐκλέξας; the reading ἤδη καὶ at 452b1, also found in Eusebius, is remarkable, but not, I think, conclusive: if these two readings are due to contamination, Bessarion may well have taken them from Eusebius, as he was thoroughly acquainted with the Fathers. The deletion of περὶ at 435e7, which is also the reading of Stobaeus (accepted by Burnet and Chambry, who did not know that this is also the reading of **N**^pc) is very noteworthy. The reading ὅτι for ὅτε at 581e6, finally, is an easy conjecture.

It cannot be proved beyond doubt that these few readings are conjectures by Bessarion and are not to be explained as the result of contamination with an ancient source, but I may remark that, if Bessarion did make use of an ancient primary witness, whose text was closely related to the text of Eusebius and/or Stobaeus, it is very strange that there are only five cases of agreement between Bessarion and these authors, while Bessarion has added hundreds of variant readings from whatever source he had at his disposal (see pp. 144 f.); the same argument could be brought against the supposition that Bessarion took these readings from Eusebius and Stobaeus directly.

I conclude that the possibility that Bessarion had access to a lost primary source cannot be excluded altogether, but is improbable; the same goes, to a lesser degree, for the hypothesis that Bessarion made use of the indirect tradition itself.

2. In the following places **N** is the principal or only MS to preserve a true reading:

413c7   αὐτοῖς ποιεῖν del. **N**pc
422e9   πολεμία **N**pc: πολέμια **D**: πολέμιαι **AF** (errat Burnet)
427b7   τε add. **N**sl
435e7   περὶ del. **N**pc: om. **Stob.**: habent **ADF**
449c1   ὅτι **N**pc: ἔτι **ADF**
454b4   μὴ add. **N**sl: om. **ADF Gal.**

The words αὐτοῖς ποιεῖν at 413c7 are quite superfluous; Adam ad loc. says: "it is difficult to see why a scribe should have introduced the words", but I do not see any objection to the hypothesis that they represent an original gloss. The reading πολεμία at 422e9 is a very easy correction of a still more easily made error; J. J. Hartman 242 proposes reading πολεμίω ἀλλήλοιν. As to the addition of τε at 427b7, Adam ad loc. rightly notes that "asyndeton is indefensible here". The deletion of περὶ at 435e7 is attractive, but not certain. The reading ὅτι for ἔτι at 449c1 is an admirable and, to my mind, certain emendation, but Richards 1893, 349, rejects it.

The text as it stands in the primary MSS and Galen at 454b4 is indefensible; the addition of μὴ is the most obvious correction, easier than the substitution of ἄλλην for αὐτὴν (Baiter); cf. Jowett-Campbell and Adam ad loc.; J. J. Hartman 250 conjectures τὴν <μὴ> for τὸ <μὴ>. Cornarius, in De Lacy's edition of Galen's *PHP*, II 554, app. crit. ad l. 1, notes: "delendum tamen est οὐ vel hoc [i.e. <μὴ>] inserendum".

3. Besides the enormous number of variant readings borrowed from other MSS, Bessarion has added a lot of readings which are not found in any other extant MS (except **N**'s apographon **E**), and which in all probability are his own conjectures. I discuss a number of these readings.

a. In some places Bessarion has added one or more words; some instances:

347d1   ἐπιτρέψαι] ἐπιτρέψαι τὴν ἀρχὴν
358d6   post βουλομένῳ add. εἴη s.l.
359e1   δακτύλιον] δακτύλιον φέρειν
459e5   post νομοθετητέαι add. ἔσονται s.l.
551e3   post ἅτε add. ὄντας s.l.

On one occasion, such an addition shows that Bessarion misinterpreted Plato's Greek: 617a4 post ἕκτον add. ὑπερβάλλειν **N**sl: the second planet (Saturn) had already been mentioned at a2; Plato actually says that the sixth planet (Venus) is second in whiteness, the whitest planet being the third (Jupiter, a3).

b. Some of the corrections are clearly intended to improve the grammar; see for instance:

349c1 βούλεται] βούλοιτο **N^sl**: Bessarion probably regarded ἀξιοῖ as an optative.

427a5 ἀνωφελῆ] ἀνωφελὲς **N^pc**: here Bessarion failed to notice that ἀνωφελῆ is said of all the specific measures of the law-givers, not of their activity as such. Moreover, the singular presents itself easily before πλέον οὐδέν, which follows immediately, but which of course has a quite different syntactical function.

459a4 παιδοποιίᾳ] παιδοποιίαις **N^sl**: a perseveration of the preceding γάμοις.

465c2 παιδοτροφίᾳ] παιδοτροφίαις **N^sl**: an anticipation of χρηματισμοῖς which follows at c3.

c. There are also a large number of other conjectures; I will discuss some of these:

336e9 οἵου γε σύ **Bekker**: οἵου τε σύ **ADF**: οἷόν γέ ἐστιν **N**: an intelligent attempt to emend the unintelligibly transmitted words οἵου τε σύ. As it stands, οἷόν γέ ἐστιν is impossible, because of the words ὦ φίλε, which are completely out of place after a sentence of this length. See the discussion of this place on pp. 211 f.

357b7-8 καὶ alterum—γίγνεται] κἂν—γίγνηται: that the second part of a relative clause is continued with a demonstrative pronoun, is quite normal Greek idiom, as Adam ad loc. points out; Bessarion's reading is an attempt to avoid this construction, which he probably felt as an anacoluthon.

358e2 τί ὄν τε] τί τε ὂν τυγχάνει **N^im**: the addition of τυγχάνει removes the anacoluthic construction of the text as it stands in **A**; see the discussion of β's reading, p. 212.

428a6 ἔτι] τι **N^im**: this reading has probably been introduced because ἔτι is pleonastic, and because of the familiarity of the phrase ἄλλο τι.

435c4 εἰς] οὐκ εἰς **N^pc**: Bessarion apparently failed to appreciate Socrates' irony here.

440e5-6 τὸ λογιστικόν] τοῦ λογιστικοῦ **N^sl**: a very attractive conjecture, accepted by Schneider and Jowett-Campbell, among others; "side with" is usually expressed by πρός + genitive (LSJ s.v. A III 2; KG I 517 even quote this place for this meaning of πρός followed by the genitive). If τοῦ λογιστικοῦ is indeed correct, then the corruption to τὸ λογιστικὸν was very easy after τίθεσθαι πρός. Even so, Adam, Burnet and Chambry may be right in retaining the reading of **ADF**; cf. Adam ad loc.

461c1 ᾧ] ἤ **N^pc**: Bessarion seems to believe that Socrates is only speaking about heterosexual love of males, but the mentioning of γυναῖκες at b9 makes it clear that ᾧ stands for both men and women, although homosexual love does not seem to be implied here.

479a3-4 ἐκεῖνος ὁ φιλοθεάμων καὶ del. **N^pc**: at first sight these words can be dispensed with, but Adam is right in remarking that "οὐδαμῇ ἀνεχόμενος by itself would be comparatively tame".

491e4 ἄκρατον] γρ. ἀκροτάτην **N^im**: a witty conjecture; yet the point being made is not so much the degree of wickedness, as its absoluteness, i.e. the complete absence of goodness.

521c7 οὖσαν del. **N^pc**: by deleting οὖσαν, Bessarion intended to combine ἀληθινήν with ἐπάνοδον, thus gravely misinterpreting the passage. See Adam's Appendix VI to book VII (II 182 f.): see also **Par.**'s reading (p. 225).

527a3 λόγοις del. **N^pc**: obviously, Bessarion was displeased with the pleonastic collocation λόγοις λεγομένοις; λόγοις is also bracketed by J. L. V. Hartman 316.

533e4-5 ἀλλ' —ψυχῇ del. **N^pc**: this phrase has puzzled many scholars, and a host of conjectures have been made (see Adam's Appendix XVI to book VII (II 192 f.); see also Schneider's note). I agree with Adam (who follows **N^pc** in deleting the words) that the whole phrase can easily be dispensed with, but I am less confident than he is about the origin of the interpolation. If it really is a gloss, its wording is very strange, to say the least.

578a7 τε] δὲ **N^pc**: τε can be missed after the first item of an enumeration, while the asyndeton is a bit harsh; therefore δέ may be correct (it is accepted by Jowett-Campbell and Adam). I do not understand how Burnet can attribute this reading to **Laur. xxxix**.

616e5 ἕκτου] πέμπτου **N^sl**; e7 πέμπτου] δευτέρου **N^sl**; e8 δευτέρου] ἕκτου **N^sl**: the reading e7 πέμπτου] δευτέρου is also found in **D**; this reading undoubtedly provided the basis for the other two readings in **N** as well. I will refrain from discussing the implications of these variant readings here, as this would involve too much detail; see Adam's notes and his Appendix VI to book X (II 470-479) (Adam did not know the variant readings in **N^sl**, which, by the way, are also found in **Ambr.**, Ficino's autograph).

9. VMatr.

1. In the following places I have noted agreement between **VMatr.** and the indirect tradition:

350c1	γε om. **V Stob.** (habet **Matr.**)
368e2-3	ἀνδρὸς ἑνός] ἑνὸς ἀνδρὸς **VMatr. Gal.** (et α)
379c2	Οὐδ'] οὐκ **VMatr. Thdt.**
379c5	οὐδένα] οὐδέν **V Eus. Procl.** (οὐδένα habet **Matr.**)
383a2	ἔφην] ἔφη **VMatr. Eus.**
425b8	οὔτ' ἄν] ὅταν **V Stobaei MA** (οὔτ' ἄν habent **Matr. Stobaei S**)
452a2	γε om. **VMatr. Gal.** (τε **ADF**: γε ci. **Richards**)
473a5	Τοῦτο] τούτῳ **V Stob.** (non ita **Matr.**)
490c2	δή] δέ **VMatr. Stob.**
599a8	ἀφεῖναι] ἐφεῖναι **VMatr. Them.**
600b6	αὖ] ἄν **V Aristidis codd. plerique** (non ita **Matr.**)

Of all these cases, I believe that only the readings at 379c5 and 599a8 deserve some interest; the other readings are simple errors or variant readings which we encounter often.

The reading οὐδέν at 379c5 is not impossible, because the causes of evil are also expressed in the neuter (ἀλλ' ἄττα—τὰ αἴτια c6-7).

Finally, ἐφεῖναι at 599a8 is only a slight modification; for the use of ἀφεῖναι in this place Jowett-Campbell aptly compare 373d9 ἀφῶσιν.

Thus I do not find any positive evidence of contamination of **VMatr.** with a lost primary source.

2. At 487c1 **VMatr.** alone preserve the manifestly correct reading φέρωσιν against φέρουσιν of the other MSS. At 558e1 ἄν is found only in **V** (not in **Matr.**, nor in **M**, as Jowett-Campbell, Adam, Burnet and Chambry wrongly report): ἄν cannot be dispensed with, and may easily have dropped out as the result of haplography (ἀναγκαῖαι follows immediately).

3. In isolated places **VMatr.** have a reading which deserves some attention; I will discuss some of these readings.

444b5 τῷ δ' οὐ δουλεύειν **Burnet**: τοῦ δ' αὖ δουλεύειν **ADF Stob.**: τῷ δ' αὖ μὴ δουλεύειν **VMatr.**: as a solution for this difficult phrase, the reading of **VMatr.** (provided, of course, that τῷ is replaced by τώ) seems to me much more attractive than the reading of **Vind.Bon.Sc.** τῶ τοῦ for τῷ δ' οὐ δουλεύειν (see p. 215) or the reading of β^pc τὼ δ' αὖ δουλεύειν ἀρχικοῦ γένους ὄντε for τῷ—ὄντι (see p. 212). But although the reading of **VMatr.** makes good sense, I believe that the words of this crux will never be established beyond any doubt.

562b6 πλούτου] τούτου: the repetition of πλούτου, immediately after b4 πλοῦτος, is a bit harsh (though not uncommon in Greek); the reading τούτου evades this repetition and is satisfactory in itself (Schneider calls it *peridoneum*); if it is a conjecture, it is a very good one.

In some cases a gloss has crept into the text at the expense of the original reading; see for instance 397c9 τύπῳ] μέρει and 499d3 εἰρημένη] ἡμετέρα.

10. αt

1. I have noted the following cases of agreement between **α** (sometimes in combination with **t**) and the indirect tradition:

330c7	ἀλλ'] ἄλλο **α Stobaei S**: ἀλλ' **Stobaei M** (ἀλλ' habent **t Stobaei A**)
365e5	παράγεσθαι] παραγενέσθαι **αt Cyr.**
368e2-3	ἀνδρὸς ἑνός] ἑνὸς ἀνδρὸς **α Gal.** (non ita **t**) (etiam **VMatr.**)
377b5-6	ὑπὸ τῶν ἐπιτυχόντων om. **αt Eus.**
380c3	αὐτὰ om. **α Thdt.** (habet **t**)
381a10	δὴ om. **α Eus.** (habet **t**)
381b11	τὸ alterum om. **α Eus.** (habet **t**)
387d2	τοὺς om. **α Stob.** (habet **t**)
399b2	καρτερούντως] καρτερῶς **α Them.** (non ita **t**)
421e6	Φαίνεται] φαίνονται **α^ac Stob.** (non ita **t**)
433c4	γε om. **α Stob.** (habet **t**)

435d3	ἄλλη habent α Gal.: ἀλλά ADF(t)
436d5	γε] τε αt Gal.
439b6	πράττοι] πράττειν αt Galeni H
441b6	ἠνίπαπε] ἠνείπαπε α Gal. (non ita t)
445d5	μὲν om. αt Stob.
451e1	ὡς] ταῖς μὲν ὡς α Galeni ed. Bas. (non ita t)
518b6	νομίσαι] νοῆσαι α Iambl. (non ita t)
525b1	γε om. α Iambl. (habet t)
531b3	κολλόπων] κολάβων αt sch. Pl. ad loc.: κολλάβων Theon Sm. Tim.
540d6	ἀξίας] ἀξίους α Stob. (non ita t)
616a1	καταβαλόντες] καταλαβόντες α[sl] Iustini D[im] (non ita t)
617a5	δὴ om. α Procl. Theon Sm. (habet t)

Of all these readings, I believe that only 435d3, 518b6 and 531b3 deserve some attention. The omissions which are common to α(t) and the indirect tradition are never significant, nor is the transposition at 368e2-3. It is remarkable that at 451e1 α agrees with the Basle edition of Galen, but here the addition is made very easily and must have originated in α and Galen's Basle edition independently (of course, contamination of α from this edition is out of the question). As to the case of 616a1, one should realize that cod. **D** of Justin is a sixteenth-century MS, which in other places shows traces of contamination with the MSS of the **Mγ**-group, e.g. 616a6-7 μή—ἀναβαίνοι] τὸν φόβον εἰ μυκήσαιτο τὸ στόμιον ὅτε ἀναβαίνοιεν **Iustini D**: this variant reading is also found (without ὅτε ἀναβαίνοιεν) in **Mγ** and their derivatives (to which αt also belong).

The reading ἄλλο at 330c7 is not surprising after οὐδὲν and followed by ἤ.

At 435d3 the reading ἄλλη, which is markedly superior to ἀλλά of **ADF**, is also found in Galen; yet I do not believe that it could not have been hit upon by an intelligent scribe, but the possibility of contamination cannot be excluded.

The reading νοῆσαι for νομίσαι at 518b6, also found in Iamblichus, may be due to contamination, but in itself νοῆσαι is just a synonym for νομίσαι, and the variant reading νοῆσαι may be the result of itacism (α has νομίσαι above the line, apparently by the first hand).

At 531b3 the reading κολάβων also occurs in Theon Smyrnaeus and Timaeus; it is also found in the **A**-scholium, but this scholium does not recur in **Mγ** and their derivatives.

On balance, I think it highly improbable that α (or αt) have undergone serious contamination with a lost primary source.

2. At 435d3, α is the only MS to preserve the almost certainly correct reading ἄλλη (with Galen) against ἀλλά of the other MSS. At 518b1 t has the correct reading εὐδαιμονίσειεν (with **Par.**P[c] and **R**) against

εὐδαιμονήσειε(ν) of the other MSS; this is a very easy correction, which may have been made unconsciously.

3. In a few places, α (sometimes in combination with t) has a reading which deserves some attention; I will also discuss some readings of α^pc.

406c6 γελοίως] γελοῖον α^1sl: an obvious attempt to bring γελοῖον into accordance with the preceding ὅ; for the meaning of γελοίως here see Jowett-Campbell and Adam ad loc.; Naber 438 proposes deleting γελοίως.

422c1 ἀναστρέφοντα] ἀναστρέφοντι αt: probably conjectured in order to avoid the slight (but quite unexceptionable) anacoluthon b10-c1 ὑποφεύγοντι—ἀναστρέφοντα.

441d12 ὅτου] ὅτῳ α^sl (altera manus, ut vid.): a possible alternative for ὅτου, but not necessarily better.

456c4 γε] τε α (deest t): a good reading, possibly authentic, which was conjectured by Bekker and accepted by many editors (Hermann, Jowett-Campbell, Adam).

515b5 ὄντα Iambl.: παρόντα **ADF**: παριόντα α^pc (altera manus, ut vid.): given the reading παρόντα of **ADF**, παριόντα is an intelligent attempt to make some sense of this notorious crux; the reading παριόντα was conjectured by Ast and accepted by Stallbaum, Hermann and Adam, who translates: "do you not suppose they would believe that they were naming these particular passing objects which they saw?" I do not believe that παριόντα has any claim to genuineness; whether ὄντα or παρόντα is read, the point being made is that the prisoners confuse shadows with reality; see also the discussion of this place on p. 76.

11. x^rec.

x itself is a (possibly direct) transcript of **F** (see pp. 190-192), and does not have any peculiar readings, except some obvious errors. Yet several later hands have occupied themselves with adding corrections, variant readings, glosses etc.; some of these readings are quite interesting and there are a few cases of agreement with the indirect tradition.

Because I have not been able to check all the readings added by later hands in **x** *in situ*, I designate all later hands as **x^pc** or, in the case of variant readings added in the margin or above the line, as **x^rec.**.

1. In the following places I have noted agreement between **x^rec.** and the indirect tradition:

351c2 σοφία] σοφίαν **x^pc** Stob.
461c6 τι] τις **x^pc** Eus. Thdt.
544c7 διαφέρουσα habent **x^pc** Stob.: διαφεύγουσα **ADF**
590e1 βούλεται habent **x^pc** Iambl. Stob.: βουλεύεται **ADF**
600e4 ἀρξαμένους] ἀρξάμενοι **x^pc** Aristid. Eus.

Of these five cases, the readings at 544c7 and 590e1 are certain corrections; the readings at 461c6 and 600e4 are easily hit upon, nor is the correction σοφίαν at 351c2 such as cannot be ascribed to conjectural emendation. Thus there are no certain indications of contamination of $x^{rec.}$ with an ancient source.

2. In the following places $x^{rec.}$ is our main MS source of a correct reading:

451b9   τότε x^{pc}: ποτε **ADF**
544c7   διαφέρουσα x^{pc} (et **Stob.**): διαφεύγουσα **ADF**
549a1   μέν τις ἄν x^{pc}: μάντις ἄν Fx^{ac}: μέν τισιν **D** et fort. A^{ac}: μέν τισ** A^{pc}
590e1   βούλεται x^{pc} (et **Iambl. Stob.**): βουλεύεται **ADF**

I believe that the readings at 451b9, 544c7 and 590e1 can be regarded as certain; for 549a1 Dr Slings proposes reading μὲν ἄν τις, which is the regular order of these words in Plato.

3. I will mention some further variant readings added by $x^{rec.}$:

a. Occasionally, one or two words have been added to clarify the sense; some instances:

389e2   ἡδονῶν] ἡδονῶν ἀπέχεσθαι $x^{rec.im}$
459c6   ἰατροῦ] ἰατροῦ. ἢ γάρ; $x^{rec.im}$
486a4   λάθῃ] λάθῃ ψυχὴ $x^{rec.im}$
516b2   ἡλίου] ἡλίου φῶς $x^{rec.im}$
558a8   περινοστεῖ] περινοστεῖ ὁ καταψηφισθεὶς $x^{rec.im}$

It is possible that some of these additions were intended as explanatory glosses, not as variant readings meant to be put into the text.

b. In some cases a variant reading facilitates or normalizes the construction of a sentence; some instances:

330b7   ἤ] ὧν $x^{rec.im}$
347c3-4 τῆς δὲ ζημίας] ζημία δὲ $x^{rec.im}$
349d9   ὁ δὲ μή] ὁ δὲ μὴ μή $x^{rec.im}$
363a3   γίγνηται] γίγνωνται $x^{rec.sl}$
519a5   ὥστε del. et ἐργαζόμενον] ἐργάσεται $x^{rec.im}$

c. Some variant readings affect the interpretation of a passage; see for instance:

437d8-9 ἢ οὔ λέγομεν] ποτοῦ λέγομεν $F^{5pc}x^{ac}$: ποτοῦ ἢ ὀλίγου x^{pc}
442e1   αὐτῷ] αὐτῇ x^{pc} (sc. τῇ ψυχῇ)
585c7   ἀεί] μὴ ἀεί x^{pc}

The correction at 585c7 has the same effect as the more elaborate correction in β: δὲ τοῦ μηδέποτε for οὖν ἀεί (see pp. 213 f.).

d. **x** has many glosses, both by the first hand and by several later hands; some instances:

392c4 τοιοῦτος] δίκαιος δὴ x^sl (x¹, ut vid.)
430a7 χαλεστραίου] νίτρου x^sl (x¹, ut vid.)
508d3 Τί μήν] καὶ μάλ' ἔφη x^im (x³, ut vid.)
534c3 ἀπτῶτι] βεβαίω x^sl (x¹, ut vid.)
559d9 δεινοῖς] πανούργοις x^5im

12. Par.^rec.

Several later hands have been at work in **Par.**; here I do not distinguish between all the different hands, because I have not been able to check all the readings discussed here *in situ*. I designate all later hands in **Par.** as **Par.**^pc or, in the case of variant readings added above the line or in the margin, as **Par.**^rec..

1. In three places I have noted agreement between **Par.**^rec. and the indirect tradition:

336e7-8 πολλῶν χρυσίων] πολλῷ χρυσίου **Par.**^rec.im **Stob.**
614a7 ἑκάτερος habent **Par.**^pc **Stob.**: ἑκάτερον **ADF Eus.**
615b3 πολλοῖς habent **Par.**^5im **Stob.**: πολλοί **AFPar.**: πολλῶν **Sc.** (deficit **D**)

These three cases of agreement are very interesting, the more so because two of them, which are probably correct, occur so close together; yet they do not seem to have been added by the same later hand: it is certain that the reading πολλοῖς at 615b3 was added by **Par.**^5 (see p. 179), but the fact that the reading ἑκάτερος at 614a7 recurs in **p** excludes the possibility that this reading is due to **Par.**^5, because in other places where I have established the identity of **Par.**^5 **p** does not follow **Par.**^5 (cf. p. 178). The reading πολλῷ χρυσίου at 336e7-8 can hardly be due to coincidence. If these three cases of agreement with the indirect tradition are the result of contamination, they may have been borrowed either from the indirect tradition itself (*i.c.* Stobaeus) or from a lost Plato MS related to Stobaeus' copy of the *Republic*.

2. In the following places **Par.**^rec. is the principal MS authority for a good or plausible reading:

518b1 εὐδαιμονίσειεν **Par.**^pc (et t**R**): εὐδαιμονήσειε(ν) **ADF**
553c5 τὸ **Par.**^rec.im: τὸν **ADF**
614a7 ἑκάτερος **Par.**^pc **Stob.**: ἑκάτερον **ADF Eus.**
615b3 πολλοῖς **Par.**^rec.im **Stob.**: πολλοί **AFPar.**: πολλῶν **Sc.** (deficit **D**)

3. A few other readings of **Par.**^(rec.) call for comment:

353d7 ἐκείνης] ἐκείνου **Par.**^(pc) (et αq²): the neuter must have been introduced to make ἐκείνου refer to ὅτῳ ἄλλῳ (d6) instead of ψυχῇ. ἐκείνης is bracketed by J. N. Madvig, *Adversaria Critica* (Copenhagen 1871), I 416.

365d8 τί καὶ ἡμῖν] καὶ ἡμῖν οὐ **Par.**^(rec.im): like **AD** and Cyrillus, **Par.** omits τί; the omission of τί makes the addition of a negative necessary; in itself the reading of β^(pc), οὐδ' ἡμῖν, is somewhat more elegant than καὶ ἡμῖν οὐ.

478a8 Δόξα] δόξαν **Par.**^(pc): after Δόξα, πέφυκεν must be supplied from a4; the reading δόξαν makes the sentence a8 δόξαν δέ φαμεν δοξάζειν self-contained.

13. Other Manuscripts

In the foregoing sections I have discussed a number of individual secondary MSS in which interesting readings can be found; yet the MSS I have mentioned are by no means the only ones containing interesting material, but they are, in my opinion, the most important. In several other MSS a plausible or even authentic reading can sometimes be found; for instance, the true reading τιμὴ μὲν at 582c4 is first found in Θ, added by a later hand; the reading δοκεῖ at 579d9, which may well be the true reading, is first found in **Lobc.**; and there are more such cases. However, these cases are so isolated that I have not thought it necessary to discuss in full the MSS in which they occur.

Conclusion

From the discussion of the individual secondary MSS it will have become clear that positive indications of contamination of one or more secondary MSS with a lost primary source are rather slight; of course, we should realize that there are great portions of the *Republic* which are not covered by the indirect tradition, but in which authentic material from a lost primary source may have been introduced into a secondary Plato MS. As I have already stated at the beginning of this chapter (p. 201), we are never able to reject the possibility of contamination of secondary MSS from a lost primary source with absolute certainty, but as far as the evidence goes, I am inclined to think, with Burnet and Dodds (and others), that the true or plausible readings which we find in our secondary MSS are for the greater part conjectures; cf. pp. 13 f., 20 f.

On the one hand, this conclusion may seem disappointing: it would certainly have been interesting to see substantial traces of ancient tradition in our medieval secondary MSS. On the other hand, it is not altogether without importance that we can now realize how intensively and with what intelligence the text of the *Republic* was worked on in the Byzantine world. Up to the present day, many scholars have believed that Byzantine scholars were not capable of anything more than removing the most obvious errors they found in their texts (cf. pp. 8, 21). From my study of the secondary MSS of the *Republic* it has become clear that this position is untenable, at least with regard to the MSS of the *Republic*. Modern scholars should not think that philological acumen is something with which only they are gifted; we should not only be grateful to our Byzantine colleagues for preserving our classical texts, we should also admire them for the intelligence with which they tried to interpret and emend these texts.

CHAPTER FIVE

THE SIXTEENTH-CENTURY EDITIONS AND CORNARIUS' ECLOGAE

1. The Aldine edition

The *editio princeps* of the Greek Plato was published in Venice by Aldus Manutius in September 1513, almost thirty years after the first edition of Ficino's translation (1484); the editorial work was done by Marcus Musurus.

It was assumed that the main source of the Aldine could be identified as **E**, Bessarion's *de luxe* copy of the complete Plato (see, e.g., Campbell 92 f., Alline 316), until Post (41-44, 58 f.) drew attention to **N**, Bessarion's working copy and the direct source of **E**) for *R.*, *Ti.*, *Criti.*, *Min.*, *Lg.*, *Epin.*, *Epp.* and to Venetus 186 for the other dialogues. Post records some readings in *R.* where the Aldine edition agrees with **NE**, or with **N** against **E** and the other MSS.

Post's conclusions are fully backed up by my collation of the MSS and the Aldine. I will first quote some places where the Aldine agrees with **NE** against the other MSS;

329b6   ἔγωγε] ἐγὼ **NE Ald.**
331b3   ἐκεῖσε ἀπιέναι] ἀπιέναι ἐκεῖσε **NE Ald.**
331d8   ἔφη] ἔφην **NE Ald.**
331e7   λέγει] λέγοι **N^sl E Ald.**
516a6   καὶ alterum om. **N^pc E Ald.**
516b9   οὗτος] οὗτός ἐστιν **N^sl E Ald.**
517c3   νοητῷ] τῷ νοητῷ **N^sl E Ald.**
519d9   ὃν om. **N^pc E Ald.**
615c6   εἴη] ἂν εἴη **NE Ald.**
617a4   τὸν ἕκτον] τὸν ἕκτον ὑπερβάλλειν **N^sl E Ald.**
618e3   ἐάσει] ἐᾶν **N^pc E Ald.**

That the Aldine goes back to **N**, and not to **E**, is proved by the following observations:

1. The Aldine does not share the (scanty) separative errors of **E**:

330c9   ἔφη habent **N Ald.**: om. **E**
391b2   σπερχειοῦ habent **N Ald.**: σπερχιοῦ **E**
518a3   μεθισταμένων habent **N Ald.**: μεθισταμένῳ **E**
616c6   ἀδάμαντος habent **N Ald.**: ἀδάνμαντος **E**

2. In some places, the Aldine agrees with **NE^ac** against **E^pc** (the corrections and variant readings in **E** were added by Bessarion, who in 1468 gave his books to the Marcian library in Venice):

332b7   γε prius habet **E^pc**: om. **NE^ac Ald.**
515e3   δύναται habet **E^pc**: δύνανται **NE^ac Ald.**

3. In some cases, the Aldine has a reading which is found in **N** and some other MSS, but not in **E**:

387c2   οἴεται] οἷόν τε **N^sl** (α^im β^pc **Vind.^pc**) **Ald.**
390e7   μήνιος] μήνιδος **N^sl** (x^pc, alii) **Ald.**
518a2   γίγνονται] γίγνοιντ' ἄν **N^sl** (**Sc.α**) **Ald.**
616b7   προελθόντες] προελθόντας **N^sl** (**Par.**) **Ald.**

4. Occasionally, the Aldine agrees with **N** against **E** and all the other MSS:

358e2   τί ὄν τε] τί τε ὂν τυγχάνει **N^im Ald.** (this reading is also found in the recent part of **b**, which stems from the first Basle edition)
403b1   αὕτη ἡ ἡδονή] αὐτῷ ἡδονὴν **N^im Ald.**
409d3   χρηστοῖς] σοφοῖς **N^sl Ald.**
465b6   ἄξουσι] ἕξουσι **N^sl Ald.**
506a6   ἂν ἑαυτῶν] εἴπερ εἰκὸς γνῶναι αὐτὰ **N^im Ald.**
581e2-3   τῆς—καὶ] τὰς δ' ἄλλας **N^im**: τῆς ἡδονῆς οὐ πάνυ πόρρω τὰς δ' ἄλλας **Ald.**

But **N** is not the only MS used by Musurus for *R*.; Alline 316 mentions three other MSS which have been consulted for the Aldine; of these, Par. 1809 does not have the *Republic*; the other two, **b** and **q**, are mentioned by Campbell 93. **b**, however, can be dismissed, because the cases of agreement between the Aldine and **b** which are mentioned by Campbell occur in the recent part of **b**, which derives from the first Basle edition; the reading which is quoted by Campbell as occurring in **q** and the Aldine is also found in **Par.βK**; it is within this group that the auxiliary MS used by Musurus is to be sought.

In a number of places, the Aldine shares a reading of **Par.**; I will quote some of these:

387b8   τὰ alterum om. **Par. Ald.**
390c7   δι'] οὐδ' **Par. Ald.**
514b6   δεικνύασιν] δεικνῦσιν **Par. Ald.**
516c6   αὑτὸν] ἑαυτὸν **Par. Ald.**
517a3   ἥκει] ἥκοι **Par. Ald.**
518a7   ἀηθείας] ἀμαθίας **Par.^pc**: ἀμαθείας **Ald.**
520c8   τοῦ] τὸ **Par. Ald.**
619a5   τῶν τοιούτων βίον] τὸν τοιοῦτον βίον **Par. Ald.**
621a6   στέγειν] στέγει **Par. Ald.**
621b6   οὐχ] οὐδὲν **Par. Ald.**

Every now and then the Aldine shares a reading added in **Par.** by a later hand, which is not found in any of the extant apographa of **Par.**; see for instance:

353d7 ἐκείνης] ἐκείνου **Par.**^pc **Ald.**
365d8 τί καὶ ἡμῖν] καὶ ἡμῖν οὐ **Par.**^im **Ald.**

This proves that Musurus used either **Par.** itself, or a lost copy of **Par.**, and not one of the extant derivatives of **Par.**

There is occasional agreement with other MSS, but in most cases this agreement may very well be coincidental; see e.g.:

383a4 ὄντας om. αtV **Ald.**
388b6 κόπρον] κόπρου βK **Ald.**
492e6 λόγου] λόγον W **Ald.**
504c3 μέτρον] μέτρου W **Ald.**
508c5 τρέπῃ] πρέπῃ V **Ald.**
601e1 αὐλῶν] αὐτῶν K **Ald.**

However, the possibility that Musurus did use some other auxiliary MS besides **Par.** cannot be discarded conclusively.

In a few places the reading of the Aldine agrees with Ficino's translation; see for instance:

499a7 καὶ alterum om. **Fic. Ald.**
540a7 αὐγὴν] ἀκτίνα **Ald.**: *radium* **Fic.**

The Aldine has a lot of separative errors of its own, besides countless printing errors; some instances:

330b7 γέ] σέ
331a7 γηροτρόφος] ἢ γηροτρόφος
386c1 οὔτε] οὔπ'
515d6 αὐτὸν] αὐτὸ
518b7 ἐπαγγελλόμενοί] ἀπαγγελλόμενοί
519b5 ἑώρα] ἐόρα
520a9 γὰρ] δὲ
618b3 ἄλλον] ἄλλων
621d2 ἦν om.

In some cases, the Aldine has a reading which does not occur in any extant MS, and which makes good sense; some of these readings may be conjectural; some instances:

488e2 οἰόμενοι] οἰομένους (accepted by Ast[3], Bekker and Stallbaum[2])
532a2 ὃν prius-περαίνει] ὁ—περαίνων
601b2 ἔχειν] ἔχει (probat Schneider)
621b8 καὶ alterum habet **Ald.**: ἀλλ' **codd.** (N. B. the reading καὶ is accepted by all modern editors, including Burnet and Chambry, but they disagree about the MS in which καὶ is to be found; actually, it is in no MS at all)

2. The first Basle edition

The first Basle edition, published by Valder in 1534, contains the complete Plato, and in addition Proclus' commentaries on the *Republic* and the *Timaeus*; the editorial work was done by Simon Grynaeus and Johannes Oporinus.

The text is based exclusively upon the Aldine edition; **Bas.**[1] shares most of the characteristic readings of the Aldine, but corrects some obvious errors, mostly printing errors; see for instance:

543a2 κοινοὺς habet **Bas.**[1]: κοινοῦς **Ald.**
551d10 ἀναγκάζεσθαι habet **Bas.**[1]: ἀνακάζεσθαι **Ald.**
579d2 βίον habet **Bas.**[1]: βίο **Ald.**

In some places an error in the Aldine has been removed conjecturally; see for instance:

477d8 τινα] τινὰς **Ald.**: τινὸς **Bas.**[1]

Bas.[1] adds some peculiar readings of its own and has a lot of printing errors; some instances:

359c1 δόντες] δέοντες
428b12 σοφή] σοφοὶ
611d5 πέτρας] πέρας
616b2 λειμῶνι] λιμῶνι

For the dependence of the recent part of **b** on **Bas.**[1] see above, p. 151.

3. The second Basle edition

The second Basle edition was published in 1556 by Henricus Petrus; the critical work was done by Arnoldus Arlenius. The text is based upon the first Basle edition, emended with the help of MSS collated in Italy by Arlenius, as is stated in the *praefatio*.

The MSS which Arlenius consulted can be identified as **T** and **E**. For **T**, this was already shown by Schanz, RhM 33 (1878), 615, who mentions some cases of agreement between **T** and the second Basle edition in *Cra.* and *Alc.1*; I will quote some readings where **Bas.**[2] agrees with **T** in *R*.:

444c8 μέν που] μέντοι **Vind.Bon.Sc.T Bas.**[2]
492c4 ἴσχειν] ἔχειν **Sc.T Bas.**[2]
493d4 πόλει] πόλεως **T Bas.**[2]
494e3 οὐ] καὶ **T Bas.**[2]
502a6 τὰς] οἱ τὰς **Sc. T Bas.**[2]
521a4 ἀγαθῆς] ἄτερ ἀγαθῆς **TW Bas.**[2]
531a3 ἀστρονόμοι] ἀστρολόγοι **T Bas.**[2]
569a1 κατέστησεν] ἔθρεψεν **Sc.T**: κατέστησεν καὶ ἔθρεψεν **Bas.**[2]

That Arlenius used **E** as well is illustrated by the following readings:

467b6   μή ποτε] μηδέποτε N^{sl}**E** Bas.²
480a7   καὶ] κἄν N^{pc}**E** Bas.²
527c2   καλλιπόλει] καλλίστῃ πόλει N^{pc}**E** Bas.²
539d5   μὴ] μηδὲν **NE** Bas.²
540d3   οὐκ ἄλλῃ ἢ] οὐ κακῶς N^{pc}**E** Bas.²
547e1   Τῷ] τὸ **E**^{pc} Bas.² (non ita **N**)
602b6   φαίνεται] ἔοικεν **NE**: φαίνεται ἔοικεν Bas.²

The reading of 547e1 shows that Arlenius used **E**, not **N**; this was only to be expected, as **E** contains the complete Plato.

The cases of 569a1 and 602b6 suggest that there was some misunderstanding between Arlenius and the printer: what had probably been intended as an alternative reading by Arlenius, was interpreted as an addition by the printer.

The second Basle edition corrects a great many errors of its predecessors, but adds some (printing) errors of its own; some instances:

477a6   ἔχει] ἔχεις
488c2   ἐπιτρέψῃ] ἐπιστρέψῃ
586e4   ἁπάσης] ἕπασης
605d7   οἰκεῖόν] οἰκόν

4. Cornarius' Eclogae

Five years after the second Basle edition, in 1561, the Latin translation of Plato by Ianus Cornarius was published. This translation was accompanied by the so-called *Eclogae*, in which Cornarius proposed a number of emendations. The *Eclogae* were edited separately by I. F. Fischer (Leipzig 1771).

The *Eclogae* appear to have some importance for the history of the text, because Cornarius in his preface states that he has used a Greek MS: (p. 4) "(...) et manu scriptum unum, quod ex Bibliotheca Hassistenia generosus Baro Henricus Vuildefelsius a Sebastiano Heroë Hassistenio mihi impetravit."

Fischer, in his preface (p. 4^r) states that this MS is identical with **Lobc.**; this is denied by Schneider (I xv), who notes that Cornarius' emendations do not significantly agree with **Lobc.**; nevertheless, Wilson 393, n. 2, again states that **Lobc.** is the MS used by Cornarius.

I have compared all emendations proposed by Cornarius with Schneider's apparatus, and I can confirm Schneider's judgement that none of Cornarius' readings is to be found in **Lobc.** exclusively. In *R.*, Cornarius never states whether a reading he proposes is to be found in his MS, or is a conjecture made by himself.

In quite a few places Cornarius' correction of the reading of the Aldine and the two Basle editions is found in most, if not all, extant MSS; some instances:

350e1 δημηγορεῖν codd. Corn.: δημηουργεῖν Ald.: δημιουργεῖν Bas.[1] Bas.[2]
430a6 ἐκκλύζειν codd. Corn.: ἐκλύζειν Ald. Bas.[1] Bas.[2]
479c2 βολῆς codd. Corn.: βουλῆς Ald. Bas.[1] Bas.[2]
544a6 κάκιστον codd. plerique Bas.[2] Corn.: κάλλιστον Ald. Bas.[1] (Par.α)

That at least some of such readings, where Cornarius agrees with the Greek MSS, are conjectural, is shown by the case of 359a1: here, the Aldine and the two Basle editions read ἐρεῖν for αἱρεῖν; Cornarius proposes reading αἱρεῖν (the reading of the MSS) or ποιεῖν (not found in any MS). Yet it is possible that some readings have been borrowed from a Greek MS.[1]

In four places Cornarius agrees with some MSS only (notably in three cases upon the addition of a negation):

330c6 καὶ] οὐ Corn.: καὶ οὐ Fa^sl
370d9 εἰ] εἰ μὴ Corn. Fγ^pc
451b1 εὖ] οὐκ εὖ Corn. β^pc
605a3 αὐτοῦ] αὐτῷ Corn. K

None of the other readings proposed by Cornarius occur in any extant MS; therefore, I agree with Schneider that there is no positive internal evidence that Cornarius' MS is identical with **Lobc.**

However, not all Cornarius' readings which are absent from the Greek tradition are conjectural; on two occasions, it is clear that he translates Ficino's Latin back into the Greek (this was already noted by Schneider ad 462c6-7), without, however, indicating his source:

399d4 τοῦτο πολυχορδότατον] τὰ πολυχορδότατα **Corn.**: *instrumenta multarum chordarum* **Fic.**
462c6-7 Κομιδῇ—ταὐτὰ om. Ald. Bas.[1] Bas.[2]: Cornarius proposes reading Καὶ μάλα γε. Ἐν ᾗτινι οὖν πόλει οἱ πλεῖστοι πρὸς ταὐτὸ κατὰ ταὐτὰ κτέ; Ficino's translation runs: *Valde. In quacunque igitur civitate complurimi ad idem secundum eadem* etc.

One of Cornarius' conjectures has been generally accepted: 437d11 ἑνὶ λόγῳ for ἐν ὀλίγῳ of the MSS and Athenaeus.

5. *Stephanus' edition*

Stephanus' famous three-volume edition of Plato appeared in 1578; it is accompanied by the Latin translation of Johannes Serranus, who also

---

[1] In my forthcoming article *The Codex Hassensteinianus of Plato* (to be published in RHT), I shall prove that **Lobc.** cannot be identical with Cornarius' MS, because some dialogues for which Cornarius quotes his MS are absent from **Lobc.**

wrote the introductions to the dialogues. In his note to the reader in volume I, Stephanus states his editorial principles, which deserve to be quoted in full:

> Ac quum varia ex veteribus libris auxilia conquisivissem, hanc in eorum usu cautionem adhibui, ut quae lectiones praecedentium editionum, Aldinae, Basiliensis, Lovaniensis (quae est duntaxat librorum De legibus) ferri posse viderentur, in ista etiam retinerentur, diversis margini adscriptis: in earum autem locum quae οὐδὲν ὑγιὲς haberent (quarum etiam nonnullae ne a Ficino quidem agnoscuntur) diversae illae ex vetustis petitae libris substituerentur. ut omittam quae ex iisdem adiecta fuerunt, ut remedia locis antea mutilis & decurtatis afferrentur. Enimvero quum in plerisque locis fidem eorundem librorum a me frustra implorari viderem, alii autem non suppeterent, ad coniecturas, tanquam ad δεύτερον πλοῦν, me convertere necesse habui. Sed quum intellegerem quam periculosae sint coniecturae, & quam fallaciter plerunque suis coniectoribus adblandiantur, ex ingenio meo profectas emendationes non in ipsum recepi contextum (ut antea etiam cum vulgo appellavi) sed partim margini adscripsi, partim Annotationibus reservavi, ubi earum rationem etiam reddere daretur.

Would it not be instructive to compare this with the principles laid down by Adam ! (Cf. p. 10)

In the passage just quoted and in the preface to the *Annotationes* in vol. III, p. 9, Stephanus states that he has consulted several *veteres libri*, by which we must understand MSS; of earlier translations and editions, he mentions Ficino's translation, and the Aldine and first Basle editions, plus the Louvain edition of the *Laws*, which is not interesting to us. Thus he makes no mention of the second Basle edition and Cornarius' translation and *Eclogae*. His reason for doing so becomes apparent upon our comparing the variant readings proposed by Stephanus with the second Basle edition and Cornarius' *Eclogae*: many readings which Stephanus claims to have found in an "old book", or which he puts forward as his own conjectures, are in fact found in the second Basle edition or Cornarius; cf. S. W. F. Hoffmann, *Bibliographisches Lexikon der gesammten Literatur der Griechen* (Leipzig 1845), III, 120 (Hoffmann also notes that in some places Stephanus translates Ficino's Latin back into the Greek; see below, p. 249).

Stephanus' plagiarizing of Cornarius was already exposed by Fischer, in the preface to his edition of the *Eclogae*:

> (...) tamen non dubitamus quin omnes gravissime reprehensuri sint taciti incredibilem Stephani audaciam et simulationem illiberalem, qua gloriatus est lectiones illas, non e Cornarii Eclogis petiisse, quas, ne fraudem ipse indicaret, nusquam laudavit, verum e veterum Codicum, nescio quorum, fonte hausisse.

I will mention some places where Stephanus plagiarizes Cornarius:

439a4 post δίψος add. ού δήτα **Corn.**: "ex quodam vet. adduntur haec" **Steph.**, *Ann.* 20
463d1 post πράττειν add. περί τε τούς άλλους **Corn.**: "scribendum est potius ex vet." **Steph.**, *Ann.* 21
532b8 πρός μέν] μέν όψις πρός et 532c1 βλέπειν] τό βλέπειν **Corn.**: "hanc eius (sc. loci) expositionem inveni" **Steph.**, *Ann.* 25

Some instances of readings in **Bas.**[2], plagiarized by Stephanus:

493d4 πόλει] πόλεως T **Bas.**[2]: "ut in uno vet." **Steph.**[im]
494e3 ού] καί T **Bas.**[2]: "in uno vet. exemplari" **Steph.**, *Ann.* 23
521a4 αγαθής] άτερ αγαθής TW **Bas.**[2]: "ex quodam vet. libro" **Steph.**, *Ann.* 24
531a3 αστρονόμοι] αστρολόγοι T **Bas.**[2]: "in quodam vet. libro" **Steph.**, *Ann.* 25
571c8 από πάσης] απάσης **Bas.**[2]: "in libro vet." **Steph.**[im]

In many places Stephanus mentions Ficino's translation, e.g.:

ad 419a3 δι' εαυτούς: "mihi venit in mentem aliquando suspicari scribendum esse κατά ταύτα δή, αύτοίς ών εστί μέν &c. Fic. quidem certe lectionem illam δι' εαυτούς non agnoscit quippe qui vertat (...)" **Steph.**, *Ann.* 20
ad 459d5 γίγνεσθαι (for which Stephanus has γενέσθαι (with **Ald.**, **Bas.**[1], **Bas.**[2])): "(...) quamvis Ficinus interpretetur Fieri, perinde acsi legisset γίνεσθαι" **Steph.**, *Ann.* 21 (which is a correct inference)
ad 559e9 έν έαυτώ: "Hic έν αύτώ Fic. legit" **Steph.**[im]

But Stephanus does not always acknowledge his debt to Ficino: he often prints a Greek text which is clearly based on Ficino's translation, without any note concerning its provenance; see for instance:

454d2 όντα] έχοντα **Steph.** (non Θ: editors have been deceived by *silentium Bekkeri*): *habentem* **Fic.**
496a8-9 ούδέ—εχόμενον] ούδέ άξιον ούδέ φρονήσεως αληθινής εχόμενον **Steph.**: *nihil dignum, nihil prudentie vere conveniens* **Fic.**
498c7 άντιτείνειν: "scribendum puto άντιτενείν **Steph.**[im]: *repugnaturos* **Fic.**
532a7 καί] καί εάν **Steph.**: (*qui*) *si* (*non destiterit prius*) **Fic.**
534b7 φαίην] ού φαίην **Steph.**: (*certe*) *non* (*aliter*) *est dicendum* **Fic.**
552e2 βία] καί βία **Steph.**: *ac vi* **Fic.**

The indications in the *Republic* that Stephanus really used one or more Greek MSS are very slight; Alline 317 argues that Stephanus used Parisini 1811 and 3009; even if this is true, it does not help us very much, because neither of these MSS contains *R*.

In a small number of places, I have noted significant agreement between Stephanus and a Greek MS; see for instance:

488c7 τούς τοιούτους] τοίς τοιούτοις V **Steph.**[im]
492c3 τό] τόν **VMatr.**: "Affertur & alia lectio, τόν λεγόμενον" **Steph.**, *Ann.*

22 (et Ficinus, ut videtur: (*adolescentem*) *illum*)

It is quite possible that Stephanus actually found these readings in (a relative of) **V**; yet the reading at 488c7 may be a conjecture (any reference to an "old book" is conspicuously absent), while in the case of 492c3 Stephanus is probably commenting on Ficino's translation.

Further, I have noted some cases of agreement with q/β:

352e9   φαμὲν] φαῖμεν **Steph.** β^{pc}q
389d2   δημιοεργοὶ habent **Steph.** q^{pc} (non ita β): δημιουργοὶ rell.
495e1   ἀποτεθρυμμένοι] ἀποτεθραυσμένοι **Steph.**^{im} βp^c: ἀποτεθρωσμένοι q
615b2   καὶ οἷον: "vel καὶ ἵνα vel οἷον sine καὶ scribendum videtur" **Steph.**^{im}: οἷον q^{pc}

I tend to regard these readings too as conjectures by Stephanus: once again, there is no reference to "old books"; the reading at 615b2 is clearly a conjecture, as appears from the fact that Stephanus gives two alternative solutions; of the three remaining readings, one does not occur in β, while another one is absent from q.

Hunger, in his catalogue, suggests that Φ was used for Stephanus' edition, but he does not say why this should be the case. At any rate, I have not found any significant cases of agreement between Φ and Stephanus.

As a rule, Stephanus follows the text of the previous editions; in the sample passages, I have noted the following places where Stephanus corrects an error found in the Aldine and the two Basle editions:

389d2   δημιοεργοὶ habet **Steph.**: δημιουργοὶ Ald. Bas.¹ Bas.² codd. praeter q^{pc}
518a2   διτταὶ habet **Steph.**: διττὰ Ald. Bas.¹ Bas.²
519e2   πράξει habet **Steph.**: πράξη Ald. Bas.¹ Bas.² (Par.)
520c8   τοῦ habet **Steph.**: τὸ Ald. Bas.¹ Bas.² (Par.)
616e3   μέσου habet **Steph.**: μέσον Ald. Bas.¹ Bas.²
619a5   τῶν τοιούτων habet **Steph.**: τὸν τοιοῦτον Ald. Bas.¹ Bas.² (Par.)
620c6   περιιοῦσαν habet **Steph.**: περιοῦσαν Ald. Bas.¹ Bas.² (Par., Mγ)

All of these cases can be accounted for as conjectural emendations.

Even if in some places Stephanus adorns himself with borrowed plumes, he has also made a number of conjectures of his own; some instances:

330c4   ταύτῃ τε δή: "fort. ταύτῃ γε δή &c." **Steph.**^{im}
387c4   θερμότεροι: "suspicor scribendum esse ἀθερμότεροι" **Steph.**^{im}
452e1   καὶ καλοῦ αὖ] ἤ
606e4   ἄξιος] ἄξιον

It is noteworthy that Stephanus does not always conform to the principles laid down in his note to the reader (see above, p. 248): in many places he prints a reading not found in any other source, without giving any note; this is the case, e.g., with the readings at 452e1 and 606e4, just quoted above.

Further, it must be noted that Stephanus occasionally refers to the indirect tradition; some instances:

ad 437c5 ἐρωτῶντος, for which Stephanus reads ὁρῶντος with **Ald. Bas.**[1] **Bas.**[2], he notes (*Ann.* 20): "In quodam vet. pro ὁρῶντος scriptum est ἐρωτῶντος. quae lectio affertur & ex Galeno, lib. sexto De dogm. Plat. & Hippocr."

ad 615c6 Ἀρδιαῖον he notes in the margin: "non Ἀρδιαῖος sed Ἀρίδαιος vocatur a Iustino martyre, afferente hunc locum"

Finally, after the harsh words I have had to say about Stephanus' intellectual integrity, I must remark that his edition is almost completely free from printing errors, and that his famous *Regii Typi Graeci* make his edition a feast for the eyes.

Stephanus' edition provided the basis for the so-called vulgate of Plato. Schneider (I xxxviiii) already noted the dependence on Stephanus of the 1590 (Lyon) and 1602 (Francfurt) editions. I have checked this in regard of the 1590 edition. Neither Schneider nor I have seen the 1713 Cambridge edition, but Stallbaum[2] LXXIX remarks: "Massey neque codd. manu scriptos consuluit, neque de suo quidquam addidit, quod sit mentione dignum". The Bipontine editors (1781-1787) too reproduced Stephanus' text, while adding some critical notes and a collation of **K**; the title of their edition runs: "Platonis philosophi quae exstant Graece ad editionem Henrici Stephani accurate expressa (...)". Ast (1804, 1814, 1822) took Stephanus' text as the basis for his editions; he sought to correct this text using the other editions and translations, by conjecture, and with the help of one or two MSS. Finally, Bekker's edition (1816-1818) inaugurated a new period of Platonic editorial activity: his edition is the first to be based on the collation of a considerable number of MSS (12).

CHAPTER SIX

THE PAPYRI

Chambry was the first editor of the *Republic* who could make use of papyri. In his time (1932-1934) only four papyri of the *Republic* were known; since then, seven more papyri have been published; six of these postdate Pack[2]. All eleven papyri are assigned to the second and third centuries A. D., to which the large majority of the Plato papyri belongs.

In listing the papyri, I will confine myself to inventory (or publication) numbers, size, date and contents; for further information the reader is referred to the editions of the papyri. The sigla Π^1 etc. have been given by me.

P. Oxy. 3509 (Π^1)

First published by R. Hübner, ZPE 30 (1978), 195-198; 9.3 × 29.8 cm.; third century A. D.; 330a2 ονομασ]τος–b4 εποιη[σεν; many gaps at the beginnings of the lines.

P. Flor. inv. 1994 (Π^2)

Provenance unknown; published by A. Carlini, in: *Scritti in onore di Orsolina Montevecchi*, a cura di E. Bresciani etc. (Bologna 1981), 85-87; 4 × 8 cm.; second-third century A. D.; 399d10 λογο]ς—e3 εκει[νου; only the ends of the lines are preserved.

P. Oxy. 455 (Π^3)

Pack[2] nr. 1418; 9 × 6.6 cm.; third century A. D.; 406a5 ει—b4 παρα]κο[λουθων; some gaps at the beginnings of the lines.

P. Oxy. 2751 (Π^4)

Consists of five fragments; fragment D measures 15 × 15.5 cm.; late second or early third century A. D.
fr. A: 412c13 τη]ς—d6 μ[η; many gaps at the beginnings and ends of the lines.
fr. B: 413d1 κα]ι—d4 γε; fragments only.
fr. C: 413e5 κα]ι alterum—e6 βασα[νιζομενον; many gaps at the beginnings and ends of the lines.

fr. D, col.i: 414a4 λαγχανο[ντα—b4 ους; many gaps at the beginnings and ends of the lines.
fr. E: 414b4 δ[η—b5 αρ]χ[οντων; some letters only.
fr. D, col. ii: 414b9 γεννα[ιον—d1 ουχ; some gaps.

P. Oxy. 456 ($Π^5$)

Pack² nr. 1419; 5.8 × 7 cm.; late second or early third century A. D.; 422c8 ει]κοτων—d2 ου[δεν; gaps at the beginnings and ends of the lines.

P. Oxy. 3679 ($Π^6$)

13.3 × 8.2 cm.; third century A. D.; col. i: 472e4 δυν]ατ[ον—473a5 διη[λθομεν, some gaps; col. ii: 473d1 νυ]ν—d5 φ[ιλε, only the beginnings of the lines are preserved.

PRIMI I 10 ($Π^7$)

Pack² nr. 1420; found in Oxyrhynchus; 6 × 6 cm.; third century A. D.; ↓ 485c10 ευροις—d6 α[λλα; → 486b10 μη—c3 ικαν[ως; gaps at the beginnings and ends of the lines.

P. Oxy. 3326 ($Π^8$)

16 × 27 cm.; second century A. D.; three consecutive columns; in the first column only the ends of the lines are preserved, in the third column only the beginnings of the lines; 545c1 ολιγαρχικο]ν—546a3 λ[υθησεται.

P. Oxy. 1808 ($Π^9$)

Pack² nr. 1421; consists of five columns; each column has a width of 4.5-5 cm.; late second century A. D.; there are some scholia; in a number of places corrections have been added by a later hand.
col. 1: 546b2 γεν]νη[σουσι—b6 ομοιο]υ[ντων; only a few letters at the ends of the lines are preserved.
col. ii: 546c4 με]ν prius—c7 κ[αι; many gaps.
col. iii: 546d5 αμελ]ειν—547a1 χαλ[κουν; only the beginnings of the lines are preserved.
col. iv: 547b6 πλουσιω—c1 ὑπ: gaps at the beginnings and ends of the last three lines.
col. v: 547c8 πα]νυ—d4 τιμα[ν; gaps at the ends of the lines.

P. Oxy. 24 (Π¹⁰)

Pack² nr. 1422; 4.6 × 7.4 cm.; third century A. D.; 607e4 γε—608a1 φανη[ναι; some gaps.

P. Oxy. 3157 (Π¹¹)

Consists of two fragments: fr. 1: 10.5 × 10 cm.; fr. 2: 2 × 3 cm.; second century A. D.
fr. 1 ↓: 610c8 αναγκαζηται—611a7 γιγνοι]το
fr. 2 ↓: 611c6 μεν—d3 συντε]τριφθαι
fr. 1 →: 611e3 αθαν]ατωι—612c7 δικ]αιον
fr. 2 →: 613a1 τε—a8 ο[ς In all fragments there are many gaps at the beginnings and ends of the lines.

In the editions of the papyri, the text offered by the papyri is compared with the editions of Burnet and/or Chambry only (the older papyri with the editions of Bekker or Baiter); as these editions do not give all the variant readings of all primary witnesses, nor of the indirect tradition, it is impossible to draw conclusions on the relation of the papyri to the primary MSS and the indirect tradition.

In order to compensate this defect, I will give a full collation of the papyri with **ADF** and the indirect tradition (N. B. variant readings in **ADF** and the indirect tradition are not recorded when the papyrus has a lacuna where its text cannot be restored).

    330a2 ὀνομαστὸς ἐγένετο **ADF Stob.**:]τος εγενετο **Π¹**: ἐγενόμην ἔνδοξος **Plu.** (hunc locum oratione recta afferens)
       a4 ὁ alterum **ADF Stob.**: om. **Π¹**
      a5-6 πάνυ—ἐπιεικὴς **Π¹AF Stob.**: om. **D**
       a5 τι **AF** (deficit **D**): om. **Π¹ Stob.**
         γῆρας **Π¹A Stob.** (deficit **D**): om. **F**
       a6 μὴ **AF Stob.** (deficit **D**):]ητε **Π¹**
         ἑαυτῷ **ADF**: ἐναυτῷ (sic) **Stob.**: εʸαυτω **Π¹** (ν s.l. a prima manu: "the scribe apparently corrected his first version ἑαυτῷ into ἐν αὐτῷ" (ed.); in fact, it is rash to assume, as the editor does, that the scribe intended αυτω to be read as αὐτῷ; ἐν αὐτῷ was conjectured by Richards 1893, 14; cf. Slings, *Papyri* 29)
    330a7 πότερον **ADF**:]οτερο[**Π¹**: πότερον ἄρα **F**ˢˡ (prima manus, ut vid.)
        ἐγώ **Π¹ᵖᶜADF**: εγ]ωι **Π¹ᵃᶜ**
        πλείω **DF**: πλει[**Π¹**: πλέω **A**
    406a5 γ' ἐννοεῖς **AD**: γε εννοει[**Π³**: γε νοεῖς **F**
       a8 μείξας] μίξας **Π³ADF**
       b1 ἔπειτ' **AD**: ε]πειτα **Π³F**
       b4 μακρόν **AD**:]κρον **Π³**: μακρὰν **F**
    412d2 δέ γ' **Π⁴AD**: δέ γε **F**: δ' **Stob.**

THE PAPYRI 255

d4 μὴν Π⁴ᵖᶜ(ν s.l.)ADF Stob.: μη Π⁴ᵃᶜ
τοῦτό Π⁴AD Stob.: τοῦ F
ᾧ AD Stob.:]ι̣ Π⁴: ὃ F
d5 καὶ alterum AD Stob. et habuit Π⁴, ut vid.: om. F
ὅταν ADF: ὅτι Stob.: deficit Π⁴: "The number of letters lost at the beginning of l. 8 is more likely to be 5 than 6, and the restoration [ὅτι] is preferable" (ed.)
413d4 γε Π⁴ᵖᶜ(prima manus)ADF: τε Π⁴ᵃᶜ Stob.
414a5 δοκεῖ μοι ὦ γλαύκων ADF:]ι̣ ω γλαυ[Π⁴: ὦ γλαύκων, δοκεῖ μοι Stob.
b3 φιλίων Π⁴ADF: φίλων Stob.
βουλήσονται Π⁴ADFᵃᶜ Stobaei M: βουλήσωνται F¹ᵖᶜ Stobaei A
δυνήσονται Π⁴AD Stobaei M: δυνήσωνται F Stobaei A
b4 δὴ νῦν A Stob.: δ[Π⁴ (ους praecedente): νῦν δὴ DF
c4 φοινικιχόν ADF Phot. Olymp.: φ[ ]νικικον Π⁴: φοινικιόν Ascl. (uno loco): φοινικόν Ascl. (altero loco) sch. Pl. ad loc.
c8 ὀκνοῦντι Π⁴A⁽ᵖᶜ?⁾: ὤκνουν τι DF (et fortasse Aᵃᶜ)
c9 δέ AD: γέ Π⁴F
μάλ' ADF: μαλ[Π⁴ (μαλ[α ed.)
422c10 συγχωρήσομαί ADF: συν[Π⁵
d1 πέμψαντες ADF: πεμ[ ]ντες Π⁵: πέμψαντες οἱ ἡμέτεροι πολῖται Bessarion
πόλιν ADF¹ᵖᶜ:]λιν Π⁵: πόλι Fᵃᶜ
472e6 τὸ μὲν τοίνυν Π⁶ADF: om. Stob.
οὕτω ADF Stob.: ουτως Π⁶
δὴ Π⁶ADF: om. Stob.
e7 τοῦτο ADF Stob.: τ[ ]υ Π⁶
δεῖ Π⁶ADF: χρὴ Stob.
e8 δυνατώτατ' ADF: δυνατωτατα Π⁶ Stob.
e9 τὰ αὐτὰ ADF Stob.: ταυτα Π⁶
διομολόγησαι A Stob.: διομολογῆσαι D: δεῖ ὁμολογῆσαι F: διωμολογηται Π⁶
473a1 τι ADF Stob.: om. Π⁶
ὡς Π⁶AᵖᶜDF: ὡ∗ Aᵃᶜ
d1 λεγόμενοι καὶ δυνασταὶ ADF Stob. (uno loco) Bessarion: λε[ ]εγ[οι και δυνασται Π⁶: om. Stob. (altero loco)
d3 πολιτικῇ AF Stob. Bessarion: πολιτικῆ D (nisi fallor): πολειτ[Π⁶
d4-5 ἐξ ἀνάγκης ADF Bessarion: om. Stob.: deficit Π⁶, sed spatium abscisum sufficit ut εξ αναγκης suppleatur
d5 ἀποκλεισθῶσιν ADF Bessarion: αποκληϊ[ ]ω[Π⁶: ἀποκαθιστῶσιν Stob.
485d1 φιλοψευδῆ ADF:]ουψευδη Π⁷
d3 φιλομαθῆ Π⁷AF: φιλομαθῆι D
486c1 τόδε AD¹ᵖᶜF:]ε Π⁷: τοῦτο Dᵃᶜ
c3 τι Π⁷AF: om. D
545c2 θεασόμεθα A: θεασώμεθα DF:]θα Π⁸: "θεασόμε]θα I think fits the space rather better than F's θεασώμεθα: similarly at i 14 (c5-GJB), where F has πειρασώμεθα" (ed.)
c3 δημοκρατικόν ADF:]κον Π⁸: "There is not enough room for δημοκρατι]κόν, the reading of the medieval MSS. δημοτι]κόν fits the

space perfectly, and I do not think there can be much doubt that it was the reading in the papyrus" (ed.)
c5 πειρασόμεθα **AD**: πειρασώμεθα **F**:]εθα **Π⁸** (cf. ad c2)
c9 ἢ **ADF**: ῆ **Π⁸**
d2 αὐτῷ **Π⁸AD¹ᵖᶜF**: αὐτὸ∗ **Dᵃᶜ**
τούτῳ **Π⁸AD¹ᵖᶜF**: ∗∗υτω **Dᵃᶜ**
ἐγγένηται **ADF**: ενγενηται **Π⁸**
d3 κἂν **Π⁸AD**: καὶ **F**
ᾗ **AD**: ηι **Π⁸**: ἤ **F**
d6 οἱ alterum **Π⁸AD**: om. **F**
ἄρχοντες **Π⁸AF**: ἄρχον **D** (corr. **D²**)
d7 ἢ **ADF**: ῆ **Π⁸**
e1 ἔμπεσε **AD**:]σε **Π⁸**: ἐμπέσῃ **F**
546a1 οὕτω **ADF**: ουτ]ως **Π⁸**
a3 μενεῖ **A**: μενεῖ **Π⁸**: μένει **Fᵃᶜ** (corr.**F¹** vel **F⁴**): μὲν εἴ **D**
c4 ἑκατὸν **AᵖᶜD**: εκατ[**Π⁹**: ἕκαστον **Aᵃᶜ**: ἕκαστὸν (sic) **F**
c5 ἑκάστων **Π⁹ADF**: εκαστου **Π⁹ˢˡ** (secunda manus)
δυοῖν **F**: δυεῖν **Π⁹AD**
c6 τριάδος **Π⁹ᵖᶜ**(secunda manus)**ADF**: om. **Π⁹**
ἀριθμὸς **ADF**: ο αριθμος **Π⁹** (sed ο puncto notatum)
c7 τοιούτου **Π⁹ˢˡ**(prima vel secunda manus)**ADF**: τουουτου **Π⁹ᵃᶜ**
547b5 πλουσίῳ **Π⁹ᵖᶜAᵖᶜDF**: πλουσίωι **AᵃᶜΠ⁹ᵃᶜ**
ἀρετὴν **Π⁹ᵖᶜADF**: αρχην **Π⁹ᵃᶜ**
b7 κατάστασιν **Π⁹ˢˡADF**: αποστασιν **Π⁹**
b8 κατανειμαμένους **Π⁹ᵖᶜADF**: κατανειμανους **Π⁹ᵃᶜ**
c9 μεταβήσεται **A**:]ταβησεται[**Π⁹**: μεταθήσεται **F**: μεταβηθήσεται **D**
οὕτω **ADF**: ουτως **Π⁹**
d1 τὰ μὲν **AD**: τα μ[**Π⁹**: τοῦ μὲν **F**
d3 ἔφη **Π⁹ᵖᶜADF**: εφηι **Π⁹ᵃᶜ**
d4 τῷ **A**:]ι **Π⁹**: τὸ **DF**
607e5 ἡγήσωνται **Π¹⁰AD¹ᵖᶜF**: ἡγήσονται **Dᵃᶜ**
e6 οὕτως **ADF**: ουτω **Π¹⁰**
τὸν **Π¹⁰AD¹ˢˡF**: om. **Dᵃᶜ**
ἐγγεγονότα **ADF**: ενγεγογοτα **Π¹⁰**
610c10 εἶναι θανάσιμον **ADF**:]ειναι **Π¹¹** (continuat τω[ ] εχοντι) (pro θανάσιμον fort. θανατήριον **Phot.**)
d2 μάλιστα **Π¹¹AᵖᶜDF**: μάλλιστα **Aᵃᶜ**
d3 μὴ **ADF**: μην **Π¹¹**
τοῦτο habent **Π¹¹βᵖᶜ**: τούτου **ADF**
d5 δί' **A**: δια **Π¹¹DF**
φανεῖται **ADF**: φανε[ ]αι **Π¹¹**: φαίνεται **Aˢˡ**
e1 ἀποκτεινύσαν (sic) **F**:]ε[**Π¹¹**: ἀποκτινύσαν **AD**
e2 μάλα **AF**: μᾶλλα (sic) **D**: μαλλον **Π¹¹**
e3 ὡς ἔοικεν **ADF**: om. **Π¹¹**
611e3 τῷ prius **A**: om. **Π¹¹DF**
οἵα **ADF**: οιωι **Π¹¹**
e4 ἐπισπομένη **AD**:]ισπομενη **Π¹¹**: ἐπισπωμένη **F**
e5 περικρουσθεῖσα **Π¹¹AD¹ᵖᶜF**: περικρουσθῆσα **Dᵃᶜ**
612a1 αὐτῇ(ι) **AD**: αυτηι **Π¹¹**: αὐτῇ **F**
a3 ἴδοι αὐτῆς **ADF**: αυτης ιδοι **Π¹¹**

b1 ἐπηινέχαμεν A^{pc}: ἐπηνέγκαμεν $A^{ac}DF$: επ[ ]μεν $Π^{11}$: ἀπηνέγκαμεν Stob.
b2 ἀλλ᾽ ADF Stob.: αλλα $Π^{11}$
b4 ἐάντε ADF Stob.: αντε $Π^{11}$
c1 οἴους AD Stob.: οιους $Π^{11}$: ὅσους F
613a5 ἐάντ(ε) ADF Stob.: α[$Π^{11}$

It can be seen that the papyri have very little to tell us: in one place a good reading is found in a papyrus against **ADF**, viz. 610d3 τοῦτο; this reading is also found in $β^{pc}$, undoubtedly as a conjecture. There are no places where a papyrus supports a variant reading with a high claim to authenticity which is not accepted by Burnet, occurring in one or more other branches of the tradition (**A**, **D**, **F**, indirect tradition)[1].

The cases of agreement in error between a papyrus and one of the primary MSS and/or the indirect tradition are very few (I discount orthographical variant radings, *scriptio plena* etc.): the only two cases of agreement in error with one or two of the primary MSS are 414c9 δέ **AD**: γέ $Π^4$**F** and 611e1 τῷ prius **A**: om. $Π^{11}$**DF**. The cases of 546c5 δυοῖν **F**: δυεῖν $Π^9$**AD** and 547b6 πλουσίω $Π^{9pc}A^{pc}$**DF**: πλουσίωι $Π^{9ac}A^{ac}$ do not tell us anything at all, in my opinion. There is agreement in error with Stobaeus at 330a5 τι om. $Π^1$ **Stob.**, 330a6 ἑαυτῷ] εν αυτω $Π^1$ (sed post correctionem) **Stob.** and 413d4 γε] τε $Π^{4ac}$ (sed correxit prima manus) **Stob.** (and possibly at 412d5: see ad loc.). None of these readings deserves any serious attention as regards the history of the text, except perhaps the reading at 330a6 (but ἑαυτῷ and ἐν αὐτῷ are often confused).

Finally, there are hardly any places where the reading of a papyrus against **ADF** and/or the indirect tradition is a serious alternative: at 545c3 $Π^8$ probably read δημοτικόν, but as Dr Slings points out, δημοτικόν may well have been an error made by the scribe himself: if he happened to notice his error, he may have added κρα above the line; in any case, I believe that the editor (M. W. Haslam) ad loc. strongly exaggerates the value of the reading δημοτι]κον in the papyrus; see Slings, *Papyri* 32-34.

I conclude that, except for the correct reading at 610d3, the papyri have hardly any importance for the constitution or the history of the text.

---

[1] The Oxyrhynchus editor states that the papyrus supports ἑκατὸν of A^{pc} **Procl.** at 546c3; Brumbaugh-Wells 4, on the contrary, say that the papyrus reads ἕκαστον with A^{ac}**DF**; both are wrong: $Π^9$, col. ii, only starts at 546c4 με]ν *prius* and does not have a word of c3; it does read εκατ[at c4.

PART THREE

THE TRANSLATIONS

CHAPTER SEVEN

THE FIFTEENTH-CENTURY LATIN TRANSLATIONS

In 1484, the translation of the complete Plato by Marsilio Ficino appeared in print[1], almost thirty years before the *editio princeps* of the Greek text, published by Aldus in 1513. Some of the dialogues were first made accessible to the Latin reader by Ficino, others had already been translated into Latin earlier. The *Republic* was first translated into Latin by Manuel Chrysoloras, who made his translation in close collaboration with his pupil Uberto Decembrio in the years 1400-1403[2]. This translation was remoulded, with the help of the Greek original, by Uberto's son Pier Candido between 1437 and 1441 (cf. Cammelli 123, n. 1). Another translation was made by Antonio Cassarino in the years 1438-1447 (cf. Garin 359). The history of these translations has been written well by Garin, Kristeller and others[3], but the translations before Ficino's have not yet been edited, nor investigated properly.

In discussing the four translations mentioned, I will indicate the Greek sources upon which they are based and add some remarks concerning their character.

1. The Chrysoloras-Uberto translation

First, I will discuss the translation by Chrysoloras and Uberto Decembrio. It appears that this translation[4] (which I shall designate **Chr.**) is closely related to **Sc.**, but not dependent on it. I will quote some readings from the sample passages which illustrate the affinity of **Chr.** with **Sc.**:

328b7   Χαρμαντίδην] χαρματίδην **TMγ**: *carmatidem* **Chr.**
328d5   σύνισθι] ξύνιθι **Sc.**: *convenies* **Chr.** (l. *convenias* ?)
331c2   αὐτὸ et εἶναι om. **Sc. Chr.**
386b6   δουλείας] δειλίας **TSc.**: *timiditate* **Chr.**
386b8   ἡμᾶς om. **Sc. Chr.**
386c6   ᾧ—εἴη om. **ATMγSc. Chr.**
388c2   εἰ δ' οὖν] εἰ δ' οὐ **Sc.**: *et si non* **Chr.**

---

[1] For this dating of the *editio princeps* of Ficino's translation see Kristeller CLIV.
[2] For a good survey of the history of the fifteenth-century Latin translations of Plato before Ficino's see Garin's article. For Chrysoloras' contact with Uberto Decembrio see Cammelli 121-127.
[3] Garin, *passim*; Kristeller CXLVII-CLV.
[4] I have read the Chrysoloras-Uberto translation in Vat. Regin. Lat. 1131 (on microfilm); for other MSS containing this translation see Kristeller CLVI; Garin 343, n. 3.

388d2 φίλε om. **Sc. Chr.**
389a8 ἐμόν] ἐμοὶ **Sc.**: *michi* **Chr.**
516c8 εἴ τινες] οἵτινες **Sc.**: *que* **Chr.**
517d2 τοῦτ'] ταῦτ' **DSc.**: *ista* **Chr.**
518a2 γίγνονται] γίγνοιντ' ἄν **Sc.**: *fierent* **Chr.**
518a7 ἀηθείας] ἀληθείας **DSc.**: *veritate* **Chr.**
614d2 διακελεύοιντό] διακελεύειν τε ΘW (deest **Sc.**): *precepisseque* **Chr.**
615b2-3 εἴ τινες] οἵτινες ΘW (deest **Sc.**): *quicumque* **Chr.**
615b3 πολλοῖς θανάτων] πολλῶν θανάτων ΘW (deest **Sc.**): *de pluribus mortibus* **Chr.**
616c2-3 εἶναι—ὑποζώματα] εἶτα *D*: *postea* **Chr.**
616e7 πέμπτου] δευτέρου *D*: *secundi* **Chr.**
618c5 διαγιγνώσκοντα] διαγιγνώσκειν καὶ ΘW (deest **Sc.**): *discernere et* **Chr.**
620b4 ἔχθρᾳ] ἐχθρὰν *D*: *inimicam* **Chr.**

But **Chr.** does not go back to **Sc.** *itself*, as is proved by the fact that **Sc.** has some separative errors against **Chr.**; some instances:

330b4 οὐσίαν] οἰκίαν **Sc.**: *divitias* **Chr.**
388d3 μή] δή **Sc.**: *non* **Chr.**
517c7 τοίνυν om. **Sc.**: *igitur* **Chr.**
614d5-6 κατὰ δὲ τὼ ἑτέρω om. ΘW (deest **Sc.**): *per alia vero duo* **Chr.**
617a7-8 αὐτῶν δὲ τούτων] αὐτὸν δὲ τοῦτον ΘW (deest **Sc.**): *de his autem* **Chr.**
618c5 ἀεὶ om. ΘW (deest **Sc.**): *usque* **Chr.**

In some places **Chr.** shows traces of contamination with the **F** tradition; some instances:

330b8 Οὖ τοι] οὗτοι **ATMγSc.**: τούτου **F**: *ideo* **Chr.**
330c6 καί] καὶ οὐ **F**: *et non* **Chr.**
386d7 οἵῳ πεπνῦσθαι] οἶος (sic) πέπνυται **F**: *solus sapit* **Chr.**
388e6 ἐφιῇ] ἐφίη **F**: *se dederit* **Chr.**: ἔφην **ATMγSc.**: ἔφη **D**
515b5 νομίζειν **F**: *opinari* **Chr.**: νομίζειν ὀνομάζειν **AD**
621b8 οὕτως **AF**: *sic* **Chr.**: οὗτος *D*

Outside the sample passages I have found a striking instance at 344e1 ὅλου **F**: *totius* **Chr.**: ἀλλ' οὐ **ATMγSc.D**

This might suggest that Chrysoloras consulted two Greek MSS simultaneously; yet this hypothesis can be discarded, because, as I will show below (pp. 265 f.), the translation by Uberto's son Pier Candido, who consulted the same Greek MS as Chrysoloras, shows traces of contamination with the **F** tradition in exactly the same places.

Therefore, I conclude that Chrysoloras' translation is based upon a gemellus of **Sc.**, which was contaminated with a MS belonging to the **F** tradition.

The fact that Chrysoloras' Greek MS was contaminated with another source might suggest that it was a derivative of **Sc.** from which **Sc.**'s errors were subsequently removed as a result of contamination. There are two arguments against this hypothesis:

1. It would seem rather surprising that Chrysoloras should have removed *all* the errors peculiar to **Sc.**, but hardly any of the distinctive readings of **AT** (up to 389d7) and **D** (after 389d7).

2. As will be illustrated below (p. 264) Chrysoloras had the habit of omitting altogether phrases which were unintelligibly corrupt; now at 392c2 **D** has the *vox nihili* ἐλεγεσθαι (*sic*) for λέγεσθαι: Chrysoloras omits 392c1-2 Οὐκοῦν—λέγεσθαι, **Sc.** has ἐλέσθαι for λέγεσθαι (an intelligent conjecture): if Chrysoloras had had ἐλέσθαι before him, he could have translated the whole phrase without any problem, and he certainly would not have omitted it.

I will now turn to the character of the Chrysoloras-Uberto translation. In the preface to his translation, Uberto himself explains the method he and his teacher Chrysoloras followed (published by Garin 343 f.). He states that Chrysoloras made a word for word translation (*verbum ex verbo redditum*) which, however, appeared to be *nimis incultum ac dissonum*; therefore Uberto set himself the task, *preceptore meo iubente et postmodum adprobante*, of shaping the translation into more elegant Latin[5].

A comparison of the translation with the Greek original shows that, as a rule, the translation is very literal and therefore in some places very obscure or even unintelligible. Thus in some cases a Greek word is not translated into Latin properly, but only transliterated; see, e.g., 386d10 ἥβην: *eben* **Chr.**; 617b6 ἕνα τόνον] ἀνὰ τόνον **D**: *anathomum* **Chr.**: (ἀνάτονον **F**).

In other cases, Greek words or phrases are translated very literally; see for instance 388e9 ἀξίους λόγου: *ratione dignos* **Chr.**; 390d1 καρτερίαι πρὸς ἅπαντα: *tollerantie ad omnia* **Chr.**

In the sample passages of book I, Chrysoloras and Uberto permitted themselves considerable liberty. The construction of a sentence is often changed drastically, e.g. 327b4-6 καί—εἴη is rendered: *ego vero postquam vestem meam puer retro apprehendit conversus ubinam polemarchus existeret sciscitabar*.

Many portions of text are omitted altogether, e.g. 327b2 κατιδών—ὡρμημένους om. **Chr.**; 328e6-7 πότερον—ἐξαγγέλλεις om. **Chr.**

Other parts are abridged, as 328c3-4 ἔκειντο—κύκλῳ: *sedilibus circumlocatis*; 329a2-3 πολλάκις—ἔχοντες: *sepe coequalibus meis convenio*. Once such a brief rendering seems to be due to prudishness on the part of

---

[5] For an analysis of Chrysoloras' opinions on the methods of translation see Cammelli 89-91 and 124 f.

Chrysoloras and/or Uberto: 329b8-c2 Πῶς—συγγίγνεσθαι is rendered by the tame *quomodo erga venerea se haberet*.

In the sample passages of books III, VII and X the translation follows the Greek much more faithfully. Omissions are rare and hardly ever affect the sense; the construction of a sentence is changed but rarely, and never so drastically as sometimes in book I.

As a possible explanation for this curious divergence in the methods of translation followed in book I and in the other books I submit that Uberto, when embarking on his task, wished to put his stamp upon the translation and therefore reworked Chrysoloras' word for word translation freely; as the work went on, he gradually contented himself with removing Chrysoloras' more glaring *peccata contra Latinitatem*.

Chrysoloras often renders Greek words or phrases for which he could not find a fitting Latin equivalent by two or more Latin words, a practice which has been regular with Latin translators since Cicero: see e.g. *Ti.* 29a2 τὸ γεγονός, which is rendered by Cicero as *id quod generatum ortumque diximus* (p. 180,15-16 Giomini). Some instances: 329d7 ἀγασθείς: *obletatus pariter et miratus*; 387e10 καὶ—σπουδαίαις: *ipsa mulieribus relinquentes, non omnibus, sed minime virtuosis*; 388a1 κακοί: *inertes et ignavi*; 519c2 σκοπὸν: *intentionem atque propositum*.

Some of the additions do not have any counterpart in the Greek, as 330b8 ἦν δ' ἐγώ: *inquam o Cephale*; 515a5 ἦν δ' ἐγώ: *inquam amice*. In one case, such an addition seems to be due to national pride on the part of Chrysoloras: 331a3 Πίνδαρος: *Pindarus noster*.

In places where a sentence is unintelligible as the result of a corruption in the Greek original, Chrysoloras leaves out the whole sentence, rather than try to restore the sense by means of conjectural emendation; see for instance: 387c2 ὡς οἴεται (undoubtedly corrupt) om. **Chr.**; 392c1-2 Οὐκοῦν—λέγεσθαι om. **Chr.** (**D** has the *vox nihili* ἐλεγεσθαι for λέγεσθαι; **Sc.** has ἑλέσθαι, which is definitely a conjectural emendation of ἐλεγεσθαι); 607a3-5 εἰδέναι—πόλιν om. **Chr.** (**D** has the *vox nihili* ὑκτέον for ὕμνους—παραδεκτέον, while **Sc.** leaves a blank).

In some places the translation is simply wrong, e.g. 327c3 ὡς: *huiusmodi*; 331e3-4 Ὅτι—ἔστι: *Quod ille inquit debita reddere cuilibet iustum esse* (Chrysoloras has wrongly understood Simonides as the subject of ἦ δ' ὅς); 515e7-8 καὶ alterum-φῶς: *nec permitteret antequam traxerit lumen solis aspicere*; 518c10 ἀνασχέσθαι: *transcendere*.

In some cases a wrong rendering by Chrysoloras seems to be due to a particular reading in the Greek original; see for instance 391c2, where τρίτου ἀπὸ Διός is rendered as *a Iove tertius* (sc. *Achilles*): possibly Chrysoloras' Greek MS read τρίτος for τρίτου.

2. *The translation by Pier Candido Decembrio*

Pier Candido's interest in Plato's *Republic* was awakened by his reading of the second book of Aristotle's *Politics*, in which a number of Platonic doctrines are expounded; wishing to compare Aristotle's account of these doctrines with the original, Pier Candido started to read book V of the *Republic* (see Garin 348 f.). Accordingly, he first translated book V; then followed books I, II, X and VI successively, followed by the remaining books (cf. Cammelli 123, n. 1)[6].

In a letter to Zenone Castiglioni (quoted by Garin 349, n. 14) Pier Candido is anxious to stress that he has translated the work from the original Greek; the charge of having plagiarized his father was brought against him by Guarino, among others (see Garin 349, n. 14, continued on p. 350; Cammelli 124, n. 1); it was to be repeated by Antonio Cassarino (see the passage from his *Isagogicon in Platonis vitam ac disciplinam*, quoted by Garin 359). J. E. Sandys, *A History of Classical Scholarship II* (Cambridge 1908), 70, 221 (followed by Alline 294 f.), states that the revision of Chrysoloras' word for word translation was begun by Uberto and continued by Pier Candido; Sandys does not add any proof in favour of this statement.

Comparison of Pier Candido's translation with the Greek MSS[7] shows that his translation is based on the same Greek original as that of Chrysoloras and his father. I will quote some readings where Pier Candido (whom I shall designate **PC**) agrees with **Sc.** and Chrysoloras:

328d5	σύνισθι] ξύνιθι **Sc.**:	*convenies* **Chr.**: *conveniens* **PC**
328e5	ἤδη om. **Sc. Chr. PC**	
386b6	δουλείας] δειλίας T**Sc.**:	*timiditate* **Chr. PC**
388d2	φίλε om. **Sc. Chr. PC**	
518a7	ἀηθείας] ἀληθείας D^ac**Sc.**:	*veritate* **Chr. PC**
615b2-3	εἴ τινες] οἵτινες ΘW (deest **Sc.**):	*quicumque* **Chr.**: *qui* **PC**
616c2-3	εἶναι—ὑποζώματα] εἶτα *D*:	*postea* **Chr.**: om. **PC**
617c5-6	τὰ prius-τῇ om. *D* **Chr. PC**	
618c5	διαγιγνώσκοντα] διαγιγνώσκειν καὶ ΘW (deest **Sc.**): *discernere et* **Chr.**: *discernere ac* **PC**

Moreover, Pier Candido shows the same traces of contamination as Chrysoloras; see for instance:

330c6	καὶ] καὶ οὐ F: *et non* **Chr.**: *non* **PC**
344e1	ὅλου F: *totius* **Chr. PC**: ἀλλ' οὐ ATMγ**Sc.**D

---

[6] For the particularities concerning the dedications of the successive books etc., see Garin 351-356.

[7] I have read Pier Candido's translation in Vat. Lat. 10669 (on microfilm); for other MSS see Garin 348, n. 11.

386d7 οἵῳ πεπνῦσθαι] οἷος (sic) πέπνυται F: *solus sapit* Chr.: *solus et ipse sapit* PC
621b8 οὕτως AF: *sic* Chr. PC: οὗτος D

Further, the comparison of Pier Candido's translation with the Chrysoloras-Uberto translation shows that Pier Candido did work from a Greek original, and that he did not simply make a revision of his father's translation: there are many cases in which Pier Candido translates words that had been omitted altogether by Chrysoloras and Uberto; see for instance:

328d2 ὡς—ὅτι om. Chr.: *nosti* PC
328e6-7 πότερον—ἐξαγγέλλεις om. Chr.: *utrum quidpiam gravius aut secus annunties* PC
329b8-c2 Πῶς—συγγίγνεσθαι: *quomodo erga venerea se haberet* Chr.: *quomodo circa venerea te habes, o Sophocles, an adhuc femine potis es comisceri* PC
330a6 εὔκολος—γένοιτο om. Chr.: *iocunde se habebit unquam* PC
515c8 πάντα δὲ ταῦτα ποιῶν om. Chr.: *hec agens omnia* PC
517c6 ὅν—δύναμαι om. Chr.: *quoad licet* PC

That Pier Candido used the same MS that had been used by Chrysoloras and not just another Greek MS, is illustrated by cases as 340e1-2: κατὰ τὸν ἀκριβῆ λόγον] κατὰ τὸν λόγον TSc. (i.e. om. ἀκριβῆ): *ratione conspecta* Chr.: *iuxta sermonem tuam* PC: both Chrysoloras and Pier Candido omit ἀκριβῆ with TSc., but Pier Candido's translation cannot possibly be based upon Chrysoloras'.

There is also an external indication that Pier Candido used the same MS as Chrysoloras: Sabbadini 59, n. 104 (continued on p. 60) quotes Traversari, *Epist.* XXIV 68, who mentions that Uberto received some Greek MSS from Chrysoloras; we may assume that the Plato MS was among these.

On the other hand, it is quite obvious that Pier Candido did make much use of his father's translation; thus he follows his father in omitting corrupt phrases like 392c1-2 and 607a3-5 altogether (cf. p. 264). Sometimes Pier Candido takes over Chrysoloras' transliterations, e.g. 617b6 ἕνα τόνον] ἀνὰ τόνον D (ἀνάτονον F): *anathomum* Chr.: *anathonon* PC.

Often it is quite obvious that Pier Candido has taken the translation of Chrysoloras and his father as his starting-point; some instances:

328e1-2 δοκεῖ—πυνθάνεσθαι: *potissime ut ab illis agnoscam* Chr.: *potissimum ut ab his agnoscam* PC
330a2-3 οὔτ' prius-'Ἀθηναῖος: *neque si essem seriphius (serephius* cod. Reg.) *famosus fuissem, nec tu si atheniensis existeres* Chr.: *Neque si ipse seriphius essem famosus nec tu si atheniensis clarus unquam fuisses* PC
515b2 Τί δὲ τῶν παραφερομένων: *quid vero illorum que penes ipsos conferuntur* Chr.: *quid autem ipsorum que penes illos conferuntur* PC

Sometimes Pier Candido takes over one or more words added by Chrysoloras, e.g. 330b8 ἦν δ' ἐγώ: *inquam o Cephale* **Chr. PC**; 390e9 νεκροῦ: *defuncti Hectoris cadaver* **Chr.**: *hectoris corpus* **PC**.

Incidentally, the agreement between Chrysoloras and Pier Candido in an obviously wrong translation may be due to an error in the Greek MS, as at 391c2, where Chrysoloras and Pier Candido connect τρίτου with Achilles, which points to the reading τρίτος (cf. p. 264).

In some cases Pier Candido corrects an error of Chrysoloras', as at 331e3-4 Ὅτι—ἐστι: *Quod ille inquit debita reddere cuilibet iustum esse* **Chr.** *falso*: *Quod debita inquit unicuique reddere iustum est* **PC** *recte*.

On the whole, when Pier Candido departs from the translation of Chrysoloras and his father, he follows Plato's Greek very closely. He shares Chrysoloras' habit of using more Latin words to render a Greek word or phrase (cf. p. 264), e.g. 515d3 ὄντος: *enti ac veritati* **PC**; 516c5 καὶ τῆς ἐκεῖ σοφίας: *eiusque prudentie que ipsis adesse consueverat* **PC**; but he does so only in isolated places. Omissions are very rare and seldom involve more than one or a few words.

In some places Pier Candido misinterprets the Greek, even when Chrysoloras' translation is correct; some instances:

331b2   ἄκοντά: *sponte* **PC**
331c1-5 τοῦτο—ποιεῖν: *iusticiamne istud simpliciter an veritatem potius dicemus: si quis a quoquam quid susceperit restituere aut id aliquando equum aliquando iniquum* **PC**
390c5-6 φίλους λήθοντε τοκῆας: *amicos proprios parentesque vitantes* **PC**
517b8-c1 ἐν—ὁρᾶσθαι: *in intelligibili supremam boni esse ideam ac vix videri* **PC**

The quotations from Homer, which occur frequently in the *Republic*, are translated into Latin hexameters by Pier Candido, which results in the translation being less literal than usual; as an instance I will quote Pier Candido's rendering of 386c5-7 (= *Od.* λ 489-491; ᾧ—εἴη is omitted by **ATMϒSc.**):

Rure prius degens malem (l. *mallem*) *servire alieno*
mancipio cunctos quam tabe et sorde peresos
defunctos regere et mundo dare iura silenti

That Pier Candido did compose his Homeric hexameters himself, and did not borrow them from an existing translation, appears from the fact that he translates 388a7-b2 as one coherent couplet, while Plato combines *Il.* Ω 10-12 with *Il.* Σ 23-24.

Occasionally, Pier Candido seems to have had recourse to conjectural emendation, as at 387c2, where he translates the undoubtedly corrupt ὡς οἴεται as *ut apparet*.

3. The translation by Antonio Cassarino

The Sicilian Antonio Cassarino[8] was a bitter opponent of Pier Candido Decembrio[9]. Sabbadini 50 tells us that he stayed in Constantinople during the years 1435-1438, in order to learn Greek; he returned with a copy of the complete Plato. He worked almost ten years (1438-1447) on his translation of the *Republic*[10].

A comparison of his translation with the Greek MSS shows that Cassarino used a MS closely related to **Mγ**; yet Cassarino's translation does not depend on **M** or **γ**, or on their common ancestor.

I will quote some readings from the sample passages which illustrate the affinity between Cassarino's translation (which I shall designate **Cass.**) and **Mγ**:

329d7	βουλόμενος] βουλόμενον **Mγ**: *volentem* **Cass.**
329e7	ὅσον οἴονται] ὅσον οἷόν τε **Mγ(F)**: *quantum est satis* **Cass.**
386c6	ᾧ—εἴη om. **ATMγ Cass.**
388e6	ἐφιῇ ἰσχυρῷ γέλωτι] ἔφην ἰσχυρῶ(ι) γέλωτι **ATMγ**: add. ἀλῶ **M**[isl]**γ**[isl]: *inquam immoderato ac nimio risu detinebitur* **Cass.**
390b6	Δία] βία **Mγ**: *vi* **Cass.**
391d1	ἄλλον] ἄλλου **AMγ**: (*ex*) *alio* (*deorum genitum*) **Cass.**
515b9	παριοῦσαν] παροῦσαν **γ** (deficit **M**): *praesens* **Cass.**
516a6	καθορῶ] καθορῶν **γ** (deficit **M**): *intuens* **Cass.**
516b9	οὗτος] αὐτὸς **Aγ** (deficit **M**): *ipse* **Cass.**
518d5	αὐτῷ τὸ ὁρᾶν] αὐτὸ τὸ ὁρᾶν **Mγ**: *visionem ipsam* **Cass.**
614d2	διακελεύοιντό] διακελεύοιτό **Mγ**: *iuberetur* **Cass.**
615a7	ὅσους] οὓς **A**[pc]**Mγ**: *quos* **Cass.**
616a6-7	μὴ—ἀναβαίνοι] εἰ μυκήσαιτο τὸ στόμιον **Mγ**[3im]: *ubi hostium* (i.e. *ostium*) *emugit* **Cass.**
617a4	τὸν ἕκτον] τῶν ἕκτων **Mγ**: *sextorum* **Cass.**
617a7-8	αὐτῶν δὲ τούτων] αὐτὸν δὲ τοῦτον **Mγ**: *ipsum autem* (*octavum*) **Cass.**
619c1	βρώσεις] βρῶσις **Mγ**: *devoratio* **Cass.**

That Cassarino's translation is not dependent on the lost exemplar of **Mγ** itself is proved by the fact that **Mγ** have some separative errors against Cassarino; some instances:

330b3	νῦν om. **Mγ**: *nunc* **Cass.**
515e3	δύναται] δύνανται **γ** (deficit **M**): *posset* **Cass.**
516a6	σκιάς] σκολιάς **γ** (deficit **M**): *umbras* **Cass.**
518c5	ᾧ] ὃ **Mγ**: *per quod* **Cass.**
617b6	ἱεῖσαν] ἰοῦσαν **Mγ**: *emittens* **Cass.**

---

[8] For information about Cassarino see Pescetti's article, *passim*; see also Vogler 195, n. 1.

[9] For an account of the quarrel between Pier Candido and Cassarino see Pescetti 34; Garin 357-359.

[10] I have read Cassarino's translation in the codex Newberry + 97 (on microfilm). This is the MS from which the beginning of book I (327a1-332d6) was published by Vogler 200-204. For further MSS see Kristeller CLVI, Pescetti 31 and Garin 357, n. 23.

There are no traces of contamination with other branches of the Greek tradition; therefore the possibility that Cassarino's translation goes back to **M**, **γ**, the exemplar of **Mγ** or a derivative of **Mγ**, which was corrected afterwards, is to be excluded.

I conclude that Cassarino's translation is based upon a gemellus of the exemplar of **Mγ**.

I will now turn to the character of Cassarino's translation. Cassarino keeps very close to the Greek original; he never omits vital phrases; he abstains from adding words or phrases, as Chrysoloras-Uberto and, in their wake, Pier Candido sometimes do (e.g. the addition of *o Cephale* at 330b8, see pp. 264, 267).

Like Chrysoloras and Pier Candido, Cassarino very frequently adopts the method of using more words to render a Greek word or phrase (cf. pp. 264, 267); some instances:

333a13   κοινωνήματα: *mutuas vitae ad invicem communicationes*
388e9   ἀξίους λόγου: *magnos et auctoritatis eximiae*
515d6   ἀπορεῖν: *dubitaturum atque hesitaturum*
614e3   ἀσπάζεσθαί: *complecti et osculari se*

Occasionally, Cassarino transliterates a word instead of translating it properly, e.g. 333a12 Συμβόλαια: *simboleis*; 387a5 νυκτερίδες: *nicterides*. Some untranslatable Greek words are paraphrased, like 387c1 ἐνέρους καὶ ἀλίβαντας: *Tartarus*.

Occasionally he renders a specific Greek expression by means of its Latin counterpart, as 329c2 Εὐφήμει: *meliora (...) ominare* and 386b3 Μὰ Δία: *me dius fidius*.

Like Pier Candido, Cassarino translates the quotations from Homer into Latin hexameters; as an instance I quote his translation of 386c5-7 (= *Od.* λ 489-491; **ATMγ** omit c6 ᾧ—εἴη):

Mallem inter superos alienas vertere glebas
cunctorum qui luce carent quam regna tenere

That Cassarino, too, composed his Homeric hexameters himself, is proved by the fact that, like Pier Candido, he translates 388a7-b2 as one coherent couplet, while Plato combines *Il.* Ω 10-12 with *Il.* Σ 23-24.

Cassarino but rarely changes the construction of a sentence, and never so drastically as Chrysoloras and Uberto had often done, at least in the first book. See for instance 327b5-6 Καὶ—ἔφη: *Conversusque ego quum ubinam is esset interrogassem hic inquit* etc.; 328e3-4 τραχεῖα—εὔπορος: *aspera an levis, facilis an difficilis*.

Sometimes his translation betrays the fact that he did not understand the Greek correctly, as at 330a7, where he translates ὧν κέκτησαι τὰ πλείω by *plura iis quae habes*: Cassarino interprets the genitive as comparative, whereas in reality it is partitive; 332a1 καίτοι γε: *nam*; 389e5 Ὁμήρῳ: *obsidi*: here Cassarino failed to recognize that Ὁμήρῳ is a proper name; 615a5 πολλοῦ χρόνου: (*multaque*) *multo tempore* (*rettulerat*).

In some places a wrong translation seems to be due to an error in his Greek MS; see for instance 390e2 ἀστέον: *audiendum* (= ἀκουστέον); 520b5 ὑμῖν: *nobis* (= ἡμῖν, a very common error). In other cases there may be a corruption in the Latin MS I have consulted, as at 387c4 φρίκης: *errore*: I think this should be *terrore*.

In places where the text of his Greek original was corrupted beyond restoration, Cassarino omits the whole phrase (as did Chrysoloras and Pier Candido also; cf. pp. 264 and 266); see for instance 359b3 τὸ μήτε ἀδικεῖν μήτε ἀδικεῖσθαι] τῶν εἴτε ἀδικεῖν εἴτε ἀδικεῖσθαι **TMγ**: om. **Cass.**

In a few places Cassarino has sought to emend the text he had before him by means of conjecture, e.g. 615b3 πολλοῖς θανάτων ἦσαν αἴτιοι] πολλοὶ θανάτων ἦσαν αἴτιοι **AMγ**: *multos occidissent* **Cass.**

Occasionally, there is remarkable agreement between Cassarino and Chrysoloras and/or Pier Candido; see for instance:

387c2 ὡς οἴεται: *ut apparet* **PC Cass.**
518c10 ἀνασχέσθαι: *transcendere* **Chr. PC**: *conscendere* **Cass.**

In the case of 387c2, it is imaginable that Pier Candido and Cassarino thought of the same conjecture independently (the reading ὡς ἔοικε is actually found in **K**), but it can hardly be coincidental that at 518c10 all three translate ἀνασχέσθαι ("endure") as *transcendere/conscendere*. I have not investigated the matter further, but I think we should at least reckon with the possibility that Cassarino made some use of the translations by Chrysoloras-Uberto and/or Pier Candido. That Cassarino knew the translations by Chrysoloras/Uberto and Pier Candido appears from the fact that he accuses Pier Candido of having plagiarized his father (cf. p. 265); but it is not impossible that Cassarino only repeated the charges made by others, without comparing the translations himself.

4. *Ficino's translation*

The circumstances under which Ficino's translation was made are well-known and need not be described here[11].

---

[11] For information about Ficino and his translation of Plato see, e.g., Marcel, *passim*; Kristeller CXLVII-CLV; Sicherl, *Platonismus* 553 f.

Not being able to consult the Florentine *editio princeps* of Ficino's translation, I have relied on the 1491 Venice edition and the text offered by Bekker; Bekker's text is based on the *editio princeps* and the Venice edition (see Bekker's *Platonis Dialogi I*, xiv), but Schneider I xxxvii states that Bekker sometimes has resort to the 1517 Venice edition or to conjecture. In all places quoted by me, Bekker agrees with the 1491 Venice edition, which I have followed in orthographical matters.

Even the comparison of a small part of the text in Ficino's translation with the Greek tradition is enough to show that Ficino did not restrict himself to using one MS only; Immisch 13, n. 3 (continued on p. 14) is therefore fully right when he states: "Nam Ficinus (...) omnino non ad unius libri manuscripti fidem Platonica convertit, sed quaecumque potuit adiumenta adhibuit infinitoque studio quae verteret partim aliunde partim de suo studebat emendare." I believe that it is possible to identify Ficino's *adiumenta* to a great extent.

Of the three primary witnesses, Ficino usually agrees with **A** against **D** and/or **F**; as Ficino did use more than one MS, as I will show, we should not consider distinctive readings in **A** which do not recur in Ficino's translation (especially when they are obviously wrong) as proof that Ficino did not use a MS of the **A**-family; the same goes for the other MSS which I shall mention in connection with Ficino. I will quote some readings which show the affinity between Ficino and the **A**-family:

327c10 ἓν λείπεται **A**³ⁱᵐ: *unum hoc subticetis* **Fic.**: ἐλλείπεται **ADF**
330e7 δειμαίνει **AD**: *extimescit* **Fic.**: ἀεὶ δειμαίνει **F**
386c6 ᾧ—εἴη **DF**: om. **A Fic.**
389c1 τοιούτους **AD**: *huiusmodi* **Fic.**: om. **F**
391d1 ἄλλον **DF**: ἄλλου **A**: *alterius* **Fic.**
516b9 οὗτος **DF**: αὐτὸς **A**: *ipsum (esse)* **Fic.**
517b1 ἅπασαν **AD**: *tota (hec imago)* **Fic.**: ἅπασι **F**
616c2-3 εἶναι—ὑποζώματα **AF**: *esse enim lumen istud celi vinculum* **Fic.**: εἶτα **D**
621a7-8 τοὺς—μέτρου **A**: *eos autem qui prudentiam ducem non habent, ultra quam deceat bibere* **Fic.**: om. **DF**

Within the **A**-family, Ficino usually sides with the **Mγ**-group; some instances:

329c8 γίγνεται] γίγνεται καὶ **Mγ**: *accidit. nam* **Fic.**
329e7 οὐ μέντοι γε ὅσον οἴονται] οὐ μέντοι γε ὅσον οἷόν τε **Mγ** (**F**): *non tamen quantum dici posset* **Fic.**
517a1 πρὶν καταστῆναι τὰ ὄμματα] πρὶν καταστῆναι τὸ ὄμμα **Mγ**: *antequam acies expurgetur* **Fic.**
616a6-7 μὴ—ἀναβαίνοι] εἰ μυκήσαιτο τὸ στόμιον **Mγ**³ⁱᵐ: *cum in ascensu mugitus excitabatur* **Fic.**
616c3 συνέχον τὴν] συνεχομένην **Mγ**: *(atque ita circumferentiam omnem) esse contentam* **Fic.**

The position of Ficino's source within the **Mγ**-group can be narrowed down to **a**, and the derivatives of **a**, especially **c**. Some instances of agreement between Ficino and **ac**:

328a6 Οὕτως, ἔφη ὁ Πολέμαρχος] οὕτως ἔφη κρείττους οὖν γένεσθε ἢ μένετε αὐτοῦ, οὐκοῦν ἦν δ' ἐγὼ ὁ Πολέμαρχος **Fa**ⁱᵐ**c**ⁱᵗ: *Ita prorsus. quare aut, addidit, potentiores sitis necesse est, aut hic maneatis. His Polemarchus tradidit* **Fic.**

389a6 ποιπνύοντα] ποι πνύοντα **a**: add. στένοντα διὰ τὸ χωλεύειν $F^{1sl}a^{im}$: add. διὰ τὸ χωλεύειν πνύοντα a^{sl}: ποι πνύοντα διὰ τὸ χωλεύειν πνύοντα c^{it}: *properantem* (...) *utpote qui claudus esset* **Fic.**
389a8 ἐμὸν] ἐμὸν τὸν λόγον $a^{sl}c^{it}$ (F^{2sl}): *meum* (...) *sermonem hunc* **Fic.**
517b5 τῆς ψυχῆς om. **ac Fic.**

It happens only rarely that Ficino takes over a variant reading in **a** which is not in **c**; in the sample passages I have noted the following cases:

517c4 αὐτή] αὕτη **AM**γ**ac**: αὐτὴ a^{sl}: *ipsa* **Fic.**
518c10 δ' om. **M**γ**ac**: add. a^{sl}: (*hoc*) *autem* **Fic.**
614d5-6 κατὰ δὲ τὼ ἑτέρω] κατὰ δὲ τὸ ἕτερον $a^{sl}c$: κατὰ δὲ τῶ ἑτέρω (sic) γ**a**: *per alias item duas* **Fic.**

Yet the agreement between Ficino and **a** (notably in all three cases in obviously correct readings) could also be the result of conjectural emendation by Ficino, or of contamination with another MS.

In the sample passages Ficino nowhere shares a separative error with **c**; in one place I have found an apparent case of agreement between Ficino and **c**: at 566c10 **c** adds τῆς πόλεως after αὐτός, while Ficino renders προστάτης ἐκεῖνος as *populi ille defensor* (omitting αὐτός); yet it is quite possible that *populi defensor* is Ficino's paraphrased translation of προστάτης (for Ficino's methods of translation, see below, pp. 276 f.).

I believe that the readings I have mentioned show sufficiently that Ficino used **a** or **c** as the primary source for his translation. But which of the two?

In 1462, Ficino received a MS with the complete Plato from Cosimo de'Medici; this MS was *in carta bona* (see Kristeller CXLVII; Marcel 253 f.; Sicherl, *Platonismus* 554). Marcel 254 identified this MS as **a**, which is one of the three extant MSS containing all Plato's works, the other two being **c** and **E**; **c** and **E** are parchment codices. Marcel states that Ficino's hand is easily identifiable in **a**, as the hand which has written many variant readings and notes; yet Sicherl, *Ficino* 53, n. 28, says that he has not noted any marks of Ficino's reading of **a**, and I myself believe that the variant readings and notes in **a** were written by the scribe himself, but after the copying of the text (see pp. 32 f., 128). On the other hand, Marcel remarks that on fol. 333^r **c** has a note in Ficino's hand *Deest hic ferme folium*; Sicherl, *Ficino* 59, confirms the presence of Ficino's hand in **c**.

In the second place, Marcel argues that **Ambr.**, an autograph of Ficino's with excerpts from many Platonic dialogues, derives from **a**; however, Sicherl, *Ficino* 51 f., thinks it more probable that **Ambr.** goes back to **c**; my study of these MSS confirms Sicherl's hypothesis: **Ambr.** does derive from **c**, and not from **a** (see p. 147).

In the third place, we have already seen that Ficino agrees with **c** at 566c10, in the addition of τῆς πόλεως; yet Ficino's translation of this place may also have been his own invention and does not prove that in this place **c** was his source. Further, it has been demonstrated that agreement of Ficino with **a** against **c** is not very significant; on the other hand, **c** has a lot of separative errors against **a** and Ficino's translation.

So there are two arguments in favour of **c** (Ficino's hand has been traced in **c** by Marcel and Sicherl; Ficino's autograph **Ambr.** depends on **c**) and two arguments in favour of **a** (Ficino says that the MS is *in carta bona*; Ficino hardly ever agrees with **c** against **a**, while **c** has separative errors against **a** and Ficino). Therefore, although it can be regarded as certain that Ficino used **c** for his excerpt MS, I tend to believe that he relied primarily on **a** for his translation; of course, it remains possible to assume, as Sicherl, *Platonismus* 554, does, that he used both **a** and **c**.

In a good many places Ficino has the correct reading against **AMγac**, **Mγac**, **γac**, **ac** or **c**; as I have already stated above (p. 271), this does not imply that these MSS were not used by Ficino[12]; the explanation is that Ficino has hit upon the correct reading by consulting other MSS or through conjecture. At any rate his diagnostic ability was great. I will quote a number of places where **Mγac** have an error against Ficino:

390b6   Δία] βία **Mγac**: *Iovem* **Fic.**
516a6   καθορῷ] καθορῶν **γac** (deficit **M**): *intuebitur* **Fic.**
518c5   ᾧ] ὅ **Mγac**: *quo* **Fic.**
617a5   στρεφόμενον] στεφόμενον **Mγac**: *volutione* **Fic.**
617a7-8 αὐτῶν δὲ τούτων] αὐτὸν δὲ τοῦτον **Mγac**: *ex his* **Fic.**
619a5   βίον] βίων **Mγac**: *vitam* **Fic.**

The study of Ficino's translation in relation to the **A**-family of the Greek tradition has already shown that Ficino did not confine himself to using one MS only. Which other MSS were available to him?

Sicherl, *Platonismus* 554, *Ficino* 59, mentions **b** and **x**; now **b** only contains *R.* up to 358d8 (the rest of book II was added by a sixteenth-century hand, who copied the first Basle edition; see p. 151) and is therefore of no account for the *Republic*. As to **x**, there are many places where Ficino agrees with the **F** tradition, sometimes with a later correction or variant reading in **F** and **x**; some instances:

349d9   ὁ δὲ μὴ ἐοικέναι] ὁ δὲ μὴ μὴ ἐοικέναι **x**[im] (manus recentior): *qui vero non talis, similis non sit* **Fic.**

---

[12] I therefore disagree with Slings 284 f., who concludes that "Ficino had a lost member of the Flor.a group before him", on the observation that **c** omits some words that are in Ficino, while **a** has some good variant readings which are not taken over by Ficino.

390a1 ὅσα ἄλλα] ὅσα ἄλλα τοιαῦτα **Fx**: *alia huiuscemodi* **Fic.**
496d6-e2 λαβών—ἔχων—πράττων—ἀποστάς—ὁρῶν—ἀγαπᾷ—αὐτὸς—
καθαρὸς—βιώσεται—αὐτοῦ—ἴλεως—εὐμενὴς—ἀπαλλάξεται] λαβόντες-
—ἔχοντες—πράττοντες—ἀποστάντες—ὁρῶντες—ἀγαπῶσιν—αὐτοὶ—
καθαροὶ—βιώσονται—αὐτῶν—ἴλεωι—εὐμενεῖς—ἀπαλλάξονται F³ˢˡx:
Hec inquam omnia quicunque diligenter animadvertunt, quietem agunt, et sua dumtaxat curant: ac velut in procella, dum et turbo agitatur at venti perflant, et offunditur pulvere celum, intra parietes tuti permanent, aliosque intuiti nequitia involutos, satis habituros se putant, si puri ipsi ab iniustitia et iniquis facinoribus vixerint, et exactis vite curriculis bona cum spe hilares piique decesserint. **Fic.**

But **x** is not the only MS besides **a/c** that was consulted by Ficino. Another MS with which Ficino has some interesting readings in common is β; I will quote some cases of striking agreement between β and Ficino:

397b8 τὴν αὐτήν] τὴν αὐτὴν ἀεὶ βᵖᶜ: *(ad) eandem (orationis formam) semper* **Fic.**
471b6 ἐναντίους] ἕλληνας βᵖᶜ: *Grecis* **Fic.**
493b3 ἐφ'οἷς ἑκάστας **Groen van Prinsterer**: ἐφ'οἷς ἕκαστος **ADF**: ἃς ἐφ'ἑκάστοις βᵖᶜ: *(voces item) quas in singulis quisque (solet exprimere)* **Fic.**

I am unable to tell whether Ficino took such readings from β itself, or from one of β's extant derivatives (**q** and **Neapol.**).

There are a number of readings in Ficino's translation which can be traced to the **Sc.**-group, esp. **TW**; some instances:

544d7 τρόπων] τρόπον **D**: τρόπον τινὰ **Sc.** (**N**ᵖᶜ): (*Totidem quoque sunt hominum) quodam modo (species* etc.) **Fic.**
561e3 παντοδαπόν] παντοδαπῶν **Sc.**: *(plenum hunc) diversis (plurimisque moribus)* **Fic.**
603a11 ὄν] οὖσα **Sc.** (**N**ᵖᶜ): *procul a veritate suum opus exercet* **Fic.**
616a3-4 ὧν ἕνεκά τε] ὧν ἕνεκά τε ταῦτα ὑπομένοιεν **TW** (**E**²ⁱᵐ**N**ⁱᵐ): *quam illi ob causam talia paterentur* **Fic.**

I do not feel quite confident, however, that these readings actually came into Ficino's translation via a MS of the **TW**-group, because three of the four readings just mentioned also occur in the MSS of Bessarion. As it is certain that Ficino used **N** (see below, p. 275), it is possible that he got some of the readings of **Sc.** via **N**; Alline 302 suggests that Ficino used **W**, which belonged to Donato Acciaiuoli, who was a member of the Platonic Academy in Florence.

As Schneider III 316 already noted, there is occasional agreement between Ficino and **αt**; I will mention some instances:

350a1 ἐν τῇ ἐδωδῇ ἢ πόσει] ἐν τῇ ἐδωδῇ ἢ ὁπόση **Mγac**: ἐν τῇ ἐδωδῇ ὁπόση αᵃᶜt: *in quantitate* **Fic.**
456a1-2 Καὶ—φιλογυμναστική] καὶ γυμναστικὴ δ'ἄρα καὶ πολεμική, ἡ δὲ ἀπόλεμος καὶ οὐ φιλογυμναστικὴ α: *et alia quidem ad exercitationes gymnasticas et rem militarem prompta, alia vero ad hec inepta* **Fic.**
499d4 οὐ—γενέσθαι] οὐ γὰρ ἀδύνατον γενέσθαι α: *fieri certe id potest* **Fic.**

However, I must add that the case of 350a1 does not seem very convincing to me; Ficino's rendering of 456a1-2 could just as well be based on the reading of β^pc, which is the same as that of α, but for the omission of δ' and the reading γυμναστική instead of φιλογυμναστική. Accordingly, I do not think that Ficino actually did make use of α.

Further, I have noted two cases of agreement between Ficino and Φ (but there may be more):

565c3 ἐκεῖνος] ἐκείνοις Φ: *illis* Fic.
565c6 περὶ ἀλλήλων] παρὰ ἀλλήλων Φ: *mutue* Fic.

Finally, Ficino consulted **N**, one of Bessarion's MSS; I will quote some instances of agreement between Ficino and **N**:

491e4 ἄκρατον] ἀκροτάτην γρ. N^im: *extremam* Fic.
497b6 ἴσχειν] ἴσχον N^pc et ἀλλὰ del. N^pc; 497b5-6 vertit Ficinus: *ita et hoc genus, propria nunc amissa virtute, in alienam speciem permutatum*
581e2-3 τῆς—καὶ] τὰς δ'ἄλλας N^im: (*vocantemque*) *alias* (*necessarias*) Fic.
581e6 εἴδους] βίου N^sl: *vite* Fic.
606c4 ὡς πονηρά del. N^pc: om. Fic.
617a4 δεύτερον δὲ λευκότητι τὸν ἕκτον] δεύτερον δὲ λευκότητι τὸν ἕκτον ὑπερβάλλειν N^sl: *secundum vero sextum albedine superare* Fic.

Many of these readings occur in **E** (a direct apographon of **N**) as well; yet it is certain that Ficino consulted **N**, and not **E**, because in some places Ficino shares a reading with **N** which is not in **E**: this is the case, e.g., with the reading at 581e2-3.

There are many places in Ficino's translation where he has obviously sought to emend by means of conjecture a text he judged corrupt. I will mention some instances:

330b1 Ποῖ'] ποῖ **AMγac**: *nonnihil* Fic. (= πόλλ')
392b9 ζητοῦμεν **Stallbaum** ex **Ficini** versione: ἐζητοῦμεν **codd.**: *querimus* Fic.
445c2 ἅ γε: *attende nunc* Fic. (= ἄγε)
498c7 ἀντιτείνειν: *repugnaturos* Fic. (= ἀντιτενεῖν)
504e4 ἄξιον τὸ διανόημα om. Fic. (secl. **Schleiermacher**)
529b6 ἤ: *nunquam* Fic. (= μὴ)
572c8 εἶδος: *mores* Fic. (= ἦθος)

Stallbaum's proposal ζητοῦμεν for ἐζητοῦμεν at 392b9, which is based on Ficino's translation, has met with general approval.

In conclusion we may say that as a textual critic Ficino has accomplished an excellent achievement: he has consulted several MSS and made a number of conjectures, some of which are felicitous.

It remains for me to discuss the character of Ficino's translation[13]. As a rule, Ficino follows Plato's Greek rather faithfully, but sometimes he changes the construction, now and then quite drastically; some instances:

387b1-2 παραιτησόμεθα—διαγράφωμεν: *bona Homeri et reliquorum poetarum venia abiiciamus*

614e4-6 καὶ—ἐκείναις: *easque omnes, tam que ex terra quam que e celo convenerint, sese ultro citroque de his que suis in locis viderint percontari sibique vicissim ad singula respondere*

Omissions do not occur very frequently, and are usually restricted to one or a few words; sometimes Ficino paraphrases a Greek expression more briefly; some instances:

329b1	τοῦ γήρως om.
331d3	ἃ ἂν λάβῃ τις: *deposita*
387c4-5	θερμότεροι καὶ om.
515c8	πάντα δὲ ταῦτα ποιῶν om.
519e3	ἀλλ'—ἐγγενέσθαι: *sed ut tota civitas* (sc. *beata sit*)
615a6-7	καὶ—ἕκαστοι om.
619a6	καὶ—ἑκατέρωσε: *missis extremis*
620b5	διὰ τὰ πάθη om.

In some cases Ficino uses more words than Plato; this is especially so when he seems to feel unable to find a fitting Latin equivalent for a Greek word or expression (we have seen the same method practised by Chrysoloras, Pier Candido and Cassarino: see pp. 264, 267, 269); some instances:

329b1	προπηλακίσεις: *convitia contumeliasque*
392b1	τὰ μέγιστα: *ea que maximi momenti sunt*
520c6	ὕπαρ: *vigilantibus recteque sentientibus*
617e3	ἀδέσποτον: *inviolabilis ac libera*

In some cases Ficino adds one or more words, for which no equivalent is found in the Greek, e.g.:

328d4	ἡδοναί: *voluptas quam ex ea re capio*
388b8	δεησόμεθα: *Homerum eundem orabimus*
616a7	ἀναβῆναι: *ascendere videbatur*

Ficino has a strong tendency to translate in an interpretative way; some instances:

621c1-2	νεκροῦ: *Hectoris cadaver* (so too Chrysoloras and Pier Candido; see p. 267)
516d7	ἐκείνως ζῆν: *in ea miseria degere*
617c6	συνεπιστρέφειν: *cum matre simul* (...) *vertere*
619c3	τὴν αἵρεσιν: *electionem noxiam*
621c1-2	τὸν τῆς Λήθης ποταμὸν: *Lethaeum, id est oblivionis fluvium*

[13] For observations on Ficino's translation of the *Phaedo* and of Plotinus, see J. Festugière, *La philosophie de l'amour de Marsile Ficin* (Paris 1941), 141-152.

In some cases such an addition shows that Ficino did not interpret the Greek correctly; see for instance:

515e7   ἀνείη: *permitteret quicquam aspicere*
519c1   παιδείᾳ: *studiis literarum* (a kind of "Freudian" mistranslation: Ficino is apparently thinking of his own studies !)
618a2-3 τῶν παρόντων: *quam que hic ad presens apparent*

Although Ficino took much trouble to establish a sound text, his translation is sometimes careless or even completely wrong. Often a mistranslation concerns only one or two words, and hardly affects the sense seriously, but in other cases Ficino demonstrably misinterpreted the text completely; some instances:

329e1-2 τοὺς πολλούς: *multos*
331b2   ἄκοντά: (*cum neque*) *invitum* (*quempiam circumvenerit*)
331d4   Πάνυ μὲν οὖν: *recte nimium dicis*
515d4   ἕκαστον: *quemque* (ἕκαστον is neuter)
516c3   μετ' ἐκεῖνα: *hisce gradibus*

In places where he read a corrupt or (to him) unintelligible text, Ficino omits the words altogether, or writes something of his own invention; some instances:

387c2   ὡς οἴεται om.
515b4-5 Εἰ—ὁρῷεν (a notorious crux): *si ergo invicem loqui liceret, nonne ista que coram viderent loqui opinarentur ?*
617e7-8 πλὴν—εἰλήχει: *neque licet cuipiam, quotus ordine sit, agnoscere, nisi cum ceperit, tunc enim duntaxat, quotus sit sortitus, intelligit*

On balance, we may conclude that Ficino's translation marks real progress in comparison with the translations of his predecessors, especially as regards the quality of the text on which he has based his translation, but it is far from perfect, because of the rather frequent cases of careless or even wrong translations.

I wish to end this chapter with some general conclusions.

In the first place, it has become clear that none of the translations permits us a glimpse of a lost primary witness: the translations of Chrysoloras-Uberto and Pier Candido are based on a gemellus of **Sc.**, that of Cassarino on a gemellus of the common source of **M** and **γ**, and that of Ficino on **a** (and/or **c**), with the help of a number of MSS, which can still be identified.

In the second place, while studying the text of a translation one should always bear in mind that a translator, in contrast to a scribe, must always make some sense of the text he has before him and that, accordingly, he is inclined to remove obvious errors instinctively. Therefore, even in places where a translator gives an especially interesting reading, we are often unable to decide whether such a reading is the result of comparison with another MS now lost, or of conjectural emendation.

Yet we have seen that Ficino paid much attention to textual criticism, and that in some cases his translation is decidedly superior to the transmitted text (e.g. at 392b9; see p. 275). I therefore conclude that in a number of places Ficino has a reading which in itself deserves some consideration on the part of an editor, if only he bears in mind that he is almost certainly pondering over a conjecture.

CHAPTER EIGHT

TRANSLATIONS INTO LANGUAGES OTHER THAN LATIN

I. Coptic translation

In codex VI of the famous Nag Hammadi library, a fragment of a Coptic translation of the *Republic* has been preserved: it runs from 588b1 (ἐπειδὴ) to 589b3 (φύεσθαι); it is edited by J. Brashler (see Bibliography), accompanied by a literal English translation which, not knowing Coptic, I have consulted. The translation is of such a poor quality that it was not even recognized as a fragment from *R*. until H.-M. Schenke (1974) identified it (cf. Brashler 325).

With regard to the quality of the translation Brashler 325 remarks: "(...) this attempt on the part of a Coptic translator to translate a summarizing excerpt from Plato's *Republic* is a disastrous failure." Brashler submits that it "was taken from a collection of edifying sayings (δοξογραφαί) said to have circulated in late antiquity as handbooks for students and others with intellectual aspirations but little philosophical sophistication. (...) If this excerpt did come from a handbook of quotations, it was separated from its original context and need not have been expressly associated with Plato."

As regards the occurrence of this fragment in a collection of Hermetic writings Brashler 326 remarks: "To characterize this tractate as gnostic or Hermetic is hazardous. Although its basic tenor is compatible with gnostic or Hermetic views, it does not betray a marked gnostic tendency, nor do the translator's errors reveal a gnosticizing approach to the text."

I have compared Brashler's English translation with the primary MSS and the indirect tradition. Because of the poor quality of the translation, it is hardly ever possible to determine what exactly the translator had before him. Yet I have noted a few places where the Coptic text deserves some attention:

588c4-5 λέγονται—γενέσθαι **AF Stob. Copt.**: om. **D Eus.**
   c7 πλάττε **ADF Eus.**: πράττε **Stob. Copt.** (*Work*)
   c9 φύειν **AD Eus. Stob.**: φύσιν **F** et fort. **Copt.** (*then it is able to cast off the first image*)

The omission of λέγονται—γενέσθαι in **D** and Eusebius at 588c4-5 is due to homoioteleuton; the error πράττε for πλάττε at c7 is remarkable, but it is one which is easily made; if the Coptic translator did read φύσιν for φύειν at c9, it may have been a majuscule error (confusion of E and Σ).

I conclude that the Coptic translation does not have any value for the history or the constitution of the text.

II. OTHER LANGUAGES

Translations into languages other than Latin and Coptic are known to have existed, but are no longer extant.

1. Arabic

M. Steinschneider, ZBB Beiheft XII (1893), 16 ff., remarks that the *Republic* was translated into Arabic by Ḥunain b. Isḥāq; however, E. I. J. Rosenthal 9, referring to G. Bergsträsser, *Ḥunain Ibn Isḥâq über die syrischen und arabischen Galen-Übersetzungen* (Leipzig 1925), 50 (Arabic text), states that Ḥunain translated Galen's synopsis of the *Republic*; E. I. J. Rosenthal plausibly suggests that Ḥunain's translation of Galen's synopsis, in its turn, was used by Averroes for his commented paraphrase of the *Republic*: see p. 288.

F. Rosenthal 393 remarks that "complete translations of Platonic Dialogues (...) were made very rarely."

2. Persian

Agathias, *Hist.* II 28, 1-2 (p. 77, 4-14 Keydell), when speaking about Chosrous, says that some Greek works were translated into Persian for Chosrous. As he goes on to mention that Chosrous was especially interested in Plato and Aristotle, and was not deterred by the most difficult dialogues, such as the *Timaeus* and the *Parmenides*, we may perhaps assume that a Persian translation of the *Republic* must have existed (but Agathias does not mention *R.* explicitly).

3. Hebrew

I. Bartoloccius, *Bibliotheca Magna Rabbinica* (Rome 1693), IV 352 f., writes: "nr. 1644. Plato celeberrimus philosophus (...). Ex iis (sc. dialogis-GJB) opus *De Republica* habetur in Vaticana Hebraice Papyr. in 4." As I have not found any notice of this Hebrew MS elsewhere, I have consulted Dr A. Sauget, Prefect of the Vatican Library. He writes me (letter of 19/12/84): "Jusqu'à présent, je n'ai trouvé *aucune trace* d'un manuscrit Hébreu de la Bibl. Vat. qui contienne en traduction le De Republica de Platon. Je dois dire qu'il serait peut-être intéressant de rechercher les sources de Bartoloccius, car je me rends compte que d'autres oeuvres citées par lui comme conservées à la Bibliothèque Vaticane posent le même problème que le De Republica. Mais un contrôle complet des citations, qui regardent la Bibl. Vat. nécessiterait une étude spéciale.''

PART FOUR

THE INDIRECT TRADITION

I. SOME GENERAL REMARKS ON THE INDIRECT TRADITION

The indirect tradition of the *Republic* is very rich, as already appears from the number of pages occupied by the *index testimoniorum* (pp. 291-365). In the following I will give a very brief survey of the Greek, Latin and Arabic indirect tradition; as I have already stated in the Introduction (see pp. XIX and XXVI), I do not undertake a full evaluation of the indirect tradition, because a comprehensive survey of the history of the text of Plato in antiquity has already been given by Carlini in his book on the text of the *Phaedo*; the state of affairs described there is basically the same with regard to the indirect tradition of the *Republic*.

1. The Greek Tradition

a. direct quotations

All in all, some 90 Stephanus pages of the *Republic* are extant in direct quotations, which is equivalent to almost exactly one-third of the complete work; in this respect, the *Republic* holds a position somewhere between other popular dialogues as the *Phaedo* (28 Stephanus pages = almost half the dialogue) and the *Gorgias* (23 Stephanus pages = about a quarter of the work)[1].

The majority of the direct quotations are to be found, as was only to be expected, in Stobaeus: he quotes some 55 pages, taken from places scattered throughout the work. The second place is held by Eusebius, who quotes *ca.* 20 pages; of course Eusebius is especially interested in theological passages; thus he quotes 377c7-383c7 in full. Iamblichus quotes about 7 pages: 514a1-517c5 and 518b6-519b5 from the Simile of the Cave, selected phrases and passages from 523a-532d and excerpts from 588e5-592a4. Galen too has some 7 pages of direct quotations, most of which come from book IV and the beginning of book V. Other authors who quote more than one Stephanus page: Theodoretus (3 pp.), Theon Smyrnaeus (2 ¼ p.), Clement (1 ½ p.), Justin Martyr (1 ¼ p.), Philoponus (1 ¼ p.), Athenaeus (1 p.).

Verbatim quotations of some length in Proclus' commentary are found only rarely. There are many literal quotations of short phrases in various authors (e.g. the lexicographers, Plutarch, Aristides, the commentators on Plato and Aristotle etc.).

---

[1] For *Grg.*, I have taken my information from the references given by Dodds in his edition; for *Phd.* I have consulted A. Carlini, *Testimonianze antiche al testo del Fedone*, SCO 16 (1967), 286-307.

b. references, imitations etc.

The number of references etc. to the *Republic* is enormous: there is hardly any page in the whole work which has not been referred to, paraphrased or imitated by some author. I will single out some favourite passages: 327a1-4 (Socrates' visit to the Piraeus), 329b7-c4 (the anecdote of Sophocles), 359d1-360b2 (the story of Gyges and his invisible-making ring), 377d-379b (God cannot be considered the cause of evil), 398a1-7 (Homer chased from the ideal state), 436a-441e (the tripartite soul), 457cd (the community of wives and children), 473c11-d6 ("let the philosophers be kings !"), 507-519 (the Similes of the Sun, Divided Line and Cave), esp. 509b9 (ἐπέκεινα τῆς οὐσίας), 546bc (the Platonic Number), 588c7-10 (the many-headed beast), and, last but not least, the Myth of Er, esp. 617d7-e5 (the Prophet's speech).

Lexicographers, of course, show a predilection for rare words, obscure phrases and proverbs, e.g. 337a3 σαρδάνιον, 430a3 δευσοποιός, 432d5 βλακικόν, 435c8 χαλεπὰ τὰ καλά, 535c1 ἄρρατον, 575c4 οὐδ' ἴκταρ βάλλει.

Countless words and phrases have been borrowed or imitated by various authors from all periods; some particularly popular phrases are 496d6-7 (the philosopher seeking protection against the rain and the storm) and 533d2 (the eye of the soul), which recur in many variations.

c. the value of the Greek indirect tradition

As a rule, direct quotations will be of greater importance to the text than references, imitations etc., but this is not always so: for instance, at 474e2 the reading μελιχλώρους of **A**im is confirmed by a paraphrase in Plutarch, an imitation by Aristaenetus and a reference in Philostratus; at 620b1 **F**'s reading εἰκοστὴν is confirmed by paraphrases in Plutarch and Proclus; at 440c7 Galen has ζητεῖ in his *verbatim* quotation (with **ADF**)[2], but in interpreting this passage he reads ζεῖ, which is certainly correct. Thus the indirect tradition in all its appearances can be important for checking and supplementing our MSS.

Dodds, *Gorgias* 65 (quoted with approval by Slings 288), states that the indirect tradition is "decidedly inferior to the direct". If this means that as a rule our MSS taken together exhibit fewer errors than the indirect tradition, then it is true; but one must realize that, in *R.*, the superiority of the direct tradition is mainly due to **A** (and, to a lesser degree, to **D**): in many passages Stobaeus presents us with a text which is much better

---

[2] That this must have been the reading in the common ancestor of the leading medieval MSS of Galen appears from the corrupt readings in these MSS: **H** reads ζητεῖται, **L** has ζητεῖν τε (see De Lacy's apparatus).

than the text of **F**. Further, the observation that **ADF** are usually right against the indirect tradition does not imply that this is always the case: at a time when the exaggerated veneration of a *codex optimus* has been rightly abandoned, we should not foster any prejudice about a *traditio optima*.

For a discussion of the frequent agreement between **F** and the indirect tradition, and the alleged "ancient vulgate" of Plato, see above, pp. 99 f., 104 f.

2. *The Latin tradition*

The Latin tradition is, of course, much less rich than the Greek.

a. *direct quotations*

Greek quotations in Latin authors are few and far between; apart from the Greek quotations in Priscianus' *Institutiones*, the only one I have found is the quotation of 583c10-d1 in a scholium on Cicero's speeches.

b. *verbatim translations*

Cicero has translated a few passages from the *Republic*: 329b7-c4, 329e7-330a3, 359d1-360b2, 562c8-563e1, 571c3-572b1; he sometimes omits or adapts a phrase. For a recent evaluation of Cicero as a translator of Plato see M. Puelma, *Cicero als Platon-Übersetzer*, MH 37 (1980), 137-178.

Ammianus Marcellinus gives a (paraphrased) translation of 329b7-c4, different from Cicero's. Hieronymus translates 389b2-9, Calcidius 571b4-572b1, Valerius Maximus 614b3-8 and Arnobius 617e3-5.

In some cases a particular reading in one of these authors deserves some attention, e.g. at 329c2, where Ammianus reads *feminis*, which corresponds to γυναιξί in Theon Smyrnaeus and Stobaeus.

c. *references, imitations etc.*

References to various passages of the *Republic* are mainly found in philosophical and Christian writers. Among pagan writers Apuleius (*Pl., Soc.*), Calcidius (*Ti.*), Cicero (*philosophica* and *Epp.*) and Macrobius (*in Somn. Scip.*) deserve mention; among Christian writers Augustine (various works), Boethius (*Cons., Arith.*), Lactantius (*Inst.*) and Tertullianus (*An., Nat.*) are prominent.

There are scattered references in various other authors, e.g. Suetonius, Ausonius, Prudentius etc.

Among Christian writers, references to the immortality of the soul are prominent.

Occasionally, a passage has been imitated by a Latin author, thus 361e-362a by Cicero.

3. *The Arabic tradition*

Up to the present day, three volumes of *Plato Arabus*, part of the ambitious project *Corpus Platonicum Medii Aevi* inaugurated by R. Klibansky in 1939, have been published. Two of these works contain some references to the *Republic*, viz. Al-Fārābī's *De Platonis Philosophia* and Galen's *Compendium Timaei Platonis*. The only other work accessible to the non-Arabist is Averroes' commented paraphrase of the *Republic*; this work is only extant in a Hebrew translation, made by Samuel ben Judah in the early fourteenth century; the Hebrew text has been translated into English by E. I. J. Rosenthal, in his *editio princeps* of the Hebrew text, and by R. Lerner; I have consulted the latter translation, because "it marks an improvement in accuracy and intelligibility over the pioneering critical edition and translation of E. I. J. Rosenthal" (Lerner, preface vii).

Averroes follows Plato's text fairly closely, starting half-way book II (369d) and ending his exposition with book IX. With regard to Averroes' source, E. I. J. Rosenthal 9 remarks:

> We know from Ḥunain b. Isḥāq that he translated Galen's *jawāmiᶜ* (summary–GJB) of the ten books of the *Republic* in two parts, of which the first contained Books I-V and the second Books VI-X. It is natural to infer that Averroes in turn summarized this Summary in three *maqālāt*, Hebrew *ma'amārīm*, "treatises". Moreover, he refers several times to Galen and accuses him of misunderstanding and misrepresenting Plato's argument, a fact which lends substance to such an assumption.

The same inference was made by Immisch 26 f.; see further Kraus-Walzer 2 ff. On p. 12, E. I. J. Rosenthal states that "there is no certainty that Averroes' source was Ḥunain's translation of Galen's *Summary of the Republic*".

It goes without saying that Averroes' summary is hardly ever of any importance for the text, especially because the text has passed through Arabic, and possibly through Syriac as well. Kraus-Walzer 18 ff. follow Immisch 25 in assuming that Ḥunain's Arabic translation goes back to an intermediary Syriac translation, but E. I. J. Rosenthal 12, n. 2, says: "this is possible but by no means certain (...). Ḥunain certainly did not always translate Greek works first into Syriac and then into Arabic."

Section I (2) of *Plato Arabus* comprises a "collection of quotations from Plato to be found in Arabic authors" (Klibansky[2] 53); but this collection has not yet been published. Prof. H. Daiber kindly gave me a copy of an article by F. Rosenthal (see Bibliography).

F. Rosenthal states (393) that "complete translations of Platonic Dialogues (...) were made very rarely." He distinguishes four ways in which the Arabs handled Plato (393-395): 1. notes taken from the doxographical tradition, esp. *De Placitis Philosophorum* attributed to Plutarch; 2. γνῶμαι, "sayings"; 3. pseudepigraphical treatises; 4. quotations, which "occupied a rather small place in Arabic literature".

Of the authors mentioned by F. Rosenthal, I will note the most prominent for the sake of curiosity; not knowing Arabic, I have not studied these authors myself: we will only be able to assess the value for the text of quotations in these authors when reliable critical editions, accompanied by translations into Latin or a current modern language, have been published.

Al-Bērūnī, in his *Books on India*, gives some verbal quotations from *Phd.*, *Lg.*, *Ti.* and *R.* (F. Rosenthal 395 f.).

The tracts of the Ikhwān aṣ-ṣafā "should be mentioned as another rather copious source" (397); it contains, among other material, the story of Gyges (359d1-360b2).

On p. 406 ff., F. Rosenthal discusses the (collections of) sayings of Plato; as an instance, he quotes some aphorisms from Abū Sulaimān's *Ṣiwān al-ḥikmah*; the twelfth and thirteenth sayings are clearly based upon *Republic* IV.

With regard to Al-Fārābī, whose *De Platonis Philosophia* has already been mentioned (p. 288), F. Rosenthal 410 notes that he did not know any Greek himself; he continues (411): "the author of these writings (the political writings of Al-Fārābī–GJB) certainly had not the original wording of Plato in front of him, and, perhaps, he was not even really acquainted with its contents. (...) That which, in these writings, may perhaps recall Plato's work to our mind, was in the age of al-Fārābī a commonplace of ancient literature never to be forgotten since the time of Plato and Aristotle" (which may also be valid for many references in Greek and Latin authors!).

On p. 417 F. Rosenthal notes that Plato's doctrine of the soul, as developed in the *Republic*, was known to such authors as Ibn Abī Yaʿqub (died 897), Thābit b. Qurrah (died 901) and their successors.

As has already been pointed out above, it will be the task of a scholar acquainted with both Arabic and Greek literature to disclose all the references in these and other authors to the classical philologist.

II. INDEX TESTIMONIORUM

I have distinguished six types of testimonia; of course I am fully aware that in many cases my choice for a particular type of testimonium is questionable; it is often impossible to draw a sharp distinction between a paraphrase and a reference, between a borrowing and an imitation. Even so, I believe that it will be convenient for the user of my index to know which type of testimonium he can approximately expect.

In the case of references and paraphrases it is often impossible to indicate where exactly the reference or paraphrase begins and ends; nevertheless I have tried to indicate this as exactly as possible, but the reader should realize that my indication involves a subjective element.

I use the following abbreviations:

AFF.   affer(un)t: a *verbatim* quotation; in each case, the first and last words of the quotation are given. I write the abbreviation AFF. in capitals, because this type of testimonium is the most interesting to the textual critic.
cit.   cita(n)t: a paraphrase in which many parts of the original can be recognized.
resp.   respici(un)t: a reference without direct quotations from the original.
imit.   imita(n)tur: an imitation of one or more words.
usurp.   usurpa(n)t: a direct borrowing of one or more words.
expl.   explica(n)t: an explanation of one or more words (this abbreviation is especially used to introduce the scholia).
interpr.   interpretatur: this abbreviation is only used to indicate the places where Proclus, in his commentary, gives an interpretation of a passage.

References in the lexicographers and in the etymologica are not preceded by any abbreviation; in all cases I give the word as it stands in Plato's text, not in the entry of the lexicon or etymologicum; the explicit mentioning of Plato is not recorded.

In quoting the authors I have as a rule conformed to the abbreviations as given in J. C. Facal-A. González, *Repertorium Litterarum Graecarum* (Madrid 1982), Lampe's *Patristic Greek Lexicon*, the *Oxford Latin Dictionary* and Blaise's *Dictionnaire Latin-Français des auteurs chrétiens*. For authors not mentioned in these works (esp. late Byzantine authors) I have invented an abbreviation of my own. For all authors I add the edition which I have consulted; the edition is designated with the initial of the editor's surname. A full list of authors occurring in the *index testimoniorum*, with abbreviations and editions, can be found on pp. 366-376.

INDEX TESTIMONIORUM 291

For the methods followed in collecting the material, I refer to the *Introduction*, pp. XXVI f.; I repeat that the reader should regard this index only as a first attempt to collect the testimonia of the *Republic*, without any claim to completeness.

LIBER PRIMUS

a1-354c3 resp. sch. Pl. *Ti. hypothes.* (277 G.)
a1-328b8 resp. Pr., *in R.* I 15,3-7 K.
a1-b8 resp. Pr., *in Ti.* I 8,30-9,2 D.
a1-5 resp. Thdt., *Affect.* XII 26 (II 426,15-427,1 C.)
a1-3 resp. Ath. Al., *Gent.* 10,35-37 (30 Th.); Eus., *PE* XIII 14,3 (II 229,15-16 M.); —, *Theoph.* II 30 (93,9-10 G.); Or., *Cels.* 6,4,2-4 (III 184-186 B.)
a1-2 resp. Max. Tyr. 5,8a (63,7-8 H.)
a1 Κατέβην—'Αρίστωνος AFF. D. H., *Comp.* 25,209 (II 133,12 U.-R.); —, *Comp. ep.* 25,133 (II 192,17-18 U.-R.); resp. Lib., *Decl.* II 25 (V 139,11-12 F.); Max. Tyr. 37,1a (426,5 H.); Pr., *in R.* I 171,6-7 K.
a1 Κατέβην—Γλαύκωνος AFF. Demetr., *Eloc.* 205 (164,13-14 R. R.)
a1 Κατέβην—Πειραιᾶ AFF. Ammon., *in Int.* 191,33 B.; Demetr., *Eloc.* 21 (78,23-24 R. R.); resp. Quint., *Inst.* 8,6,64 (II 476,5-6 W.)
a1 Κατέβην χθὲς AFF. Pr., *in Ti.* I 9,10 D.; sch. Pl. *Ti. hypothes.* (277 G.); Sud. χ 323 (IV 808,18-19 A.)
a1 Πειραιᾶ resp. Anon., *Prol. Plat.* V 16,46 (33 W.); expl. sch. Pl. ad loc. (187 G.)
a2-5 resp. Pr., *in R.* I 18,8-12 K.
a2 τὴν ἑορτὴν expl. sch. Pl. ad loc. (188 G.)
a3 ἅτε—ἄγοντες AFF. Demetr., *Eloc.* 21 (78,24 R. R.)
a4-b1 resp. Pr., *in R.* I 19,21-23 K.
a4-5 πομπὴν ἔπεμπον Phot. II 99 N.
b2-328b3 (de Polemarcho) resp. Herm., *in Phdr.* 208,13-15 C.
b2 Πολέμαρχος Harp. 252,13 D.
b7-8 'Αλλὰ—Γλαύκων AFF. Phot. I 254 N.; Sud. η 100 (II 553,31 A.)
b8 (et alibi) ἦ Did., *Plat.* 399 M.
c6 (et alibi) ἦν δ' ἐγώ Zonar. I 997 T.
c12 (et alibi) ἦ δ' ὅς A. D., *Pron.* 8,5-6 et 56,18 S.

a2 λαμπὰς—θεῷ AFF. Simp., *in Ph.* 892,1-2 D.
a3-4 λαμπάδια—ἵπποις AFF. Simp., *in Ph.* 892,2-3 D.
a3-4 fort.imit. Meth., *Symp.* VI 4 (68,15-16 B.)
a3 λαμπάδια Harp. 189,10-11 D.; Sud. λ 86 (III 232,12 A.)
b4-5 resp. Pr., *in Ti.* I 21,2-4 D.
b6 Θρασύμαχον resp. Cic., *Or.* XII 39 (12,10 W.); Philostr., *VS* 13,497 (II 15,10 K.)
b7 Παιανιᾶ expl. sch. Pl. ad loc. (188 G.)
b8-331d9 (de Cephalo) resp. Herm., *in Phdr.* 13,21-22 C.
c1 ἑωράκη Did., *Plat.* 404 M.; Phot. I 242 N.
c1 καθῆστο Poll. III 89 (I 183,19 B.)
c5-331d9 resp. Cic., *Att.* IV 16,3 (89, II 108-110 S. B.)
c6 θαμίζεις Phot. I 272 N.; expl. sch. Pl. ad loc. (188 G.)
c7-8 εἰ—ῥᾳδίως AFF. sch. Hom. *Od.* θ 186 (I 371,1-2 D.)
c7 χρῆν expl. sch. Pl. ad loc. (188 G.)
c7 ἦ Hdn. Gr., *Affection.* III ii 326,32-34 L.
d2-330a6 ὡς—γένοιτο AFF. Stob. IV 50a,31 (V 1033,1-1035,13 H.)
d2-4 εὖ—ἡδοναί AFF. Clem., *Strom.* III 3,18,4 (II 204,10-12 S.); Thdt., *Affect.* XII 38

(II 431,6-8 C.); usurp. Anaximen. 72F38 (IIA 126,27-28 J.); resp. sch. Pl. ad loc. (189 G.)
d3 ἀπομαραίνονται usurp. Meth., *Symp.* V 2 (55,15 B.)
d5-6 ἀλλὰ—φοίτα AFF. Thom. Mag., *Ecl.* 191,1-3 R.
d7-e7 resp. Theod. Metoch. 111 (747 M.)
e4 σοῦ—πυθοίμην imit. Zach. Mit., *Opif.* 96,39 C.; —, — 111,505 C.
e5 ἐνταῦθα—ἡλικίας usurp. Chor., *Decl.* 5,68 (246,4-5 F.-R.)
e6 ἐπὶ γήραος οὐδῷ usurp. Aen. Gaz., *Thphr.* 31,10 C.: Chor., *Or.* 6,33 (108,17 F.-R.)

329 a3 διασώζοντες—παροιμίαν usurp. Chor., *Or.* 7,7 (111,23-24 F.-R.)
a3 τὴν παλαιὰν παροιμίαν expl. sch. Pl. ad loc. (189 G.)
a4-d1 resp. Gal., *PHP* IX 6,52 (II 582,29 L.)
a7 (et alibi) ἀγανακτοῦσιν *AB* I 334,22; *An. Bachm.* I 19,9-10; *EM* 7,13 G.
b1 προπηλακίσεις expl. sch. Pl. ad loc. (189 G.)
b2 ὑμνοῦσιν *EM* 777,13-14 G.; Phot. II 239 N.: Sud. υ 112 (IV 640,9-10 A.); expl. sch. Pl. ad loc. (189 G.)
b4 αἴτιον αἰτιᾶσθαι usurp. Chor., *Decl.* 9,49 (403,3 F.-R.)
b5 ἐπεπόνθη Phot. I 242 N.
b7-c4 Σοφοκλεῖ—ἀποδράς AFF. Theon, *Prog.* 158-159 (II 66,3-9 S.); cit. Plu., *Mor.* 525a (III 337,3-5 P.-S.); —, — 788e (V 1,34,15-17 H.-P.-D.); latine cit. Amm. Marc. XXV 4,2 (I 360,21-25 S.); Cic., *Sen.* 14,47 (24,25-25,3 S.); resp. Clem., *Paed.* II x 95,1 (I 214,18-20 S.); Olymp., *in Grg.* 5,10 (44,8-9 W.); Plu., *Mor.* 1094e (VI 2,144,2-4 P.-W.); fort.resp. Ath. XI 506d (III 119,21-22 K.)
c2-4 Εὐφήμει—ἀποδράς AFF. Clem., *Strom.* III 3,18,5 (II 204,13-14 S.)
c2-4 Εὐφήμει—δεσπότην AFF. Clem., *Paed.* II x 95,1 (I 214,19-20 S.); Thdt., *Affect.* XII 39 (II 431,9-11 C.)
c2-3 Εὐφήμει ὦ ἄνθρωπε usurp. Chor., *Dial.* 6,2 (151,11 F.-R.)
c3-4 cit. Philostr., *VA* I XIII 16 (I 13,10 K.); fort.resp. Clem., *QDS* 25,4 (III 176,10 S.)
c3 ἀσμενέστατα —ἀπέφυγον AFF. Olymp., *in Alc.* 98,19-20 (65 W.)
c3 ἀσμενέστατα μέντοι *EM* 31,18-19 G.; *Et. Sym.* α 244 (110,1 S.)
c3 ἀσμενέστατα Philox. Gramm. 337,11 (246 Th.) et 337,25 (247 Th.); Sud. α 4188 (I 386,13-15 A.)
c6-7 τῶν τοιούτων ἐλευθερία imit. Chor., *Decl.* 5,50 (240,25 F.-R.)
c7 παύσωνται κατατείνουσαι usurp. Chor., *Or.* 1,12 (6,1-2 F.-R.)
e4-5 τοῖς—εἶναι AFF. Pr., *In Ti.* I 42,20-21 D.
e6-7 καὶ—οἴονται imit. Areth., *Scr. Min.* I (I 9,15-16 W.); —, — XII (I 117,10-11 W.); —, — XXIV (I 224,31 W.); —, — XXXVII (I 292,17 W.); —, — XLI (I 298,5-6 W.); —, — LIV (I 335,2-3 W.); —, — LXVII (II 57,28-29 W.); Chor., *Or.* 12,15 (157,24-25 F.-R.); usurp. Pr., *in Alc.* 12,10-11 (5 W.)
e7-330a3 cit. Or., *Cels.* 1,29,33-39 (I 154 B.); Plu., *Vit.* 121a (I 1,179,3-6 Z.); latine cit. Cic., *Sen.* 3,8 (6,17-21 S.)
e8 Σεριφίῳ expl. sch. Pl. ad loc. (189 G.)

330 b1-c6 fort.resp. Chor., *Decl.* 6,3 (254,3-4 F.-R.)
b1-7 fort.resp. Clem., *Protr.* X 89,1 (I 66,6-8 S.)
b2 χρηματιστὴς expl. sch. Pl. ad loc. (189 G.)
b8-331c1 Οὖ—Κέφαλε AFF. Stob. IV 31d,118 (V 774,18-776,20 H.)
c3-6 fort.resp. Chor., *Decl.* 6,2 (253,21-254,1 F.-R.)
d4-331b7 resp. Chrysipp., *Stoic.* III 77,21-22 A.
d5-331a9 ἐπειδὰν—κυβερνᾷ AFF. Iust. Phil., *Coh. Gent.* 26 (III 90 O.)
d6 εἰσέρχεται—φροντὶς AFF. Prisc., *Inst.* XVIII 199 (303,13-14 H.); usurp. Chor., *Decl.* 8,2 (316,9 F.-R.)
d6 εἰσέρχεται δέος usurp. Chor., *Decl.* 1,24 (137,16 F.-R.)
d6 δέος καὶ φροντὶς usurp. Chor., *Decl.* 12,76 (532,3 F.-R.)
e1-331a9 imit. Chor., *Or.* 6,3 (100,9-14 F.-R.)

INDEX TESTIMONIORUM 293

e1-2 στρέφουσιν τὴν ψυχὴν usurp. Chor., *Decl.* 7,69 (304,7 F.-R.); —, *Or.* 3,22 (54,20 F.-R.)
e4 ὑποψίας—γίγνεται usurp. Chor., *Decl.* 4,14 (203,1-2 F.-R.)
e5 ἀναλογίζεται—σκοπεῖ usurp. Chor., *Decl.* 11,49 (490,20-21 F.-R.)
e6-331a3 ὁ—λέγει AFF. Niceph. Greg., *in Syn.* 610
e7 δειμαίνει *An. Bachm.* I 189,30; Hsch. δ 777 (I 412 L.); Phot. δ 117 (I 382 Th.); Sud. δ 326 (II 30,24 A.)

a1-9 resp. Them., *Or.* 8,101b (I 154,2-7 D.-N.)
a1 ζῇ μετὰ κακῆς ἐλπίδος cit. Clem., *Strom.* IV 22,144,2 (II 312,13 S.); usurp. Chor., *Decl.* 6,28 (261,28 F.-R.)
a1 μετὰ κακῆς ἐλπίδος AFF. Thdt., *Affect.* VIII 45 (II 326,6 C.)
a2 cit. Olymp., *in Alc.* 23,14-15 (17 W.)
a4-7 ὅτι—γηροτρόφος AFF. Niceph. Greg., *in Syn.* 610
a6-9 γλυκεῖα—κυβερνᾷ AFF. Synes., *Insomn.* XIII 147a (172,14-17 T.); Apostol. 5,52a (II 347,15-16 L.-S.); resp. Chrys., *adv. oppugn.* II (*PG* 47,347); Dexipp., *in Cat.* III 1 (64,10 B.); Mich. Acom., *Ep.* I 266,14 L.; Niceph. Greg., *Hist. Byz.* 8,8 (337,11 B.); —, *in Syn.* 610; Plu., *Mor.* 477b (III 219,1-2 P.-S.); —, — 480c (III 226,20-21 P.-S.); ps.-Arist., *Oec.* II 654,167 R. (latine); Theod. Metoch. 350 M.; — 695 M.; imit. Gr. Naz., *Vit.* 1942 (148 J.)
a7 cit. Olymp., *in Alc.* 23,14-15 (17 W.)
a7 ἀτάλλοισα expl. sch. Pl. ad loc. (190 G.)
a7 συναορεῖ expl. sch. Pl. ad loc. (190 G.)
b3-4 ἔπειτα—συμβάλλεται AFF. Niceph. Greg., *in Syn.* 610
c1-354c3 resp. Averr., *in R.* 47,29-30 R.; Pr., *in R.* I 7,12-14 K.
c1-335a5 fort.resp. sch. Hes. *OD* 709 (217,3-5 P.)
c1-d3 resp. sch. Pl. ad loc. (190 G.)
c1-9 fort.resp. Ph., *Cher.* 5,15 (I 173,22-23 C.-W.); —, *Plant.* 23,101 (II 153,4-5 C.-W.); —, *Spec.* IV 3,66 (V 224,1-2 C.-W.)
c5-9 cit. *Exc. Par.* 298,26-299,3 R.; Ioh. Sard. (?), *in Hermog. Stat.* 326,16-19 R.; Marcellin. (?), *in Hermog. Stat.* 283,3-7 R.; resp. Phlp., *in de An.* 555,21-23 H.
d2 (et alibi) ἄρα *AB* I 441,19; *An. Bachm.* I 139,28-29; Phot. α 2763 (I 253 Th.); Zonar. I 310 T.
d4-332a8 resp. Demetr. Cyd., *Ep.* 70,5-6 (I 102 L.)
d4-5 resp. Chor., *Dial.* 15,2 (282,7-8 F.-R.)
d5-332c3 resp. sch. Hes. *OD* 709-710 (217,14-16 P.)
d8 ἔφη sc. Πολέμαρχος sch. Pl. ad loc. (190 G.)
e3-332a8 resp. sch. Pl. ad loc. (190 G.)
e5 ἀπιστεῖν Zonar. I 261 T.
e8-332a6 cf. ad 331c5-9
e9-332a1 resp. Phlp., *in de An.* 555,21-23 H.

a9-335d13 resp. Them., *Or.* 7,95a (I 143,3-5 D.-N.); —, — 34,XXVI (II 230,13-15 D.-N.)
a9-335b1 resp. Ammon., *in APr.* 42,12-15 W.
d1 usurp. Chor., *Dial.* 9,2 (196,10 F.-R.)
d4-333b6 resp. sch. Pl. ad loc. (190 G.)
e6 Εἶεν expl. sch. Pl. ad loc. (190 G.)
e7 (et alibi) ἄχρηστος *AB* I 475,17; *An. Bachm.* I 176,20-21; Phot. α 3456 (I 316 Th.)

a13 Συμβόλαια resp. (ση) sch. Pl. ad loc. (190 G.)
c7-e2 resp. sch. Pl. ad loc. (191 G.)
d11 ἀχρηστίᾳ *AB* I 78,13

b1-3 resp. Lib., *Decl.* I 95 (V 67,12 F.)
b8-e5 resp. sch. Pl. ad loc. (191 G.)

c1-2 δοκοῦντας—ὄντας imit. Chor., Or. 6,4 (100,18 F.-R.)
e10-335d13 resp. sch. Pl. ad loc. (191 G.)

335 b2-d13 fort.resp. sch. Aristid. 3,166 (546,13-14 D.)
b6-c3 resp. Pr., in R. I 30,1-3 K.
b8-11 imit. Them., Or. 1,5c (I 9,1-2 D.-N.)
c12 ἀφίππους expl. sch. Pl. ad loc. (191 G.)
d3-12 resp. Eus., PE IV 22,8 (I 212,7-8 M.); Hierocl. ap. Stob. II 9,7 (II 181,24-27 W.); Plu., Mor. 1102d (VI 2,161,15-16 P.-W.); Porph., Abst. II 41 (170,19-21 N.); Pr., in Ti. I 375,23-25 D.
d3 resp. S. E., M. XI 70 (II 391 M.-M.)
d7 resp. Sen., Ira I 3,6,5 (46,15-16 R.)
d11-12 resp. sch. Pl. ad loc. (191 G.)
e9 usurp. Dam., Isid. 244 (201,1 Z.); Marin., Procl. 36 (169,11 C.); Plot. III 7,1,14 (I 368 H.-S.); — III 7,7,11-12 (I 378 H.-S.)

336 b1-354a11 (de Thrasymacho) resp. Bas., Ep. 135,1,26 (II 50 C.); Epict. IV 5,3 (402,17 S.); Ephipp. 14,3 (II 257 K.); Hsch. Mil., Vir. Ill. LV (46,10 F.); Lib., Decl. II 25 (V 139,14-15 F.); Olymp., in Alc. 61,8-9 (41 W.); Pr., in Alc. 295,10-11 (137 W.); —, in Prm. 691,25-26 C.; —, — 655,10-12 C.; —, in R. I 274,2 K.; Procop. Gaz., Ep. 33 (544,6 H.)
b1-2 fort.resp. Pr., in Ti. I 284,13-14 D.
b3-4 διακοῦσαι τὸν λόγον usurp. Chor., Dial. 4,10 (83,20 F.-R.)
b4 διεπαυσάμεθα usurp. Lib., Ep. 19,2 (X 11,9 F.)
c1 εὐηθίζεσθε expl. sch. Pl. ad loc. (191 G.)
d4 ὕθλους Hsch. υ 117 (IV 195 S.)
d5-7 resp. Them., Or. 21,253c (II 33,11-13 D.-N.)
d6-e3 resp. Or., Cels. 1,17,19-21 (I 120 B.)
d6-7 resp. Gp. 15,1,8 (432,21-24 B.)
d7-8 νῦν—πρότερος AFF. Prisc., Inst. XVIII 281 (356,8-9 H.)
e1 ὑποτρέμων usurp. Meth., Res. I 27,1 (254,10 B.)
e4-9 μὴ—αὐτό AFF. Stob. III 9,24 (III 355,10-15 H.)
e7 resp. Pr., in R. I 7,28 K.

337 a3-c2 resp. Them., Or. 21,252b (II 31,4 D.-N.)
a3 ἀνεχάγχασέ usurp. Chor., Dial. 4,22 (87,13 F.-R.); —, Or. 8,93 (365,11 F.-R.); Lib., Ep. 758,6 (X 685,2 F.); Phot. α 1829 (I 180 Th.)
a3 μάλα σαρδάνιον usurp. Zach. Mit., Opif. 131,1127 C.
a3 σαρδάνιον Hsch. σ 202 (IV 11 S.); — σ 204 (IV 11 S.); Phot. II 146-147 N.; Poll. VI 200 (II 50.19 B.); Tim. 192 R.-K.; Zen. V 85 (I 154,1-156,15 L.-S.); resp. Philox. Gramm. 591,2 (352 Th.); imit. Iul., Or. VII 222b4-5 (II 1,67-68 R.); expl. sch. Pl. ad loc. (192-194 G.)
a4-8 resp. Psell., Orat. Min. 17,43-44 (63 L.)
a4 ῏Ω Ἡράκλεις expl. sch. Pl. ad loc. (194 G.)
a4 αὕτη-Σωκράτους AFF. Olymp., in Alc. 52,22 (135 W.)
a4 εἰρωνεία expl. sch. Pl. ad loc. (194 G.)
d3-5 fort.resp. sch. D. Ol. Γ 35,29 (VIII 132,4-7 D.)
e3 λαμβάνῃ λόγον AB I 106,17
e5-7 ἔπειτα—ἐρεῖ AFF. Thom. Mag., Ecl. 253,9-11 R.

338 c1-347a6 resp. sch. Pl. ad loc. (194 G.)
c1-344c8 resp. Pr., in R. I 110,11 K.; sch. Hes. OD 207-212 (76,3-4 P.)
c1-339e8 resp. Gal., Hist. Phil. 10 (605,21-606,2 D.)
c1-2 resp. Pr., in R. I 27,4-5 K.
c2 resp. Calc., Ti. V (59,5-6 W.); Str. I 1,18 (I 1,80,19-20 A.)
c7 Πουλυδάμας fort.resp. Bas., Leg. Lib. Gent. VIII 22 (53 B.); Max. Tyr. I 5b (8,11 H.); expl. sch. Pl. ad loc. (194 G.)

INDEX TESTIMONIORUM 295

c7 παγκρατιαστής resp. sch. Pl. ad 333e4 (191 G.); expl. sch. Pl. ad loc. (194-195 G.)
c8 τὰ βόεια κρέα fort.resp. Anon. Lond. XV 14 (62 J.)
d3 resp. Pr., in R. I 159,28-160,1 K.

a3-b8 (de Clitophonte) resp. Olymp., in Alc. 105,13 (70 W.); Pr., in Ti. I 20,19 D.
d1 Συκοφάντης Sud. σ 1329 (IV 454,23 A.); expl. sch. Pl. ad loc. (195 G.)
d2-e6 resp. Aristid., Or. 2,251 (I 2,215,14-18 L.-B.)
d5 (et alibi) ἁμαρτίαν AB I 79,7
e3-4 ἐπιλειπούσης—δημιουργός AFF. Stob. II 8,38 (II 163,14-15 W.)
e4-5 resp. D. L. III 63 (I 147,2-3 L.)

a5 συκοφαντεῖν Phot. II 184 N.
b5 ὡς ἔπος εἰπεῖν expl. sch. Pl. ad loc. (195 G.)
c1-2 ξυρεῖν—λέοντα resp. Aristid., Or. 3,97 (I 2,324,2 L.-B.); Philostr., VS 13,497 (II 15,12-13 K.); fort.usurp. Ioseph. Kaloth., Ath. 22 (480,871 T.); expl. sch. Pl. ad loc. (195 G.)
c4-342e11 resp. Epicur. 397 (267,17-19 U.); Gal., PHP IX 5,1 (II 564,10-13 L.); Pr., in R. I 208,10-11 K.
c9-11 fort.resp. Alb., Intr. XXX 3 (147 L.)

b3-4 resp. Plot. II 3,16,39-40 (I 181 H.-S.)
d2 Συνωμολόγησε usurp. Zach. Mit., Opif. 101,182 C.
d6-10 fort.resp. Aristid., Or. 2,146 (I 2,189,3-4 L.-B.)
e6-11 resp. Cic., Off. I 25,85 (38,8-10 A.); Pr., Th. Pl. I 16 (I 77,12-15 S.-W.)

a1-4 Ἐπειδὴ—Σώκρατες AFF. Alex. Aphr., in SE 118,1-2 W.
a3-9 fort.resp. Areth., Scr. Min. XXI (I 208,19-20 W.); —, — LIV (I 334,12-13 W.)
a3-4 ὦ—τίτθη cit. Demetr. Cyd., Ep. 5,58-59 (I 28 L.)
a4 τίτθη Hsch. τ 987 (IV 160 S.); Phot. II 211 et 217 N.; Tim. 214 R.-K.; expl. sch. Pl. ad loc. (195 G.)
a7 κορυζῶντα expl. sch. Pl. ad loc. (196 G.)
b1-344c8 resp. Pr., in R. I 24,25-27 K.
b1-c1 resp. Gal., PHP IX 5,1 (II 564,13-15 L.)
c3 fort.resp. Arist., EN V 1,1130a3 B.; —, — V 6,1134b5-6 B.
d1-2 imit. Meth., Res. I 53,2 (309,4-5 B.)

a1-c4 resp. Pr., in R. II 176,7-9 K.
a3-4 imit. Meth., Res. I 53,2 (309,5-6 B.)
a8 ὅσια expl. sch. Pl. ad loc. (196 G.)
b3-4 imit. Plot. IV 4,31,52-53 (II 122 H.-S.)
b3 τοιχωρύχοι Hsch. τ 1080 (IV 163 S.)
b4 κατὰ μέρη ἀδικοῦντες expl. sch. Pl. ad loc. (196 G.)
c4-8 resp. sch. Pl. ad loc. (196 G.)
d1-345b6 resp. Alex. Aphr., in SE 118,3-6 W.
d1-3 resp. Areth., Scr. Min. LXIX (II 85,17-18 W.)
d1 Ταῦτα—ἀπιέναι AFF. Alex. Aphr., in SE 118,2-3 W.
d2 βαλανεὺς Moer. 85 P.-K.
e5 κήδεσθαι Hsch. κ 2462 (II 470 L.)

a1-2 οὗτοι—εὐεργετήσῃς AFF. Them., Or. 26,330c (II 149,15-16 D.-N.)
b4-5 εἰ—ποιήσω AFF. Alex. Aphr., in SE 118,6 W.
b5-6 ἢ—λόγον AFF. An. Ox. III 209,25; usurp. An. Ox III 209,27-28
b7-e2 resp. Gal., PHP IX 5,2 (II 564,15-18 L.); —, — IX 5,8 (II 564,33-566,1 L.)
b9-e3 νῦν—ἄρχειν AFF. Eus., PE XII 44,2 (II 133,21-134,11 M.)
c1-d1 resp. Synes., Regn. V 5d (12,18-13,5 T.)
c3-d1 resp. Them., Or. 13,171cd (I 246,10-12 D.-N.)
c5-6 resp. D. Chr., Or. I 13 (I 3,8-9 A.)

346   c9 ἀρνυμένους *AB* I 446,2; expl. sch. Pl. ad loc. (196 G.)
      c12-d1 resp. Calc., *Ti.* V (59,7-8 W.)
      e1 προῖκα Hsch. π 3499 (III 379 S.); expl. sch. Pl. ad loc. (197 G.)
      e3-347a6 οὐκοῦν—ἀρχῃ AFF. Eus., *PE* XII 9,2-3 (II 98,9-18 M.)

347   a5 ζημίαν expl. sch. Pl. ad loc. (197 G.)
      b1-3 ἤ—ἔστιν AFF. Stob. III 10,72 (III 427,3-4 H.)
      b3 λέγεταί τε καὶ ἔστιν imit. Zach. Mit., *Opif.* 107,373 C.
      b5-9 resp. Them., *Or.* 24,304c (II 103,24 D.-N.)
      b9-c5 resp. Boet., *Cons.* I 4,17-21 (7 B.)
      c4 τὸ—ἄρχεσθαι AFF. sch. Pl. ad 347a5 (197 G.)
      c7 εὐπαθήσοντες *AB* I 94,28
      d1 ἐπιτρέψαι expl. sch. Pl. ad loc. (197 G.)
      d8 πράγματα expl. sch. Pl. ad loc. (197 G.)
      e5 (et alibi) ἀληθεστέρως *AB* I 78,23

348   a7 ἀντικατατείναντες expl. sch. Pl. ad loc. (197 G.)
      b8-350c12 resp. Alex. Aphr., *in Top.* 166,25-27 W.; —, — 325,11-13 W.; Ammon., *in APr.* 73,6-10 W.; Pr., *in R.* I 26,18-21 K.; sch. Pl. ad loc. (197 G.)
      b8-349c10 resp. Olymp., *in Alc.* 86,2-4 (57 W.); Pr., *in Alc.* 218,17-18 (101 W.)
      c2-d2 resp. Alex. Aphr., *in Top.* 361,3-6 W.
      c11-12 resp. Plot. I 6,1,47-48 (I 106 H.-S.)
      c12 γενναίαν εὐήθειαν resp. Pr., *in Alc.* 323,2 (150 W.)
      e5-350c11 Τοῦτο—κακός AFF. Stob. III 9,58 (III 381,18-384,16 H.)

349   a9-10 imit. Meth., *Res.* I 29,3 (259,13-14 B.)
      b1-350c11 cit. Pr., *in Alc.* 323,9-324,14 (150-151 W.); resp. Alex. Aphr., *in APr.* 275,15-19 W.; —, — 279,10-12 W.
      b4 ἀστεῖος expl. sch. Pl. ad loc. (197 G.)
      b5 (et alibi) εὐήθης *AB* I 91,28
      b11 'Ἀλλ' οὐ τοῦτο imit. Zach. Mit., *Opif.* 111,492 C.
      e10-350b12 resp. Herm., *in Phdr.* 222,19-20 C.
      e11-12 ἐπιτάσει καὶ ἀνέσει usurp. Alb., *Intr.* XXX 1 (145 L.); Niceph. Greg., *Ep.* 46,47 (II 159 L.)

350   d2-3 imit. Meth., *Res.* I 30,2 (262,5 B.)
      d3 εἶδον Θρασύμαχον ἐρυθριῶντα resp. Aristid., *Or.* 3,616 (I 3,497,9-10 L.-B.); Pr., *in Ti.* III 341,9-10 D.; Synes., *Calv.* IV 66a (195,15 T.)
      d3 εἶδον ἐρυθριῶντα usurp. Niceph. Greg., *Flor.* 92,826 L.
      d3 ἐρυθριῶντα imit. Zach. Mit., *Opif.* 131,1127 C.
      d4-7 ἐπειδὴ—ἀδικίαν AFF. Stob. III 9,59 (III 384,18-21 H.)
      d4-6 ἐπειδὴ—κείσθω AFF. Stob. III 10,73 (III 427,6-8 H.)
      d6-352b4 resp. sch. Pl. ad loc. (197 G.)

351   a5 resp. Alb., *Intr.* XXIX 4 (143 L.)
      a5 (et alibi) ἀμαθία Zonar. I 146 T.
      a7-354a9 ἀλλὰ—δικαιοσύνης AFF. Stob. III 9,60 (III 385,2-390,11 H.)
      b1-352a4 resp. sch. Hes. *OD* 274-280 (94,6-10 P.)
      c8-352a9 cit. et interpr. Pr., *in R.* I 20,7-24,24 K.
      c8-352a4 resp. Pr., *de Mal. Subs.* 52,10-12 (250,251 B.)
      d4-5 resp. Chrysipp., *Stoic.* III 70,31-32 A.
      d5-6 fort.resp. Epicur. 397 (270,15-16 U.)
      d5-6 ὁμόνοιαν καὶ φιλίαν usurp. Chor., *Decl.* 1,57 (143,20-21 F.-R.)
      e9-352a9 fort.resp. Epicur. 397 (272,15-16 U.)

352   a1 ἀδύνατον—πράττειν expl. sch. Pl. ad loc. (198 G.)

INDEX TESTIMONIORUM 297

a10-b2 resp. Mich., *in EN* 47,18 Ha.; —, — 66,5-7 Ha.; fort.resp. Meth., *Symp.* VIII 16 (105,19-106,2 B.)
a10 fort.resp. Plu., *Mor.* 1102f (VI 2,162,8 P.-W.)
b3 Εὐωχοῦ expl. sch. Pl. ad loc. (198 G.)
c3 κομιδῇ expl. sch. Pl. ad loc. (198 G.)
d2-354a11 resp. sch.Pl. ad loc. (198 G.)
d5-6 οὐ-λόγος imit. Plat. V 3,10,7-8 (II 315 H.-S.)
d2-354a11 resp. sch.Pl. ad loc. (198 G.)
d5-6 οὐ-λόγος imit. Plot. V 3,10,7-8 (II 315 H.-S.)
d8-354a11 cit. et interpr. Pr., *in R.* I 24,27-26,17 K.
d8-353b1 fort.resp. Them., *Or.* 26,327b (II 144,14-15 D.-N.)

a1-5 resp. Pr., *in Cra.* LXI (26,29-30 P.)
a1 σμίλη Hsch. σ 652 (IV 30 S.); expl. sch. Pl. ad loc. (198 G.)
b6-c2 imit. Plot. I 7,3,2-3 (I 120 H.-S.)
d3-5 cit. Pr., *Th. Pl.* III 6 (III 23,18-19 S.-W.)
e7-8 fort.resp. Meth., *Symp.* VIII 16 (107,8-9 B.)

a1-5 resp. Boet., *Cons.* IV 1,25-26 (65 B.)
a10 εἰστιάσθω imit. Bas., *Hex.* III 10 (242 G.)
a11 Βενδιδίοις Hsch. β 514 (I 323 L.); resp. Anon., *Prol. Plat.* V 16,38-39 (33 W.); Pr., *in R.* I 19,21-23 K.; —, *in Ti.* I 8,31 D.; Str. X 3,18 (VII 78,1-2 L.)
b1-3 imit. Iul., *Or.* III 15,34-36 (I 1,141 B.)
b8 οὐκ prius-ἐλθεῖν AFF. *Lex. Vind.* α 79 (15,11-12 N.); Prisc., *Inst.* XVIII 192 (299,10-11 H.)

LIBER SECUNDUS

a3-4 καὶ prius-ἀπεδέξατο AFF. Phryn., *PS* 47,10-11 B.
a4 ἀπόρρησιν Poll. II 127 (I 123,1-2 B.); Tim. 38 R.-K.
b4-d2 resp. Apul., *Pl.* II 10,235 (87-88 B.); expl. sch. Pl. ad loc. (198 G.)
c1-d2 fort.resp. Nemes. 17 (224 M.)
c6 (et alibi) ἰατρεύεσθαι *AB* I 100,10

a1-3 resp. sch. Pl. ad 367a5 (202 G.)
b7-c1 ἐπανανεώσομαι—λόγον AFF. Thom. Mag., *Ecl.* 114,6-7 R.
c7 διατεθρυλημένος τὰ ὦτα Phot. α 811 (I 87 Th.); — δ 462 (I 409 Th.); Sud. δ 782 (II 74,16 A.); imit. Them., *Or.* 34,XVII (II 224,9-10 D.-N.); Zach. Mit., *Opif.* 96,52 C.; usurp. Aen. Gaz., *Thphr.* 12,4 C.; Chor., *Decl.* 7,75 (306,3-4 F.-R.); —, *Or.* 1,53 (16,8-9 F.-R.); —, — 8,128 (373,25 F. R.)
d3 διὸ—ἐρῶ AFF. Phot. I 323 N.; Sud. κ 818 (III 61,1-2 A.)
e3-359b5 resp. Anon., *in EN* 178,11-13 H.; Herm., *in Phdr.* 9,21-22 C.; Pr., *in R.* I 220,13-18 K.; sch. Pl. ad loc. (199 G.)
e3-5 expl. sch. Pl. ad loc. (199 G.)

b6-d7 resp. sch. Pl. ad loc. (199 G.)
d1-360b2 cit. Eudoc., *Viol.* CCXLVII (169 F.); latine cit. Cic., *Off.* III 9,38 (96,26-97,8 A.); resp. Aristid., *Or.* 2,239 (I 2,212,21-23 L.-B.); Demetr. Cyd., *Ep.* 14,25 (I 42 L.); Gr. Naz., *Carm. Mor.* 10,31-32 (*PG* 37,683); —, *Carm. Semet* 88,7-12 (*PG* 37,1435); —, *Or.* 43,21 (*PG* 36,524b); Ioseph. Kaloth., *Ath.* 15 (471,602 L.); Luc., *Nav.* 42 (IV 119,9 M.); Pr., *in R.* II 111,4 K.; sch. Pl. ad loc. (ση) (199 G.); Theon, *Prog.* 159 (II 66,17-18 S.)
d1 resp. Pr., *in R.* II 111,4 K.
d4 χάσμα Hsch. χ 223 (IV 276 S.)
e5 σφενδόνην Hsch. σ 2872 (IV 114 S.); Phot. II 192 N.

360 b5-6 καὶ—ἀλλοτρίων AFF. Prisc., *Inst.* XVIII 192 (299,11-12 H.)
e1-362c8 resp. sch. Pl. ad loc. (199 G.); imit. Cic., *Rep.* III 17,27 (94,1-16 Z.)
e6-362c8 resp. David, *in Cat.* 23a B.; expl. sch. Pl. ad loc. (199 G.)

361 a4-5 ἐσχάτη—ὄντα AFF. Plu., *Mor.* 50e (I 101,6 P.-W.-P.-G.); —, — 613f-614a (IV 5,19-20 H.); —, — 854e (V 2,2,6,6-7 H.); Stob. III 10,71 (III 427,1 H.); resp. Bas., *Leg. Lib. Gent.* VI 25-26 (50 B.)
a4-5 ἐσχάτη ἀδικία Phot. I 218 N.; Suid. α 3250 (II 432,6 A.)
a7 imit. Chor., *Or.* 6,4 (100,18 F.-R.)
b5-d1 τοῦτον—βίου AFF. Eus., *PE* XII 10,2-3 (II 99,1-9 M.); Thdt., *Affect.* XII 30-31 (II 428,9-19 C.)
b6-d1 ἄνδρα—βίου AFF. Georg. Mon., *Chron.* I 356,9-357,1 B.
b6-7 resp. Synes., *Ep.* 131 (225,15 G.)
b7-8 resp. Bas., *Leg. Lib. Gent.* VI 24 (50 B.); Clem., *Strom.* I 1,6,3 (II 6,8-9 S.); Dam., *Isid.* 56 (45,9 Z.); sch. A. *Th.* 593-594 (264,20-29 S.); fort.resp. Gr. Naz., *Or.* 7,6,77 (*PG* 35,761); —, — 43,60,87 (*PG* 36,576)
b7 resp. sch. Pl. ad loc. (200 G.); usurp. Chor., *Or.* 6,4 (100,18 F.-R.)
c4-d3 fort.resp. Clem., *Strom.* VII 7,45,3 (III 34,12-13 S.)
c6 μὴ—κακοδοξίας AFF. Phryn., *PS* fr. 361 (179,11 B.); Phot. II 203 N.
c6 τέγγεσθαι Hsch. τ 300 (IV 135 S.); expl. sch. Pl. ad loc. (200 G.)
d5 ὥσπερ ἀνδριάντα usurp. Meth., *Res.* I 25,1 (250,8 B.); Pr., *Th. Pl.* I 1 (I 6,22 S.-W.)
d5 ἀνδριάντα *AB* I 82,11; — I 210,15; — I 211,14
e1-362a3 λεκτέον—ἐθέλειν AFF. Eus., *PE* XII 10,4 (II 99,11-15 M.)
e1 ἀγροικοτέρως expl. sch. Pl. ad loc. (200 G.)
e3-362a2 οὕτω—ἀνασχινδυλευθήσεται AFF. Clem., *Strom.* V 14,108,3 (II 398,21-23 S.); Eus., *PE* XIII 13,35 (II 211,12-13 M.); Thdt., *Affect.* VIII 50 (II 328,9-12 C.); imit. Cic., *Rep.* III 17,27 (94,6-10 Z.)
e4-362a1 cit. Clem., *Strom.* IV 7,52,1 (II 272,11-12 S.); Epict. IV 1,172 (388,1-4 S.); *Mart. Apoll.* 40 (100,21-23 M.); imit. Epict. II 1,38 (118,17 S.); Lib., *Decl.* XXI 29 (VI 334,15-16 F.)

362 a2-3 resp. Clem., *Strom.* I 1,6,3 (II 6,8-9 S.)
a2 ἀνασχινδυλευθήσεται Hsch. α 4583 (I 160 L.); Phot. α 1662 (I 167 Th.); — II 162 N.; Phryn., *PS* 48,1 B.; Suid. α 2071 (I 186 A.); usurp. Clem., *Strom.* IV 11,78,1 (II 283,5 S.); expl. sch. Pl. ad loc. (200 G.)
a8-b1 resp. sch. A. *Th.* 593-594 (264,20-29 S.)
a8 ἄλοκα—καρπούμενον cit. Dam., *Isid.* 56 (45,10 Z.)
b3 ὁπόθεν ἂν βούληται usurp. Niceph. Greg., *Ep.* 88,18 (II 279 L.)
d6 ἀδελφὸς—παρείη Apostol. I 36 (II 248 L.-S.); Diogenian. I 91 (II 16 L.-S.); Macar. I 29 (II 137 L.-S.); Suid. α 442 (I 47 A.); expl. sch. Pl. ad loc. (200 G.)

363 a7-c2 resp. Them., *Or.* 30,351ab (II 185,13-19 D.-N.)
c3-d2 resp. Plu., *Vit.* 521b (I 1,419,24-26 Z.)
c4-d2 resp. Aen. Gaz., *Thphr.* 42,6-9 C.
d3 παῖδας παίδων usurp. Aristid., *Or.* 30,10 (204,11-205,1 K.); expl. sch. Pl. ad loc. (201 G.)
d5-6 resp. Gr. Naz., *Or.* 25,15,4-5 (192 M.-L.)

364 a1 ἐξ ἑνὸς στόματος Poll. II 102 (I 116,9 B.)
a2-3 resp. Chor., *Or.* 6,8 (102,6-7 F.-R.)
a5 ὡς—πλῆθος expl. sch. Pl. ad loc. (201 G.)
b5 ἀγύρται Hsch. α 866 (I 33 L.); expl. sch. Pl. ad loc. (201 G.)
c1 ἀκεῖσθαι Phot. α 730 (I 80 Th.); Phryn., *PS* 48,13-15 B.; imit. Porph., *Abst.* II 31 (161,14 N.); expl. sch. Pl. ad loc. (201 G.)
c7-d2 resp. sch. Pl. ad loc. (201 G.)
d2-3 resp. Gal., *Pecc. Dign.* 5,23 (60,9-10 B.)

INDEX TESTIMONIORUM 299

d3 τραχεῖαν καὶ ἀνάντη resp. Them., *Or.* 21,246a (II 21,26-22,1 D.-N.); imit. Meth., *Symp. prooem.* 5 (5,4 B.)
d3 ἀνάντη expl. sch. Pl. ad loc. (201 G.)
d4-5 τὸν "Ομηρον μαρτύρονται AFF. Phot. I 407 N.; Sud. μ 237 (III 332,16-17 A.)
d6 λιστοί expl. sch. Pl. ad loc. (201 G.)
e3-4 fort.resp. Pr., *in R.* I 72,3-5 K.
e3 βίβλων ὅμαδον usurp. Dam., *Isid. Epit.* 37 (62,8 Z.); Them., *Or.* 2,32b (I 42,7 D.-N.)
e3 βιβλων expl. sch. Pl. ad loc. (201 G.)
e3 ὅμαδον expl. sch. Pl. ad loc. (202 G.)
e4 θυηπολοῦσιν Phot. I 284 N.

a2 ἅς—καλοῦσιν resp. (ση) sch. Pl.ad loc. (202 G.)
b3-4 Πότερον—ἀναβὰς AFF. Max. Tyr. 12,1a (145,13-14 H.) (e Pindaro, non e Platone)
c1-2 resp. (ση) sch. Pl. ad loc. (202 G.)
c2 κύριον expl. sch. Pl. ad loc. (202 G.)
c3 πρόθυρα καὶ σχῆμα imit. Meth., *Res.* I 27,4 (256,15 B.)
c4 σκιαγραφίαν ἀρετῆς imit. Chor., *Or.* 8,35 (352,18 F.-R.)
c4 σκιαγραφίαν Hsch. σ 967 (IV 44 S.)
c5-6 fort.resp. Bas., *Leg. Lib. Gent.* X 134 (59 B.)
c5 ἀλώπεκα ἑλκτέον ἐξόπισθεν usurp. Them., *Or.* 279a (II 69,20-21 D.-N.)
c5 ἀλώπεκα Tim. 214 R.-K.
d2 ταύτῃ ἰτέον AFF. Olymp., *in Alc.* 201,14 (127 W.)
d2 ἴχνη τῶν λόγων usurp. Niceph. Greg., *Ep.* 103,98 (II 269 L.); —, *Flor.* 70,330 L.
d6-e5 Ἀλλά—ἀναπειθόμενοι AFF. Cyr., *adv. Iul.* 617ab
e4-5 θυσίαις τε καὶ ἀναθήμασιν usurp. Aen. Gaz., *Thphr.* 34,5 C.

a7 λύσιοι θεοί Phot. I 398 N.
c7 θείᾳ φύσει imit. Alb., *Intr.* XXXI 1 (151 L.)

a6 fort.resp. Olymp., *in Alc.* 105,14 (70 W.)
b2 κατατείνας λέγω resp. sch. Pl. ad loc. (202 G.)
d1-2 ἀγαθὰ γόνιμα Phryn., *PS* 56,3 B.
d5 τῶν μὲν ἄλλων expl. sch. Pl. ad loc. (202 G.)
e5-368a5 resp. Pr., *in Prm.* 665,1-8 C.
e7 ἀτὰρ expl. sch. Pl. ad loc. (202 G.)

a2 ἐλεγείων expl. sch. Pl. ad loc. (203 G.)
a3 Μεγαροῖ expl. sch. Pl. ad loc. (203 G.)
a4 παῖδες—γένος AFF. sch. Aristid. 2,304 (420,2-3 D.); resp. Aristid., *Or.* 2,304 (I 2,235,4-5 L.-B.); —, — 4,18 (I 3,534,14-535,1 L.-B.)
b7-c2 resp. Pr., *in Alc.* 313,14-17 (146 W.)
c7-369a3 εἶπον—ἐπισκοποῦντες AFF. Gal., *PHP* IX 2,7-11 (II 546,8-22 L.); resp. Pr., *in R.* I 210,15-20 K.
d1-369a3 cit. Averr., *in R.* 48,2-8 R.; resp. Elias, *in Porph.* 33,33-34,1 B. (22,14 W.); Olymp., *in Alc.* 75,22-23 (50 W.); —, — 193,24-25 (122 W.); —, — 225,18-19 (140 W.); —, — 228,27 (142 W.); —, *in Mete.* 100,19-24 S.
d2-7 resp. Olymp., *in Alc.* 182,21-22 (115 W.); —, — 186,21-22 (118 W.); —, — 194,9 (122 W.); Pr., *in R.* I 7,15-17 K.; —, — I 12,9-15 K.; —, — I 13,14-15 K.; —, — I 217,9-10 K.
d6 ἕρμαιον expl. sch. Pl. ad loc. (203 G.)
d8-e1 resp. Pr., *in R.* I 7,28 K.
e2-369b4 resp. Gal., *Inst. Log.* XVIII 2-4 (45,14-46,11 K.); Pr., *in R.* I 217,10-18 K.
e2-369a3 resp. Alfar., *Plat. Phil.* VI 25 (14 R.-W.); Arist., *Pol.* H 1,1323b33-36 B.; Averr., *in R.* 48,1-2 R.; Phlp., *Aet.* VI 27 (216,19-22 R.); Pr., *in Alc.* 223,8-11 (103 W.)
e2-8 resp. Pr., *in R.* I 14,12 K.

369 **a5-412b7** resp. Max. Tyr. 37,1a (426,5-14 H.)
a5-10 resp. Phlp., *Aet.* VI 21 (188,7-9 R.); —, — VI 27 (224,2-4 R.)
b5-374a2 resp. Averr., *in R.* 48,8-9 R.
b5-372d3 resp. Or., *Cels.* 5,43,17-19 (III 127 B.); Pr., *in R.* I 217,18-21 K.
b5-372c1 resp. Alb., *Intr.* XXXIV 1 (167 L.)
b5-371e11 resp. Averr., *in R.* 22,18-30 R.; —, — 27,28-30 R.
b5-7 resp. (ση) sch. Pl. ad loc. (203 G.)
d1-371e7 resp. Arist., *Pol.* Δ 4,1291a11-19 B.
e2-370a4 resp. Arist., *MM* A 33,1194a5-12 B.; Pr., *in R.* II 360,21-361,3 K.
e4-5 τετραπλάσιον—κοινωνεῖν AFF. Thom. Mag., *Ecl.* 220,1-3 R.

370 **a3** καὶ—ἔχειν AFF. Thom. Mag., *Ecl.* 220,4-5 R.
c3-5 πλείω—πράττῃ AFF. Stob. II 31,106 (II 220,4-6 W.)
d1 σμινύην Phot. II 168 N.; expl. sch. Pl. ad loc. (203 G.)
d2 οἰκοδόμος Poll. VII 117 (II 84,24-25 B.)

371 **b8** resp. Elias, *in Porph.* 16,4 W.
d5 καπήλους resp. sch. Pl. ad loc. (203 G.)
d7 πλανήτας resp. sch. Pl. ad loc. (203 G.)
e7 imit. Aristid., *Or.* 29,19 (197,1 K.)

372 **a7** (et alibi) οἰκοδομησάμενοι *AB* I 110,19
b2 ἄλφιτα expl. sch. Pl. ad loc. (203 G.)
b3 τὰ μὲν—τὰ δὲ expl. sch. Pl. ad loc. (204 G.)
b3 πέψαντες expl. sch. Pl. ad loc. (204 G.)
b3 μάξαντες expl. sch. Pl. ad loc. (204 G.)
b5 κατακλινέντες usurp. Plu., *Mor.* 616b (IV 10,17 H.)
c2-d3 ἄνευ—παραδώσουσιν AFF. Ath. IV 138ab (I 313,2-11 K.)
c5-d1 resp. Plu., *Mor.* 664a (IV 127,18-22 H.)
c5-6 resp. Clem., *Paed.* II i 15,1 (I 164,23-24 S.)
c5 βολβοὺς expl. sch. Pl. ad loc. (204 G.)
c7 resp. Clem., *Paed.* II i 15,3 (I 165,4-5 S.)
c7 τραγήματά expl. sch. Pl. ad loc. (204 G.)
c8 σποδιοῦσιν Phot. II 169 N.; expl. sch. Pl. ad loc. (204 G.)
d1 μετρίως ὑποπίνοντες imit. Plu., *Mor.* 615e (IV 9,17 H.)
d5 ἐχόρταζες imit. Plu., *Mor.* 616b (IV 10,17 H.)
e2-376c6 resp. Alb., *Intr.* XXXIV 1 (167 L.)
e5-373e8 resp. Pr., *in R.* I 217,21-23 K.
e8 φλεγμαίνουσαν πόλιν resp. Apul., *Pl.* II 24,256 (102 B.); Phot. II 265 N.; Plu., *Vit.* 64d (III 2,60,10-11 Z.)
e8 φλεγμαίνουσαν expl. sch. Pl. ad loc. (204 G.)

373 **a4** πέμματα Phot. II 72 N.; expl. sch. Pl. ad loc. (204 G.)
b5-c1 fort.resp. Calc., *Ti.* CXLVII (198,10-11 W.)
b6 σχήματα καὶ χρώματα usurp. Niceph. Greg., *Flor.* 100,1018 L.
b7 ῥαψῳδοί expl. sch. Pl. ad loc. (205 G.)
b8 ἐργολάβοι Phot. I 208 N.; Poll. VII 182 (II 102,4-5 B.)
c3 κομμωτριῶν expl. sch. Pl. ad loc. (205 G.)
c4-7 fort.imit. Plot. III 1,6,9-10 (I 263 H.-S.)
c4-6 expl. sch. Pl. ad loc. (205 G.)
c4 fort.resp. Clem., *Strom.* II 20,105,1 (II 170,22 S.)
d4-374a2 resp. Averr., *in R.* 26,28-27,1 R.
d7-e8 resp. Dam., *in Phd.* I 110,7-9 (71 W.)
e9-376c7 resp. Pr., *in R.* I 217,23-218,18 K.

INDEX TESTIMONIORUM 301

a6 ἀδύνατον—τέχνας usurp. Them., Or. 21,250d (II 28,21 D.-N.)
d8-e2 resp. Averr., in R. 28,5-6 R.
d8 (et alibi) φυλάκων resp. Eust., Ep. 57 (355,73-74 T.); Max. Tyr. 37,1a (426,12 H.)
e6-417b9 resp. Aristid., Or. 3,136 (I 2,335,19-336,4 L.-B.)
e6-412b7 resp. Theod. Prodr., Epith. 349,12-13 G.
e6-376a10 Ἡμέτερον—δῆλον AFF. Stob. IV 1,154 (IV 103,5-105,13 H.)
e10 (et alibi) φαῦλον An. Bachm. I 412,10-12
e11 imit. Aristid., Or. 35,3 (254,1 K.)

a2-376c6 resp. Anon., in EN 193,20-21 H.; Averr., in R. 29,6-8 R.; Pr., in R. I 240,1-12 K.; —, — I 240,17-19 K.; Synes., Ep. 131 (225,15-17 G.); —, Regn. XIII 13a (26,14-16 T.); —, — XIX 21b (43,14-15 T.); expl. sch. Pl. ad loc. (205 G.)
a2-e7 cit. Averr., in R. 28,6-23 R.
a6 διωκάθειν Tim. 74 R.-K.; expl. sch. Pl. ad loc. (205 G.)
a11-e8 resp. Mich. Ital., Or. 44 (282,9-10 G.)
a11 (et alibi) θυμοειδής Hsch. θ 886 (II 335 L.)
c1-4 resp. Arist., Pol. H 7,1327b39-40 B.
c6-7 cit. Chor., Or. 3,8 (51,13-14 F.-R.); resp. Asp., in EN 119,6-7 H.
d10-376c6 resp. David, in Cat. 23b B.
e1-376b7 breviter cit. Olymp., in Grg. 10,7 (64,2-6 W.)
e1-4 resp. Them., Or. de virtute (III 65 D.-N.)
e9-376c6 cit. Averr., in R. 28,24-29,5 R.; resp. Ammon., in Cat. 2,7 B.; Olymp., Prol. 3,30 B.

a5-8 resp. Plu., Mor. 276f (II 1,303,24-25 N.-S.-T.); —, — 355b (II 3,11,4-5 N.-S.-T.)
a9-10 resp. Pr., in Prm. 712,18-20 C.
a11 (et alibi) κομψόν AB I 102,23; expl. sch. Pl. ad loc. (205 G.)
b3-c3 resp. Plu., Mor. 969bc (VI 1,36,23-26 H.-D.)
b5 φιλομαθές usurp. Plot. I 3,3,7 (I 75 H.-S.)
b8-c6 Ἀλλὰ—ἔφη AFF. Stob. IV 1,112 (IV 57,2-9 H.)
b8-c3 resp. sch. Pl. ad loc. (206 G.)
b11-c5 resp. Aristid., Or. 3,680 (I 3,519,6-7 L.-B.)
c2 resp. Niceph. Greg., in Syn. 522a
c4-6 Φιλόσοφος—ἔφη AFF. Stob. IV 1,155 (IV 105,15-17 H.)
c7-412b7 resp. Olymp., in Grg. 32,4 (166,9-11 W.)
c7-377a5 resp. Pr., in R. I 218,18-24 K.
c7-e5 resp. Averr., in R. 29,9-12 R.
d5 προὔργου expl. sch. Pl. ad loc. (206 G.)
e2-412b7 resp. Pr., in R. II 4,3 K.
e2-383c7 resp. Pr., Th. Pl. I 4 (I 21,18-28 S.-W.)
e2-377c5 Τίς—ἐκβλητέον AFF. Stob. II 31,110ᵛ (II 225,26-226,25 W.)
e2-4 resp. Ammon., in Porph. 13,28-30 B.
e3-4 resp. Pr., in R. I 59,27-29
e6-403c8 resp. Olymp., in Grg. 5,4 (41,13-24 W.); —, — 41,2 (208,6-14 W.)
e6-392c5 resp. Olymp., in Grg. 5,4 (41,17-21 W.); —, — 6,11 (49,29-50,3 W.); Pr., in R. I 219,22-26 K.
e6-7 resp. Averr., in R. 29,13-14 R.
e11-377b4 resp. Hermog., Prog. 1 (2,4 R.)
e11-377a8 Λόγων—ταῦτα AFF. Eus., PE XII 4,1 (II 90,10-14 M.)

a4-383c7 resp. Anon., Prol. Plat. II 7,20-27 (15 W.)
a4-5 resp. Averr., in R. 29,20 R.; —, — 29,25 R.
a4 resp. Hermog., Prog. 1 (1,3 R.)
a12-378e3 resp. Averr., in R. 30,14-21 R.
a12-c5 Οὐκοῦν—ἐκβλητέον AFF. Eus., PE XII 5,1-3 (II 90,22-91,6 M.)
a12-b3 ἀρχή—ἑκάστῳ AFF. Stob. II 31,110ⁿ (II 223,21-23 W.); resp. Them., Or. 21,244b (II 19,2 D.-N.)

a12-b1 ἄλλως τε expl. sch. Pl. ad loc. (206 G.)
a12 resp. Gal., *PHP* IX 1,9 (II 542,1-2 L.); fort.resp. D. H., *Rh.* III 243 (II 267,2-3 U.-R.)
b1 resp. Hermog., *Prog.* 1 (1,5 R.)
b4 Κομιδῇ expl. sch. Pl. ad loc. (206 G.)
b11-378e3 resp. Thom. Mag., *Subd. Off.* 24 (*PG* 145,541c)
b11-d10 Πρῶτον—τοῦτο AFF. Phlp., *Aet.* XVIII 10 (640,17-641,8 R.)
b11-c5 resp. Plu., *Mor.* 3ef (I 6,6-9 P.-W.-P.-G.)
c7-383c7 Ἐν—χρώμην AFF. Eus., *PE* XIII 3,1-36 (II 167,11-174,17 M.)
c7-d6 Ἐν—λέγουσι AFF. Eus., *PE* XIII 14,6 (II 230,9-14 M.)
d4-398b4 resp. *An. Ox.* III 225,22-31; Aug., *Civ.* II 14,6-11 (45 D.-K.); Eus., *Theoph.* II 41 (96,32-35 G.); Max. Tyr. 17,4a (212,19-213,2 H.); — 18,5ad (222,8-223,15 H.); Or., *Cels.* 4,50,34-35 (II 314 B.); Pr., *in R.* I 44,6-15 K.; —, — I 47,16-17 K.; —, — I 65,20-25 K.; Tert., *Nat.* II 7,11 (52,9-10 B.)
d4-378d3 resp. Calc., *Ti* CXXVIII (171,12-16 W.)
d4-6 resp. Pr., *in R.* I 72,1-3 K.
d4 Ἡσίοδός resp. Aristid., *Or.* 4,45 (I 3,547,10 L.-B.)
d8-e3 Ὅπερ—γράψαι AFF. Eus., *PE* XIII 14,12 (II 231,18-21 M.)
d9 resp. Dam., *in Phd.* I 466,3-4 (241 W.)
e6-378e3 resp. D. Chr., *Or.* LIII 2 (II 110,7-10 A.); fort.resp. Bas., *Leg. Lib. Gent.* IV 15-18 (45 B.)
e6-378d6 Πρῶτον—ὑπονοιῶν AFF. Eus., *PE* II 7,4-7 (I 97,13-98,15 M.); breviter cit. Thdt., *Affect.* II 7 (I 138,19-21 C.)
e6-378a5 Πρῶτον—ἀκούειν AFF. Thdt., *Affect.* III 38 (I 180,7-14 C.); resp. Pr., *Th. Pl.* V 3 (254 P.)
e6-378a2 resp. Pr., *in R.* I 72,21-22 K.; —, — I 82,4-5 K.
e6-378a1 Πρῶτον—αὐτόν AFF. Eus., *PE* XIII 14,12 (II 231,23-25 M.)
e8-378a1 resp. Lib., *Decl.* I 121 (V 82,6 F.); Pr., *in R.* I 82,16 K.

378
a1-2 resp. Pr., *in R.* I 82,14 K.
a2-5 resp. Pr., *in R.* I 83,7-10 K.
a3-4 resp. Pr., *in R.* I 186,17-18 K.
a4-6 δι'—θῦμα AFF. Pr., *in R.* I 80,14-16 K.
a5-6 θυσαμένους—θῦμα AFF. Clem., *Strom.* V 10,66,4 (II 370,22-23 S.)
a7-c6 καὶ—αὐτῶν AFF. Thdt., *Affect.* III 39-40 (I 180,15-181,9 C.)
b4 πρωτοί (hoc sensu) *AB* I 111,16
b8-d3 resp. D. Chr., *Or.* LIII 2 (II 110,7-15 A.); Pr., *in R.* I 87,11-15 K.
b8-c6 resp. Lib., *Decl.* I 121 (V 82,5 F.)
b8-c1 resp. Pr., *in Ti.* I 172,21-23 D.
c3 πολλοῦ δεῖ expl. sch. Pl. ad loc. (206 G.)
c6-e4 ἀλλ'—λόγον AFF. Stob. II 31,110ʷ (II 226,27-227,11 W.)
d3-e3 resp. Olymp., *in Grg.* 46,5 (238,25-239,2 W.)
d3-6 Ἥρας—ὑπονοιῶν AFF. Thdt., *Affect.* III 41 (I 181,10-14 C.)
d3-4 resp. Pr., *in R.* I 72,3 K.; —, — I 82,3 K.; —, — I 82,10 K.
d3 Ἥρας—νέος AFF. Phot. I 266 N.; Sud. η 481 (II 584,30 A.)
d7-e5 resp. Pr., *in R.* I 50,2-11 K.
d7-e3 ὁ—ἀκούειν AFF. Pr., *in R.* I 79,29-80,4 K.; fort.resp. Bas., *Leg. Lib. Gent.* V 6-8 (46 B.)
d7-e1 resp. Anon., *Prol. Plat.* II 7,32-33 (17 W.); David, *in Porph.* 106,10-12 B.
d7-8 ὁ—μή cit. Pr., *in R.* I 186,15-16 K.
d7 resp. Pr., *in R.* I 44,16-17 K.
d8-e1 cit. Elias, *in Porph.* 28,32-33 B.
d8-e1 δυσέκνιπτά τε καὶ ἀμετάστατα imit. Them., *Or.* 21,249c (II 26,22-23 D.-N.)
d8 δυσέκνιπτά usurp. Chor., *Decl.* 9,104 (419,16 F.-R.)
e1 ἀμετάστατα usurp. Chor., *Or.* 8,140 (376,22 F.-R.)
e4-383c7 resp. Pr., *Th. Pl.* I 17 (I 80,23-25 S.-W.)

a5-6 resp. Pr., *Th. Pl.* I 3 (I 12,8 S.-W.)
a7-383c7 resp. Pr., *in R.* I 41,6-9 K.
a7-380c10 resp. Pr., *Th. Pl.* I 17 (I 81,14-17 S.-W.)
a7-c8 resp. sch. Pl. ad loc. (206 G.)
b1-380c10 fort.resp. Gal., *Hist. Phil.* 16 (609,9-10 D.)
b1-d6 Οὐκοῦν—ἐσθλῷ AFF. Thdt., *Affect.* V 34-35 (I 237,5-238,6 C.)
b1-c7 resp. Averr., *in R.* 30,22-26 R.; Iambl., *Myst.* 57,2-3 (71 P.); —, — 189,7-11 (151-152 P.); Porph., *Marc.* 12 (112,14-15 P.); Pr., *in R.* II 355,29-356,1 K.; —, *in Ti.* I 359,23-24 D.; sch. Pl. ad loc. (206 G.); S. E., *M.* XI 70 (II 391 M.-M.); Sext., *Sent.* 113 et 114 (26 Ch.); —, — 390 (56 Ch.); Theod. Daphn., *Ep.* 5,80 (63 D.-W.)
b1-c1 cit. Pr., *in R.* I 28,26-29 K.; resp. Boet., *Cons.* III 12,64-70 (61 B.)
b1-14 resp. Olymp., *in Phd.* 5,2,7-8 (91 W.)
b1-5 cit. sch. Hom. *Il.* Ω 527b (V 607,9-11 E.)
b1 ἀγαθός—ὄντι cit. Georg. Mon., *Chron.* I 85,4-6 B.
b1 resp. Pr., *in R.* I 27,13 K.; —, — I 28,11 K.
b5-6 cit. Pr., *in R.* I 29,16-17 K.
b7-8 cit. Pr., *in R.* I 29,27-28 K.
b9-10 cit. Pr., *in R.* I 30,21-22 K.
b15-c7 resp. Clem., *Strom.* V 14,136,4 (II 418,13-14 S.); Thdt., *Affect.* VI 57 (I 274,18 C.)
b15-16 cit. Georg. Mon., *Chron.* I 85,4-6 B.; fort.resp. Anast. Sin., *VD* II 3,34 (33 U.); Clem., *Strom.* VII 4,22,2 (III 16,13-14 S.)
b16 cit. Pr., *in R.* I 31,1-2 K.
b16 τῶν κακῶν ἀναίτιον cit. Pr., *Th. Pl.* I 21 (I 99,23 S.-W.)
c2-380c10 resp. et interpr. Pr., *in R.* I 31,2-32,3 K.
c2-d4 resp. Pr., *in R.* I 96,7-15 K.
c2-7 resp. Apul., *Pl.* I 12,205 (71 B.); Bess., *in Cal. Pl.* 160,36-40 M.; Max. Tyr. 5,1g (53,13-14 H.); Phot., *Amphil.* 1,572 (20 W.)
c5-7 resp. Pr., *in Prm.* 830,19-21 C.; —, *in Ti.* I 375,20-22 D.; fort.resp. Plot. VI 7,19,19 (III 239 H.-S.)
c5-7 τῶν alterum-θεόν AFF. Pr., *de Prov.* 13,4-5 (120 B.)
c5-6 τῶν alterum-ζητεῖν AFF. Phlp., *Aet.* XVI 1 (566,14-16 R.); resp. Pr., *in R.* I 99,18-19 K.
c6-7 cit. Pr., *de Mal. Subs.* 34,13-14 (216 B.); —, — 34,14-15 (217 B.); —, — 47,13-14 (240,241 B.); resp. Pr., *de Mal. Subs.* 41,10-11 (230,231 B.); —, *in R.* I 38,8-9 K.; sch. Pl.ad loc. (206 G.)
c9-e2 resp. Them., *Or.* 6,79c (I 117,19-22 D.-N.); —, — 15,194ab (I 280,1-3 D.-N.)
d3-e2 fort.resp. Plu., *Mor.* 369c (II 3,45,18-22 N.-S.-T.); —, — 600c (III 515,4-8 P.-S.)
d3-4 δοιοί—δειλῶν AFF. Plu., *Mor.* 24a (I 47,27-28 P.-W.-P.-G.); Pr., *in R.* I 96,14-15 K.; resp. sch. Pl. ad loc. (207 G.)
d8 βούβρωστις expl. sch. Pl. ad loc. (207 G.)
e1-2 fort.resp. Them., *Or.* 9,126c (I 191,8-9 D.-N.)
e3-5 resp. Pr., *in R.* I 100,21-27 K.
e5-380a1 resp. Pr., *in R.* I 106,15-18 K.

a3-4 θεός—θέλῃ AFF. Plu., *Mor.* 17b (I 33,14-15 P.-W.-P.-G.)
b6-c9 κακῶν—ἀγαθῶν AFF. Thdt., *Affect.* V 36 (I 238,8-17 C.)
c2 resp. Pr., *Th. Pl.* I 17 (I 81,4 S.-W.)
c10 ἀπόχρη fort.resp. Phot. α 2722 (I 250 Th.)
d1-383c7 resp. et interpr. Pr., *in R.* I 33,9-37,2 K.; resp. Pr., *Th. Pl.* I 20 (I 94,13 S.-W.)
d1-382c5 resp. Averr., *in R.* 30,32-31,4 R.
d1-381e11 resp. Apul., *Soc.* XII 146 (32 B.); Pr., *Th. Pl.* I 19 (I 88,12-15 S.-W.); sch. Pl. ad loc. (207 G.); sch. Pl. ad *Sph.* 216a (bis) (41 et 446 G.)
d1-6 resp. Bess., *in Cal. Pl.* 160,36-40 M.
d5-6 resp. Pr., *Inst.* 127 (112,25-34 D.)

d5 resp. Pr., *Th. Pl.* I 20 (I 94,12 S.-W.)
d8-e5 οὐκ—πόνων AFF. Simp., *in Cael.* 289,16-19 H.
e3-381b7 cit. et interpr. Pr., *in R.* I 33,25-35,5 K.
e5 imit. Plot. I 8,14,7 (I 137 H.-S.)
e5 εἰλήσεών expl. sch. Pl. ad loc. (207 G.)

381 b1-e11 resp. Alb., *Intr.* X 7 (63 L.)
b8-c10 cit. et interpr. Pr., *in R.* I 35,6-17 K.
b8-c2 Ἀλλ᾽—εἶναι AFF. Simp., *in Cael.* 289,19-23 H.
c7-9 resp. Pr., *in R.* I 27,24 K.; —, *in Ti.* I 421,18-19 D.
c8-9 ἀλλ᾽—μορφῇ AFF. Pr., *Th. Pl.* I 19 (I 89,18-20 S.-W.); Simp., *in Cael.* 289,24-26 H.
c9 ἕκαστος—μορφῇ AFF. Pr., *Th. Pl.* I 20 (I 94,16-17 S.-W.)
d1-383a1 cit. et interpr. Pr., *in R.* I 36,10-27 K.
d1-e1 resp. Pr., *in R.* I 109,15-21 K.
d4 παντοῖοι—πολῆας AFF. Plot. VI 5,12,31-32 (III 176 H.-S.)
d7 ἀγείρουσαν Tim. 9 R.-K.
e1-2 μηδ᾽—ἐκδειματούντων AFF. Thom. Mag., *Ecl.* 396,15-16 R.
e2 ἐκδειματούντων expl. sch. Pl. ad loc. (207 G.)
e3-383a6 resp. Pr., *Th. Pl.* I 21 (I 97,8-10 S.-W.)

382 a1-383c7 resp. sch. Pl. ad loc. (207 G.)
a4 τὸ ὡς ἀληθῶς ψεῦδος resp. Dam., *Pr.* 7 (I 15,12-14 W.); Pr., *in Alc.* 108,3-4 (48 W.); imit. Pr., *in Ti.* I 179,24-25 D.; Plot. II 5,5,23-24 (I 208 H.-S.)
b8-9 expl. sch. Pl. ad loc. (207 G.)
c6-d3 resp. Or., *Cels.* 4,18,7-10 (II 224 B.)
d9 ἔνι expl. sch. Pl. ad loc. (207 G.)
e6 ἀψευδὲς τὸ θεῖον cit. Pr., *in R.* I 41,11-13 K.; —, *Th. Pl.* I 21 (I 97,9 S.-W.)

383 a2 resp. Pr., *Th. Pl.* I 17 (I 81,4 S.-W.)
a7-8 resp. Pr., *in R.* I 115,4-9 K.
b2 μακραίωνας Phot. I 403 N.
b4 παιᾶν᾽ expl. sch. Pl. ad loc. (207 G.)
b5-9 κἀγώ—ἐμόν AFF. Athenag., *Suppl.* 21,5 (48 S.)
b7-8 αὐτὸς—κτανών AFF. Plu., *Mor.* 16e (I 32,18-19 P.-W.-P.-G.)
c1-5 resp. Pr., *in R.* I 51,7-14 K.
c2 χορὸν οὐ δώσομεν Sud. χ 408 (IV 815,18 A.); resp. Pr., *in R.* I 51,20 K.; —, — I 61,1 K.; expl. sch. Pl. ad loc. (207-208 G.)
c6 resp. Pr., *Th. Pl.* I 17 (I 81,4 S.-W.)

LIBER TERTIUS

386 a1-388e4 resp. sch. Pl. ad loc. (208 G.)
a1 τοιαῦτ᾽ ἄττα Did., *Plat.* 400 M.
a6-398b4 resp. Cic., *TD* II 11,27 (293,24-294,3 P.)
a6-392c5 resp. Pr., *in R.* I 66,9-17 K.
a6-392a2 resp. Pr., *in R.* II 313,2-4 K.
a6-388e4 resp. Pr., *in R.* I 106,1-3 K.
a6-b7 resp. Averr., *in R.* 31,26-32,9 R.; sch. Aristid. 3,165 (545,29-546,1 D.)
b4-387c8 resp. D. Chr., *Or.* LIII 2 (II 110,12-18 A.); Pr., *in R.* I 118,5-17 K.
b5-6 αἱρήσεσθαι πρὸ δουλείας θάνατον cit. sch. Aristid. 3,277 (628,8-10 D.)
c3-388e4 resp. Averr., *in R.* 31,30-32,9 R.
c3-5 Ἐξαλείψομεν—ἄλλῳ AFF. Eus., *PE* XIII 14,7 (II 230,17-19 M.)
c3 Ἐξαλείψομεν usurp. Aristid., *Or.* 3,653 (I 3,508,14 L.-B.); —, — 4,41 (I 3,544,12 L.-B.)

INDEX TESTIMONIORUM

c5-7 resp. Pr., *in R.* I 120,1-2 K.
d2 resp. Pr., *in R.* I 122,7-9 K.
d7 οἵῳ—ἀΐσσουσι AFF. Bas., *Leg. Lib. Gent.* VI 7 (49 B.)
d9-10 resp. Pr., *in R.* I 119,27 K.

a5-8 resp. Pr., *in R.* I 120,6-9 K.
b2 διαγράφωμεν Moer. 110 P.-K.
b5-6 fort.resp. Cic., *Fam.* XIII 77,1 (213, II 58 S. B.)
b5 δουλείαν—πεφοβημένους usurp. Aristid., *Or.* 3,277 (I 2,387,3 L.-B.)
c1 ἐνέρους expl. sch. Pl. ad loc. (208 G.)
c1 ἀλίβαντας Hsch. α 2986 (I 105 L.); *Lex. Seg.* X B.; resp. Plu., *Mor.* 736a (IV 303,16 H.); —, — 956a (VI 1,2,13-14 H.-D.); expl. sch. Pl. ad loc. (208 G.)
d1-388e4 resp. Pr., *in R.* I 50,26-29 K.
d1-388a3 resp. Chor., *Or.* 6,29 (107,21-22 F.-R.)
d1-388a1 Καὶ—ἀνδρῶν AFF. Stob. IV 44,84 (V 992,2-18 H.)
d5 resp. sch. Hom. *Il.* Σ 22-35a (IV 440,47-49 E.)
d12 αὐτὸς αὐτῷ αὐτάρκης imit. Them., *Or.* 15,189d (I 274,26-27 D.-N.)
e9-10 resp. Pr., *in R.* I 63,25-26 K.

a5-392a2 resp. Cyr., *adv. Iul.* 561bc
a5-b4 resp. Olymp., *in Grg.* 5,4 (41,18-19 W.)
a5-8 Πάλιν—ὕπτιον AFF. Eus., *PE* XIII 14,8 (II 230,21-24 M.)
a6-b2 resp. Pr., *in R.* I 123,9-12 K.
b1 resp. sch. Hom. *Il.* Σ 22-35a (IV 440,47-49 E.)
b4-7 resp. Pr., *in R.* I 123,7-8 K.
c1 ὤμοι—δυσαριστοτόκεια AFF. Max. Tyr. 18,5c (223,8-9 H.)
c2-d1 resp. Pr., *in R.* I 123,16-20 K.
c7 αἲ αἲ—ἀνδρῶν AFF. Max. Tyr. 18,5c (223,4-6 H.)
d2-7 resp. Pr., *in R.* I 123,23-28 K.
d3 σχολῇ expl. sch. Pl. ad loc. (208 G.)
d5 ἐπιπλήξειεν expl. sch. Pl. ad loc. (208 G.)
e5-389b1 resp. Averr., *in R.* 32,10-13 R.; Pr., *in R.* I 50,26-29 K.; sch. Pl. ad loc. (208 G.)
e5-389a1 Ἀλλὰ—θεούς AFF. Stob. III 1,53 (III 21,2-6 H.)
e5-7 σχεδὸν—τοιοῦτον AFF. Apostol. XIII 41b (II 584,23-24 L.-S.); cit. Averr., *in R.* 32,10-11 R.

a3-7 resp. sch. Pl. ad loc. (208 G.)
a5-6 resp. Max. Tyr. 18,5c (223,1 H.); Pr., *in R.* I 126,14-16 K.
b2-d6 Ἀλλὰ—τελῆται AFF. Stob. IV 5,95 (IV 228,2-21 H.); cit. Averr., *in R.* 32,13-21 R.; resp. sch. Pl. ad loc. (209 G.)
b2-9 latine AFF. Hieron., *Ruf.* I 18,6-17 (17 L.); resp. Gal., *in R.* 2 (100 K.-W.); fort.resp. Ph., *Cher.* 5,15 (I 173,16-21 C.-W.); —, *Deus* 13,65 (II 71,6-8 C.-W.)
b2-5 fort.resp. Clem., *Strom.* VII 9,53,2 (III 39,14-16 S.)
b4-8 resp. Anon., *in Tht.* 59,9 (39 D.-S.)
b4-5 resp. Or., *Cels.* 4,18,7-10 (II 224 B.)
b4 ὡς—εἴδει usurp. Anon., *in EN* 137,7-8 H.; imit. Plu., *Mor.* 6e (I 12,5 P.-W.-P.-G.)
c3 παιδοτρίβην expl. sch. Pl. ad loc. (209 G.)
d7-390d6 resp. Averr., *in R.* 32,24-33,2 R.; Pr., *in R.* I 129,8-13 K.; sch. Pl. ad loc. (209 G.)
d7-390c8 expl. sch. Pl. ad loc. (209 G.)
d7-e3 Τί—δοκεῖ AFF. Stob. III 5,11 (III 258,11-15 H.)
d9-e2 cit. Bess., *in Cal. Pl.* 424,34-35 M.
e6-390d6 cit. Bess., *in Cal. Pl.* 424,35-426,15 M.
e12-390c8 resp. Pr., *in R.* I 130,1-2 K.
e12-390a2 resp. Olymp., *in Grg.* 46,4 (238,5-8 W.)
e13-390a1 resp. Pr., *in R.* I 129,13-17 K.

390 **a2** νεανιεύματα Phot. I 441 N.
a8-c8 fort.resp. Bas., *Leg. Lib. Gent.* IV 15-18 (45 B.)
a8-b4 resp. Pr., *in R.* I 129,17-26 K.
a10-b2 resp. Max. Tyr. 18,5c (223,1 H.)
b5 λιμῷ—ἐπισπεῖν AFF. Lib., *Decl.* XXVIII 24 (VI 587,3 F.); resp. Demetr. Cyd., *Ep.* 332,24 (II 264 L.)
b6-c7 ἤ—τοιαῦτα AFF. Eus., *PE* XIII 14,9 (II 231,1-8 M.)
b6-c6 resp. Max. Tyr. 18,5c (222,16 H.); Olymp., *in Grg.* 46,4 (237,30-238,2 W.); Pr., *in R.* I 132,15-22 K.
b6-7 resp. Pr., *in R.* I 72,20 K.
b6 καθευδόντων τῶν ἄλλων usurp. Pr., *in Ti.* I 2,12 D.; —, *ibid.* II 36,26 D.
c1-2 resp. sch. Hom. *Il.* Ξ 176b (III 599,97-99 E.); — Ξ 342-351 (III 646,62-64 E.)
c5-6 φίλους λήθοντε τοκῆας AFF. Pr., *in R.* I 139,21 K.
c6-7 resp. Max. Tyr. 18,5c (222,17-18 H.); Pr., *in R.* I 140,19-23 K.
d4-5 στῆθος—ἔτλης AFF. Gal., *PHP* III 3,9 (I 186,23-24 L.)
d5 τέτλαθι—ἔτλης AFF. Olymp., *in Grg.* 5,4 (41,19-21 W.)
d7-392a2 resp. Pr., *de Mal. Subs.* 21,3-6 (200 B.)
d7-391a2 resp. sch. Pl. ad loc. (209 G.)
d7-8 imit. Them., *Or.* 21,259d-260a (II 43,7-8 D.-N.)
e3 δῶρα—βασιλῆας AFF. Paus. Gr. δ 31 (174,15-16 E.); Sud. δ 1451 (II 135,12-14 A.)
e4-391a2 resp. Pr., *in R.* I 143,18-23 K.
e7 ἀξιώσομεν (hoc sensu) *An. Bachm.* I 107,22-23

391 **a3-c7** resp. sch. Pl. ad loc. (209 G.)
a3 ὀκνῶ expl. sch. Pl. ad loc. (209 G.)
a5-b5 resp. Pr., *in R.* I 146,9-17 K.
a5-7 resp. Max. Tyr. 18,5c (223,2-3 H.)
a5 καὶ αὖ ὡς expl. sch. Pl. ad loc. (210 G.)
b1-2 resp. Pr., *in R.* I 148,25-26 K.
b2-4 resp. Pr., *in R.* I 149,15-17 K.
b5 ἕλξεις *AB* I 94,19
b6 resp. Pr., *in R.* I 151,24 K.
b7-c3 resp. Pr., *In R.* I 150,4-11 K.
c1-6 resp. Pr., *in R.* I 153,14-17 K.
c2-3 καὶ alterum-τεθραμμένος AFF. *EM* 769,35 G.; Phot. II 229 N.; Sud. τ 1061 (IV 597,13 A.)
c2-3 ὑπὸ—τεθραμμένος Zonar. II 1748 T.
c5 (et alibi) ἀνελευθερίαν *AB* I 78,10
c8-392a2 resp. sch. Pl. ad 391c8 sqq. (210 G.)
c8-e3 resp. Pr., *in R.* II 331,10-14 K.; —, *Th. Pl.* I 9 (I 37,10-12 S.-W.)
c8-d1 resp. Pr., *in R.* I 153,22-24 K.
d5 resp. Pr., *Th. Pl.* I 9 (I 37,11-12 S.-W.)
d6-7 resp. Pr., *in Alc.* 75,18-76,2 (33 W.)
e4-8 πᾶς—ἐγγύς AFF. Bess., *in Cal. Pl.* 426,17-19 M.
e7-8 ἀγχίσποροι Ζηνός cit. Luc., *Dem. Enc.* 13 (III 268,1-2 M.)
e7 θεῶν ἀγχίσποροι resp. Dam., *Isid.* 30 (27,8 Z.)
e7 ἀγχίσποροι Phot. α 299 (I 37 Th.); expl. sch. Pl. ad loc. (210 G.)
e8-9 ὤν—ἔστ' AFF. Str. XII 8,20 (IX 148,18-19 L.)
e12-392a1 ἕνεκα—πονηρίας AFF. Bess., *in Cal. Pl.* 426,19-21 M.

392 **a3-c5** resp. sch. Pl. ad loc. (210 G.)
a8-397d5 resp. Pr., *in R.* I 47,17-19 K.
b4 ἀπερεῖν expl. sch. Pl. ad loc. (210 G.)
b8-c6 expl. sch. Pl. ad loc. (210 G.)
c6-398b9 resp. Olymp., *in Grg.* 5,4 (41,22 W.); Pr., *in Ti.* I 66,5-7 D.
c6-394c6 resp. Averr., *in R.* 33,8-15 R.; Pr., *in R.* II 14,19-26 K.

INDEX TESTIMONIORUM 307

c6-8 Τὰ—ἐσκέφεται AFF. Ammon., *in Int.* 13,11-13 B.
d5-397d5 resp. Pr., *in R.* I 44,1-6 K.
d7 imit. Meth., *Res.* I 29,8 (260,23 B.)
d8 Γελοῖος expl. sch. Pl. ad loc. (210 G.)

a1 κατεύχεσθαι Phot. I 327 N.
b4 Ἰθάκη expl. sch. Pl. ad loc. (210 G.)
c11-d3 resp. sch. Hom. *Il.* B 494-877 (I 289,5-8 E.)
d7-8 ὧδέ πως Hsch. ω 44 (IV 319 S.)
d8 οὐ—ποιητικός resp. Chor., *Dial.* 6,5 (152,8 F.-R.); Socr., *Ep.* 15,3 (622 H.); usurp. Chor., *Dial.* 8,2 (194,8-9 F.-R.); —, *Or.* 6,35 (109,4 F.-R.); Max. Tyr. 35,1d (403,1 H.)
e2 οἱ expl. sch. Pl. ad loc. (210 G.)
e8 (et alibi) οὗ A. D., *Pron.* 76,2 S.

b3-398b5 resp. Anon., *Prol. Plat.* IV 14,12-13 (27 W.); Olymp., *in Grg. prooem.* 1 (1,7-12 W.); —, — 33,3 (172,6-10 W.)
c2 τραγῳδία et κωμῳδία expl. sch. Pl. ad loc. (211 G.)
c3 διθυράμβοις expl. sch. Pl. ad loc. (211 G.)
c7-8 ὅτι—εἶναι AFF. Prisc., *Inst.* XVIII 234 (324,6-7 H.)
d1 χρείη expl. sch. Pl. ad loc. (211 G.)
e1-398b5 resp. Pr., *in R.* I 66,19-26 K.
e1-396a7 resp. Averr., *in R.* 33,20-34,8 R.
e3-6 εἴς—ἐλλόγιμος AFF. Stob. II 31,110ʳ (II 224,10-12 W.)
e3-4 ὅτι—οὖ AFF. Prisc., *Inst.* XVIII 200 (304,15-16 H.)
e8-9 πολλὰ—δυνατός AFF. Stob. II 31,108 (II 220,16 W.)

a1-b7 resp. Pr., *in R.* I 51,29-52,6 K.
a3-5 resp. Pr., *in R.* I 41,16-22 K.; —, — I 53,21-23 K.
a5-8 resp. Anon., *Contra Phil.* I 1084-1086 (38 A.)
a8 ῥαψῳδοί Hsch. ρ 167 (III 424 S.)
b3-4 resp. Areth., *Scr. Min.* XXIV (I 223,5-10 W.)
b4 κατακεκερματίσθαι Phot. I 317 N.; Poll. IX 88 (II 172,11 B.); usurp. Niceph. Greg., *Flor.* 73,416 L.; Pr., *in R.* I 53,1 K.
b5 ἢ αὐτὰ ἐκεῖνα expl. sch. Pl. ad loc. (211 G.)
b8-398b5 resp. Pr., *in R.* I 160,16-25 K.; sch. Pl. ad loc. (211 G.)
b8-d4 Εἰ—ὅς AFF. Stob. IV 1,156 (IV 105,19-106,9 H.)
c2-d4 οὐδὲν—ὅς AFF. Stob. II 31,110ʸ (II 227,23-228,2 W.)
c3-396a6 ἐὰν—μιμητέον AFF. Bess., *in Cal. Pl.* 426,24-428,2 M.
d1-3 resp. Pr., *in R.* I 49,23-24 K.
d5-398b5 resp. Averr., *in R.* 30,3-5 R.
d5-396e3 fort.resp. Bas., *Leg. Lib. Gent.* IV 15-18 (45 B.)
d6-7 γυναῖκα—ὄντας resp. Pr., *in R.* I 63,24-25 K.
e7-396a6 resp. Aristid., *Or.* 3,616 (I 3,497,7-8 L.-B.)

a8-397b3 resp. Averr., *in R.* 34,8-13 R.
b5-7 resp. D. Chr., *Or.* LIII 5 (II 111,6-7 A.)
b5 μυκωμένους Phot. I 431 N.
b10-e10 resp. sch. Pl. ad loc. (211 G.)
c3 φὺς καὶ τραφείς usurp. Niceph. Greg., *Flor.* 89,760 L.

a4-b2 resp. Plu., *Mor.* 18c (I 35,22-24 P.-W.-P.-G.)
b7 resp. Pr., *in R.* I 63,28-29 K.
c3-398b5 resp. Pr., *in R.* I 49,20-25 K.; —, — I 63,1-2 K.
d4 ἡ ἐμὴ νικᾷ expl. sch. Pl. ad loc. (212 G.)
d7 πολύ—παισί AFF. Prisc., *Inst.* XVIII 271 (348,23 H.)
d8 αἴρῃ expl. sch. Pl. ad loc. (212 G.)
d10-e9 resp. Pr., *in R.* I 48,28-49,11 K.

e1 διπλοῦς ἀνήρ fort.imit. Aristid., *Or.* 27,13 (145,19 K.)
e2 πολλαπλοῦς Poll. IV 47 (I 215,12 B.)

398
a1-7 (Homerus fugatus) resp. Aristid., *Or.* 3,165 (I 2,348,4-5 L.-B.); —, — 3,605 (I 3,493,21-494,1 L.-B.); —, — 4,38 (I 3,543,12-13 L.-B.); Bas. Min., *in Greg.* 1168a; D. Chr., *Or.* LIII 2 (II 110,12-13 A.); D. H., *Pomp.* 13 (II 225,12-17 U.-R.); Gr. Naz., *Or.* 25,6,3-4 (168 M.-L.); Heracl., *All. Hom.* 4 (298,6-9 M.); —, — 12 (307,29-308,1 M.); —, — 17 (311,24 M.); —, — 76 (358,15-16 M.); —, — 76 (358,21 M.); I., *Ap.* II 256 (104 R.); Iust. Phil., *Apol.* 2,10 (I 226 O.); Max. Tyr. 17,5g (215,17-18 H.); —, 18,5b (222,12-15 H.); Mich. Acom., *Ep.* 111,40 (II 220,12-13 L.); Minuc. Fel., *Oct.* 23,2 (20,18-19 K.); Niceph. Greg., *Ep.* 22,65-67 (II 74 L.); Or., *Cels.* 4,36,30-32 (II 274 B.); Pr., *in Cra.* LXX (29,15-16 P.); —, *in R.* I 47,23-26 K.; —, — I 161,9-10 K.; —, — I 204,12-13 K.; sch. Aristid. 3,165 (545,24-26 D.); —, — (545,29-546,1 D.); — 3,605 (719,7-8 D.); Suet., *Cal.* XXXIV 2 (II 88 A.); Tert., *Nat.* II 7,11 (52,9-10 B.); Thdt., *Affect.* II 6 (I 138,15-18 C.); —, — X 37 (II 372,11-12 C.); Zach. Mit., *Opif.* 110,473-480 C.; fort.resp. *An. Ox.* III 225,22-31; Niceph. Chumn., *Ep.* 44 (VI 60 B.)
a4 resp. Pr., *in R.* I 48,1-2 K.
a5-7 imit. Demetr. Cyd., *Ep.* 71,21-23 (I 103 L.)
a6-8 cit. D. Chr., *Or.* LIII 5 (II 111,7 A.): imit. Max. Tyr. 17,3g (212,11-12 H.)
a6-7 resp. et interpr. Pr., *in R.* I 48,11-26 K.
a7 μύρον—καταχέαντες resp. Pr., *in R.* I 42,4-5 K.; Thdt., *Affect.* V 9 (I 228,14 C.); fort.resp. Areth., *Scr. Min.* LXVI (II 52,29-30 W.); imit. Aristid., *Or.* 4,48 (I 3,548,11 L.-B.)
a7 μύρον κατὰ τῆς κεφαλῆς expl. sch. Pl. ad loc. (212 G.)
a7 ἐρίῳ στέψαντες AFF. Phot. I 211 N.; Sud. ε 3001 (II 409,21-22 A.); resp. Pr., *in R.* I 42,7 K.; imit. Areth., *Scr. Min.* XXXII (I 269,5 W.); Clem., *Protr.* I 2,2 (I 4,5 S.); Nicet. Chon., *Or.* 15 (151,13 D.)
a8 αὐστηροτέρῳ usurp. Pr., *in R.* I 47,7 K.
c1-401a9 resp. Olymp., *in Grg.* 5,4 (41,23-24 W.)
c1-400c6 resp. Herm., *in Phdr.* 247,4-10 C.; Pr., *in R.* I 54,3-7 K.; —, — I 59,20-27 K.; —, — I 60,1 K.; —, — I 66,26-67,6 K.
c1-399c6 resp. Averr., *in R.* 34,29-35,19 R.; sch. Pl. ad loc. (212 G.)
d1-2 expl. sch. Pl. ad loc. (212 G.)
d4-400d5 resp. Pr., *in R.* I 43,3-6 K.
d4-400c6 resp. Phld., *Mus.* 18. XXXVI,14-27 (95 K.)
d4-399e3 fort.resp. Aristid. Quint. II 6 (62,20-22 W.-I.)
d8-9 resp. Pr., *in R.* I 63,28-29 K.; —, — I 64,2-4 K.; fort.resp. Plot. V 9,11,11 (II 424 H.-S.)
d11-12 imit. Them., *Or.* 20,233d (II 2,20 D.-N.)
e1-400c6 resp. Boet., *Mus.* I 1 (181,20-23 F.); Pr., *in R.* I 41,22-28 K.
e1-399c6 resp. Pr., *in R.* I 61,19-24 K.; —, — I 131,18-20 K.; expl. sch. Pl. ad loc. (212 G.)
e1-399a4 resp. Boet., *Mus.* I 1 (181,14-16 F.); Plu., *Mor.* 1136e (VI 3,14,5-8 Z.-P.); —, — 1138c (VI 3,18,1-3 Z.-P.)
e1-10 resp. Plu., *Mor.* 1136c (VI 3,13,1-4 Z.-P.)
e1-4 resp. Plu., *Mor.* 822bc (V 1,118,2-6 H.-P.-D.)
e1-2 cit. Aristid. Quint. I 9 (19,3-4 W.-I.)
e1 σὺ γὰρ μουσικός AFF. Pr., *in R.* I 54,7 K.
e1 resp. Pr., *in R.* I 55,17-18 K.
e9 resp. Pr., *in R.* I 55,17-18 K.
e10-399a4 fort.resp. Them., *Or.* 27,336a (II 159,23-24 D.-N.)
e10 cit. Aristid. Quint. I 9 (19,4-5 W.-I.)

399
a1-5 resp. Arist., *Pol.* Θ 7,1342a32-b1 B.
a3-4 κινδυνεύει—φρυγιστί AFF. Aristid. Quint. I 9 (19,6-7 W.-I.); expl. sch. Pl. ad loc. (213 G.)

a3 fort.resp. Niceph. Greg., *Antirrh.* I 1,1,4 (127,11 B.)
a5-c4 resp. Pr., *in R.* I 55,19-25 K.; fort.resp. Aristid. Quint. II 6 (60,3-6 W.-I.)
b2-3 καρτερούντως—τύχην imit. Them., *Or.* 24,309a (II 111,7-8 D.-N.)
b2-3 resp. Iambl. *VP* 32,220 (119,6-8 D.)
b6 μεταπείθοντι expl. sch. Pl. ad loc. (213 G.)
c1-400c4 resp. Pr., *in Ti.* II 169,8-11 D.
c5 ἃς νυνδὴ expl. sch. Pl. ad loc. (213 G.)
c7-d10 resp. Plu., *Mor.* 827a (V 1,129,16-19 H.-P.-D.)
c7-d6 resp. Pr., *in R.* I 63,2-7 K.
c7-d1 Οὐκ—πολυαρμόνια AFF. Ath. IV 182f (I 399,4-8 K.)
c7 παναρμονίου Hsch. π 313 (III 264 S.)
c10-d6 resp. Pr., *in Alc.* 197,10 (91 W.)
c10 πηκτίδων Phot. II 88 N.
d3-6 resp. Anon., *Prol. Plat.* IV 14,10-11 (27 W.); Arist., *Pol.* Θ 7,1342a32-b1 B.
d3-4 resp. Poll. IV 67 (I 221,14-15 B.)
d7-8 Λύρα—πόλιν AFF. Demetr., *Eloc.* 185 (154,28-29 R. R.)
d7 resp. Anon., *Prol. Plat.* IV 14,11-12 (27 W.); Synes., *Ep.* 148 (265,16-18 G.)
e1 Οὐδὲν καινὸν usurp. Aen. Gaz., *Thphr.* 39,16 C.
e2 πρὸ Μαρσύου expl. sch. Pl. ad loc. (213 G.)
e5 νὴ τὸν κύνα expl. sch. Pl. ad loc. (213 G.)
e8-403c8 resp. sch. Pl. ad loc. (213 G.)
e8 καθαίρωμεν Phot. I 302 N.
e9 ποικίλους resp. Anon., *Prol. Plat.* IV 14,9-10 (27 W.)

a2-c6 resp. Pr., *in R.* I 55,27-56,3 K.
b1-c6 resp. Pr., *in R.* I 61,2-11 K.
b1 (et alibi) Δάμωνος resp. Anon., *Prol. Plat.* I 2,30 (7 W.); Olymp., *in Alc.* 2,44 (3 W.); —, — 138,13-14 (90 W.); Pr., *in R.* I 56,9-10 K.
b4-5 ἐνόπλιόν et ἡρῷόν expl. sch. Pl. ad loc. (214 G.)
b6 διακοσμοῦντος AFF. Pr., *in R.* I 62,15 K.
c7-d5 resp. sch. Pl. ad loc. (213 G.)
d11-e3 Εὐλογία—διάνοιαν AFF. Gal., *in Hipp. Progn.* 332,7-10 H.
e1 ὑποκοριζόμενοι Phot. II 247 N.; usurp. Chor., *Dial.* 3,56 (192,18 F.-R.); expl. sch. Pl. ad loc. (214 G.)

b1-d3 resp. Averr., *in R.* 34,23-28 R.
b1-c3 Ἀρ'—ψυχῇ AFF. Bess., *in Cal. Pl.* 428,30-430,4 M.
c8-d1 imit. Meth., *Symp. prooem.* 8 (6,10 B.)
d6 καταδύεται Hsch. κ 1082 (II 423 L.)
d7 ἐρρωμενέστατα ἅπτεται usurp. Niceph. Greg., *Ep.* 42,22-23 (II 145 L.); —, *Flor.* 97,956-957 L.
e3 ἐκεῖ expl. sch. Pl. ad loc. (214 G.)
e4-403a9 fort.resp. Plu., *Mor.* 1146a (VI 3,35,8-19 Z.-P.)

b9-e1 resp. Averr., *in R.* 35,20-26 R.
b9-c8 Ἀρ'—μελέτης AFF. Theon Sm. 10,18-11,7 H.
c3 ἐλευθεριότητος usurp. Alb., *Intr.* XXX 4 (149 L.)
d1-403a12 Οὐκοῦν—προσοιστέον AFF. Stob. IV 21ᵃ,18 (IV 488,14-489,17 H.)
e2 παιδικὰ expl. sch. Pl. ad loc. (214 G.)
e3-403c8 resp. Averr., *in R.* 35,27-36,4 R.
e3-403a11 resp. Bess., *in Cal. Pl.* 430,4-8 M.

b4-6 resp. Max. Tyr. 18,4d (221,6-7 H.)
b7 σπουδάζοι Sud. σ 967 (IV 420,24-25 A.)
c2 ἀπειροκαλίας expl. sch. Pl. ad loc. (214 G.)
c5 οἵ expl. sch. Pl. ad loc. (215 G.)

c6-7 resp. Aristid. Quint. III 18 (118,27-28 W.-I.); Plot. I 3,2,1 (I 74 H.-S.)
c9-410b9 resp. Alb., Intr. XXVIII 4 (139 L.); Averr., in R. 36,6-10 R.
c9-404e6 expl. sch. Pl. ad loc. (215 G.)
c9-d8 Μετά—ἀκριβολογεῖσθαι AFF. Stob. II 31,110ˣ (II 227,13-21 W.)
d7-410a10 cit. Averr., in R. 36,24-38,1 R.
e5-6 μή—ἐστιν resp. Plot. VI 5,9,29-30 (III 170 H.-S.)
e7 imit. Iul., Or. III 28,42 (I 1,163 B.)

404   a1-5 fort.resp. Clem., Paed. II i 2,1-2 (I 154,17-25 S.)
a1 ἡ ἀσκητῶν ἕξις fort.resp. Simp., in Cat. 173,33-34 K.
a4-b2 resp. Plu., Vit. 357c (II 2,3,17-19 Z.)
a4-7 resp. Gal., Bon. Hab. IV 753 K.; fort.resp. Plu., Mor. 128e (I 266,1-2 P.-W.-P.-G.);
—, — 134f-135a (I 277,23-27 P.-W.-P.-G.); —, Vit. 614de (III 2,236,17-19 Z.)
a10 ἀγρύπνους (φύλακας) usurp. Chor., Decl. 2,54 (165,13 F.-R.); —, Or. 8,34 (352,12 F.-R.)
b2 ἀκροσφαλεῖς Lex. Seg. IX B.; expl. sch. Pl. ad loc. (215 G.)
b12-c1 resp. D. Chr., Or. II 47 (I 26,8 A.)
b12 resp. sch. Hom. Il. Π 407b (IV 252,95 E.)
c6 ἡδυσμάτων expl. sch. Pl. ad loc. (215 G.)
d1-9 Συρακοσίαν—εὐπαθείας AFF. Ath. XII 527d (III 164,1-5 K.)
d1-2 Σικελικὴν—ὄψου fort.resp. Philostr., Gymn. 44 (II 285,15 K.)
d1 Συρακοσίαν τράπεζαν Phot. II 190 N.
d1 fort.resp. Socr., Ep. 9 (616 H.); imit. Iul., Or. IX 203a7 (II 1,172 R.); Them., Or. 20,238c (II 11,4 D.-N.); —, — 24,301b (II 98,13 D.-N.); Max. Tyr. 21,5d (261,6 H.); — 32,3b (370,3 H.)
d8 πεμμάτων expl. sch. Pl. ad loc. (215 G.)
d9 εὐπαθείας AB I 94,28; Phot. I 232 N.
d12 παναρμονίῳ Phot. II 50 N.
e3-405a4 resp. Str. VI 1,8 (III 139,21-140,2 L.)
e3-5 expl. sch. Pl. ad loc. (215 G.)
e3 ποικιλία resp. Anon., Prol. Plat. IV 14,9-10 (27 W.)

405   a1-c7 resp. sch. Pl. ad loc. (215 G.)
a4 σπουδάζωσιν Phot. II 172 N.; Sud. σ 967 (IV 420,24-25 A.)
b5-c7 Πάντων—αἴσχιον AFF. Stob. III 2,43 (III 189,3-13 H.)
b9 καλλωπίζεσθαι Phot. I 309 N.
c2 λυγιζόμενος Phot. I 395 N.; Sud. λ 771 (III 291,19 A.); sch. Pl. ad loc. (216 G.)
c8-406e5 resp. sch. Pl. ad loc. (216 G.)
d3-408c4 resp. sch. Pl. ad loc. (216 G.)
d4 κομψούς AB I 102,23; Hsch. κ 3486 (II 507 L.); Moer. 190 P.-K.
d5 ἄτοπα expl. sch. Pl. ad loc. (216 G.)
e1 ὑεῖς Hsch. υ 25 (IV 195 S.)
e2 οἶνον Πράμνειον expl. sch. Pl. ad loc. (216 G.)

406   a5-e3 fort.resp. Max. Tyr. 4,2b (42,1-6 H.); Pr., in R. I 55,3-5 K.
a5-c5 fort.resp. Anon. Lond. 14,12-15,31 D.
a5-b8 resp. Plu., Mor. 554c (III 410,15-19 P.-S.)
a5-7 resp. Gal., Thras. 33 (78,20-22 H.)
a7-b2 resp. Gal., in Hipp. Epid. VI 177,10-12 W.-P.; Ioh. Alex., in Hipp. Epid. VI 132a1-2 (171 P.)
a7 Ἡρόδικον resp. Olymp., in Grg. 2,13 (22,1-2 W.); sch. Pl. ad loc. (216 G.); sch. Pl. Grg. 448b (459 G.); Them., Or. 23,290a (II 84,5 D.-N.)
b1 ἀπέκναισε Did., Plat. 400 M.; resp. sch. Luc. Cat. 16 (49,4-5 R.); expl. sch. Pl. ad loc. (216 G.)
b5 (et alibi) θανασίμῳ AB I 99,9
b6-8 imit. Lib., Decl. XV 37 (VI 138,9-10 F.)

c1-407b7 resp. Averr., *in R*. 38,3-14 R.
c5 σχολή expl. sch. Pl. ad loc. (216 G.)
d2-3 καύσει ἢ τομῇ usurp. Them., *Or*. 11,148c (I 224,7 D.-N.); —, — 22,277a (II 67,5 D.-N.)
e3 πραγμάτων expl. sch. Pl. ad loc. (216 G.)

a8 ὅταν—ᾖ imit. Gr. Naz., *Ep*. 190,8 (138,12 G.)
a11 πότερον μελετητέον τοῦτο expl. sch. Pl. ad loc. (217 G.)
b2 ἐμπόδιον expl. sch. Pl. ad loc. (217 G.)
b4-c5 Ναὶ—σώματος AFF. Gal., *Thras*. 36 (82,5-15 H.)
c2 ἰλίγγους Hsch. ε 893 (II 29 L.)
c7-408c4 resp. Olymp., *in Grg*. 6,11 (49,1-3 W.); —, — 23,5 (127,1-2 W.)
c7-e2 resp. Elias, *in Porph*. 15,10-13 B.
d4-e2 resp. Olymp., *in Phd*. 1,8,11-14 (49 W.)

b1 κυκεῶνα expl. sch. Pl. ad loc. (217 G.)
b2 νοσώδη—ἀκόλαστον expl. sch. Pl. ad loc. (217 G.)
b4-5 Μίδου πλουσιώτεροι expl. sch. Pl. ad loc. (217 G.)
b8 Ἀπόλλωνος—Ἀσκληπιὸν expl. sch. Pl. ad loc. (217 G.)
c3-4 cit. Alex. Aphr., *in APr*. 22,8-9 W.
c5-410a6 ἀλλὰ—πέφανται AFF. Stob. IV 5,96 (IV 229,2-231,8 H.)
d10-e6 resp. Averr., *in R*. 38,22-25 R.; Plu., *Mor*. 1072a (VI 2,90,29-91,1 P.-W.)

a1-410a10 resp. Averr., *in R*. 38,25-39,5 R.
a1-c1 resp. Averr., *in R*. 25,5-9 R.
a6 ἀκέραιον usurp. Pr., *in Ti*. II 118,13 D.
b4 γέροντα resp. (ση) sch. Pl. ad loc. (217 G.)
b5 ὀψιμαθῆ usurp. Chor., *Decl*. 3,57 (193,3 F.-R.)
b8-c1 ἐπιστήμη, οὐκ ἐμπειρίᾳ usurp. Aen. Gaz., *Thphr*. 37,20 C.
c4 καχύποπτος Poll. II 57 (I 100,16 B.)
d3 ἀμαθέστερος Zonar. I 140 T.

b1-412a8 resp. Pr., *in Alc*. 194,1-16 (89-90 W.)
b3 ὅτι μὴ ἀνάγκη expl. sch. Pl. ad loc. (217 G.)
b5-8 Αὐτά—μεταχειριεῖται AFF. Gal., *Thras*. 36 (82,18-83,1 H.)
b10-412b1 resp. Averr., *in R*. 36,10-24 R.; Thdt., *Affect*. XII 53 (II 435,16-19 C.)
b10-e4 resp. Clem., *Strom*. IV 4,18,1 (II 256,20-23 S.)
c5-6 resp. Thdt., *Affect*. V 14 (I 230,7-9 C.)
d2 ἡμερότητος Hsch. η 476 (II 283 L.)
d4-5 μαλακώτεροι—αὑτοῖς AFF. Prisc., *Inst*. XVIII 222 (318,16-17 H.)
e2 μαλακώτερον τοῦ δέοντος usurp. Chor., *Decl*. 8,60 (330,26-27 F.-R.)
e8 fort.resp. S. E., *M*. VI 13 (III 165,23-24 M.-M.)

a3 ἄγροικος *Lex. Rhet. Cant*. 10,11-13 H.
a5-b4 fort.resp. Bas., *Hex*. IV 1 (244 G.)
a5-6 ὅταν—ὤτων AFF. Demetr., *Eloc*. 51 (94,29-96,1 R. R.)
a6 καταχεῖν διὰ τῶν ὤτων usurp, Bas., *Leg. Lib. Gent*. IX 38-39 (56 B.)
a7-8 γλυκείας καὶ μαλακὰς ἁρμονίας usurp. Them., *Or*. 22,265b (II 52,25-53,1 D.-N.)
a7 νυνδὴ ἡμεῖς ἐλέγομεν AFF. Demetr., *Eloc*. 183 (154,18 R. R.)
a8-9 μινυρίζων—ὅλον AFF. Demetr., *Eloc*. 184 (154,19-20 R. R.)
a8-9 μινυρίζων—ᾠδῆς AFF. Phot. I 425 N.
a8 μινυρίζων καὶ γεγανωμένος usurp. Plu., *Mor*. 42c (I 85,7 P.-W.-P.-G.)
a8 μινυρίζων Sud. μ 1103 (III 399,23-24 A.); expl. sch. Pl. ad loc. (217 G.)
a8 γεγανωμένος expl. sch. Pl. ad loc. (218 G.)
a9-10 τὸ—ἐμάλαξεν AFF. Demetr., *Eloc*. 184 (154,20-21 R. R.)
a10-b1 imit. Them., *Or*. 1,7c (I 11,11-12 D.-N.)

a10 fort.imit. Gr. Naz., *Vit.* 1473-1474 (126 J.)
b3 ἐκτήξῃ τὸν θυμὸν imit. Them., *Or.* 13,176d (I 253,5 D.-N.)
b3 resp. Plu., *Mor.* 449f (III 150,3-4 P.-S.); —, — 457bc (III 168,22-23 P.-S.)
b4-c2 resp. Plot. II 3,11,6 (I 174 H.-S.)
b6 ἄθυμον *AB* I 350,12; *An. Bachm.* I 37,29
b8 ὀξύρροπον Phot. II 21 N.
c1-2 resp. Plu., *Mor.* 454b (III 160,20-22 P.-S.)
c1 ἀκράχολοι *AB* I 77,9; usurp. Them., *Or.* 22,269d (II 58,10 D.-N.); expl. sch. Pl. ad loc. (218 G.)
c6 φρονήματος καὶ θυμοῦ usurp. Chor., *Decl.* 9,113 (422,3 F.-R.)
e4-6 expl. sch. Pl. ad loc. (218 G.)

412
a9-415c6 resp. Gal., *PHP* IX 2,12 (II 546,23-25 L.)
b8-416d2 resp. Alb., *Intr.* XXXIV 1 (167 L.); Pr., *in R.* I 218,24-27 K.
b8-414b6 τὸ—δόγμασιν AFF. Stob. IV 1,157 (IV 106,11-109,20 H.)
c9-414b7 cit. Averr., *in R.* 39,6-24 R.
c9-10 resp. Plu., *Mor.* 620c (IV 20,4-5 H.); Pr., *in R.* I 219,15-16 K.
c13 κηδεμόνας τῆς πόλεως usurp. Chor., *Or.* 2,24 (34,16-17 F.-R.)
d2-e3 resp. Bess., *in Cal. Pl.* 520,34-35 M.
d9-e4 resp. sch. Pl. ad loc. (218 G.)
e5-8 resp. Pr., *in R.* II 367,19-21 K.
e8 δόξαν expl. sch. Pl. ad loc. (218 G.)
e10-413a10 φαίνεταί—στερίσκεσθαι AFF. Stob. I 59,3 (I 499,5-15 W.); resp. Olymp., *in Grg.* 10,3 (62,15-16 W.)
e10-413a1 expl. sch. Pl. ad loc. (218 G.)

413
a4-c4 cit. Clem., *Strom.* I 8,42,2-4 (II 28,8-16 S.); resp. Bess., *in Cal. Pl.* 520,36-40 M.
a9-c4 expl. sch. Pl. ad loc. (218 G.)
c2 ὑφ' ἡδονῆς κηληθέντες imit. Meth., *Symp.* VIII 1 (81,17 B.)
c7-414a8 expl. sch. Pl. ad loc. (219 G.)
c7-d1 τηρητέον—ἀποχριτέον AFF. Bess., *in Cal. Pl.* 522,1-3 M.
d4-5 Καὶ—τηρητέον AFF. Bess., *in Cal. Pl.* 522,3-4 M.
d7-e3 cit. Bess., *in Cal. Pl.* 522,5-9 M.; resp. Bess., *in Cal. Pl.* 430,8-12 M.
d8-9 resp. D. Chr., *Or.* LIII 2 (II 110,17-18 A.)
d10-e4 resp. Aristid. Quint. II 6 (59,24-25 W.-I.)
e2-3 δυσγοήτευτος—ἀγαθὸς AFF. Bess., *in Cal. Pl.* 430,11-12 M.
e5-414a7 resp. Apul., *Pl.* II 7,230 (85 B.)

414
a1-3 ἀκήρατον—τελευτήσαντι AFF. Bess., *in Cal. Pl.* 522,9-11 M.
a2-3 resp. Aristid., *Or.* 3,136 (I 2,336,2 L.-B.); Demetr. Cyd., *Ep.* 7,13 (I 32 L.); sch. Aristid. 3,196 (566,34-567,2 D.)
a4 γέρα *AB* I 87,22
a4 τὸν—ἀποχριτέον AFF. Bess., *in Cal. Pl.* 522,11-12 M.
a5 ἐκλογὴ fort.resp. *AB* I 94,17
a6 ὡς ἐν τύπῳ usurp. Niceph. Greg., *Ep.* 6,32 (II 37 L.)
b1-7 expl. sch. Pl. ad loc. (219 G.)
b5 ἐπικούρους resp. Aristid., *Or.* 3,142 (I 2,339,13 L.-B.)
b8-e7 cit. Olymp., *in Grg.* 44,3 (229,8-16 W.)
c4 Φοινικικὸν Phot. II 267 N.; resp. Ascl., *in Metaph.* 135,4-7 H.; —, — 354,2-3 H.; expl. sch. Pl. ad loc. (219 G.)
c9 μάλ' εἰκότως Hsch. μ 145 (II 624 L.); Phot. I 403 N.
d1-415d5 cit. Averr., *in R.* 39,24-41,4 R.; fort.resp. Averr., *in R.* 32,21-22 R.
d1-e6 fort.resp. Lact., *Inst.* III 21,2 (248,11-13 B.)
e7 (et alibi) Οὐκ ἐτός Did., *Plat.* 399 M.; Phot. II 37; expl. sch. Pl. ad loc. (219 G.)

a1-c7 ἀλλ'—μηχανήν AFF. Eus., *PE* XII 43,2-4 (II 132,33-133,10 M.)
a2-c6 resp. Ascl., *in Metaph.* 354,3-5 H.; Clem., *Strom.* V 14,133,6 (II 416,14-16 S.); Plu., *Mor.* 1b (I 1,17-20 P.-W.-P.-G.)
a2-7 ἐστὲ—δημιουργοῖς AFF. Clem., *Strom.* V 14,98,2 (II 390,21-25 S.); (ex Clemente) Eus., *PE* XIII 13,18 (II 203,11-14 M.)
a2-3 ἐστὲ—ἀδελφοί AFF. Clem., *Strom.* V 14,133,6 (II 416,15 S.); (ex Clemente) Eus., *PE* XIII 13,63 (II 227,10 M.); fort.resp. Eus., *Theoph.* I 38 (56,7 G.)
a4-7 resp. Pr., *in R.* II 77,20-26 K.
a4-5 resp. Clem., *Strom.* IV 2,4,2 (II 249,24-25 S.); sch. Aristid. 3,197 (567,33-34 et 568,5-6 D.)
b3-c6 resp. Pr., *in R.* I 249,4-6 K.
b3-7 resp. Pr., *in R.* II 56,5-6 K.
c3 ὑπόχρυσος usurp. Pr., *in R.* II 99,6 K.
d2 οἱ ὕστερον expl. sch. Pl. ad loc. (219 G.)
d6-416a1 resp. Averr., *in R.* 41,5-10 R.
d6 ἀγάγῃ expl. sch. Pl. ad loc. (219 G.)
d8-9 fort.imit. Aristid., *Or.* 2,273 (I 2,222,13-14 L.-B.)

a2-417b9 cit. Averr., *in R.* 41,10-42,24 R.
a2-7 imit. Iul., *Or.* III 28,38-40 (I 1,163 B.); —, — III 29,13-16 (I 1,164 B.)
a4-7 fort.resp. Synes., *Regn.* XV 15d (31,18-32,1 T.)
b9-417b6 ὃ—πόλις AFF. Stob. IV 1,158 (IV 109,22-111,12 H.)
c2-3 resp. Lyd., *Mens.* 4,88 (136,16-17 W.)
d3-417b9 resp. Arist., *Pol.* H 10,1329b41-1330a1 B.; Aristid., *Or.* 3,103 (I 2,326,5-9 L.-B.); —, — 3,136 (I 2,336,5-8 L.-B.); Averr., *in R.* 29,5-6 R.; Pr., *in R.* I 161,25-26 K.; —, — II 9,8 K.; sch. Pl. *Lg. hypothes.* (296 G.)
d3-e4 resp. Apul., *Pl.* II 25,257 (103 B.)
d4-417b9 resp. sch. Pl. ad loc. (220 G.)
d4-5 latine cit. Lact., *Inst.* III 21,2 (248,11-13 B.)
d5-6 ἂν μὴ πᾶσα ἀνάγκη expl. sch. Pl. ad loc. (220 G.)
d7-e3 resp. Pr., *in R.* I 131,24-29 K.
e2 περιεῖναι Hsch. π 1625 (III 312 S.)
e4-417a5 resp. Aristid., *Or.* 3,335 (I 3,406,3-4 L.-B.); Plu., *Mor.* 820a (V 1,112,4-8 H.-P.-D.); sch. Aristid. 3,335 (657,2-3 D.)

LIBER QUARTUS

a1-445e4 resp. Averr., *in R.* 22,30-23,12 R.
a1-421c7 resp. Averr., *in R.* 42,24-32 R.
a10 ἀτεχνῶς expl. sch. Pl. ad loc. (220 G.)

a2-3 καὶ prius-ἄλλοι AFF. Ath. VI 247a (II 51,10-12 K.)
a2 ἐπισίτιοι expl. sch. Pl. ad loc. (220 G.)
b3-8 resp. Cic., *Off.* I 25,85 (38,10-12 A.); Pr., *in Ti.* I 43,29-31 D.
b3 Τὸν αὐτὸν οἶμον usurp. Pr., *in Ti.* I 95,20 D.
b6-8 resp. Pr., *de Decem Dub.* 38,3-6 (60 B.)
c4-d5 cit. Herm., *in Phdr.* 241,24-29 C.; imit. Plot. III 2,11,9-12 (I 285 H.-S.)
c4-8 fort.resp. Plu., *Mor.* 618a (IV 15,12-13 H.)
c5 ἀνδριάντα *AB* I 82,11; — I 210,15; — I 211,14
c6 φάρμακα expl. sch. Pl. ad loc. (220 G.)
e2 ξυστίδας expl. sch. Pl. ad loc. (220 G.)

a3-6 νευρορράφοι—ἀπολλύασιν AFF. Stob. IV 1,159 (IV 11,14-17 H.)
a3 νευρορράφοι expl. sch. Pl. ad loc. (221 G.)

314 THE INDIRECT TRADITION

d1-422a4 Τούς—ἔφη AFF. Stob. IV 1,160 (IV 11,19-112,13 H.); cit. Averr., *in R.* 43,1-44,9 R.
d6-e6 fort.resp. Aristid., *Or.* 3,360 (I 3,417,7-8 L.-B.)
d6 χυτρεύς Sud. χ 616 (IV 836,19-20 A.); expl. sch. Pl. ad loc. (221 G.)
e4-5 fort.resp. Apul., *Pl.* II 4,225 (82 B.)
e7-422a3 Ἕτερα—νεωτερισμῷ AFF. Eus., *PE* XII 35,1 (II 129,4-7 M.)

422 **a4-423c5** cit. Averr., *in R.* 44,9-46,22 R.
a6-7 ἄλλως—πολεμεῖν AFF. Bess., *in Cal. Pl.* 542,13-14 M.
c4 Ἀμέλει expl. sch. Pl. ad loc. (221 G.)
d1-7 Τί—ἁπαλοῖς AFF. Bess., *in Cal. Pl.* 542,20-25 M.
e3-423a2 resp. Bess., *in Cal. Pl.* 542,14-18 M.
e3 Εὐδαίμων εἶ ὅτι usurp. Aen. Gaz., *Thphr.* 7,18 C.; —, — 66,8 C.
e7-8 resp. Plu., *Mor.* 678d (IV 163,15-16 H.)
e7 (et alibi) Μειζόνως *AB* I 107,26
e8-9 πόλις, τὸ τῶν παιζόντων resp. Phot. II 97 N.; expl. sch. Pl. ad loc. (221 G.)
e8 resp. Olymp., *in Grg.* 15,3 (88,6-7 W.)

423 **a5-b2** resp. Apul., *Pl.* II 24,256 (102 B.); sch. Pl. ad loc. (221 G.)
a6-b1 σωφρόνως—εὑρήσεις cit. Bess., *in Cal. Pl.* 542,26-28 M.
b9-10 resp. Plu., *Mor.* 678d (IV 163,15-16 H.)
c5-6 Καὶ—φαυλότερον AFF. *EM* 789,44-45 G.; Phot. II 259 N.; Sud. φ 140 (IV 705,12-13 A.)
c5 φαῦλόν expl. sch. Pl. ad loc. (221 G.)
c6-424a3 resp. Averr., *in R.* 46,22-32 R.
d2-6 resp. Pr., *in R.* II 361,14-17 K.
d8-425a2 Οὗτοι—ἔφη AFF. Stob. IV 1,161 (IV 112,15-114,17 H.)
e6-425e2 resp. Apul., *Pl.* II 25,258 (104 B.)
e6-424d2 resp. sch. Pl. *Lg. hypothes.* (296 G.)
e6-424a2 resp. sch. Pl. ad loc. (222 G.)

424 **a1-2** κοινὰ τὰ φίλων AFF. Apostol. IX 88 (II 481,16 L.-S.); Diogenian. V 76 (I 266,1 L.-S.); Greg. Cypr. Leid. II 54 (II 76,14 L.-S.); Zen. IV 79 (I 106,5-8 L.-S.); resp. Demetr. Cyd., *Ep.* 27,15 (I 57 L.); Niceph. Greg., *Ep.* 64,2-3 (II 91 L.); Plu., *Mor.* 767d (IV 385,19 H.); usurp. Aen. Gaz., *Ep.* VI 4 (42 P.); expl. sch. Pl. ad loc. (222 G.)
a4-425a7 resp. Averr., *in R.* 47,1-5 R.
a5-b1 τροφὴ—ζῴοις AFF. Clem., *Strom.* I 6,33,4 (II 22,7-10 S.)
c3-e4 resp. Cic., *Leg.* II 15,38-39 (70,22-71,11 Z.)
c3-6 resp. Boet., *Mus.* I 1 (180,22-23 F.)
c5-6 resp. Cic., *Leg.* III 14,32 (103,16-17 Z.)
d8 ἐπιτηδεύματα usurp. Alb., *Intr.* V 5 (25 L.)

425 **a3-c5** Ὅταν—τοὐναντίον AFF. Stob. IV 1,97 (IV 38,6-23 H.)
a8-427c5 cit. Averr., *in R.* 47,5-29 R.
b1-5 fort.resp. Anon. Gnom. II 468 B.
b3 ἀμπεχόνας *Lex. Seg.* XII B.
b7 εὔηθες Ael. Dion. ε 70 (120,9 E.); *Et. Gud.* II 555,4-6 S.; Phot. I 225 N.; Sud. ε 3460 (II 448,3 A.)
b10-c2 Κινδυνεύει—παρακαλεῖ AFF. Stob. II 31,110° (II 223,25-27 W.)
c2 resp. Pr., *in Ti.* I 246,17 D.
c10-427a7 resp. Olymp., *in Grg.* 32,2 (164,5-7 W.)
d2 αἰκίας An. Bachm. I 49,20-21

426 **a1** χαριέντως expl. sch. Pl. ad loc. (222 G.)
b1-2 fort.usurp. Alex. Aphr., *Fat.* 174,21-24 B.; Eus., *PE* VI 9,24 (I 332,12-14 M.)
d8-e1 imit. Plot. II 9,9,60-61 (I 237 H.-S.)

INDEX TESTIMONIORUM 315

e8 Ὕδραν τέμνουσιν Sud. υ 57 (IV 635,19 A.); usurp. Lib., Or. LIX 165 (IV 292,16 F.); Meth., Res. I 62,9 (329,4 B.); Plu., Vit. 844c (III 1,459,30-460,1 Z.); expl. sch. Pl. ad loc. (222 G.)

b2-434d1 resp. Or., Cels. 5,43,17-19 (III 127 B.)
b3 Δελφοῖς expl. sch. Pl. ad loc. (222 G.)
b6-7 imit. Aristid., Or. 27,14 (128,18-19 K.)
b7-c4 resp. Aristid., Or. 3,316 (I 3,399,15-20 L.-B.)
c1-4 imit. Them., Or. 26,330cd (II 150,3-6 D.-N.)
c2 cit. Eus., PE IV 34,3 (I 285,3 M.) (= Oenom. II 376 M.); resp. Olymp., in Alc. 175,3-4 (111 W.)
c2 πατρίῳ expl. sch. Pl. ad loc. (222 G.)
c3-4 fort.resp. Plot. VI 1,14,5-6 (III 28 H.-S.)
c3-4 ἐν μέσῳ τῆς γῆς resp. (ση) sch. Pl. ad loc. (222 G.)
c6-445e4 resp. et interpr. Pr., in R. I 206,1-235,21 K.; resp. Chrys., de Inani Gloria 69,788-794 (162-164 M.); D. L. III 90-91 (I 157,11-19 L.); —, Div. 28 (48,20-49,5 M.); Saloust. X 3 (16 R.)
c6-444a9 resp. Olymp., in Grg. prooem. 5 (4,13-17 W.); —, in Phd. 4,3,3-4 (79 W.)
d1-7 resp. Plot. I 4,16,10-13 (I 97 H.-S.)
e6-429a7 cit. Averr., in R. 48,10-29 R.
e10-11 usurp. Arist., Pol. H 1,1323b33-36 B.

a11-445e4 resp. Averr., in R. 23,18-24,10 R.
a11-432a9 resp. Alb., Intr. XXIX 1 (141 L.)
b3-433c3 resp. Plu., Mor. 1034c (VI 2,5,8-10 P.-W.)
b3-d10 resp. Pr., in R. I 212,8-11 K.; —, — I 216,1-5 K.; —, — I 219,21-22 K.
d11-429b7 resp. Gal., PHP IX 2,12 (II 546,23-25 L.)

a2 μεταλαγχάνειν Hsch. μ 1002 (II 654 L.)
a8-430c2 cit. Averr., in R. 49,1-17 R.; resp. Apul., Pl. II 6,229 (84 B.); Or., Cels. 5,47,17-20 (III 136 B.); Pr., in R. I 212,16-20 K.; —, — I 216,5-8 K.; —, — I 219,28-230,2 K.
b1-c2 resp. Averr., in R. 49,18-22 R.
c5-430b9 Σωτηρίαν—καλεῖν AFF. Stob. IV 1,98 (IV 39,2-40,15 H.)
c7-d2 cit. Theon Sm. 13,1-4 H.
c7-8 resp. Alb., Intr. XXIX 3 (143 L.)
c9-d1 fort.imit. Plot. I 1,1,1-2 (I 49 H.-S.); — III 6,3,1-2 (I 338 H.-S.)
d4-e6 οἱ—γελοῖα cit. Theon Sm. 13,4-14,4 H.
d4 βαφῆς resp. Cyr., Gloss. βαφ 1 (77 D.)
e1-2 fort.resp. Areth., Scr. Min. LXVI (II 54,22 W.)
e1 δευσοποιὸν Did., Plat. 403 M.; EM 348,41 G.; Harp. 88,16-17 D.; Hsch. δ 735 (II 421 L.); usurp. Gr. Naz., Or. 2,11,1 (104 B.); expl. sch. Pl. ad loc. (223 G.)
e2 ῥυμμάτων Hsch. ρ 499 (III 435 S.); expl. sch. Pl. ad loc. (223 G.)

a3 δευσοποιὸς δόξα An. Ox. II 361,28-29; Et. Parv. ε 40 (43,207-209 P.)
a7 χαλεστραίου Did., Plat. 403 M.; Moer. 379 P.-K.; Poll. X 135 (II 230,13 B.); Tim. 227 R.-K.; expl. sch. Pl. ad loc. (223 G.)
b1 fort.imit. Plot. I 1,1,1-2 (I 49 H.-S.); — III 6,3,1-2 (I 338 H.-S.)
b1 κονίας Poll. VII 40 (II 62,24 B.); expl. sch. Pl. ad loc. (223 G.)
b2-5 resp. Clem., Strom. II 18,79,5 (II 154,17-18 S.)
c3-7 resp. Plot. I 2,1,16-19 (I 62-63 H.-S.)
c8-432b6 cit. Averr., in R. 49,23-50,10 R.
d4 πραγματευώμεθα expl. sch. Pl. ad loc. (223 G.)
d6-432a9 resp. Apul., Pl. II 6,229 (84 B.)
d8 εἰ—χαρίζεσθαι imit. Aen. Gaz., Thphr. 4,16 C.
e3-432b1 resp. Pr., in R. I 212,11-15 K.; —, — I 212,20-26 K.; —, — I 216,13-18 K.; —, — I 220,2-5 K.

e3-9 resp. Clem., *Strom.* I 25,165,4 (II 103,21-22 S.)
e6-432b1 Κόσμος—συνδοχεῖ AFF. Stob. IV 1,99 (IV 40,17-43,2 H.)
e6-7 resp. Alb., *Intr.* XXIX 2 (141 L.); Iambl. *ap.* Stob. III 5,48 (III 271,18-20 H.)
e6 Κόσμος ἡ σωφροσύνη resp. Meth., *Symp.* VII 2 (73,4 B.)
e11-431a1 resp. Plu., *Mor.* 450d (III 151,21-23 P.-S.)

431 a5 ἔνι expl. sch. Pl. ad loc. (223 G.)
a7 ὑπὸ τροφῆς κακῆς usurp. Bess., *in Cal. Pl.* 158,13-14 M.
a7 (et alibi) ὁμιλίας *AB* I 110,7
e4-432a9 resp. Plot. I 2,1,18-19 (I 63 H.-S.)
e7 ἐπιεικῶς expl. sch. Pl. ad loc. (223 G.)
e8 resp. Porph., *Sent.* 32 (23,9-10 L.)

432 a3 διὰ πασῶν fort.resp. Lacap., *Ep.* 27,1 (169,1-2 L.); usurp. Hierocl., *in CA* 10,1 (34,26 K.)
b8 κύκλῳ περιίστασθαι imit. Them., *Or.* 22,271b (II 60,15-16 D.-N.)
c3 Εἰ γὰρ ὤφελον expl. sch. Pl. ad loc. (224 G.)
c7-8 δύσβατος, ἐπίσκιος, δυσδιερεύνητος imit. Them., *Or.* 21,254d (II 35,10-12 D.-N.)
c7-8 δύσβατος, ἐπίσκιος imit. Them., *Or.* 1,3b (I 6,6 D.-N.)
d2 Ἰοὺ ἰού expl. sch. Pl. ad loc. (224 G.)
d2 ἰού Phot. I 294 N.
d4 Εὖ ἀγγέλλεις fort.resp. Phryn., *Ecl.* 232 (84,20-21 F.)
d5 βλακικόν—πάθος AFF. *EM* 199,7 G.; *Et. Sym.* β 131 (71,13 B.); Paus. Gr. β 10 (168,19 E.); Phot. β 150 (I 334 Th.); Sud. β 315 (I 474,9 A.)
d5 βλακικόν expl. sch. Pl. ad loc. (224 G.)
d7-8 πρὸ ποδῶν κυλινδεῖσθαι imit. Them., *Or.* 4,52c (I 75,11 D.-N.)
d9-e1 resp. Poll. IV 2 (I 204,9-10 B.)
e8 imit. Aristaenet. I 13,5-6 (31 M.); Meth., *Res.* I 28,4 (257,14 B.)

433 a1-434d1 cit. Averr., *in R.* 50,11-51,2 R.; resp. Alb., *Intr.* XXXIV 2 (169 L.); Apul., *Pl.* II 7,229 (84 B.); Averr., *in R.* 27,28-30 R.; Pr., *in R.* I 214,3-7 K.; —, — I 216,24-217,3 K.; —, — I 220,5-9 K.; —, — II 360,21-361,3 K.
a1-434a2 Ἀλλ᾽—ταῦτα AFF. Stob. IV 1,100 (IV 43,4-44,21 H.); resp. Gal., *Inst. Log.* XVIII 2 (45,14-46,11 K.)
b8 φρόνησις (pro σοφία) usurp. Alb., *Intr.* XXIX 1 (141 L.)
c4-e2 resp. Pr., *in R.* I 220,23-25 K.; —, — I 220,28 K.
c7-8 ἡ—σωτηρία cit. Alb., *Intr.* XXIX 3 (143 L.)
d1-2 τοῦτο μάλιστα expl. sch. Pl. ad loc. (224 G.)

434 a3-c6 resp. Pr., *in R.* I 220,25-28 K.
a3-b8 resp. Gal., *PHP* IX 2,12 (II 546,23-25 L.)
a6 μεταλλαττόμενα expl. sch. Pl. ad loc. (224 G.)
c1-436a7 cit. Averr., *in R.* 51,3-17 R.
c7-435c2 resp. Olymp., *in Alc.* 75,23-24 (50 W.); Pr., *in Alc.* 223,8-11 (103 W.)
c7-10 resp. Clem., *Strom.* I 25,165,4 (II 103,21-22 S.); Olymp., *in Grg. prooem.* 7 (6,16-17 W.); Porph., *Sent.* 32 (23,11-12 L.)
c8 οἰκειοπραγία usurp. Plot. I 2,1,20 (I 63 H.-S.)
d2-445b4 resp. Dam., *in Phd.* I 75,5 (59 W.); —, — I 140,3-5 (87 W.); —, — I 149,6-7 (91 W.)
d2-435b3 resp. Pr., *in R.* I 221,9-12 K.

435 a1-2 resp. Ascl., *in Metaph.* 137,28-138,1 H.
a4 καθ᾽ ὁδόν usurp. Pr., *Th. Pl.* III 7 (III 29,8 S.-W.)
b1-7 expl. sch. Pl. ad loc. (224 G.)
c3 Πᾶσα ἀνάγκη usurp. Zach. Mit., *Opif.* 101,195 C.
c4 σκέμμα Hsch. σ 912 (IV 42 S.)

INDEX TESTIMONIORUM 317

c8 χαλεπὰ τὰ καλά AFF. Apostol. XVIII 7 (II 717,10-17 L.-S.); *App. Prov.* V 22 (I 462,4-12 L.-S.); Greg. Cypr. Leid. III 30 (II 89,10-17 L.-S.); Hsch. χ 44 (IV 269 S.); Tz., *in pr. Il.* 443,12-13 M.; Zen. VI 38 (I 172,12-13 L.-S.); usurp. Chor., *Or.* 7,7 (111,24 F.-R.); Greg. Akind., *Ep.* 5,27 (*ap.* Niceph. Greg., *Ep.* II 393 L.); Lib., *Prog.* XIII 22 (VIII 557,11-12 F.); Them., *Or.* 22,270c (II 59,12 D.-N.); expl. sch. Pl. ad loc. (224-225 G.)
c9-d3 καὶ—ὁδός AFF. Gal., *PHP* V 7,6-7 (I 338,1-3 L.)
e1-436a3 Ἀρ'—ἥκιστα AFF. Stob. I 47,10 (I 306,6-15 W.); resp. D. H., *Rh.* XI 403 (II 379,11-17 U.-R.); Pr., *in R.* I 221,12-16 K.
e4-7 fort.usurp. Arist., *Pol.* H 7,1327b23-24 B.
e4-6 resp. Pr., *in R.* I 221,21 K.
e6-7 resp. Pr., *in R.* I 221,20 K.
e6 fort.resp. Gal., *PHP* III 3,6 (I 186,1 L.)

a1-2 resp. Pr., *in R.* I 221,21 K.
a8-441e7 (de anima tripartita) resp. Aët. Doxogr. IV 4,1 (389a10-390a4 D.); Alb., *Intr.* V 2 (23 L.); —, — XXXIV 1 (167 L.); Ambr., *Luc.* VII 139,1492-1496 (262 A.); Anast. Sin., *VD* II 7,56-59 (63 U.); Anon. Lond. XVI 33-36 (66 J.); Apul., *Pl.* I 13,207 (73 B.); Calc., *Ti.* CCXXIX (244,13-16 W.); —, — CCXXXIII (246,24-247,17 W.) (= Porph., *in Ti.* 103,18-33 S.); Chrysipp., *Stoic.* II 239,9 A.; Cic., *Luc.* 39,124 (89,21-22 P.); —, *TD* I 10,20 (227,25-228,2 P.); —, — IV 5,10 (366,11-17 P.); Clem., *Paed.* III i 1,2 (I 236,4-8 S.); —, *Strom.* V 8,53,1 (II 362,8-9 S.); D. L. III 67 (I 148,17-20 L.); — III 90 (I 157,3-10 L.); *EM ap.* Miller, *Mélanges* 161; Epiphan. I (587,10 D.); — III 22 (591,19 D.); Gal., *Corp. Compl.* 2 (35,2-36,8 M.); —, *Hist. Phil.* 24 (615,1-2 D.); —, *PHP* IX 2,12 (II 546,25-28 L.); Gr. Naz., *Or.* 44,7 (*PG* 36,613c); Gr. Nyss., *V. Mos.* II (VII 1,62,9-12 M.); Hieron., *in Math.* II 13,33 (109,899-903 H.-A.); Luc., *Salt.* 70 (III 48,9-12 M.); Nicet. Chon., *Or.* 17 (176,15 D.); Or., *Pr.* III 4,1 (264,7-11 K.); Ph., *Conf.* 7,21 (II 233,20-22 C.-W.); —, *Leg.* I 22,71 (I 79,22-23 C.-W.); —, — III 38,115 (I 138,27-29 C.-W.); —, *Her.* 45,225 (III 50,22-23 C.-W.); —, *Spec.* IV 2,92 (V 229,26-27 C.-W.); Phlp., *in de An.* 565,20-30 H.; —, — 571,20-572,15 H.; —, — 573,22-31 H.; —, — 574,5-6 H.; —, — 574,24-26 H.; Plot. IV 4,28,64-65 (II 115 H.-S.); — IV 7,14,9 (II 220 H.-S.); Plu., *Mor.* 441e-442b (III 131,2-17 P.-S.); —, — 759e (IV 364,10-11 H.); —, — 1008b (VI 1,134,7-12 H.-D.); Pr., *in R.* I 11,14-18 K.; —, — I 177,14-178,5 K.; —, — I 207,10-11 K.; —, — I 223,1-3 K.; —, — I 229,4-5 K.; sch. Hom. *Il.* Σ 113b (IV 459,59-61 E.); sch. Pr. *in R.* II 370,3 K.; Simp., *in An.* 287,27-29 H.; —, — 289,9 H.; —, — 289,16-17 H.; —, — 299,22 H.; Sophon., *in An.* 139,32 H.; Synes., *Regn.* X 10ab (21,7-9 T.); Tert., *An.* XIV 2 (17,28-29 W.); —, — XVI 1 (20,9-10 W.)
a8-b4 Τόδε—ἔφη AFF. Stob. I 49,30 (I 360,12-17 W.)
a10-11 ἐπιθυμοῦμεν—γέννησιν AFF. Phot. II 229 N.; Sud. τ 1061 (IV 597,11 A.)
b8-437a3 resp. Pr., *in R.* I 223,7-13 K.
b8-9 Δῆλον—ἅμα AFF. Gal., *PHP* V 7,12 (I 338,22-24 L.); —, — IX 9,23 (II 602,22-23 L.)
b8-9 ταὐτὸν prius-ταὐτὸν AFF. Gal., *PHP* IX 9,39 (II 606,33-34 L.)
b8-9 fort.resp. Clem., *Strom.* VII 11,65,5 (III 47,6-7 S.)
c5-6 Ἑστάναι—δυνατόν AFF. Gal., *PHP* IX 9,24 (II 602,26 L.); resp. Alb., *Intr.* XXIV 1 (113 L.)
c8-d3 Ἔτι—οὕτω AFF. Gal., *PHP* IX 9,25-26 (II 602,28-32 L.)
d4-e6 Οὐκοῦν—ἑστάναι AFF. Gal., *PHP* IX 9,27 (II 604,1-9 L.)
d4 χαριεντίζοιτο expl. sch. Pl. ad loc. (225 G.)
d5-7 resp. Gal., *PHP* IX 9,32 (II 604,28-29 L.)
d6 κέντρον (hoc sensu) usurp. Alb., *Intr.* XIV 7 (85 L.)
d7 κύκλῳ περιιὸν usurp. Them., *Or.* 8,105a (I 159,14 D.-N.)
e4 εὐθυωρίαν Phot. I 228 N.
e8-437a2 Οὐδὲν—ποιήσειεν AFF. Gal., *PHP* IX 9,28 (II 604,10-13 L.); resp. Alb., *Intr.* XXIV 1 (113 L.)

437   a8 ἤ expl. sch. Pl. ad loc. (225 G.)
       b1-d1 ῎Αρ'—οὖ AFF. Gal., *PHP* V 7,13-15 (I 338,25-340,6 L.)
       b1-c1 resp. Gal., *PHP* VI 1,27 (II 366,27-28 L.)
       b1-4 ῎Αρ'—παθημάτων AFF. Gal., *PHP* VI 1,25 (II 366,14-16 L.)
       b7-c10 Τί—θήσομεν AFF. Gal., *PHP* VI 1,26 (II 366,18-25 L.)
       c8 ἀβουλεῖν *AB* I 322,6; *An. Bachm.* I 4,15; Phot. α 45 (I 12 Th.); Sud. α 61 (I 8,28 A.)
       d9-e6 ἐπιθυμία—βρώματος AFF. Ath. III 123cd (I 281,20-282,5 K.)

438   a1-3 Μήτοι—σίτου AFF. Gal., *PHP* IX 9,36 (II 606,9-11 L.)
       a1 Μήτοι—θορυβήσῃ AFF. Gal., *PHP* IX 9,37 (II 606,17-18 L.)
       a7-b2 resp. Olymp., *in Grg.* 22,3 (122,10-13 W.); Simp., *in Ph.* 247,30-248,20 D.
       (= Porph., *in Ti.* 118,2-4 S.)
       a7-b1 ᾿Αλλά—τινός AFF. Simp., *in Cat.* 159,19-20 K.
       b2 τά—μόνον AFF. Gal., *PHP* IX 9,36 (II 606,16 L.)
       b4-c5 resp. Simp., *in Cat.* 189,30 K.; —, — 196,32 K.
       b4-5 resp. D. L. III 109 (I 163,20-23 L.)
       d11 φάθι Hsch. φ 34 (IV 226 S.)

439   a1-441c3 resp. Pr., *in R.* I 223,22-224,19 K.
       a9-440a7 Τοῦ—ἔφη AFF. Stob. I 49,30 (I 360,18-361,28 W.)
       a9-d8 Τοῦ—ἑταῖρον AFF. Gal., *PHP* V 7,36-40 (I 344,21-346,7 L.)
       b3-442b10 cit. Averr., *in R.* 51,18-52,5 R.
       b3-d8 resp. Alb., *Intr.* XXIV 1 (113 L.); —, — XXIV 3 (115 L.)
       b3 ἀνθέλκει Hsch. α 5109 (I 176 L.)
       b5 τῷ αὐτῷ expl. sch. Pl. ad loc. (225 G.)
       d5-6 resp. Hierocl., *in CA* 1,19 (13,16 K.)
       d7 περί...ἐπτόηται usurp. Chor., *Decl.* 5,5 (227,29 F.-R.); —, — 6,58 (271,13-14 F.-R.);
       —, — 9,51 (403,13 F.-R.); —, — 11,45 (489,24 F.-R.)
       e2-440a7 Ταῦτα—ἔφη AFF. Gal., *PHP* V 7,45-47 (I 346,26-348,5 L.)
       e6-440d3 fort.resp. Alb., *Intr.* XXIV 3 (115 L.); —, — XXV 7 (123 L.)

440   a3 κακοδαίμονες expl. sch. Pl. ad loc. (225 G.)
       a3 ἐμπλησθῆτε τοῦ καλοῦ θεάματος imit. Them., *Or.* 34,XXIV (II 228,3-4 D.-N.)
       a8-441c2 resp. Apul., *Pl.* II 24,257 (102 B.)
       a8-b8 Οὐκοῦν—ἔφη AFF. Gal., *PHP* V 7,53-54 (I 350,2-8 L.); resp. Pr., *in R.* I 211,18-23
       K.; —, — I 214,15-17 K.
       b1-7 fort.resp. Plot. IV 4,28,45-46 (II 114 H.-S.)
       b4 αὐτὸν κοινωνήσαντα expl. sch. Pl. ad loc. (225 G.)
       b6 τοῦ τοιούτου expl. sch. Pl. ad loc. (225 G.)
       c1-d3 Τί—πραϋνθῇ AFF. Gal., *PHP* V 7,62-63 (I 352,7-16 L.)
       c7 ζεῖ resp. Alb., *Intr.* XXIII 2 (111 L.)
       d2 imit. Them., *Or.* 11,154a (I 230,16-17 D.-N.)
       e2-441a3 resp. Alb., *Intr.* XXXIV 1 (167 L.)
       e4 πολλοῦ δεῖν expl. sch. Pl. ad loc. (226 G.)
       e8-441c3 ῎Αρ'—λέγεις AFF. Stob. I 49,31 (I 362,2-22 W.); resp. Clem., *Strom.* VIII
       4,10,3 (III 85,29-86,1 S.)
       e8-441a6 resp. Ph., *Virt.* 3,13 (V 269,19-270,3 C.-W.)
       e8-10 ῎Αρ'—ἐπιθυμητικόν AFF. Gal., *PHP* VI 2,11 (II 370,16-17 L.)
       e10-441a3 ἤ—διαφθαρῇ AFF. Gal., *PHP* V 7,72 (I 354,16-19 L.); expl. sch. Pl. ad loc.
       (226 G.)

441   a2-3 resp. Gal., *Aff. Dign.* 6,1 (19,14-15 B.)
       a7-c2 καί—θυμουμένῳ AFF. Gal., *PHP* V 7,75-76 (I 354,30-356,4 L.)
       a7-b1 fort.resp. Gal., *PHP* III 3,6 (I 186,2-3 L.)
       b2-3 resp. Alb., *Intr.* XXIV 1 (113 L.)
       b3-c2 resp. Gal., *PHP* III 3,13 (I 188,15-16 L.)

INDEX TESTIMONIORUM 319

c4-445b8 Ταῦτα—ἀποκμητέον AFF. Stob. III 9,61 (III 390,13-397,18 H.)
c4 διανενεύκαμεν Phot. δ 394 (I 404 Th.); usurp. Clem., *Strom.* V 14,140,4 (II 420,27 S.); Them., *Or.* 23,297b (II 92,19-20 D.-N.); expl. sch. Pl. ad loc. (226 G.)
c9-444a9 resp. Pr., *in R.* I 228,7-27 K.
d5-442b4 resp. Gal., *Inst. Log.* XVIII 2-4 (45,14-46,11 K.)
d5-e2 resp. Dam., *in Phd.* I 36,2 (45 W.)
d12-444a2 resp. Apul., *Pl.* II 24,256 (102 B.)
d12-e2 resp. Anon., *in EN* 254,24-25 H.; Mich., *in EN* 72,5-6 Ha.
e4-6 resp. Elias, *in Cat.* 121,28-29 B.; Pr., *in R.* I 216,10-13 K.; Them., *Or.* 7,87d (I 133,2-4 D.-N.); —, — 11,149a (I 224,18-19 D.-N.); fort.resp. Chor., *Decl.* 1,70 (146,15-16 F.-R.)
e6 resp. Them., *Or.* 7,98b (I 147,21 D.-N.)

a1 τρέφουσα λόγοις imit. Lib., *Ep.* 1306,2 (XI 370,3 F.)
a5-7 fort.resp. Alb., *Intr.* XXV 7 (123 L.)
b5-d3 resp. Gal., *PHP* VII 1,25-26 (II 434,3-9 L.)
b11-d6 resp. Averr., *in R.* 52,6-12 R.
e6 παρακαταθήκην Phryn., *Ecl.* 286 (90,89-90 F.)

a9 ἀθεραπευσίαι *AB* I 78,17
b1-5 resp. Porph., *Sent.* 32 (23,11-12 L.); —, — 40 (52,3-4 L.)
b2 ἀρχῆς—ἄρχεσθαι usurp. Plot. I 2,1,20-21 (I 63 H.-S.)
c4-5 resp. Porph., *Sent.* 40 (52,5-6 L.)
c9-444a9 resp. Anon., *in EN* 254,24-25 H.; Gal., *PHP* VII 1,25-26 (II 434,3-9 L.); Mich., *in EN* 72,5-6 Ha.; Olymp., *in Alc.* 75,23-24 (50 W.); Plot. VI 8,6,20-21 (III 279 H.-S.); Pr., *in Alc.* 223,8-11 (103 W.)
c9-e6 resp. Alb., *Intr.* XXIX 3 (143 L.)
c9-e2 resp. Pr., *in R.* I 230,5-9 K.
c9-d5 resp. Olymp., *in Grg. prooem.* 7 (6,18-19 W.)
c9-d3 resp. Iambl., *Myst.* 187,14 (150 P.)
d3-e2 resp. Olymp., *in Grg. prooem.* 5 (5,1-4 W.); Plu., *Mor.* 1007e (VI 1,133,6-9 H.-D.)
d6 νεάτης τε καὶ ὑπάτης expl. sch. Pl. ad loc. (226 G.)
d7 resp. Pr., *in R.* I 231,10 K.

b1-445c6 cit. Averr., *in R.* 52,13-20 R.
b1-445b4 resp. D. L., *Div.* 3 (42,5-10 M.)
b1-8 resp. Apul., *Pl.* II 4,225 (82 B.)
b2 ἀλλοτριοπραγμοσύνην *AB* I 81,2
c5-445b4 resp. Zonar. I 42-43 T.
c5-e2 resp. Ph., *Virt.* 3,13 (V 269,19-270,3 C.-W.)
d13-e2 resp. Clem., *Strom.* V 14,97,5 (II 390,9-10 S.); Max. Tyr. 27,3b (323,1-2 H.); — 28,4f (338,1 H.)
e1-2 resp. Apul., *Pl.* II 17,244 (94 B.); Plot. I 8,14,1 (I 137 H.-S.)
e1 αἶσχος Hsch. α 2150 (I 77 L.)
e4 ἐπιτηδεύματα (hoc sensu) usurp. Alb., *Intr.* V 5 (25 L.)

c1-e3 Δεῦρό—διήλθομεν AFF. Stob. IV 1,101 (IV 44,23-45,16 H.)
c1 Δεῦρό (hoc sensu) *AB* I 88,19
c4 ὥσπερ ἀπὸ σκοπιᾶς usurp. Niceph. Greg., *Ep.* 57,29 (II 176 L.); —, *Flor.* 72,379-380 L.; Ph., *Spec.* III (1) 2 (V 150,14 C.-W.); Pr., *Th. Pl.* I 7 (I 31,1 S.-W.); —, *in Ti.* III 247,27 D.
c4 ἀπὸ σκοπιᾶς usurp. Pr., *in Ti.* II 113,24 D.
c6-e4 resp. Averr., *in R.* 52,20-26 R.
c9-10 imit. Them., *Or.* 2,35a (I 47,14-15 D.-N.)
d1-e3 resp. D. L. III 82-83 (I 154,6-20 L.)
d1 resp. Arist., *Pol.* Δ 7,1293a42-b1 B.; Herm., *in Phdr.* 164,29 C.
d3-e3 resp. Olymp., *in Grg.* 42,2 (221,14-15 W.)

LIBER QUINTUS

449 **a1-5** resp. Alb., *Intr.* XXXIV 3 (169 L.); sch. Aeschin. *in Tim.* 4 (8,27 D.)
a7 ἦα Phot. I 251 N.; expl. sch. Pl. ad loc. (226 G.)
b2 καθῆστο Poll. III 89 (I 183,19 B.)
c5 κοινὰ τὰ φίλων vide ad 424a1-2

450 **a7** ἐπιλαβόμενοί μου *AB* I 93,23
a8 resp. Gr. Naz., *Or.* 4,113 (270 B.)
b1 ἑσμὸν usurp. Aristid., *Or.* 37,16 (308,10 K.); Synes., *Ep.* 95 (160,1 G.); Them., *Or.* 1,5a (I 8,10 D.-N.)
b3-4 Τί—ἀκουσομένους AFF. Harp. 308,2-5 D.
b3 Τί—χρυσοχοήσοντας AFF. Greg. Cypr. Leid. III 39 (II 91,13 L.-S.); Sud. χ 586 (IV 833,30 A.)
b3 χρυσοχοήσοντας usurp. Chor., *Dial.* 5,2 (129,8-9 F.-R.)
b6-7 imit. Plu., *Mor.* 1098e (VI 2,153,2-3 P.-W.)
c7 (et 457d4) ἀπιστίας Zonar. I 242 T.
d1 ὄκνος expl. sch. Pl. ad loc. (226 G.)
d3 ἀγνώμονες *AB* I 329,30; — I 334,8; *An. Bachm.* I 13,21-22; — I 18,27-29; Hsch. α 674 (I 26 L.); *Lex. Rhet. Cant.* 10,9 H.; *Lex. Seg.* VIII B.; *Lex. Vind.* α 41 (8,15 N.); Phot. α 217 (I 29 Th.); Sud. α 284 (I 30,16-17 A.); Zonar. I 38 T.
d3 ἄπιστοι Zonar. I 234 T.
d5 ἦ που expl. sch. Pl. ad loc. (226 G.)
d8-451a4 fort.resp. Gal., *Ven. Sect.* 6 (XI 224 K.)
d10-451a1 ἐν—ὀφλεῖν AFF. Stob. III 1,78 (III 32,14-17 H.)

451 **a4** προσκυνῶ δὲ 'Αδράστειαν imit. Lib., *Or.* I 160 (I 1,158,5 F.); expl. sch. Pl. ad loc. (227 G.)
b9-457b5 resp. Apul., *Pl.* II 25,258 (103-104 B.)
c1-3 resp. Chor., *Or.* 8,16 (348,7-8 F.-R.)
d4-457c3 resp. Averr., *in R.* 53,2-54,17 R.; Pr., *in R.* I 236,5-9 K.
d4-452a5 τὰς—ταὐτά AFF. Gal., *PHP* IX 3,3-4 (II 552,9-19 L.)
d4-9 resp. Olymp., *in Alc.* 189,6-7 (119 W.); —, — 194,21-22 (122 W.); Pr., *in R.* I 239,28-241,1 K.; fort.resp. Clem., *Strom.* IV 8,62,3 (II 276,25-27 S.)
d4 τὰς—κυνῶν usurp. Chor., *Decl.* 2,25 (159,18-19 F.-R.)
e1-2 resp. Chor., *Decl.* 2,15 (157,25-158,1 F.-R.)

452 **a7-b3** Ἴσως—φιλογυμναστῶσιν AFF. Eus., *PE* XIII 19,1 (II 245,7-12 M.); resp. Pr., *in R.* I 83,11-15 K.
a10-e3 resp. Pr., *in R.* I 243,11-244,11 K.; —, — I 251,13-252,1 K.
a10-b3 resp. Pr., *in R.* I 242,20-28 K.
b2 ῥυσοί Tim. 191 R.-K.
b7 τὰ τῶν χαριέντων σκώμματα usurp. Lib., *Ep.* 1449,2 (XI 486,12 F.)
b7 χαρίεντων expl. sch. Pl. ad loc. (227 G.)
c2 ὀχήσεις Hsch. ο 2023 (II 803 L.)
d6-e2 ὅτι—ἀγαθοῦ AFF. Stob. III 1,56 (III 21,14-22,3 H.)
e4-457b6 resp. Pr., *in R.* I 238,15-21 K.
e4-455e3 resp. Pr., *in R.* I 236,10-11 K.
e4-453a6 resp. Chor., *Decl.* 2,15 (157,25-158,1 F.-R.); Syr., *in Hermog.* II 180,19-26 R.
e5 φιλοπαίσμων expl. sch. Pl. ad loc. (227 G.)

453 **a7-c6** Βούλει—ἀπολογεῖσθαι AFF. Gal., *PHP* IX 3,6-8 (II 552,23-34 L.)
b2-455e3 resp. Pr., *in R.* I 252,1-21 K.
b2-c5 resp. Pr., *in R.* I 242,28-243,9 K.
d5 κολυμβήθραν Poll. VII 138 (II 90,4 B.)
d7 νεῖ expl. sch. Pl. ad loc. (227 G.)

d9 νευστέον expl. sch. Pl. ad loc. (227 G.)
d10 δελφῖνά τινα expl. sch. Pl. ad loc. (227-228 G.)
e2-455e3 resp. Pr., *in R.* 244,11-245,12 K.

a1 Ἦ expl. sch. Pl. ad loc. (228 G.)
a11 μῶν expl. sch. Pl. ad loc. (228 G.)
b1-456b11 κινδυνεύομεν—οὖν AFF. Gal., *PHP* IX 3,10-23 (II 554,1-556,25 L.)
b5 ἀνδρείως expl. sch. Pl. ad loc. (228 G.)
c1-5 resp. Pr., *in R.* I 245,6-8 K.
c9 ἐκεῖνο τὸ εἶδος expl. sch. Pl. ad loc. (228 G.)
d7-e4 resp. Olymp., *in Grg.* 18,9 (105,25-26 W.)

a9-457b6 resp. sch. Pl. *Alc.1* 127a (bis) (103 et 453 G.)
a9 (et 539c8) ἀντιλέγοντος Zonar. I 218 T.
b4-c3 Ἴθι—φήσει AFF. Stob. I 47,11 (I 306,17-25 W.)
b7 εὑρετικὸς usurp. Alb., *Intr.* XXXVI (173 L.)
c4-456c3 resp. Pr., *in R.* I 245,14-246,3 K.
c4-456b3 Οἶσθά—φύσιν AFF. Eus., *PE* XII 32,2-6 (II 126,17-127,11 M.)
c4-d1 resp. Pr., *in R.* I 256,6-10 K.
c7 ποπάνων et ἐψημάτων expl. sch. Pl. ad loc. (228 G.)
d2-e2 resp. Chor., *Decl.* 1,15 (135,27-136,2 F.-R.)
d2-5 resp. Chor., *Decl.* 2,15 (157,25-158,1 F.-R.)
d6-457b6 resp. Aristid., *Or.* 3,332 (I 3,405,9-11 L.-B.)
d6-e3 resp. Olymp., *in Alc.* 188,13-15 (119 W.); —, — 189,4 (119 W.); —, — 194,18-19 (122 W.); Pr., *in R.* I 236,16-19 K.
e6-456b7 resp. Pr., *in R.* I 241,24-25 K.

a5 ἄθυμός *AB* I 350,12; *An. Bachm.* I 37,29; Phot. α 487 et 488 (I 57 Th.); Sud. α 765 (I 72,24 A.)
b8-10 resp. Pr., *in R.* I 240,19-21 K.
b12 εὐχαῖς ὅμοια usurp. Pr., *in R.* I 238,19 K.; expl. sch. Pl. ad loc. (228 G.)
c9-457a5 resp. Pr., *in R.* I 246,22-247,15 K.

a6-b5 Ἀποδυτέον—αἰσχρόν AFF. Stob. IV 1,102 (IV 45,18-46,2 H.)
a6-10 resp. Averr., *in R.* 54,17-18 R.
a6-7 ἀρετὴν ἀντὶ ἱματίων usurp. Bas., *Leg. Lib. Gent.* V 32 (47 B.); imit. Clem., *Strom.* VII 11,61,2 (III 44,21-23 S.)
a10-b3 ὁ—γελᾷ AFF. Eus., *PE* XIII 19,2 (II 245,14-16 M.); Thdt., *Affect.* IX 38 (II 347,14-17 C.)
b4-6 κάλλιστα—οὖν AFF. Stob. III 1,83 (III 34,13-15 H.)
b4-5 κάλλιστα—αἰσχρόν AFF. Stob. III 1,208 (III 173,2-3 H.)
b4 λελέξεται resp. Cyr., *Gloss.* λελ 11 (131 D.)
b7-d5 Τοῦτο—ὠφελίμου AFF. Phlp., *Aet.* IX 3 (325,16-326,6 R.)
b7 κῦμα διαφεύγειν imit. Lib., *Ep.* 1027,2 (XI 155,10 F.)
b7 κῦμα usurp. Clem., *Strom.* V 14,140,4 (II 420,27 S.)
c7-d8 Τούτῳ—παῖδας AFF. Stob. IV 1,103 (IV 46,4-13 H.)
c7-d3 Τούτῳ—γονέα AFF. Eus., *PE* XIII 19,14 (II 248,19-22 M.)
c10-462c9 resp. Pr., *in R.* II 367,13-14 K.; Thdt., *Affect.* XII 77 (II 441,9-10 C.)
c10-462a1 resp. Apul., *Pl.* II 25,258 (103 B.); Averr., *in R.* 52,26-29 R.
c10-d3 Τάς—γονέα AFF. Thdt., *Affect.* IX 44 (II 349,14-17 C.); resp. Arist., *Pol.* B 21,1274b9-11 B.; Hieron., *Ep.* LXIX 3 (III 196,6-7 L.); Pr., *in R.* II 365,26-366,5 K.; sch. Pl. *Lg. hypothes.* (296 G.); Them., *Or.* 26,324a (II 139,8-9 D.-N.)
c10-d1 Τάς—συνοικεῖν AFF. Phlp., *Aet.* IX 3 (326,13-15 R.); resp. Agath., *Hist.* IV 27,7 (158,17-22 K.); Aristid., *Or.* 4,39 (I 3,543,21 L.-B.); Clem., *Strom.* III 2,10,2 (II 200,16-17 S.); —, — VI 2,24,5 (II 441,13 S.); Clem. *Recogn.* X 5,6-7 (327,15-19 R.-P.); D. L. VII 131 (II 353,1-4 L.); Epict. II 4,8 (125,1 S.); — fr. XV (466 S.) (= Stob. III 6,58

(III 301,1-2 H.)); Epiphan. III 22 (591,20-21 D.); Gell., *NA* XVIII 2,8 (II 234,22-24 H.); Lact., *Inst.* III 21,4 (248,18-19 B.); Luc., *Conv.* 39 (I 159,8-9 M.); —, *Fug.* 18 (III 213,8-10 M.); Phot., *Ep.* 165 (II 26,29-30 L.-W.); sch. Aristid. 3,332 (655,29 D.); sch. Hom. *Il.* Ω 371 (V 586,78-80 E.); sch. Luc. *VH* II 19 (22,9-10 R.); sch. Pl. ad loc. (ση) (229 G.); S. E.,*P.* III 205 (I 189 M.-M.); Syr., *in Hermog.* II 180,26-181,3 R.; Thpl. Ant., *Autol.* III 6 (106 G.)
d1-3 resp. Pr., *in R.* I 161,26-27 K.; —, — II 9,7 K.

458 c6-460b6 resp. Averr., *in R.* 52,29-53,2 R.
c6-e5 resp. Averr., *in R.* 54,18-25 R.
c6-d7 Σὺ—λέων AFF. Eus., *PE* XIII 19,15 (II 249,1-9 M.); Thdt., *Affect.* IX 45 (II 349,17-350,7 C.)
d5-7 resp. (ση) sch. Pl. ad loc. (229 G.)
d5 cit. Plu., *Vit.* 48c (III 2,22,20-21 Z.)
d5 γεωμετρικαῖς ἀνάγκαις usurp. Nicet. Mag., *Ep.* 23,5 (113 W.); Plu., *Mor.* 1122d (VI 2,205,3 P.-W.); Pr., *in Ti.* I 332,7 D.; Zach. Mit., *Opif.* 116,665 C.
e3-4 resp. Pr., *in Ti.* I 49,15-16 D.; imit. Them., *Or.* 21,248ab (II 24,20-22 D.-N.)

459 a1-460b11 cit. Averr., *in R.* 54,28-55,28 R.
a1-b6 imit. Them., *Or.* 21,248b (II 25,2-8 D.-N.)
c8-d2 resp. Cels., *ap.* Or., *Cels.* 4,18,7-10 (II 224 B.); Clem., *Strom.* VII 9,53,2 (III 39,14-16 S.); Pr., *in R.* I 116,12-16 K.
d4-461c7 fort.resp. Gell., *NA* XVIII 2,8 (II 234,24-26 H.)
d4-e3 Ἐν—ἔσται AFF. Phlp., *Aet.* IX 3 (320,22-321,5 R.)
d7-460b6 resp. Thpl. Ant., *Autol.* III 6 (106 G.)
e3 ἀγέλη fort.resp. *AB* I 336,29; *An. Bachm.* I 22,1-2
e6 θυσίαι resp. Pr., *in R.* II 66,10 K.

460 c1-d5 cit. Averr., *in R.* 56,1-4 R.
c1-7 Τὰ—ἔσεσθαι AFF. Phlp., *Aet.* IX 3 (321,9-15 R.)
c9 σπαργῶσι Hsch. σ 1113 (IV 62 S.); Phot. II 170 N.; expl. sch. Pl. ad loc. (229 G.)
d3 θηλάσονται *AB* I 99,13
d4 τίτθαις expl. sch. Pl. ad loc. (229 G.)
d8-461a2 τὸ—φρονήσεως AFF. Stob. IV 50^b,86 (V 1052,18-1053,5 H.)
d8 ἐφεξῆς διέλθωμεν usurp. Meth., *Symp.* III 14 (45,11 B.)
e1-7 resp. Averr., *in R.* 55,8-9 R.; Pr., *in R.* II 366,18-19 K.
e4-7 Γυναικὶ—πεντεκαιπεντηκονταέτους AFF. Eus., *PE* XIII 19,17 (II 249,18-20 M.); Thdt., *Affect.* IX 50 (II 351,8-10 C.)
e5-7 resp. sch. Hes. *OD* 695-698 (212,16-18 P.)

461 a5 φιτύοντος expl. sch. Pl. ad loc. (229 G.)
a6 θυσιῶν vide ad 459e6
b1-2 ὑπὸ σκότου γεγονώς Phot. II 249 N.
b6 ἀνέγγυον Phot. I 239 N.
b9-e4 cit. Averr., *in R.* 56,4-57,4 R.
b9-c7 Ὅταν—τοιούτῳ AFF. Phlp., *Aet.* IX 3 (321,22-322,6 R.)
b9-c1 Ὅταν—ἐθέλωσι AFF. Eus., *PE* XIII 19,18 (II 249,22-23 M.); Thdt., *Affect.* IX 51 (II 351,13-15 C.)
c4-7 διακελευσάμενοι—τοιούτῳ AFF. Eus., *PE* XIII 19,18 (II 250,2-4 M.); Thdt., *Affect.* IX 51 (II 351,15-352,2 C.)
c5 κύημα Hsch. χ 4436 (II 542 L.)
d2-e3 resp. Pr., *in R.* II 366,10-20 K.
d7 τηθάς expl. sch. Pl. ad loc. (229 G.)
e2-3 resp. (ση) sch. Pl. ad loc. (230 G.)
e3 resp. Aristid., *Or.* 3,617 (I 3,497,17 L.-B.)
e5-465e3 Ἡ—χαλά AFF. Stob. IV 1,104 (IV 46,15-53,5 H.)
e5-462e3 cit. Averr., *in R.* 57,5-25 R.

INDEX TESTIMONIORUM

a2-b7 resp. Pr., *in R.* II 365,1-8 K.
a3-4 resp. Pr., *Th. Pl.* I 4 (I 21,5-6 S.-W.)
a9-e2 resp. Bess., *in Cal. Pl.* 494,39-496,6 M.
a9-b2 resp. Pr., *in R.* II 361,14-17 K.
b1-c10 resp. Iambl., *VP* 30,167 (94,18-22 D.)
b4-c9 resp. Pr., *in R.* II 78,26-29 K.
b8 ἰδίωσις *AB* I 100,20
c3-8 resp. Cic., *Rep.* IV 5,5 (110,8-10 Z.); Plu., *Mor.* 140d (I 288,11-14 P.-W.-P.-G.); —, — 484b (III 236,2-3 P.-S.); —, — 767d (IV 385,17-18 H.); Pr., *in R.* II 365,9-26 K.
c3-5 resp. Stob. IV 23,43 (IV 582,17-583,3 H.)
c10-e3 resp. Pr., *in R.* II 361,3-13 K.
c10-d5 resp. Synes., *Insomn.* II 132c (147,7-10 T.); fort.resp. Chor., *Decl.* 9,42 (401,1-8 F.-R.)

a10-b3 resp. Olymp., *in Grg.* 32,4 (166,11-14 W.)
b14-c1 οἰκεῖον et ἀλλότριον usurp. Alb., *Intr.* V 1 (21 L.)
c5-d8 resp. Averr., *in R.* 57,25-30 R.
c5-7 resp. Lact., *Inst.* III 21,7 (249,11-13 B.)
d3 κηδεμονίας Phot. I 338 N.; usurp. Meth., *Symp.* X 3 (126,4 B.)

a1-2 μετά—κοινῇ AFF. Phlp., *Aet.* IX 3 (326,17-20 R.)
b1-465e3 cit. Averr., *in R.* 58,1-14 R.
b1-3 resp. Pr., *in R.* II 361,3-13 K.
b8-d6 resp. Phlp., *Aet.* IX 3 (326,22-23 R.)
e4 αἰκίας *An. Bachm.* I 49,20-21; expl. sch. Pl. ad loc. (230 G.)

c4 πάντως expl. sch. Pl. ad loc. (230 G.)
c5 οἰκέτας expl. sch. Pl. ad loc. (230 G.)
d3 ὀλυμπιονῖκαι expl. sch. Pl. ad loc. (230-231 G.)
d9 ἀναδοῦνται expl. sch. Pl. ad loc. (231 G.)
e5 ὅτου expl. sch. Pl. ad loc. (231 G.)

c2-3 τὸν Ἡσίοδον—παντός ad Hesiodi *OD* (40) refert sch. Pl. ad loc. (231 G.)
c6-467e8 cit. Averr., *in R.* 58,15-59,4 R.
d3 παρὰ φύσιν usurp. Alb., *Intr.* IX 2 (53 L.)
e4 resp. Aristid., *Or.* 3,332 (I 3,405,9-11 L.-B.)

a1 διακονεῖν τὰ περὶ τὸν πόλεμον imit. Chor., *Decl.* 3,27 (186,19 F.-R.)
a10-b1 Ἀλλὰ—τέχῃ AFF. Stob. IV 24a,13 (IV 603,6-7 H.)
c1-3 expl. sch. Pl. ad loc. (231 G.)
c5-e7 resp. Iul., *Or.* I 11 (I 1,23,7-10 B.); —, — I 12 (I 1,23,20-27 B.)
c7 ἢ γάρ expl. sch. Pl. ad loc. (231 G.)
c10 ὅσα ἄνθρωποι expl. sch. Pl. ad loc. (231 G.)
e6 ἀσφαλέστατα fort.resp. *An. Bachm.* I 156,31; Phot. α 3037 (I 280 Th.)

a1-b1 cit. Averr., *in R.* 59,4-7 R.
a6 κάκην Moer. 206 P.-K.
b2-e3 resp. Averr., *in R.* 59,11-15 R.
b11-c8 resp. Gell., *NA* XVIII 2,8 (II 234,24-26 H.); Plu., *Mor.* 11f (I 22,18-20 P.-W.-P.-G.)
b12 Πάντων, ἔφη, μάλιστα expl. sch. Pl. ad loc. (231 G.)
c5-8 expl. sch. Pl. ad loc. (232 G.) (ad Hom. *Il.* A (317-318) referens)
c10-d5 Ἀλλὰ—αὐξήσει AFF. Hermog., *Id.* II 4 (336,18-23 R.)
d7 ταὐτά γε expl. sch. Pl. ad loc. (232 G.)
e4-469b3 τῶν—κριθῶσιν AFF. Eus., *PE* XIII 11,1 (III 189,16-190,3 M.); cit. Averr., *in R.* 59,15-19 R.

e4-7 τῶν—μάλιστα AFF. Clem., Strom. IV 4,16,1 (II 255,31-256,2 S.); Thdt., Affect. VIII 46 (II 326,11-14 C.)
e5-6 usurp. Dam., Isid. 30 (27,7-8 Z.); fort.usurp. Clem., Strom. IV 2,4,2 (II 249,24-25 S.)
e8-469b3 resp. Pr., in Alc. 74,13-15 (33 W.)
e8-469a3 'Αλλ'—οὖν AFF. Hermog., Id. II 4 (337,1-5 R.)
e8-469a1 resp. Bess., Ep. 19 (459,10-11 M.)

469   a1-2 οἱ—ἀνθρώπων AFF. (e Platone) Aristid., Or. 3,188 (I 2,355,12-13 L.-B.); imit. Them., Or. 20,240b (II 14,7-8 D.-N.)
a7-b3 Τί—κριθῶσιν AFF. Thdt., Affect. VIII 46 (II 326,14-18 C.)
a8-b3 τὸν—κριθῶσιν AFF. Cyr., adv. Iul. 812bc
b5-471c3 fort.resp. Averr., in R. 27,1-3 R.
c3 "Ὅλῳ καὶ παντί expl. sch. Pl. ad loc. (232 G.)
c4-7 Μηδὲ—ἀπέχοιντο AFF. Eus., PE XII 37,1 (II 130,6-8 M.)
c8-e6 cit. Averr., in R. 59,8-10 R.
d6-e6 'Ανελεύθερον—Δία AFF. Stob. IV 57,16 (V 1140,9-16 H.)
d6-9 fort.resp. Pr., in Alc. 214,6-10 (98-99 W.)
e1-2 resp. Arist., Rh. Γ 4,1406b32-34 B.
e4 τῶν ἀναιρέσεων expl. sch. Pl. ad loc. (232 G.)
e7-471c3 resp. Averr., in R. 59,20-60,2 R.

470   a9-b9 'Εμοὶ μὲν τοίνυν κτέ resp. sch. Pl. ad loc. (232 G.)
b4-9 Φαίνεταί—πόλεμος AFF. Stob. IV 1,105 (IV 53,7-12 H.)
b10 ἀπὸ τρόπου expl. sch. Pl. ad loc. (232 G.)
c7-d1 resp. Aristid., Or. 7,28 (I 3,610,14-15 L.-B.)
d6 ἀλιτηριώδης expl. sch. Pl. ad loc. (232 G.)
d7-8 τροφὸν καὶ μητέρα usurp. Chor., Or. 2,14 (31,33 F.-R.)
e4-5 resp. Aristid., Or. 3,616 (I 3,497,14-15 L.-B.)

471   a1-b8 resp. Aristid., Or. 3,137 (I 2,336,23-25 L.-B.)
a9-b5 resp. Averr., in R. 60,5 R.
b9-d3 Τιθῶμεν—ὑεῖς AFF. Stob. IV 1,106 (IV 53,14-54,2 H.)
c6-7 fort.resp. Niceph. Greg., Ep. 15,61-63 (II 56 L.)

472   a3-4 imit. Lib., Ep. 873,1 (XI 30,15-16 F.); Plu., Mor. 549e (III 398,16-17 P.-S.)
a4 τριχυμίας resp. Pr., in R. I 18,1 K.; usurp. Them., Or. 3,43a (I 61,16 D.-N.); —, — 34,XXIV (II 228,19 D.-N.)
b2 μὴ διάτριβε expl. sch. Pl. ad loc. (233 G.)
b4-5 cit. Bess., in Cal. Pl. 506,30-31 M.
b7-c2 ἀλλ'—μετέχῃ AFF. Bess., in Cal. Pl. 506,31-34 M.
d4-7 ὅς—ἄνδρα AFF. Bess., in Cal. Pl. 506,35-37 M.; fort.resp. Bas., Leg. Lib. Gent. VI 9-10 (49 B.)
e3-4 μὴ—ἐλέγετο AFF. Bess., in Cal. Pl. 508,1-2 M.
e6-473d2 Τὸ—φιλοσοφήσωσι AFF. Stob. IV 1,111 (IV 55,20-56,26 H.)

473   a1-b1 expl. sch. Pl. ad loc. (233 G.)
a1 φύσιν ἔχει expl. sch. Pl. ad loc. (233 G.)
c8-e5 σκόπει—δημοσίᾳ AFF. Stob. IV 1,107 (IV 54,4-17 H.)
c11-e2 'Εὰν—δυνατὸν AFF. Bess., in Cal. Pl. 502,4-11 M.
c11-d6 (philosophos regnare necesse est) resp. Agap. Diac., Ecth. XVII (PG 86,1,1169); Agath., Hist. II 30,3 (80,14-15 K.); Alb., Intr. XXXIV 1 (167 L.); —, — XXXIV 2 (169 L.); Alfar., Plat. Phil. VI 25 (14 R.-W.); Anon., in Hermog. Stat. 343,21-22 R.; Apul., Pl. II 24,257 (102 B.); Areth., Scr. Min. LXI (II 24,27-30 W.); Aristid., Or. 3,135 (I 2,335,14-17 L.-B.); —, — 3,408 (I 3,433,7 L.-B.); Aurel. Vict., Caes. 15,3 (94,6-7 P.); Auson., Tetrast. ad Marc. Aurel. 1-2 (209 P.); Averr., in R. 60,17-19 R.; Bas. Min., in

Greg. 1097b; Boet., *Cons.* I 4,15-17 (7 B.); Cic., *Quint.* I 1,29 (1,29-30 S. B.); Demetr. Cyd., *Ep.* 6,4 (I 31 L.); —, — 239,14-15 (II 141 L.); —, — 259,25 (II 164 L.); —, — 430,10 (II 386 L.); *Gnomol. Vat.* 443 (166 S.); Greg. Cypr., *Encom. Andr. Pal.* I 387 B.; Gr. Naz., *Ep.* 24,4 (23,20-22 G.); —, *Or.* 4,45,9-11 (146 B.); Hierocl., *Prov.* II *ap.* Phot., *Bibl.* 464a13-15 (VII 200 H.); Hieron., *in Ion.* iii,6/9 (408,171-172 A.); Ioh. Can. 3,6-10 L.; Iust. Phil., *Apol.* I 3 (I 10 O.); Lact., *Inst.* III 21,6 (249,5-6 B.); Lib., *Decl.* XXIII 32 (VI 394,2 F.); —, *Ep.* 758,2 (X 684,4 F.); Muson. *ap.* Stob. IV 7,67 (IV 285,2-4 H.); Niceph. Greg., *Ep.* 83,65 (II 228 L.); Ph., *Mos.* II 1,2 (IV 200,9-11 C.-W.); Plu., *Vit.* 73d (III 2,82,2-8 Z.); —, — 887d (I 2,371,19-20 Z.); Plb. XII 28,2 (III 229,19-21 B.-W.); Prud., *Symm.* I 30-32 (186 C.); Rut. Lup., *Fig.* I 6 (10,1-2 B.); sch. Aristid. 3,408 (687,31-33 D.); sch. Pl. ad loc. (ση) (233 G.); Synes., *Regn.* VII 7b (15,19-16,2 T.); —, — XXIX 32a (61,15-17 T.); Syr., *in Hermog.* II 17,6-8 R.; Them., *Or.* 2,34b (I 46,7-9 D.-N.); —, — 2,40a (I 56,9-10 D.-N.); —, — 8,107c (I 162,21-23 D.-N.); —, — 13,166b (I 239,14 D.-N.); —, — 17,214a (I 306,21 D.-N.); —, — 34,VII (II 217,7-8 D.-N.); Thom. Mag., *Reg. Off.* 30 (*PG* 145,496c); Troil., *in Hermog. Stat.* 50,12-13 R.; Val. Max. VII ii *ext.* 4 (329,1-4 K.)

c11-d3 Ἐὰν—φιλοσοφία cit. Bess., *in Cal. Pl.* 584,14-16 M.
d2 φιλοσοφήσωσι γνησίως usurp. Clem., *Strom.* V 9,58,2 (II 365,11 S.)
d6 τῷ ἀνθρωπίνῳ γένει expl. sch. Pl. ad loc. (233 G.) (S., *Ph.* 386 afferens)

a4 (et alibi) τῷ ὄντι Hsch. τ 1756 (IV 190 S.)
a4 τωθαζόμενος Hsch. θ 7 (II 303 L.); expl. sch. Pl. ad loc. (233 G.)
b3-480a13 resp. Pr., *in R.* I 258,6-11 K.
b3-476b3 resp. Bess., *in Cal. Pl.* 502,12-19 M.
c2 ἡγεμονεύειν *AB* I 98,23; Phot. I 252 N.
c5 ἀμῇ γέ πῃ expl. sch. Pl. ad loc. (234 G.)
d4-475a2 cit. Plu., *Mor.* 44f-45a (I 90,5-10 P.-W.-P.-G.)
d7-475a2 cit. Plu., *Mor.* 56c (I 112,27-113,4 P.-W.-P.-G.); resp. Plu., *Mor.* 84e (I 169,12-13 P.-W.-P.-G.); imit. Aristaenet. I 18,20-29 (45 M.)
d8-e2 resp. Lib., *Ep.* 114,2 (X 114,10-11 F.); —, — 795,2 (X 715,8-9 F.)
d8-9 σιμός et γρυπὸν imit. Plot. V 9,12,6 (II 426 H.-S.)
d9 γρυπὸν βασιλικόν fort.resp. Ioseph. Gen., *Reg.* III 3,92-93 L.-W.—Th.
e1-2 fort.resp. *Gp.* 16,2,2 (455,14-15 B.)
e2-4 resp. sch. Pl. ad 485b7 (236 G.)
e2 cit. Mich. Ital., *Or.* 44 (282,1-2 G.); resp. Nicet. Chon., *Or.* 5 (37,16 D.)
e2 μελιχλώρους resp. Philostr., *Imag.* A 4,768 (II 300,9-10 K.)
e3 ὑποκοριζομένου expl. sch. Pl. ad loc. (234 G.)

a3-6 resp. Averr., *in R.* 61,31 R.
a5-7 imit. Aristaenet. I 18,29-30 (45 M.)
a9-10 resp. sch. Pl. ad 485b7 (236 G.)
a10 τριττυαρχοῦσιν expl. sch. Pl. ad loc. (234 G.)
b4-9 resp. Plu., *Vit.* 861e (III 2,313,29-314,2 Z.)
b8-480a13 resp. Averr., *in R.* 60,21-25 R.
b8-9 imit. Them., *Or.* 27,335c (II 159,11-13 D.-N.)
c4 κακόσιτον expl. sch. Pl. ad loc. (234 G.)
d1-8 resp. Ammon., *in EN* 117,4-6 H.
d2 φιλοθεάμονες Hsch. φ 494 (IV 244 S.); Phot. II 264 N.; usurp. Clem., *Strom.* V 4,19,2 (II 338,23 S.); Zach. Mit., *Opif.* 96,48 C.
d3 φιλήκοοι Phot. II 263 N.
d7 Διονυσίοις expl. sch. Pl. ad loc. (234 G.)
d8-e4 τούτους—φιλοθεάμονας AFF. Clem., *Strom.* I 19,93,3 (II 59,26-60,4 S.); Cyr., *adv. Iul.* 773d; Thdt., *Affect.* I 33 (I 112,17-21 C.)
d8-e1 resp. Pr., *in R.* I 262,8-11 K.
e3-4 Τοὺς—φιλοθεάμονας AFF. Clem., *Strom.* V 3,16,2 (II 336,6-7 S.)
e4-480a13 resp. Pr., *in Prm.* 926,14-16 C.

e4 τοὺς τῆς ἀληθείας φιλοθεάμονας cit. Pr., *in Alc.* 29,5 (13 W.); fort.resp. Clem., *Strom.* IV 17,108,2 (II 195,30 S.); imit. Cyr., *adv. Iul.* 764a; Pr., *Th. Pl.* I 10 (I 40,23-24 S.-W.); —, — I 10 (I 44,22 S.-W.); usurp. Clem., *Strom.* II 5,24,3 (II 125,29 S.); —, — VII,18,109,1 (III 76,31-77,1 S.); Dam., *Isid.epit.* 31 (54,1-2 Z.); Dion. Ar., *CH* 85 R.-H.-G.; Iambl., *Myst.* 172,10-11 (141 P.); Pr., *Th. Pl.* I 9 (I 35,1-2 S.-W.); —, — II 4 (II 34,9-10 S.-W.); —, — III 27 (III 97,6 S.-W.); —, — IV 26 (IV 78,2-3 S.-W.); resp. (ση) sch. Pl. ad loc. (234 G.); vide etiam ad 475d2
e6-476a7 resp. Pr., *in R.* I 258,11-25 K.

476 **a4-7** resp. sch. Pr. *in R.* II 374,14-15 K.
a7 resp. Dam., *in Phlb.* 46,1-2 (25 W.)
b4 φιλήκοοι καὶ φιλοθεάμονες usurp. Plu., *Mor.* 394f (III 25,20 P.-S.)
b10-d4 resp. Simp., *in Cat.* 70,14-19 K.
c2-480a13 resp. Alb., *Intr.* IV 3 (13 L.)
d5-6 resp. Gal., *in Hipp. Off.* 3 (XVIII 2,656-657 K.)
d8-9 Τί—γιγνώσκειν AFF. Simp., *in Ph.* 13,2-3 D.
e4-477b2 resp. Pr., *in Prm.* 1041,30-33 C.; —, *in R.* I 261,6-8 K.; —, — I 264,24-29 K.

477 **a1** resp. Pr., *in R.* I 265,15-16 K.
a2-b8 resp. Pr., *in Prm.* VII 44,22-25 K.-L.; —, *in R.* I 265,30-266,5 K.; —, *in Ti.* I 228,1-4 D.
a2-3 resp. sch. Pr. *in R.* II 376,3-4 K.
a3-4 resp. sch. Pr. *in R.* II 375,21-22 K.; fort.resp. Dam., *Pr.* 92,8-9 R.
a3 ὂν γνωστόν resp. Dam., *in Prm.* II 297,11 R.
a3 μὴ ὂν resp. Clem., *Strom.* V 13,89,6 (II 385,9 S.)
a9-478e5 resp. Apul., *Pl.* II 4,224 (81 B.)
c1-d6 resp. Pr., *in R.* I 238,28-239,4 K.
c1 δυνάμεις—ὄντων AFF. Pr., *in R.* I 266,17 K.; —, — I 266,23 K.
c6-8 resp. Pr., *in R.* I 267,21-22 K.
c9-d5 resp. Pr., *in R.* I 266,28-30 K.; sch. Pr. *in R.* II 376,12-14 K.
d7-478d12 resp. Pr., *in R.* I 261,11-20 K.
d7-8 fort.resp. Olymp., *in Alc.* 36,15-16 (25 W.); —, — 55,18 (37 W.); Pr., *in Alc.* 155,8-9 (71 W.)

478 **b3-c9** resp. Pr., *in R.* I 280,21-22 K.
b6-c9 resp. Ammon., *in Int.* 212,34-213,1 B.
b10 resp. Pr., *in R.* I 261,15 K.
b12 resp. Pr., *in Prm.* VII 46,17 K.-L.
d3 resp. Pr., *in Ti.* I 250,11-12 D.

479 **a5-d6** resp. Ascl., *in Metaph.* 33,14-15 H.
b11-c3 Τοῖς—βαλεῖν AFF. Ath. X 452cd (II 483,13-17 K.)
b11 ἐπαμφοτερίζουσιν Tim. 91 R.-K.
c1-2 νυκτερίδος αἶνος Phot. I 450 N.
c1 παιδῶν αἰνίγματι expl. sch. Pl. ad loc. (235 G.)
d3-5 expl. sch. Pl. ad loc. (235 G.)
d7-8 Προωμολογήσαμεν—λέγεσθαι AFF. Simp., *in Ph.* 13,4-5 D.
d9-10 resp. Pr., *in R.* I 263,24 K.
e7-480a13 resp. Pr., *in R.* I 261,29-262,7 K.
e7-8 resp. Pr., *in R.* I 263,25 K.
e10-480a1 ἀσπάζεσθαί—δόξα AFF. Clem., *Strom.* V 14,98,1 (II 390,25-391,1 S.); Eus., *PE* XIII 13,19 (II 203,15-16 M.)

LIBER SEXTUS

b4 resp. Pr., *in R.* I 263,25 K.
b6-7 cit. Bess., *in Cal. Pl.* 502,20 M.
b9-d4 cit. Bess., *in Cal. Pl.* 502,20-25 M.

a4-487a6 resp. Pr., *in Alc.* 133,18-19 (60 W.)
a10-487a6 cit. Averr., *in R.* 61,20-62,22 R.
a10-b3 resp. sch. Pl. ad loc. (235 G.); imit. Them., *Or.* 21,250c (II 28,13-16 D.-N.)
b2-3 cit. Bess., *in Cal. Pl.* 502,29-30 M.
b5-9 resp. sch. Pl. ad 485a10 sqq. (235 G.)
b10-487a6 resp. Matth. Eph., *Ep.* 19,99 (II 419 L.)
b10-d5 resp. sch. Pl. ad 485a10 sqq. (235 G.)
c3-5 imit. Them., *Or.* 21,257c (II 39,13-15 D.-N.)
c3-4 fort.resp. Boet., *Cons.* I 4,71-73 (9 B.); expl. sch. Pl. ad loc. (236 G.)
c3-4 μηδαμῇ προσδέχεσθαι τὸ ψεῦδος usurp. Alb., *Intr.* I 2 (3 L.)
c3 ἑκόντας expl. sch. Pl. ad loc. (236 G.)
c7 του expl. sch. Pl. ad loc. (236 G.)
d6-e6 resp. sch. Pl. ad 485a10 sqq. (235 G.)
d6-e1 resp. Alb., *Intr.* I 2 (5 L.)
d6-8 imit. Them., *Or.* 21,260a (II 43,9-10 D.-N.)
d6 ὅτῳ—ῥέπουσιν imit. Them., *Or.* 22,269d (II 58,15-16 D.-N.)
d10-e1 resp. (ση) sch. Pl. ad loc. (236 G.)
d12-e1 εἰ—εἴη AFF. Bess., *in Cal. Pl.* 502,32 M.
e3-5 resp. Pr., *in Alc.* 110,17-111,1 (50 W.)

a1-b5 resp. sch. Pl. ad 485a10 sqq. (235 G.)
a1-6 imit. Them., *Or.* 22,269b (II 57,17-20 D.-N.)
a4-5 ἀνελευθερίας et σμικρολογία expl. sch. Pl. ad loc. (236 G.)
a4 Μή—ἀνελευθερίας AFF. Anon., *in Tht.* 13,8-12 (10 D.-S.)
a5-6 resp. Elias, *in Porph.* 11,20 W.; fort.resp. Psell., *Orat. Min.* 13,21 (49 L.)
a5 σμικρολογία imit. Meth., *Symp.* I 1 (9,15 B.)
a6 θείου τε καὶ ἀνθρωπίνου resp. Alb., *Intr.* I 2 (3 L.); —, — I 3 (5 L.)
a8-b2 ᾿Ηι—γε AFF. M. Ant. VII 35 (64,5-8 D.)
a8 μεγαλοπρέπεια expl. sch. Pl. ad loc. (237 G.)
b6-13 resp. sch. Pl. ad 485a10 sqq. (235 G.)
b6-8 imit. Them., *Or.* 22,269b (II 58,5-7 D.-N.)
b7 ἀλαζών *AB* I 374,20
b11-12 ἥμερος et ἀγρία usurp. Alb., *Intr.* XXXII 4 (157 L.)
b11-12 δυσκοινώνητος et ἀγρία usurp. Them., *Or.* 21,254b (II 34,16-17 D.-N.)
c1-d12 resp. Olymp., *in Grg.* 13,10 (80,11-14 W.)
c1-6 resp. sch. Pl. ad 485a10 sqq. (235 G.)
c3-d2 resp. Alb., *Intr.* I 3 (5 L.)
c7-d3 resp. sch. Pl. ad 485a10 sqq. (235 G.)
d4-12 resp. sch. Pl. ad 485a10 sqq. (235 G.)

a2-5 resp. Nicet. Chon., *Or.* 5 (37,12-14 D.); Pr., *in Prm.* 854,23-25 C.; Them., *Or.* 8,104d (I 159,5-7 D.-N.); expl. sch. Pl. ad loc. (237 G.)
a4-5 μνήμων—σωφροσύνης resp. Greg. Cypr., *Encom. Andr. Pal.* I 387 B.; usurp. Marin., *Procl.* 9,2-4 C.; imit. Them., *Or.* 3,46a (I 65,7-10 D.-N.); —, — 4,62a (I 88,5-7 D.-N.); —, — 17,215c (I 308,11 D.-N.); —, — 34,XVI (II 223,20-21 D.-N.)
a6 resp. Areth., *Scr. Min.* XIV (I 174,11-12 W.); Or., *Cels.* 4,47,14-15 (II 304 B.); imit. Aristaenet. I 1,47 (3 M.); usurp. Chor., *Dial.* 7,14 (178,15 F.-R.); —, *Or.* 2,56 (42,2-3 F.-R.); Greg. Cypr., *Antilog.* 47 (*ap.* Lib. VII 166,4 F.); Lib., *Decl.* XV 19 (VI 127,4 F.)
b1-d5 resp. Pr., *in R.* I 202,17-19 K.; expl. sch. Pl. ad loc. (237 G.)
c1 σφεῖς expl. sch. Pl. ad loc. (237 G.)
c4-e3 resp. Averr., *in R.* 63,5-9 R.

328   THE INDIRECT TRADITION

d2 ἀλλοκότους *AB* I 378,32; expl. sch. Pl. ad loc. (237 G.)
e1-3 vide ad 473c11-d6
e4 Ἐρωτᾷς ἐρώτημα imit. Meth., *Symp.* II 4 (19,6-7 B.)

488   **a1-489c8** cit. Averr., *in R.* 63,9-26 R.
a1-489a3 resp. Anon., *Prol. Plat.* XI 27,29-32 (51 W.); fort.resp. Bas., *Leg. Lib. Gent.* VIII 7-12 (52 B.); sch. Aristid. 2,369 (427,6-9 D.); Socr., *Ep.* 1,10 (611 H.); imit. Gr. Nyss., *Ep.* XVII 19 (55,22-24 P.)
a2 εἰκάζω expl. sch. Pl. ad loc. (237 G.)
a8-b1 resp. Arist., *Rh.* Γ 3,1406b34-35 B.
b3-4 resp. Cic., *Off.* I 25,87 (39,2-4 A.)
b8-c6 imit. Them., *Or.* 26,326b (II 143,1-3 D.-N.)
b8 ἑτοίμους κατατέμνειν usurp. Them., *Or.* 21,245a (II 20,14-15 D.-N.)
c3 ἀλλὰ ἄλλοι μᾶλλον expl. sch. Pl. ad loc. (238 G.)
c4-5 imit. Gr. Nyss., *Benef.* IX 95,17 H.
c4 μανδραγόρᾳ Phot. I 405 N.; expl. sch. Pl. ad loc. (238 G.)

489   **a1** ἀδολέσχην expl. sch. Pl. ad loc. (238 G.)
a5-6 πρός—ἔοικεν AFF. Phot. δ 317 (I 398 Th.)
b3-c7 fort.imit. Them., *Or.* 26,326a (II 142,18-20 D.-N.)
b3-5 resp. Them., *Or.* 34,XVI (II 223,14-15 D.-N.)
b8 κομψευσάμενος expl. sch. Pl. ad loc. (238 G.)
c6 μετεωρολέσχας Hsch. μ 1086 (II 657 L.); Phot. I 419 N.

490   **a8-9** πρὸς τὸ ὂν ἁμιλλᾶσθαι usurp. Pr., *Th. Pl.* I 9 (I 39,23 S.-W.); Them., *Or.* 21,254c (II 35,3 D.-N.)
a9 ἁμιλλᾶσθαι usurp. Meth., *Symp.* I 1 (8,13 B.)
b2 ἴοι—ἔρωτος usurp. (verbatim) Them., *Or.* 21,256b (II 37,13 D.-N.)
b2 ἀμβλύνοιτο usurp. Meth., *Res.* I 27,4 (256,1 B.)
b2 ἀπολήγοι τοῦ ἔρωτος imit. Pr., *Th. Pl.* II 8 (II 57,1 S.-W.)
b3 ᾧ προσήκει expl. sch. Pl. ad loc. (238 G.)
b3 resp. Iambl., *Myst.* 26,13 (53 P.)
b5-7 fort.imit. Plot. V 3,17,16-17 (II 330 H.-S.)
b5-6 γεννήσας νοῦν καὶ ἀλήθειαν imit. Pr., *Th. Pl.* I 23 (I 105,13-14 S.-W.); —, — III 22 (III 79,21 S.-W.)
b7 λήγοι ὠδῖνος imit. Pr., *Th. Pl.* II 8 (II 57,1 S.-W.)
c2-3 Ἡγουμένης—ἀκολουθῆσαι AFF. Stob. III 11,27 (III 435,6-7 H.)
e2-496a10 resp. Averr., *in R.* 63,27-64,23 R.
e2-491e7 resp. Alb., *Intr.* I 4 (5 L.)
e2-4 expl. sch. Pl. ad loc. (238 G.)
e4-491a5 expl. sch. Pl. ad loc. (239 G.)

491   **a8-b2** τοιαύτην—ὀλίγας cit. Bess., *in Cal. Pl.* 502,39-41 M.
c1-4 resp. D. L. III 78 (I 152,17-19 L.)
d1-e6 Παντός—ἔσεσθαι AFF. Stob. II 31,110ᵍ (II 222,10-22 W.); resp. Marin., *Procl.* 21,2-3 C.; Pr., *de Decem Dub.* 56,13 (90 B.)
d1-5 resp. Ammon., *in Int.* 253,23-26 B.
d1-2 ἐγγείων—ζῴων resp. Plu., *Mor.* 911c (V 3,1,4 H.-P.-D.)
d4-5 ἀγαθῷ—ἀγαθῷ AFF. Ammon., *in Int.* 253,25-26 B.; usurp. Meth., *Symp.* XI (130,27 B.)
d7-8 τὴν—φαύλης AFF. Bess., *in Cal. Pl.* 502,42-43 M.
e1-492a5 fort.resp. Mich. Gabr., *Ep.* 245,33 (II 399 F.); —, — 462,49 (II 710 F.)
e1-6 resp. Paus. 7,17,3 (II 186,14-17 R.-P.)
e1-3 καὶ—γίγνεσθαι AFF. Bess., *in Cal. Pl.* 502,43-504,1 M.
e2 παιδαγωγίας Poll. II 20 (I 86,22 B.)
e3-6 τὰ—ἔσεσθαι AFF. Bess., *in Cal. Pl.* 504,1-3 M.; resp. Plu., *Mor.* 552bc (III 405,9-12 P.-S); —, *Vit.* 889c (III 1,2,25-26 Z.)

INDEX TESTIMONIORUM 329

2   **a3-4** σπαρεῖσά τε καὶ φυτευθεῖσα imit. Them., *Or.* 27,339a (II 164,4 D.-N.)
    b5-c8 imit. Plu., *Mor.* 41c (I 83,10-12 P.-W.-P.-G.)
    b5-c2 ἀθρόοι—ἐπαίνου AFF. Bess., *in Cal. Pl.* 504,4-10 M.
    c6 φερομένην κατὰ ῥοῦν usurp. Manuel II Pal., *Ep.* 67,81-82 (191 D.)
    c6 κατὰ ῥοῦν Phot. I 322 N.
    e5-493a2 resp. Averr., *in R.* 64,14-15 R.; Bess., *in Cal. Pl.* 504,20-22 M.
    e5-6 expl. sch. Pl. ad loc. (239 G.)

3   **a6-c8** imit. Plu., *Mor.* 51e-52a (I 309,9-17 P.-W.-P.-G.)
    a9 θρέμματος expl. sch. Pl. ad loc. (239 G.)
    a10-b1 τὰς—κατεμάνθανεν AFF. *AB* I 319,26-27
    b7 διδασκαλίαν usurp. Alb., *Intr.* XXIV 4 (115 L.)
    d3 τούτοις expl. sch. Pl. ad loc. (239 G.)
    d6 ἡ Διομηδεία ἀνάγκη imit. Them., *Or.* 21,251c (II 30,2 D.-N.); expl. sch. Pl. ad loc. (239 G.)

4   **a4** Φιλόσοφον—εἶναι AFF. Clem., *Strom.* V 3,17,4 (II 337,10-11 S.)
    d1-2 ὑψηλὸν—ἐμπιμπλάμενον imit. Them., *Or.* 21,251b (II 29,16 D.-N.)

5   **a4-8** Ὁρᾷς—παρασκευή AFF. Stob. II 31,110^h (II 222,24-28 W.)
    b2 ἄλλως expl. sch. Pl. ad loc. (240 G.)
    d8 λελώβηνται fort.resp. Cyr., *Gloss.* λελ 9 (131 D.)
    e1 ἀποτεθρυμμένοι Tim. 39 R.-K.; resp. Apostol. III 60d (II 301,16 L.-S.); expl. sch. Pl. ad loc. (240 G.)
    e2 βαναυσίας expl. sch. Pl. ad loc. (240 G.)
    e4-8 resp. Aristid., *Or.* 3,686 (I 3,521,1 L.-B.); Them., *Or.* 5,64c (I 94,8-11 D.-N.); —, — 21,246d (II 22,24-23,1 D.-N.)
    e5 χαλκέως φαλακροῦ resp. Aen. Gaz., *Ep.* XXI 3 (51 P.)

6   **b6-c3** resp. Alex. Aphr., *in Top.* 232,20-22 W.
    c1-3 cit. Ael., *VH* 4,15 (69,7-10 D.); Aen. Gaz., *Thphr.* 21,8-10 C.
    c1-2 ἐκπεσεῖν φιλοσοφίας usurp. Plu., *Mor.* 47c (I 94,28 P.-W.-P.-G.); —, — 52d (I 104,25 P.-W.-P.-G.)
    c3-5 fort.resp. Them., *Or.* 21,246b (II 22,2-3 D.-N.)
    c5-497a5 resp. Averr., *in R.* 64,23-27 R.
    c5-e2 imit. Olymp., *in Grg.* 26,18 (143,7-9 W.); —, — 41,2 (208,2-5 W.); —, — 45,2 (234,13-14 W.)
    d2 imit. Olymp., *in Grg.* 32,4 (165,21-23 W.)
    d5-9 cit. Them., *Or.* 8,104bc (I 158,12-22 D.-N.)
    d6-8 οἷον—ἀποστάς AFF. Phot. I 244 N.; Sud. ζ 13 (II 499,25-500,1 A.); resp. *Gnomol. Vat.* 430 (161 S.); imit. Plot. I 4,8,4-5 (I 90 H.-S.); Them., *Or.* 24,308a (II 109,11-12 D.-N.)
    d6-7 οἷον—φερομένου AFF. *EM ap.* Miller, *Mélanges* 139
    d6 λογισμῷ λαβών usurp. Aristid., *Or.* 8,12 (I 3,619,6 L.-B.); Chor., *Or.* 5,50 (99,3 F.-R.)
    d7-8 cit. Bas., *Ep.* 3,1,15-16 (I 14 C.); Max. Tyr. 15,10d (195,13-15 H.)
    d7 imit. Plu., *Mor.* 97f (I 198,18-19 P.-W.-P.-G.); —, — 126c (I 261,12-13 P.-W.-P.-G.); —, — 751e (IV 343,18 H.)
    d7 ζάλης ὑπὸ πνεύματος imit. Gal., *Praecogn.* 1,11 (72,18 N.)
    d7 ζάλης resp. Pr., *in R.* I 18,1 K.
    d8 ὑπὸ τειχίον ἀποστάς imit. Meth., *Symp.* II 3 (18,5 B.)

7   **a4** αὐξήσεται *Lex. Sabb.* 40,3 P.-K.; Phot. α 3185 (I 293 Th.)
    b1-511e5 resp. Averr., *in R.* 64,28-74,12 R.
    b1-c3 ἀλλά—ἐπιτηδευμάτων AFF. Stob. IV 1,108 (IV 54,19-55,6 H.)
    d10 τὰ καλὰ χαλεπά vide ad 435c8
    e3-4 expl. sch. Pl. ad loc. (240 G.)

330   THE INDIRECT TRADITION

498 a7-b1 τοῦ Ἡρακλειτείου ἡλίου expl. sch. Pl. ad loc. (240-241 G.)
b1 resp. Plot. II 1,2,11-12 (I 147 H.-S.)
b3-4 μειρακιώδη παιδείαν expl. sch. Pl. ad loc. (241 G.)
b5-6 ἐπιμελεῖσθαι—κτωμένους usurp. Them., Or. 21,260a (II 43,12 D.-N.)
b6 ὑπηρεσίαν—κτωμένους AFF. Bas., Leg. Lib. Gent. IX 63-64 (56-57 B.)
c9-d4 resp. Pr., in Alc. 90,6-9 (40 W.)
c9 Μὴ—Θρασύμαχον AFF. Lex. Sabb. 48,13 P.-K.; Phot. δ 291 (I 396 Th.)
d3 προὔργου expl. sch. Pl. ad loc. (241 G.)
d5 Εἰς μικρόν expl. sch. Pl. ad loc. (241 G.)
e1-2 expl. sch. Pl. ad loc. (241 G.)
e2 ἀπὸ τοῦ αὐτομάτου expl. sch. Pl. ad loc. (242 G.)
e3 παρισωμένον imit. Dam., in Phd. I 207,6 (125 W.)

499 a1 ἑτέρᾳ τοιαύτῃ expl. sch. Pl. ad loc. (242 G.)
a8-9 πόρρωθεν ἀσπαζομένων usurp. Them., Or. 16,211b (I 302,6 D.-N.)
b2-c2 cf. ad 473c11-d6
b6 κατηκόῳ expl. sch. Pl. ad loc. (242 G.)
c4-5 εὐχαῖς ὅμοια λέγοντες expl. sch. Pl. ad loc. (242 G.)
c7-d5 Εἰ—λέγομεν AFF. Eus., PE XII 26,1 (II 116,23-117,3 M.)
c9-d1 imit. Them., Or. 13,177d (I 254,17 D.-N.)

500 a3-4 expl. sch. Pl. ad loc. (242 G.)
a5 ἄφθονόν AB I 81,29
a8 ἀμέλει expl. sch. Pl. ad loc. (242 G.)
b3 οὐ προσῆκον ἐπεισκεκωμακότας expl. sch. Pl. ad loc. (242 G.)
b4 φιλαπεχθημόνως Hsch. φ 455 (IV 243 S.)
c1-2 φθόνου ἐμπίμπλασθαι imit. Them., Or. 21,249c (II 26,24 D.-N.)
c2-5 resp. Pr., in R. I 269,6-7 K.
c4-d1 cit. Bess., in Cal. Pl. 504,33-37 M.
c9-501c2 Θείῳ—ποιήσειαν AFF. Eus., PE XII 19,2-9 (II 109,16-110,13 M.)
c9-d1 resp. Alb., Intr. XXVIII 3 (139 L.)
d5 μελετῆσαι εἰς ἀνθρώπων ἤθη usurp. Alb., Intr. II 3 (7 L.)
e2-501c2 cit. Hierocl., Prov. II, ap. Phot., Bibl. 464a16-27 (VII 200-201 H.)
e2-4 fort.imit. Meth., Symp. I 4 (13,4 B.)
e3-4 fort.resp. Alb., Intr. IX 1 (51 L.)

501 a2 ὥσπερ πίνακα imit. Meth., Symp. I 4 (13,7 B.)
a11 Τί μήν expl. sch. Pl. ad loc. (243 G.)
b1 ἀποβλέποιεν expl. sch. Pl. ad loc. (243 G.)
b5 ἀνδρείκελον Hsch. α 4739 (I 165 L.)
b5 ἀπ' ἐκείνου expl. sch. Pl. ad loc. (243 G.)
b7 θεοειδές resp. Lact., Inst. II 10,4 (147,11-12 B.)
b7 θεοείκελον usurp. Gr. Nyss., Hom. in Cant. XIV (421,4 L.); Them., Or. 6,79a (I 117,7 D.-N.)
b9-c2 resp. Alb., Intr. XXVIII 3 (139 L.)
d1 resp. Bess., in Cal. Pl. 470,7-8 M.
d2 ἀληθείας ἐραστὰς usurp. Clem., Strom. VII 16,94,5 (III 67,3 S.); —, — VIII 1,2,5 (III 81,5 S.); Pr., Th. Pl. III 27 (III 96,23 S.-W.)
d4 τὴν φύσιν αὐτῶν expl. sch. Pl. ad loc. (243 G.)
d9 οὓς expl. sch. Pl. ad loc. (243 G.)
e2-3 πρὶν—γένηται AFF. Bess., in Cal. Pl. 506,4 M.

502 b4-5 cit. Bess., in Cal. Pl. 506,6-8 M.
c6-7 resp. Bess., in Cal. Pl. 494,38 M.; —, — 504,25-27 M.

INDEX TESTIMONIORUM 331

a6 βασανιζόμενον expl. sch. Pl. ad loc. (243 G.)
a9-b1 παρεξιόντος λόγου usurp. Plu., Mor. 758d (IV 361,12-13 H.)
b3 Ὄκνος expl. sch. Pl. ad loc. (243 G.)
b4-5 resp. Pr., in R. II 73,13 K.
b7-c8 resp. Greg. Cypr., Encom. Andr. Pal. I 387 B.
c2-7 resp. Pr., in R. II 74,19 K.
c6-7 cit. Bess., in Cal. Pl. 494,38 M.
d4 χάσμης usurp. Them., Or. 5,68c (I 100,13 D.-N.)
e4 δυνατή expl. sch. Pl. ad loc. (243 G.)

c9-505a4 resp. Pr., in R. I 269,7-12 K.
d1 οὐχ—γυμναζομένῳ AFF. Stob. II 31,110ᵉ (II 222,4 W.)
d5 ὧν διήλθομεν expl. sch. Pl. ad loc. (244 G.)
d8-e3 imit. Meth., Symp. I 1 (9,16-20 B.)

a2-b3 resp. Pr., Th. Pl. II 7 (II 47,11-14 S.-W.)
a2-4 ἐπεί—γίγνεται AFF. Syr., in Metaph. 55,18-20 K.
a2-4 ὅτι—γίγνεται AFF. Pr., in R. I 272,11-14 K.
a2-3 resp. Dam., Pr. 25² (I 65,8 W.)
a2 resp. Pr., in R. I 280,15 K.; —, — I 281,5 K.; —, — I 282,27-28 K.
a2 ἡ τοῦ ἀγαθοῦ ἰδέα resp. Anon., Prol. Plat. II 9,6-7 (19 W.); —, — II 12,7 (25 W.); Amphis 6,3 (II 237 K.)
a2 μέγιστον μάθημα AFF. Pr., in Prm. VII 62,26-27 K.-L.; usurp. Plot. I 4,13,5-6 (I 95 H.-S.); — VI 7,36,4-5 (III 260 H.-S.)
a4-c5 resp. Pr., in R. I 269,14-18 K.
a5-6 ὅτι—ἴσμεν prius AFF. Pr., in R. I 272,14 K.
b5-c5 resp. Dam., in Phlb. 12,1-3 (9 W.); Pr., in R. I 271,13-14 K.; —, — I 272,21-273,4 K.
b8-10 resp. Plot. V 5,12,23-24 (II 358 H.-S.)
d5-6 δίκαια—δοκοῦντα AFF. Pr., in R. I 273,8-9 K.
d7-8 ἀγαθά—ζητοῦσιν AFF. Pr., in R. I 273,9-10 K.
d11-e1 cit. Pr., in R. I 273,12-14 K.
e1 ἀπομαντευομένη τι εἶναι usurp. Plot. III 5,7,7-8 (I 328 H.-S.)

b5 πάλαι καταφανής expl. sch. Pl. ad loc. (244 G.)
c6-509a5 resp. Dam., Pr. 34 (I 106,5-8 W.)
c6-9 Τί—δοξάζοντες AFF. Stob. II 8,35 (II 162,19-22 W.)
d1 παρ' ἄλλων expl. sch. Pl. ad loc. (244 G.)
d3-5 resp. Pr., in R. I 269,22-24 K.
d6-507a6 resp. Pr., in R. I 273,16-21 K.
d6 καὶ μάλα ἀρκέσει expl. sch. Pl. ad loc. (244 G.)
d7 ὅπως μή expl. sch. Pl. ad loc. (244 G.)
d8-511e5 resp. Aug., Acad. III 17,37 (76,7-13 K.)
d8-509b10 resp. Dam., Pr. 29¹ (I 83,16 W.); Pr., Th. Pl. II 5 (II 37,15-17 S.-W.); —, — III 7 (III 29,20-22 S.-W.)
d8-e7 ἀλλ'—διήγησιν AFF. Bess., in Cal. Pl. 96,7-11 M.
d8-e3 ἀλλ'—νῦν AFF. Pr., in R. I 273,23-26 K.; resp. Alb., Intr. XXVII 1 (129 L.)
e1-3 expl. sch. Pl. ad loc. (244 G.)
e1 resp. Pr., Th. Pl. II 6 (II 40,5 S.-W.); —, — III 7 (III 29,18-20 S.-W.)
e3-4 resp. Pr., in Ti. I 393,18 D. (= Porph., in Ti. 36,18 S.)
e3 resp. Pr., Th. Pl. II 7 (II 44,12 S.-W.)

a1-511e5 fort.resp. Pr., in Prm. 880,20 C.
a1-509b10 resp. sch. Pl. Grg. 506c (166 G.)
a3-5 resp. Pr., in R. I 274,16-18 K.
a3-4 resp. Syr., in Metaph. 90,30-31 K.

a3 ἔκγονον τοῦ ἀγαθοῦ usurp. Pr., *Th. Pl.* II 7 (II 45,19 S.-W.)
a7-b8 resp. Pr., *Th. Pl.* II 7 (II 45,26 S.-W.)
b2-11 resp. Pr., *in R.* I 275,16-24 K.
b5-7 Καὶ—προσαγορεύομεν AFF. Pr., *Th. Pl.* II 7 (II 46,22-25 S.-W.); resp. Plot. V 8,5,24-25 (II 390 H.-S.)
b9-509b10 resp. Plu., *Mor.* 433de (III 111,18-23 P.-S.); —, — 1006f-1007a (VI 1,131,4-9 H.-D.)
b9-508d10 resp. Pr., *Th. Pl.* II 7 (II 46,1 S.-W.)
b9-c5 resp. Pr., *Th. Pl.* II 7 (II 43,26 S.-W.)
b9-10 Καὶ—οὗ AFF. Pr., *in R.* I 275,18-20 K.; resp. Aug., *Retract.* I 3,8 (20,5-6 K.); Pr., *Th. Pl.* II 7 (II 47,11-14 S.-W.)
c1-509a5 resp. Sym. Seth, *Consp.*, II 79,10-17 D.
c1 Τῷ expl. sch. Pl. ad loc. (244 G.)
c6-508c2 resp. Pr., *Th. Pl.* II 7 (II 44,4 S.-W.)
c6-8 resp. Phlp., *in de An.* 323,27-29 H.
c9 Οὐ πάνυ expl. sch. Pl. ad loc. (244 G.)
d8-e5 resp. Plu., *Mor.* 436cd (III 118,1-3 P.-S.); Pr., *in Ti.* II 8,3-6 D.
d11-e2 resp. Iul., *Or.* XI,134c2-3 (II 2,106 L.)

508

a4-c2 resp. Alb., *Intr.* X 5 (61 L.); Plot. V 5,8,7-8 (II 350 H.-S.); Plu., *Mor.* 372a (II 3,51,23 N.-S.-T.); Pr., *in R.* I 272,4-5 K.; —, *in Ti.* III 66,16-17 D.
a9-509b10 expl. sch. Pl. ad loc. (245 G.)
a11-c2 fort.resp. *Corp. Herm.* X 4 (I 115,3 N.-F.)
a11-b4 resp. Dam., *Pr.* 34 (I 106,1-2 W.); Plot. VI 7,16,26 (III 234 H.-S.)
b3-4 resp. Calc., *Ti.* CCXLII (258,7-11 W.) (= Porph., *in Ti.* 106,29-30 S.); Gal., *de Usu Part.* III 10,242 (I 177,17-20 H.); Plot. I 6,9,31 (I 117 H.-S.); — II 4,5,10 (I 187 H.-S.); imit. Iul., *Or.* VIII,172d1-2 (II 1,121 R.)
b3 ἡλιοειδέστατόν resp. Pr., *Phil. Chal.* 3,28-29 J.; usurp. Pr., *Th. Pl.* I 22 (I 102,4 S.-W.); —, — II 4 (II 33,13 S.-W.); —, — VI 12 (380 P.)
b9-509b10 resp. Pr., *Th. Pl.* II 4 (II 32,1-5 S.-W.)
b9-c2 Ἄρ'—ὁρώμενα AFF. Bess., *in Cal. Pl.* 96,12-16 M.; Eus., *PE* XI 21,3 (II 47,14-18 M.); resp. Pr., *in Ti.* I 393,16-18 D.
b12-509b10 resp. Dam., *Pr.* 25² (I 64,16-17 W.); —, — 26 (I 70,2-5 W.); Pr., *in R.* I 275,29-276,6 K.; Synes., *Ep.* 154 (275,15-20 G.)
b12-509a5 resp. Pr., *in R.* I 276,25-277,6 K.
b12-d10 resp. Pr., *in R.* I 274,25-26 K.
b12-c2 Τοῦτον—ὁρώμενα AFF. Iul., *Or.* XI,133a3-8 (II 2,104 L.); resp. Calc., *Ti.* CCXLII (258,7-11 W.) (= Porph., *in Ti.* 106,28-29 S.); Gr. Naz., *Or.* 28,30,1-2 (168 G.-J.); Pr., *in Prm.* 1200,38-40 C.; —, *Th. Pl.* II 7 (II 44,12 S.-W.); —, — II 7 (II 48,3 S.-W.); —, — II 7 (II 48,25 S.-W.); —, — VI 12 (377 P.); —, *in Ti.* I 393,16 D. (= Porph., *in Ti.* 36,16-18 S.); Them., *in An.* 103,35-36 H.; fort.resp. Ascl. 18 (*Corp. Herm.* II 317,13-15 N.-F.)
b12-13 resp. Bess., *in Cal. Pl.* 120,41-122,1 M.; Pr., *in Cra.* CCLXXVI (101,11-12 P.); —, *in Prm.* 1044,29-30 C.; —, *Th. Pl.* VI 12 (380 P.); —, — VI 12 (381 P.); ad Gregorium Theologum refert sch. Pl. ad loc. (245 G.)
b13-c2 usurp. Gr. Naz., *Or.* 21,1 (*PG* 35,1084a); expl. sch. Pl. ad loc. (245 G.)
b13 resp. Pr., *in Prm.* 1193,26-28 C.; —, *in R.* II 351,3-4 K.; —, *Th. Pl.* III 7 (III 29,18-20 S.-W.)
c1 τῷ νοητῷ τόπῳ imit. Plot. II 9,6,39 (I 231 H.-S.); usurp. Plot. V 6,6,14 (II 368 H.-S.); — V 8,13,23-24 (II 408 H.-S.); — VI 2,4,28-29 (III 61 H.-S.); — VI 4,16,18-19 (III 158 H.-S.); — VI 7,35,5 (III 258 H.-S.); — VI 7,35,41 (III 259 H.-S.)
c4-d10 resp. Pr., *Th. Pl.* II 7 (II 44,7 S.-W.)
c4-d1 Ὀφθαλμοί—ὁρῶσι AFF. Pr., *in R.* I 277,29-278,2 K.
c5 ἡμερινὸν φῶς *AB* I 98,29
d1-e4 resp. Dam., *Pr.* 26 (I 70,9-12 W.)
d4-509a5 resp. Alb., *Intr.* XXVII 2 (129 L.); Dam., *in Phlb.* 238,2 (113 W.); Pr., *Th. Pl.* III 4 (III 16,19-21 S.-W.)

d4-9 resp. Pr., *in Prm.* 903,20-22 C.; —, *Th. Pl.* II 7 (II 48,3 S.-W.)
d4-8 Οὕτω—ἀμβλυώττει AFF. Pr., *in R.* I 278,4-8 K.
d4-6 resp. Plot. III 9,1,9-10 (I 412 H.-S.)
d8 ἀμβλυώττει *Lex. Seg.* XI B.
e1-509b10 resp. Dam., *Pr.* 26 (I 70,15-18 W.); Iul., *Or.* XI,132d3-9 (II 2,103 L.); Or., *Cels.* 7,45,20-25 (IV 122 B.); Phlp., *in Ph.* 72,14-16 V.; —, — 162,5-17 V.; —, — 166,22 V.; —, — 219,6-7 V.; —, — 480,2 V.; Pr., *de Prov.* 46,12-13 (157 B.); —, *in R.* I 276,16-22 K.; —, *Th. Pl.* II 7 (II 42,5 S.-W.); —, — II 7 (II 46,3 S.-W.); —, — II 7 (II 47,24-27 S.-W.); —, *in Ti.* I 347,23-24 D.; fort.resp. Gr. Nyss., *Hom. in Cant.* I (31,4-5 L.); —, — (36,18-20 .); —, — III (85,20 L.); —, — (87,2-3 L.); —, — (91,2-3 L.); —, — V (157,14-15 L.); —, *Hom. in Eccl.* VII (406,13-17 McD.-A.)
e1-509a5 resp. Dam., *Pr.* 34 (I 99,12-14 W.); —, — 40 (I 122,14-15 W.); —, — 40 (I 122,20-22 W.); Pr., *Th. Pl.* II 7 (II 44,9 S.-W.)
e1-3 Τοῦτο—εἶναι AFF. Bess., *in Cal. Pl.* 96,16-18 M.; Eus., *PE* XI 21,4 (II 47,20-21 M.); resp. Eus., *PE* XI 22,9 (II 51,4 M.); Pr., *in Prm.* VII 44,27 K.-L.; —, *Th. Pl.* I 21 (I 100,13-15 S.-W.); —, — II 7 (II 47,17-18 S.-W.)
e3 resp. Pr., *Th. Pl.* II 6 (II 40,5 S.-W.); —, — II 7 (II 48,3-4 S.-W.)
e4 resp. Pr., *in R.* I 272,3 K.
e5 resp. Pr., *Th. Pl.* II 7 (II 48,3 S.-W.)
e6-509b10 resp. Pr., *in R.* I 285,11-14 K.; —, — I 285,18-19 K.
e6-509a5 resp. Alb., *Intr.* XXVII 1 (129 L.); Pr., *in R.* I 277,9-11 K.; —, — I 279,14-15 K.

9 **a1-2** usurp. Gr. Naz., *Or.* 21,1 (112 M.-L.)
a1 resp. Pr., *Th. Pl.* II 4 (II 33,13 S.-W.); —, — III 4 (III 16,24 S.-W.); —, — VI 12 (380 P.)
a2-5 resp. Pr., *Th. Pl.* II 7 (II 47,11-14 S.-W.)
a3 resp. Porph., *Sent.* 32 (26,10 L.)
a3 ἀγαθοειδῆ usurp. Plot. I 2,4,12 (I 68 H.-S.); — III 8,11,16 (I 410 H.-S.); — V 3,16,18 (II 328 H.-S.); — V 6,5,13 (II 366 H.-S.); — VI 7,15,9 (III 233 H.-S.); — VI 8,15,19 (III 295 H.-S.); Pr., *in R.* I 280,8 K.; —, *Th. Pl.* III 4 (III 16,27 S.-W.)
a5 τὴν τοῦ ἀγαθοῦ ἕξιν AFF. Pr., *in R.* I 272,1 K.
a6 Ἀμήχανον κάλλος usurp. Plot. I 6,8,2 (I 115 H.-S.); — II 9,17,36 (I 251 H.-S.); — V 5,3,8 (II 343 H.-S.); — V 8,3,19 (II 382 H.-S.)
a9 Εὐφήμει expl. sch. Pl. ad loc. (245 G.)
b2-10 Τὸν—ὑπερέχοντος AFF. Bess., *in Cal. Pl.* 96,18-24 M.; Eus., *PE* XI 21,5 (II 47,23-48,4 M.); Pr., *Th. Pl.* II 4 (II 32,13-22 S.-W.); resp. Alex. Aphr., *de An.* 89,1-3 B.; Bess., *in Cal. Pl.* 120,41-122,1 M.; Pr., *in Prm.* 1240,20-26 C.; —, — VII 28,13-18 K.-L.; —, *in R.* I 271,18-20 K.; —, — I 278,17-22 K.; —, *Th. Pl.* II 7 (II 44,7 S.-W.); —, — V 29 (310 P.); —, — VI 12 (379,380 P.) —, *in Ti.* I 230,26-27 D.; fort.resp. Iust. Phil., *Coh. Gent.* 5 (III 32 O.)
b2-8 resp. Plot. VI 7,16,22-25 (III 233 H.-S.); Pr., *in R.* I 295,1-2 K.
b2-4 resp. Pr., *in Ti.* I 429,11-13 D.
b2-3 usurp. Gr. Naz., *Or.* 21,1 (112 M.-L.)
b3 αὔξην Phot. α 3187 (I 294 Th.)
b6-10 τοῖς—ὑπερέχοντος AFF. Thdt., *Affect.* IV 36 (I 213,14-214,1 C.); resp. David, *in Cat.* 26a B.; Pr., *in Prm.* VII 44,25-27 K.-L.; —, — VII 64,25-27 K.-L.; —, *in R.* I 279,2-4 K.; —, *Th. Pl.* II 7 (II 48,3 S.-W.); fort.resp. Dam., *Pr.* 46 (I 92,8-9 R.); Plu., *Mor.* 413c (III 67,10-11 P.-S.)
b6-8 Καὶ—οὐσίαν cit. Pr., *in R.* I 279,20-22 K.
b6-7 resp. Pr., *in R.* I 280,14-15 K.
b7-8 resp. Pr., *Th. Pl.* III 9 (III 37,6-9 S.-W.)
b8-c2 resp. Pr., *in R.* I 274,3-6 K.
b8-10 οὐκ—ὑπερέχοντος AFF. Pr., *in R.* I 280,11-13 K.; resp. Dam., *Pr.* 22 (I 55,23-24 W.); fort.resp. Gr. Nyss., *Hom. in Eccl.* VII (411,8-9 McD.-A.)
b8-9 resp. Plot. VI 2,17,7 (III 78 H.-S.)

b9-10 resp. Alb., *Intr.* X 2 (57 L.); Syr., *in Metaph.* 166,5-7 K.; imit. Gr. Nyss., *Hom. in Cant.* VI (174,6-7 L.); Iul., *Or.* XI,132c8-9 (II 2,103 L.)
b9-10 πρεσβείᾳ καὶ δυνάμει ὑπερέχοντος usurp. Pr., *Th. Pl.* II 7 (II 46,19-20 S.-W.)
b9 ἐπέκεινα—δυνάμει cit. Anon., *in Prm.* XIV 3-4 (108 H.); resp. Plot. VI 7,37,23-24 (III 262 H.-S.); usurp. Or., *Cels.* 6,64,20 (III 340 B.)
b9 ἐπέκεινα τῆς οὐσίας cit. Anon., *in Prm.* XII 23 (104 H.); Dam., *Pr.* 41 (I 126,18-19 W.); Pr., *in Prm.* 1060,28-29 C.; —, — 1097,12-13 C.; —, — 1240,20-22 C.; —, *in R.* I 270,6-8 K.; latine cit. Calc., *Ti.* CLXXVI (204,7 W.); resp. Iust. Phil., *Dial.* 4 (II 18 O.); Pr., *in R.* I 271,25-26 K.; —, — I 277,23-24 K.; —, — I 278,12-13 K.; —, — I 282,20-21 K.; —, — I 286,20-21 K.; —, — I 292,20-21 K.; —, — I 295,4-5 K.; —, *in Ti.* I 305,10 D.; imit. Gr. Nyss., *Hom. in Cant.* VIII (246,9 L.); Plot. I 3,5,7 (I 77 H.-S.); — II 4,16,25 (I 201 H.-S.); — III 9,9,1 (I 416 H.-S.); — IV 4,16,27 (II 94 H.-S.); — V 5,6,11 (II 347 H.-S.); — VI 2,17,22-23 (III 78 H.-S.); — VI 6,5,37 (III 183 H.-S.); — VI 8,9,27-28 (III 284 H.-S.); usurp. Iambl., *Myst.* I 5,15,5 (46 P.); Or., *Cels.* 7,38,1 (IV 100 B.); Plot. I 7,1,19 (I 119 H.-S.); — I 8,6,28 (I 128 H.-S.); — V 1,8,8 (II 280 H.-S.); — V 4,1,10 (II 332 H.-S.); — V 3,17,13 (II 331 H.-S.); — V 6,6,29-30 (II 369 H.-S.); — VI 7,40,26 (III 266 H.-S.); — VI 8,16,34 (III 297 H.-S.); — VI 8,19,13 (III 302 H.-S.); — VI 9,11,42 (III 327 H.-S.).
b9 ἐπέκεινα usurp. Plot. I 6,9,41 (I 117 H.-S.); — III 8,9,2 (I 406 H.-S.); — V 3,11,28-29 (II 318 H.-S.); — V 3,12,47 (II 320 H.-S.); — V 3,13,2 (II 322 H.-S.); — V 3,17,13 (II 331 H.-S.); — V 8,1,3-4 (II 374 H.-S.); — V 9,2,24 (II 413 H.-S.)
b9 πρεσβείᾳ καὶ δυνάμει usurp. Pr., *in R.* I 177,24 K.; —, *Th. Pl.* IV 6 (IV 23,28-24,1 S.-W.); —, *in Ti.* I 70,3 D.; —, — I 100,14 D.
c1-2 Ἄπολλον, δαιμονίας ὑπερβολῆς AFF. Pr., *in R.* I 265,21-22 K.
c1 μάλα γελοίως AFF. Pr., *in R.* I 265,24 K.
c1 γελοίως expl. sch. Pl. ad loc. (245 G.)
c1 Ἄπολλον expl. sch. Pl. ad loc. (245 G.)
c7-10 resp. Pr., *in R.* I 274,7-9 K.; —, — I 286,5-6 K.
d1-511e5 resp. Anon., *Prol. Plat.* VIII 20,11-14 (37 W.); Archyt., *ap.* Iambl., *Comm. Math.* VIII (36,3-37,19 F.); Ascl., *in Introd.* I ιγ,2-9 (28 T.); Cic., *Luc.* 46,142 (99,23-26 P.); D. L. III 9-10 (I 124,25-125,6 L.); Pr., *in Alc.* 21,14-22,3 (9-10 W.); —, *in Ti.* I 228,4-5 D.
d1-510a3 resp. Pr., *in R.* I 289,21-28 K.
d1-4 resp. Pr., *in R.* I 270,9-11 K.; —, *Th. Pl.* II 7 (II 44,12 S.-W.); —, — III 8 (II 53,25 S.-W.)
d2-3 resp. Dam., *in Phd.* I 14,3-4 (35-37 W.)
d2 resp. Pr., *in R.* I 51,12 K.; —, — I 271,4-7 K.; —, — II 45,12 K.; usurp. Plot. I 8,2,8-9 (I 122 H.-S.); — V 3,12,42 (II 320 H.-S.)
d3-4 fort.resp. Calc., *Ti.* XCVIII (150,15-16 W.)
d3 fort.resp. Bas., *Hex.* III 8 (230 G.)
d6-511e5 resp. Ascl., *in Metaph.* 142,8-13 H.; Dam., *in Phd.* I 80,5 (61 W.); Plu., *Mor.* 1001c (VI 1,118,2-12 H.-D.); Pr., *in Euc.* 1,14-2,8 F.; —, — 10,19-11,9 F.; —, — 131,9-11 F.; —, *in Prm.* 1081,7-8 C.; —, *Inst.* 108,29-110,3 D.; —, *de Prov.* 50,7-10 (160,161 B.); Syr., *in Metaph.* 4,16 K.; —, — 55,31-33 K.; —, — 82,22-25 K.; —, — 101,5 K.
d6-8 resp. Pr., *in R.* I 287,22-23 K.; —, — I 288,8-9 K.; —, — 288,18-29 K.; —, — I 289,6-9 K.; —, — I 289,16-18 K.
d7 resp. Pr., *in R.* I 290,23-24 K.
d8 resp. Simp., *in Cat.* 76,25 K.
e1-510a3 resp. Pr., *in R.* I 289,21-28 K.
e1 τὸ—εἰκόνες cit. Pr., *in R.* I 289,19-20 K.
e1 εἰκόνες usurp. Alb., *Intr.* VII 5 (47 L.)

510 **a1** τὰ ἐν τοῖς ὕδασι φαντάσματα usurp. Plot. VI 2,22,39-40 (III 86 H.-S.); imit. Pr., *in Euc.* 11,2 F.
a1 fort.resp. Clem., *Strom.* I 19,94,7 (II 61,4-5 S.); Gr. Naz., *Or.* 2,74,9-10 (186 B.)

a5-6 ᾧ—γένος AFF. Pr., *in R.* I 291,2-3 K.
b2-511e5 resp. Pr., *in R.* I 291,12-21 K.; fort.resp. Averr., *in R.* 75,19-33 R.
b4-d3 expl. sch. Pl. ad loc. (246 G.)
b4-9 cit. Pr., *in R.* I 283,7-11 K.
b4-6 resp. Pr., *in R.* I 283,4-5 K.
b4-5 cit. Pr., *in R.* I 291,19-21 K.
b4 τοῖς τότε μιμηθεῖσιν AFF. Pr., *in R.* I 291,15-16 K.
b4 μιμηθεῖσιν AFF. Pr., *in R.* I 291,18 K.
b6-7 ἐπ'—ἰοῦσα cit. Alb., *Intr.* V 4 (25 L.)
b7 resp. Pr., *in Prm.* 1033,34-35 C.
b7 ἀρχὴν ἀνυπόθετον resp. Pr., *in R.* I 283,18 K.; —, — I 283,24 K.; —, — I 284,15 K.; —, — I 284,20 K.; —, — I 292,5-6 K.
b7 ἀνυπόθετον usurp. Alb., *Intr.* XXXIV 1 (167 L.); Them., *Or.* 26,327b (II 145,1 D.-N.)
c2-511b2 resp. Pr., *in Euc.* 11,10-16 F.; —, — 11,26-12,9 F.; —, — 30,8-9 F.
c4-5 γωνιῶν τριττὰ εἴδη AFF. Pr., *in Euc.* 131,9-10 F.
d5-511e5 expl. sch. Pl. ad loc. (246 G.)
d5-511c2 resp. Pr., *in Euc.* 31,11-22 F.; —, — 57,3-4 F.
e2-3 resp. Plot. VI 4,10,12-13 (III 150 H.-S.)

a3-8 fort.resp. Lyd., *Mens.* 2,8 (27,13-14 W.)
b3-c2 resp. Ammon., *in Cat.* 3,5-7 B.; Arist., *EN* I 4,1095a32-b1 B.; Ascl., *in Metaph.* 142,23-24 H.; Eustr., *in EN* 31,16-19 H.
b5-6 resp. Asp., *in EN* 9,28-29 H.
b6-8 resp. Pr., *in Prm.* 655,30-656,2 C.
b6-7 cit. Pr., *in Euc.* 31,15-16 F.
b6-7 τοῦ—ἀρχὴν resp. Alb., *Intr.* V 4 (25 L.)
b6 ἐπιβάσεις usurp. Plot. VI 7,36,9 (III 260 H.-S.)
b6 μέχρι τοῦ ἀνυποθέτου usurp. Pr., *Th. Pl.* I 9 (I 39,13-14 S.-W.)
b8 resp. Pr., *in Euc.* 31,19 F.
d2-5 resp. Pr., *in Euc.* 57,3-4 F.
d6-e5 resp. Pr., *in Ti.* I 246,32-247,2 D.; —, — I 346,5-6 D.
d8-e2 resp. Pr., *in R.* I 283,27-284,4 K.
e1-2 fort.resp. Clem., *Strom.* II 4,16,1 (II 120,18 S.)
e2-4 resp. Syr., *in Metaph.* 98,7-9 K.
e2 (et alibi) εἰκασίαν Poll. IV 9 (I 205,9 B.)

LIBER SEPTIMUS

a1-521c9 resp. sch. Pl. ad loc. (246 G.)
a1-519b6 resp. Alb., *Intr.* XXVII 5 (133 L.); Averr., *in R.* 74,14-75,1 R.
a1-517c5 Μετά—δημοσίᾳ AFF. Iambl., *Protr.* 15 (78,1-82,4 P.); resp. Ph., *Prob.* 1,5 (VI 2,7-11 C.-W.)
a1-517a7 resp. Aen. Gaz., *Thphr.* 6,10-11 C.
a1-516c3 resp. Boet., *Cons.* III 1,15-17 (37 B.); Gr. Naz., *Ep.* 165,8 (120,20-22 G.); —, *Ep.* 228,1 (164,18 G.); —, *Or.* 24,19,10-13 (82 M.-L.); Hierocl., *in CA* 27,1 (119,10 K.); Luc., *Philops.* 16 (II 185,18 M.)
a1-515e5 resp. Plot. II 9,6,8-10 (I 230 H.-S.); imit. Greg. Magn., *Dial.* IV 1,3 (III 20,22-32 V.-A.)
a1-515c2 resp. Aug., *Qu. Ev., app.* XI (127,75-76 M.); Calc., *Ti.* CCCXLIX (340,14 W.); Gr. Naz., *Ep.* 178,8 (129,6 G.); Pr., *in R.* II 31,5 K.; —, *in Ti.* I 153,7 D.; —, — I 208,11 D.; sch. Pl. ad loc. (246 G.); imit. Gr. Nyss., *Hom. in Cant.* V (162,1-2 L.); —, — (169,1-2 L.); fort.imit. Gr. Nyss., *Hom. in Cant.* IV (108,9-10 L.); —, — V (148,10-11 L.)
a1-b6 imit. Meth., *Symp.* II 4 (19,12 B.)
a1-2 ἀπείκασον—φύσιν AFF. Pr., *in R.* I 292,25 K.

a2-5 ἰδὲ—σπήλαιον AFF. Porph., Antr. 8 (61,22-62,3 N.)
a2-3 ἰδὲ—σπηλαιώδει AFF. Pr., in R. I 293,10-11 K.
a2 παιδείας—ἀπαιδευσίας AFF. Pr., in R. I 292,27-28 K.
a2 ἰδὲ expl. sch. Pl. ad loc. (247 G.)
a3 οἰκήσει σπηλαιώδει resp. Pr., in Alc. 153,7 (70 W.); imit. Plot. IV 8,1,33 (II 228 H.-S.); — IV 8,3,4 (II 233 H.-S.); — IV 8,4,28 (II 238 H.-S.); — IV 8,5,3 (II 240 H.-S.); usurp. Gr. Nyss., Hom. in Cant. VII (212,8 L.)
b1-2 fort.usurp. Chor., Decl. 7,8 (287,12 F.-R.)
b3-4 μεταξὺ—ὁδόν AFF. Pr., in R. I 293,13-14 K.

515 a4 Ἄτοπον λέγεις εἰκόνα AFF. Porph., Antr. 8 (62,4 N.)
c4-516b8 resp. Pr., in R. I 293,23-25 K.; sch. Pl. ad 532a3 (252 G.); fort.resp. Or., Pr. I 1,5 (20,9-15 K.); Plot. I 6,9,1-2 (I 116 H.-S.).
c4-5 resp. Aen. Gaz., Thphr. 6,11-12 C.
c4 resp. Plot. IV 8,1,35 (II 228 H.-S.); — IV 8,4,29 (II 238 H.-S.)
e1-516b8 fort.resp. Corp. Herm. X 4 (I 115,3 N.-F.); Gr. Naz., Vit. 331-332 (70 J.); imit. Gr. Naz., Or. 28,3,15-18 (106 G.-J.)
e1-4 resp. Dam., Pr. 29[1] (84,7-10 W.); Gr. Naz., Or. 20,10,18-22 (78 M.-L.); fort.imit. Plu., Mor. 36e (I 74,15-16 P.-W.-P.-G.)
e7 τραχείας καὶ ἀνάντους imit. Meth., Symp. prooem. 5 (5,4 B.)

516 a5-b7 imit. Gr. Nyss., Hom. in Cant. III (90,10-11 L.); —, — IV (104,11-12 L.); —, — VIII (257,1-3 L.)
a8-b2 resp. Pr., in R. I 294,4-5 K.
b4-c3 resp. Pr., in R. I 294,25-28 K.
b4-7 imit. Gr. Nyss., Hom. in Cant. III (86,8 L.)
e3-518b5 resp. Pr., in Ti. I 19,13-16 D.
e8 γνωματεύοντα usurp. Plot. V 8,11,15 (II 402 H.-S.); expl. sch. Pl. ad loc. (247 G.)

517 a8-b6 imit. Meth., Symp. II 5 (21,1-2 B.)
a8-b4 Ταύτην—δυνάμει AFF. Porph., Antr. 8 (62,5-9 N.)
a8-b1 resp. Pr., in R. I 294,25-28 K.
b1-6 expl. sch. Pl. ad loc. (247 G.)
b4-5 resp. Plot. IV 8,1,35-36 (II 228 H.-S.); — IV 8,4,29 (II 238 H.-S.)
b5 τὸν νοητὸν τόπον vide ad 508c1
b7-c5 resp. Alb., Intr. XXVII 1 (129 L.); Alex. Aphr., de An. 89,9-11 B.; Dam., in Prm. II 96,25 R.
b8-c1 ἐν—ὁρᾶσθαι cit. Pr., in R. I 295,7-8 K.; resp. Pr., Th. Pl. I 9 (I 39,24 S.-W.)
c2 ὀρθῶν—αἰτία cit. Pr., in R. I 296,9 K.
c3-4 cit. Pr., in R. I 296,10-11 K.
c8 ἐνταῦθα expl. sch. Pl. ad loc. (247 G.)
d5 ἀσχημονεῖ Hsch. α 7978 (I 270 L.)
d8-9 περὶ τῶν τοῦ δικαίου expl. sch. Pl. ad loc. (247 G.)

518 a1-b4 resp. Or., Cels. 6,66,9-11 (III 344 B.); Pr., in Ti. I 22,28-31 D.
a1-3 resp. Dam., Pr. 29[1] (84,7-10 W.)
a2-3 resp. Porph., Qu. Hom. I 47,8-12 S.
a2 ἐπιταράξεις ὄμμασιν Poll. II 65 (I 103,9 B.)
a8 φανότερον Phot. II 255 N.
b3 ἧττον—εἴη usurp. Clem., Paed. II v 47,1 (I 186,11-12 S.)
b5 μετρίως expl. sch. Pl. ad loc. (247 G.)
b6-519b5 Δεῖ—τέτραπται AFF. Iambl., Protr. 16 (82,10-83,19 P.)
b6-d1 resp. Hero, Def. 136,2 (IV 110,3-16 H.); Pr., in Ti. I 41,2-4 D.
c2 ὄψιν ἐντιθέντες usurp. Clem., Strom. V 3,19,2 (II 338,23-24 S.)
c4-d7 imit. Gr. Nyss., Hom. in Cant. II (48,12-14 L.)
c7-8 fort.resp. Boet., Cons. III 2,45-46 (39 B.)

c9 εἰς τοῦ ὄντος τὸ φανότατον AFF. Pr., *de Mal. Subs.* 24,11 (203 B.)
c9 τοῦ—φανότατον usurp. Pr., *Th. Pl.* II 7 (II 48,9 S.-W.)
d1 resp. Pr., *Th. Pl.* II 6 (II 40,5 S.-W.)
d4 περιαγωγῆς usurp. Alb., *Intr.* I 1 (3 L.)
d9-e3 fort.resp. Eustr., *in EN* 400,30-32 H.; expl. sch. Pl. ad loc. (247 G.)
d10 ἐγγύς—σώματος AFF. Plot. VI 8,6,24-25 (III 279 H.-S.)
e1 ἔθεσι καὶ ἀσκήσεσιν AFF. Plot. VI 8,6,25 (III 279 H.-S.); usurp. Plot. I 1,10,12-13 (I 58 H.-S.); imit. Alb., *Intr.* XXIV 4 (115 L.); —, — XXX 3 (147 L.)

9   a2-3 δριμὺ—ψυχάριον usurp. Iul., *Or.* VIII,161b7 (II 1,106 R.)
a8-b3 fort.imit. Clem., *Strom.* IV 4,15,1 (II 255,9-11 S.)
b1-4 resp. Gal., *PHP* IX 6,52 (II 582,29 L.)
b1-2 imit. Plot. III 4,2,15 (I 311 H.-S.)
b1 resp. Or., *Cels.* 7,5,5 (IV 22 B.)
b1 μολυβδίδας fort.imit. Plu., *Mor.* 1096c (VI 2,147,13 P.-W.-P.-G.)
b3 resp. Max. Tyr. 10,3e (115,3-7 H.)
b7-521b11 resp. Synes., *Ep.* 129 (221,6-9 G.)
c1 μήτε τοὺς ἐν παιδείᾳ κτέ resp. (ση) sch. Pl. ad loc. (247 G.)
c5 ἐν μακάρων νήσοις expl. sch. Pl. ad loc. (247 G.)
c8-521a9 resp. Alb., *Intr.* XXXIV 1 (167 L.); Cic., *Off.* I 9,28 (13,15-24 A.)
c8-520a4 resp. Alb., *Intr.* II 3 (7 L.)
c8-d2 resp. Ascl., *in Metaph.* 20,8-10 H.; —, *in Introd.* I ια,66-70 (27 T.)
c8-d1 τάς—ἀνάβασιν AFF. Clem., *Strom.* V 14,133,4 (II 416,9-11 S.); Eus., *PE* XIII 13,63 (II 225,5-7 M.)
c9-10 resp. Dam., *Pr.* 25² (I 65,8 W.)
d1 fort.resp. Plot. VI 8,7,7 (III 280 H.-S.)
d4-6 resp. Plot. VI 9,7,26-27 (III 319 H.-S.)
e1-520a4 resp. Pr., *de Decem Dub.* 38,3-6 (60 B.)
e1-3 resp. Cic., *Off.* I 25,85 (38,10-12 A.)
e3 μηχανᾶται expl. sch. Pl. ad loc. (248 G.)

0   a6-521b11 resp. Pr., *in R.* I 209,10-13 K.
a6-e3 resp. Ascl., *in Metaph.* 20,7-11 H.
a6-c1 resp. Olymp., *in Grg.* 32,4 (166,15-18 W.)
b1 τοιοῦτοι expl. sch. Pl. ad loc. (248 G.)
b2-6 imit. Them., *Or.* 2,36a (I 49,11-13 D.-N.); —, — 19,233a (I 339,7-8 D.-N.)
b5-6 resp. Dam., *in Phd.* I 114,2-3 (73 W.); fort.imit. Them., *Or.* 4,53d (I 77,2-3 D.-N.)
c6-7 imit. Aristaenet. II 19,5 (95 M.); Max. Tyr. 37,1a (426,12-13 H.)
d1-4 τὸ—οἰκεῖσθαι AFF. Stob. IV 1,109 (IV 55,8-10 H.); resp. Them., *Or.* 66d (I 97,19-98,3 D.-N.)
d2-4 resp. Pr., *in R.* II 4,2 K.
e4-521a4 expl. sch. Pl. ad loc. (248 G.)

1   a2-8 ἐν—πόλιν AFF. Stob. IV 1,110 (IV 55,12-18 H.)
a4 ζωῆς ἔμφρονος usurp. Plot. IV 7,10,5-6 (II 214 H.-S.); — V 5,10,12 (II 355 H.-S.); — VI 7,20,10-11 (III 239 H.-S.); — VI 8,16,34 (III 297 H.-S.)
b1-2 expl. sch. Pl. ad loc. (248 G.)
c1-541b5 resp. Apul., *Pl.* II 20,247 (96 B.)
c1-539d7 resp. Pr., *in R.* II 4,3 K.
c1-534d2 resp. Averr., *in R.* 29,21-22 R.; —, — 29,26-29 R; Elias, *in Porph.* 18,17 W.; Pr., *in Alc.* 194,1-2 (89 W.)
c1-532d1 resp. Hero, *Def.* 136,2 (IV 110,3-16 H.)
c1-531c5 resp. Olymp., *in Grg.* 32,4 (166,9-11 W.)
c2 imit. Iul., *Ep.* 59 (I 2,137,5 B.)
c2 ἀνάξει usurp. Pr., *Th. Pl.* I 9 (I 39,10 S.-W.)
c5-531d6 resp. Pr., *in R.* I 60,2-6 K.

c5-d4 Τοῦτο—ὄν AFF. Iambl., *Comm. Math.* 6 (23,4-10 F.)
c5-8 Τοῦτο—εἶναι AFF. Clem., *Strom.* V 14,133,5 (II 416,11-14 S.); Eus., *PE* XIII 13,63 (II 227,7-9 M.)
c5 ὀστράκου περιστροφή Phot. II 32 N.; expl. sch. Pl. ad loc. (248 G.)
c6-7 cit. Clem., *Strom.* IV 6,28,2 (II 260,18-19 S.)
c6 νυκτερινῆς ἡμέρας resp. Clem., *Strom.* V 14,105,2 (II 396,26-27 S.); Eus., *PE* XIII 13,32 (II 209,11-12 M.)
c7 τοῦ ὄντος ἐπάνοδον resp. Alb., *Intr.* VII 2 (43 L.)
c10-531d6 resp. sch. Pl. ad 514a1 (246 G.)
c10-522b1 resp. sch. Pl. ad loc. (248 G.)
d3-535a2 resp. Pr., *in Ti.* I 41,25-42,6 D.
d3-531d4 resp. Averr., *in R.* 75,1-14 R.
d3-522b6 Τί—οὔ AFF. Eus., *PE* XIV 13,1-4 (II 291,18-292,15 M.)
d3 resp. Pr., *in Ti.* I 41,2 D.
d3 (et alibi) ὁλκὸν *AB* I 111,1; Phot. II 12 N.
e4 τετεύτακεν Ael. Dion. τ 11 (144,13 E.); Phot. II 210 N.; Sud. τ 431 (IV 534,18-19 A.); Tim. 212 R.-K.; expl. sch. Pl. ad loc. (248 G.)

522 c1-531d4 resp. Phlp., *in de An.* 456,19-20 H.; Plu., *Mor.* 1001e (VI 1,119,1-5 H.-D.); Them., *Or.* 34,V (II 215,10-13 D.-N.)
c1-7 resp. Plot. I 3,6,3-4 (I 77 H.-S.)
c1 Οἷον τοῦτο τὸ κοινόν expl. sch. Pl. ad loc. (248 G.)
c5-527c11 resp. Gal., *Constit.* 6 (I 244 K.); fort.resp. Dam., *in Prm.* II 67,19 R.
d1-8 resp. Aristid., *Or.* 3,479 (I 3,457,1-7 L.-B.)
d1-7 Παγγέλοιον—ἠπίστατο AFF. Theon Sm. 4,2-8 H.
e4 ἐπαΐειν Hsch. ε 4090 (II 134 L.)

523 a1-526b10 resp. Pr., *in Ti.* I 392,17-19 D.
a1-3 Κινδυνεύει—οὐσίαν AFF. Theon Sm. 4,8-11 H.
a10-524d5 cit. Theon Sm. 4,11-19 H.
a10-b4 Δείκνυμι—ποιούσης AFF. Iambl., *Comm. Math.* 6 (23,10-14 F.); resp. Pr., *Th. Pl.* IV 5 (IV 19,25 S.-W.); expl. sch. Pl. ad loc. (249 G.)
a10 τὰ μὲν expl. sch. Pl. ad loc. (249 G.)
b2 τὰ δὲ expl. sch. Pl. ad loc. (249 G.)
b7 Οὐ πάνυ expl. sch. Pl. ad loc. (249 G.)
b9-525b3 Τὰ—εἴη AFF. Iambl., *Comm. Math.* 6 (23,14-26,3 F.)
b9-524a4 expl. sch. Pl. ad loc. (249 G.)
c10-d6 resp. Pr., *in Ti.* III 89,19-20 D.
e6 ἁφή Hsch. α 8628 (I 291 L.)

524 a6-525a11 resp. D. L. III 10 (I 125,2-3 L.)
c10 ἐντεῦθέν ποθεν usurp. Alb., *Intr.* XI 3 (67 L.)
d9-525a2 fort.resp. Plot. VI 6,4,23-24 (III 182 H.-S.)

525 a1 ἀγωγῶν resp. Hero, *Def.* 136,3 (IV 110,19-20 H.)
a3-530b4 resp. Plot. VI 3,16,20-24 (III 113 H.-S.)
a9-526c3 resp. Alb., *Intr.* VII 2 (43 L.)
b1 ἀγωγὰ resp. Theon Sm. 4,19-20 H.
b3-6 cit. Iambl., *Comm. Math.* 6 (26,4-9 F.)
b3-4 resp. Alb., *Intr.* VII 2 (43 L.)
b5-6 γενέσεως ἐξαναδύντι usurp. Clem., *Strom.* IV 25,159,2 (II 319,1 S.)
b10 Τί μήν expl. sch. Pl. ad loc. (249 G.)
c1-6 ἀνθάπτεσθαι—οὐσίαν cit. Theon Sm. 4,20-5,4 H.
c5 resp. Clem., *Strom.* IV 6,28,2 (II 260,18-19 S.)
c8-d8 cit. Iambl., *Comm. Math.* 6 (26,10-14 F.)
d5-8 Τοῦτό—διαλέγηται AFF. Theon Sm. 5,5-7 H.
d5 Τοῦτό γε expl. sch. Pl. ad loc. (249 G.)

d6 ἀναγκάζει expl. sch. Pl. ad loc. (249 G.)
d8-e1 fort.resp. Dam., Pr. 46 (I 92,8-9 R.)
d9-e1 αὐτὸ τὸ ἕν expl. sch. Pl. ad loc. (249 G.)
d9 τοὺς περὶ ταῦτα δεινοὺς expl. sch. Pl. ad loc. (249 G.)
e1-4 resp. Plot. VI 2,2,39-40 (III 59 H.-S.)
e2 κερματίζῃς expl. sch. Pl. ad loc. (249 G.)

6 a6-c3 cit. Iambl., Comm. Math. 6 (26,14-21 F.)
b5-9 τόδε—γίγνεσθαι AFF. Theon Sm. 5,8-10 H.; resp. Olymp., in Grg. 21,4 (117,3-5 W.)
b6 Theaetetum nominat exempli gratia sch. Pl. ad loc. (250 G.)
c1-3 expl. sch. Pl. ad loc. (250 G.)
c8 δεύτερον κτέ resp. sch. Pl. ad loc. (250 G.)
c10-527c11 resp. Alb., Intr. VII 2 (43 L.); Pr., in Ti. I 50,8-9 D.
d1-6 resp. Averr., in R. 76,23-26 R.
d2-3 πρὸς—στρατιᾶς AFF. Theon Sm. 5,10-13 H.
d9-e7 σκοπεῖσθαι—προσήκει AFF. Iambl., Comm. Math. 6 (26,22-28 F.)

7 a6-b6 cit. Iambl., Comm. Math. 6 (27,2-3 F.)
a6-b1 ὡς γὰρ κτέ expl. sch. Pl. ad loc. (250 G.)
b9-11 Ὁλκὸν—ἔχομεν AFF. Iambl., Comm. Math. 6 (27,4-6 F.)
b9 Ὁλκὸν πρὸς ἀλήθειαν usurp. Pr., Th. Pl. IV 34 (IV 101,21-22 S.-W.)
b9 Ὁλκὸν resp. Theon Sm. 4,19-20 H.
b11 οὐ δέον expl. sch. Pl. ad loc. (250 G.)
c2 καλλιπόλει usurp. Them., Or. 21,248a (II 24,18 D.-N.)
c6 πρὸς—ἀποδέχεσθαι AFF. Simp., in Ph. 510,28 D.
c7 ὅλῳ καὶ παντὶ expl. sch. Pl. ad loc. (250 G.)
d1-530c1 resp. Alb., Intr. VII 3 (43 L.)
d1 Τί δὲ; τρίτον expl. sch. Pl. ad loc. (250 G.)
d2-4 resp. Averr., in R. 76,27 R.
d5-e3 Ἡδὺς—ὁρᾶται AFF. Nicom., Ar. I 3,7 (8,19-9,4 H.); Theon Sm. 3,8-15 H.
d5 Ἡδὺς Phot. I 255 N.; expl. sch. Pl. ad loc. (250 G.)
d6-528a3 resp. Pr., in Euc. 20,10-11 F.; —, — 29,6-30,5 F.
d6-e3 resp. Bess., in Cal. Pl. 598,15-20 M.
d7-e6 ἐν—ὠφελίαν AFF. Iambl., Comm. Math. 6 (22,19-23,4 F.)
d7-e3 resp. Elias, in Porph. 23,5 W.; Max. Tyr. 10,3e (115,3-7 H.)
d7-e2 cit. Pr., in Euc. 20,18-21 F.
d7-8 imit. Gr. Nyss., Mort. 54,18 H.
d8-e3 resp. Plu., Mor. 718d (IV 261,24-27 H.)
d8-e2 cit. Alb., Intr. XXVII 3 (131 L.); Andron. Call., Def. 192,25-28 M.; Pr., in Euc. 20,18-21 F.
d8-e1 resp. Iambl., VP 16,70 (40,6-8 D.); Pr., in Alc. 194,18-195,3 (90 W.); imit. Clem., Strom. I 6,33,3 (II 22,5-6 S.)
d8 ἑκάστου expl. sch. Pl. ad loc. (250 G.)
d8 ἐκκαθαίρεταί resp. Hero, Def. 136,3 (IV 110,19-20 H.); usurp. Meth., Symp. IX 4 (118,9 B.)
e1 τυφλούμενον resp. Pr., in Ti. III 352,9 D.; Syr., in Metaph. 96,13 K.
e2-3 κρεῖττον—ὁρᾶται cit. Boet., Arith. I 1 (10,3-6 F.)
e2-3 μόνῳ—ὁρᾶται imit. Iambl., Comm. Math. 6 (27,6 F.)
e2 κρεῖττον—ὀμμάτων AFF. Iambl., VP 16,70 (40,8-9 D.); cit. Pr., in Euc. 30,2-3 F.

8 a7 τὸ ἑξῆς expl. sch. Pl. ad loc. (250 G.)
a9-b2 cit. Alb., Intr. VII 3 (43 L.)
a9 expl. sch. Pl. ad loc. (250 G.)
b2-3 resp. D. L. VIII 83 (II 431,23 L.)
b4-5 δοκεῖ οὔπω ηὑρῆσθαι expl. sch. Pl. ad loc. (251 G.)

c3-4 cit. Iambl., *Comm. Math.* 6 (27,7 F.)
c4-8 resp. Stob. IV 18ª,10 (IV 414,18-21 H.) (= Plu., fr. 147 (VII 90 S.))
c5 κολουόμενα expl. sch. Pl. ad loc. (251 G.)
c6-7 ὅμως—αὐξάνεται AFF. Plu., *Mor.* 1094d (VI 2,143,11-12 P.-W.)
c7 χάριτος expl. sch. Pl. ad loc. (251 G.)
d1 ἐπίχαρι—ἔχει usurp. Iambl., *Comm. Math.* 6 (27,9 F.)
d2-3 resp. Pr., *in Euc.* 116,20-22 F.
d3 πραγματείαν usurp. Alb., *Intr.* VI 3 (29 L.)
d5 ἀστρονομίαν expl. sch. Pl. ad loc. (251 G.)
d9 γελοίως ἔχει expl. sch. Pl. ad loc. (251 G.)

529   a1-2 αὕτη—ἄγει AFF. Theon Sm. 5,16-17 H.
a2 εἰς τὸ ἄνω ὁρᾶν imit. Meth., *Symp.* V 4,118 (57,19-20 B.)
a3-530c1 resp. Pr., *Hyp.* I 1 (2,1-5 M.)
b3-c3 resp. Gal., *de Usu Part.* III 3,183 (I 134,3-6 H.)
b4 ἄνω—βλέπειν usurp. Iambl., *Comm. Math.* 6 (27,9 F.)
b5 cit. Iambl., *Comm. Math.* 6 (27,11 F.)
c2 ἐξ ὑπτίας νέων Poll. VII 138 (II 89,26-27 B.)
c4 Δίκην expl. sch. Pl. ad loc. (251 G.)
c7-530c1 resp. Plot. VI 3,16,20-24 (III 113 H.-S.)
c7-d5 resp. Simp., *in Cat.* 265,8-10 K.
d1-4 resp. Pr., *in Prm.* 736,14-16 C.
d2-4 resp. Pr., *in Cra.* CXXVI (74,18-20 P.)
d2-3 ἐν—ἀριθμῷ AFF. Plot. VI 6,4,20-21 (III 182 H.-S.); resp. Pr., *in R.* II 18,2 K.; —, *in Ti.* III 19,17-18 D.
e1 Δαιδάλου expl. sch. Pl. ad loc. (251 G.)
e5-530a1 ἐπισκοπεῖν—συμμετρίας AFF. Iambl., *Comm. Math.* 6 (27,13-16 F.)

530   a3-b4 expl. sch. Pl. ad loc. (251 G.)
b1-4 οὐκ—λαβεῖν AFF. Iambl., *Comm. Math.* 6 (27,16-19 F.)
b2-3 cit. Plot. II 1,2,9-10 (I 147 H.-S.)
d4 ἀντίστροφον αὐτοῦ expl. sch. Pl. ad loc. (251 G.)
d6-9 resp. Theon Sm. 205,2-4 H.
d6-7 cit. Alb., *Intr.* VII 4 (45 L.)
d7-8 αὗται—Πυθαγόρειοί cit. Theon Sm. 6,1-2 H.
e3-6 ἡμεῖς—ἀφήκειν AFF. Iambl., *Comm. Math.* 6 (27,20-22 F.)
e5-531c4 Μή—ἑκάτεροι AFF. Eus., *PE* XIV 13,5-8 (II 292,17-293,8 M.)
e6 οἵ expl. sch. Pl. ad loc. (252 G.)
e6 ἀφήκειν Phot. α 3335 (I 305 Th.); expl. sch. Pl. ad loc. (252 G.)

531   a1-b4 τὰς—στρεβλοῦντας AFF. Theon Sm. 6,2-10 H.
a4-b1 resp. Plu., *Mor.* 389d (III 12,24-25 P.-S.)
a5-6 οἷον—θηρευόμενοι imit. Panaet. *ap.* Porph., *in Harm.* 66,13 D.
a5-6 ἐκ—θηρευόμενοι AFF. Theon Sm. 17,1 H.
b1 ὦτα—προστησάμενοι AFF. Pr., *in Euc.* 41,1-2 F.; usurp. Pr., *in Ti.* II 170,10 D.
b1 προστησάμενοι usurp. Pr., *in R.* I 177,26 K.
b2-3 ταῖς—παρέχοντας cit. Theon Sm. 17,1-2 H.; imit. Aristaenet. I 14,5 (35 M.)
b3 κολλόπων Tim. 135 R.-K.; expl. sch. Pl. ad loc. (252 G.)
c3 τίνες prius-οὔ AFF. Theon Sm. 6,11-12 H.
c6-d4 Χρήσιμον—ἀνόνητα AFF. Iambl., *Comm. Math.* 6 (27,22-28,1 F.)
c6-7 Χρήσιμον—ἄχρηστον cit. Theon Sm. 6,12-7,1 H.
c9-d3 καὶ—πραγματείαν AFF. Theon Sm. 7,1-4 H.
d7-541b5 resp. sch. Pl. ad 514a1 (246 G.); — ad loc. (252 G.)
d7-8 resp. Alb., *Intr.* VII 4 (45 L.)
d9 οἱ—διαλεκτικοί AFF. Theon Sm. 7,4-5 H.
e4-5 cit. Theon Sm. 7,5-6 H.

INDEX TESTIMONIORUM 341

a3 ἐλέγομεν expl. sch. Pl. ad loc. (252 G.)
a5-b2 cit. Clem., *Strom.* V 11,74,2 (II 375,25-376,2 S.); Theon Sm. 7,6-7 H.; resp. Pr., *in Alc.* 29,4-5 (13 W.); expl. sch. Pl. ad loc. (252 G.)
b4 τὴν πορείαν usurp. Pr., *Th. Pl.* I 9 (I 39,21 S.-W.)
b6-d1 Ἡ—τόπῳ AFF. Iambl., *Comm. Math.* 6 (28,1-14 F.); imit. Gr. Nyss., *Hom. in Cant.* II (48,12-14 L.); expl. sch. Pl. ad loc. (252 G.)
b6-7 resp. Clem., *Strom.* IV 6,28,2 (II 260,18-19 S.)
c1 φαντάσματα καὶ σκιὰς imit. Meth., *Symp.* VIII 3 (83,21-22 B.)
c3-d1 cit. Theon Sm. 7,7-8 H.
d5 ἐπανιτέον Hsch. ε 4296 (II 137 L.)
d8-e3 expl. sch. Pl. ad loc. (252 G.)
d8 τῆς τοῦ διαλέγεσθαι δυνάμεως imit. Alb., *Intr.* VI 10 (37 L.)
e3 ἀνάπαυλα καὶ τέλος usurp. Plot. VI 9,8,43 (III 322 H.-S.)
e3 ἀνάπαυλα usurp. Aen. Gaz., *Thphr.* 8,1 C.
e3 τέλος τῆς πορείας usurp. Plot. I 3,1,16-17 (I 73 H.-S.); — VI 9,11,45 (III 328 H.-S.)

b1-e3 resp. Averr., *in R.* 75,15-18 R.
b1-c6 resp. Ascl., *in Metaph.* 150,17-19 H.; Pr., *in Euc.* 29,18-24 F.; Simp., *in An.* 276,34-277,1 H.; —, *in Cat.* 229,32 K.; —, *in Ph.* 12,8-9 D.
b4 πρὸς δόξας ἀνθρώπων usurp. Pr., *Th. Pl.* I 9 (I 39,17-18 S.-W.)
b6-c3 cit. Alb., *Intr.* VII 4 (45 L.)
c3-4 ᾧ—οἶδεν AFF. Pr., *in Euc.* 29,21-22 F.; cit. Phlp., *in Cat.* 141,19-20 B.; Simp., *in An.* 276,35-37 H.; resp. Pr., *in Euc.* 30,8-9 F.; —, *in Prm.* 1034,2-5 C.
c7-534a8 resp. Pr., *in Ti.* III 167,5-8 D.
c7-e2 resp. Dam., *in Phd.* II 37,2-3 (309 W.)
c7-d7 Οὐκοῦν—ὡρισάμεθα AFF. Stob. II 2,1 (II 15,15-16,8 W.)
c7 διαλεκτικὴ expl. sch. Pl. ad loc. (253 G.)
c8 τὰς ὑποθέσεις ἀναιροῦσα imit. Alb., *Intr.* VII 3 (43 L.)
c8 ἀναιροῦσα imit. Meth., *Arbitr.* VI 7 (162,5 B.)
d1-2 cit. Andron. Call., *Def.* 192,25-28 M.; resp. Bas., *Leg. Lib. Gent.* IX 61-62 (56 B.); Clem., *Paed.* II ix 81,1 (I 206,31-207,1 S.); imit. Clem., *Strom.* II 20,118,5 (II 177,8-9 S.); Plot. I 8,13,24-25 (I 136 H.-S.)
d2-3 imit. Clem., *Protr.* VI 68,4 (I 52,15-16 S.)
d2 τὸ τῆς ψυχῆς ὄμμα resp. Elias, *in Porph.* 23,5 W.; Pr., *in Ti.* III 352,9 D.; fort.resp. Anast. Sin., *VD* II 5,67-68 (54 U.); usurp. (latine) Apul., *Pl.* II 11,236 (89 B.); —, — II 22,251 (99 B.); (latine) Boet., *Arith.* I 1 (10,3 F.); Clem., *Paed.* II i 1,2 (I 154,7 S.); —, *Strom.* I 1,10,1 (II 8,2 S.); Dam., *Pr.* 117 (I 302,5-6 R.); Eus., *Or. Const.* XI (165,22 H.); Or., *Lib. Arb.* 25,2 (220,37 J.); Ph., *Decal.* (14) 68 (IV 284,16 C.-W.); —, *Det.* (8) 22 (I 263,13 C.-W.); —, *Deus* (37) 181 (II 93,17 C.-W.); —, *Ebr.* (11) 44 (II 178,24 C.-W.); —, — (12) 58 (IV 14,11 C.-W.); —, — (15) 70 (IV 17,10 C.-W.); —, *Her.* (17) 89 (III 21,13 C.-W.); —, *Migr.* (8) 39 (III 276,4 C.-W.); —, — (9) 49 (II 278,2 C.-W.); —, — (30) 167 (III 300,27 C.-W.); —, — (34) 191 (III 305,25 C.-W.); —, *Mos. I* (33) 185 (IV 164,20 C.-W.); —, — (52) 289 (IV 189,6 C.-W.); —, *Mut.* (1) 3 (III 156,13 C.-W.); —, — (37) 203 (III 191,22 C.-W.); —, *Plant.* (5) 22 (II 138,9-10 C.-W.); —, *Post.* (2) 8 (II 2,20-21 C.-W.); —, *Praem.* (6) 37 (V 344,6 C.-W.); —, *Sacr.* (6) 36 (I 217,7 C.-W.); —, — (19) 69 (I 230,10 C.-W.); —, — (22) 78 (I 234,13 C.-W.); —, *Sobr.* (1) 3 (II 215,16 C.-W.); —, *Somn. I* (19) 117 (III 230,9 C.-W.); —, — (26) 164 (III 240,3 C.-W.); —, — II (23) 160 (III 284,21 C.-W.); —, *Spec. I* (5) 37 (V 10,5 C.-W.); —, — III (1) 4 (V 151,7 C.-W.); —, — IV (1) 140 (V 240,13 C.-W.); Pr., *in Alc.* 194,18 (90 W.); —, *in Euc.* 20,18 F.; —, *Th. Pl.* I 9 (I 39,12 S.-W.); —, *in Ti.* I 206,21 D.; Simp., *in Cat.* 8,5 K.; imit. Aen. Gaz., *Thphr.* 28,23-24 C.; Alb., *Intr.* XXVII 3 (131 L.); *Corp. Herm.* VII 1 (I 81,6 N.-F.); Gr. Naz., *Carm. semet* 211 (*PG* 37,986); Gr. Nyss., *Hom. in Cant.* I (4,4 L.); —, — V (170,1 L.): —, *Melet.* (442,11-12 S.); —, *Mort.* IX (47,11 J.); Meth., *Symp.* VII 2,153 (72,21 B.); Ph., *Conf.* (20) 92 (II 246,23 C.-W.); —, — (21) 100 (II 248,12-13 C.-W.); —, *Ios.* (20) 106 (IV 83,16 C.-W.); —, *Opif.* (23) 71 (I 24,7 C.-W.); —, *Plant.* (13) 58 (II 145,10 C.-W.); —, — (41) 169 (II 167,21 C.-W.);

—, Post. (6) 18 (II 4,22 C.-W.); —, — (34) 118 (II 26,11 C.-W.); —, — (48) 167 (II 37,7 C.-W.); —, Prob. (1) 5 (VI 2,8 C.-W.); —, Somn. (34) 129 (III 247,24 C.-W.); —, Spec. I (6) 49 (V 12,16-17 C.-W.); —, — III (1) 2 (V 150,14 C.-W.); —, — III (1) 6 (V 151,17 C.-W.); —, — IV(8) 191 (V 253,6-7 C.-W.); Psell., Orat. Min. 8,107 (33 L.); Synes., Ep. 154 (275,16 G.)
d2 ὄμμα κατορωρυγμένον imit. Clem., Protr. XI 113,2 (I 79,32 S.); —, — XI 114,1 (I 80,16 S.)
d2 κατορωρυγμένον resp. Syr., in Metaph. 96,13 K.; usurp. Clem., Strom. VI 6,44,3 (II 453,27 S.); Nicom., Ar. I 3,7 (9,1 H.); imit. Syn., Ep. 137 (233,9-10 G.)
d3-4 resp. Alex. Aphr., in Metaph. 122,4-5 H.
d3 συνερίθοις Tim. 202 R.-K.; resp. Ascl., in Metaph. 104,16 H.
d4-e2 resp. Pr., in Ti. I 249,7-9 D.
d5-e2 expl. sch. Pl. ad loc. (253 G.)
d5-6 resp. Pr., in Euc. 11,16-19 F.
d6-e2 resp. Alb., Intr. VII 5 (47 L.)
d7-534a8 resp. Calc., Ti. CCXXXI (254,13-14 W.); —, — CCCXLII (334,18-20 W.)
d7-e5 resp. Gal., Anat. Adm. VI 13 (II 581 K.); —, in Hipp. Art. 15 (XVIII 1,685 K.); —, Meth. Med. 12 (X 772 K.); —, Simpl. Medic. 5 (XI 717 K.)
e1-2 resp. Gal., Diff. II 7 (VII 354 K.)
e7-534a8 vide ad 509d6-511e5; resp. sch. Pl. ad loc. (253 G.)
e7-534a1 resp. Calc., Ti. CCXXXI (254,14 W.) (= Porph., in Ti. 102,25-26 S.)
e8-534a2 resp. Plot. V 9,7,3-5 (II 420 H.-S.)

534   **a1** fort.resp. Clem., Strom. II 4,16,1 (II 120,28 S.)
a5-7 resp. Pr., in R. I 287,27-288,2 K.
a5 πίστιν et εἰκασίαν usurp. Alb., Intr. VII 5 (47 L.)
a7-8 imit. Meth., Res. I 26,2 (254,4-5 B.)
b3-535a1 resp. Pr., in Prm. 622,22-24 C.
b3-6 resp. Anon., Prol. Plat. II 11,2-4 (23 W.); Plot. I 3,4,2 (I 76 H.-S.)
b3-4 resp. sch. Pl. ad loc. (253 G.)
b8-d10 resp. Alb., Intr. XXXIV 1 (167 L.)
b8-d1 ὅς—ἐπικαταδαρθεῖν AFF. Stob. II 8,36 (II 162,24-163,7 W.); resp. Pr., in R. I 285,6-8 K.
b9-c1 cit. Pr., in Prm. VII 58,23-24 K.-L.; resp. Pr., in Prm. VII 64,17-19 K.-L.
b9 ἀφελών usurp. Plot. IV 7,10,30 (II 215 H.-S.)
c1-2 resp. Pr., in Prm. 698,26-29 C.
c3 ἀπτῶτι λόῳ usurp. Pr., in R. I 285,30 K.
c4-d1 imit. Clem., Paed. II x 106,1-2 (I 220,15-22 S.)
c4-5 resp. Phlp., in Cat. 141,19-20 B.
c6 δόξῃ, οὐκ ἐπιστήμῃ usurp. Plot. I 3,4,8-9 (I 76 H.-S.)
c7-d1 εἰς Ἅιδου ἀφικόμενον ἐπικαταδαρθεῖν usurp. Plot. I 8,13,25-26 (I 136 H.-S.)
d1 ἐπικαταδαρθεῖν Did., Plat. 401 M.; expl. sch. Pl. ad loc. (253 G.)
d8-535a1 resp. Pr., in Prm. 989,11-13 C.
e2-535a1 Ἆρ'—μαθημάτων AFF. Stob. II 2,2 (II 16,10-13 W.); resp. Pr., in Ti. I 42,3-4 D.
e2-3 θριγκὸς—διαλεκτική resp. Elias, in APr. 136,5 W.; —, — 137,1 W.; Mich. Acom., Or. 3 (I 73,3-4 L.); usurp. Clem., Strom. VI 10,81,4 (II 472,17-18 S.)
e2-3 θριγκὸς τοῖς μαθήμασιν cit. Pr., in Cra. II (1,16 P.); —, in Enc. 42,9-11 F.; —, — 44,10-11 F.; —, in Prm. 649,11-12 C.; —, — 995, 22-23 C.; —, de Prov. 29,5 (138 B.); —, — 49,13 (158 B.); —, Th. Pl. I 9 (I 39,10 S.-W.); resp. Alex. Aphr., in Top. 1,14-15 W.; Olymp., Prol. 14,22 B.
e2 θριγκὸς Phot. I 283 N.; Sud. τ 966 (IV 589,13-14 A.); resp. Phlp., Aet. VI 19 (181,7-8 R.); Pr., in R. I 283,13 K.; sch. Iambl., Comm. Math. 4 (18,4 F.) (101,11 F.); fort.resp. Epict. III 26,15 (348,19 S.); usurp. Alb., Intr. VII 5 (47 L.); Them., Or. 21,257c (II 39,16 D.-N.); expl. sch. Pl. ad loc. (253 G.)

INDEX TESTIMONIORUM 343

a3-536a7 resp. sch. Pl. ad loc. (254 G.)
b5-c3 resp. Alb., *Intr.* I 3 (5 L.)
b5 δριμύτητα expl. sch. Pl. ad loc. (254 G.)
b6-9 πολύ—σώματος AFF. Stob. II 31,110^q (II 224,6-8 W.)
c1 ἄρρατον *AB* I 446,15; *An. Bachm.* I 145,21; Did., *Plat.* 400 M.; Phot. α 2869 (I 264 Th.); Tim. 43 R.-K.; Zonar. I 301 T.; expl. sch. Pl. ad loc. (254 G.)
c5-8 fort.imit. Synes., *Ep.* 129 (221,9 G.)
d1-7 Πρῶτον—φιλοπονίαν AFF. Stob. III 29,81 (III 653,1-7 H.)
d9-e5 Οὐκοῦν—μολύνηται AFF. Stob. III 12,22 (III 449,8-13 H.)
d9-e1 ἀνάπηρον ψυχὴν Phot. α 1597 (I 162 Th.)

a7 οἱ δὲ ἄρχουσι expl. sch. Pl. ad loc. (254 G.)
b1-5 ὡς—καταντλήσομεν AFF. Iambl., *Comm. Math.* 6 (22,13-18 F.)
c3 προπεπηλακισμένην expl. sch. Pl. ad loc. (254 G.)
d1-3 Σόλωνι—πόνοι AFF. Stob. II 31,110^m (II 223,17-19 W.)
d1 Σόλωνι versum Solonis affert sch. Pl. ad loc. (254 G.)
d3 cit. Olymp., *in Alc.* 191,5-6 (120 W.); resp. sch. Pl. ad loc. (254 G.)
d5-537a2 Τά—πέφυκεν AFF. Stob. II 31,110² (II 228,4-14 W.)
e3-4 ψυχῇ κτέ expl. sch. Pl. ad loc. (254 G.)
e6-539d7 resp. Averr., *in R.* 77,13-78,1 R.
e6-537a2 Μή—πέφυκεν AFF. Stob. II 31,110^p (II 224,2-4 W.)

a4-7 resp. Iul., *Or.* I 11 (I 1,23,7-10 B.); —, — I 12 (I 1,23,20-27 B.)
a6-7 imit. Them., *Or.* 9,121d (I 183,23-24 D.-N.)
a10-11 εἰς ἀριθμόν ad Hom. (*Od.* λ 449) refert sch. Pl. ad loc., versum partim afferens (254 G.)
a10 ἐντρεχέστατος *AB* I 94,30
b4-5 κόποι—πολέμιοι AFF. *Mantiss. Prov.* III 34 (II 778,4-5 L.-S.); Plu., *Mor.* 8c (I 15,22-23 P.-W.-P.-G.); Stob. II 31,42 (II 209,4 W.)
b8-c3 ἐκ—φύσεως AFF. Theon Sm. 2,22-3,3 H.
c1-5 τά—ἐγγένηται AFF. Iambl., *Comm. Math.* 6 (22,5-9 F.)
c1-3 τά—φύσεως AFF. Stob. II 31,43 (II 209,6-8 W.)
c2 σύνοψιν οἰκειότητός Poll. VI 159 (II 42,1 B.)
c7 resp. Simp., *in Cat.* 70,20 K.
d2-e4 resp. Pr., *in Prm.* 648,10-15 C.; —, — 676,16-19 C.
d5-7 ὀμμάτων—ἰέναι AFF. Iambl., *Comm. Math.* 6 (22,9-11 F.)
e1-539d2 resp. Pr., *in Prm.* 648,12-15 C.; —, — 991,14-20 C.
e9 ὑποβολιμαῖος Hsch. υ 576 (IV 211 S.)

a6 ᾔδει Did., *Plat.* 405 M.
c3 μέλειν τὸ μηδέν expl. sch. Pl. ad loc. (254 G.)

b1-7 resp. Pr., *in Prm.* 648,10-15 C.; —, — 676,16-19 C.; fort.resp. Plu., *Mor.* 769e (IV 391,8-9 H.)
b1-2 resp. sch. Pl. ad loc. (254 G.)
b5-6 χαίροντες—σπαράττειν AFF. Plu., *Mor.* 78e (I 157,5-7 P.-W.-P.-G.)
b6-7 resp. Theophyl. Achr., *ad Disc.* 2 (157,28-29 G.)
c5-d1 resp. sch. Pl. ad loc. (254 G.)
d8-540c2 resp. Averr., *in R.* 78,2-9 R.
e2 Ἀμέλει expl. sch. Pl. ad loc. (255 G.)

a7-8 resp. Pr., *in R.* I 280,27-281,3 K.
a7 cit. Pr., *in Prm.* 997,28-30 C.; —, — VII 58,19-20 K.-L.; resp. Dam., *Pr.* 25² (I 65,5-6 W.); —, — 34 (I 106,3-5 W.); —, — 41 (I 125,10 W.)
b7-c9 resp. Averr., *in R.* 78,10-16 R.
b7-c2 resp. Aristid., *Or.* 3,316 (I 3,399,15-20 L.-B.); Demetr. Cyd., *Ep.* 7,13 (I 32 L.); sch. Aristid. 3,316 (646,35-647,2 D.)

c1 ἐάν—συναναιρῇ AFF. Aristid., *Or.* 2,41 (I 2,156,21 L.-B.); resp. Aristid., *Or.* 3,616 (I 3,497,17 L.-B.)
c5-8 fort.resp. Pr., *in Ti.* III 291,2-4 D.
c5 τὰς ἀρχούσας resp. (ση) sch. Pl. ad loc. (255 G.)
d1-541a8 πόλεώς—ὀνήσειν AFF. Stob. IV 1,113 (IV 57,11-58,4 H.); resp. Averr., *in R.* 78,17-25 R.

541 a3 τρόποισι expl. sch. Pl. ad loc. (255 G.)
b2 ἅδην Did., *Plat.* 400 M.; expl. sch. Pl. ad loc. (255 G.)

LIBER OCTAVUS

543 a1-569c9 resp. Averr., *in R.* 79,24-80,16 R.
a1-b4 Εἶεν—πᾶσι AFF. Stob. IV 1,116 (IV 67,16-68,2 H.)
b8 ἀθλητὰς πολέμου usurp. Clem., *Strom.* VI 14,112,2 (II 488,2-3 S.)
c4-5 ἀλλ'—ἐξετραπόμεθα AFF. Thom. Mag., *Ecl.* 390,10-11 R.
c5 πόθεν δεῦρο ἐξετραπόμεθα imit. Them., *Or.* 2,34b (I 46,7 D.-N.); —, — 4,57c (I 82,13 D.-N.)
c7-544e6 σχεδὸν—Τί μήν AFF. Stob. IV 1,117 (IV 68,4-69,9 H.)
c7-544c7 resp. Theod. Metoch. 98 (639 M.)

544 a1-e2 resp. sch. Pl. ad loc. (255 G.)
a1-3 resp. Alb., *Intr.* XXXIV 3 (169 L.)
b2 ἀναλαβὼν τὸν λόγον usurp. Niceph. Greg., *Flor.* 90,776 L.
b5 Πάλιν—παλαιστής usurp. Them., *Or.* 2,36a (I 49,4 D.-N.)
b5 λαβὴν resp. Cyr., *Gloss.* λαβ 1 (105 D.)
b5 ὥσπερ παλαιστής expl. sch. Pl. ad loc. (255 G.)
b9-e6 resp. Herm., *in Phdr.* 164,29 C.
b10 resp. Arist., *Pol.* Δ 7,1293a42-b1 B.; sch. Aeschin. *in Tim.* 4 (8,27 D.)
c1-577b9 resp. Pr., *in R.* I 13,23-29 K.
c1-569c9 resp. Arist., *Pol.* E 12,1316a20-23 B.; D. L. III 82-83 (I 154,6-20 L.); Olymp., *in Grg.* 1,13 (14,7-21 W.); Plb. VI 5,1 (II 244,12-14 B.-W.)
c1-d4 resp. Averr., *in R.* 80,17-23 R.
c2 ὑπὸ τῶν πολλῶν expl. sch. Pl. ad loc. (256 G.)
c3 resp. Demetr. Cyd., *Ep.* 4,8 (I 26 L.); Plb. VI 45,1 (II 295,7-11 B.-W.); sch. Aristid. 3,131 (518,25-26 D.); — 3,380 (678,27-29 D.); sch. D. *ad Lept.* 490,21 (IX 506,27-507,2 D.); fort.resp. Max. Tyr. 16,4k (203,10-11 H.)
d6-7 imit. Plu., *Mor.* 826c (V 1,128,4-5 H.-P.-D.); Them., *Or.* 2,35a (I 47,14-15 D.-N.)
d6 καὶ ἀνθρώπων εἴδη expl. sch. Pl. ad loc. (256 G.)
d7-8 ἐκ—πέτρας cit. Pr., *in R.* I 221,16-17 K.; expl. sch. Pl. ad loc. (256 G.)
e1 ῥέψαντα Hsch. ρ 226 (III 426 S.)

545 a2-580c8 resp. Apul., *Pl.* II 14,240-16,242 (91-93 B.); —, — II 28,262-263 (106-107 B.)
a2-569c9 resp. Pr., *in Ti.* III 282,14-18 D.
a2-550b7 resp. Pr., *in Alc.* 138,10-11 (62-63 W.)
a2-3 resp. Olymp., *in Alc.* 167,3 (106 W.)
a3 resp. sch. D. *ad Lept.* 490,21 (IX 506,27-507,2 D.)
c8-548c7 resp. Alb., *Intr.* XXXIV 3 (169 L.); sch. Pl. ad 543a1 (255 G.); sch. Pl. ad loc. (256 G.)
d1-2 expl. sch. Pl. ad loc. (256 G.)
d5-592b6 resp. Alfar., *Plat. Phil.* VI 25 (14 R.-W.)
d5-547a5 resp. Anon., *Prol. Plat.* XI 27,9 (51 W.); Pr., *in Euc.* 23,21-26 F.; —, *in R.* I 15,25-26 K.; —, — II 1,1-80,27 K.; —, *in Ti.* I 193,13-14 D.; —, — III 242,3 D.; —, — III 244,3 D.

d5-546d8 resp. Ascl., *in Introd.* II λβ,63-73 (68 T.); Pr., *in Euc.* 8,12-20 F.
d5-546c6 resp. Boet., *Arith.* II 46 (151,23-25 F.)
d5-546a3 resp. Cic., *Div.* II 2,6 (79,19-22 G.); Olymp., *in Alc.* 2,6-9 (1 W.)
d5-e3 resp. Nicom., *Ar.* II 24,11 (131,8-10 H.)
d8-e1 ὅπως—ἔμπεσε AFF. Pr., *in R.* II 4,6-7 K.; —, — II 79,29 K.; imit. Plot. III 7,11,7 (I 386 H.-S.); expl. sch. Pl. ad loc. (256 G.)
e2 imit. Aristid., *Or.* 50,56 (439,29-30 K.)
e2 ἐρεσχηλούσας Did., *Plat.* 401 M.
e3 ὑψηλολογουμένας cit. Pr., *in R.* II 7,27 K.; —, *in Ti.* III 200,5-6 D.

a1-547a5 resp. Arist., *Pol.* E 12,1316a1-2 B.; sch. Pl. ad loc. (256 G.)
a1-b3 resp. Pr., *Th. Pl.* IV 29 (IV 87,10-11 S.-W.)
a1-3 χαλεπὸν—λυθήσεται AFF. Simp., *in Cael.* 300,18-19 H.; resp. Averr., *in R.* 87,20-21 R.; Pr., *in Ti.* I 287,25-27 D.
a1 resp. et partim AFF. Pr., *in R.* II 8,25-28 K.
a2-b3 resp. Pr., *in R.* II 7,10-13 K.
a2-3 οὐδ'—χρόνον AFF. Pr., *in R.* II 11,17-18 K.
a2 γενομένῳ—ἔστιν AFF. Phlp., *Aet.* VI (120,6 R.); cit. Olymp., *in Alc.* 2,8 (1 W.); Pr., *in Ti.* I 296,4-5 D.; resp. Epict. II 5,12 (127,9 S.); Phlp., *Aet.* XVII (589,8-9 R.); Pr., *in Ti.* I 287,26 D.; —, — I 293,18 D.; —, — III 212,25-28 D.; imit. Phlp., *Opif.* 221,13 R.
a3 τὸν ἅπαντα μενεῖ χρόνον expl. sch. Pl. ad loc. (256-257 G.)
a4-7 resp. Pr., *in Alc.* 121,13-15 (55 W.)
a4-6 resp. Pr., *in Euc.* 150,3-5 F.
a4-5 resp. Dam., *Pr.* 81 (I 184,17 R.)
a4 resp. Pr., *in R.* II 12,15-16 K.
a4 οὐ μόνον φυτοῖς AFF. Pr., *in R.* II 12,20-21 K.
a4 φυτοῖς ἐγγείοις fort.resp. Plu., *Mor.* 911c (V 3,1,4 H.-P.-D.)
a4 ἐγγείοις expl. sch. Pl. ad loc. (257 G.)
a5 resp. Pr., *in R.* II 13,4-5 K.; —, — II 19,7-8 K.; —, — II 20,15 K.; —, — II 31,20-21 K.; —, *in Ti.* I 162,30 D. (= Porph., *in Ti.* 13,5-6 S.); imit. Eus., *PE* VI 6,44 (I 307,3-5 M.)
a6-8 resp. Pr., *in Ti.* III 93,30-94,1 D.
a7-b2 γένους—τεύξονται AFF. Pr., *in R.* II 29,24-25 K.; resp. Pr., *Th. Pl.* IV 29 (IV 87,10-11 S.-W.)
a7 resp. Pr., *in R.* II 14,3-7 K.; —, *in Ti.* I 116,19-20 D.
a8 resp. Pr., *in Ti.* I 162,29-30 D.; —, — I 288,4 D.
b1-2 οὐδὲν—τεύξονται cit. Pr., *in R.* II 29,27-28 K.
b3-547a5 resp. Iambl., *in Nic.* 82,20-24 P.-K.; —, — 83,13-18 P.-K.
b3-c6 resp. Apul., *Pl.* II 25,258 (103 B.); Cic., *Att.* VII 13,5 (136, IV 16 S. B.); Plu., *Mor.* 373f (II 3,56,5-7 N.-S.-T.); sch. Pl. ad loc. (257 G.)
b3-6 resp. Pr., *in R.* II 79,19-24 K.
b3-4 ἔστι—τέλειος AFF. Plu., *Mor.* 1017c (VI 1,155,17-18 H.-D.); Pr., *in Ti.* III 54,21-22 D.; cit. Pr., *Th. Pl.* IV 34 (IV 102,11-13 S.-W.); —, *in Ti.* III 93,23-25 D.; resp. Pr., *in Ti.* III 89,5-6 D.; —, *Th. Pl.* IV 29 (IV 87,7-9 S.-W.); —, — IV 34 (IV 102,7-9.21-22 S.-W.)
b3-4 θείῳ—τέλειος AFF. Pr., *in R.* II 14,24-25 K.
b3-4 θείῳ—περίοδος resp. Pr., *in Ti.* III 278,12-13 D.
b3 θείῳ γεννητῷ resp. Pr., *in R.* II 14 sqq. *passim*; —, *in Ti.* I 125,24-25 D.; —, — I 292,7-8 D.; —, — III 233,17-18 D.; Tz., *H.* X 520-526 (409 L.); expl. sch. Pl. ad loc. (257 G.)
b3 γεννητῷ resp. Pr., *in R.* II 9,19 K.; —, — II 9,27 K.; —— II 10,15 K.
b4 περίοδος usurp. Plot. V 7,1,23 (II 371 H.-S.)
b4 ἀριθμὸς τέλειος resp. Pr., *in R.* II 16,3 K.
b5-c2 resp. et interpr. Pr., *in R.* II 36,3-43,19 K.
b5-6 τρεῖς ἀποστάσεις resp. Pr., *in R.* II 36,22 K.

b5 δυνάμεναί τε καὶ δυναστευόμεναι resp. Pr., *in R.* II 36,24-25 K.; —, — II 37,1 K.; usurp. Pr., *in Euc.* 8,13-14 F.
b6-7 ὁμοιούντων τε καὶ ἀνομοιούντων resp. Pr., *in R.* II 36,13-15 K.; —, — II 36,25-26 K.
b7-547c5 resp. Pr., *in R.* II 173,27-174,12 K.
b7-c1 πάντα—ἀπέφηναν resp. Pr., *in R.* II 36,23-24 K.; —, *in Ti.* I 17,5 D.; —, — II 25,30 D.; imit. Pr., *in Ti.* II 210,23 D.; —, — II 230,26-27 D.
b7 αὐξόντων καὶ φθινόντων resp. Pr., *in R.* II 36,16-17 K.; —, — II 36,28 K.
c1-6 resp. Pr., *in R.* II 174,3-7 K.
c1-2 ὧν—παρέχεται AFF. Arist., *Pol.* E 12,1316a6-7 B.
c1-2 ἐπίτριτος—αὐξηθείς cit. Pr., *in R.* II 39,26-27 K.; resp. Pr., *in R.* II 37,21-22 K.
c1-2 ἐπίτριτος—παρέχεται cit. Iambl., *VP* 27,131 (74,20-21 D.)
c1-2 ἐπίτριτος—συζυγεὶς AFF. Aristid. Quint. III 23 (124,25-26 W.-I.)
c1 ὧν—πυθμὴν AFF. Pr., *in R.* II 37,3 K.
c1 πυθμὴν Hsch. π 4302 (III 407 S.); resp. Pr., *in R.* II 36,29 K.
c3-4 fort.resp. Pr., *in R.* II 75,25 K.
c3 ἴσην ἰσάκις resp. Pr., *in R.* II 37,26 K.; —, — II 38,4 K.
c3 ἑκατὸν τοσαυτάκις AFF. Pr., *in R.* II 37,19 K.; —, — II 37,27 K.
c4 προμήκη δέ expl. sch. Pl. ad loc. (257 G.)
c5 resp. Pr., *in Euc.* 61,14-17 F.
c6-547a5 resp. et interpr. Pr., *in R.* II 70,21-72,27 K.
c6-7 resp. Pr., *de Decem Dub.* 32,11-12 (52 B.)
c6 fort.resp. Psell., *Chron.* II 176,1 R.
c6 ἀριθμὸς γεωμετρικός resp. Pr., *in R.* II 36,3 K.
c7 κύριος—γενέσεων AFF. Pr., *in R.* II 19,4 K.; cit. Pr., *in R.* II 70,22-24 K.; resp. Pr., *in Euc.* 23,22 F.; —, *in R.* II 5,21 K.
c7 ἀμεινόνων—γενέσεων AFF. Pr., *in R.* II 55,8-9 K.; —, *Th. Pl.* IV 34 (IV 102,23-24 S.-W.); Syr., *in Metaph.* 190,34 K.
c7 ἀμεινόνων—χειρόνων AFF. Pr., *in R.* II 19,22 K.; —, — II 19,25-26 K.; —, II 20,7 K.; —, — II 22,18 K.; cit. Pr., *in R.* II 21,1-2 K.
d1-547a5 resp. Averr., *in R.* 87,22-29 R.; Pr., *in R.* II 100,11-12 K.
d1-8 resp. Pr., *in R.* II 79,13-17 K.
d3-8 resp. Pr., *in R.* I 219,8-12 K.

547
a1 resp. Pr., *in R.* II 77,20-26 K.
a2-5 resp. Pr., *in R.* II 78,12-13 K.
a2-4 resp. Plu., *Mor.* 484c (III 234,11-13 P.-S.); Pr., *in R.* II 77,29-78,3 K.; —, — II 79,6-11 K.
a4-5 ταύτης—γίγνηται AFF. Pr., *in R.* II 79,28-80,1 K.
a4-5 ταύτης τοι γενεῆς usurp. Plot. V 1,7,27 (II 278 H.-S.)
b2-569c9 resp. Phlp., *in de An.* 565,32-37 H.
b2-550b7 resp. Apul., *Pl.* II 15,241 (92 B.)
b2-548d5 cit. Averr., *in R.* 87,30-88,23 R.; resp. sch. Pl. ad loc. (258 G.)
b2-c4 resp. Pr., *in R.* II 3,11-12 K.; —, — II 3,25-4,1 K.; —, — II 7,13-16 K.
b6-7 ἀρχαίαν κατάστασιν usurp. Plot. IV 7,9,28 (II 214 H.-S.)
c1 ἰδιώσασθαι Phot. I 289 N.
d4-8 resp. sch. Pl. ad loc. (258 G.)
e1-548a3 resp. sch. Pl. ad loc. (258 G.)

548
c1-2 πρεσβυτέρως τετιμηκέναι usurp. Gal., *Praecogn.* 1,13 (72,23-24 N.)
c5-7 resp. sch. Pl. ad loc. (258 G.)
d6-550b7 cit. Averr., *in R.* 88,24-89,32 R.; expl. sch. Pl. ad loc. (258 G.)

549
c2-550b7 resp. sch. Pl. ad loc. (258 G.)
e1 ὑμνεῖν expl. sch. Pl. ad loc. (258 G.)

550
a5-7 expl. sch. Pl. ad loc. (258 G.)
b1-7 fort.resp. Synes., *Regn.* X 10ab (21,7-9 T.)

b6 τῷ μέσῳ expl. sch. Pl. ad loc. (258 G.)
b7 ὑψηλόφρων τε καὶ φιλότιμος imit. Them., Or. 2,27d (I 33,20 D.-N.)
c4-553a2 cit. Averr., in R. 89,33-91,12 R.; resp. Alb., Intr. XXXIV 3 (169 L.)
c11 Τὴν ἀπὸ τιμημάτων expl. sch. Pl. ad loc. (258-259 G.)
d3-551b8 resp. sch. Pl. ad loc. (259 G.)
d6 καὶ τυφλῷ δῆλον usurp. Niceph. Greg., Ep. 49,9 (II 162 L.); Plu., Mor. 1098f (VI 2,153,11-12 P.-W.)
d9-551a10 resp. Arist., Pol. E 12,1316a39-b1 B.
e4-551d2 Τοὐντεῦθεν—Φαίνεται AFF. Stob. IV 1,145 (IV 90,15-91,23 H.)
e4-551a6 Τοὐντεῦθεν—Οὕτω AFF. Stob. IV 31c,82 (V 761,5-12 H.)
e7 πλάστιγγι Hsch. π 2462 (III 341 S.); usurp. Them., Or. 22,275b (II 65,5 D.-N.)

1   a4 Ἀσκεῖται—ἀτιμαζόμενον AFF. Lib., Or. LXII 15 (IV 354,9-10 F.); Them., Or. 15,195d (I 282,5-6 D.-N.); —, — 31,353a (II 189,2-3 D.-N.); cit. Them., Or. 16,204a (I 293,16-17 D.-N.); usurp. Them., Or. 4,54d (I 78,19 D.-N.)
a7 φιλοχρηματισταὶ expl. sch. Pl. ad loc. (259 G.)
c2-5 imit. Them., Or. 1,12b (I 17,14-16 D.-N.)
d5-6 resp. Arist., Pol. E 12,1316b6-7 B.

2   b2 ὀλιγαρχουμέναις Phot. II 11 N.
c2 ὡς ἐν κηρίῳ κηφὴν imit. Meth., Res. II 2,7 (333,6 B.)
c2 κηφὴν usurp. Synes., Ep. 143 (251,5 G.); Them., Or. 23,285d (II 79,18 D.-N.); expl. sch. Pl. ad loc. (259 G.)
c6-d1 resp. Plu., Mor. 818c (V 1,108,13-14 H.-P.-D.)
c7 ἐνίους expl. sch. Pl. ad loc. (259 G.)

3   a6-555b2 cit. Averr., in R. 91,13-92,12 R.
a6-554a8 resp. Apul., Pl. II 15,241 (92 B.)
a6-d9 resp. sch. Pl. ad loc. (259 G.)
a10-b1 ἴχνη—ἕρματι imit. Them., Or. 23,285d (II 79,16-17 D.-N.)
b7-d7 fort.resp. Synes., Regn. X 10ab (21,7-9 T.)
c3 γλίσχρως Phot. α 438 (I 51 Th.); fort.resp. An. Bachm. I 185,26; expl. sch. Pl. ad loc. (259 G.)
c4-7 resp. sch. Pl. ad loc. (260 G.); imit. Them., Or. 24,306c (II 106,18-21 D.-N.)
c4-6 εἰς τὸν θρόνον ἐγκαθίζειν usurp. Aristid., Or. 3,653 (I 3,508,13 L.-B.)
c6 τιάρας Phot. II 213 N.; expl. sch. Pl. ad loc. (260 G.)
c7 στρεπτοὺς καὶ ἀκινάκας expl. sch. Pl. ad loc. (260 G.)
e1-555a6 resp. (ση) sch. Pl. ad loc. (260 G.)

4   a10 Αὐχμηρός expl. sch. Pl. ad loc. (260 G.)
b5 τυφλὸν expl. sch. Pl. ad loc. (260 G.)
d2 οὐ πείθων expl. sch. Pl. ad loc. (260 G.)
d9-e5 resp. Apul., Pl. II 4,225 (82 B.); —, — II 5,227 (83 B.)
e7 (et alibi) ἀνταγωνιστής Phot. α 2053 (I 198 Th.)

5   b3-558c6 cit. Averr., in R. 92,13-94,4 R.; resp. Alb., Intr. XXXIV 3 (169 L.); sch. Pl. ad loc. (261 G.)
b5-6 παραστησώμεθ'—κρίσιν AFF. Phot. II 60 N.; Sud. π 448 (IV 42,28 A.); cit. Poll. VIII 39 (II 118,9-10 B.)
b8-558c6 resp. sch. Pl. ad loc. (261 G.)
d2 Ἐπιεικῶς expl. sch. Pl. ad loc. (261 G.)
d3 (et 590a5, 591a6) ἀκολασταίνειν AB I 80,31; — I 368,27; An. Bachm. I 58,15-16; Phot. α 783 (I 85 Th.)
e3-556a2 resp. Arist., Pol. E 12,1316b14-17 B.

556   a4 οὔτε γ' ἐκείνη expl. sch. Pl. ad loc. (261 G.)
      c10 θεωρίας expl. sch. Pl. ad loc. (261 G.)
      d3 ἡλιωμένος Phot. I 259 N.
      d5 αὐτὸν expl. sch. Pl. ad loc. (261 G.)

557   b5 μεστὴ παρρησίας usurp. Niceph. Greg., Flor. 82,594 L.
      c6-7 expl. sch. Pl. ad loc. (261 G.)
      d8 παντοπώλιον Poll. VI 163 (II 43,3 B.); resp. Plu., Vit. 981d (II 1,131,14-15 Z.)

558   a8 περινοστεῖ Hsch. π 1772 (III 316 S.)
      b5-c1 resp. sch. Pl. ad loc. (261 G.)
      c5-6 fort.resp. Plu., Mor. 643b (IV 75,21-22 H.)
      c8-562a3 cit. Averr., in R. 94,5-25 R.; resp. Apul., Pl. II 15,241 (92 B.); sch. Pl. ad loc. (261 G.)
      d5 χρηματιστικαὶ expl. sch. Pl. ad loc. (261 G.)
      d8-559c7 expl. sch. Pl. ad loc. (261 G.)

559   a11-c2 ῏Αρ'—οὖν AFF. Ath. XII 511ef (III 129,22-130,7 K.)
      a11 ὑγιείας τε καὶ εὐεξίας imit. Zach. Mit., Opif. 131,1141-1142 C.
      d8 γεύσηται μέλιτος usurp. Niceph. Greg., Ep. 75,3 (II 214 L.); —, Flor. 63,183 L.
      d9 αἴθωσι expl. sch. Pl. ad loc. (262 G.)
      e4-560b10 fort.imit. Gr. Nyss., Hom. in Eccl. VIII (429,6-433,15 McD.-A.)

560   a1-2 fort.resp. Gr. Nyss., Hom. in Eccl. VI (383,21 McD.-A.)
      b7-c3 imit. Plu., Mor. 38b (I 77,5-8 P.-W.-P.-G.)
      b7-8 ψυχῆς ἀκρόπολιν resp. Alb., Intr. XXIII 1 (111 L.); usurp. Cic., TD I 10,20 (227,26-27 P.); imit. Gr. Nyss., Hom. in Eccl. VIII (430,8 McD.-A.); Max. Tyr. 16,4e (202,11-12 H.); Niceph. Greg., Flor. 77,502 L.; Ph., Leg. II 23,91 (I 109,2 C.-W.); —, Somn. I 31 (III 211,19 C.-W.); —, Spec. III 8,49 (V 220,1 C.-W.)
      c2 (et c7-8) ἀλάζονες λόγοι resp. Iambl., Myst. 91,14-15 (92 P.); usurp. Zach. Mit., Opif. 100,147-148 C.
      c5 Λωτοφάγους expl. sch. Pl. ad loc. (262 G.)
      d2-6 expl. sch. Pl. ad loc. (262 G.)
      d2-3 ἠλιθιότητα, σωφροσύνην resp. Plot. I 6,1,46-47 (I 106 H.-S.)
      e4-561a4 expl. sch. Pl. ad loc. (262 G.)
      e5 ἀσωτίαν usurp. Alb., Intr. XXX 1 (145 L.)

561   a9 ἐκβακχευθῇ expl. sch. Pl. ad loc. (263 G.)
      b2 ἐνδῷ Tim. 86 R.-K.
      c3 ἀνανεύει Hsch. α 4456 (I 155 L.)

562   a7-587e4 resp. Apul., Pl. II 4,225 (82 B.)
      a7-569c9 cit. Averr., in R. 94,29-98,6 R.; resp. Alb., Intr. XXXIV 3 (169 L.); sch. Pl. ad loc. (263 G.)
      a7-566d3 resp. sch. Pl. ad loc. (263 G.)
      b6-c2 expl. sch. Pl. ad loc. (263 G.)
      b6-10 resp. Pr., in Cra. XXXIV (11,24-26 P.)
      c8-563e1 latine AFF. Cic., Rep. I 43,66-67 (40,23-42,2 Z.)
      c8-d6 ῞Οταν—προπηλακίζει AFF. Ath. X 443f-444a (II 465,15-22 K.)
      c8-d3 imit. Plu., Mor. 295d (II 1,345,17-18 N.-S.-T.)
      c8-d2 ῞Οταν—μεθυσθῇ AFF. Ath. XI 505d (III 117,7-9 K.)
      d2 ἀκράτου usurp. Plot. IV 4,17,30 (II 95 H.-S.)
      d6 προπηλακίζει Hsch. π 3631 (III 384 S.)
      e9 μέτοικον expl. sch. Pl. ad loc. (263 G.)

INDEX TESTIMONIORUM 349

3   **a8** εὐτραπελίας expl. sch. Pl. ad loc. (263 G.)
    a8 χαριεντισμοῦ expl. sch. Pl. ad loc. (263 G.)
    b6 ἐωνημένοι Hsch. ε 7741 (I 255 L.)
    c1-2 κατ'—στόμα AFF. Plu., *Mor.* 763b (IV 373,16 H.); imit. Them., *Or.* 4,52b (I 75,3 D.-N.)
    c5-7 resp. Clem., *Paed.* III x 73,3 (I 276,19 S.)
    c5 ἐνταῦθα expl. sch. Pl. ad loc. (263 G.)
    c6-7 fort.usurp. Lib., *Or.* XVIII 133 (II 293,9-10 F.); —, — XLVIII 38 (III 446,21-447,1 F.)
    c6 proverbium affert sch. Pl. ad loc. (264 G.)
    d2 usurp. Iul., *Ep.* 50 (I 2,186,6 B.)
    d7-8 οὐδὲ—φροντίζουσιν expl. sch. Pl. ad loc. (264 G.)
    d8 resp. D. L. III 85 (I 155,19-20 L.)
    e3-568d3 latine cit. Cic., *Rep.* I 44,68 (42,5-43,4 Z.)
    e9 τὸ ἄγαν τι ποιεῖν expl. sch. Pl. ad loc. (264 G.)

4   **a3-7** Ἡ—δημοκρατίας AFF. Stob. IV 1,118 (IV 69,11-14 H.)
    b5-7 expl. sch. Pl. ad loc. (264 G.)
    b10 περὶ—χολή imit. Plot. I 8,14,24 (I 138 H.-S.)
    c6-7 ἵν'—βουλόμεθα usurp. Meth., *Res.* I 33,3 (270,17 B.)
    d1-565a3 expl. sch. Pl. ad loc. (264 G.)
    e4 ἀποκρίνεται fort.resp. *An. Bachm.* I 116,19; Phot. α 2325 (I 219 Th.)
    e10 βλίττει *EM* 200,34 G.; *Et. Gen.* β 150 (81 B.); *Et. Gud.* 274,9 S.; Hsch. β 752 (I 332 L.); Sud. β 343 (I 477,10-12 A.); Tim. 54 R.-K.; expl. sch. Pl. ad loc. (264 G.)
    e13 κηφήνων βοτάνη usurp. Plu., *Mor.* 42a (I 84,15 P.-W.-P.-G.)

5   **c6** Εἰσαγγελίαι expl. sch. Pl. ad loc. (265 G.)
    d4-566c3 resp. sch. Pl. ad loc. (265 G.)
    d4-e1 resp. Plb. VII 13,7 (II 326,19-23 B.-W.)
    d6-7 resp. sch. Pl. ad loc. (265 G.)
    e3-569c9 resp. Cic., *Att.* X 8,6 (199, IV 246 S. B.)

6   **a1** χρεῶν ἀποκοπὰς usurp. Them., *Or.* 7,91c (I 138,12 D.-N.)
    a4 imit. Plot. III 2,8,26-27 (I 280 H.-S.)
    b5-11 expl. sch. Pl. ad loc. (265 G.)
    b5 πολυθρύλητον Phot. II 98 N.
    c5-6 expl. sch. Pl. ad loc., oraculum afferens (265-266 G.)
    d4 μέλλει Phot. I 414 N.; expl. sch. Pl. ad loc. (266 G.)
    d8-e4 resp. sch. Pl. ad loc. (266 G.)
    e1 ὑπισχνεῖταί Hsch. υ 553 (IV 210 S.)

7   **a7-10** expl. sch. Pl. ad loc. (266 G.)
    b12-c3 fort.resp. Cic., *Off.* I 25,87 (39,5-7 A.)

8   **a8-c6** resp. Averr., *in R.* 101,15-18 R.
    a8 Οὐκ ἐτός expl. sch. Pl. ad loc. (266 G.) (vide etiam ad 414e7)
    b1 σοφοὶ συνουσίᾳ AFF. Aristid., *Or.* 3,585 (I 3,488,8 L.-B.); Them., *Or.* 6,72c (I 107,13 D.-N.); Zen. V 98 (I 159,10-12 L.-S.); expl. sch. Pl. ad loc., versum Sophocli tribuens (266 G.)
    c3 καλὰς φωνάς expl. sch. Pl. ad loc. (266 G.)
    c3 πιθανάς Hsch. π 2264 (III 334 S.)
    d2 fort.imit. Plu., *Mor.* 77a (I 153,13 P.-W.-P.-G.)

9   **a3** συγκλύδων Phot. II 182 N.; Hsch. σ 2174 (IV 91 S.)
    b8-c1 usurp. Demetr. Cyd., *Ep.* 32,14 (I 63 L.); Niceph. Greg., *Antirrh.* I 1,8,15 (191,26 B.)

LIBER NONUS

571   **a1-580c8** resp. Apul., *Pl.* II 15-16,242 (92-93 B.); —, — II 18,246 (95 B.)
a1-577b9 cit. Averr., *in R.* 98,7-101,2 R.
a1-573c10 resp. sch. Pl. ad loc. (267 G.)
b4-572b7 τῶν—ἔνδηλον AFF. Stob. III 1,57 (III 22,5-23,20 H.)
b4-572b1 latine AFF. Calc., *Ti.* CCLIII (261,15-262,17 W.) (= Porph., *in Ti.* 108,16-109,17 S.)
b4-d4 resp. Bess., *in Cal. Pl.* 430,13-15 M.
c3-572b1 latine AFF. Cic., *Div.* I 29,60-61 (38,3-23 G.); resp. Apul., *Pl.* I 13,207 (73 B.); Plu., *Mor.* 83a (I 165,19-25 P.-W.-P.-G.)
c9-d1 μητρί—μείγνυσθαι AFF. Plu., *Mor.* 101a (I 206,13 P.-W.-P.-G.)
d6-572b1 resp. Cic., *Div.* II 58,119 (134,10-13 G.)
d8 ἑστιάσας λόγων usurp. Bas., *Hex.* III 10 (242 G.); Chor., *Dial.* 1,5 (2,14 F.-R.); —, *Or.* 2,72 (45,24 F.-R.); imit. Synes., *Ep.* 101 (170,11-12 G.)
d8 ἑστιάσας usurp. Zach. Mit., *Opif.* 125,940 C.

572   **a5-6** ἀλλ'—ἐγγίγνεται AFF. Gal., *PHP* VI 2,12 (II 370,18-19 L.)
e2 βοηθοῦντά τε expl. sch. Pl. ad loc. (267 G.)
e5-6 expl. sch. Pl. ad loc. (267 G.)

573   **a4** βομβοῦσαι Sud. β 374 (I 479,16-17 A.)
a7 πόθου resp. Alb., *Intr.* XXXII 3 (157 L.)
a8-b1 imit. Synes., *Ep.* 101 (171,18-19 G.)
d1 σὺ καὶ ἐμοὶ ἐρεῖς expl. sch. Pl. ad loc. (267 G.)
d3 καὶ κῶμοι καὶ θάλειαι AFF. Did., *Plat.* 401 M.
d3 κῶμοι expl. sch. Pl. ad loc. (267 G.)
d4-5 διακυβερνᾷ τὰ τῆς ψυχῆς imit. Meth., *Symp.* X 1 (121,24-25 B.)
e3-4 resp. Longin. 44,7,21-22 R.
e6-7 ὑπ'—ἡγουμένου AFF. Phot. I 252 N.

574   **c2** ἄωρόν Hsch. α 8993 (I 304 L.)
c3 πληγαῖς expl. sch. Pl. ad loc. (267 G.)
d4-5 ἱερόν τι νεωκορήσει AFF. Phot. I 290 N.; Sud. ι 187 (II 617,3 A.)
d5 νεωκορήσει Phot. I 445 N.; expl. sch. Pl. ad loc. (267 G.)
d6 τὰς δικαίας expl. sch. Pl. ad loc. (267 G.)
d7-8 δορυφοροῦσαι τὸν Ἔρωτα imit. Meth., *Symp.* X 6 (128,24 B.)
d7 δορυφοροῦσαι expl. sch. Pl. ad loc. (267 G.); usurp. Alb., *Intr.* XVII 4 (97 L.)
e2 ὑπὸ Ἔρωτος expl. sch. Pl. ad loc. (268 G.)
e3 ὀλιγάκις expl. sch. Pl. ad loc. (268 G.)

575   **c4** οὐδ' ἴκταρ βάλλει AFF. Did., *Plat.* 401 M.; Hsch. ι 504 (II 358 L.); *Lex. Vind.* ι 8 (104,9 N.); Paus. Gr. ο 36 (202,14-15 E.); Zen. V 55 (I 143,7-11 L.-S.)
c4 ἴκταρ *EM, ap.* Miller, *Mélanges* 236; Eust., *Od.* 1936,12 (292 D.); Moer. 176 P.-K.; sch. Luc. *Lex.* 21 (202,1-2 R.); expl. sch. Pl. ad loc. (268 G.)
d7 μητρίδα τε, Κρῆτές φασι fort.resp. Plu., *Mor.* 792e (V 1,45,7 H.-P.-D.)
d7 μητρίδα Phot. I 422 N.; fort.resp. Synes., *Ep.* 94 (156,13 G.); expl. sch. Pl. ad loc. (268 G.)

576   **a4-e5** resp. Plu., *Mor.* 827b (V 1,130,5-6 H.-P.-D.)
b4 Κεφαλαιωσώμεθα usurp. Zach. Mit., *Opif.* 104,275 C.
b10 διαδεξάμενος τὸν λόγον usurp. Niceph. Greg., *Flor.* 100,1027-1028 L.
b11-588a11 resp. Pr., *in R.* II 81,1-83 K.
c3 πολλὰ expl. sch. Pl. ad loc. (268 G.)
d8-e5 μὴ—εὐδαιμονεστέρα AFF. Stob. IV 1,119 (IV 69,16-22 H.)

INDEX TESTIMONIORUM 351

c1-587e4 resp. Pr., *in Ti.* III 344,14-19 D.
c1-580c8 cit. Averr., *in R.* 101,3-103,12 R.; resp. Pr., *in R.* II 81,6-7 K.; —, — II 81,14-27 K.
e2 ὡς—ψυχῆς expl. sch. Pl. ad loc. (268 G.)

b3-580a8 ῎Αρ'—ἀντερεῖ AFF. Stob. IV 8,34 (IV 319,7-320,15 H.)
e4 διὰ-σφαδασμῶν AFF. *EM* 737,18 G.
e4 σφαδασμῶν Hsch. σ 2830 (IV 112 S.)

a9-c4 ῎Ιθι—πόλεως AFF. Stob. IV 1, 120 (IV 69,24-70,13 H.)
a9-b1 διὰ πάντων κριτής Hsch. δ 1201 (I 438 L.)
b8-c8 resp. Dam., *in Phlb.* 250,2 (119 W.); David, *in Cat.* 23a B.; Elias, *in Cat.* 110,23-28 B.
c6-7 ἐάντε—θεούς imit. Plu., *Mor.* 528a (III 345,4-5 P.-S.)
d3-587a1 cit. Averr., *in R.* 103,16-104,23 R.; resp. Nemes. 18 (223 M.)
d3-581e4 resp. D. L., *Div.* 39 (53,7-54,9 M.); Pr., *in R.* II 81,10-11 K.; fort.resp. Synes., *Regn.* 10ab (21,7-9 T.)
d7-8 resp. Bess., *in Cal. Pl.* 430,16 M.

b9 κατὰ τρόπον usurp. Alb., *Intr.* XXXIV 2 (169 L.)
e6-582a2 ῞Οτε—λέγει AFF. Gal., *PHP* VI 2,12 (II 370,19-23 L.)

a4-586b4 resp. Plu., *Mor.* 1091d (VI 2,136,21-24 P.-W.)
a4-583a11 resp. Pr., *in R.* II 81,7-8 K.; —, — II 81,27-82,16 K.
a4-5 καλῶς κριθήσεσθαι expl. sch. Pl. ad loc. (268 G.)
a6 κριτήριον usurp. Alb., *Intr.* III 5 (11 L.)
c7-8 τῆς δὲ τοῦ ὄντος θέας usurp. Alb., *Intr.* III 1 (9 L.)

a1-3 Τριῶν—ἥδιστος AFF. Bess., *in Cal. Pl.* 430,18-20 M.
b2-588a11 resp. Pr., *in R.* II 81,8-10 K.; —, — II 82,17-83,2 K.
b2-3 τὸ—'Ολυμπίῳ AFF. Ael. Dion. τ 25 (145,14-15 E.); Apostol. XVII 28 (II 693,2-3 L.-S.); Phot. II 227 N.; Sud. τ 1024 (IV 594,26 A.); resp. sch. Pl. *Phlb.* 66d (55 G.)
b2 τὸ—'Ολυμπικῶς resp. Pr., *in R.* I 228,1 K.; expl. sch. Pl. ad loc. (269 G.)
b3-5 cit. Bess., *in Cal. Pl.* 430,20-22 M.
c3-587b10 resp. *An. Par.* I 230,20-21 (= sch. Arist. *EN* 1172b3)
c3-584a10 resp. Apul., *Pl.* II 12,238 (90 B.)
c10-d1 ῎Αρ'—ὄν AFF. sch. Cic. *Mil.argum.* (60,1-4 H.)
e9-10 resp. Alb., *Intr.* XXXII 1 (155 L.); —, — XXXII 5 (159 L.)

d3-4 expl. sch. Pl. ad loc. (269 G.)

a8-587a2 resp. Did., *ap.* Stob. II 7,3[f] (II 49,21-22 W.)

a1-b4 Οἱ—πιμπλάντες AFF. Bess., *in Cal. Pl.* 430,22-23 M.; fort.resp. Anast. Sin., *VD* II 5,137-138 (58 U.); imit. Clem., *Paed.* II i 9,3-4 (I 160,4-11 S.)
a1-b3 Οἱ—ἀπληστίαν AFF. Longin. 13,1,2-11 R.
a7-8 imit. Meth., *Res.* I 60,4 (325,4 B.)
a7 fort.imit. Gr. Naz., *Vit.* 26 (54 J.)
b1 κυρίττοντες Hsch. κ 4688 (II 552 L.); Phot. I 361 N.
b6 χρησμωδεῖς usurp. Meth., *Symp. prooem.* 8 (6,14 B.)
c4 Ἑλένης εἴδωλον resp. Demetr. Cyd., *Ep.* 44,21 (I 78 L.)
c4 Στησίχορός resp. sch. Pl. ad loc. (269 G.)

a7-e4 resp. Plu., *Mor.* 827b (V 1,130,5-6 H.-P.-D.)
d3-e4 expl. sch. Pl. ad loc. (269-270 G.)
d3-10 resp. Pr., *in Euc.* 24,17-20 F.

d6-7 τὸν τοῦ μήκους ἀριθμὸν resp. Anon., *Prol. Plat.* I 5,10-11 (11 W.)
d10-11 fort.resp. Synes., *Regn.* V 5d (13,6-7 T.)

588 b1-591a4 Εἶεν—ἦ δ' ὅς AFF. Stob. III 9,62 (III 397,20-402,2 H.)
b6-589b7 Νῦν—ἐπαινῶν AFF. Eus., *PE* XII 46,2-6 (II 135,6-136,10 M.)
c2-589b7 fort.resp. Synes., *Regn.* XI 11a (13,1-3 T.)
c2 Χιμαίρας, Σκύλλης, Κερβέρου expl. sch. Pl. ad loc. (270 G.)
c7-e2 resp. Gal., *PHP* VI 2,4 (II 368,15-20 L.); Mich., *in EN* 483,2-6 He.
c7-10 (de bestia multiformi) resp. Gal., *in Ti.* 12,4-6 S.-K.; Gr. Nyss., *Ep.* XX 11 (70,26-28 P.); Herm., *in Phdr.* 53,9-10 C.; Iambl., *Protr.* 3 (14,1 P.); Olymp., *in Grg.* 34,3 (175,10 W.); —, — 35,3 (180,6 W.); Phlp., *in de An.* 565,35-36 H.; Plot. I 1,7,20-21 (I 55 H.-S.); Pr., *in Alc.* 43,11 (19 W.); —, — 160,3 (73 W.); —, — 244,3 (113 W.); —, *de Prov.* 47,7 (157 B.); —, *in R.* I 225,17-18 K.; —, — I 226,10 K.; —, — I 227,25 K.; — — I 292,29-293,2 K.; Them., *Or.* 13,169c (I 243,12 D.-N.); fort.resp. Pr., *in R.* I 17,19 K.; Synes., *Regn.* X 10a (21,6-7 T.); imit. Meth., *Symp.* VIII 12 (97,5-6 B.)
d1-2 εὐπλαστότερον κηροῦ usurp. Pr., *in Cra.* LXXVII (36,22 P.)
d10-e1 imit. Gr. Nyss., *Hom. Creat.* I 12,12-13 H.; —, — 13,5-6 H.; —, — II 46,11 H.
e5-589b6 cit. Iambl., *Protr.* 5 (31,19-32,5 P.)

589 a7-b1 ὁ ἐντὸς ἄνθρωπος cit. Plot. V 1,10,10 (II 284 H.-S.); resp. Pr., *in Ti.* I 16,15-16 D.; usurp. Dor., *Doct.* I 6,3 (154 R.-P.); Plot. I 1,10,15 (I 58 H.-S.)
b2-3 ἥμερα et ἄγρια resp. Alb., *Intr.* XXXII 4 (157 L.)
c3 ψέκτης *AB* I 116,25; Poll. V 117 (I 294,6 B.)
d7-e5 cit. Iambl., *Protr.* 5 (32,9-12 P.)
e4-5 fort.resp. Clem., *Paed.* II x 100,4 (I 217,20-23 S.)

590 a1 Ἐριφύλη expl. sch. Pl. ad loc. (270 G.)
a5-b9 cit. Iambl., *Protr.* 5 (32,13-22 P.)
a9-b1 resp. Plot. I 1,7,20-21 (I 55 H.-S.)
a9 τὸ λεοντῶδές usurp. Aen. Gaz., *Thphr.* 12,22 C.
b9 resp. Plot. I 1,7,20-21 (I 55 H.-S.); fort.resp. Gr. Naz., *Vit.* 408-409 (74 J.)
c1-d6 cit. Iambl., *Protr.* 5 (32,22-33,1 P.)
c2 χειροτεχνία Poll. II 149 (I 129,2 B.)
c8-d6 resp. Apul., *Pl.* II 18,245 (95 B.)
e1-591a3 Δηλοῖ—ἀφίεμεν AFF. Iambl., *Protr.* 5 (33,1-7 P.)

591 b2-3 fort.resp. Gr. Naz., *Vit.* 1224 (112 J.)
b3-6 ὅλη—κτωμένη AFF. Bess., *in Cal. Pl.* 430,32-34 M.
c1-592a4 Οὐκοῦν—δημοσίᾳ AFF. Iambl., *Protr.* 5 (33,7-27 P.)
c1-2 cit. Bess., *in Cal. Pl.* 430,31-32 M.
c5-d3 Ἔπειτά—φανεῖται AFF. Bess., *in Cal. Pl.* 430,34-39 M.
c7 ζήσει *AB* I 97,28; Phot. I 247 N.
d1-3 resp. Georg. Mon., *Chron.* I 359,2 B.; Sud. υ 652 (IV 681,13-14 A.); Thdt., *Affect.* V 14 (I 230,7-9 C.); —, — XII 53 (II 435,16-19 C.)
d6-e5 resp. Pr., *in R.* I 12,22-23 K.
e1 resp. Pr., *in R.* I 12,19-21 K.

592 b2-5 cit. Phlp., *Aet.* II 4 (35,16-23 R.)
b2-4 resp. Pr., *in R.* II 98,8-11 K.; —, *in Ti.* I 197,12-14 D.
b2 resp. Anon., *Prol. Plat.* II 10,43 (23 W.); Apul., *Pl.* II 25,258 (104 B.); Boet., *Cons.* I 4,12-13 (7 B.); Clem., *Strom.* IV 26,172,3 (II 325,4-5 S.); Demetr. Cyd., *Ep.* 5,38 (I 27 L.); Olymp., *in Grg. prooem.* 5 (5,5-6 W.); —, — 39,2 (199,14-15 W.); Or., *Cels.* 5,43,17-19 (III 127 B.); Pr., *in R.* I 162,5-6 K.; —, — I 247,21-22 K.; —, — I 269,6-7 K.; —, — II 326,1-2 K.; —, —, *in Ti.* I 4,22 D.; —, — I 28,13 D.; —, — I 127,7-8 D.; —, — III 109,5 D.; Th. *Pl.* V 24 (299 P.)

LIBER DECIMUS

a1-608b3 resp. Averr., *in R.* 105,11-14 R.; Pr., *in R.* I 173,7-8 K.; —, — I 177,9-13 K.; —, — II 85,3-5 K.
a1-7 Καὶ—φαίνεται AFF. Pr., *in R.* I 196,25-197,3 K.
a5 cit. Pr., *in R.* I 197,17-18 K.
b3-c4 'Ως—ἔφη AFF. Eus., *PE* XII 49,1-2 (II 138,19-26 M.)
b3-6 'Ως—διανοίας AFF. Pr., *in R.* I 197,4-7 K.
b3 'Ως πρὸς ὑμᾶς εἰρῆσθαι usurp. Meth., *Res.* I 27,1 (254,11 B.)
b9-10 fort.imit. Plot. II 9,10,3 (I 238 H.-S.)
b10-c3 ἔοικε—ἀνήρ AFF. Pr., *in R.* I 204,23-26 K.
c1 τραγικῶν expl. sch. Pl. ad loc. (271 G.)
c2-3 ἀλλ'—ἀνήρ AFF. Iust. Phil., *Apol.* II 3 (I 206 O.); resp. Aristid., *Or.* 4,40 (I 3,544,4-5 L.-B.); Greg. Cor., *Dial.* 5 S.; Thdt., *Affect.* IX 49 (II 351,5-6 C.); fort.resp. Eun., *Hist.* 28 (I 231,3 D.)
c7-598d6 resp. Pr., *in R.* II 86,5-87,6 K.
c9 Ἦ που expl. sch. Pl. ad loc. (271 G.)

a10-603b2 fort.resp. Synes., *Calv.* IX 72c (207,1-2 T.)
a10-597d10 resp. Pr., *in Cra.* LIII (22,30-23,2 P.); —, *in Ti.* I 344,8-10 D.; Syr., *in Metaph.* 105,6-7 K.
b7 πρὸς τὴν ἰδέαν βλέπων resp. Alb., *Intr.* XII 1 (67 L.)
d2-e3 resp. Pr., *in Cra.* CLIX (89,2-3 P.)
d8-e1 imit. Iul., *Or.* VIII 163d7 (II 1,109 R.)
d9-e3 resp. (ση) sch. Pl. ad loc. (271 G.)
e4 φαινόμενα—ἀληθείᾳ AFF. *EM* 790,2 G.; Phot. II 254 N.; Sud. φ 172 (IV 708,22-23 A.)

b5-598a9 resp. Pr., *in Prm.* 827,28-30 C.
b5-7 fort.resp. Gr. Naz., *Carm. Dogm.* 4,21-23 (*PG* 37,417)
c1-d3 fort.resp. Gr. Naz., *Carm. Dogm.* 4,21-23 (*PG* 37,417)
c7-9 resp. Pr., *in Ti.* I 443,2-3 D.
e1-10 resp. Pr., *in R.* I 197,24-26 K.; —, — I 198,26-28 K.
e3-4 τὸν—καλεῖς AFF. Pr., *in R.* I 197,27-28 K.
e6-8 Τοῦτ'—μιμηταί AFF. Pr., *in R.* I 197,30-198,2 K.; resp. Pr., *in Alc.* 12,11 (5 W.); —, — 21,18 (9-10 W.); —, *in R.* I 190,27-191,1 K.; —, — I 199,2-3 K.
e6-7 Τοῦτ'—πεφυκώς AFF. Pr., *in R.* I 204,26-28 K.
e7 τρίτος τις ἀπὸ τῆς ἀληθείας cit. Pr., *in Ti.* I 344,2 D.; resp. Herm., *in Phdr.* 165,32 C.; Iambl., *Myst.* 168,14-15 (139 P.); Meth., *Symp.* V 7 (62,9 B.); Pr., *in R.* I 58,8 K.; —, — I 70,21 K.; —, — I 157,26-158,1 K.; —, — I 199,2-6 K.; —, — I 204,11 K.; —, — I 205,3-5 K.; —, — I 205,10 K.; —, *Th. Pl.* I 29 (I 124,7 S.-W.); usurp. Clem., *Strom.* IV 6,30,2 (II 261,18 S.)
e10-598b5 Τὸν—ἔφη AFF. Pr., *in R.* I 191,4-18 K.

a1-2 πότερα—δημιουργῶν AFF. Prisc., *Inst.* XVIII 273 (350,17-18 H.)
b3-5 resp. Pr., *in R.* I 189,2-3 K.; —, — I 191,2-3 K.
b6 Πόρρω—ἐστιν AFF. Pr., *in R.* I 198,4-5 K.
b8 εἴδωλον resp. Pr., *in R.* I 70,26-27 K.
d7-601b8 resp. Pr., *in R.* II 87,7-88,3 K.
d7-599a4 Οὐκοῦν—λέγειν AFF. Pr., *in R.* I 203,12-26 K.
d8 resp. Hermog., *Meth.* 33 (450,3-4 R.); —, — 36 (454,17-18 R.)

a6-b1 cit. Pr., *in R.* I 199,14-18 K.; imit. Them., *Or.* 21,251b (II 29,19-22 D.-N.)
a8-b1 προστήσασθαι τοῦ βίου usurp. Them., *Or.* 7,99b (I 149,7 D.-N.)
b9-601b5 Τῶν—ἔφη AFF. Eus., *PE* XII 49,3-14 (II 139,2-141,5 M.)
c6-e4 resp. Niceph. Greg., *Ep.* 22,58-64 (II 74 L.); Pr., *in R.* I 200,5-8 K.
d2-600e6 Ὧ—ἅπτεσθαι AFF. Aristid., *Or.* 4,43 (I 3,544,18-546,17 L.-B.)

354 THE INDIRECT TRADITION

d2-3 resp. Iust. Phil., *Coh. Gent.* 5 (III 34 O.)
d2 vide ad 597e7
d7-e3 resp. sch. Aristid. 3,162 (543,27-29 D.)
d7 Λυκοῦργον expl. sch. Pl. ad loc. (271 G.)
e2 Χαρώνδαν expl. sch. Pl. ad loc. (271 G.)
e3 Σόλωνα expl. sch. Pl. ad loc. (271-272 G.)

600 **a6** Θάλεώ expl. sch. Pl. ad loc. (272 G.)
a6 'Ανάχαρσιος expl. sch. Pl. ad loc. (272 G.)
b2-5 fort.resp. Eus., *Or. Const.* XVII (177,20-23 H.)
b2 Πυθαγόρας expl. sch. Pl. ad loc. (272-273 G.)
b6-9 resp. Aristid., *Or.* 4,39 (I 3,543,18 L.-B.)
b6-7 ὁ—ἑταῖρος AFF. Phot. I 351 N.
b6 Κρεώφυλος resp. Aristid., *Or.* 4,40 (I 3,544,1 L.-B.); expl. sch. Pl. ad loc. (273 G.)
c2-602b11 imit. Meth., *Res.* I 28,2 (257,4-13 B.)
c7 Πρόδικος expl. sch. Pl. ad loc. (273 G.)
d4 ἐπὶ ταῖς κεφαλαῖς περιφέρουσιν usurp. Them., *Or.* 21,254a (II 34,9 D.-N.)
d6 Ἡσίοδον resp. Aristid., *Or.* 4,45 (I 3,547,10 L.-B.)
e4-5 resp. Aristid., *Or.* 4,46 (I 3,547,16-17 L.-B.)

601 **a1** ἐπαΐων Hsch. ε 4106 (II 134 L.)
b2-3 resp. Arist., *Rh.* Γ 4,1406b36 B.
b9-603b8 resp. Pr., *in R.* II 88,4-20 K.
c3 ἡμίσεως *AB* I 98,30
c6-602a10 resp. Averr., *in R.* 23,12-15 R.; Pr., *in R.* I 200,27-201,4 K.
d1-2 expl. sch. Pl. ad loc. (274 G.)
d8-602a10 expl. sch. Pl. ad loc. (274 G.)

602 **a8-9** οὔτε prius-πονηρίαν AFF. Pr., *in R.* I 191,30-192,3 K.; resp. Pr., *in R.* I 200,24-27 K.; —, — I 205,10-11 K.
a8-9 οὔτε alterum-πονηρίαν AFF. Pr., *in R.* I 198,6-7 K.
d2 σκιαγραφία usurp. Pr., *in R.* I 179,25 K.
d2 ἐπιθεμένη expl. sch. Pl. ad loc. (274 G.)

603 **b1** ἑταίρα Phot. I 219 N.
b2 ὑγιεῖ οὐδ' ἀληθεῖ fort.usurp. Niceph. Greg., *Ep.* 3,167 (II 26 L.)
b6-606d8 resp. Olymp., *in Grg.* 33,3 (172,6-10 W.)
b9-608b3 resp. Pr., *in R.* II 88,21-89,5 K.
e3-604d11 'Ανήρ—οὖν AFF. Stob. IV 56,43 (V 1134,19-1136,11 H.)
e3-8 resp. Dam., *in Phd.* I 75,5 (59 W.)

604 **b9-e4** Λέγει—καταμαθεῖν AFF. Stob. IV 45,10 (V 995,5-996,8 H.)
b9-d2 ἡσυχίαν—ἀφανίζοντα AFF. Plu., *Mor.* 112e (I 232,15-24 P.-W.-P.-G.)
c5-7 resp. Plu., *Mor.* 467a (III 193,14-16 P.-S.)
e2 (et **605a5**) ἀγανακτητικόν *AB* I 334,28; *An. Bachm.* I 19,15-16; Phot. α 102 (I 18 Th.)

605 **a2-5** Ὁ—ἦθος AFF. Pr., *in R.* I 201,27-30 K.
a4 εὐδοκιμήσειν ἐν τοῖς πολλοῖς imit. Gal., *Praecogn.* 1,2 (68,7-8 N.); —, — 1,12 (72,21 N.)
a9 ἀντίστροφον expl. sch. Pl. ad loc. (274 G.)
c3 εἴδωλα εἰδωλοποιοῦντα resp. Anon., *Prol. Plat.* X 25,22-23 (47 W.)
c10-d5 resp. Pr., *in R.* II 106,1-3 K.; fort.resp. Max. Tyr. 17,4f (214,5-9 H.)
d7 χῆδος Hsch. χ 2471 (II 470 L.); expl. sch. Pl. ad loc. (274 G.)

606 **b8** (et alibi) ἐλεινὸν *AB* I 92,10
c2-9 resp. Pr., *in Prm.* 715,16-17 C.
c7 βωμολοχίας expl. sch. Pl. ad loc. (274 G.)

d5 αὐχμεῖν Hsch. α 8518 (I 288 L.)
e1-608b2 resp. Greg. Akind., *Ep.* 10,234-238 (48 H.)
e1-607a8 vide ad 398a1-7

a5-6 εἰ—βασιλεύσετον AFF. Pr., *in R.* I 204,16-18 K.; fort.resp. Boet., *Cons.* I 1,23 (2 B.)
b6 λακέρυζα Phot. I 370 N.; expl. sch. Pl. ad loc. (275 G.)

a3 ἐπᾴδοντες ἡμῖν αὐτοῖς imit. Plu., *Mor.* 920c (V 3,31,12 H.-P.-D.)
c1 ἐπίχειρα usurp. Gal., *Praecogn.* 1,9 (72,1 N.)
d3-611a3 (de immortalitate animae) resp. Alex. Aphr., *in APr.* 272,7-8 W.; Ammon., *in APr.* 71,37-72,1 W.; Ascl., *in Metaph.* 90,28-29 H.; Averr., *in R.* 105,14-15 R.; Bess., *in Cal. Pl.* 150,27-35 M.; Did., *ap.* Stob. II 7,3^f (II 49,21-22 W.); Firm., *Math.* I 1,7 (I 5,16-17 K.-S.); Luc., *Dem. Enc.* 47 (III 285,4-5 M.); Nemes. 2 (124 M.); Phlp., *in APr.* 256,23-24 W.; Pr., *in Alc.* 317,5-7 (147 W.); —, *de Mal. Subst.* 5,1-4 (178,179 B.); —, — 13,15-16 (193 B.); —, *in Prm.* 699,9-10 C.; —, *in R.* II 85,5-7 K.; —, — II 89,7-8 K.; —, — II 89,9-92,19 K.; —, *in Ti.* I 227,24-27 D.; —, *Th. Pl.* I 26 (I 116,14-16 S.-W.); Simp., *in An.* 318,30-31 H.
e3-4 resp. Pr., *in R.* I 270,22-24 K.
e4 ὠφελοῦν τὸ ἀγαθόν imit. Meth., *Symp.* VIII 16 (106,2-3 B.)

a2 ἐρυσίβην Hsch. ε 6111 (II 201 L.); Phot. I 214 N.; expl. sch. Pl. ad loc. (275 G.)
a2 ἰόν fort.resp. *Corp. Herm.* XIV 7 (II 224,19 N.-F.)
a9-b1 resp. Gal., *Capt.* 96,11-12 E.; Herm., *in Phdr.* 103,17 C.
c2-611a3 resp. Alb., *Intr.* XXV 4 (121 L.)
c5-d11 resp. Pr., *in R.* II 2,15-16 K.

a2 ἔμφυτον κακόν usurp. Gr. Naz., *Vit.* 816-817 (94 J.)
c3-5 ὡς—γίγνονται AFF. Bess., *in Cal. Pl.* 152,2-3 M.
c6 imit. Meth., *Res.* II 4,1 (335,9 B.)
c9 ἀξιώσομέν—λέγων imit. Meth., *Res.* II 4,1 (335,13-14 B.)
c10 (et alibi) θανάσιμον *AB* I 99,9; Phot. I 272 N.
d5-7 Μὰ—κακῶν AFF. Bess., *in Cal. Pl.* 152,5-6 M.; resp. Pr., *de Mal. Subs.* 39,36-37 (229 B.); —, — 39,38-40 (228 B.)
e7 σχολῇ expl. sch. Pl. ad loc. (275 G.)
e10-611b10 Οὐκοῦν—ἄν AFF. Stob. I 49,29 (I 359,19-360,8 W.)

a1-2 (de immortalitate animae; vide etiam ad 608d3-611a3) resp. Aët. Doxogr. IV 7,1 (392a12-13 D.); Alexis 158,1-3 (II 355 K.); Aug., *Trin.* XIV xix 57-59 (458-459 M.-G.); D. L. III 67 (I 148,14-15 L.); Eus."Gall.", *Hom.* XXVII 7 (316,89-90 G.); —, *Serm.* 2,12 (833,137-138 G.); Favor., *Ex.* IX 3-4 (384 B.); Gal., *Hist. Phil.* 24 (613,15 D.); Herm., *Irris.* 2 (6 0.); Minuc. Fel., *Oct.* 34,6 (32,21-24 K.); Thpl. Ant., *Autol.* III 7 (108 G.)
a4-9 resp. Pr., *in R.* II 91,19-92,3 K.
a10-613e5 resp. Pr., *in R.* II 92,4-19 K.
a10-612a7 resp. Pr., *in R.* II 89,8-9 K.
b5-6 resp. Heliod., *in EN* 611,28-30 H.
b5 resp. Plot. I 1,12,11 (I 59 H.-S.)
b9-d8 resp. Anon., *Prol. Plat.* II 10,22-23 (21 W.); Dam., *in Phd.* I 63,2-4 (53 W.)
b10 λελωβημένον usurp. Plot. IV 7,10,25 (II 215 H.-S.)
c3 καθαρὸν γιγνόμενον fort.imit. Plot. V 1,2,45 (II 265 H.-S.)
c7-d1 τεθεάμεθα—ὁρῶντες AFF. Plot. I 1,12,13-14 (I 59 H.-S.)
d1-5 resp. Phlp., *in de An.* 70,22-23 H.; Pr., *in Alc.* 224,9-10 (103 W.)
d1 τὸν θαλάττιον Γλαῦκον expl. sch. Pl. ad loc. (275 G.)
d2 ἀρχαίαν φύσιν usurp. Plot. VI 5,1,16 (III 161 H.-S.); — VI 9,8,14-15 (III 320-321 H.-S.)

d4-5 προσπεφυκέναι—ψυχία AFF. Ath. III 92f (I 214,2-3 K.)
d5 resp. Dam., *in Phd.* I 63,3-4 (53 W.); fort.resp. Clem., *Protr.* IX 86,2 (I 64,28 S.)
e1-612a4 cit. Plot. I 1,12,14-17 (I 59-60 H.-S.)
e2-3 fort.imit. Plot. IV 7,10,1-2 (II 214 H.-S.)
e5 τοῦ πόντου usurp. Pr., *in R.* II 69,17 K.

612 **a1** γεηρὰ usurp. Plot. IV 7,10,48 (II 216 H.-S.)
a3 ἑστιάσεων usurp. Plot. VI 7,36,10 (III 260 H.-S.)
a4 πολυειδὴς Phot. II 98 N.
a4 μονοειδής resp. Dam., *in Prm.* II 259,17-18 R.
a8-614a6 Οὐκοῦν—περιμένει AFF. Stob. III 9,63 (III 402,4-405,7 H.)
a8-b5 resp. D. L. III 78 (I 152,16-17 L.)
b3-4 resp. Tz., *in Il.* 76,8 L.
b4-5 resp. Socr., *Ep.* 14,2 (619 H.); Lib., *Or.* LXIV 36 (IV 442,8-10 F.)
b4 resp. Demetr. Cyd., *Ep.* 14,25 (I 42 L.)
b5 ῎Αιδος κυνῆν resp. Dam., *in Phd.* I 348,4 (191 W.); Olymp., *in Grg.* 46,4 (246,4-5 W.); expl. sch. Pl. ad loc. (275 G.)

613 **a4-b1** resp. D. L. III 79 (153,6-8 L.)
a7-b1 οὐ—θεῷ AFF. Alb., *Intr.* XXVIII 1 (137 L.); resp. Mich., *in EN* 66,5-7 Ha.; Them., *Or.* 15,189a (I 274,2-3 D.-N.)
b1 cit. Thdt., *Affect.* XI 9 (II 394,4-5 C.); resp. Apul., *Pl.* II 23,252 (100 B.); Clem., *Paed.* I ii 4,2 (I 91,26 S.); D. L. III 78 (I 152,15-16 L.); Eus., *Theoph.* II 30 (92,27-93,2 M.); Muson. *ap.* Stob. IV 50,94 (V 1057,19 H.); Plot. I 2,1,3-4 (I 62 H.-S.); — I 4,16,12 (I 97 H.-S.); — I 6,6,20 (I 112 H.-S.); Stob. II 7,3ᶠ (II 49,9 W.); Them., *Or.* 2,32d (I 43,6-7 D.-N.); —, — 34,XXX (II 232,18 D.-N.); fort.resp. Alb., *Intr.* XXVIII 3 (137-139 L.); Clem., *Strom.* I 11,52,3 (II 34,12 S.); —, — II 22,131,5 (II 185,23-24 S.); —, — VII 3,13,2-3 (III 10,18 et 23 S.); Gr. Naz., *Ep.* 165,8 (120,22 G.); Ioseph. Kaloth., *Andr.* 3 (439,107 T.); Sext., *Sent.* 45 (16 Ch.); —, — 381 (56 Ch.); usurp. Didym., *in Gen.* 145,6-7 (I 332 N.); imit. Gr. Nyss., *Hom. in Cant.* I (25,8-9 L.)
c1 τὰ—ἔχοντες AFF. Phot. II 202 N.; Sud. τ 100 (IV 503,5 A.)
c2-e4 fort.resp. Ptol., *Tetr.* γ 14,8-9 (157,13-158,2 B.)
c2-3 resp. Demetr. Cyd., *Ep.* 6,14 (I 31 L.)

614 **a5-d3** Ταῦτα—τόπῳ AFF. Eus., *PE* XI 35,1-5 (II 73,12-74,7 M.)
a5-8 resp. Pr., *in R.* II 97,11-18 K.
b2-621d3 resp. et interpr. Pr., *in R.* II 96,1-368,18 K.; resp. Averr., *in R.* 105,15-16 R.; Dam., *in Phd.* I 471,2-3 (241 W.); —, — II 85,4-5 (335 W.); D. L. III 80 (I 153,9-10 L.); Gr. Naz., *Or.*27,10,3-5 (94 G.-J.); Macrob., *in Somn. Scip.* 2,17,13 (II 153,6-10 W.); Olymp., *in Grg.* 46,8-9 (241,4.12.26, 242,4 W.); —, *in Mete.* 144,33 S.; Pr., *in R.* I 15,26-27 K.; —, — II 85,7-11 K.; —, *Th. Pl.* I 6 (I 28,24-25 S.-W.); sch. Luc. *VH* I 4 (18,17-19 R.); Theon, *Prog.* 159 (II 66,20-21 S.)
b2-616c2 Ἀλλ'—τεταμένα AFF. Stob. I 49,64 (I 451,4-454,9 W.)
b2-616b1 resp. Anon., *in Rh.* 329,13-15 R.; Elias, *in Porph.* 33,16-18 B.; Pr., *in R.* II 92,21-24 K.
b2-d3 Ἀλλ'—τόπῳ AFF. Thdt., *Affect.* XI 43-44 (II 406,18-407,12 C.)
b2-8 resp. Aristid., *Or.* 26,69 (110,22-111,3 K.)
b2-7 Ἀλλ'—ἀνεβίω AFF. Anon., *in Rh.* 328,31-35 R.
b2-4 cit. Pr., *in R.* I 169,18-20 K.; resp. Pr., *in R.* II 109,4-6 K.; expl. sch. Pl. ad loc. (276 G.)
b2-3 resp. et interpr. Pr., *in R.* II 111,18-112,7 K.; resp. Pr., *in R.* II 111,8 K.
b2 Ἀλκίνου ἀπόλογον resp. Anon., *in Rh.* 324,12 R.
b3-8 latine cit. Val. Max. I viii *ext.* 1 (51,5-9 K.); resp. Aen. Gaz., *Thphr.* 64,7-8 C.; Clem., *Strom.* V 14,103,3 (II 395,21-23 S.); Cyr., *adv. Iul.* 881c; Or., *Cels.* 2,16,25-27 (I 328 B.); Tert., *An.* LI 2 (69,4-6 W.)

INDEX TESTIMONIORUM 357

b3-4 Ἡρὸς—Παμφύλου AFF. Clem., *Strom.* V 14,103,2 (II 395,17-18 S.); Eus., *PE* XIII 13,30 (II 208,4-5) (ex Clemente); resp. Plu., *Mor.* 740b (IV 314,3-4 H.); Pr., *in R.* II 96,2-4 K.; —, — II 103,2 K.
b3 Ἡρὸς τοῦ Ἀρμενίου resp. Anon., *in Rh.* 324,13 R.; Clem., *Strom.* V 9,58,6 (II 365,19 S.)
b3 Ἀρμενίου resp. Pr., *in R.* II 110,12.15 K.
b4-8 resp. Aug., *Civ.* XXII 28,7 (855 D.-K.)
b4-7 ὅς—ἀνεβίω cit. Pr., *in R.* II 113,1-4 K.
b4-5 resp. Pr., *in R.* II 127,13 K.
b6-7 δωδεκαταῖος—ἀνεβίω cit. Pr., *in R.* II 188,17-19 K.
b6 δωδεκαταῖος resp. Pr., *in R.* II 354,2 K.
b7-c1 ἀναβιοὺς—δαιμόνιον AFF. Pr., *in R.* II 122,12-14 K.
b8-621b4 resp. Pr., *in R.* I 168,11-17 K.
b8-616b1 resp. Gal., *Hist. Phil.* 24 (614,8-10 D.)
b8-c7 resp. Pr., *in R.* II 131,11-14 K.
b8-c4 cit. Pr., *in R.* II 132,22-23 K.
b8-c1 resp. Pr., *in R.* II 127,4-5 K.; —, — II 127,11-12 K.
c1-d1 resp. Numen. *ap.* Pr., *in R.* II 128,16-129,4 K.; Pr., *in R.* II 155,23-28 K.
c1-4 resp. Pr., *in R.* II 132,1-2 K.
c1-3 resp. et interpr. Pr., *in R.* II 136,21-144,11 K.; resp. Pr., *in R.* II 93,13-18 K.; —, — II 130,18-20 K.; —, — II 131,18-20 K.
c1 τόπον δαιμόνιον resp. Pr., *in R.* II 128,3 K.
c2-e1 resp. Porph., *Antr.* 22 (71,17 N.); —, — 29 (76,21-23 N.); —, — 31 (77,16-18 N.)
c2-d1 resp. Pr., *in R.* II 139,12-18 K.
c2-4 ἐν—καθῆσθαι AFF. Pr., *in R.* II 136,17-20 K.
c2 δύ' εἶναι χάσματα resp. Plu., *Mor.* 1104b (VI 2,165,13 P.-W.); Pr., *in R.* II 129,13 K.; —, — II 130,2-3 K.; —, — II 138,9 K.; Psell., *Orat. Min.* 11,9 (44 L.)
c3-621d3 resp. Pr., *in R.* I 7,29-8,4 K.
c3-616b1 resp. D. L. III 79 (I 153,8-9 L.); Eus., *Theoph.* II 30 (92,25-27 G.); Pr., *in R.* II 100,20-23 K.; —, — II 104,7-8 K.
c3-d3 resp. Pr., *in R.* II 353,12-14 K.
c3 καταντικρύ resp. Pr., *in R.* II 139,26-140,13 K.
c3 δικαστὰς resp. Pr., *in Ti.* III 323,23-25 D.
c4-7 οὕς—πρόσθεν AFF. Pr., *in R.* II 144,13-16 K.
c6-d1 resp. Pr., *in R.* II 93,25-29 K.
c6 σημεῖα resp. Pr., *in R.* II 151,4-5 K.; —, *in Ti.* III 120,27-30 D.
c8-d1 πάντων ὧν ἔπραξαν AFF. Pr., *in R.* II 144,16 K.
d1-3 ἑαυτοῦ—τόπῳ AFF. Pr., *in R.* II 153,1-4 K.; resp. Pr., *in R.* II 153,12-18 K.
d3-616a7 resp. Pr., *de Mal. Subs.* 16,11-15 (196 B.)
d3-e1 resp. Pr., *in R.* II 93,18-25 K.
d3-5 ὁρᾶν—γῆς AFF. Pr., *in R.* II 155,19-20 K.
d6-7 resp. Pr., *in R.* I 118,28 K.; —, — II 327,1 K.
d7-e1 resp. Dam., *in Phd.* II 100,5 (343 W.); fort.imit. Meth., *Symp.* II 5 (21,5 B.)
e1-3 resp. et interpr. Pr., *in R.* II 158,8-159,19 K.; resp. Pr., *in R.* II 93,29-94,3 K.; —, — II 159,19-20 K.; Psell., *Omnif. Doctr.* 198,8-10 (97 W.)
e2-3 καὶ—κατασκηνᾶσθαι AFF. Pr., *in R.* II 155,20-22 K.; resp. Pr., *in R.* II 160,13 K.
e2 resp. Herm., *in Phdr.* 161,7-9 C.; Pr., *in Alc.* 256,15 (118 W.); —, *in R.* II 132,16-133,3 K.; —, — II 139,11 K.
e3-615a3 cit. Pr., *in R.* II 327,16-18 K.
e3-6 καὶ—ἐκείναις AFF. Pr., *in R.* II 163,13-16 K.
e3 οἷον—κατασκηνᾶσθαι cit. Pr., *in R.* II 158,4-5 K.
e4-615a4 resp. Pr., *in R.* II 163,28-164,7 K.
e6-615c1 resp. Herm., *in Phdr.* 168,1-3 C.

a2-3 cit. Pr., *in R.* II 161,1 K.; resp. Calc., *Ti.* CXXXVI (176,17-177,1 W.); Pr., *in R.* II 94,3-5 K.

a3 τὴν πορείαν χιλιέτη resp. et interpr. Pr., *in R.* II 172,20-174,12 K.; resp. Aristid., *Or.* 4,39 (I 3,543,21 L.-B.); Pr., *in R.* II 161,11 K.; —, — II 168,28 K.; —, — II 172,12 K.; —, — II 172,23 K.; —, — II 188,21-22 K.; —, — II 327,7 K.; —, — II 328,20-21 K.; Thpl. Ant., *Autol.* III 29 (146 G.)
a3 εὐπαθείας *AB* I 94,28
a4-616a7 resp. Pr., *de Mal. Subs.* 19,21-29 (199 B.); —, *in Ti.* III 238,12-13 D.
a4-6 τὰ—εἶναι AFF. Pr., *in R.* II 171,22-23 K.
a4 καὶ—κάλλος AFF. Pr., *in R.* II 163,16 K.
a4 θέας—κάλλος cit. Pr., *in R.* II 168,18 K.; imit. Iambl., *Protr.* 12 (60,21-22 P.)
a8-b1 resp. Herm., *in Phdr.* 168,9-10 C.
a8 resp. Pr., *in R.* II 172,6-10 K.
b2-c1 resp. Pr., *in R.* II 174,29-175,23 K.
c1-2 resp. Pr., *in R.* II 175,10-18 K.
c2-4 εἰς—διηγεῖτο AFF. Pr., *in R.* II 171,24-26 K.
c3 resp. Pr., *in R.* II 174,13-29 K.
c5-616b1 Ἔφη—ἀντιστρόφους AFF. Iust. Phil., *Coh. Gent.* 27 (III 92-94 O.)
c5-616a4 resp. Aen. Gaz., *Thphr.* 42,9-10 C.; Anon., *in Rh.* 324,14 R.; Herm., *in Phdr.* 169,8-10 C.; Olymp., *in Mete.* 144,34-35 S.; Pr., *in R.* II 102,28 K.; —, — II 326,28-29 K.; Synes., *Ep.* 43 (178,11-16 G.)
c5-6 Ἔφη—μέγας AFF. Pr., *in R.* II 175,29-176,1 K.
c5 resp. Pr., *in R.* II 177,16-178,1 K.
c6 Ἀρδιαῖος resp. Pr., *in R.* II 97,21 K. (et *passim*)
c8 resp. Pr., *in R.* II 176,25-26 K.
d1 resp. Pr., *in R.* II 177,4-5 K.
d3 Οὐχ—δεῦρο AFF. Pr., *in R.* II 178,1-2 K.
d4-e4 cit. Pr., *in R.* II 179,28-180,8 K.
e1-4 fort.resp. Plu., *Mor.* 591c (III 496,6 P.-S.)
e2-616a4 resp. Pr., *in R.* I 118,26-28 K.
e2-3 fort.resp. Ph., *Spec.* III 15,88 (V 175,7-9 C.-W.)
e2 resp. Pr., *in R.* II 97,20 K.; —, — II 106,6 K.
e2 τὸ στόμιον resp. Pr., *in R.* II 94,5-8 K.; —, *in Ti.* III 352,27-28 D.
e2 ἐμυκᾶτο resp. Pr., *in R.* II 142,2 K.
e3 ἀνιάτως ἐχόντων resp. Pr., *in R.* II 178,2-179,2 K.
e4-616a4 resp. et interpr. Pr., *in R.* II 179,11-184,10 K.; resp. Calc., *Ti.* CXXXVI (177,5-6 W.); Elias, *in Porph.* 41,28-33 W.; Pr., *in R.* II 100,24-28 K.; —, *in Ti.* III 323,23-25 D.
e4-616a3 ἐνταῦθα—κνάμπτοντες AFF. Clem., *Strom.* V 14,90,5 (II 385,27-386,4 S.); Eus., *PE* XIII 13,5 (II 199,12-15 M.); Thdt., *Affect.* XI 18 (II 396,17-397,1 C.)
e4-5 resp. Plu., *Mor.* 828f (V 1,134,13-14 H.-P.-D.); Pr., *in R.* II 181,9 K.; —, — II 182,1-4 K.; —, *in Ti.* III 154,5-9 D.
e4 διάπυροι resp. Pr., *in R.* II 104,20 K.; —, — II 106,6 K.; —, — II 180,11 K.
e5 cit. Pr., *in R.* II 142,1-2 K.; resp. Pr., *in R.* II 181,23 K.
e6-616a4 resp. Pr., *in R.* II 97,21 K.
e6-616a1 resp. et interpr. Pr., *in R.* II 182,9-16 K.
e6 διαλαβόντες resp. Pr., *in R.* II 182,6-8 K.

616 **a1-2** resp. et interpr. Pr., *in R.* II 182,16-22 K.
a2-3 resp. et interpr. Pr., *in R.* II 182,28-183,6 K.; resp. Pr., *in R.* II 104,21 K.; —, — II 180,12 K.
a2 resp. et interpr. Pr., *in R.* II 182,22-28 K.
a2 ἀσπαλάθων expl. sch. Pl. ad loc. (276 G.)
a3-4 resp. Pr., *in R.* II 180,13 K.; —, — II 183,6-11 K.
a3 κνάμπτοντες Phot. I 347 N.
a4-7 cit. Pr., *in R.* II 183,27-29 K.; resp. Pr., *in R.* II 183,27-184,10 K.
a4 resp. Pr., *in R.* II 183,11-25 K.
a7 καὶ—ἀναβῆναι AFF. Pr., *in R.* II 176,2-3 K.

INDEX TESTIMONIORUM 359

a8-b1 καὶ prius-ἀντιστρόφους AFF. Pr., *in R.* II 184,11-13 K.
a8 resp. et interpr. Pr., *in R.* II 184,14-185,18 K.
b1-621b8 resp. Pr., *Th. Pl.* I 5 (I 24,21-23 S.-W.)
b1-617d1 resp. Pr., *in R.* II 92,25-29 K.
b1-617b7 ἐπειδή—συμφωνεῖν AFF. Theon Sm. 143,19-146,2 H.
b1-c2 cit. Pr., *in R.* II 188,8-14 K.
b1-4 ἐπειδή—τεταρταίους AFF. Clem., *Strom.* V 14,106,2 (II 397,9-11 S.); Eus., *PE* XIII 13,33 (II 209,21-22 M.)
b1-3 ἐπειδή—πορεύεσθαι AFF. Pr., *in R.* II 185,19-21 K.
b1 resp. Pr., *in R.* II 97,22 K.
b3-c2 resp. Pr., *in R.* II 120,11-15 K.
b4-617b3 resp. Pr., *in R.* II 104,9-10 K.; —, — II 105,2-6 K.
b4-c4 διά—περιφοράν cit. Pr., *in R.* II 193,26-194,1 K.; resp. Pr., *in R.* II 193,21-199,21 K.
b4 διά—οὐρανοῦ cit. Pr., *in Ti.* II 6,29 D.
b5-c4 resp. Pr., *in R.* II 94,8-11 K.
b5-6 resp. Pr., *in R.* II 195,5-6 K.; —, — II 199,6 K.; Simp., *in Ph.* 612,36 D.; —, — 615,32-33 D.
b5-6 τῇ ἴριδι προσφερῆ cit. Pr., *in Ti.* II 6,29-31 D.
b5 τεταμένον—κίονα AFF. Phot. II 208 N.
b5 τεταμένον resp. Pr., *in R.* II 198,30 K.
b5 οἷον κίονα resp. Pr., *in R.* II 199,1 K.; —, — II 199,27-200,12 K.; —, — II 202,14 K.
b6-621a1 resp. Paul. Nol., *Ep.* XVI 4 (118,8-12 H.)
b7-c1 καὶ—φῶς AFF. Pr., *in R.* II 199,24-25 K.
c1-617b7 resp. Iambl., *Theol. Ar.* 81,19-22 F.
c1-4 resp. Pr., *in R.* II 200,13-201,2 K.
c1-2 resp. et interpr. sch. Pr., *in R.* II 381,4-9 K.; resp. Pr., *in R.* II 195,26-27 K.; —, — II 199,10-11 K.; —, — II 202,9-10 K.
c2-4 resp. Pr., *in R.* II 196,5-6 K.
c2 resp. Pr., *in R.* II 199,4-5 K.
c3-4 οἷον—περιφοράν AFF. Pr., *in R.* II 199,25-26 K.; —, — II 202,23-24 K.; resp. Pr., *in R.* II 199,2 K.
c3-4 οὕτω—περιφοράν AFF. Pr., *in R.* II 185,21-22 K.
c3 οἷον—τριήρων AFF. Pr., *in R.* II 200,24.29 K.
c4-617d1 resp. Max. Tyr. 4,4f (45,2-4 H.); Plu., *Mor.* 745f (IV 328,13-15 H.)
c4-617b7 resp. Demetr. Cyd., *Ep.* 33,52 (I 65 L.); Iambl., *Theol. Ar.* 81,19-22 F.
c4-6 resp. Pr., *in Ti.* III 147,22-24 D.
c4-5 ἐκ—περιφοράς AFF. Pr., *in R.* II 202,5-6 K.; resp. Pr., *in Ti.* III 138,22-23 D.
c4 Ἀνάγκης ἄτρακτον Phot. α 1427 (I 148 Th.); resp. Pr., *in R.* II 202,10-11 K.
c4 Ἀνάγκης resp. et interpr. Pr., *in R.* II 204,25-208,25 K.; resp. Pr., *in Ti.* I 397,10 D.
c4 ἄτρακτον resp. et interpr. Pr., *in R.* II 203,3-204,22 K.; resp. Plot. II 3,9,1 (I 171 H.-S.); Pr., *in R.* II 240,23 K.
c5-6 resp. et interpr. Pr., *in R.* II 209,31-213,12 K.
c5 δι'—περιφοράς AFF. Pr., *in R.* II 202,4-5 K.; resp. et interpr. Pr., *in R.* II 202,16-22 K.
c6-7 τὸν—γενῶν AFF. Pr., *in R.* II 202,5-6 K.
c6 resp. et interpr. Pr., *in R.* II 208,26-209,29 K.; resp. Pr., *in R.* II 200,4 K.
c6 ἄγκιστρον *AB* I 335,21; *An. Bachm.* I 20,15; Phot. α 182 (I 26 Th.)
c7-e3 τὴν—ἐληλάσθαι resp. et interpr. Pr., *in R.* II 213,16-217,18 K.
c7-d2 τὴν—ἐνθάδε AFF. Pr., *in R.* II 213,13-14 K.
c7-d1 resp. Ptol., *Hyp.* II 4 (II 113,31 H.)
c7 σφόνδυλον resp. Pr., *in R.* II 240,23 K.
d1-617b3 resp. Pr., *in R.* II 97,23 K.; —, — II 102,1 K.
d1-e3 resp. Pr., *in R.* II 189,13-17 K.
d1-6 resp. Theon Sm. 189,2-3 H.
d1-4 resp. Pr., *in R.* II 213,9-214,25 K.

d3 ἐξεγλυμμένῳ resp. Pr., in R. II 215,6-7 K.
d5 resp. Pr., in R. II 216,5-6 K.
d6-e3 resp. Pr., in Ti. III 56,31-33 D.
d6-7 ὀκτώ—σφονδύλους resp. et interpr. Pr., in R. II 216,18-217,18 K.; resp. Pr., in R. II 203,8 K.; —, in Ti. II 268,12-13 D.
d6 resp. Phlp., Opif. 15,23-24 R.
e1 resp. Pr., in R. II 189,13 K.; —, — II 203,22-23 K.; —, — II 215,4-5 K.; —, — II 216,8 K.
e2-8 resp. Pr., in R. I 282,9 K.
e2-3 ἐκείνην—ἐληλάσθαι AFF. Pr., in R. II 213,14-15 K.
e3-617d1 resp. Pr., in Ti. III 70,20-30 D.
e3-8 resp. et interpr. Pr., in R. II 217,22-222,23 K.; varias lectiones cit. Pr., in R. II 218,1-219,20 K.
e3-5 τὸν—ἔχειν AFF. Pr., in R. II 217,19-20 K.
e3 διαμπερὲς ἐληλάσθαι resp. Pr., in R. II 214,26-27 K.; —, — II 215,1 K.
e5 resp. Pr., in Ti. III 61,1-2 D.
e8-617a4 cit. Pr., in R. II 222,29-223,16 K.; resp. et interpr. Pr., in R. II 222,27-225,27 K.; resp. Simp., in Cael. 474,16-18 H.
e8-9 καὶ—λαμπρότατον AFF. Pr., in R. II 222,24-25 K.
e8 ὄγδοον—δευτέρου AFF. Pr., in R. II 217,21 K.
e9 λαμπρότατον usurp. Plot. II 1,7,22 (I 155 H.-S.)

a4-b4 resp. et interpr. Pr., in R. II 226,3-236,15 K.
a4-7 resp. Anon., Prol. Plat. X 25,7-9 (47 W.); Macrob., in Somn. Scip. 2,3,1 (II 103,31 W.) (= Porph., in Ti. 59,11-12 S.); Plot. III 4,6,49-51 (I 317 H.-S.)
a4-6 κυκλεῖσθαι—φοράν AFF. Pr., in R. II 225,30-226,1 K.; fort.resp. Them., Or. 26,327c (II 145,6-7 D.-N.)
a4 δεύτερον—ἕκτον AFF. Pr., in R. II 222,25-26 K.
a5-6 resp. Pr., in R. II 226,14-15 K.
a6-b3 resp. Pr., in Ti. I 264,28-30 D.
a7-b3 αὐτῶν—δεύτερον AFF. Simp., in Cael. 475,16-18 H.
a7 resp. Pr., in R. II 226,24 K.
b3 resp. Pr., in R. II 94,15-18 K.
b4-d1 cit. Calc., Ti. XCV (148,7 W.); resp. et interpr. Pr., in R. II 226,27-227,22 K.; resp. Macrob., in Somn. Scip. 2,3,1 (II 103,29-32 W.) (= Porph., in Ti. 59,11-12 S.); Plu., Mor. 1029c (VI 1,186,10-14 H.-D.); Pr., in R. II 97,24 K.; —, — II 98,21-22 K.; —, — II 100,6-8 K.; —, — II 194,7-8 K.
b4-7 resp. et interpr. Pr., in R. II 236,20-239,14 K.; resp. Heracl., All. Hom. 12 (308,1-4 M.); Mythogr. III 11,9 (234,14-17 B.); Pr., in R. II 236,16-19 K.; —, in Ti. II 208,12-14 D.; fort.resp. Pr., in Alc. 204,14-15 (94 W.)
b4 στρέφεσθαι—γόνασιν AFF. Pr., in R. II 226,1-2 K.; resp. Pr., in Ti. I 397,11 D.; —, Th. Pl. VI 23 (405 P.)
b5-7 resp. Plu., Mor. 1147a (VI 3,35,29-36,3 Z.-P.); Pr., in R. II 100,8-11 K.
b5-6 cit. Pr., in R. I 69,10-11 K.
b6-7 resp. Pr., in R. II 250,16-20 K.
b6 φωνήν—τόνον AFF. Pr., in R. I 69,11-12 K.
b6 φωνήν μίαν ἱεῖσαν resp. Plot. IV 3,12,24-25 (II 30 H.-S.)
b6 ἕνα τόνον resp. Pr., in R. II 236,27 K.; —, — II 237,1 K.; —, — II 238,15 K.
b7-620e6 fort.resp. Max. Tyr. 5,5e (60,2-5 H.)
b7-d1 resp. Plu., Mor. 568e (III 446,16-18 P.-S.); —, — 745bc (IV 326,24-327,4 H.); Pr., in Prm. 692,21-22 C.; —, — 1234,14-18 C.; —, — 1238,39-1239,2 C.; —, in R. II 94,18-21 K.; —, in Ti. II 234,22-25 D.; —, — III 182,17-19 D.
b7-c5 resp. Pr., in R. II 102,2 K.
b7-c3 resp. et interpr. Pr., in R. II 249,23-26 K.
b7-c2 ἄλλας—'Ανάγκης AFF. Pr., in R. II 239,15-16 K.
c1-2 resp. et interpr. Pr., in R. II 245,4-246,4 K.; resp. Bess., in Cal. Pl. 180,27-28 M.;

INDEX TESTIMONIORUM 361

Nicet. Chon., *Or.* 3 (18,23 D.); Pr., *in R.* II 207,15-16 K.; —, *Th. Pl.* VI 23 (406 P.)
c1 resp. et interpr. Pr., *in R.* II 247,22-249,21 K.
c2-3 resp. et interpr. Pr., *in R.* II 247,3-21 K.; resp. Pr., *Th. Pl.* VI 23 (410 P.)
c2 resp. et interpr. Pr., *in R.* II 246,5-247,2 K.
c4-5 cit. Pr., *in R.* II 249,29-31 K.; resp. et interpr. Pr., *in R.* I 249,29-251,17 K.; resp. Pr., *Th. Pl.* VI 23 (407 P.); expl. sch. Pl. ad loc. (276 G.)
c5-d1 resp. et interpr. Pr., *in R.* II 251,18-253,17 K.; resp. Pr., *Th. Pl.* VI 12 (381 P.); —, — VI 23 (406 P.)
c5-8 resp. Pr., *Th. Pl.* VI 23 (408 P.)
c6-8 resp. Pr., *Th. Pl.* VI 24 (411 P.)
c7 διαλείπουσαν χρόνον resp. et interpr. Pr., *in R.* II 252,7-13 K.; resp. Pr., *in R.* II 244,8 K.; —, — II 252,4 K.; —, *Th. Pl.* VI 23 (406 P.); —, — VI 23 (407 P.)
c8-d1 τὴν—ἐφάπτεσθαι AFF. Pr., *in R.* II 239,17-18 K.; resp. et interpr. Pr., *in R.* II 239,19-253,17 K.; resp. Dam., *in Prm.* II 213,14 R.; Pr., *in R.* II 341,21-22 K.
d1-620d5 resp. Pr., *in R.* II 92,29-93,5 K.
d1-5 resp. et interpr. Pr., *in R.* II 253,21-268,2 K.
d1-2 σφᾶς—Λάχεσιν AFF. Pr., *in R.* II 253,18-19 K.
d2-619b6 resp. Pr., *in R.* II 98,22-26 K.
d2-e8 resp. Pr., *in Ti.* III 323,17-18 D.
d2-e5 resp. Plot. II 3,15,1-5 (I 178-179 H.-S.); Pr., *in Ti.* III 154,5-9 D.; —, — III 242,3-4 D.; —, — III 244,3-4 D.; —, — III 303,3-5 D.
d2-5 resp. Clem., *Strom.* I 15,69,2 (II 43,8-10 S.); Pr., *in R.* II 94,22-24 K.; —, — II 341,26-28 K.
d4-5 resp. Pr., *Th. Pl.* VI 23 (409 P.)
d4 resp. et interpr. Pr., *in R.* II 263,4-268,26 K.; resp. Pr., *in Alc.* 143,9-11 (65 W.); —, *in R.* II 257,27-30 K.
d5 ἀναβάντα—εἰπεῖν AFF. Pr., *in R.* II 253,19-20 K.; usurp. David, *in Cat.* 23a B.
d5 ἀναβάντα—ὑψηλὸν cit. Pr., *in Ti.* III 200,6-7 D.; resp. et interpr. Pr., *in R.* II 256,22-257,25 K.
d6-621a1 resp. Cass., *Hist. Trip.* VI 46,7,25 (370 J.-H.); Epiphan. II (588,21-22 D.); Hieron., *Ep.* LXXXIV 6 (IV 132,2 L.); Minuc. Fel., *Oct.* 34,6 (32,21-24 K.); Socr. Sch., *HE* III 21 (162 B.); Thpl. Ant., *Autol.* III 7 (108 G.)
d6-619b1 resp. Alb., *Intr.* XXVI 1 (125 L.); Herm., *in Phdr.* 69,28-31 C.
d6-618b6 resp. Herm., *in Phdr.* 164,24-25 C.
d6-e5 resp. et interpr. Pr., *in R.* II 269,1-279,6 K.; resp. Aët. Doxogr. I 27,3 (322a5-8 D.)
d6-7 Ἀνάγκης—θανατηφόρου AFF. Pr., *in R.* II 268.27-29 K.
d6-7 Ψυχαὶ ἐφήμεροι AFF. Pr., *in R.* II 98,26 K.; —, — II 270,14 K.; resp. et interpr. Pr., *in R.* II 270,14-19 K.; usurp. Pr., *de Mal. Subs.* 12,4 (192 B.)
d6 Ἀνάγκης—λόγος AFF. Plu., *Mor.* 568cd (III 445,15 P.-S.); Pr., *in R.* II 269,15-16 K.; —, — II 323,2-3 K.; cit. Pr., *in R.* II 254,29-255,1 K.; resp. et interpr. Pr., *in R.* II 269,16-270,13 K.; resp. Pr., *Th. Pl.* VI 23 (409 P.)
d6 Ἀνάγκης—Λαχέσεως resp. et interpr. Pr., *in R.* II 207,5-7 K.
d7-e1 resp. Pr., *in R.* II 255,2-4 K.
d7 ἀρχὴ—θανατηφόρου cit. Pr., *in R.* II 270,19-20 K.; resp. et interpr. Pr., *in R.* II 270,21-271,6 K.
e1-5 resp. Aug., *Pecc. Or.* XXXI 36 (*PL* 44,403)
e1-3 resp. Cyr., *adv. Iul.* 621b; Pr., *in R.* II 94,24-26 K.; imit. Iul., *Or.* X 335d1-2 (II 2,70 L.)
e1 οὐχ—αἱρήσεσθε AFF. Apostol. XVII 54 (II 700,10-11 L.-S.); Bess., *in Cal. Pl.* 188,33-34 M.; Dam., *in Phd.* II 103,1-2 (343 W.); Herm., *in Phdr.* 69,30-31 C.; Olymp., *in Alc.* 45,4 (30 W.); —, — 104,12-13 (69 W.); Pr., *in R.* II 323,3-4 K.; cit. (latine) Calc., *Ti.* CLIV (189,6-8 W.) (= Porph., *in Ti.* 86,15-18 S.); cit. Pr., *in R.* II 271,6-8 K.; resp. et interpr. Pr., *in R.* II 271,8-273,5 K.; resp. Apul., *Soc.* XVI 155 (36 B.); Olymp., *in Alc.* 49,23-24 (33 W.); Or., *Cels.* 8,34,22 (IV 248 B.); Pr., *in R.* II 100,15-19 K.; —, — II 104,23-24 K.; —, — II 244,25 K.

e1 οὐχ—λήξεται AFF. Pr., in R. II 271,27 K.
e1 ὑμεῖς—αἱρήσεσθε AFF. Pr., in R. II 266,3 K.; resp. Plot. III 4,3,8-9 (I 313 H.-S.)
e2-3 πρῶτος prius-ἀνάγκης AFF. Porph. ap. Stob. II 8,39 (II 164,6 W.)
e2-3 ᾧ—ἀνάγκης AFF. Pr., in R. II 266,8-9 K.; —, — II 274,23 K.; resp. et interpr. Pr., in R. II 274,22-275,20 K.
e2 πρῶτος prius-βίον AFF. Pr., in R. II 265,16-17 K.; resp. et interpr. Pr., in R. II 273,6-274,21 K.
e3-5 ἀρετή—ἀναίτιος AFF. (latine) Arn., Gent. II 64 (99,22-24 R.); usurp. Clem., Strom. V 14,136,4 (II 418,12-13 S.)
e3-4 ἀρετή—ἕξει AFF. Bess., in Cal. Pl. 188,30-31 M.; Pr., in R. II 275,26-28 K.; Porph. ap. Stob. II 8,39 (II 164,23-24 W.); Thdt., Affect. VI 57 (I 274,16-17 C.); resp. et interpr. Pr., in R. II 275,28-279,6 K.
e3 ἀρετή ἀδέσποτον AFF. (latine) Calc., Ti. CLIV (189,5 W.); Plot. IV 4,39,2 (II 133 H.-S.); cit. Philostr., Ep. 15,390 (I 349,29-30 K.); Plu., Mor. 740d (IV 314,17 H.); resp. Alb., Intr. XXXI 1 (151 L.); Ap. Ty., Ep. 15 (113,20 H.); Aristid. Quint. III 27 (133,20-21 W.-I.); Gnomol. Vat. 423 (158 S.); Iul., Ep. 59 (I 2,135,6 B.); Nemes. 28 (306 M.); Nicet. Chon., Or. 15 (161,9 D.); Olymp., in Alc. 226,15-16 (140 W.); Plot. II 3,9,17 (I 172 H.-S.); — VI 8,5,31 (III 278 H.-S.); Pr., in Ti. I 93,17 D.; —, — I 201,15 D.; fort.resp. Or., Cels. 4,3,48-49 (II 194 B.); usurp. Aen. Gaz., Thphr. 21,2 C.; Alb., Intr. XXVI 2 (127 L.); Pr., de Prov. 23,2 (132 B.); —, — 23,3 (133 B.); —, — 23,18 (132,133 B.)
e4-5 αἰτία—ἀναίτιος AFF. (latine) Calc., Ti. CLIV (189,4-5 W.) (= Porph., in Ti. 86,12-13 S.); Clem., Paed. I viii 69,1 (I 130,14-15 S.); Hipp., Haer. I 19,19 (III 23,3-4 W.); IG XIVa,1196 (316 K.); Iuln. Ar., Hiob 38,7 (256,16-17 H.); Iust. Phil., Apol. I 44 (I 122 O.); Luc., Merc. Cond. 42 (II 236,2-3 M.); Max. Tyr. 41,5a (482,1 H.); Nemes. 28 (306 M.); Olymp., in Alc. 45,3 (30 W.); Phlp., Aet. XVI 1 (566,17 R.); Pr., in R. II 268,29-30 K.; —, — II 277,9 K.; —, — II 288,29-289,1 K.; —, — II 323,5 K.; —, — II 355,27 K.; —, in Ti. III 303,5 D.; Thdt., Affect. VI 57 (I 274,17-18 C.); cit. Bess., in Cal. Pl. 158,13-14 M.; Corp. Herm. IV 8 (I 52,7-8 N.-F.); Hierocl., in CA 25,15 (109,10-11 K.); resp. et interpr. Pr., in R. II 277,9-279,6 K.; resp. Gr. Naz., Or. 4,47 (148 B.); Hierocl., in CA 11,8 (44,24-25 K.); —, — 11,38 (54,28 K.); —, — 25,17 (110,1 K.); Iust. Phil., Qu. et Resp. 8 (V 14 O.); fort.resp. Anast. Sin., VD II 3,34 (33 U.); Clem., QDS 14,4 (III 168,31-169,3 S.); usurp. Clem., Strom. I 1,4,1 (II 4,26-27 S.); —, — IV 23,150,4 (III 315,10-11 S.); Eus., PE VI 6,50 (I 308,10 M.); Porph., Marc. 12 (112,15-16 P.); —, — 24 (119,23-25 P.); imit. Gr. Nyss., Mort. 37,15-16 H.; Meth., Symp. VIII 16 (109,14 B.)
e4 αἰτία ἑλομένου AFF. Plot. III 2,7,19-20 (I 278 H.-S.); resp. Plu., Mor. 740d (IV 314,16-17 H.); Pr., de Decem Dub. 39,5 (60 B.); —, — 39,5-6 (61 B.)
e5 θεὸς ἀναίτιος resp. Clem., Strom. I 17,84,1 (II 54,16 S.); —, — II 16,75,3 (II 152,27 S.); usurp. Aen. Gaz., Thphr. 25,8 C.; Clem., Strom. VII 2,12,1 (III 9,26 S.)
e6-621b4 resp. Ruf., Greg. IX 10 (275,14-18 E.)
e6-618a1 resp. Plot. III 4,5,15-17 (I 315 H.-S.)
e6-8 resp. Pr., in R. II 94,26-29 K.; —, — II 97,24 K.; —, — II 353,15-17 K.
e7 πλὴν οὗ Phot. II 4 N.; Sud. ο 3 (IV 614,10 A.)

618   a1-620d5 resp. Pr., in R. II 97,25-26 K.
a1-b6 resp. Alb., Intr. XXV 6 (123 L.); Herm., in Phdr. 164,10-12 C.; Pr., in R. I 104,17-19 K.; —, — II 94,29-95,1 K.
a1-4 resp. Pr., in R. II 333,1-2 K.
a4-5 τυραννίδας διατελεῖς Phot. δ 465 (I 409 Th.)
b2-3 ψυχῆς—ἐνεῖναι AFF. Pr., in R. II 310,24-25 K.; cit. Pr., in R. II 323,12 K.; —, — II 331,2-4 K.; resp. Pr., in Alc. 70,8 (31 W.)
b6-619b1 resp. et interpr. Pr., in R. II 285,25-288,6 K.
b6-7 ἔνθα—ἀνθρώπῳ AFF. Pr., in R. II 285,22-23 K.
b6-7 ἔνθα—κίνδυνος imit. Iul., Or. VII,230d7 (II 1,79 R.)
b6 καὶ μεσοῦν τούτων AFF. Pr., in R. II 285,4-5 K.

INDEX TESTIMONIORUM 363

b7-c6 μάλιστα—αἱρεῖσθαι AFF. Stob. III 1,24 (III 11,2-7 H.)
d3 resp. Pr., *in R.* II 286,21-23 K.
e4-619a1 ἀδαμαντίνως—ἰέναι AFF. Olymp., *in Phd.* 6,14,3 (105 W.); —, — 8,17,9-10 (127 W.); cit. David, *in Cat.* 23a B.; Elias, *in Cat.* 110,18-20 B.; resp. Pr., *in R.* II 287,6 K.

a6 τὰ ὑπερβάλλοντα ἑκατέρωσε cit. Pr., *in R.* II 287,26-27 K.
a7-b1 οὕτω—ἄνθρωπος AFF. Pr., *in R.* II 285,24 K.; —, — II 287,29 K.
b2-e5 resp. Alb., *Intr.* XXVI 1 (125 L.)
b2-6 resp. et interpr. Pr., *in R.* II 288,9-290,24 K.; resp. Pr., *in Ti.* III 242,3-4 D.
b2-3 Καὶ prius-εἰπεῖν AFF. Pr., *in R.* II 288,7-8 K.
b3-5 Καὶ—κακός AFF. Pr., *in R.* II 289,1-3 K.; —, — II 321,8-10 K.; —, — II 323,6-7 K.
b5-6 μήτε prius-ἀθυμείτω AFF. Pr., *in R.* II 289,25-26 K.
b5-6 μήτε alterum-ἀθυμείτω AFF. Pr., *in R.* II 288,8-9 K.
b7-e5 resp. Pr., *in R.* II 95,2-4 K.; —, *in Ti.* III 237,7 D.; —, — III 238,12 D.
b7-d7 resp. Pr., *in Alc.* 99,11-13 (44 W.); —, — 137,4-15 (62 W.)
b7-d1 resp. et interpr. Pr., *in R.* II 290,28-292,22 K.; resp. Pr., *in Ti.* I 70,30-71,2 D.
b7-8 Εἰπόντος—ἑλέσθαι AFF. Pr., *in R.* II 290,25-26 K.; resp. Pr., *in R.* II 300,1 K.
b8-c6 resp. Pr., *in R.* II 295,24-27 K.
b9 λαιμαργίας Phot. I 370 N.; usurp. Pr., *in Ti.* III 235,18 D.
c1 excursum de παίδων αὐτοῦ βρώσεις dat Pr., *in R.* II 292,23-298,6 K.
c4-6 resp. Pr., *in Alc.* 292,17-19 (135 W.)
c6-d1 resp. et interpr. Pr., *in R.* II 300,4-301,7 K.; resp. Pr., *in R.* II 161,9-11 K.; —, — II 300,2-3 K.; —, — II 325,20-24 K.
c7-d1 ἔθει—μετειληφότα AFF. Dam., *in Phd.* I 529,4 (269 W.); Pr., *in R.* II 290,27 K.; resp. Pr., *in R.* II 326,9 K.
c7-d1 ἔθει ἄνευ φιλοσοφίας AFF. Pr., *in R.* II 161,9 K.
d1-5 resp. et interpr. Pr., *in R.* II 301,12-302,8 K.
d1-3 ὡς—ἥκοντας AFF. Pr., *in R.* II 301,8-9 K.; resp. Pr., *in Prm.* 693,16-18 C.
d4-5 fort.resp. Lyd., *Mens.* 4,7 (73,13-15 W.); —, — 4,100 (140,21-23 W.)
d5-e5 resp. et interpr. Pr., *in R.* II 302,12-304,17 K.
d5-7 διὸ—τύχην AFF. Pr., *in R.* II 302,9-11 K.
d5 οὐκ—ποιεῖσθαι AFF. Pr., *in R.* II 301,6 K.
d7-e5 resp. Psell., *Orat. Min.* 25,174-175 (93 L.)
d7 τὴν τοῦ κλήρου τύχην fort.resp. Plot. IV 8,1,39 (II 228 H.-S.)
d8-e2 resp. Pr., *in R.* II 304,24-26 K.
e1-5 cit. Pr., *in R.* II 302,23-26 K.
e4-5 οὐκ—οὐρανίαν AFF. Sud. χ 326 (IV 808,24-25 A.)
e4 χθονίαν resp. Pr., *in R.* II 93,21 K.; —, — II 94,4 K.
e5 ἀλλὰ λείαν τε καὶ οὐρανίαν AFF. Pr., *in R.* II 302,11 K.
e6-620d5 resp. Alb., *Intr.* XXV 6 (123 L.); Pr., *in R.* II 95,4-7 K.; —, — II 104,28-105,2 K.
e6-620a3 Ταύτην—αἱρεῖσθαι AFF. Pr., *in R.* II 304,18-22 K.; resp. et interpr. Pr., *in R.* II 304,23-312,5 K.

a2-3 cit. Pr., *in R.* I 120,21-22 K.; resp. Pr., *in R.* II 326,11-13 K.
a2-3 τοῦ προτέρου βίου fort.resp. Plot. III 4,5,5-6 (I 314 H.-S.); — IV 3,8,9-10 (II 22 H.-S.)
a3-d5 ἰδεῖν—μείγνυσθαι AFF. Eus., *PE* XIII 16,9-11 (II 236,7-25 M.); resp. et interpr. Pr., *in R.* II 312,10-341,4 K.; resp. Epiphan. I (587,12-13 D.); fort.resp. Herm., *Irris.* 2 (6 O.)
a3-c3 resp. et interpr. Pr., *in R.* II 308,7-312,5 K.
a3-6 cit. Aen. Gaz., *Thphr.* 11,12-14 C.
a3-5 ἰδεῖν—γένους AFF. Pr., *in R.* II 312,6-8 K.
a3 resp. Pr., *in R.* II 305,12 K.

a4-5 μίσει—γένους AFF. Pr., in R. II 314,15 K.
a4 Ὀρφέως resp. Pr., in R. II 103,1 K.
a4 κύκνου resp. Pr., in R. II 311,1 K.; —, — II 340,26-27 K.
a7-8 resp. Pr., in R. II 321,21-23 K.
a7 ἀηδόνος resp. Pr., in R. II 311,2 K.
b1-3 cit. Plu., Mor. 739f (IV 313,4-6 H.)
b1 εἰκοστὴν resp. Pr., in R. II 318,8 K.
b1 λέοντος resp. Pr., in R. II 311,2 K.
b2 Αἴαντος resp. Pr., in R. II 103,1 K.
b5-c2 resp. Pr., in R. II 321,24-28 K.
b5 resp. Plot. III 4,2,25-26 (I 312 H.-S.)
b5 ἀετοῦ resp. Pr., in R. II 311,2 K.
c1-2 εἰς—φύσιν cit. Pr., in R. II 311,9-10 K.
c2-3 resp. Aen. Gaz., Thphr. 11,15-18 C.; Pr., in Ti. III 295,7-8 D.
c3 resp. Olymp., in Phd. 7,3,10-12 (107 W.)
c3 πίθηκον resp. Pr., in R. II 311,3 K.
c4 Ὀδυσσέως resp. Pr., in R. II 103,1 K.
c5-6 πόνων—ἀπράγμονος cit. Pr., in R. II 305,15-17 K.
c5 πόνων—λελωφηκυῖαν AFF. Pr., in R. II 320,11-12 K.
c6 βίον ἀπράγμονος resp. Pr., in Ti. III 196,1 D.
d2-5 resp. Pr., in R. II 321,28-322,4 K.
d3-5 καὶ—ἥμερα AFF. Pr., in R. II 321,18-19 K.
d4-5 resp. et interpr. Pr., in R. II 322,12-328,18 K.
d4 fort.resp. Plot. II 4,2,18 (I 312 H.-S.)
d5-621a5 fort.resp. Pr., in R. II 244,25-29 K.
d5 καὶ—μείγνυσθαι AFF. Pr., in R. II 312,8 K.; resp. Pr., in R. II 322,4-11 K.
d6-621d3 resp. Pr., in R. II 93,5-10 K.
d6-621b1 cit. Porph. ap. Stob. II 8,39 (II 164,6-19 W.)
d6-621a3 Ἐπειδὴ—πεδίον AFF. Stob. I 5,21 (I 82,12-23 W.)
d6-621a1 resp. et interpr. Pr., in R. II 341,13-345,26 K.
d6-e1 Ἐπειδὴ—αἱρεθέντων AFF. Clem., Strom. V 14,91,4 (II 386,16-19 S.); Eus., PE XIII 13,6 (II 200,6-8 M.); resp. Dam., in Prm. II 213,14 R.; Plot. II 3,15,1-5 (I 178-179 H.-S.)
d6-7 Ἐπειδὴ—Λάχεσιν AFF. Pr., in R. II 341,9-11 K.
d6 Ἐπειδὴ—ᾑρῆσθαι AFF. Pr., in R. II 323,23-24 K.
d7-e1 cit. Pr., in R. II 341,22-26 K.
d8-e1 resp. Apul., Soc. XVI 155 (36 B.); Dam., in Phd. I 491,4-5 (251 W.); —, — II 105,3 (345 W.); Plot. III 4,5,8-9 (I 314 H.-S.); Pr., in R. II 323,26 K.
d8 resp. Plot. III 5,7,35 (I 329 H.-S.)
e1-6 resp. Pr., Th. Pl. VI 23 (410 P.)
e1 ἀποπληρωτὴν τῶν αἱρεθέντων cit. Plot. III 4,5,25 (I 315 H.-S.)
e2-3 ὑπὸ—δίνης AFF. Pr., in R. II 342,11-12 K.
e3-4 cit. Pr., in R. II 341,21-22 K.
e5 τὴν τῆς Ἀτρόπου νῆσιν Poll. VII 30 (II 60,12 B.)
e6-621a6 resp. Pr., Th. Pl. VI 23 (408 P.)
e6-621a1 ἀμεταστρεπτὶ—θρόνον AFF. Pr., in R. II 342,21-22 K.; resp. Pr., in Prm. 692,21-24 C.; —, in R. II 344,5-6 K.; —, — II 344,19-20 K.; —, in Ti. III 277,30 D.
e6 ἀμεταστρεπτὶ Hsch. α 3614 (I 126 L.); Lex. Seg. XI B.

a1-b4 resp. Pr., in Ti. III 323,18-20 D.
a1-4 ἐπειδὴ—φύει cit. Pr., in R. II 346,16-19 K.
a1-3 καὶ—πεδίον AFF. Pr., in R. II 345,27-29 K.
a1 resp. Pr., de Mal. Subs. 24,13-14 (203 B.)
a2-b1 resp. Iren. Lugd. II 33,2 (II 2,346,24-31 R.-D.)
a2-5 resp. Pr., in R. II 93,7 K.
a2-3 τὸ τῆς Λήθης πεδίον resp. Demetr. Cyd., Ep. 160,7 (II 31 L.); Pr., de Mal. Subs. 24,14 (203 B.); —, in R. II 31,6 K.; —, — II 95,7-9 K.

a4-b1 resp. et interpr. Pr., *in R.* II 347,20-350,22 K.; resp. Pr., *in Ti.* I 126,16 D.; —, — III 325,28-29 D.
a4-5 σκηνᾶσθαι—ποταμόν AFF. Pr., *in R.* II 347,17-18 K.
a4 καὶ—φύει AFF. Pr., *in R.* II 345,29 K.; resp. et interpr. Pr., *in R.* II 346,1-347,16 K.
a5-6 τὸν—στέγειν cit. Pr., *in R.* II 348,2-3 K.
a5 τὸν ᾿Αμέλητα ποταμὸν resp. *An. Ox.* III 245,13; Iambl., *Myst.* 148,14-15 (127 P.); Plot. IV 3,26,55 (II 55 H.-S.); Porph., *Gaur.* 35,1 K.; Pr., *de Mal. Subs.* 24,18 (203 B.); —, *Phil. Chal.* 2,21 J.; —, *in R.* II 95,9-12 K.; —, *in Ti.* III 323,23 D.
a6-7 μέτρον—πιεῖν resp. Pr., *de Mal. Subs.* 21,15-16 (200 B.)
b1-4 resp. Pr., *in R.* II 104,8 K.; resp. et interpr. Pr., *in R.* II 350,26-353,7 K.
b1-2 ἐπειδή—γενέσθαι prius AFF. Pr., *in R.* II 350,23 K.
b1 πάντων ἐπιλανθάνεσθαι AFF. Pr., *in R.* II 347,18-19 K.; resp. Pr., *in R.* II 95,19-21 K.
b2 resp. Pr., *in R.* II 95,12-14 K.
b3-4 εἰς—ἀστέρας AFF. Pr., *in R.* II 350,24 K.; cit. Pr., *in R.* II 352,21-22 K.
b3 resp. Pr., *in R.* II 95,14-15 K.
b4-c2 resp. et interpr. Pr., *in R.* II 353,10-355,7 K.
b4-5 αὐτός—πιεῖν AFF. Pr., *in R.* II 353,8 K.; resp. Pr., *in R.* II 353,17-20 K.
b4 ἄττοντας ὥσπερ ἀστέρας resp. Pr., *in R.* II 93,8 K.; —, — II 95,15-18 K.; imit. Gr. Naz., *Ep.* 241,1 (172,3 G.)
b4 ἄττοντας resp. Pr., *in Ti.* III 265,3 D.
b4 ὥσπερ ἀστέρας AFF. Pr., *in R.* II 352,11 K.; —, — II 352,20 K.
b6-7 cit. Pr., *in R.* II 354,1-2 K.
b7 ἐπὶ τῇ πυρᾷ resp. sch. Pl. ad loc. (276 G.)
b8-d3 resp. Pr., *in R.* I 8,1-4 K.
b8-c2 cit. Pr., *in R.* II 354,10-15 K.
b8-c1 cit. Herm., *in Phdr.* 64,21-22 C.
b8 μῦθος ἐσώθη Phot. I 431 N.; expl. sch. Pl. ad loc. (276 G.)
c1-2 τὸν τῆς Λήθης ποταμὸν vide ad 621a5
c2 καὶ—μιανθησόμεθα AFF. Pr., *in R.* II 353,9 K.
c7-d1 resp. Plu., *Mor.* 1105c (VI 2,168,10-14 P.-W.)
d1 ὥσπερ—περιαγειρόμενοι AFF. Did., *Plat.* 403 M.; Phot. II 77 N.; Sud. ω 241 (III 626,25 A.); — π 1054 (IV 90,9-10 A.)
d1 νικηφόροι περιαγειρόμενοι Tim. 180 R.-K.
d2 τῇ χιλιέτει πορείᾳ vide ad 615a3

III. INDEX AUCTORUM PLATONIS REMPUBLICAM LAUDANTIUM

A. D., *Pron.* = Apollonius Dyscolus, *De Pronominis Appellationibus*, ed. R. Schneider (*Grammatici Graeci* 2,1), Leipzig 1878
AB = *Anecdota Graeca*, ed. I. Bekker, Berlin 1814-1821
Ael., *VH* = Aelianus, *Varia Historia*, ed. M. R. Dilts, Leipzig 1974
Ael. Dion. = Aelius Dionysius, ed. H. Erbse, *Untersuchungen zu den attizistischen Lexika*, Berlin 1950
Aen. Gaz., *Ep.* = Aeneas Gazaeus, *Epistulae*, ed. L. M. Positano, Naples 1962[2]
——, *Thphr.* = —, *Theophrastus*, ed. M. E. Colonna, Naples 1958
Aët. Doxogr. = Aëtius Doxographus, ed. H. Diels, *Doxographi Graeci*, Berlin 1879
Agap. Diac., *Ecth.* = Agapetos Diaconos, *Ecthesis*, PG 86,1
Agath., *Hist.* = Agathias Myrinaeus, *Historiae*, ed. R. Keydell, Berlin 1967
Alb., *Intr.* = Albinus, *Introductio in Platonem*, ed. P. Louis, Paris 1945
Alex. Aphr., *de An.* = Alexander Aphrodisiensis, *De Anima Liber*, ed. I. Bruns (*CAG Suppl.* 2,1), Berlin 1887
——, *Fat.* = —, *De Fato*, ed. I. Bruns (*CAG Suppl.* 2,2), Berlin 1892
——, *in APr.* = —, *In Aristotelis Analyticorum Priorum Librum I Commentarium*, ed. M. Wallies (*CAG* 2,1), Berlin 1883
——, *in Metaph.* = —, *In Aristotelis Metaphysica Commentaria*, ed. M. Hayduck (*CAG* 1), Berlin 1891
——, *in SE* = —, *In Aristotelis Sophisticos Elenchos Commentarium*, ed. M. Wallies (*CAG* 2,3), Berlin 1898
——, *in Top.* = —, *In Aristotelis Topicorum Libros Octo Commentaria*, ed. M. Wallies (*CAG* 2,2), Berlin 1891
Alexis = Alexis, ed. T. Kock, *Comicorum Atticorum Fragmenta II*, Leipzig 1884
Alfar., *Plat. Phil.* = Alfarabius, *De Platonis Philosophia*, edd. F. Rosenthal—R. Walzer (*Plato Arabus* II), London 1943
Ambr., *Luc.* = Ambrosius, *Expositio Evangelii secundum Lucam*, ed. M. Adriaen (*CChr., Ser. Lat.* 14), Turnhout 1957
Amm. Marc. = Ammianus Marcellinus, *Historiae*, ed. W. Seyfarth, Leipzig 1978
Ammon., *in APr.* = Ammonius, *In Aristotelis Analyticorum Priorum Librum I Commentarium*, ed. M. Wallies (*CAG* 4,6), Berlin 1889
——, *in Cat.* = —, *In Aristotelis Categorias Commentarius*, ed. A. Busse (*CAG* 4,4), Berlin 1895
——, *in Int.* = —, *In Aristotelis de Interpretatione Commentarius*, ed. A. Busse (*CAG* 4,5), Berlin 1897
——, *in Porph.* = —, *In Porphyrii Isagogen sive V Voces*, ed. A. Busse (*CAG* 4,3), Berlin 1891
Amphis = Amphis, ed. T. Kock, *Comicorum Atticorum Fragmenta II*, Leipzig 1884
An. Ath. = *Anecdota Atheniensia*, ed. A. Delatte, Paris 1927-1939
An. Bachm. = *Anecdota Graeca e cod. Mss. Bibl. Reg. Parisin.*, ed. L. Bachmann, Leipzig 1829
An. Boiss. = *Anecdota Graeca e cod. Regiis*, ed. J. F. Boissonade, Paris 1829-1833, 1844
An. Matr. = *Anecdota Graeca*, ed. P. Matranga, Rome 1850-1851
An. Ox. = *Anecdota Graeca e cod. Mss. Bibl. Oxon.*, ed. J. A. Cramer, Oxford 1835-1837
An. Par. = *Anecdota Graeca e cod. Mss. Bibl. Reg. Parisiensis*, ed. J. A. Cramer, Oxford 1839-1841
Anast. Sin., *VD* = Anastasius Sinaita, *Viae Dux*, ed. K.-H. Uthemann (*CChr., Ser. Gr.* 8), Turnhout 1981
Anaximen. = Anaximenes Lampsacenus, ed. F. Jacoby, *Die Fragmente der griechischen Historiker* IIA, Berlin 1926
Andron. Call., *Def.* = Andronicus Callistus, *Defensio Theodori Gazae*, ed. L. Mohler, *Aus Bessarions Gelehrtenkreis*, Paderborn 1942

Anon., *Contra Phil.* = Anonymus, *Contra Philosophos*, ed. D. Aschoff, (*CChr., Ser. Lat.* 58A), Turnhout 1975
——, *in EN* = ——, *In Ethica Nicomachea Commentaria*, ed. G. Heylbut (*CAG* 20), Berlin 1892
——, *in Hermog. Stat.* = ——, *In Hermogenis de Statibus Commentarius*, ed. H. Rabe, *Prolegomenon Sylloge*, Leipzig 1931
——, *in Prm.* = ——, *Commentarius in Platonis Parmenidem*, ed. W. Kroll, RhM 47 (1892), 599-627; quoted from P. Hadot, *Porphyre et Victorinus* II, Paris 1968, 60-113
——, *in Rh.* = ——, *In Artem Rhetoricam Commentaria*, ed. H. Rabe (*CAG* 21,2), Berlin 1896
——, *in Tht.* = ——, *Commentarius in Platonis Theaetetum*, edd. H. Diels—W. Schubart (*BKT* 2), Berlin 1905
——, *Prol. Plat.* = ——, *Prolegomena ad Platonis Philosophiam*, ed. L. G. Westerink, Amsterdam 1962
Anon. Gnom. = Anonymus Gnomologus, in *An. Boiss.*
Anon. Lond. = Anonymus Londinensis, ed. H. Diels (*CAG Suppl.* 3,1), Berlin 1893; ed. W. H. S. Jones, Cambridge 1947
Ap. Ty., *Ep.* = Apollonius Tyaneus, *Epistulae*, ed. R. Hercher, *Epistolographi Graeci*, Paris 1873
Apostol. = Apostolius, edd. E. L. von Leutsch—F. G. Schneidewin, *Paroemiographi Graeci*, Göttingen 1839
App. Prov. = *Appendix Proverbiorum*, edd. E. L. von Leutsch—F. Schneidewin, *Paroemiographi Graeci*, Göttingen 1839
Apul., *Pl., Soc.* = Apuleius, *De Platone et eius Dogmate, De Deo Socratis*, ed. J. Beaujeu, Paris 1973
Archyt. = Archytas, *ap.* Iamblichum, *Comm. Math.*
Areth., *Scr. Min.* = Arethas, *Scripta Minora*, ed. L. G. Westerink, Leipzig 1968-1972
Arist., *EN, MM, Pol., Rh.* = Aristoteles, *Ethica Nicomachea, Magna Moralia, Politica, Rhetorica*, ed. I. Bekker, Berlin 1831
Aristaenet. = Aristaenetus, *Epistulae*, ed. O. Mazal, Leipzig 1971
Aristid., *Or.* = Aristides, *Orationes*, 1-16 edd. F. W. Lenz—C. A. Behr, Leiden 1976-1980; 17-53 ed. B. Keil, Berlin 1898
Aristid. Quint. = Aristides Quintilianus, *De Musica*, ed. R. P. Winnington-Ingram, Leipzig 1963
Arn., *Gent.* = Arnobius, *Adversus Nationes*, ed. A. Reifferscheid (*CSEL* 4), Vienna 1875
Ascl. = Asclepius, in *Corp. Herm.*
Ascl., *in Introd.* = Asclepius, *Commentaria in Nicomachi Geraseni Pythagorei Introductionem Arithmeticam*, ed. L. Tarán, Philadelphia 1969
——, *in Metaph.* = ——, *In Aristotelis Metaphysicorum Libros A-Z Commentaria*, ed. M. Hayduck (*CAG* 6,2), Berlin 1888
Asp., *in EN* = Aspasius, *In Ethica Nicomachea Commentaria*, ed. G. Heylbut (*CAG* 19,1), Berlin 1889
Ath. = Athenaeus, *Dipnosophistae*, ed. G. Kaibel, Leipzig 1887-1890
Ath. Al., *Gent.* = Athanasius Alexandrinus, *Contra Gentes*, ed. R. W. Thomson, Oxford 1971
Athenag., *Leg.* = Athenagoras, *Supplicatio pro Christianis*, ed. W. R. Schoedel, Oxford 1972
Aug., *Acad.* = Augustinus, *Contra Academicos*, ed. P. Knöll (*CSEL* 63), Vienna-Leipzig 1922
——, *Civ.* = ——, *De Civitate Dei*, edd. B. Dombart—A. Kalb (*CChr., Ser. Lat.* 47-48); Turnhout 1955
——, *Pecc.or.* = ——, *De Peccato Originali*, PL 44
——, *Qu.ev.* = ——, *Quaestiones Evangelicae*, ed. A. Mutzenbecher (*CChr., Ser. Lat.* 44B), Turnhout 1980
——, *Retract.* = ——, *Retractationes*, ed. P. Knöll (*CSEL* 36), Vienna-Leipzig 1902
——, *Trin.* = ——, *De Trinitate*, edd. W. J. Mountain—F. Glorie (*CChr., Ser. Lat.* 50A), Turnhout 1968
Aurel. Vict., *Caes.* = Aurelius Victor, *Liber de Caesaribus*, ed. F. Pichlmayr, Leipzig 1966

Auson., *Tetrast. ad Marc. Aurel.* = Ausonius, *Tetrastichon ad Marcum Aurelium*, ed. S. Prete, *Ausonius, Opuscula*, Leipzig 1978
Averr., *in R.* = Averroes, *In Platonis Rempublicam Commentarii*, ed. (cum versione anglica) E. I. J. Rosenthal, Cambridge 1956
Bas., *Ep.* = Basilius Caesariensis Cappadociae, *Epistulae*, ed. Y. Courtonne, Paris 1957-1966
——, *Hex.* = ——, *Homiliae in Hexaemeron*, ed. S. Giet (*SC* 26), Paris 1950
——, *Leg. Lib. Gent.* = ——, *De Legendis Libris Gentilium*, ed. F. Boulenger, Paris 1935
Bas. Min., *in Greg.* = Basilius Minimus, *Scholia in Gregorium Theologum*, *PG* 36
Bess., *Ep., in Cal. Pl.* = Bessarion, *Epistulae, In Calumniatorem Platonis*, ed. L. Mohler, Paderborn 1942, 1927
Boet., *Arith.* = Boethius, *De Institutione Arithmetica*, ed. G. Friedlein, Leipzig 1867
——, *Cons.* = ——, *De Consolatione Philosophiae*, ed. L. Bieler (*CChr., Ser. Lat.* 94), Turnhout 1957
——, *Mus.* = ——, *De Institutione Musica*, ed. G. Friedlein, Leipzig 1867
Calc., *Ti.* = Calcidius, *Timaeus*, ed. J. H. Waszink (*Plato Latinus* IV), London-Leiden 1962
Cass., *Hist. Trip.* = Cassiodorus-Epiphanius, *Historia Ecclesiastica Tripartita*, edd. W. Jacob—R. Hanslik (*CSEL* 71), Vienna 1952
Chor., *Decl., Dial., Or.* = Choricius Gazaeus, *Declamationes, Dialexes, Orationes*, edd. R. Foerster—E. Richtsteig, Leipzig 1929
Chrys., *adv. oppugn.* = Iohannes Chrysostomus, *Adversus Oppugnantes*, *PL* 47
——, *de Inani Gloria* = ——, *De Inani Gloria*, ed. A. M. Malingrey (*SC* 188), Paris 1972
Chrysipp., *Stoic.* = Chrysippus, ed. H. von Arnim, *Stoicorum Veterum Fragmenta*, Leipzig 1903-1924
Cic., *Att.* = Cicero, *Epistulae ad Atticum*, ed. D. R. Shackleton Bailey, Cambridge 1965-1970
——, *Div.* = ——, *De Divinatione*, ed. R. Giomini, Leipzig 1975
——, *Fam.* = ——, *Epistulae ad Familiares*, ed. D. R. Shackleton Bailey, Cambridge 1977
——, *Leg.* = ——, *De Legibus*, ed. K. Ziegler, Heidelberg 1963[2]
——, *Luc.* = ——, *Lucullus*, ed. O. Plasberg, Leipzig 1922
——, *Off.* = ——, *De Officiis*, ed. C. Atzert, Leipzig 1963
——, *Orat.* = ——, *Orator*, ed. R. Westman, Leipzig 1980
——, *Quint.* = ——, *Epistulae ad Quintum Fratrem*, ed. D. R. Shackleton Bailey, Cambridge 1980
——, *Rep.* = ——, *De Republica*, ed. K. Ziegler, Leipzig 1964
——, *Sen.* = ——, *De Senectute*, ed. L. Simbeck, Stuttgart 1917
——, *TD* = ——, *Tusculanae Disputationes*, ed. M. Pohlenz, Leipzig 1918
Clem., *Paed., Protr., QDS, Strom.* = Clemens Alexandrinus, *Paedagogus, Protrepticus, Quis Dives Salvetur, Stromata*, ed. O. Stählin, (*GCS* 17,52), Leipzig 1909, Berlin 1960[3], Berlin 1972[3]
Clem. Recogn. = Ps.-Clemens Romanus, *Recognitiones*, edd. B. Rehm—F. Paschke (*GCS* 51), Berlin 1965
Corp. Herm. = *Corpus Hermeticum*, edd. A. D. Nock—A.-J. Festugière, Paris 1945-1954
Cyr., *adv. Iul.* = Cyrillus Alexandrinus, *Adversus Iulianum*, *PG* 76
——, *Gloss.* = ——, *Glossarium*, partim ed. A. B. Drachmann, *Die Überlieferung des Cyrillglossars*, Copenhagen 1936
D. Chr., *Or.* = Dio Chrysostomus, *Orationes*, ed. H. von Arnim, Berlin 1893
D. H., *Comp., Comp.ep., Pomp., Rh.* = Dionysius Halicarnassensis, *De Compositione Verborum, De Compositione Verborum Epitome, Ad Pompeium Geminum, Ars Rhetorica*, edd. H. Usener—L. Radermacher, Leipzig 1899-1904
D. L. = Diogenes Laertius, *Vitae Philosophorum*, ed. M. S. Long, Oxford 1964
——, *Div.* = ——, *Divisiones*, ed. H. Mutschmann, Leipzig 1906
Dam., *in Phd.* = Damascius, *In Platonis Phaedonem Commentaria*, ed. L. G. Westerink, Amsterdam 1977
——, *in Phlb.* = ——, *In Platonis Philebum Commentaria*, ed. L. G. Westerink, Amsterdam 1959

——, *in Prm.* = ——, *In Platonis Parmenidem Commentaria*, ed. Ch. A. Ruelle, *Damascius Diadochus, Dubitationes et Solutiones in Platonis Parmenidem* II, Paris 1889
——, *Isid.* = ——, *Vita Isidori*, ed. C. Zintzen, Hildesheim 1967
——, *Pr.* = ——, *De Primis Principiis*, 1-42 ed. L. G. Westerink, Paris 1986; cetera ed. Ch. A. Ruelle, *Damascius Diadochus, Dubitationes et Solutiones in Platonis Parmenidem* I, Paris 1889
David, *in Cat.* = David, *In Aristotelis Categorias Scholia*, ed. C. A. Brandis, *Scholia in Aristotelem*, Berlin 1836
——, *in Porph.* = ——, *In Porphyrii Isagogen Commentarium*, ed. A. Busse (*CAG* 18,2), Berlin 1904
Demetr., *Eloc.* = Demetrius, *De Elocutione*, ed. W. Rhys Roberts, Cambridge 1902
Demetr. Cyd., *Ep.* = Demetrius Cydonès, *Epistulae*, ed. R.-J. Loenertz, Vatican City 1956-1960
Dexipp., *in Cat.* = Dexippus, *In Aristotelis Categorias Commentarium*, ed. A. Busse (*CAG* 4,2), Berlin 1888
Did., *Plat.* = Didymus, *De Dubiis apud Platonem Lectionibus*, ed. E. Miller, *Mélanges de littérature grecque*, Paris 1868; et *ap.* Stobaeum
Didym., *in Gen.* = Didymus, *In Genesin*, ed. P. Nautin (*SC* 233), Paris 1976
Diogenian. = Diogenianus, edd. E. L. von Leutsch—F. Schneidewin, *Paroemiographi Graeci*, Göttingen 1839
Dion. Ar., *CH* = Dionysius Areopagita, *De Caelesti Hierarchia*, edd. R. Roques—G. Heil—M. de Gandillac (*SC* 58), Paris 1958
Dor., *Doct.* = Dorotheus Gazaeus, *Doctrinae Diversae*, edd. L. Regnault—J. de Préville (*SC* 92), Paris 1963
Elias, *in APr.* = Elias, *In Aristotelis Analytica Priora Commentarius*, ed. L. G. Westerink, Mnem. IV 14 (1961), 134-139
——, *in Cat.* = ——, *In Aristotelis Categorias Commentaria*, ed. A. Busse (*CAG* 18,1), Berlin 1900
——, *in Porph.* = ——, *In Porphyrii Isagogen Commentaria*, ed. A. Busse (*CAG* 18,1), Berlin 1900; ed. L. G. Westerink, Amsterdam 1967
EM = *Etymologicum Magnum*, ed. T. Gaisford, Oxford 1848; et *ap.* E. Miller, *Mélanges de littérature grecque*, Paris 1868
Ephipp. = Ephippus, ed. T. Kock, *Comicorum Atticorum Fragmenta* II, Leipzig 1884
Epict. = Epictetus, *Dissertationes*, ed. H. Schenkl, Leipzig 1916[2]; et *ap.* Stobaeum
Epicur. = Epicurus, ed. H. Usener, *Epicurea*, Leipzig 1887
Epiphan. = Epiphanius, ed. H. Diels, *Doxographi Graeci*, Berlin 1879
Et. Gen. = *Etymologicum Genuinum*, β ed. G. Berger, Meisenheim am Glan 1972
Et. Gud. = *Etymologicum Gudianum*, ed. A. de Stefani, Leipzig 1909-1920
Et. Parv. = *Etymologicum Parvum*, ed. R. Pintaudi, Milan 1973
Et. Sym. = *Etymologicum Symeonis*, α ed. H. Sell, Meisenheim am Glan 1968; β ed. G. Berger, Meisenheim am Glan 1972
Eudoc., *Viol.* = Eudocia Augusta, *Violarium*, ed. H. Flach, Leipzig 1880
Eun., *Hist.* = Eunapius, *Historiae*, ed. L. Dindorf, *Historici Graeci Minores*, Leipzig 1870-1871
Eus., *Or. Const.* = Eusebius Caesariensis, *Constantini Oratio ad Sanctorum Coetum*, ed. I. A. Heikel (*GCS* 7), Leipzig 1902
——, *PE* = ——, *Praeparatio Evangelica*, ed. K. Mras (*GCS* 43,1-2), Berlin 1954-1956
——, *Theoph.* = ——, *Theophania*, ed. H. Gressmann (*GCS* 11,2), Leipzig 1904
Eus."Gall.", *Hom.* = Eusebius "Gallicanus", *Homiliae*, ed. F. Glorie (*CChr., Ser. Lat.* 101), Turnhout 1970
——, *Serm.* = ——, *Sermones*, ed. F. Glorie (*CChr., Ser. Lat.* 101B), Turnhout 1971
Eust., *Ep.* = Eustathius, *Epistulae*, ed. T. L. F. Tafel, *Eustathii Opuscula*, Francfurt 1832
——, *Od.* = ——, *In Odysseam Commentarii*, ed. M. Devarius, Leipzig 1825-1829
Eustr., *in EN* = Eustratius, *In Ethica Nicomachea Commentaria*, ed. G. Heylbut (*CAG* 20), Berlin 1892
Exc. Par. = *Excerpta Parisiensia*, ed. H. Rabe, *Prolegomenon Sylloge*, Leipzig 1931

Favor., *Ex.* = Favorinus, *De Exilio*, ed. A. Barigazzi, Florence 1966
Firm., *Math.* = Firmicus Maternus, *Mathesis*, edd. W. Kroll—F. Skutsch, Leipzig 1897-1913
Gal., *Aff. Dign.* = Galenus, *De Affectuum Dignotione*, ed. W. de Boer (*CMG* 5.4.1.1), Leipzig-Berlin 1937
——, *Anat. Adm.* = —, *De Anatomicis Administrationibus*, ed. C. G. Kühn, *Galeni Opera Omnia*, Leipzig 1821-1833, II
——, *Bon. Hab.* = —, *De Bono Habitu*, IV Kühn
——, *Capt.* = —, *De Captionibus*, ed. R. B. Edlow, Leiden 1977
——, *Comp. Ti.* = —, *Galeni Compendium Timaei Platonis*, edd. P. Kraus—R. Walzer (*Plato Arabus* I), London 1951
——, *Constit.* = —, *De Constitutione Artis Medicinae*, I Kühn
——, *Corp. Compl.* = —, *Quod Animi Mores Corporis Temperamenta Sequantur*, ed. I. Müller (*Scripta Minora* II), Leipzig 1893
——, *de Usu Part.* = —, *De Usu Partium Libri XVII*, ed. G. Helmreich, Leipzig 1907-1909
——, *Diff.* = —, *De Differentiis Febrium*, VII Kühn
——, *Fac.* = —, *De Facultatibus*, XI Kühn
——, *Hist. Phil.* = —, *De Historia Philosophica Liber Spurius*, ed. H. Diels, *Doxographi Graeci*, Berlin 1879
——, *in Hipp. Art.* = —, *In Hippocratis De Articulis Liber et Galeni in eum Commentarii Quattuor*, XVIII 1 Kühn
——, *in Hipp. Epid. VI* = —, *Commentarii Sex in Hippocratis Librum Sextum Epidemiarum*, edd. E. Wenkebach—F. Pfaff (*CMG* 5.10.2.2), Berlin 1956
——, *in Hipp. Off.* = —, *In Hippocratis De Officina Medici Commentarii Tres*, XVIII 2 Kühn
——, *in Hipp. Progn.* = —, *In Hippocratis Prognosticum Commentaria Tria*, ed. J. Heeg (*CMG* 5.9.2), Leipzig-Berlin 1915
——, *in R.* = —, *In Platonis Rempublicam Commentariorum Fragmenta*, edd. P. Kraus—R. Walzer, *Galeni Compendium Timaei Platonis* (*Plato Arabus* I), London 1951
——, *in Ti.* = —, *In Platonis Timaeum Commentariorum Fragmenta*, ed. H. O. Schroeder, appendicem arabicam add. P. Kahle (*CMG Suppl. I*), Leipzig 1934
——, *Inst. Log.* = —, *De Institutione Logica*, ed. K. Kalbfleisch, Leipzig 1896
——, *Meth. Med.* = —, *De Methodo Medendi*, X Kühn
——, *Pecc. Dign.* = —, *De Peccatorum Dignotione*, ed. W. de Boer (*CMG* 5.4.1.1), Leipzig-Berlin 1937
——, *PHP* = —, *De Placitis Hippocratis et Platonis*, ed. Ph. de Lacy (*CMG* 5.4.1.2), Berlin 1978-1979
——, *Praecogn.* = —, *De Praecognitione*, ed. V. Nutton (*CMG* 5.8.1), Berlin 1979
——, *Simpl. Medic.* = —, *De Simplicium Medicamentorum Temperamentis ac Facultatibus*, XI Kühn
——, *Thras.* = —, *Thrasybulus*, ed. G. Helmreich (*Scripta Minora* III), Leipzig 1893
——, *Ven. Sect.* = —, *De Venae Sectione*, XI Kühn
Gell., *NA* = Gellius, *Noctes Atticae*, ed. C. Hosius, Leipzig 1903
Georg. Mon., *Chron.* = Georgius Monachus, *Chronicon*, ed. C. de Boor, Leipzig 1904
Gnomol. Vat. = *Gnomologium Vaticanum*, ed. L. Sternbach, WS 9 (1887), 175-206; 10 (1888), 1-49, 211-260; 11 (1889), 43-64, 192-242; repr. Berlin 1963
Gp. = *Geoponica*, ed. H. Beckh, Leipzig 1895
Gr. Naz., *Carm. dogm., mor., semet* = Gregorius Nazianzenus, *Carmina Dogmatica, Moralia, De semet ipso*, PG 37
——, *Ep.* = —, *Epistulae*, ed. P. Gallay (*GCS* 53), Berlin 1969
——, *Or.* = —, *Orationes*, PG 35-36; 1-3 ed. J. Bernardi (*SC* 247), Paris 1978; 20-23 edd. J. Mossay—G. Lafontaine (*SC* 270), Paris 1980; 24-26 edd. J. Mossay—G. Lafontaine (*SC* 284), Paris 1981; 27-31 edd. P. Gallay—M. Jourjon (*SC* 250), Paris 1978
——, *Vit.* = —, *De Vita sua*, ed. C. Jungck, Heidelberg 1974
Gr. Nyss., *Benef.* = Gregorius Nyssenus, *De Beneficentia*, ed. A. van Heck (vol. 9 Jaeger), Leiden 1967
——, *Ep.* = —, *Epistulae*, ed. G. Pasquali (vol. 8.2 Jaeger), Leiden 1959[2]

——, *Hom. Creat.* = —, *Homiliae de Creatione Hominis*, ed. H. Hörner (*Suppl.* Jaeger), Leiden 1972
——, *Hom. in Cant.* = —, *Homiliae in Canticum Canticorum*, ed. H. Langerbeck (vol. 6 Jaeger), Leiden 1960
——, *Hom. in Eccl.* = —, *Homiliae in Ecclesiasten*, edd. J. McDonough—P. Alexander (vol. 5 Jaeger), Leiden 1962
——, *Melet.* = —, *In Meletium*, ed. A. Spira (vol. 9 Jaeger), Leiden 1967
——, *Mort.* = —, *De Mortuis*, ed. G. Heil (vol. 9 Jaeger), Leiden 1967
——, *V. Mos.* = —, *De Vita Moysis*, ed. H. Musurillo (vol. 7.1 Jaeger), Leiden 1964
Greg. Akind., *Ep.* = Gregorius Akindynos, *Epistulae*, ed. A. C. Hero, Washington 1983
Greg. Cor., *Dial.* = Gregorius Corinthius, *De Dialectis Linguae Graecae*, ed. G. H. Schaefer, Leipzig 1811
Greg. Cypr. = Gregorius Cyprius, edd. E. L. von Leutsch—F. Schneidewin, *Paroemiographi Graeci*, Göttingen 1839
——, *Antilog.* = —, *Antilogiae, ap.* Libanium
——, *Encom. Andr. Pal.* = —, *Encomium Andronici Palaeologi*, in *An. Boiss.*
Greg. Magn., *Dial.* = Gregorius Magnus, *Dialogi*, edd. A. de Vogüé-P. Antin (*SC* 251 etc.), Paris 1978-
Harp. = Harpocration, ed. W. Dindorf, Oxford 1853
Hdn. Gr. = Herodianus Grammaticus, *De Affectionibus*, ed. A. Lentz (*Grammatici Graeci* III ii), Leipzig 1868
Heliod., *in EN* = Heliodorus, *In Ethica Nicomachea Paraphrasis*, ed. G. Heylbut (*CAG* 19,2), Berlin 1889
Heracl., *All. Hom.* = Heraclides, *Allegoriae Homericae*, in *An. Matr.*
Herm., *in Phdr.* = Hermias Alexandrinus, *In Platonis Phaedrum Scholia*, ed. P. Couvreur, Paris 1901
Herm., *Irris.* = Hermias, *Irrisio Gentilium Philosophorum*, ed. J. C. Th. Otto (*Corp. Apol. Graec.* 9), Wiesbaden 1872
Hermog., *Id., Meth., Prog.* = Hermogenes Tarsensis, *De Ideis, Methodi Gravitatis, Progymnasmata*, ed. H. Rabe, Leipzig 1913
Hero, *Def.* = Hero Alexandrinus, *Definitiones*, ed. J. L. Heiberg, Leipzig 1914 (vol. IV Teubner)
Hierocl. = Hierocles Platonicus, *ap.* Stobaeum
——, *in CA* = —, *In Aureum Pythagoreorum Carmen*, ed. F. G. Koehler, Stuttgart 1974
——, *Prov.* = —, *De Providentia, ap.* Photium, *Bibliotheca* 251
Hieron., *Ep.* = Hieronymus, *Epistulae*, ed. J. Labourt, Paris 1949-1963
——, *in Ion.* = —, *Commentarii In Ionam*, ed. M. Adriaen (*CChr., Ser. Lat.* 76), Turnhout 1969
——, *in Math.* = —, *Commentarii in Matheum*, edd. D. Hurst—M. Adriaen (*CChr., Ser. Lat.* 77), Turnhout 1969
——, *Ruf.* = —, *Apologia contra Rufinum*, ed. P. Lardet (*CChr., Ser. Lat.* 79), Turnhout 1982
Hipp., *Haer.* = Hippolytus Romanus, *Refutatio Omnium Haeresium*, ed. P. Wendland (*GCS* 3), Leipzig-Berlin 1916
Hsch. = Hesychius, α—ο ed. K. Latte (Copenhagen 1953-1966); π—ω ed. M. Schmidt, Jena 1861-1864
Hsch. Mil. = Hesychius Milesius, *De Viris Illustribus*, ed. H. Flach, Leipzig 1880
I., *Ap.* = Flavius Iosephus, *Contra Apionem*, ed. Th. Reinach, Paris 1930
Iambl., *Comm. Math.* = Iamblichus, *De Communi Mathematica Scientia*, ed. N. Festa, Leipzig 1891
——, *in Nic.* = —, *In Nicomachi Arithmeticam Introductionem Liber*, edd. H. Pistelli—U. Klein, Stuttgart 1975[2]
——, *Myst.* = —, *De Mysteriis*, ed. E. des Places, Paris 1966
——, *Protr.* = —, *Protrepticus*, ed. H. Pistelli, Leipzig 1888
——, *Theol. Ar.* = —, *Theologumena Arithmeticae*, edd. V. de Falco—U. Klein, Stuttgart 1975[2]

——, *VP* = ——, *De Vita Pythagorica*, ed. L. Deubner, Leipzig 1937
IG = *Inscriptiones Graecae* XIVa, ed. G. Kaibel, Berlin 1890
Ioh. Alex. = Iohannes Alexandrinus, *Commentaria in Sextum Librum Hippocratis Epidemiarum* ed. C. D. Pritchet, Leiden 1975
Ioh. Can. = Iohannes Canabutzes, *Ad Principem Aeni et Samothraces in Dionysium Halicarnassensem Commentarius*, ed. M. Lehnerdt, Leipzig 1890
Ioh. Sard., *in Apht. Prog.* = Iohannes Sardianus, *In Aphtonii Progymnasmata Commentaria*, ed. H. Rabe, Leipzig 1928
Ioh. Sard.(?), *in Hermog. Stat.* = Iohannes Sardianus (?), *In Hermogenis De Statibus Commentarius*, ed. H. Rabe, *Prolegomenon Sylloge*, Leipzig 1931
Ioseph. Gen., *Reg.* = Iosephus Genesius, *Regum Libri IV*, edd. A. Lesmueller-Werner—I. Thurm, Berlin 1978
Ioseph. Kaloth., *Andr., Ath.* = Iosephus Kalothetos, *Ad Andream Cretensem, Vita Athanasii*, ed. D. G. Tsami, Thessaloniki 1980
Iren. Lugd., *Haer.* = Irenaeus Lugdunensis, *Adversus Haereses* II 2 (*SC* 294), edd. A. Rousseau—L. Doutreleau, Paris 1982
Iul., *Ep., Or.* = Iulianus, *Epistulae, Orationes*, I 1,2 ed. J. Bidez, Paris 1932; II 1 ed. G. Rochefort, Paris 1963; II 2 ed. C. Lacombrade, Paris 1964
Iuln. Ar., *Hiob* = Iulianus Arianus, *In Hiob*, ed. D. Hagedorn, Berlin-New York 1973
Iust. Phil., *Apol., Coh. Gent., Dial., Qu. et Resp.* = Iustinus Martyr, *Apologia, Cohortatio ad Gentiles, Dialogus cum Tryphone, Quaestiones et Responsa*, ed. J. C. Th. Otto (*Corp. Apol. Graec.* 1-5), Wiesbaden 1876-1881[3]
Lacap., *Ep.* = Georgius Lacapenus, *Epistulae*, ed. S. Lindstam, Uppsala 1910
Lact., *Inst.* = Lactantius, *Divinae Institutiones*, ed. S. Brandt (*CSEL* 19), Prague-Vienna-Leipzig 1890
Lex. Rhet. Cant. = *Lexicon Rhetoricum Cantabrigiense*, ed. E. O. Houtsma, Leiden 1870
Lex. Sabb. = *Lexicon Sabbaiticum*, ed. A. Papadopoulos-Kerameus, Petersburg 1892-1893
Lex. Seg. = *Lexicon Seguerianum*, ed. C. Boysen, Marburg 1891-1892
Lex. Vind. = *Lexicon Vindobonense*, ed. A. Nauck, Petersburg 1867
Lib., *Decl., Ep., Or., Prog.* = Libanius, *Declamationes, Epistulae, Orationes, Progymnasmata*, ed. R. Foerster, Leipzig 1903-1927
Longin. = Longinus, *De Sublimitate*, ed. D. A. Russell, Oxford 1968
Luc., *Cat., Conv., Dem. Enc., Fug., Lex., Merc. Cond., Nav., Philops., Salt., VH* = Lucianus, *Cataplus, Convivium, Demosthenis Encomium, Fugitivi, Lexiphron, De Mercede Conductis, Navigium, Philopseudes, De Saltatione, Verae Historiae*, ed. M. D. MacLeod, Oxford 1972-1987
Lyd., *Mens.* = Iohannes Lydus, *De Mensibus*, ed. R. Wuensch, Leipzig 1898
M. Ant. = Marcus Antoninus, *Ad se ipsum*, ed. J. Dalfen, Leipzig 1979
Macar. = Macarius, edd. E. L. von Leutsch—F. Schneidewin, *Paroemiographi Graeci*, Göttingen 1839
Macrob., *in Somn. Scip.* = Macrobius, *Commentarii In Somnium Scipionis*, ed. J. Willis, Leipzig 1963
Mantiss. Prov. = *Mantissa Proverbiorum*, edd. E. L. von Leutsch—F. Schneidewin, *Paroemiographi Graeci*, Göttingen 1839
Manuel II Pal., *Ep.* = Manuel II Palaeologus, *Epistulae*, ed. G. T. Dennis, Washington 1977
Marcellin.(?), *in Hermog. Stat.* = Marcellinus (?), *Prolegomena in Hermogenis De Statibus*, ed. H. Rabe, *Prolegomenon Sylloge*, Leipzig 1931
Marin., *Procl.* = Marinus, *Vita Procli*, ed. V. Cousin, *Procli Philosophi Platonici Opera Inedita*, Paris 1864
Mart. *Apoll.* = *Martyrium Apollonii*, ed. H. Musurillo, *The Acts of the Christian Martyrs*, Oxford 1972
Matth. Eph., *Ep.* = Matthaeus Ephesius, *Epistulae*, ap. Nicephorum Gregoram, *Epistulae*
Max. Tyr. = Maximus Tyrius, *Philosophumena*, ed. H. Hobein, Leipzig 1910
Meth., *Arbitr., Res., Symp.* = Methodius, *De Libero Arbitrio, De Resurrectione, Symposium*, ed. G. N. Bonwetsch (*GCS* 27), Leipzig-Berlin 1917

Mich., *in EN* = Michael Ephesius, *In Ethica Nicomachea Commentaria*, edd. G. Heylbut (*CAG* 20), Berlin 1892; M. Hayduck (*CAG* 22,3), Berlin 1901
Mich. Acom., *Ep., Or.* = Michael Acominas, *Epistulae, Orationes*, ed. Sp. P. Lambros, Athens 1879-1880
Mich. Gabr., *Ep.* = Michael Gabras, *Epistulae*, ed. G. Fatouros, Vienna 1973
Mich. Ital., *Or.* = Michael Italikos, *Orationes*, ed. P. Gautier, Paris 1972
Minuc. Fel., *Oct.* = Minucius Felix, *Octavius*, ed. B. Kytzler, Leipzig 1982
Moer. = Moeris, edd. J. Pierson—G. A. Koch, Leipzig 1830
Muson. = Musonius, *ap.* Stobaeum
Mythogr. = *Scriptores Rerum Mythicarum Latini Tres Romae Nuper Reperti*, ed. G. H. Bode, Celle 1834
Nemes. = Nemesius, *De Natura Hominis*, ed. C. F. Matthaei, Halle 1802
Niceph. Chumn., *Ep.* = Nicephorus Chumnas, *Epistulae*, in *An. Boiss.*
Niceph. Greg., *Antirrh.* = Nicephorus Gregoras, *Antirrhetika*, ed. H. V. Beyer, Vienna 1976
——, *Ep.* = —, *Epistulae*, ed. P. L. M. Leone, Lecce 1982-1983
——, *Flor.* = —, *Florentius*, ed. P. L. M. Leone, Naples 1975
——, *Hist. Byz.* = —, *Historia Byzantina*, ed. L. Schopen, Bonn 1829
——, *in Syn.* = —, *Scholia in Synesii De Insomniis*, *PG* 149
Nicet. Chon., *Or.* = Nicetas Choniates, *Orationes*, ed. J.-L. van Dieten, Berlin 1972
Nicet. Mag., *Ep.* = Nicetas Magister, *Epistulae*, ed. L. G. Westerink, Paris 1973
Nicom., *Ar.* = Nicomachus Gerasenus, *Arithmetica Introductio*, ed. R. Hoche, Leipzig 1866
Numen. = Numenius, *ap.* Proclum, *In Platonis Rempublicam Commentaria*
Oenom. = Oenomaus, *ap.* Eusebium, *Praeparatio Evangelica*; fragmenta ed. F. W. A. Mullach, *Fragmenta Philosophorum Graecorum*, Paris 1860-1867
Olymp., *in Alc.* = Olympiodorus, *In Platonis Alcibiadem Commentaria*, ed. L. G. Westerink, Amsterdam 1956
——, *in Grg.* = —, *In Platonis Gorgiam Commentaria*, ed. L. G. Westerink, Leipzig 1970
——, *in Mete.* = —, *In Aristotelis Meteora Commentaria*, ed. W. Stüve (*CAG* 12,2), Berlin 1900
——, *in Phd.* = —, *In Platonis Phaedonem Commentaria*, ed. L. G. Westerink, Amsterdam 1976
——, *Prol.* = —, *Prolegomena*, ed. A. Busse (*CAG* 12,1), Berlin 1902
Or., *Cels.* = Origenes, *Contra Celsum*, ed. M. Borret (*SC* 132, 136, 147, 150, 227), Paris 1967-1976
——, *Lib. Arb.* = —, *De Libero Arbitrio*, ed. E. Junod (*SC* 226), Paris 1976
——, *Pr.* = —, *De Principiis*, ed. P. Koetschau (*GCS* 22), Leipzig 1913
Panaet. = Panaetius, *ap.* Porphyrium, *In Ptolemaei Harmonica*
Paul. Nol., *Ep.* = Paulinus Nolanus, *Epistulae*, ed. G. von Hartel (*CSEL* 29), Prague-Vienna-Leipzig 1894
Paus. = Pausanias Periegeta, *Graeciae Descriptio*, ed. M. H. Rocha-Pereira, Leipzig 1973-1981
Paus. Gr. = Pausanias Atticista, ed. H. Erbse, *Untersuchungen zu den attizistischen Lexika*, Berlin 1950
Ph., *Cher., Conf., Decal., Det., Deus, Ebr., Her., Ios., Leg., Migr., Mos., Mut., Opif., Plant., Post., Praem., Prob., Sacr., Sobr., Somn., Spec., Virt.* = Philo Alexandrinus, *De Cherubim, De Confusione Linguarum, De Decalogo, Quod Deterius Potiori Insidiari Soleat, Quod Deus Sit Immutabilis, De Ebrietate, Quis Rerum Divinarum Heres Sit, De Iosepho, Legum Allegoriae, De Migratione Abrahami, De Vita Moysis, De Mutatione Nominum, De Opificio Mundi, De Plantatione, De Posteritate Caini, De Praemiis et Poenis, Quod Omnis Probus Liber Sit, De Sacrificiis Abelis et Caini, De Sobrietate, De Somniis, De Specialibus Legibus, De Virtutibus*, edd. L. Cohn—P. Wendland, Berlin 1896-1930
Philostr., *Ep., Gymn., Imag., VA, VS* = Philostratus, *Epistulae, De Gymnastica, Imagines, Vita Apollonii, Vitae Sophistarum*, ed. C. L. Kayser, Leipzig 1870-1871
Philox. Gramm. = Philoxenus Grammaticus, ed. Chr. Theodoridis, Berlin-New York 1976

Phld., *Mus.* = Philodemus, *De Musica*, ed. I. Kemke, Leipzig 1884
Phlp., *Aet.* = Iohannes Philoponus, *De Aeternitate Mundi contra Proclum*, ed. H. Rabe, Leipzig 1899
——, *in APr.* = ——, *In Aristotelis Analytica Priora Commentaria*, ed. M. Wallies (*CAG* 13,2), Berlin 1905
——, *in Cat.* = ——, *In Aristotelis Categorias Commentarium*, ed. A. Busse (*CAG* 13,1), Berlin 1898
——, *in de An.* = ——, *In Aristotelis de Anima Libros Commentaria*, ed. M. Hayduck (*CAG* 15), Berlin 1897
——, *in Ph.* = ——, *In Aristotelis Physica Commentaria*, ed. G. Vitelli (*CAG* 16-17), Berlin 1887-1888
——, *Opif.* = ——, *De Opificio Mundi*, ed. G. Reichardt, Leipzig 1897
Phot. = Photius, *Lexicon*, α—δ ed. Chr. Theodoridis, Berlin-New York 1982; ε—ω ed. S. A. Naber, Leiden 1864-1865
——, *Amphil.* = ——, *Amphilochia*, ed. L. G. Westerink, Leipzig 1986
——, *Bibl.* = ——, *Bibliotheca*, ed. R. Henry, Paris 1959-1978
——, *Ep.* = ——, *Epistulae*, edd. B. Laourdas—L. G. Westerink, Leipzig 1979-
Phryn., *Ecl.* = Phrynichus Atticista, *Eclogae*, ed. E. Fischer, Berlin 1974
——, *PS* = ——, *Praeparatio Sophistica*, ed. I. de Borries, Leipzig 1911
Plb. = Polybius, *Historiae*, ed. T. Buettner-Wobst, Leipzig 1889-1905
Plot. = Plotinus, edd. P. Henry—H. R. Schwyzer, Bruxelles 1951-1973
Plu., *Mor.* = Plutarchus, *Moralia*, I edd. W. R. Paton—J. Wegehaupt—M. Pohlenz—H. Gärtner, Leipzig 1925; II edd. W. Nachstädt—W. Sieveking—J. B. Titchener, Leipzig 1935; III edd. W. R. Paton—M. Pohlenz—W. Sieveking, Leipzig 1929; IV ed. C. Hubert, Leipzig 1938; V 1 edd. C. Hubert—M. Pohlenz—H. Drexler, Leipzig 1960; V 2,1 ed. J. Mau, Leipzig 1971; V 2,2 ed. B. Häsler, Leipzig 1978; V 3 edd. C. Hubert—M. Pohlenz—H. Drexler, Leipzig 1960[2]; VI 1 edd. C. Hubert—H. Drexler, Leipzig 1959[3]; VI 2 edd. M. Pohlenz—R. Westman, Leipzig 1959[3]; VI 3 edd. K. Ziegler—M. Pohlenz, Leipzig 1966[3]; VII ed. F. H. Sandbach, Leipzig 1967
——, *Vit.* = ——, *Vitae*, ed. K. Ziegler, I 1, Leipzig 1969[4]; I 2, Leipzig 1964[3]; II 1, Leipzig 1964[2]; II 2, Leipzig 1968[2]; III 1, Leipzig 1971[2]; III 2, Leipzig 1973[2]
Poll. = Pollux, *Onomasticon*, ed. E. Bethe, Leipzig 1900-1931
Porph. = Porphyrius Tyrius, *ap.* Stobaeum
——, *Abst.* = ——, *De Abstinentia*, ed. A. Nauck, *Porphyrii Opuscula*, Leipzig 1886[2]
——, *Antr.* = ——, *De Antro Nympharum*, ed. A. Nauck, *Porphyrii Opuscula*, Leipzig 1886[2]
——, *Gaur.* = ——, *Ad Gaurum*, ed. T. Kalbfleisch, Berlin 1895
——, *in Harm.* = ——, *In Ptolemaei Harmonica*, ed. I. Düring, Göteborg 1932
——, *in Ti.* = ——, *In Platonis Timaeum Commentariorum Fragmenta*, ed. A. R. Sodano, Naples 1964
——, *Marc.* = ——, *Epistula ad Marcellam*, ed. E. des Places, Paris 1982
——, *Qu. Hom.* = ——, *Quaestiones Homericae I*, ed. A. R. Sodano, Naples 1970
——, *Sent.* = ——, *Sententiae*, ed. E. Lamberz, Leipzig 1975
Pr., *de Decem Dub., de Mal. Subst., de Prov.* = Proclus, *De Decem Dubitationibus, De Malorum Subsistentia, De Providentia*, ed. H. Boese, *Procli Diadochi Tria Opuscula*, Berlin 1960
——, *Hyp.* = ——, *Hypotyposis Astronomicarum Positionum*, ed. C. Manitius, Leipzig 1909
——, *in Alc.* = ——, *In Platonis Alcibiadem Commentaria*, ed. L. G. Westerink, Amsterdam 1954
——, *in Cra.* = ——, *In Platonis Cratylum Commentaria*, ed. G. Pasquali, Leipzig 1908
——, *in Euc.* = ——, *In Primum Euclidis Elementorum Librum Commentarii*, ed. G. Friedlein, Leipzig 1873
——, *in Prm.* = ——, *In Platonis Parmenidem Commentarii*, ed. V. Cousin, *Procli Philosophi Platonici Opera Inedita*, Paris 1864; librum VII edd. R. Klibansky—C. Labowsky (*Plato Latinus* III), London 1953
——, *in R.* = ——, *In Platonis Rempublicam Commentarii*, ed. W. Kroll, Leipzig 1899-1901
——, *in Ti.* = ——, *In Platonis Timaeum Commentarii*, ed. E. Diehl, Leipzig 1903-1906

———, *Inst.* = ———, *Institutio Theologica*, ed. E. R. Dodds, Oxford 1963[2]
———, *Phil. Chal.* = ———, *De Philosophia Chaldaica*, ed. A. Jahn, Halle 1891
———, *Th. Pl.* = ———, *Theologia Platonica*, I-IV edd. H. D. Saffrey—L. G. Westerink, Paris 1968-1981; V-VI ed. A. Portus, Hamburg 1618
Prisc., *Inst.* = Priscianus, *Institutiones*, ed. M. Hertz (*Grammatici Latini* III), Leipzig 1859
Prisc. Lyd. = Priscianus Lydus, *Metaphrasis in Theophrastum*, ed. I. Bywater (*CAG Suppl.* 1,2), Berlin 1886
Procop. Gaz., *Ep.* = Procopius Gazaeus, *Epistulae*, ed. R. Hercher, *Epistolographi Graeci*, Paris 1873
Prud., *Symm.* = Prudentius, *Contra Symmachum*, ed. M. P. Cunningham (*CChr., Ser. Lat.* 126), Turnhout 1966
ps.-Arist., *Oec.* = Ps.-Aristoteles, *Oeconomicus*, ed. V. Rose, *Aristoteles Pseudepigraphus*, Leipzig 1863
Psell., *Chron.* = Michael Psellus, *Chronographie*, ed. E. Renauld, Paris 1926-1928
———, *Omnif. Doctr.* = ———, *De Omnifaria Doctrina*, ed. L. G. Westerink, Nijmegen 1948
———, *Orat. Min.* = ———, *Oratoria Minora*, ed. A. R. Littlewood, Leipzig 1985
Ptol., *Hyp.* = Ptolemaeus, *Hypotheses*, ed. J. L. Heiberg, Leipzig 1907
———, *Tetr.* = ———, *Tetrabiblos*, edd. F. Boll—E. Boer, Leipzig 1940
Quint., *Inst.* = Quintilianus, *Institutio Oratoria*, ed. M. Winterbottom, Oxford 1970
Ruf., *Greg.* = Rufinus, *De Arrianis*, ed. A. Engelbracht (*CSEL* 46), Vienna-Leipzig 1910
Rut. Lup., *Fig.* = Rutilius Lupus, *De Figuris Sententiarum et Elocutionum*, ed. E. Brooks, Leiden 1970
S. E., *M., P.* = Sextus Empiricus, *Adversus Mathematicos, Pyrrhonicae Institutiones*, edd. H. Mutschmann—I. Mau, Leipzig 1912-1961
Saloust. = Saloustios, *De Deis et Mundo*, ed. G. Rochefort, Paris 1960
sch. A. = *Scholia in Aeschylum* II 2, ed. O. L. Smith, Leipzig 1982
sch. Aeschin. = *Scholia in Aeschinem*, ed. W. Dindorf, *Scholia Graeca in Aeschinem et Isocratem*, Leipzig 1852
sch. Aristid. = *Scholia in Aristidem*, ed. W. Dindorf, Leipzig 1829
sch. Cic. = *Scholia in Ciceronis Orationes Bobiensia*, ed. P. Hildebrandt, Leipzig 1907
sch. D. = *Scholia in Demosthenem*, ed. W. Dindorf, Oxford 1851 (= voll. VIII-IX)
sch. Hes. *OD* = *Scholia in Hesiodi Opera et Dies*, ed. A. Pertusi, Milan 1956
sch. Hom. *Il.* = *Scholia in Homeri Iliadem*, ed. H. Erbse, Berlin 1969-1977
sch. Hom. *Od.* = *Scholia Graeca in Homeri Odysseam*, ed. W. Dindorf, Oxford 1855
sch. Luc. = *Scholia in Lucianum*, ed. H. Rabe, Leipzig 1906
sch. Pl. = *Scholia in Platonem*, ed. W. C. Greene, Haverford 1938
sch. Pr. *in R.* = *Scholia in Procli In Platonis Rempublicam Commentarios*, ed. W. Kroll, *Proclus Diadochus, In Platonis Rempublicam Commentarii* II, Leipzig 1901
Sen., *Ira* = Seneca, *De Ira*, ed. L. D. Reynolds, *Senecae Dialogi*, Oxford 1977
Sext., *Sent.* = Sextus Gnomologus, *Sententiae*, ed. H. Chadwick, Cambridge 1959
Simp., *in An.* = Simplicius, *In Libros Aristotelis de Anima Commentaria*, ed. M. Hayduck (*CAG* 11), Berlin 1882
———, *in Cael.* = ———, *In Aristotelis de Caelo Commentaria*, ed. J. L. Heiberg (*CAG* 7), Berlin 1894
———, *in Cat.* = ———, *In Aristotelis Categorias Commentarium*, ed. C. Kalbfleisch (*CAG* 8), Berlin 1907
———, *in Ph.* = ———, *In Aristotelis Physica Commentaria*, ed. H. Diels (*CAG* 9-10), Berlin 1882-1895
Socr., *Ep.* = Socratis et Socraticorum *Epistulae*, ed. R. Hercher, *Epistolographi Graeci*, Paris 1873
Socr. Sch., *HE* = Socrates Scholasticus, *Historia Ecclesiastica*, ed. W. Bright, Oxford 1893
Sophon., *in An.* = Sophonias, *In Libros Aristotelis de Anima Paraphrasis*, ed. M. Hayduck (*CAG* 23,1), Berlin 1883
Stob. = Iohannes Stobaeus, *Anthologium*, edd. C. Wachsmuth—D. Hense, Berlin 1958[2]
Str. = Strabo, *Geographia*, edd. G. Aujac, F. Lasserre etc., Paris 1966-
Sud. = Suidas, *Lexicon*, ed. A. Adler, Leipzig 1928-1938

Suet., *Cal.* = Suetonius, *Vita Caligulae*, ed. H. Ailloud, *Suétone, Vies des douze Césars* II, Paris 1932
Sym. Seth, *Consp.* = Symeon Seth, *Conspectus*, in *An. Ath.*
Synes., *Calv., Insomn., Regn.* = Synesius Cyrenensis, *Laus Calvitiae, De Insomniis, Oratio de Regno*, ed. N. Terzaghi, Rome 1944
——, *Ep.* = ——, *Epistulae*, ed. A. Garzya, Rome 1979
Syr., *in Hermog.* = Syrianus, *In Hermogenem Commentaria*, ed. H. Rabe, Leipzig 1892-1893
——, *in Metaph.* = ——, *In Metaphysica Commentaria*, ed. W. Kroll (*CAG* 6,1), Berlin 1902
Tert., *An.* = Tertullianus, *De Anima*, ed. J. H. Waszink, Amsterdam 1947
——, *Nat.* = ——, *Ad Nationes*, ed. J. G. Ph. Borleffs (*CChr., Ser. Lat.* 1), Turnhout 1954
Thdt., *Affect.* = Theodoretus, *Graecarum Affectionum Curatio*, ed. P. Canivet (*SC* 57), Paris 1958
Them., *in An.* = Themistius, *In Libros Aristotelis de Anima Paraphrasis*, ed. R. Heinze (*CAG* 5,3), Berlin 1899
——, *Or.* = ——, *Orationes*, edd. G. Downey—A. F. Norman, Leipzig 1965-1971
Theod. Daphn., *Ep.* = Theodorus Daphnopates, *Epistulae*, edd. J. Darrouzès—L. G. Westerink, Paris 1978
Theod. Metoch. = Theodorus Metochita, *Miscellanea Philosophica et Historica*, ed. C. G. Müller, Leipzig 1821
Theod. Prodr., *Epith.* = Theodorus Prodromos, *Epithalamus, ap.* Nicephorum Bryennium, *Historiarum Libri IV*, ed. P. Gautier, Bruxelles 1975
Theon, *Prog.* = Theon, *Progymnasmata*, ed. H. Spengel, *Rhetores Graeci* II, Leipzig 1854
Theon Sm. = Theon Smyrnaeus, *Expositio Rerum Mathematicarum ad Platonem Legendum Utilium*, ed. E. Hiller, Leipzig 1878
Theophyl. Achr., *ad Disc.* = Theophylactus Achridensis, *Ad Discipulos*, ed. P. Gautier, Thessaloniki 1980
Thom. Mag., *Ecl.* = Thomas Magister, *Ecloga Vocum Atticarum*, ed. F. Ritschl, Halle 1832
——, *Reg. Off., Subd. Off.* = ——, *Oratio de Regis Officiis, Oratio de Subditorum Officiis*, *PG* 145
Thpl. Ant., *Autol.* = Theophilus Antiochenus, *Ad Autolycum*, ed. R. M. Grant, Oxford 1970
Tim. = Timaeus, *Lexicon Platonicum*, edd. D. Ruhnken—G. A. Koch, Leipzig 1828
Troil., *in Hermog. Stat.* = Troilus, *In Hermogenis de Statibus Commentarius*, ed. H. Rabe, *Prolegomenon Sylloge*, Leipzig 1931
Tz., *H.* = Iohannes Tzetzes, *Historiarum Variarum Chiliades*, ed. P. L. M. Leone, Naples 1968
——, *in Il.* = ——, ed. A. Lolos, *Der unbekannte Teil der Ilias-Exegesis des Iohannes Tzetzes*, Königstein/Ts. 1981
——, *in pr. Il.* = ——, *In Primum Librum Iliadis Commentaria*, in *An. Matr.*
Val. Max. = Valerius Maximus, *Factorum et Dictorum Memorabilium Libri Novem*, ed. C. Kempf, Leipzig 1888[2]
Zach. Mit., *Opif.* = Zacharias Scholasticus, *De Mundi Opificio*, ed. M. M. Colonna, Naples 1973
Zen. = Zenobius, edd. E. von Leutsch—F. G. Schneidewin, *Paroemiographi Graeci*, Göttingen 1839
Zonar. = Zonaras, *Lexicon*, ed. J. A. H. Tittmann, Leipzig 1808

BIBLIOGRAPHY

The bibliography consists of three sections: in the first section I will list the major editions of the *Republic*; I have not aimed at mentioning all the editions which have been published up to the present day, but I only record those editions which in some respect are interesting to the student of the text. In the second section I will mention the catalogues of manuscripts. The third section contains those studies (books and articles) which I have quoted more than once; I have not included such well-known works of reference as Kühner-Gerth, LSJ etc.; in referring to scholarly journals I usually adopt the abbreviations employed in *L'Année Philologique* (but for Mnemosyne I use the abbreviation Mnem.).

A) Editions

Aldina (Marcus Musurus), Venice 1513
First Basle edition (Simon Grynaeus, Johannes Oporinus), Basle 1534
Second Basle edition (Arnoldus Arlenius), Basle 1556
Stephanus, Paris 1578
Lyon 1590
Francfurt 1602
E. Massay, Cambridge 1713
Bipontine edition, Strassburg 1781-1787 (*R.* 1785)
Fr. Ast, Jena 1804 (= Ast^1), repr. 1820
Fr. Ast, Leipzig 1814 (= Ast^2)
I. Bekker, Berlin 1816-1818 (*R.* 1817); critical notes in *Commentaria critica in Platonem a se edita*, Berlin 1823
Fr. Ast, Leipzig 1822 (= Ast^3)
G. Stallbaum, Leipzig 1819-1827 (*R.* 1823) (= Stallbaum^1)
G. Stallbaum, *Platonis Dialogi Selecti* III 1-2, Gotha-Erfurt 1829-1830 (= Stallbaum^2)
C. E. C. Schneider, *Platonis Civitas*, Leipzig 1830-1833, supplemented by his *Additamenta ad Civitatis Platonis Libros X*, Leipzig 1854
J. G. Baiter—J. C. Orelli—A. W. Winckelmann, Zürich 1839
C. E. C. Schneider, Vratislava 1841
C. E. C. Schneider, Paris 1846 (Didot)
J. G. Baiter, Zürich 1847
G. Stallbaum, Gotha-Erfurt 1848-1849 (= Stallbaum^3)
C. F. Hermann, Leipzig 1852 (Teubner)
B. Jowett—L. Campbell, Oxford 1894
J. Adam, Cambridge 1897
T. G. Tucker, London 1900 (books I-II 368c only)
J. Adam, Cambridge 1902
J. Burnet, Oxford 1902
J. Burnet, Oxford 1905 (OCT)
P. Shorey, London 1930-1935 (Loeb Classical Library)
E. Chambry, Paris 1932-1934 (Budé)
J. M. Pábon—M. F. Galiano, Madrid 1949

B) Catalogues of manuscripts

De Andrés = G. de Andrés, *Catálogo de los Códices Griegos de la real Biblioteca de El Escorial*, II, Madrid 1965; III, Madrid 1967
Bandini = A. M. Bandini, *Catalogus Codicum Graecorum Bibliothecae Laurentianae*, II, Florence 1768; III, Florence 1770

Coxe, *Bodl.* = H. O. Coxe, *Catalogus Codicum MSS. Bibliothecae Bodleianae I*, Oxford 1893
——, *Ox.* = ——, *Catalogus Codicum MSS. qui in Collegiis Aulisque Oxoniensibus hodie asservantur II*, Oxford 1852
Cyrillus = S. Cyrillus, *Codices Graeci MSS. Regiae Bibliothecae Borbonicae II*, Naples 1832
Feron-Battaglini = E. Feron—F. Battaglini, *Codices MSS. Graeci Ottoboniani*, Rome 1892
Franchi de'Cavalieri-Muccio = P. Franchi de'Cavalieri—G. Muccio, *Index Codicum Graecorum Bibliothecae Angelicae*, SIFC 4 (1896), 33-184
Hardt = I. Hardt, *Catalogus Codicum Manuscriptorum Graecorum Bibliothecae Regiae Bavaricae*, III, Munich 1806; V, Munich 1812
Hunger, *Katalog* = H. Hunger, *Katalog der griechischen Handschriften der österreichischen Nationalbibliothek I*, Vienna 1961
——, *Supplementum* = ——, *Supplementum Graecum*, Vienna 1957
Iriarte = J. Iriarte, *Regiae Bibliothecae Matritensis Codices Graeci MSS*, Madrid 1769
Lambros = Sp. P. Lambros, *Catalogue of the Greek Manuscripts on Mount Athos II*, Cambridge 1900
Lilla = S. Lilla, *Codices Vaticani Graeci 2162-2254*, Vatican City 1985
Martini-Bassi = A. Martini—D. Bassi, *Catalogus Codicum Graecorum Bibliothecae Ambrosianae I-II*, Milan 1906
Mercati-Franchi de'Cavalieri = G. Mercati—P. Franchi de'Cavalieri, *Codices Vaticani Graeci 1-329*, Rome 1923
De Meyier = K. A. de Meyier, *Codices Vossiani Graeci et Miscellanei*, Leiden 1955
Mioni, *Ital.* = E. Mioni, *Catalogo di manoscritti greci esistenti nelle biblioteche Italiane I*, Rome 1964
——, *Ven. Ant.* = ——, *Bibliothecae Divi Marci Venetiarum Codices Graeci Manuscripti. Thesaurus Antiquus I*, Rome 1981
——, *Ven. App.* = ——, *Bibliothecae Divi Marci Venetiarum Codices Graeci Manuscripti I 2*, Rome 1972 (= *Appendix*)
Olivier-Monégier du Sorbier = J.-M. Olivier—M.-A. Monégier du Sorbier, *Catalogue des manuscrits grecs de Tchécoslovaquie*, Paris 1983
Olivieri-Festa = A. Olivieri—A. N. Festa, *Indice dei codici greci delle Biblioteche Universitaria e Comunale di Bologna*, SIFC 3 (1895), 385-595
Omont, *Inventaire* = H. Omont, *Inventaire sommaire des MSS. grecs de la Bibliothèque Nationale II*, Paris 1888
Papadopoulos-Kerameus = A. Papadopoulos-Kerameus, Ἱεροσολυμιτικὴ Βιβλιοθήκη I, Petersburg 1891
Rostagno-Festa = E. Rostagno—A. N. Festa, *Indice dei codici greci Laurenziani non compresi nel Catalogo del Bandini*, SIFC 1 (1893), 131-232
Rud = Th. Rud, *Codicum Manuscriptorum Ecclesiae Cathedralis Dunelmensis Catalogus Classicus*, Durham 1825
Samberger = C. Samberger, *Catalogi Codicum Graecorum qui in minoribus bibliothecis Italicis asservantur*, I, Leipzig 1965; II, Leipzig 1968
Stevenson = H. Stevenson, *Codices MSS. Palatini Graeci Bibliothecae Vaticanae*, Rome 1885
Stornajolo = C. Stornajolo, *Codices Urbinates Graeci*, Rome 1895
Vitelli = G. Vitelli, *Indice de' codici greci Riccardiani, Magliabechiani e Marucelliani*, SIFC 2 (1894), 471-570
Warner-Gilson = G. F. Warner—J. P. Gilson, *Catalogue of Western Manuscripts in the old Royal and King's Collections II*, London 1921

C) GENERAL

Adam, *Burnet* = J. Adam, *Burnet's Republic of Plato*, CR 16 (1902), 215-219
Allen = T. W. Allen, *Palaeographica III*, JPh 21 (1893), 48-55
Alline = H. Alline, *Histoire du texte de Platon*, Paris 1915
Andrieu = J. Andrieu, *Le dialogue antique*, Paris 1954
Apelt = O. Apelt, *Review of Adam's 1902 edition*, WKPh 20 (1903), 337-350

Berti = E. Berti, *Contributo allo studio dei manoscritti platonici del Critone*, SCO 15 (1966), 210-220
Bluck = R. S. Bluck, *Plato's Meno*, Cambridge 1961
Brashler = J. Brashler, ed., *Nag Hammadi Codex VI 5*, in: D. M. Parrott (volume editor), *Nag Hammadi Codices V 2-5 and VI with Papyrus Berolinensis 8502, 1 and 4*, Leiden 1979, 325-339
Brumbaugh-Wells = R. S. Brumbaugh—R. Wells, *The Plato Manuscripts, A New Index*, New Haven-London 1968
Burnet, *Neglected MS* = J. Burnet, *A neglected MS. of Plato*, CR 16 (1902), 98-101
——, *Vind. F* = —, *Vindobonensis F and the text of Plato*, CR 17 (1903), 12-14
——, *Platonica I* = —, *Platonica I*, CR 18 (1904), 199-204
——, *Platonica II* = —, *Platonica II*, CR 19 (1905), 99-101
——, *Vindiciae I* = —, *Vindiciae Platonicae I*, CQ 8 (1914), 230-236
Cammelli = G. Cammelli, *I dotti bizantini e le origini dell'umanesimo, I, Manuele Crisolora*, Florence 1941
Campbell = L. Campbell, *On the text of this edition of Plato's Republic*, in the edition by B. Jowett and L. Campbell (Oxford 1894), II, 67-131
Carlini = A. Carlini, *Studi sulla tradizione antica e medievale del Fedone*, Rome 1972
Clark = A. C. Clark, *The Descent of Manuscripts*, Oxford 1918
Cobet = C. G. Cobet, *De Platonis Codice Parisino A*, Mnem. II 3 (1875), 157-208
Cornarius = I. Cornarius, *Eclogae*, Basle 1561 (I have consulted the edition by I. F. Fischer, Leipzig 1771)
Deneke = E. Deneke, *De Platonis dialogorum libri Vindobonensis F memoria*, diss. Göttingen 1922
Diller, *Petrarch* = A. Diller, *Petrarch's Greek Codex of Plato*, CPh 59 (1964), 270-272
——, *Codex T* = —, *Codex T of Plato*, CPh 75 (1980), 322-324
Dodds, *Notes* = E. R. Dodds, *Notes on some Manuscripts of Plato*, JHS 77 (1957), 24-30
——, *Gorgias* = —, *Plato Gorgias*, Oxford 1959
Fonkič = B. L. Fonkič, *Notes paléographiques sur les manuscrits grecs des bibliothèques italiennes*, Thesaurismata 16 (1979), 153-169
Gadelle = L. Gadelle, *Quaestiones Platonicae*, Strassburg 1910
Garin = E. Garin, *Ricerche sulle traduzioni di Platone nella prima metà del sec. XV*, in: *Medioevo e Rinascimento. Studi in onore di Bruno Nardi I* (Florence 1955), 339-374
Giorgetti = G. P. Giorgetti, *Review of Carlini's Studi sulla tradizione antica e medievale del Fedone*, JHS 95 (1975), 202-204
Greene = W. C. Greene, *Scholia Platonica*, Haverford 1938
J. J. Hartman = J. J. Hartman, *Ad Platonis Rempublicam*, Mnem. II 42 (1914), 223-256
J. L. V. Hartman = J. L. V. Hartman, *Ad Platonis Rempublicam*, Mnem. II 46 (1918), 38-52, 302-319
Immisch = O. Immisch, *Philologische Studien zu Plato II. De recensionis platonicae praesidiis atque rationibus*, Leipzig 1903
Jachmann = G. Jachmann, *Der Platontext*, NGG, Phil.-Hist. Klasse (1941), Nr. 7, 225-389
Jordan, *Cod. Auct.* = A. Jordan, *De Platonis codicum auctoritate*, NJPhP Suppl. 7 (1873-1875), 607-640
——, *Republik* = —, *Zu den Handschriften des Plato IV. Zu den Handschriften der Republik*, Hermes 13 (1878), 474-481
Klibansky[2] = R. Klibansky, *The Continuity of the Platonic Tradition during the Middle Ages*, London 1981[2]
Král = J. Král, *Über den Platocodex der Wiener Hofbibliothek suppl. phil. gr. 7*, WS 14 (1892), 161-208
Kraus-Walzer = P. Kraus—R. Walzer, *Galeni Compendium Timaei Platonis (Plato Arabus I)*, London 1951
Kristeller = P. O. Kristeller, *Supplementum Ficinianum I*, Florence 1937
Lenz = F. Lenz, *Der Vaticanus gr. 1, eine Handschrift des Arethas*, NGG, Phil.-Hist. Klasse, 1933, Fachgr. 1, Nr. 17, 193-218

Lerner = R. Lerner, *Averroes on Plato's Republic*, translated, with an Introduction and Notes, by R. Lerner, Ithaca and London 1974
Maas = P. Maas, *Textkritik*, Leipzig 1959[4]
Marcel = R. Marcel, *Marsile Ficin*, Paris 1958
Marg = W. Marg, *Timaeus Locrus, De natura mundi et animae*, Leiden 1972
Morelli = I. Morelli, *Bibliotheca Manuscripta Graeca et Latina I* (all published), Bassano 1802
Müller = G. Müller, *Review of Dodds' edition of the Gorgias*, Gnomon 36 (1964), 120-136
Naber = S. A. Naber, *Platonica*, Mnem. II 36 (1903), 216-288
Nielsen = G. R. Nielsen, *Review of Immisch' Philologische Studien zu Plato*, NTF 12 (1903), 130 ff.
Omont, *Parisinus* = H. Omont, *Œuvres philosophiques de Platon: fac-similé en phototypie, à la grandeur exacte de l'original du Ms. grec 1807 de la Bibliothèque Nationale*, Paris 1908
Pack[2] = R. A. Pack, *The Greek and Latin Literary Texts from Greco-Roman Egypt*, Ann Arbor 1965[2]
Pasquali = G. Pasquali, *Storia della tradizione e critica del testo*, Florence 1952[2]
Pescetti = L. Pescetti, *Appunti su Antonio Cassarino e la sua traduzione della 'Repubblica' di Platone*, BASP 7 (1929), 23-45
Des Places = E. des Places, *Platon, Les Lois, tôme I*, Paris 1951
Post = L. A. Post, *The Vatican Plato and its Relations*, Middletown 1934
Reynolds-Wilson = L. D. Reynolds—N. G. Wilson, *Scribes and Scholars*, Oxford 1974[2]
Richards 1893 = H. Richards, *Critical Notes on the Republic of Plato*, CR 7 (1893), 14 f., 251-254, 349-352 (reprinted in his *Platonica*, London 1911)
— 1894 = —,—, CR 8 (1894), 22-25, 192-195, 292-294, 393-395 (reprinted in his *Platonica*, London 1911)
E. I. J. Rosenthal = E. I. J. Rosenthal, *Averroes' Commentary on Plato's Republic*, Cambridge 1956
F. Rosenthal = F. Rosenthal, *On the Knowledge of Plato's Philosophy in the Islamic World*, Islamic Culture 14 (1940), 387-422
Rostagno = E. Rostagno, *De Cod. 4 Plutei XXVIII, qui Caesenae in Bibl. Malatestiana asservatur*, in the edition by B. Jowett and L. Campbell (Oxford 1894), II, 157-164
Sabbadini = R. Sabbadini, *Le scoperte dei codici latini e greci ne'secoli XIV e XV*, Florence 1967[2]
Sauvantidis = G. P. Sauvantidis, Ἀπὸ τὴ χειρόγραφη παραδόση τῆς Πολιτείας τοῦ Πλάτωνος. Σχέση τοῦ κώδ. Τ (Venetus App. Cl. IV,1) μὲ τὸν κώδ. Α (Parisinus 1807). Διόρθωση στὸ 509d τῆς Πολιτείας, Ioannina 1970
Schanz, *Mittheilungen I* = M. Schanz, *Mittheilungen über platonische Handschriften*, Hermes 10 (1876), 171-177
——, *Mittheilungen II* = —, *Mittheilungen über platonische Handschriften*, Hermes 11 (1876), 104-117
——, *Untersuchungen* = —, *Untersuchungen über die platonischen Handschriften*, Philologus 35 (1876), 643-670
——, *Republik* = —, *Über die kritische Grundlage der platonischen Republik*, Hermes 12 (1877), 173-181
——, *Platocodex* = —, *Über den Platocodex der Markusbibliothek in Venedig*, Append. Class. 4, Nr. 1, Leipzig 1877
——, *Parisinus* = —, *Über den Platocodex Nr. 1807 der Nationalbibliothek in Paris*, RhM 33 (1878), 303-307
——, *Nachträge* = —, *Untersuchungen über die platonischen Handschriften, Nachträge*, Philologus 38 (1879), 359-365
——, *Stichometrie* = —, *Zur Stichometrie*, Hermes 16 (1881), 309-315
Sicherl, *Ficino* = M. Sicherl, *Neuentdeckte Handschriften von Marsilio Ficino und Johannes Reuchlin*, Scriptorium 16 (1962), 50-61
——, *Platonismus* = —, *Platonismus und Textüberlieferung*, JOeByzG 15 (1966), 201-229; reprinted with additions in D. Harlfinger, ed., *Griechische Kodikologie und Textüberlieferung*, Darmstadt 1980, 535-576; I quote from the reprint.
Slings = S. R. Slings, *A Commentary on the Platonic Clitophon*, diss. Vrije Universiteit Amsterdam 1981

——, *Papyri* = ——, *Some Recent Papyri of the Politeia*, Mnem. IV 40 (1987), 27-34
Stuart Jones = H. Stuart Jones, *The 'ancient vulgate' of Plato and Vind. F*, CR 16 (1902), 388-391
Tarán = L. Tarán, *Academica: Plato, Philip of Opus, and the Pseudo-Platonic Epinomis*, Philadelphia 1975
Vogler = E. Vogler, *Plato's Republik, lateinisch von Antonio Cassarino aus Sicilien*, Philologus 13 (1858), 195-204
Vollgraff = W. Vollgraff, *Observationes criticae in Platonis Rempublicam*, Mnem. II 44 (1916), 1-17, 133-148
Vretska = K. Vretska, *Platonica*, WS 66 (1953), 76-91
Wallies = M. Wallies, *Textkritisches zu Platons Staat*, BPhW 42 (1922), 41-47
West = M. L. West, *Textual Criticism and Editorial Technique*, Stuttgart 1973
Wilamowitz = U. von Wilamowitz-Moellendorf, *Plato II*, Berlin 1962[3]
Wilson = N. G. Wilson, *A List of Plato Manuscripts*, Scriptorium 16 (1962), 386-395
——, *Scholars* = ——, *Scholars of Byzantium*, London 1983
Wohlrab = M. Wohlrab, *Die Platonhandschriften und ihre gegenseitigen Beziehungen*, NJPhP Suppl. 15 (1887), 641-728

INDEX LOCORUM POTIORUM

This index comprises those places which are interesting with regard to textual criticism. It contains all the places occurring in the chapter on the secondary MSS, and a selection of places occurring in the other chapters. I have also included those places where there is agreement between secondary MSS and the indirect tradition.

327c14	208	345a7	217
328b4	222	345c3	106
328d5	217	346a5	224
328d7	70	346a6	71, 98
328e3	209	346e4-5	207
328e7	90	347c3-4	238
329c2	287	347d1	232
329c3	225	347d3	208
329c7	230	348c7	75
329d1	230	349b8	222
329d6	185	349b9	76
329e7	217	349c1	233
330a5	109	349d9	238
330b1	275	350c1	234
330b7	238	351a6	208
330b8	70	351b9	204
330c4	250	351c2	237
330c6	109	352a1	70
330c7	235	352e9	212
331a3	204	353c8	204
332e3	106	353d7	240
332e5	226	354a11	204
333b8	71, 98	354b3	65, 219
333e1	90	354b4	209
333e3	106	354b8	226
333e6	211	357b7-8	233
335a8-9	76	358a2	226
336e7-8	239	358b7	217
336e9	65, 211, 233	358d6	232
337a3	216, 222, 223	358e2	212, 233
337a6	222	359d1	165
337a7	206	359d8	73
337b4	206	359e1	232
337c5	70	360a8	209
339a1	99	360b2	75
340a6	88	360b6	106
341c4	222, 223	361b8	204
341d11	207	361c7	216
342a4	206	362a1	204, 226, 228
342b5	226	362a2	210, 226, 228
343a3	204	362c1	106
343c1	226	363a1	185
344a3	109, 224	363a3	238

INDEX LOCORUM POTIORUM 383

364a1	217	399b3	217
365b5	79, n. 3	399c3	219
365d8	212, 240	400a6	225
365e3	76	400d4	208
365e5	235	401a7	74
366b3	106	403a6	217
366e1	99	403a11	216
366e6	75, 109	403b1,3	210
368e2-3	234, 235	403c9	224
368e8-369a1	106	405b3	109
370a6	65, 206	405c2	226
370b2	116, 226	406c6	237
370d3	71, 98	407a7	109
370e12	206	407c1	66, 224
373a1	206	407c2	103
374a3	98	407c6	74
374b7-8	71, 98	407c7	208
375a5	207	407e4	220
375d1	208	408a5	212
375d7	204	409a1	208
376a5	109	410c10-d1	207
376a6	216	410d2	209
376c8	109	410e5-6	221
377b5-6	235	411a6	221
379c2	234	411c1	71
379c5	234	411c2	103
379d6	222	411d2	224
380c3	235	411e4	66
381a10	235	412a9	209
381b4	71	413c6	204
381b11	235	413c7	232
381c9	216	413e5	214
382c6	106	414a4	225
383a2	234	414b3	222
386b5	210	414e2	217
386d4	65, 226	414e3	206
386d7	109, 138, 139	415a2	231
387a7	174	415a6	214
387b4	210	416c2	216
387c2	66	416d1	225
387c4	250	420b5	90
387d2	235	420c7-8	217
388e6	76, 174	421a8	210
389e2	238	421e6	235
391c2	264, 267	422a2	75
392b2	76	422c1	237
392b9	275	422e9	71, 232
392c2	219	423c6	214
392c4	239	423e7	215
393e2	230	425b8	234
393e8	222	425c2	226, 228
394c7	217	425d2	224
394c8	217	425d4	229
397c9	235	426a3	215
398e10	220	426b8	208
399b2	235	427a1	79, n. 3

427a5	233	451e1	236
427b7	232	452a2	234
428a6	233	452b1	231
428b4	209	452c9	225
428c12	229	452e1	209, 220, 250
428d11	75	452e4	206
429a2	99	454b4	232
429c7	66, 206	454d1	204, 206
429d8	214, 223	454d2	212, 215
430a7	226, 229, 239	454e5	75
431b6	66, 206	456a1-2	212
433c1	216	456c4	237
433c4	235	457a7	217
433c8	226, 229	457b1	216, 226, 228
435b7	220	457c6	209
435c4	233	457d1	97
435d3	66, 236	458a5	215
435e7	231, 232	458c7	231
436a9	209	459a4	233
436a11	230	459b11	210
436c2	212	459c6	238
436d5	236	459e5	232
436d7	216	460b2	210
436d8	204, 206	460c6	219
436e5	204	461a6	219
436e6	204, 206	461b10	66
437d8-9	238	461c1	233
437d11	66, 247	461c6	237
438b2	223	461d6	214
439a2	209	462a6	214
439b3	230	462b2	214
439b4	223, 224	462e6	204
439b6	236	464e6	223, 224
439e6	226, 229	465c2	233
440a2	210	465d2	226, 229
440a5	214	466a4	210
440c7	66, 204, 206, 286	467e3	215
440e5-6	233	468a10	66
441b6	236	469a6	208
441c5	223, 225	469c9	230
441c6	214, 218, 219	469e1	216
441d8	204	469e5	230
441d12	237	471b4	221
442b2	204, 210	471b6,9	213
442b6	206	471c8	215
442e1	238	472a2	104
443a1	204	472a6-7	79, n. 3
444a1	223	472a8	71
444b5	66, 212, 215, 235	472b1	230
445c1	214, 226, 229	472d5	211
445c2	275	473a5	234
445d5	236	473b2	214
445e1	204, 210	474e2	286
449c1	232	475b1	230
451b1	209	475e2	223, 225
451b9	66, 238	476b7	215

INDEX LOCORUM POTIORUM

477a9	209	524a7	204, 227
478a8	240	525b1	236
479a3-4	233	526d5	75
479a6	213	526d9	71
479c8-d1	207	527a3	234
486a4	238	527c2	219, 222
486a8	204	527d5	223
487c1	235	529b5-6	208
488e2	244	529b6	275
489e4	222	530a3	208
490c2	234	530c1	76, 77, 90
491e4	233	530d7	106
492a6	209	530d8	221
493b3	66	531b3	236
494b5	66	532a2	244
494b6	230	533e4-5	234
495e1	210, 221	534c3	239
496a1	230	535d2	75
496c5	230	535d4	230
497a5	230	536c3	211
497c8	229	537a11	211
498c1	206	538d8	90
498c7	275	540d3	208
499d3	235	540d6	236
501a5	206	541b2	222, 223
502b11	225	543c4	71
503b5	222	544a4	208
503c5	222	544b9	75
504c6	66, 224	544c6	213
504e4	275	544c7	66, 124, 237, 238
505a3	221	544e1	227
506a6	211	545c6	222
506a7	208	545d3	211
508b9	109	546c3	257, n. 1
508b12	211	547a5	227, 229, 230
508b13	220	547b4-5	221
508d2	220	547c9	224
508d3	239	548a3	229
508d6	211	548d9	206
510b4	99	549a1	238
510b7	224	549a5	74
511c3	90	549b1	222
514a1	211	550e2	230
514b4	99	550e8	218
515b5	76, 237	551a1	218
516b2	238	551e3	232
517e2-3	207	552c1	74
518a2	222	553b2	66, 229
518a4	220	553c4	219, 222
518b1	236, 239	553c5	239
518b6	236	554b5	213
519a3	211	554b6	66, 213
519a5	238	557c7	208
519b2	223	558a1	224
521c7	225, 234	558a8	238
523d5	227	558c2	229

558e1	235	600a5	204
559b4	206	600b6	234
559d9	239	600d6	227
559d10-e1	219	600e4	237
559e4	90	601b2	244
560b10	74	601b3	204
561b2	71	603a12	225
562b6	235	604a1	214
563a4	106	604c7	66, 204, 206
564b6	223	604d2	204, 206
566c10	272	606c7	219
567e3	213, 221	606e4	250
568d8	90	607a4	207, 224
569a1	222	607b1	219
571b2	66, 229	607d4	90
572a7	218	608c7	208
572a8	218, 223	609a3	214
572b2	218	610d3	66, 204, 206, 257
572c8	275	611c3	206, 229
573e3	211	612c8	211
574c9	74	612d6	218
575c4	106	614a7	239
576d2	90	614b3	223, 224
578a4	229	614b8	218
578a7	234	614c2	211
579d9	240	614d6	227, 229
580d1	222	615b3	179, 239, 270
580d4	66, 182, 219	615c3	218
580d10	220	615d3	222
581d10	66	616a1	236
581e1	220	616a3	227
581e6	231	616a4	220, 223
582a1	210, 222	616a6-7	227
582c4	240	616b7	223
585c7	213, 238	616e5-8	234
586a4	223	617a4	232
586e1	211	617a5	236
588c7	279	617b1	204, 205, 206
588e3	227	618a3-4	210
590e1	66, 237, 238	619e4	230
591c7	227, 228, 229	619e6-620d5	210
596d3	222	620b1	286
597a6	73	620e5	227
599a8	234	621a7-8	74
599b1	211	621b8	244
599c2	220	621d3	225